The ANATOMY *of An* HORSE

The ANATOMY *of An* HORSE

ANDREW SNAPE

A Faithful Reproduction of the 1683 Edition
With Commentary by David W. Ramey, D.V.M.

HOWELL BOOK HOUSE
NEW YORK

Howell Book House
A Simon & Schuster Macmillan Company
1633 Broadway
New York, NY 10019

Library of Congress Cataloging-in-Publication Data

Snape, Andrew, b. 1644.
The anatomy of an horse / Andrew Snape.
p. cm.
Originally published: 1683.
Includes bibliographical references.
ISBN 0-87605-607-9
1. Horses—Anatomy—Early works to 1800. I. Title.
SF765.S63 1997 97–9779
636.1'0891—dc21 CIP

Manufactured in the United States of America

10 9 8 7 6 5 4 3 2 1

CONTENTS

INTRODUCTION

IT is the seventeenth century. In many ways, your life is just like it is today. You work; you play. You marry, have a family, and want the best for your children.

If you are a man, you work. Your work is most likely that of your father's. If you are a woman, few choices are open to you. You are probably fulfilling the traditional role of mother and wife. Of course you do not have any modern conveniences—no running water, no electricity, no central air conditioning.

You have animals. Animals provide you with companionship. Your dogs help you hunt and help protect your home. Your cows provide meat and milk. If you are lucky enough, you have a horse. If you have many horses, you are privileged, perhaps even of royal blood.

Your horse is a blessing. With him, you have a method of transportation that lets you cover distances far greater than you could travel on foot. You have a beast of burden to pull and carry loads. You can plow fields. What a luxury; what a necessity.

Your life may be good, but that's not to say that it is easy. You most likely have as many children as you can afford; to help around the house, to work if and where needed. Not all of your children are likely to survive to adolescence, much less adulthood.

Adulthood ends all too soon. If you are fifty years of age, you are old. Life can be hard.

You thank your Creator for health. Health is a mystery and something to cherish. Your Creator is a constant. He provides the only answers to life's questions.

Sickness is fear: fear for the health, safety, and life of you and your family. All too often, sickness brings death. Should you lose a child, it is a tragedy, something you and your friends may have suffered many times. Should your animals become sick, however, everyone's life can change. Your whole family can be affected. You can lose food, a working partner, or a friend. To cure sickness, you pray. You may also turn to doctors.

Doctors do their best to help. Many doctors work on both people and animals. After all, medicine is medicine (as it is today). Unfortunately, most doctors have a bad name. They so rarely seem to be able to help. Perhaps this is unavoidable; the best of seventeenth-century medicine is not very good.

Should your horse get sick, there are some men who specialize in the care of horses. These men are called farriers. (The word farrier is derived from the Latin for "iron"; the English word is a borrowing from the Middle French word for "blacksmith," *ferrier*). In the seventeenth century, unlike today, farriers are the experts in all aspects of horse care. There are no trained veterinarians who only attend to the health of a horse. The first veterinary schools begin to open sixty years after the close of the seventeenth century.

It is the seventeenth century. You practice "modern" medicine. You are a farrier.

Seventeenth-century medicine is a far cry from what it is today. It is in no way modern. Medical practitioners, doctors, and farriers alike are still in the grip of medical notions that have held sway for over fifteen hundred years.

Here is what you have been taught:

You take for granted the existence of an all-knowing Creator. He does nothing at random. There is a reason for the existence of all things and that reason can be explained. (Later, this line of thought will be called teleology.)

"Classic" medical knowledge, the anatomy and physiology that you must know to cure your patients, has been most eloquently described by Galen, a Roman physician born of Greek parents. Galen lived circa A.D. 130–200. He was said to have written over five hundred medical treatises (over a hundred of them survive to this day).

Galen's anatomy is an anatomy of analogy. Roman custom at the time did not allow Galen to actually dissect human bodies. His external anatomy was performed on monkeys and his internal anatomy on pigs. He then assumed that humans were the same. Predictably, in many areas, Galen's anatomy bears little relation to reality.

Even though Galen did not dissect horses, in the seventeenth century, Galen's ideas of the internal anatomy of all creatures hold powerful influence. It may be the only anatomy you know (if you know any at all). If you have any true knowledge of the internal anatomy of horses, it is most likely knowledge that you have gained through your own experience.

You may believe that Galen's physiology (the study of how the body works) is also largely accurate. For Galen the body organs are in charge of life. The brain rules sensation and motion, the heart is in charge of the passions, and the liver provides nutrition.

Galen's description of the forces responsible for life begins with three *pneuma* (souls), which Plato said controlled the body. Air is inhaled into the lungs and is changed into pneuma; the life process changes one kind of pneuma into another. *Chyle* from the intestines is changed by the liver into a "natural spirit" that waxes and wanes like the moon. Some of this natural spirit enters the heart where it becomes the "vital spirit." The vital spirit rises to the brain, where it is again changed, this time into the "animal spirit." This animal spirit, the highest form of pneuma, is distributed throughout the body by the nerves (which Galen said were hollow).

The center of Galen's physiology is the heart and its heat. "Innate heat," as described by Hippocrates and Aristotle, distinguishes the living from the dead. The heat is innate because it comes from life itself. The heat is generated by the heart. Thus, the heart is the hottest organ in the body, a sort of internal furnace that were it not for the cooling power of the lungs would consume itself. You may even believe that you can burn yourself by touching blood that comes directly out of the heart.

You have been taught that health is a balance of the four body *humors*. (Humor comes from the Latin *umor*, meaning "fluid" or "moisture"). There are four humors—blood, choler (or bile), phlegm, and black choler (or melancholy)—and they exist in a specific balance for each individual.

The balance of the humors is more than medical theory; it is a general theory of the nature of being. Certain individuals normally have one fluid that dominates their system. The balance of the humors is responsible for one's "temperament," and an individual being may be "choleric," "melancholic," "phlegmatic" or "sanguine," depending on which humor predominates. Even the body temperature is affected by the balance of the body's humors. In fact, there is no "normal" temperature for a living being; each individual's temperature is a direct reflection of his temperament. The terms *temperament* and *temperature* are synonymous.

You believe that if the body's humors become unbalanced, disease results. Disease is "distemper," a disruption of the normal temperament. To restore the balance, the "normal" fluid levels must be restored. Hence, in fever, for example, there is too much blood. Blood must be let out of the system to restore the body's balance. (Bleeding will remain part of standard medical practice for hundreds of years.) Other "treatments" that you will use include purging and sweating. Like bleeding, these also are designed to remove bodily fluids and to restore the healthy balance of the body's humors.

Over the centuries, Galenic medicine has become dogma; Galen's texts have become sacred. In times past, individuals who disagreed with Galen were banished or executed. Even in the seventeenth century, individuals whose ideas differ from Galen's are sometimes persecuted. (This is the height of irony; Galen himself urged his followers to learn from information that came before their own studies and to use their own experience to expand on and improve the sum of knowledge.)

In spite of formidable obstacles, medical knowledge is changing rapidly. In the seventeenth century you, as a medical practitioner, are in the midst of a whirlwind of new ideas. Galen's anatomy has been challenged (by Vesalius). His theories of circulation are questioned (by Harvey and Waleus). The humoral theories have been ridiculed (by Paracelsus). What you have known to be true may no longer be true; the medical world is being turned upside down. You try to hold to the old truths, but you are forced to acknowledge the truth of what is being discovered, truth that you can see with your own eyes.

Andrew Snape was the farrier to King Charles II. Almost nothing is known of his life, not even the date of his death. He was born in 1644. He may have succeeded his father as farrier to the king (he refers to himself as the "junior").

What can be known about Snape must be gleaned from reading this book. He must have been a man of great imagination and curiosity. He must have had a desire to learn and to improve himself. He experimented and made some wonderful observations. He may have been arrogant and judgmental; his book certainly shows him to be intolerant and disdainful of the relative ignorance of farriers who did not subscribe to his views of the current state of medical knowledge and did not share his thirst for learning. He was certainly educated and he evidently read Latin and Greek.

He took pains that his son, also called Andrew, be educated, too. His son would become chaplain to Queen Anne and subsequently to King George I. Snape must have been quite a character. He was at once an original observer, a respectful admirer of medical investigation, and a documented plagiarist. Some of his ideas are new and challenging; others hold to the old beliefs. However, in the seventeenth century, many of his observations contradict much of what was previously believed to be true.

The Anatomy of An Horse is the first book on the anatomy of the horse ever published in the English language. The first edition of the book was published in 1683. This facsimile edition is taken from the second edition, published in 1687. The two texts are identical.

Modern technology makes possible an authentic reproduction of this seventeenth-century book, which was typeset, printed, and bound by hand. Variations in inking, the occasional blurred lines due to printing on paper not completely smooth, and foxing—blemishes caused by age—do not detract from the appeal or readability of the book.

Snape's is not the first book on horse anatomy; that book was written by an Italian, Carlo Ruini, at the end of the sixteenth century. To Snape's discredit, almost half of the engraved plates in his book are taken directly from Ruini's book, *Anatomia del Cavallo.* To his historical chagrin, all of the plates are reversed. Thus, in the drawings of the horse's abdomen, the positions of the viscera (the liver, the intestines, and the like) are reversed from their actual positions. Snape was therefore dishonest when he asserted in his introduction that no one else had preceded him in the study of equine anatomy or "shewed me the way." Nonetheless, the merits of his book are considerable.

The Anatomy of An Horse is a treasure box full of veterinary history. You will be amazed that the anatomical terminology of Snape's day remains largely the same today. The words you use to describe your horse are those that have been used for literally hundreds of years! In some sections, Snape tries to explain where some of the terms used in anatomy come from; even when he is wrong, his explanations are a delight to the modern reader.

Snape was a scientist. He tries to give reasons for everything. He believes that there is a Creator who has done nothing by accident. With that in mind, he tries to understand the reasons for all things, in health and disease, that concern the horse. He relies on the then-current state of medical knowledge and references many of his contemporaries in his book. He is curious—searching—looking for answers. He is exactly like the scientists of today.

Snape's book describes a variety of the treatments and ideas that were in vogue in the seventeenth century (and holds many of them up to ridicule). For example, while at times you may think that your horse's behavior indicates that he doesn't have a brain, he does; in the seventeenth century many people believed that the horse did not have a brain at all! Many other interesting and delightful errors are found in the text. In many ways, you will see how far veterinary medicine has come; in others, you will find that it is largely unchanged since *The Anatomy of An Horse* was written.

Snape's writing style is accessible. He deliberately tries to avoid using too much Latin and Greek. He is writing to a specific audience—farriers—whose education he describes as "mean" and which he hopes to improve. Although his language is a bit flowery (in the style of the time), it is easy to follow. He's not trying to write over anyone's head; he wants to improve the "current" state of knowledge.

Two major differences between the printed (and written) English writing of Snape's day and today are apparent in the book. First, there is the *f*. What we call the "f" (it looks like the modern letter *f* without the crossbar) is actually called the "long s." The *s* that you are familiar with is called a "short s." Both printed letters are actually just different versions of the same letter. In books printed between 1500 and 1700, the short *s* was used at the end of a word, in capitals and especially before the letters *f, b,* and *k*. The long *s* was used everywhere else. It's not that confusing and your eye gets used to this old style rather quickly.

Second, you will notice that all of the nouns are capitalized. Interestingly, this is still done in German language writing. In English, it must have gotten lost along the way.

The Anatomy of An Horse is also noteworthy for its artistic merits. Of course, any book of anatomy without drawings would be almost incomprehensible. Still, the many plates of this book are beautifully rendered (even if some of them are plagiarized and reversed). The number of engravings must have made the book expensive. That could account for the fact that even though the book was designed for the "working" farrier, it apparently had a relatively small circulation at the time. However, the fact that the drawings are in many cases themselves incorrect, or in other cases not labeled correctly, in no way detracts from their beauty.

Following this introduction is the text of the book. *The Anatomy of An Horse* is divided into five books. These books are treatises that, in order of appearance in the book, describe "The Lowest Belly or Paunch," "The Middle Venter or Chest," "The Head," "The Muscles," and "The Bones." Snape's chief interest seems to lie in the circulation, the functioning of the bowels, the nervous system, and in generation and development. Accordingly, the first three books are the most detailed and descriptive; the last two books deal with their subjects in a somewhat more superficial manner.

The original book contains two appendices that are not included with this facsimile edition. These deal with "Generation, Development, the Circulation of the Blood, and Movements of the Chyle." The content of the appendices is largely reiterated in various places in the text and clarified in the author's Commentary. Snape's writing in this area is not original and is an "up-to-date" summation of seventeenth-century knowledge.

The Commentary is not intended to be a criticism of the knowledge and ideas of the day. Accordingly, it makes little effort to provide the correct anatomy, although it does point out some significant discrepancies between Snape's anatomy and what actually exists. If you are interested in the correct anatomy of the horse, there are numerous books to which you can refer to get all of the right names. Besides, an anatomy book that exists just to correct another anatomy book would be terribly boring, don't you think?

Instead, the Commentary tries to highlight the beliefs of the day, and to point out their similarities to modern thought as well as show some of the differences. In some ways, Andrew Snape is an "everyman" in medicine. He is trying to make sense of the body's functions. He is trying to explain what is happening to his patients when they get sick. He is trying to make them better. He is trying to expand the scope of knowledge for all of his fellow practitioners.

Today, with four hundred years of hindsight, it is easy to find errors in seventeenth-century thinking. Even with the obvious errors aside, it is remarkable to see how the terminology and beliefs about horses have changed. Hopefully, the Commentary that follows *The Anatomy of An Horse* is not so much a criticism as it is a celebration of the spirit and will to learn and the curiosity that leads to discovery. That spirit and curiosity has remained a constant in humans through the ages.

David W. Ramey, DVM

THE ANATOMY OF AN HORSE.

CONTAINING

An exact and full Defcription of the *Frame*, *Situation* and *Connexion* of all his *Parts*, (with their *Actions* and *Ufes*) expreft in Forty nine Copper-plates.

To which is Added

An APPENDIX,

Containing two Difcourfes:

The one, of the

GENERATION of ANIMALS;

And the other, of the

MOTION of the CHYLE,

AND THE

CIRCULATION of the BLOUD.

By *ANDREW SNAPE*, Jun. Farrier to His MAJESTY.

LONDON,

Printed by *M. Flefher* for the Authour, and are to be fold by *T. Flefher* at the *Angel* and *Crown* in S. *Paul's* Church-yard. *An. Dom.* 1683.

TO

His Most Sacred Majesty,

CHARLES II.

KING of Great *BRITAIN*, *FRANCE* and *IRELAND*, &c.

May it please Your Majesty.

NOTHING could have excused, or induc'd me unto, the Presumption of this Address unto Your MAJESTY, if Your Royal Bounty towards me, had not made such an Application my Duty. For being a Son of that Family that hath had the honour to serve the Crown of this Kingdom in the Quality of *Farriers* for these two Hundred Years, and being my self retain'd by Your MAJESTY's Favour in that capacity;

As these hereditary and personal Engagements were the first Motives that put me upon dissecting of Horses, that I might be more capable of serving Your MAJESTY in my Station; so do they entitle Your MAJESTY to the Discoveries I have made, as being but the effects of such Obligations. And I do the rather flatter my self with the hope of Your MAJESTY's Pardon in this Particular, in regard that this Essay has something in it that is *new*, and withall of *Publick* and *Common Benefit*, which Your Royal Goodness hath been pleased upon all occasions to Honour with Your Princely Encouragement and Approbation. For the Intention of publishing this Treatise being to instruct Farriers in the Frame, Situation and Use of the Parts of an Horse, which is the Subject of their Care; They will thereby, I hope, become more skilfull in applying and administring proper Remedies to the Distempers of that Generous Animal, which yields Your MAJESTY and Your Subjects that great service both in Peace and War.

May

May God Almighty long continue Your MAJESTY's Gracious Reign over a Loyal and Obedient People: And that Your MAJESTY will vouchsafe Your Royal Pardon for the boldness of this Dedication, is the humble Petition of

Your MAJESTY's

Most Loyal and

Obedient Subject

and Servant,

A. Snape.

The Introduction.

THERE is nothing gives a greater check to the progress of an Art, than to believe it is already perfected by those that have gone before us, and so to content our selves with their determinations: For had our ancient Artists been thus supinely credulous, and thought it sufficient to have traced their predecessors, limiting their wits within other mens bounds, never had time brought to light such discoveries in our Profession, nor had the mysteries of our Art been so far communicated to posterity as they already are.

This consideration induced me to make an attempt for the cultivating and improving our Art *to a greater perfection than it had as yet attain'd to: In order to which considering the several parts of it, and observing that our profession has such a correspondence with that of a Physician, that they differ not at all saving in the subject they act upon; I begun to think, whosoever would excel in the knowledge of the one, must arrive at it by the same method as the others do. Now he that once bends his mind toward the practice of Physick, first applies himself to the study of Anatomy, to understand all the Parts (with their actions and uses) of that Body which is to be the subject whereupon his Art is to be exercised; without which no wise man will think him capable of that profession. And yet how rare amongst the greatest part of those that think themselves no mean Farriers, is the knowledge of that Creature they practise upon? whereas it is plain, seeing they know not the situation and use of the parts, they can make but wide guesses at the seat or nature of the distemper, and so must administer their* Medicines *at random and at all adventures, and be in the most opprobrious sense* Horse-doctors.

Nay I will be bold to say something more (which I hope I may speak without the envy of Physicians, for whom I have a profound respect) that in some regards Anatomy is more neces-

ſary to Farriers than to them, in order to find out diſeaſes: For beſides the pulſe and the urine, and the pathognomonick ſigns (as they call them) of each diſtemper, they are aſſiſted in their enquiry moreover (not to ſay chiefly) by the complaints and relations of the Patients themſelves: whereas a Farrier having to do with a dumb creature, muſt be very curious in his knowledge of the parts with their offices, and of the ſympathy or conſent that one part hath with another; or elſe, ſeeing all his information muſt be of his own hammering out, he's like to make but a ſhort diſcovery of the diſtemper.

How neceſſary the knowledge of the parts is to the diſcerning of diſeaſes.

Now there are two things chiefly neceſſary to the judging or diſcerning of a diſeaſe, namely the Affection *or diſtemper, and the* part Affected *or diſtempered; the ſignes of which are many, but eſpecially from the* action *of the part affected: As for example, he that knows the action of the Stomach to be concoction or digeſtion, if the concoction be impaired or hindred, he may eaſily judge that the Stomach is ill affected. So likewiſe he that knows the ſituation of the* Liver *to be on the right ſide, and the* Spleen *on the left; if the right ſide be ſore or do ſwell, he cannot but know that the Liver and not the Spleen is affected, and will therefore apply his remedies accordingly. Now he that is ignorant of the parts of the Body ſhall ill know either the ſituation or action of either theſe parts mentioned or any other: and there is no way to come to the underſtanding of them but by Anatomy.*

Seeing then the profit and neceſſity of underſtanding Anatomy is ſuch and of ſo great uſe to us, I thought I could not ſpend my time and endeavours on any thing more conducing to the advancement of our profeſſion, than by applying my ſelf unto it *in the firſt place; wherein having none that have gone before me or ſhew'd me the way, I hope all ingenuous men will be favourable to my undertaking, and not be over ſevere Cenſors of any Imperfections they may poſſibly meet with in the following Treatiſe; and I hope alſo that having broken the Ice, as we ſay, all deſerving Artiſts will be excited to Emulation.*

A definition of Anatomy.

This Treatiſe then deſigning to teach the Anatomy of an Horſe, we muſt in the firſt place let you know what Anatomy *is: "It "is an opening or cutting up of the Body of any Animal or living "Creature whatſoever, whether frequenting the land or water,*

whereby

"whereby the knowledge of the frame of its body, and the use of "its parts may be attained unto.

Now this knowledge may be obtained two ways, namely by Inspection, *or by* Instruction; *both which ways are very necessary, but the first is the more certain, though the latter carrieth more grace and state.* How it is taught.

The first, which is Inspection, *is to look into either the Figures of the parts of Horses onely, or into the bodies of Horses themselves.*

The latter, which is Instruction, *is by the Voice of a Teacher or Instructor, or by the Writings of famous and renowned men.*

As to the Figures *of the parts, they are thus far necessary,* viz. *they daily represent to us such parts as we have not the opportunity to see in the bodies themselves: For it is not easy to find in all places (nor at such times when we stand in most need of them) such a store of dead bodies as is necessary for us to practise upon; wherefore to supply the want of such bodies, I do think these Figures usefull, and have therefore accordingly by a curious draught or delineation represented to you such observations as are made in true dissections, not by copying out* every *part, but chiefly those that are most necessary for us to understand, omitting those of less consideration, lest I should make this Volume swell too big, and become too chargeable, whereby such would be discouraged from buying it, for whom I chiefly intend it.* The Figures of the parts how far necessary.

But although I approve of these Figures as necessary, to be by *us, upon occasion; yet this caution I must give to the Student, that he do not trust too much to these* Copies, *as I may call them, without practising upon the* original *body it self: For as it is not possible to make a good Commander by viewing onely representative Armies, without practice and experience in real Engagements; so is it vain for you to think to attain to the exact knowledge of Anatomy by minding the Figures onely.* A Caution.

Neither would I have any that undertakes this study to be discouraged, for fear they should not get such bodies as I have *mentioned (I mean Horſes bodies) ſufficient for them to practiſe upon; for they may, to ſupply the want of ſuch, take the bodies of Aſſes or Mules, of Sheep and Oxen, Hogs or Dogs, any of which come near the bodies you deſire, eſpecially as to the ſituation and uſe, as alſo hidden* motions *of the* Internal *parts: for if thoſe motions be the ſame in Beaſts as in Men, as by a very worthy* * *Authour they are affirmed to be, (who ſaith that the motions of the Heart, the Arteries, the Midriff, the Brain and Guts are the ſame in Beaſts as in Men) they muſt certainly be the ſame in one Beaſt as in another.*

* See Doctor *Crooke*, lib. 1. chap. 9.

The method of Anatomy.

Next we come to ſhew after what manner *you are to take in hand the diſſection of any of theſe Creatures, and that you muſt not doe confuſedly nor diſorderly, but with due courſe of proceeding. For the doing of which take theſe following Rules.*

Firſt then, you muſt begin with that which is beſt known and moſt eaſie, which are the external or outward parts; for as much as the knowledge of them is moſt neceſſary, as to Cures Chirurgical: and theſe parts are commonly diſtinguiſhed into two kinds; one of which are called ſpermatical *and ſolid, which are ſuppoſed to be bred of ſeed, and ſuch are Bones, Griſtles and Ligaments; and the other* ſanguineous, *ſaid to be generated of bloud, as Muſcles.*

I ſhall not in this place give you any particular inſtructions for the anatomiſing any of theſe parts, referring you for them to the book it ſelf: onely advertiſe you of this, that when you deſire a Body for examining the ſolid parts, the bodies of old and lean Horſes are the fitteſt, in regard the fleſh and fat will not ſo much hinder, nor hide the parts from you, as in fat Horſes they will.

You are alſo to obſerve that there is a two-fold way of proceeding in diſſection: The one is where there is a plenty, the other where there is a ſcarcity of dead bodies. If there be a plenty, then you may look into the Muſcles of one, into the Entrails of another, and into the Veſſels of a third, &c. *not mattering though you ſpoil one part in diſcovering another: but where they are ſo ſcarce that you can get but one body and that ſeldome too, then if you would ſee all in that body, great skill muſt be uſed to ſhew every thing in its order and place.*

Now

The INTRODUCTION.

Now order of dissection requires that you should first begin with the Head, it being the most noble and excellent part; next to that the Chest, and lastly the Belly: but this (as I have said) is not to be done where there is but one body, for there you must begin with those parts that are most subject to Corruption, wherefore you must first cut up the Lower Belly, then the Chest, and lastly the Head; both which ways are often used; the first being called the way of dignity, and the other of diuturnity; the one being more noble, and the other of a longer durance.

I shall not here treat of any of the parts contained in these three Regions or Venters, but will leave them till I come to speak of them in their order in the following Treatise, my design being to be as brief as may be, and not to repeat any thing over several times, as I have seen some Authours have done. Therefore I shall put an end to this Introduction when I shall have informed you, that all the parts which fall under the Anatomists knife to be examined are commonly reduced to two heads, namely, simple *or similar, and* compound *or dissimilar.*

The division of the parts, into 1. Simple,

Those that are generally accounted simple *parts, are in number ten, namely, a Bone, a Gristle, a Ligament, a Membrane, a Fibre, a Nerve, an Artery, a Vein, Flesh and Skin. These are called* simple *or* similar, *because every particle of them is of the same name and substance; as every part of a bone is bone,* &c.

Yet three of these ten, though they are generally accounted simple parts, if strictly taken cannot be truly reputed so; for first, Veins are made of a coat, fibres and valves; secondly, Arteries are made of two coats or skins different from one another; and for Nerves, their inner substance is medullar or marrowey, and the outward, membranous or skinny: so that of truly similar or simple parts, there are onely seven, namely, Bones, Gristles, Ligaments, Membranes, Fibres, Flesh and Skin.

2. Compound.

The Dissimilar or compound *parts are those, which, contrary to the* simple, *may be divided into several particles or parcels of unlike or different substance and denomination: As for*

for example, A Leg may be cut into ſeveral pieces, yet not into ſeveral Legs, but into Fleſh, Bones, Veins and other things which it is compounded of; whereas, as was ſaid, a ſimilar part though it be divided into parcels, yet thoſe are ſtill like one another, and of the ſame nature: for ſuppoſe a Ligament be cut into many pieces, every piece partakes onely and truly of the nature of a Ligament, and all remain what they were before, their length or other accident onely excepted.

Thus much for the Introduction, *wherein I mainly intended to ſhew the method of Anatomy, and to hint the reaſon of my undertaking; It now remains that I addreſs my ſelf to the Work it ſelf, which ſhall be writ with the greateſt plainneſs its nature is capable of, that I may thereby attain to that wiſhed end I ſet before me, namely, the benefiting of my Reader.*

THE

In Feilds nor Pastures, Woods nor Forests wide,
Does any Beast So Noble as thus Reside. ~
His Nostrills raise a Tempest when he blows;
His Feet produce an Earthquake when he goes.

Runs he: the Swiftest Winds behind retire, ~
Whilst from his Eyes, flow streams of flaming fire.
Wouldst know his Parts: the following Book peruse,
Which shews of each the Figure, Seat and Use.

THE ANATOMY OF AN HORSE.

BOOK I.

Of the Lowest Belly or Paunch.

CHAP. I.

Of the Parts investing the whole Body, and first of the Hair.

BEFORE I take in pieces this Goodly Creature, It will not be amiss if I first give you an account of all these Parts as they lie in order, beginning with that which first appeareth to our View, and that is the Scarf-skin adorned with hairs, wherein (as in a Case) Nature hath wrapped this stately Beast; besides which there are other four, that, with this, are *common* to the whole body, which are, first, the true skin, which lieth next under it; then the fleshy pannicle; under that the fat; and lastly the common membrane of the Muscles. Besides these five, there are other Investing parts, but they are onely *proper* to particular parts of the body, to which I will speak in their due place, and onely of the *common* ones here.

First then I will begin with the *Hairs*, because they meet first with the Sense. They are said to be ingendred of a clammy and earthy Excrement of the third concoction, so that themselves are reputed not so properly to be called parts of the body, as Excrements. They are void of sense and of animal life, yet they have a vegetative life, such as Plants have, to which they owe their growth. *Whereof Hairs are ingendred.*

These

How nourished. These Hairs are by some thought to have for their *nourishment* a proportionable quantity of that juice of which they are generated, continually ministred unto them. Others think that the Hairs being hollow and porous are nourished as the Feathers of Fowl are, and that is by bloud; for if one pull off a Feather from a young Bird that is unfledged, a pretty deal of its stem will appear bloudy. But though we should grant that the matter of their nourishment were made of bloud, yet certainly it must be very much altered and degenerate from its own nature, before it can be adapted to the hair, seeing the hair of a Man's head (for example) grows not onely in living persons, whose bloud runs briskly in their Arteries and Veins, whereby it is kept from corruption, but also in the dead, in whom the whole mass of bloud is devoid of all nutritive power, as has been often observed in bodies preserved unburied. But whatsoever the humour be that nourishes them, it is thrust through the skin by the pores thereof, the action and heat of the body assisting thereunto, where the purer part of it enters the roots of the hair, but the more earthy not being able to enter such almost unperceivable pores, is driven out amongst the hair where it becomes dust; which dust is that that is brought forth with the Curry-combe when a Horse is drest. From hence then it is, that a Horse, though he be never so well dressed one morning, and never so clean kept till the next, he shall notwithstanding be as full of dust as he was the morning before; for the cleaner the skin of a Horse is kept, the more open are its pores to transmit a more plentifull nourishment to the hair, whence also there is a greater collection of this excrementitious dust.

How the Hair comes to fall off. And hence may be gathered a reason of the *shedding* of the hair, which is observed to happen in many Horses that have ill keeping, such as your Cart-horses that seldom have any labour bestowed upon them, for want of which dressing, to remove the dust which lieth upon the mouths of the pores or at the roots of the hairs, the passages, through which the juice should come that nourishes the hair, are obstructed or stopped, and so like dead Leaves from a Tree in Autumn they drop off, or as untimely Fruit falls before the season of the year requireth it.

Reasons for the different colour of the hairs. As for the *Colours* of the hairs, they are various, according as is the humour which doth predominate in the body: for such as the humour is which is driven forth towards the skin for their nourishment, such will the colour of the hair be. As for Instance:

If the cholerick humour doth most predominate, then are the hairs of a black, a Sorrel or a Chestnut colour; If bloud most predominate, then will the Horse be a bright Bay or Roan; If flegme, then the Horse will be of a milk-white or yellow-dun; If melancholy, then will the Horse be of an Iron-gray or Mouse-dun. Thus much for the colour of the hairs, next I come to the use of them.

Their use. The *use* of the hairs is, first, to cover the skin; secondly, to defend it; thirdly, to be an ornament to it; and lastly, as I have before shewed, to suck up that excrementitious superfluous juice which through the pores of the skin is sent from all parts of the body to them.

CHAP.

CHAP. II.

Of the Cuticle or Scarf-skin.

THE Hide on which the hairs already ſpoken of do grow, conſiſts of two Skins, the outer of which is called the *Scarf-skin*, ſerving to defend the Body from outward Injuries, and for that intent is of it ſelf Inſenſible, that it may the better indure the violence of the weather, or other harms which many times happen to it. And for that cauſe, Nature hath ſo ordered it, that if at any time it happeneth to be rubb'd off, as often it is by an ill Saddle, and many other ways, it groweth again without a ſcar or blemiſh, provided the Parts under it (as particularly the true Skin) be not alſo violated; for they being ſpermatical Parts, or made of Seed, cannot eaſily be reſtored, which is the reaſon that moſt Wounds will not heal up without a ſcar. Now this Scarf-skin having its matter (of which it is made) from the true Skin and the Veſſels that terminate in it, which are of all ſorts, both Veins, Arteries and Nerves, none of which reach any farther than the true Skin, it is apparent that this Skin is without ſenſe, it being their office alone to communicate both life, ſenſe and motion to all parts of the Body. And that this Skin is void of ſenſe, may be ſeen by the cutting of it; as thus, If you cut onely through this Skin, when you go to Rowel a Horſe, you ſhall not find the Horſe move for it, neither will it bleed; but if you cut ſo far as to touch the true Skin under it, you will find him both ſtir and bleed, for then you touch the little threads of the Veſſels, and by violating them, you cauſe the Horſe to feel pain, and alſo bloud to iſſue forth. *The Scarf-skin.*

The *uſe* of this Skin, beſides being a covering to the whole Body, is to cover the mouths of thoſe ſmall hairy Veſſels already ſpoken of, that the bloud, ſpirits, or other ichorous or watery Matter do not iſſue from them, which otherwiſe they would. Yet its Pores are ſo large as to permit the vapourous moiſture that is thruſt out of all parts of the Body to it, to paſs through them, either in the form of ſweat, or by inſenſible tranſpiration. Theſe Pores being many times obſtructed or conſtringed by a ſudden cold taken after hard riding, by giving the Horſe cold Water too ſoon after it, or by waſhing him too high in cold Water when he is hot, the Vapours are thereby hindered from coming forth, and ſo are detained between the two Skins, and there generate evill Diſtempers, or at leaſt fall from thence into the Limbs, and there cauſe Inflammations and breakings out, which we call *Greaſe in the heels* or *Scratchets.* *Its uſe.*

CHAP. III.

Of the Cutis or true Skin.

The true Skin. Its ſubſtance. UNder this Scarf, lieth the *true Skin,* which the Latines call *Cutis.* Its *ſubſtance,* as I have before ſhewed, is ſaid to be ſpermatical, ſuch as being once loſt, cannot be reſtored as formerly it was, but is reunited by a cicatrice or ſcar, that is bred of the dried and conſtringed fleſh under it; which is the reaſon no hairs will grow upon that part of the Skin where the ſcar is, becauſe it is callous and deſtitute of Pores in which they ſhould grow. This Skin doth encompaſs the whole Body as well as the Scarf, and hath the ſame paſſages for the receiving in, and letting out, for the eaſe and relief of the Body, as that hath.

Veſſels. It hath for its nouriſhment, life, and ſenſe, *Veſſels* of all ſorts, Veins, Arteries and Nerves, divaricated and branched through it in the ſmalleſt hair-like threads, all which terminate in it, none of them being inſerted into the Cuticle.

Colour. As for its *colour,* it varieth as do the humours in the Body; for that humour which moſt abounds, coloureth it with its proper reſpective colour; as for example, If bloud moſt abound, then is it moſt red; if choler do moſt predominate, then is it yellowiſh; and ſo for the other humours.

Uſe. Its *uſe* is principally to inveſt and defend the Body, as I have ſaid before of the Scarf-skin: for as that keeps it from the violent impreſſion of either exceſſive heat, or cold; ſo doth this Skin reſtrain, and, as it were, wall in (as in a Caſtle) all the ſpirits and natural heat, which would otherwiſe in hot weather, or in violent exerciſe be ſo faſt ſpent, that they would leave the vital parts deſtitute, which would occaſion the loſs of your Beaſt. But though Nature has made this proviſion to hinder the diſſipation of the ſpirits, yet has ſhe framed the Skin (as well as the Scarf-skin) full of ſmall Pores, through which upon violent exerciſe do iſſue in great plenty hot and moiſt vapours, which are that we call *ſweat*; yea though the Beaſt be at reſt, if the Air be any whit mild or temperate, warm ſteams are continually a paſſing through them by inſenſible tranſpiration.

It's alſo as ſerviceable in cold weather, for then the more fiercely it is beſieged by the cold, the narrower do the aforeſaid Pores purſe up themſelves, whereby the internal heat is detained within, and the external cold kept out.

CHAP.

CHAP. IV.

Of the fleſhy Pannicle.

The names of the fleſhy Pannicle.

NEXT to the true Skin, lieth the fleſhy Pannicle, called *membrana Carnoſa*, or *panniculus carnoſus*, becauſe in moſt parts of the Body, it comes near to the nature of fleſh, and is truly muſcular.

Its ſituation, and extent.

In Man this Membrane is ſaid to lie under the Fat, though ſome very curious Anatomiſts deny that Man has any ſuch Membrane at all, ſave in the Forehead; and of this opinion is Dr. *Gliſſon*. I will not intermeddle in that Controverſie, as being not proper for me; but in Horſes it lies immediately under the Skin, above the Fat, and is more like to a Muſcle than a Membrane. In fleying off the Skin, you muſt be very carefull and curious, or elſe you will take this Pannicle off along with it, it is ſo cloſely knit to it by Fibres and innumerable Veſſels that go between. It is of the ſame extent and figure as the true Skin, inveſting the whole Body as that does; but in ſome Parts it is almoſt wholly fleſhy, and in others altogether membranous.

Its Veſſels.

It has *Veſſels* of all ſorts as the Skin has, for before they can reach the Skin, they muſt pierce through this Membrane; and as they paſs through, they ſend forth many ſmall twigs into it, both Veins, Arteries and Nerves, but eſpecially Nerves to aſſiſt its motion, whence it is by ſome called the nervous Membrane.

Its Uſe.

The *uſe* of it is chiefly to ſerve for a Muſcle to move the Skin, whereby the Beaſt ſhakes off the Flies, or any other thing that offends him. It ſerves alſo to defend the neighbouring Parts, and to ſtrengthen in their paſſage the Veſſels which are diſſeminated into the true Skin. It alſo hinders the Fat from being melted and ſpent by the continual motion of the Muſcles. And laſtly, it helpeth to heal or cloſe up the Skin when it is cut or otherwiſe hurt; for the Skin being a ſpermatick Part cannot be bred anew, and therefore this fleſhy Membrane helps to glew as it were the ſides of it together again, growing into one body with it, and making what we call a *Scar*.

CHAP. V.

Of the Fat, and Common Membrane of the Muſcles.

Fat, its difference and matter.

FAT is of two ſorts, and is diſtinguiſhed by two ſeveral Names as well in Latin as Engliſh. That which we are to ſpeak of in this Chapter is called in Latin *pinguedo*, and in Engliſh *Fat*; but that which is within the Belly and makes up the Caul and Meſentery and covers the Kidneys, is named *ſevum*, Suet or *Tallow*. The former will not congeal ſo quickly or ſo hard as this latter will. Both the one and the other are made of an oily part of the bloud; and this we are to treat of here, is congealed between the Carnous Membrane deſcribed in the foregoing Chapter, and the Common Membrane of the Muſcles.

How generated.

This Fat is the fourth common covering of the whole Body, for there is no Part which has the reſt of the common coverings, but has this alſo, if the Horſe be not extreme lean; though the fatteſt have it not in any great plenty. Now as all Food that is eaten, conſiſts of ſeveral parts or principles, which the Chymiſts can ſeparate one from another, namely Salt, Spirit and Oyl; ſo the Food, that conſiſts of theſe ſeveral principles, when it is taken into the Body, and concocted in the Stomach (which is natural Chymiſtry, as I may call it) has them ſo looſened one from another, that each principle paſſes into the nouriſhment and increaſe of that part that is of the ſame nature with it. Amongſt the reſt the oily part, (which is otherwiſe called the Sulphureous, becauſe it will flame like Brimſtone) ſweating as it were through the pores of the Veſſels and ſubjacent parts towards the ſurface of the Body, is ſtopt by the cloſeneſs and compactneſs of the fleſhy Membrane, and there congeals into Fat. Now this Fat is not one continued body as Butter or (what we call) tryed Suet is; but is included in innumerable membranous partitions or cells, almoſt like Honey-combs, (which it is likely are borrowed from the fleſhy Pannicle) which makes the Fat to appear ſomewhat ſpongy. It is not eaſie to give a reaſon of this oily humour's turning into Fat; for it cannot be by cold, ſeeing the Beaſt is always actually warm; much leſs can it be by heat, which is apter to melt Fat into Oyl, than to harden Oyl into Fat: therefore ſome make a moderate heat to be the efficient of it. 'Tis true indeed that the Beaſt is moderately hot, and we ſee by experience that Fat is generated; but that *that* is the cauſe of *this*, I dare not affirm. My apprehenſion of it is this: That when the oily Matter iſſues out of the Veins and Arteries, &c. there paſſes along with it much thin watry humour; And when they both come to the fleſhy Membrane, this latter being thin, evaporates through it and is evacuated by ſweat or inſenſible tranſpiration; but the other being thicker and more clammy, is forced to ſtay behind, and loſing by degrees that wheyiſh humour that before kept it liquid, it curdles into Fat.

The uſes of Fat.

The uſe of the Fat is, like a Garment, to keep the Body warm, and cheriſh the natural heat, which by its clammineſs it hinders from evaporating too much; and on the other ſide by its thickneſs it ſtoppeth the Pores ſo, that the cold cannot enter in.

It alſo fills up the empty ſpaces between the Muſcles, and the wrinkles of the Skin, by which the Horſe is made plump, ſmooth and beautifull; and therefore old, lean and decrepit Horſes are deformed for want of Fat.

It ſerves alſo as a pillow or bulwark againſt any violence, either from blows, bruiſes or heavy weights, and the like.

Finally, it relieveth ſuch Creatures as abound with it, in time of ſcarcity or want of ſuſtenance, by being converted into nouriſhment; for it ſerves as aliment, and holdeth the parts of the Body in play, till the Creature attain its proper Food.

The common membrane of the Muſcles.

The fifth and laſt common Covering of the Body, is the *Common Membrane of the Muſcles.* This is ſpread over all the Muſcles (immediately under the Fat) and is knit by Fibres to that Membrane which is proper to each Muſcle, but ſomewhat looſely, that it might not hinder their

their motion by inveſting them too cloſely. It is ſaid to ariſe from the Back-bone, becauſe it cleaves moſt firmly to the Spine thereof, and is ſtronger there, than in its other Parts. In an Horſe it is as thick as Parchment, and very ſtrong. And its uſe is to confirm and ſtrengthen the Muſcles in general in their proper ſituation, and to be as it were a Caſe for them to move glibly in, and to defend them from injuries.

CHAP. VI.

Of the Inveſting Parts proper to the Lower Belly.

HAVING ſhewed you what are the *common inveſting* or containing parts of the whole Body, I come now to ſhew which are thoſe that are *proper* to the Lower Belly in particular, and thoſe are onely two, beſides thoſe common ones already ſpoken of, namely the *Muſcles* of the Paunch, and the *Rim of the Belly*.

Now by the *Lower Belly* we underſtand all that cavity (and onely that) which is below the Midriff, and is encompaſſed by the ſhort Ribs, the point of the Breaſt-bone, Loins, Haunch-bones, and Share-bones, and is filled with the Guts and other Entrails.

The Muſcles of the Abdomen or Paunch.

The *Muſcles* are in all Horſes of a like number, which is on each ſide four. The firſt pair that ſhew themſelves are called the *External oblique* pair; the next are the *Internal oblique* pair; the third are the two *right* or *ſtreight* Muſcles; and under theſe are the two *tranſverſe* Muſcles, ſo called from their going croſs the Belly.

But before I proceed any further in deſcribing theſe Muſcles, I will firſt ſhew what a *Muſcle* is, and whereof it is compounded, and alſo the ſeveral uſes of the Muſcles in general.

What a Muſcle is.

The Muſcles, if you take them in a large ſignification, are all that which we call Fleſh; which Fleſh may be divided into many pieces or parcels without cutting or breaking any of them, if with care undertaken; and each piece ſo ſeparable, is named a Muſcle.

Muſcles are the inſtrument of voluntary motion.

Now theſe pieces have each their ſeveral diſtinct Epithets, appellations or names from ſeveral conſiderations, as from their ſituation, ſhape, uſe, &c. but are all called Muſcles, their office being to perform the *voluntary motion:* which motion is performed ſix ſeveral ways, namely, upwards, downwards, forwards, backwards, to the right hand and to the left. All which motions are performed in this manner.

You muſt know that all or moſt of the Muſcles of the Body have each their Oppoſite or Antagoniſt, ſo that the one being contracted or drawn together, (which is its proper motion) the oppoſite at the ſame time is relaxed or looſned; and contrarily when that which upon the former motion was relaxed, does it ſelf enter upon motion, it is contracted, whilſt that which was before contracted, is now relaxed. As for example, when you ſtretch out either your Arm, or Leg, that motion is performed by one of theſe Muſcles; and when you draw your Arm, or Leg back again, that is performed by the other.

But

But here let none so far misunderstand me as to think that either an Arm or Leg can be either stretcht forth or drawn back by the help of *one* Muscle alone; but *as* to either of the before-mentioned Limbs there are several parts belonging, *so* do the distinct Muscles of every part perform (at the same time) the offices aforesaid.

Neither can this voluntary motion be performed without the help of a Sinew or Nerve, by which the Spirits are brought from the Brain which give the Muscles their moving faculty.

Involuntary or natural motion is performed without Muscles, properly so called.

Now there are other motions of the Body which are not performed by the Muscles, such as is (according to some) the pulsation of the Heart and Arteries, the peristaltick motion of the Stomach and Guts, of the passage of the Gall, and of the Ureters, and several other Parts which have their continual motions whether the Horse be sleeping or waking, and will perform their several motions as well in Men as Beasts, whether we will or not. Wherefore these are called *not Voluntary*, or *Natural.*

I shall in the next place shew what parts the Muscles are compounded of, and those are agreed upon by all Authours of Anatomy to be these.

A Muscle is an organical and dissimilar part.

Of what simple parts it consists.

A Muscle being an organical Part is composed of Nerves, Flesh, Fibres, Veins and Arteries, all covered or invested with a proper Coat or Skin. It is called *organical*, because it is the instrument or organ of an action, to wit, motion. And that it is also dissimilar, the several kinds of parts whereof it is made, do evidently prove. The several uses of the parts that make up a Muscle are these: The Fibres and Tendon are the immediate instruments of its action; The Flesh properly so called filleth up the interstices or distances between the Fibres; The Arteries by importing vital spirit and bloud do conserve the inbred heat, and help to nourish it; The Veins do convey back to the Heart all that bloud that remains from the nourishment of the Muscle; The Nerves convey animal Spirit to the Fibres and Tendon, whereby they are enabled for their action; and the Membrane or Skin which incompasseth the Muscle, doth keep it together, and distinguishes one from another.

Why called a Muscle.

Having shewed what a Muscle is, and the several simple parts whereof it is made, I shall next shew you why it is so called. It is called *mus*, or *musculus*, by the Latins, for that it is like a fley'd Mouse, or a Fish which is called *musculus*; and by some Authours it is called by the name of *lacertus*, from its similitude with a Creature called a Lizard. Yet there can be no one certain figure whereby to resemble it, by reason of its sundry shapes; but that it is like a fley'd Mouse in colour, cannot be denied.

Whence Muscles have distinct names.

Now the Muscles being many in number have accordingly many names, which names they take from either their Figure, their Situation, or their Action, and many times from their Use; also sometimes from their Insertion, and sometimes from their Magnitude.

And although there be such difference in the Muscles, in respect of their Figures, their Magnitude, their Situation, and the like, yet are they so united or conjoyned together through the whole Body, in so close a manner, that in many places they are hard to be separated, except at some times, when either wind, some wheyish humour or some other matter gets between them, and then many times they will gape, and are at some distance the one from the other.

Yet are they not so closely united neither, but that by a carefull and expert Dissector they may be separated, and one divided from another;

after

after which, to see the several parts of a Muscle severally, you must divide it also, which is on this manner.

Some divide a Muscle into two parts, which are a fleshy and a tendinous part; Again, they divide it into other three parts, namely, the Head, the Middle and the Tail. By the *Head* is to be understood the beginning or original of a Muscle, which is one while ligamentous and nervous, and otherwhiles fleshy: By the *Middle* is that part meant which is absolutely fleshy; and by the *Tail*, the Tendon, consisting of the numerous Fibres that are extended through the Muscle, and the Membrane that invests it, which grow by little and little into one body, and compose this Tendon, that is the tail of the Muscle. It is sometimes round, sometimes broad; other times long, and otherwhiles short, thicker or slenderer according to the part it appertains to, or according to the use it is put to; it being but necessary that those Parts which are moved most strongly or vehemently, should have thicker and stronger Tendons. Thus much for the Muscles in general. *A Muscle divided into parts.*

Now I come to the particular Muscles, the first of which are the Muscles of the *Abdomen* or Paunch, of which I have spoken something in the beginning of this Chapter, the which I shall now further prosecute, and let you know how they are situated. The pair that in dissection first offer themselves are called the *Oblique* (or slanting) *Descending External* pair, which pair are the broadest of all the rest, though it is by many Authours said that the oblique internal are equal in figure, magnitude, strength and action. The original or rise of these Muscles is from the side of the Breast-bone, the lower edge of five or six of the lowest Ribs, and from the tips of the cross or transverse processes of the Joints of the Rack-bone in the Loins. Their rise from the Ribs imitates the teeth of a Saw; for springing with a narrow point from the lower side of the Rib, every such point grows broader and broader, till it unite with the two next it on each side, so that there is a space of above an inch between every point, into which empty spaces the greater Saw-like Muscle of the Breast ends with like points. From their rise they run sloping downwards toward the *white line* (so called) in the middle of the Belly; but before they reach half way thither, they lose their fleshy substance, and become tendinous, and their Tendon is so united to the common Membrane of the Muscles, described in the foregoing Chapter, that it seems to become one with it, and running over the streight Muscles is inserted into the foresaid white Line, down even to the very Share-bone, into which also it is inserted. *The Oblique descending external pair.*

The next to these are the *Oblique Ascending Internal* pair, so called because of the contrary course of their Fibres to those of the External; for as those *descend* obliquely or aslant, so do these *ascend* in like manner. Their rise is from the Rib of the Haunch-bone, and from the processes of the *vertebræ* of the Loins and *os sacrum*; and their Tendon is extended to the short Ribs partly, and partly to the white line, above the Navel, adhering to the common Membrane of the Muscles as was said before of the oblique descending, where it is not cover'd by the Tendon of that Muscle. These have a different *action* from the former; for whereas the External pair do draw the lower part of the Belly towards the Breast, where they have their original; these on the contrary draw down the Chest with a kind of slanting motion towards the Hips; it being the action of all Muscles to draw towards their original, and the original of these Muscles is (as was said) at the Rib of the Haunch-bone. *The Oblique ascending internal pair.* *Their Action.*

The right or streight pair. After these follow the *Right* or *Streight* Pair, so called because their Fibres run streight down the Belly as do the Muscles themselves: for their original is at the sides of the sword-fashioned Gristle at the end of the Breast-bone, and from the gristly ends of the bastard Ribs, whence they go all along the eminentest part of the Belly streight to the Share-bone where they terminate. Now in these Muscles there are several Inscriptions or tendinous Interstices, which are, according to the bigness of the Horse, more or fewer in number, but most commonly there are in each Muscle eight, not so fair indeed as in Humane Bodies, but yet so plain, that they do distinguish the Muscles into nine parts or more, as there are eight of these inscriptions or more; and besides, each part has a distinct Nerve: and yet notwithstanding, because they cannot be easily separated one from another, they do by most Anatomists go for onely one pair. On the inside of these Muscles are to be seen the Epigastrick Arteries and Veins ascending, and the Mammary Arteries and Veins descending, which by an ancient Tradition have been held in Humane Bodies to inosculate one with another, the Arteries with the Arteries, and the Veins with the Veins: but later and more inquisitively curious Anatomists have discovered it to be a meer fancy, invented to support the erroneous Opinion, That whilst the Young was in the Womb, it was nourished with bloud carried to it by the Hypogastrick Arteries and Veins; but after the birth, the bloud altering its course, regurgitated up from the Womb, by the Epigastrick Vessels, which inosculating with the Mammary, conveyed it to the Breasts, where it was converted into Milk. This I say was the opinion as to Women, which has in several particulars been detected of errour: and may receive a further confutation in Mares, from the different situation of their Udders from the Breasts in Women; whereas these Vessels have the same Course in both. The *action* of these Muscles is to shorten the Belly by drawing the Breast and Share-bone towards one another, whereby it is drawn as it were on a heap, to squeez forth the Excrements or Urine, whence Dogs that strain so hard to dung, have these Muscles arising as high up as the Channel-bones.

Their Action.

The pyramidal Muscles. There are other two Muscles (sometimes to be found) which do rest upon the Tendons of the Right Muscles at the lower end of them, which I have not yet spoken of, and these are called the *pyramidal* Muscles. They are of a triangular figure, and their use is to assist the streight Muscles in their squeezing forth the Excrements, saith *Fallopius*. I believe these Muscles are so seldom found, that they ought to be accounted *lusus Naturæ*, a sport of Nature; for I do not remember that ever I have observed any other here, but what ought to be accounted the lowest part or portion of the streight Muscles before described.

The transverse or overthwart Muscles. Under all these lie the transverse or overthwart Muscles, so called from their own and their Fibres running cross or overthwart the Belly. They are of a quadrangular or foursquare figure, and do stick so close to the Rim of the Belly (which is under them) that they cannot easily be separated.

Their Original is from the one or two lowest bastard Ribs, the transverse processes of the Joints or *vertebræ* of the Loyns, and the Haunch-bones; and their Tendons reach to the white line, where they terminate.

Their Action. Their *Action* is to press the Guts for the expulsion of Excrements.

Now

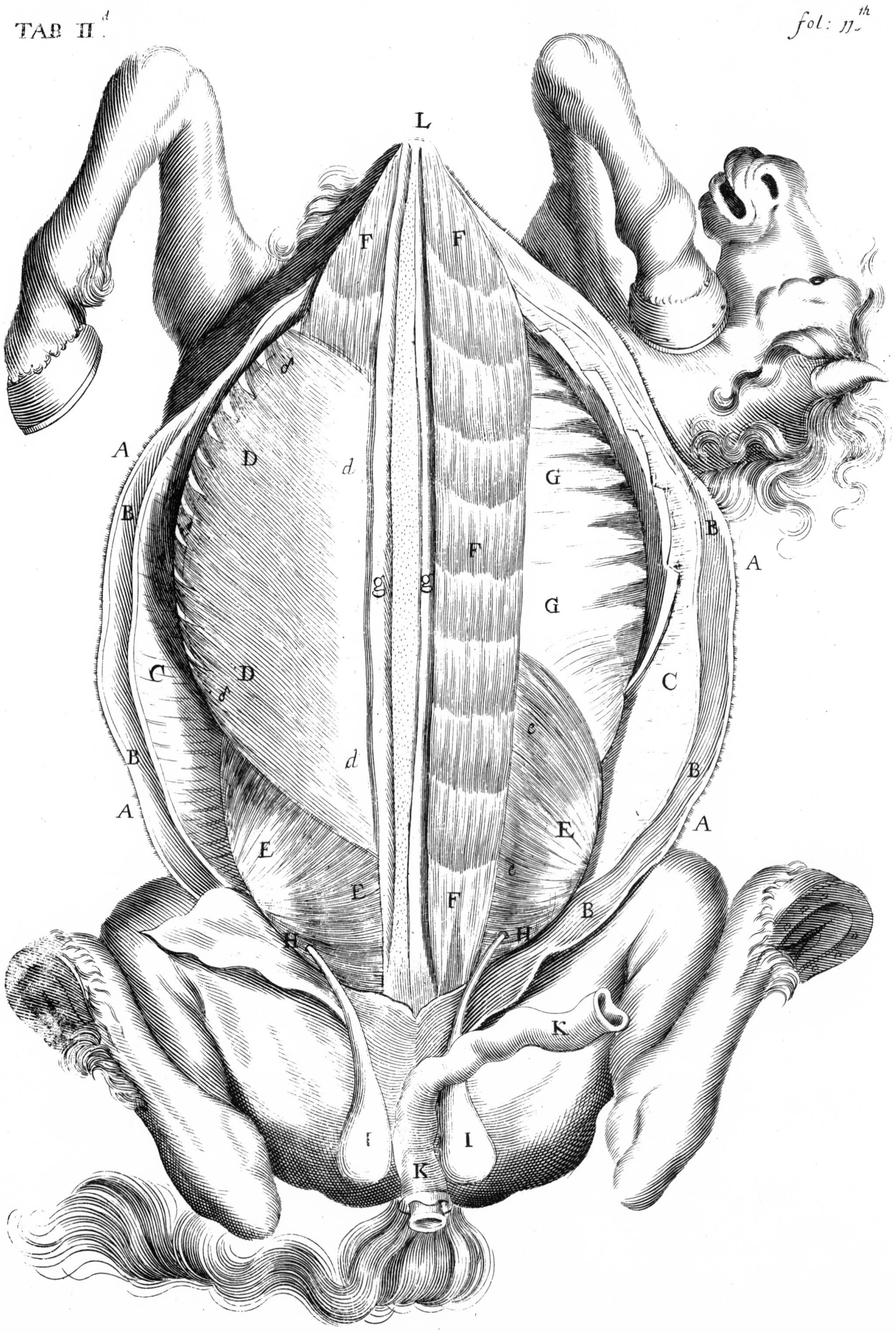
L
F
F
d
A
D
d
G
B
B
F
A
g
g
G
C
D
C
d
e
B
d
B
A
A
E
E
E
e
F
B
H
H
K
I
I
K

Now as each Muscle has a peculiar action to it self, which is that already ascribed to each, so have all these ten Muscles two Actions general to them all conjoinedly, which are these; The *first* is, that they serve for a defence or bulwark for all the Parts underneath them, and do by their flesh (which pretty much aboundeth in them) cherish their natural heat and assist concoction; The *next* is, that they do all assist together in the compressing of the Guts for the voiding of the excrements, the Midriff assisting thereunto, by whose help the excrements are thrust downwards, which otherwise would be onely squeezed together, and not thrust any more downward than upward.

The action of all these Muscles together.

I think it not amiss in this place to explain what it is I call the *white Line*, for fear the naming of it so often as I have done in this Chapter, without shewing what it is, should puzzle the Reader.

The *white Line* is nothing else, but the extremities or tendinous endings of these Muscles of the Paunch, and is called *white* from its colour, becoming so, because it consists of Tendons and Fibres onely, wherewith no fleshy part or particle is interwoven, whereby to change or alter the colour. It distinguisheth the Belly into two parts, a right and a left, and is placed all along the middle of the Belly both below and above the Navel, running from the sword-pointed Gristle of the Breast as low as to the Share-bone.

The white *Line what it is.*

Now the *Udder* being an external part of the Belly in Mares, I might in this place (in order) treat of it; but because its Action, to wit the making of Milk, has so near relation to the Foal, for which it provides nourishment, I shall omit it in this place, and describe it at the latter end of this *first* Book, after I have done with the generative parts of Mares, and the breeding, nourishing, &c. of the Young in the Womb.

The *Second* Table representeth all the Investing parts of the *Abdomen*, as well proper as common.

AA *Shew the Skin and Scarf-skin turn'd back.*

BB *The fleshy Membrane likewise turn'd back, with a little sprinkling of Fat on its inside.*

CC *The Common Membrane that invests the Muscles, in like manner turn'd back.*

DD *The obliquely descending Muscle expressed* in situ *on the right side.*

dd *The Tendon of the same running to the white Line.*

δδ *Its saw-like origine from the Ribs.*

EE *The obliquely ascending Muscle, with its Tendon* e e, *on the same side, likewise* in situ.

FF *The Streight exprest to the full on the left side, but onely in part on the right, because the Tendons of the obliquely descending, and ascending Muscles run over it.*

GG *The transverse Muscle exprest to the full on the left side, but hid on the right by the two oblique.*

gg *The* white Line *and outer Skin of the Rim of the Belly cut in sunder, that the Fat contained between the outer and inner Skin of the Rim may appear.*

HH *The perforations in the obliquely ascending Muscles, by which the spermatick Vessels do pass out of the* Abdomen *into the Cod.*

II *The Stones.* K *The Yard.* L *The* Sternum *or Breast-bone.*

CHAP. VII.

Of the Rim of the Belly, called the Peritonæum.

THE Muſcles of the Paunch being all removed, as alſo their Tendons which make the white Line before ſpoken of, the *Peritonæum* or Rim of the Belly comes next into ſight.

What the Peritonæum is. This *Peritonæum* is of a ſpermatick ſubſtance (as are all other Membranes or Skins) and is of an oval Figure, or like a long faſhioned Egg, for it compaſſeth all the Lower Belly and ingirts all the Parts therein contained, and alſo ſtrengthneth them, from whence it hath its name, from its office of *ſpreading* and *ſtretching about*. It is thin and ſoft, that it might not be either heavy or burthenſom; yet is it very ſtrong and compact, that it might be ſtretched without danger, when the Belly is full of Meat, or the Womb is full of the Burthen. Its inſide is ſmooth, and by reaſon of the Guts is daubed with moiſture; but its outſide is rough, which makes it ſtick ſo cloſe to the Muſcles that lie above it, that they can hardly be ſeparated, as I have before ſhewed.

Its original. It takes its *original* from the *vertebræ* or joints of the Loins, where it is very thick, and is therefore believed to proceed from the Membrane that inveſts the Marrow in the Back-bone, and is propagated from the double Membrane of the Brain. It is in all places double, and betwixt its Membranes I have always obſerved good ſtore of Fat, which Anatomiſts do not ſpeak of in other Creatures. The Veſſels run along this Fat between the Membranes, that they may be the better ſecured and defended, and may with more ſafety diſperſe their branches all over it; and for that purpoſe it is *perforated* in ſeveral places, ſo wide as is proportionably neceſſary to the largeneſs of the Veſſels that are to go through, and no larger, leſt in diſtentions or ſtrains they ſhould tear, as too apt they are to do, as Experience daily teſtifies in Men and Children, when vehement coughs or long and ſtraining cries do, in ſome, open the orifice of the Navel, and in others the orifices in the Groin, where the ſpermatick or ſeminary Veſſels go forth to the Stones, ſo that the wideneſs gives liberty for the ſmall Guts to fall out of their places into the outward parts, which cauſeth Ruptures and broken Bellies. The like I have ſeen in Horſes. *Its perforations.*

The outmoſt Skins of all the parts of the Lower Belly, have their original from this. From the inner Membrane of this Rim of the Belly, all the outmoſt Skins or Coats which cover every Part contained in the Lower Belly do proceed, and from it have their original, ſome thicker and ſome thinner, according to the neceſſity or uſe of the Part reſpectively. As for Example, the Common Membrane of the Kidneys, the proper one of the Liver and Spleen (each of which have but one) are but very thin, for ſeeing they are never (naturally) extended, there was no neceſſity for their being otherwiſe; but the Common Skin of the Stomach, the Guts, the Bladder and the Womb are ſomewhat thicker, but much ſtronger and more compact, becauſe the uſes they are put to require it, that they may without danger be ſtretched, when there is occaſion. Now as the Entrails are many and of divers kinds, and alſo ſituated in ſeveral places different from one another, ſo does their outward Inveſting Membrane take

take its original from that part of this *Peritonæum* or Rim of the Belly which is next to them; as the upper Entrails, which are the Stomach, the Liver, the Spleen, &c. borrow it from that part of the Rim which makes the under Membrane of the Midriff; so do the lower Entrails (as the Bladder, Womb, &c.) borrow it from that part of the Rim, which cleaveth to the Share-bone, it being the nearest to them.

From this *Peritonæum* or Rim of the Belly do also proceed two double Membranes or Skins, which are those of the Caul and of the Mesentery; as also several Ligaments, of which the most remarkable are those of the Liver and Guts.

This *Peritonæum* is composed of membranous and nervous Fibres which are very small. The Vessels that are dispersed through it are small branches of Veins and Arteries which it hath from the Midriff, and other neighbouring Parts, as the Seminary and Mammary; and for Nerves, it hath them from the branches which are carried to the Muscles of the Lower Belly. *Its Composition.*

Its *Uses* are several, the first of which is, to cover and contain all the Parts or Entrails of the Lower Belly; secondly, to further the expulsion of the Excrements by pressing the Stomach and Guts before and on the sides, as the Midriff doth above. Again, it binds with its Ligaments all the Guts in their proper places by mediation of the Mesentery, that no violent motion (such as running or leaping) should move them out: By Ligaments proceeding from it, is the Liver also suspended in its place. Its last use is to be a safeguard to the Vessels that run through it, which being but small and having a long course to run, would be in danger of breaking, were they not secured between its two Skins. *Its Uses.*

CHAP. VIII.

Of the Omentum *or Caul.*

HAVING according to the order of dissection, removed all the *investing* or *containing* Parts of the Lower Belly, and shewed which, and what they are; it now follows that I shew which are the parts *invested* or *contained*. And because the *Caul* appears first in dissection, I will first treat of it.

This *Caul* is in Latin called *Omentum*, from *Omen*, because the Roman Soothsayers pretended by it to foretell things. It is also called *mappa ventris*, the Map or Dish-clout of the Belly, because it seemeth to lick up the superfluities thereof. It doth cover all or most of the Guts in many Creatures; but in a Horse it is most times removed from all the lower parts of the Belly, and lieth in wrinkles or folds near and about the Stomach. The reason of its being removed, I do suppose, is the hard labour and violent Exercise a Horse undergoeth; for whilst he is young, and before he comes to his labour, it is spread as far over his Entrails as in other Creatures, as hath been observed by the Learned *Marcus Aurelius Severinus*, who did in a She-foal which he dissected at *Naples*, see the *The Caul what it is.* *How far it spreads over the Guts.*

Caul ſpread all over the Guts as far as to the bottom of the Womb, to which it was alſo joined with a ſtrait connection.

It is ſometimes the cauſe of barrenneſs. It ſometimes happeneth that the Caul falleth between the bottom of the Bladder and the neck of the Womb in Women, and then it ſo compreſſeth the mouth of the Womb, that it leaveth very little or no paſſage for the Man's ſeed to enter in, which when it ſo happeneth is a cauſe of barrenneſs. But I believe no ſuch thing can happen in Mares.

Its connexion or origine. It is compoſed of two Membranes, the uppermoſt or formoſt of which ariſeth at the bottom of the Stomach to which it is faſtned, as alſo to the hollow ſide of the Liver and Spleen: The inner or backer Membrane ſprings from the *Peritonæum*, immediately under the Midriff towards the Back, and is tied to that part of the Gut *Colon* that paſſeth under the Stomach lengthways, as likewiſe to the Sweetbread and to the beginning of the ſmall Gut, next to the lower Orifice of the Stomach. Theſe Membranes are larded with plentifull Fat.

Figure. It is in figure like a Purſe-net, or Faulkner's Bag, conſiſting as is ſaid of a double Coat, ſeparate at the top, but knit together at the bottom, where it is round ſometimes, and ſometimes unequal, but at its upper part or orifice it is orbicular.

Its Veſſels. It has Veſſels of all ſorts, which do run through the ſubſtance thereof. It hath its Veins and Arteries from the Cœliacal and Meſenterical branches, and Nerves from a double branch of the Intercoſtal pair.

Its Fat. In Horſes it has much Fat, eſpecially in thoſe that are ſound and have not waſted it by either ſickneſs or long faſting, for in ſuch it conſiſts of little but the Membranes and Veſſels, the Fat ſerving for a ſubſidiary nouriſhment to the natural heat to feed upon when the Beaſt eats nothing. Now this Fat is not diſtributed equally to all the parts of the Caul, but runs here and there in ſtreaks accordingly as the larger Bloud-veſſels do, the ſpaces between being wholly membranous and ſeemingly tranſparent, ſo that it imitates a Net, whence in ſome Countries they call it ſo. Now the Fat adhering to and accompanying the Veſſels in this manner, it ſeems to be bred of an unctuous or oily part of the Bloud that ſweats through the Veſſels, but is detained by the cloſeneſs or denſeneſs of the Membrane, by whoſe reſpective coldneſs alſo it is curdled or congealed into Fat. But very unlikely it is that it ſhould be made of I know not what Vapours ſteaming out of the Parts contained in the Lower Belly, and condenſed by theſe Membranes; for not to mention the many abſurdities of this Opinion, if it were ſo bred, then would all the Membranes be evenly and equally beſmeared with it, which it is obvious to any Eye that they are not.

The uſe of its Fat. The uſe of this plentifull Fat is to cheriſh and heat the bottom of the Stomach, the upper part of which has no need of its warmth, it being covered with the Liver, whoſe Lobes hang over it and lie upon it. It ſerves alſo to moiſten the Guts, which have great need of being kept ſlippery and glib, that they may the better perform their continual periſtaltick motion.

The uſe of its Membranes or Skins. The uſe of the Membranes or Skins beſides their congealing and including the Fat, is to prop up and ſuſtain all the branches of the Veſſels which lie between and paſs through them, to the Stomach, the Spleen, the beginning of the ſmall Gut, and *Colon*, &c.

The

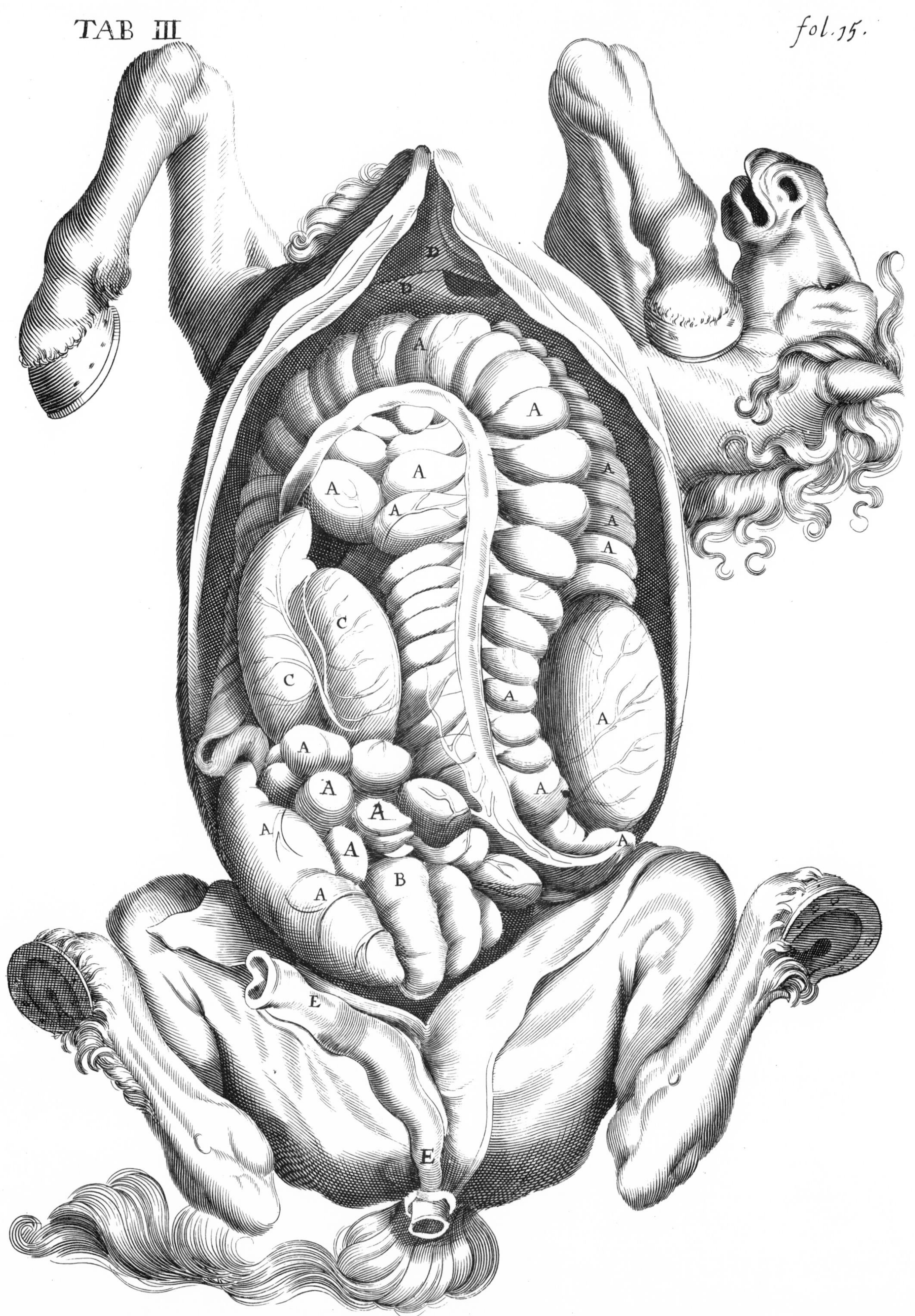
D
D
A
A
A
A
A
A
A
A
C
C
A
A
A
A
A
A
A
A
A
B
E
E

The *Third* Table repreſenteth the Guts *in ſitu*, as they appear after the Caul is taken away.

AAAA *Sheweth the Gut* Colon *or Colick Gut with its Convolutions or Folds, as alſo what parts of the lower Belly it takes up.*
BB *The ſtreight or Arſe-gut.*
CCC *The Gut* Cæcum *or blind Gut.*
DDD *The Diaphragm or Midriff.*
EE *The Horſes Tard.*

CHAP. IX.

Of the Gullet and Stomach.

AFTER the Caul is removed, the Inteſtins or Guts do appear in their natural ſituation, as is ſhewed in the foregoing Figure; but there is another Part that lies abſconded under them, which muſt firſt be ſpoken of according to the order of diſſection, and that is the Stomach. It is ſingle in an Horſe as it is in Man, though ſuch Creatures as have Horns, as Beeves, Sheep, *&c.* and ſuch as having no Horns yet chew the Cud, as Camels, Hinds, *&c.* have four. This is the Kitchin of the Body and receptacle of Meat and Drink; as alſo the ſeat of Appetite, by reaſon of the Nerves that are diſperſed chiefly in its upper Orifice, but run in ſmall twigs alſo through its whole ſubſtance. It is called in Latin *ventriculus*, which is as much as to ſay a little Belly; and is placed or ſeated juſt under the Midriff between the Liver and the Spleen, almoſt in the very middle of the Body, inclining a little towards the left Side that it might ballance the Body againſt the Liver, which is much bigger and heavier than the Spleen.

But before we enter upon the Stomach it is convenient firſt to deſcribe the *Gullet* which is an Appendage to it, and ſerves as a Tunnel to convey the Food out of the Mouth into it, though the greateſt part of it be contained in the Neck and Breaſt. *The Gullet.*

It is an organical or diſſimilar Part, hollow and round, beginning at the root of the Tongue, behind the head of the Windpipe, and paſſeth down from thence directly between the Windpipe and the Joints of the Neck and of the Cheſt, about the fifth or ſixth Joint of which latter it turneth a little to the right ſide, to give way to the trunk of the great Artery, but about the ninth Joint it turns toward the left again and climbs upon the great Artery, and paſſing through the Midriff at an hole proper to it ſelf it is inſerted into the Stomach toward its left ſide, as you may ſee in the following Figure. *Its origine and deſcent.*

It conſiſts of three Membranes or Skins. The *outermoſt* is *common*, which it hath from the *Pleura* or from the ligaments of the Joints of the Neck and Breaſt on which it reſteth: This inveſteth the two *proper*. The *middle* or firſt proper one is thick and fleſhy, conſiſting of two ranks of fleſhy *Its ſubſtance.*

fleſhy Fibres, obliquely or ſlopingly aſcending and deſcending, ſo that they croſs one another like an X. The innermoſt or ſecond proper is membranous, and hath onely ſtreight Fibres.

Its Veſſels. It has *Veins* in the Neck from the Jugulars, in the Breaſt from the *Vein without a fellow*; and where it is joined to the Stomach, from the coronary branch of the *Porta*. *Arteries* in the Neck it has from the *Carotides*, in the Breaſt from the Intercoſtals; and where it joins to the Stomach, from the cœliack coronary branch. It hath *Nerves* from that pair that is commonly called the ſixth.

Its Kernels. It has two notable Glands or Kernels at its beginning in the Throat, called Almonds from their ſhape, which ſeparate a kind of flegmatick humour to keep the inſide of the Gullet moiſt and glib, that the Food may eaſilier deſcend down by it.

Its Uſe. Its *uſe* is, to convey Meat after it is chewed in the Mouth, as likewiſe Drink, down into the Stomach, there to be turned into chyle.

The Stomach. Having done with the Gullet, we now return to the *Stomach*.

Its figure, Its *figure* is round and ſomewhat long, reſembling a Bag-pipe; though on the left ſide and at the bottom it is bunching and more capacious than on the right ſide; for there it is by little and little narrowed that it might give place to the Liver.

And magnitude. Its *magnitude* is divers according to the largeneſs of the Horſe, or according to the quantity of Meat or Drink (be it little or much) that is in it; for it contracteth or diſtendeth it ſelf as there is occaſion. As for example, if there be a great quantity of Meat and Drink let into it, it doth extend it ſelf to that largeneſs as to contain it; and as that Meat is by little and little concocted, and then let forth through the lower Orifice into the ſmall Guts to be there ſuckt up by the milky Veins, the Stomach doth accordingly by little and little contract or draw it ſelf up ſo cloſe to that which remains, that it embraceth it on all ſides, ſo that there is never any cavity or hollowneſs to ſpeak of to be found in the Stomach; whence we ſee in Tripes, that the inſide is by ſuch contracting always rugged or in wrinkles, whereas the outſide is ſmooth and plain. Onely this we may note as to its bigneſs, that in conſideration of the bigneſs of an Horſes Body or the largeneſs of his Guts, it is far leſs in him than in moſt Animals.

Its Orifices. The Stomach hath two *Orifices*, a left and upper, which is to receive in Meat; and a right which is the lower, to let it out after concoction. The firſt being the uppermoſt I will firſt ſpeak of, which is much wider and larger than the other, becauſe it admits the Meat, many times not half chewed, into the Stomach (and for that cauſe is much thicker and alſo ſtronger than the other) whereas all is reduced into a fluid ſubſtance, before it paſs out at the other.

The upper and left Orifice of the Stomach. This Orifice being a continuation of the Gullet is called the *mouth* of the Stomach, and hath an exquiſite ſenſe of feeling becauſe of the Nerves which encompaſs it, and by which it the ſooner perceives the emptineſs and want of Meat, and therefore ſtirs up the Horſe to ſeek Food to ſatisfy his want. It is near the middle of the Stomach, and not ſo near the left ſide of it as in Men.

Its Uſes. It is furniſhed with fleſhy and circular Fibres, that it may naturally ſhut up and ſtraiten it ſelf after the Meat is received in, and alſo may intercept or hinder the Vapours from coming forth, which would by their aſcent up to the Brain be very injurious, by breeding diſeaſes and evil

diſtempers

diſtempers in the Head; which Vapours would be alſo wanted in the Stomach to further concoction: for as it is an uſual cuſtom when Meat is over the fire for the Pot-lid to be put on to keep the Vapours or Reek from coming forth; ſo likewiſe it is requiſite in this caſe that the Vapours of the Stomach ſhould be kept in, that Concoction ſhould be thereby furthered, or the Food be ſooner digeſted, the Vapours aſſiſting thereunto.

The lower Orifice, and its office. The lower and right Orifice is called *pylorus*, which is to ſay, the Porter, from its office, which is to open and ſhut as occaſion ſerves; to open, when the chyle is let forth and ſent into the Gut *duodenum*, and then to contract or draw it ſelf cloſe up again, that nothing may paſs through it which is not fully concocted. Which contraction is performed by tranſverſe or overthwart Fibres, with which it is plentifully furniſhed for that purpoſe; as alſo a thick and compact circle doth encompaſs it round, which circle is in ſhape like the ſphincter Muſcle of the Fundament. By theſe Fibres and this Circle the action of the Porter, or lower Orifice, is performed, that is to ſay, it is either opened or ſhut, widened or ſtraitned as there is occaſion, as I have ſaid before. And theſe are the offices of the Orifices of the Stomach.

The compoſition of the Stomach. Now I proceed to the *compoſition* of it, which is of three Membranes or Skins, the firſt or outmoſt of which it hath from the *Peritonæum*, or Rim of the Belly. The ſecond and middlemoſt is more fleſhy than the former, conſiſting of fleſhy Fibres, which do mightily ſtrengthen the Stomach and by their heat do further concoction. The third and inmoſt is nervous, into which all the Veſſels do terminate or end. This Coat or Skin is continued with the Gullet up to the Mouth, that the Mouth ſhould not admit or receive in any thing that is offenſive to the Stomach.

Its Veſſels. 1. Veins. The Stomach is furniſhed with *Veſſels* of all ſorts. *Veins* it hath *firſt* from the Splenick branch, as 1. The *vas breve*, or ſhort Vein, which is inſerted into the bottom of the Stomach, whence afterwards it creeps up between the Coats towards the upper Orifice, but is obliterated before it comes quite to it. 2. The two Gaſtrick Veins (the greater and leſs) which creep along the bottom of the Stomach, and in their courſe ſpread many branches into it; but the largeſt branch of the greater of theſe two is that which is called the Crown-vein, that encompaſſes the upper Orifice of the Stomach. 3. A Vein that is common to the left ſide of the Stomach and the Caul. *Secondly*, it hath another common to its right ſide and the Caul, from the Meſenterick branch. And *laſtly*, its lower or right Orifice has a ſmall Vein from the trunk of the *Porta* it ſelf, which is called *pylorica* or Porter-vein. Now before the circulation of the bloud was found out, it was believed that all theſe Veins brought bloud to the Stomach for its nouriſhment: but ſince that was diſcovered by Dr. *Harvey*, every one knows that they carry nothing to the Stomach, but bring back from it ſo much of the Arterial bloud as is not ſpent upon its nouriſhment. But beſides the bloud ſome learned Men have entertained an opinion that they ſuck out of the Stomach a thinner and more ſpirituous part of the chyle, which paſſes along with the bloud to the Heart by a far ſhorter paſſage than if it deſcended into the Guts and entred into the milky Veins, &c. (as ſhall afterwards be fullier declared.) And this they think it reaſonable to ſuppoſe, becauſe of the ſudden and quick refreſhment that Creatures receive from Cordial Drinks, and the like. I ſhall not pretend to decide the controversie betwixt those that affirm this, and others that deny it, but do think this opinion to be very probable, because of the very speedy revival of Horses (that I have observed) which being ready to faint away, have suddenly grown brisk upon the giving them some comfortable draught: unless we should think with some, that the Nerves of the Stomach do imbibe some spirituous parts of such potions, and so the refreshment should come that way.

2. *Arteries.* The Stomachal *Arteries* are twigs from the Cœliacal branch of the *Arteria magna* or great Arterie, and these do accompany the Veins in all their course, and bestow nourishment and vital heat upon it. For the Stomach is not nourished with the Chyle, any more than any other part, but with arterial bloud which by these Arteries is brought from the Heart.

3. *Nerves.* It hath two notable *Nerves* from the sixth pair (reckoned by Dr. *Willis* to be the eighth) propagated from those branches which make the recurrent Nerves. These do encompass the upper Orifice, and then are carried, in oblique or slanting lines, cross one another over most part of it; the right branch compassing the foremost and left part, and the left branch compassing the hindermost and right part thereof.

Its Action. The Stomach has several *Actions,* as first Hunger and Thirst, which are the sense that it has of the want of Meat and Drink, and an Appetite that is excited in it for the obtaining of them. Secondly, it has an action of retention, whereby it contracts it self close about the Food that is taken in, and detains it so long till it is throughly concocted or turned into a thin juice called Chyle. Thirdly, it has a motion that is called peristaltick, such as the Guts also have, resembling the motion of a Worm, whereby its parts contracting themselves successively from above downwards, thrust out the chyle into the Guts gently and by degrees. But the chief and most considerable action of the Stomach, is, fourthly, Chylification, or turning the aliment into a whitish liquor commonly known by the name of Chyle, which being expelled out of the Stomach into the Guts, is, the *thinner* part of it, suckt up by a sort of Vessels called *milky* Veins, (so called from that colour which this liquor gives them) that are inserted every where into the Guts, and which carry it towards the Heart, by those ways that hereafter shall be described: but the thicker and more dreggy part is driven along the Guts and cast out at the Fundament as excrement.

How it concocts. Now there are several things that concur to this last and principal action of the Stomach, *viz.* Concoction. As *first*, the very numerous Arteries that are dispersed through it which much foster and encrease its *heat*, which though it be not the main instrument of concoction, yet much furthers it. And this heat is also encreased by the Liver which covers the upper and fore-part of its right side, as also by the Caul which by its two Membranes invests its bottom. But *secondly*, that to which concoction is mainly owing is a certain ferment in the Stomach, which is compounded *partly* of the slaver with which the Horses mouth always abounds for the moistening and softning of his Meat while he chews it, and part of which is continually swallow'd down into his Stomach together with the Food; and *partly* of an acid or sharp and salt liquor bred in the Stomach, as is most likely, of salt and acid steams evaporating out of the stomachal Arteries, and condensed in it into this juice: And this liquor is that which dissolves and melts as it were the solid Meats that are

swallowed

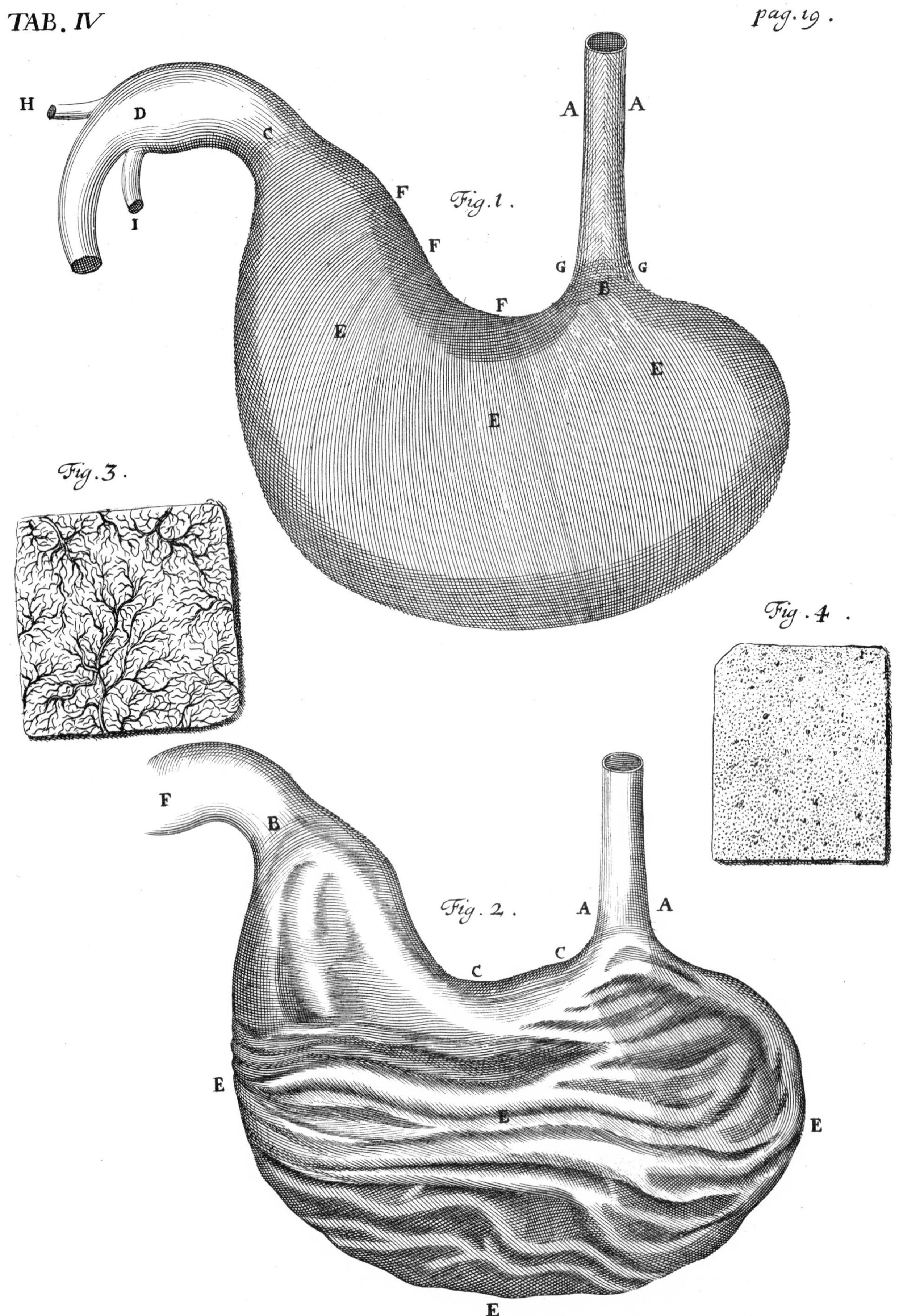
H
D
C
I
A
A
F
Fig. 1.
F
G
G
B
F
E
E
E
Fig. 3.
Fig. 4.
F
B
Fig. 2.
A
A
C
C
E
E
E
E

ſwallowed (ſomething like as *Aqua fortis* diſſolves Steel) and reduces the whole maſs into fluid ſubſtance, which then paſſes down into the Guts, as abovesaid. This acid Juice was formerly thought to come from the Spleen by a Vein called *the ſhort Veſſel*; but later Anatomiſts have diſcovered from the circulation of the Bloud, that that Vein brings nothing from the Spleen to the Stomach, but contrariwiſe carries the Bloud, that is ſuperfluous to the nouriſhment of the Stomach, from it into the ſplenick Vein, by which it goes to the Liver, and from thence to the Heart in its circulation. So that no ſuch original or ſpring of this ferment is to be imagined.

The *Fourth* Table expreſſeth the ſecond or middle, and the innermoſt Coats of the Stomach.

Fig. I. Sheweth the Stomach freed from its outmoſt nervous Coat, that the outer or convex ſurface of the middle Coat may appear with its fleſhy Fibres.

AA *The Gullet.*
B *The Mouth or upper Orifice of the Stomach.*
C *Its lower Orifice called* Pylorus.
D *A portion of the ſmall Gut.*
EEE *The circular Fibres encompaſſing the Stomach depthways.*
FFF *The top or upper part of the Stomach, where theſe Fibres ariſe.*
GG *The circular fleſhy Fibres that encompaſs the upper Orifice or Mouth of the Stomach, which contracting themſelves ſhut or purſe it up as occaſion ſerves.*
H *The Gall-paſſage inſerted into the ſmall Gut.*
I *The Pancreatick duct inſerted into the ſmall Gut.*

Fig. II. Sheweth the Stomach turned inſide out, that its woolly cruſt with its wrinkles and folds may appear.

AA *The left Orifice or Mouth of the Stomach.*
B *The right or lower Orifice, to which the ſmall Gut is knit.*
CC *The top or ſummity of the Stomach between its two Orifices.*
EEEE *The ſides, ends and bottom of the inſide of the Stomach, with its woolly cruſt and wrinkles or folds.*
F *A portion of the ſmall Gut.*

Fig. III. Repreſents a piece of the inmoſt nervous Coat, wherein the woolly cruſt being taken off, the inner or concave ſurface with a very thick ramification of Veſſels doth appear.

Fig. IV. Shews a piece of the woolly cruſt, which looks like a fourth Coat, wherein its outer ſurface, whereby it ſticks to the nervous Coat, appears very full of glands and the mouths of Veſſels.

CHAP. X.

Of the Guts in general.

The Guts. Their Name, Figure and Length. THE Guts are called in Latin *Inteſtina*, becauſe they are placed in the inmoſt part of the Body, as you ſee them placed in the Third Figure, which ſhews their natural poſition or ſituation, they taking up the moſt part of the cavity or hollowneſs of the Lower Belly. They are oblong, round, hollow Bodies, in number ſix, and are bigger or leſſer as is the bigneſs of the Horſe. They are the Inſtruments of diſtribution of the Chyle and expulſion of the Ordure, being continued with the *Pylorus* or Porter of the Stomach and reaching to the Fundament. They are in length about thirty ſix yards, a little under or over according to the largeneſs of the Horſe; wherefore they are neceſſarily girded and wound into manifold convolutions or folds, that the cavity of the Lower Belly might be capable of containing them, which otherwiſe it could not do.

How knit together. They are gathered up and entwiſted in the folds of the Meſentery, by which coming between they are alſo knit to the Back: all which is to keep them from falling out of their places or rolling upon one another, which would have often hapned, had not Nature ſo well provided for the contrary, eſpecially in violent exerciſe, as hunting, running, leaping and the like; and if it had hapned, the weight of the one lying upon the other would have obſtructed the paſſage of the Excrements, and ſo caus'd exceſſive pains, as gripings, ſtrainings to dung, and the like, and upon the continuance of ſuch ſtoppage, death it ſelf.

The Guts are on the outſide moſt times fat, but on the inſide they are covered with a ſlimy or ſnotty ſubſtance, for the more free and glib paſſage of the Dung.

Their Coats. They have *three Coats*, like as the Stomach hath. The *outermoſt* or common one is nervous, ſpringing mediately from the Rim of the Belly, but immediately from the Membranes of the Meſentery; ſaving that of the beginning of the firſt Gut, and of that part of the *Colon* which runneth under the Stomach, where it immediately proceedeth from the Caul adhering to thoſe Parts. The *middle* is thicker and fleſhy, having two ranks of Fibres, the outer of them ſtreight, and the inner tranſverſe or overthwart. The *innermoſt* is alſo nervous like the outmoſt, but on its inſide it is cruſted over with a kind of ſpongy ſubſtance, that ſerves as a ſtrainer for the Chyle to paſs through out of the Guts into the milky Veins. This Coat has all ſorts of Fibres, and is very wrinkled, to prevent the too quick gliding away of the Chyle. The Fibres of this and the middle Coat ſerve to perform the periſtaltick or worm-like motion of the Guts, by which whatſoever is contained in them is gently driven along downwards towards the Fundament.

Veſſels. 1. Veins. Viz. firſt, Bloud-veins. The Guts have all ſorts of Veſſels. As 1. *Veins.* Theſe they have from ſeveral branches of the *Porta*, but the moſt come from that branch of it that is called the Meſenterick. The uſe of which Veins was by the Ancients thought to be, both to carry Bloud to them from the Liver for their nouriſhment, and to bring back from them the Chyle to the Liver, there

there to be turned into bloud. But as to the firſt, the circulation of the Bloud makes it evident, that they carry no bloud to the Guts, but all that is contained in them, is received from the Arteries that are inſerted into the Inteſtins, and returns by them to the Liver, through which it paſſes into the Vein called *Cava*, and by it aſcends to the Heart. And as to the latter uſe aſſigned to theſe Veins, namely the bringing of Chyle from the Guts to the Liver, there was another ſort of Veſſels found out by one *Aſellius* about threeſcore years agoe, that perform this office, called by him (from their colour) *milky Veins*. But neither do theſe conveigh the Chyle to the Liver, as the firſt Inventor of them thought, but running from the circumference of the Meſentery they unite and diſcharge themſelves into one common receptacle near its centre at the Back-bone, from whence the Chyle paſſes up along the ſide of the Back-bone as high as the Collar-bone by a proper pipe, where it is emptied into the ſubclavian Vein, in which being mixed with the Bloud it glides along with it immediately into the Heart. I ſay then the uſe of the Bloud-veins of the Guts, is onely to receive ſo much of the Arterial bloud as is ſuperfluous from their nouriſhment. *Secondly, milky Veins.*

A *ſecond* ſort of Veſſel diſperſed through the Guts are the *Arteries*, which ſpring partly from the Cœliack branch, and partly from the Meſenterick. Theſe afford both Vital heat and nouriſhment to the Guts, and beſides upon adminiſtring a Drench to ſcour your Horſe, they diſcharge the impurities and bad humours flowing in the maſs of bloud, into the Guts, to be thrown out in the draught. *2. Arteries.*

3. Their *Nerves* are from that pair that has commonly been called the ſixth, but according to Dr. *Willis*'s diſtinction is now generally reputed for the ninth pair, and otherwiſe called the *Intercoſtal*, becauſe as it deſcends down the Cheſt, it ſends out a ſmall twig between every Rib. Theſe contribute to the Guts their ſenſe of feeling, and furniſh their Fibres with animal Spirits, whereby they are enabled to perform their worm-like motion. *3. Nerves.*

As for the *milky Veins*, we have mention'd them before, and ſhall treat further of them in the Chapter of the *Meſentery*.

CHAP. XI.

Of the Guts in particular.

NOW though the Guts be one continued Body from the lower Orifice of the Stomach to the Fundament, yet they are wont to be diſtinguiſhed into ſeveral; In Men they are divided into ſix, three ſmall, and three thick: but in a Horſe we cannot ſo well follow this diviſion, there being not any difference in the ſmall Guts ſo conſiderable as to ground a diſtinction upon. However, becauſe the ſecond of the thick Guts ſeems to have three partitions, we ſhall make three of it, and ſo will they anſwer to the number in Men, and be reckoned *ſix*. *The Guts are in number ſix.*

1. The ſmall Gut. The firſt we ſhall diſtinguiſh onely by the name of the *ſmall Gut*. This is twenty ſix or twenty ſeven yards in length, ſomething narrower at a foot and half diſtance from the Stomach than towards its ending, but through the whole it is wider than in an Oxe, being about two inches or two and an half over. Preſently at its beginning it bends under the Stomach towards the Back-bone, ſtreight along which it deſcends a pretty way, being annexed firmly to it by a ſtrong Membrane (that ſeems to be borrow'd of the Caul here knit to it) which is all the eſtabliſhment it has. But by and by it leaves this hold, and beginning to wind about, is received into the folds of the Meſentery, whereby it is admirably kept from twiſting and entanglement. Now there are far more of the *milky Veins* inſerted into this Gut than into all that follow; and beſides thoſe Veſſels which are common to it with the thick Guts, namely Veins, Arteries and Nerves, it has two other Veſſels inſerted into it, one from the Liver and another from the Sweet-bread. By the firſt is yellow Choler, and by the latter a peculiar Juice from the Sweet-bread (called the *pancreatick Juice*) diſcharged into it. Theſe two Liquors flowing into it from the aforeſaid Bowels about a foot below the Stomach, within an inch or two one of another, make a notable ferment in it, which mixing with the Chyle that is paſſing down this way, cauſes it alſo to ferment, whereby it comes to work it ſelf ſomething clearer, as I may ſay, even as Ale or Beer in a Barrel does. For by this fermentation the impurer and more earthy or dreggy part of the Chyle, is ſeparated and precipitated as it were from the more pure and ſpirituous, whereby this latter part is made capable of being received in at the ſmall mouths of the milky Veins that gape in abundance into this Gut, whilſt the thicker and excrementitious part is thruſt along the Guts by their worm-like motion, and makes the Dung. This Gut for about two hands breadth at its beginning from the *Pylorus* is wider, and for the like ſpace at its end before it is joined to the following, is a little narrower, than in its other parts.

2. The Cæcum or blind Gut. Having done with the *ſmall Gut*, we next come to the *thick* ones, in number five, of which the firſt is called *Cæcum* or the *blind Gut*, becauſe it has but one paſſage for the Excrements both into and out of it, which come into it out of the ſmall Gut, and go out of it into the next thick Gut. It is not round in ſhape like the ſmall Gut, but as it were four-ſquare, which figure it comes to have from four Ligaments that run along it, one on each ſide, which contain it in that ſhape; and theſe Ligaments being ſhorter than its Coats, make them bag out in many Cells as the *Colon* does in other Creatures. It is almoſt a yard long, and unequal in breadth: for though at its mouth, where it joyns to the ſmall Gut and the *Colon*, it be near a quarter of a yard over, yet towards its cloſe end it grows ſo by degrees narrower, that it is not above three inches. This Gut is very inconſiderable for its bigneſs in moſt Creatures, particularly in Man, in whom it is not ordinarily above four inches long, and hardly ſo thick as ones little Finger: onely in a Rabbit it bears much the ſame proportion with the reſt of the Guts, as it does in an Horſe. In ſuch Creatures as have it ſo very ſmall, its uſe is very obſcure; but in an Horſe where it is ſo very large, its uſe is apparent to be, to ſtay the too quick paſſage of the Excrements by receiving them into it ſelf as it were into an Inn, whereas if they kept directly the ſtreight Road of the reſt of the Guts without turning in here, they would come too ſoon to their journeys end, namely the Fundament: I mean the Horſe would be continually

a-ſcouring,

a-scouring, and so fall from his flesh and languish, by reason that the *milky Veins* would not have time to suck up all the Chyle out of the Guts to turn into his nourishment; besides that it would be troublesome to the Horse, and offensive to his Rider to have him always a-dunging. Its connexion to the small Gut and *Colon* you may better conceive of by the following Figure, in which it is well expressed, than by my description of it in words.

That which is the second thick Gut and in Man is called the *Colon*, seems in an Horse to be divided into three, to which I shall not take upon me to assign distinct names, but onely call them three *Colons*. The *first* of them is about a yard and a half in length, and for the most part of it a quarter of a yard over. The *second* is as wide as the first, but onely about a yard in length. These two are divided one from the other by a narrow *neck* about half a yard long, and four inches over. The *first* of these two wide *Colons*, is that which in its upper part joyns with the blind Gut above described, where it has a Valve, consisting of a loose Membrane or Skin that hangs round its mouth, which permits any thing to come into the *Colon* out of the *Cæcum* or out of the small Gut, but when any thing would pass out of that into these, then the edges of this loose Skin flap close one against another and hinder it, whereby Nature has prevented the return of the Excrements back out of the *Colon* into the small Gut. And the lower end of the *latter* of these two wide *Colons* joins to the *third*, which is very narrow in comparison of *them*, but yet is more than twice as long as both of them, namely about six yards. Now all these three *Colons* are contracted into Cells by two Ligaments, one of which runs along the upper part, and the other on the lower side of them: and besides these two which are common to them all, the larger ones have somewhere other two that run along their sides, but especially so has the Neck that divides them whereby it is made foursquare like the blind Gut. The reason why these *Colons* (as well as they are in other Creatures, and the *Cæcum* also in this) are contracted into Cells, is for the slower passage of the Excrements, that what of the Chyle was not drunk in by the milky Veins of the small Gut, might be leisurely suckt up by those that are inserted into these thick ones; for though we call their Contents *Excrements*, yet that is onely because the much greater part is so, for all the Chyle is not clear imbibed from them till they come towards the end of the last *Colon*, though the milky Veins are not a tenth part so numerous in these as in the small Gut. *Three Colons.*

To the lower end of the small *Colon* is joined the last Gut called *Rectum* or the *streight* Gut, because it runs streight along without any windings. It is also called the *Arse-gut*, because it reacheth to the Fundament. The Coats of this Gut, especially the middle, are much thicker than any of the other, and the whole seems fleshy and muscular. It is but about half a yard long, and betwixt three and four inches over. This is not gathered in the foldings of the Mesentery, but instead of that, is from its beginning at the lower end of the Loins, to its ending at the Arse-hole, fast tied by a Membrane to the Back and Rump-bones, which keep it from falling out upon straining to dung. At its lower end at the Arse-hole it has a round Muscle that encompasses it, called the *sphincter* Muscle, whereby it is pursed up so, that nothing can pass out, except when the Beast loosens it of his own accord when he goes to dung, and then at the same time he squeezes the Guts by help of the Muscles that environ his Paunch, *6. The streight Gut.*

Paunch, which we deſcribed above in *chap.* 6. and ſo forces the Dung to iſſue out at the Fundament.

And thus we have finiſhed the Hiſtory of the Guts, not needing to add any thing of the uſe of them, becauſe their uſe is all along interwoven in their deſcription, and therefore we ſhall paſs on to the other parts.

The *Fifth* Table repreſenteth the Gullet, Stomach and Guts taken out of the Body.

A *The Gullet.*

B *The upper Orifice of the Stomach.*

CC *The two external Nerves of the ſixth pair (otherwiſe reckon'd for the eighth) diſperſed through the upper part of the Stomach.*

DDD *The three different Coats of the Gullet, a little turned down, to ſhew them the plainer.*

E *The lower Orifice of the Stomach called the* Pylorus.

F *The outermoſt Coat of the Stomach turned back.*

G *The entrance of the* porus bilarius *or Choler-paſſage into the beginning of the ſmall Gut.*

H *The entrance of the pancreatick duct or paſſage of the Sweet-bread into the ſame Gut.*

IIIIIIII *The ſmall Gut.*

K *The* Inteſtinum cæcum *or blind Gut.*

LL *The firſt* Colon.

M *The ſmall neck that divides the firſt* Colon *from the ſecond.*

NN *The ſecond or middle* Colon.

OO *One of the Ligaments that contracts the blind Gut and* Colons *into Cells.*

PP *The third and laſt* Colon, *far ſmaller than the two former, but longer.*

QQ *The* Inteſtinum rectum *or Arſe-gut.*

R *The two Muſcles called* levatores Ani, *or openers of the Fundament.*

S *The ſphincter Muſcle that contracts or purſes up the Arſe-hole.*

T *The middle Coat of the Stomach through which the two branches of Nerves are diſperſed.*

U *The third or inmoſt Coat of the Stomach.*

XX *The branchings of the Bloud-veſſels, as they appear on the outſide of the Stomach.*

YY *The ſeveral Gaſtrick Veſſels inſerted into the bottom of the Stomach.*

CHAP.

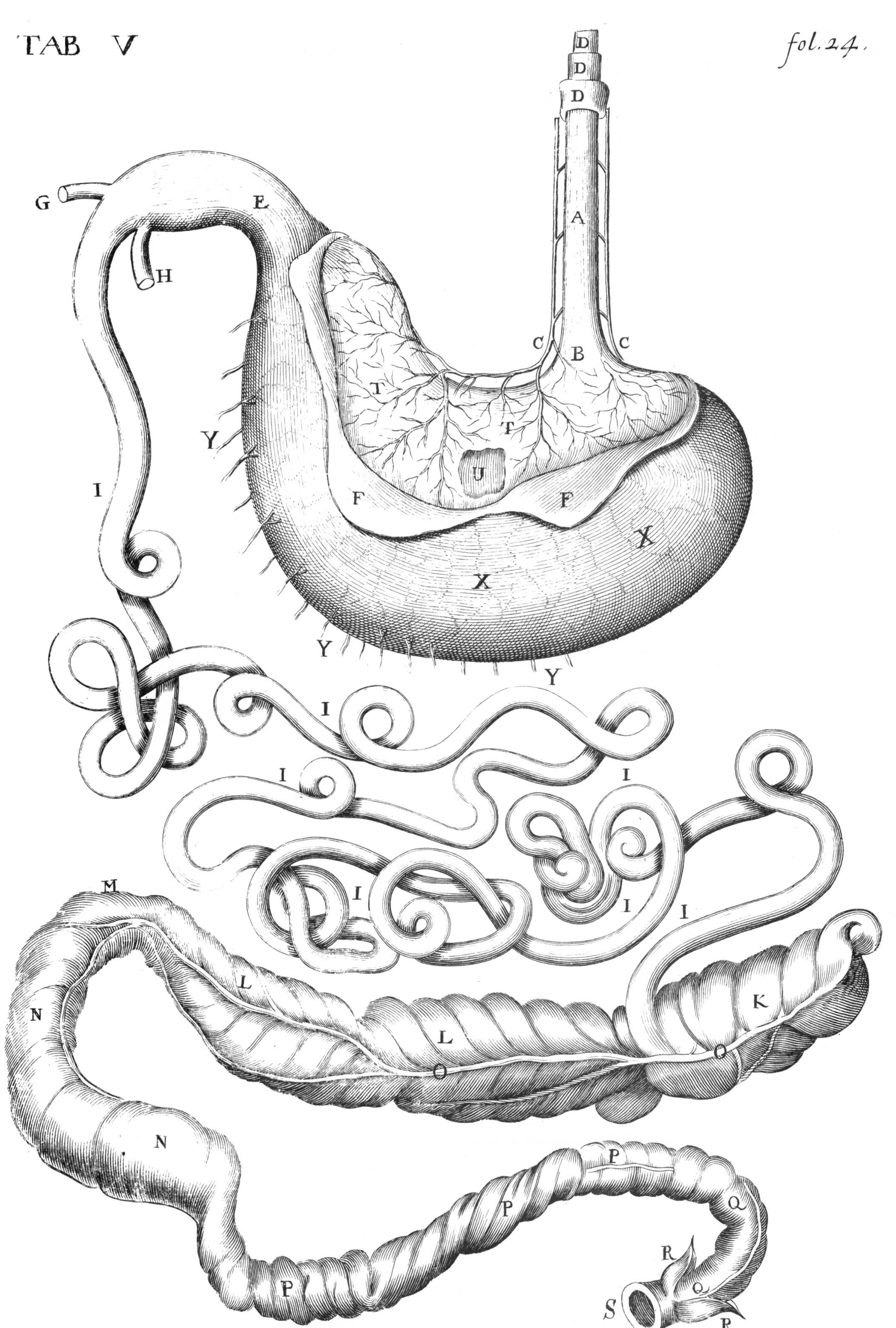
D
D
D
G
E
A
H
C
B
C
T
T
Y
U
I
F
F
X
X
Y
Y
I
I
I
I
M
I
I
I
L
N
K
L
O
O
N
P
P
Q
P
R
Q
S
R

CHAP. XII.

Of the Mesentery.

THE *Mesenterium* or *Mesentery* is so called from its being placed in the middle of the Guts, which it embraces round, gathering them together in form of a Globe, but is it self gathered into folds. This Mesentery is of a circular figure, composed of a double Coat, between which do run many Vessels and those of all sorts, and betwixt which also there is a collection of much fat. Dr. *Wharton* says that in *Man* there is a third Membrane betwixt the two commonly known, in which are seated the Glands or Kernels, and through which the Vessels run. If so, 'tis likely there is the same in an *Horses* Mesentery, which abounds with Glands. 'Tis a little above a quarter of a yard broad from its centre to its circumference. *The* Mesentery *why so called.*

Now its *centre* or *rise* is at the first and third Rack-bone of the Loins, where membranous Fibres are produced from the Rim of the Belly, and spread into the two investing Coats or Skins of the Mesentery. *Its rise.*

The *fat* with which these Membranes are stuft, is collected in the same manner as that of the Caul above-described in *chap.* 8. namely the oily part of the Bloud sweating out of the Arteries that run in abundance between these Membranes, is stopt by them, (they being more compact and close than the Coats of the Arteries) and by their respective coldness is congealed into fat. *Its Fat.*

There are almost innumerable Vessels running through it, but such as are rather sustained and conducted by it, than for its own use. *Its Vessels.*

The first sort are the *Veins*, to which it gives the denomination of *Mesaraick*. These are all branches of the *Porta*, and their office is to receive so much of the Arterial bloud as is not spent on the nourishment of the Guts and Mesentery, and to convey it to the Liver, and from thence to the Heart. Before the *milky Veins* were found out, it was believed they brought the Chyle to the Liver; but that opinion is now out of doors, as we have more fully shewn before in the tenth Chapter. *1. Veins.*

Its *Arteries* also from its name are called *Mesaraick* or *Mesenterick*; these run in great numbers through it to the Guts, to which what office they perform was likewise declar'd above, *chap.* 10. And besides the uses there ascribed to them, they continually supply new oily Vapours for the maintenance of the fat of the Mesentery. *2. Arteries.*

Its *Nerves* are very numerous, and spring from that pair which is now (from Dr. *Willis*) commonly called the *Intercostal*, and reckoned for the ninth pair, but was formerly reputed the sixth. *3. Nerves.*

All the *venæ lacteæ* or *milky Veins* run through it from the Guts towards its centre. These are very slender and almost transparent Vessels, having but one single Coat, and gaping with their mouths in the inmost Coat of the Guts do there suck up the Chyle, and take the nearest course thence to those Glands or Kernels of the Mesentery that are next to them, several smaller in their passage growing into one greater. From the several smaller Glands they proceed to the greatest that is placed at the Back at the centre of the Mesentery, and from thence to the common receptacle that *4. Milky Veins.*

that is seated betwixt the Kidneys. What course it takes from thence the Reader may see in the already twice mentioned tenth Chapter.

5. Lymphe-ducts. Besides all these sorts of Vessels there was a fifth sort found out by *Thomas Bartholin* (a Dane) some thirty years ago, which indeed are to be found in most parts of the Body, but most abound in the Mesentery, and are called *Lympheducts*, as much as to say, Water-passages. Their Coat is single as that of the milky Veins, but more transparent; and the *lympha* or water that is contained in them, is very clear. This Liquor differs from the *serum* or wheyish watery part of the Bloud, which one may discover by this Experiment; If you take a little of this Liquor into a Spoon, it will soon thicken into a gelly of its own accord, which the *serum* of the Bloud will not do unless you heat it over the fire. It is supposed to be made of thin moist Vapours of the Bloud, which being condensed into water, are imbibed by these Vessels. All those that run through the Mesentery discharge their water into the common receptacle of the Chyle above-mentioned, so that it passes together with the Chyle up the passage that ascends by the Back towards the Shoulders, and there mixes with the Bloud in the subclavian Vein.

Its Glands. In the middle Membrane of the Mesentery (first found out by Doctor *Wharton* as abovesaid) there are a great many *Glands* or *Kernels*, into which the milky Veins as they pass through the Mesentery are inserted, and then rise out of them again, continuing their course to the one great Gland at its centre, in which they all meet together, and from it hold on their way to the common receptacle as was above-declared. By these Glands the said Veins are supported and strengthened in their passage.

Its Use. Now the *use* of the Mesentery is to be as it were a tie or band to the Guts to bind or gather them together, and to fasten them to the Back, that their great weight do not cause them in violent motion either to break or twist or roll confusedly one over the other, whereby their gentle worm-like motion would be hindred, if not perverted or abolished. And besides by its Membranes and Glands it does guard and sustain the several Vessels whose way lies through it.

CHAP. XIII.

Of the Pancreas or Sweet-bread.

The Pancreas *why so called.* THE *Sweet-bread* is an unshapely body, of a glandulous yet flesh-like substance, from whence it hath its name *Pancreas* which signifies *all flesh*.

Its situation. In dissection it is at the end of the Liver and bottom of the Stomach; but while the Horse is living, it is situated on the backside of the bottom of the Stomach, and lies cross the Belly lengthways as that does.

Its substance. Its proper flesh is white and soft, but the little Kernels with which it is plentifully stored, are of a more reddish colour. It is covered with a single Membrane which it has from the Rim of the Belly, as all the Bowels of the Lower Belly have, of which it is almost the least.

It

It has *Veins* from that branch of the *Porta* that runs to the Spleen, and is called the Splenick. Its *Arteries* ſpring from the Cœliacal; and its *Nerves* from the Intercoſtal or ninth pair. This Bowel for its bigneſs has very many of thoſe Lympheducts that we deſcribed in the foregoing Chapter running through the Meſentery. *Its Veſſels.*

Beſides theſe Veſſels which are common to it with other parts, it has a pipe or paſſage peculiar to it ſelf, which was firſt found out at *Padua* in an humane Body about forty years ago. This paſſage is membranous, and though it be but one in its going out, yet within the Sweet-bread it is divided firſt into two, and thoſe two into innumerable ſmall branches which are diſperſed all over its Body, but their extremities terminate in the aboveſaid reddiſh Kernels with which the Sweet-bread abounds. *Its proper paſſage.*

Before this paſſage was found out, ſome thought the *uſe* of the Sweet-bread to be only to ſerve as a Cuſhion (being very ſoft) for the Stomach to bolſter upon, and to ſuſtain the Veſſels that run through it; and others, that it ſent a ferment to the Stomach to aſſiſt concoction. As to this latter uſe it muſt needs be onely imaginary, ſeeing there is no paſſage from it to the Stomach. And as to the former, though it doe thoſe offices mentioned, yet from its proper paſſage (which opens into the beginning of the ſmall Gut very near the ſame place where the Gall-paſſage enters) it gives ſuſpicion that it has a further uſe. Now ſome have been ſo curious as to open Dogs alive, and cutting off this paſſage where it is inſerted into the Gut, to receive its end into a narrow-mouth'd Veſſel, (you may ſee the manner of it in *Barthol.* Anat. *l.* 1. *c.* 13.) into which Veſſel in a few hours time there has a Spoonfull of Juice deſtilled out of it. And this Juice, to diſtinguiſh it from all other Liquors in the Body, they call the *Pancreatick juice*, from the name *Pancreas* whereby the Sweet-bread is otherwiſe called. So that it ſeems there is a peculiar Liquor ſeparated from the Arteries into this paſſage in the little Kernels or Glands above-ſpoken of, which thoſe that have taſted it, ſay, is of a ſaltiſh and ſomewhat ſowriſh taſte. Now this Juice paſſing by its Pipe into the beginning of the ſmall Gut, meets there with the Gall, with which it ferments, and cauſes ſome fermentation in the Chyle as it deſcends that way, whereby its purer parts are ſeparated from the more impure and earthy, as was diſcourſed more fully in the eleventh Chapter, when we were deſcribing the ſmall Gut, (to which the Reader may pleaſe to turn back.) *Its Uſe.* *The Pancreatick Juice.*

As for the *figure* of the Sweet-bread, you have it expreſt in the next Table but one, namely in that wherein the Spleen is alſo deſcribed.

CHAP. XIV.

Of the Liver.

HAVING now done with the Parts that minister to the first concoction, namely *Chylification*, we proceed to those other that in some measure, some more some less, assist *Sanguification*, of which the *Liver* was esteemed by the Ancients the principal, nay almost the onely instrument. Which errour of theirs was founded on this mistake in Anatomy, That having not then found out the milky Veins which we have before described, they thought that the Chyle was received out of the Guts by the Mesaraick Veins, which being branches of the *Porta*, all run to the Liver; And the *Cava* or large hollow Vein that arises out of the Liver, and is the trunk whence all the branches of Veins in the whole Body spring, containing nothing in it but bloud, it necessarily follow'd that if the Chyle came to the Liver, it must by it be turned into bloud before it departed from it again. Yea so deep was this Opinion of the Liver's making bloud fixed in Mens Brains, that for some while after the milky Veins were found out, they would needs have *them* to convey the Chyle to the Liver, though they were forced to a thousand shifts to apologize for their non-appearance between the great Gland of the Mesentery, (whither they might be easily traced) and the Liver. But this prejudice was soon overcome when about thirty years ago the common Receptacle (described before in the tenth and twelfth Chapters) was found out, and a new office was invented for the Liver, which yet may in some sort be said to assist Sanguification: and what this office is, shall be shewn by and by in this and the next Chapters.

Its substance, situation and figure. The *substance* of it is like concrete or congealed Bloud, for which cause it is called *Parenchyma*, which is to say an affusion or shedding forth of bloud. It is one in number, and situated in the Lower Belly in the upper part thereof on the right side under the short Ribs, near to the *Diaphragma* or Midriff, in its upper side, and its lower lies upon the right and foreside of the Stomach. It is divided into several Lobes or Flaps, in Horses, otherwise than in Men, in whom it is one continued body. These Lobes do cover the Stomach, grasping of it (as it were) as one should grasp any thing with their hand by spreading their fingers about it. This covering the Stomach stands in great need of, for thereby is the heat thereof much cherished for the furthering concoction. As for its *shape*, you cannot so well conceive it by any description, as by the figure of it annexed at the end of this Chapter, which you may please to take a view of.

Its Ligaments and investing Membrane. It is tied in its place by three Ligaments: the strongest of which is that which is called its *suspensory* Ligament. This springs from the *Peritonæum* where it is spread over the under side of the Midriff. It is very strong and membranous, and arising from the Midriff somewhat towards its right side, it is inserted into the upper or bunching side of the Liver, into which it enters a little way; but in its entrance it loses one of its Membranes, which dilating or spreading it self makes the skin that en-

wraps

wraps the whole Liver; for the Liver is onely covered with one thin skin which it has from this Ligament. There is a *second* Ligament which seems to spring from this skin of the Liver, and is inserted into the sharp-pointed Gristle at the bottom of the Breast-bone. By these two is the Liver kept from falling lower down into the Belly, or from slipping out of its place sideways. The *third* Ligament is not one originally, but when the Foal is in the Womb it supplies the place of a Vein, running from the Navel to the lower or hollow side of the Liver, and by it is nourishment brought from the Dam to the Foal. But as soon as it is foaled, and it begins to take its nourishment by the mouth onely, and not any longer at all this way, this Vein dries and closes up, and so degenerates into a Ligament, whereby the Liver is kept from ascending or bearing up against the Midriff, as it might have done in an Horses leaping or the like. This is just opposite to the *Suspensory* one, entring in at the lower side over against where that does on the upper.

It hath two sorts of *Veins*. The *first* are the roots of the *Vena cava* or large hollow Vein, which spreading themselves through all its parts, do receive into them the bloud that is brought into the Liver by the *Porta*; which having done, the smaller roots two or three of them grow into one, and this one uniting with two or three of the like kind into another larger root, they do at last all of them meet in one trunk and make the hollow Vein, which issuing out of the upper part of the Liver presently enters the Midriff, and so ascends up to the Heart. The *second* sort of Vein is the *Porta*, all whose branches coming from the Guts, Spleen, Stomach, &c. and uniting into one trunk enter the Liver on its lower or hollow side, into which it is no sooner entred, but presently it disperses it self into innumerable branches through all the Lobes of the Liver, affording nourishment unto it, in that regard supplying the place of an Artery, which it resembles the more, because within the Liver it has two Coats, the outer whereof it receives from that skin that cloaths the Liver, in its entrance into it. Now so much of the bloud that is imported by the *Porta*, as is not spent on the nourishment of the Liver, is drunk in by the roots of the *hollow Vein* before-mentioned, and returned to the Heart. This Vein is called *Porta* or *Vena portæ*, the Gate-vein, from two bunchings out, of the Liver, (called *gates* by *Hippocrates*) between which it enters it. *Veins.*

Yet is not the Liver, at least all the parts of it, onely nourished by the bloud that is brought in by the *Porta*; for there is a branch which comes from the Cœliack Artery that ascends to its hollow side just by the *Porta*, which sends forth twigs all over its Coat, as likewise through the Coats of the *Porta* and the Choler-Vessels: but whether any of them enter into its parenchyma or substance, is not discovered. These twigs of Arteries bring vital heat and nourishment to those parts through which they run. *Arteries.*

Its *Nerves* spring from the Intercostal pair, *viz.* partly from the stomachick and partly from the mesenterick branch thereof. These onely are communicated to those parts to which the Arteries are dispersed, so that the substance of the Liver has very little sense. *Nerves.*

We shew'd before how that for some while after the milky Veins were found out, they were believ'd to convey the Chyle to the Liver: and all the colour for this Opinion was a few small clear, limpid and almost transparent Vessels, that run between the Mesentery and it. But as on *Lympheducts.*

the one hand they are too few in number for that office (eſpecially being ſo ſlender) being ſcarce one for ten of the milky Veins in the Meſentery: ſo on the other, they are neither of the ſame colour (as being much clearer) nor does the Liquor they contain come from the Meſentery to the Liver, but runs from this to that, as has been obſerved in Live-diſſections, in which having been tied they have ſwelled on that ſide of the Ligature toward the Liver, and grown empty toward the Meſentery. They are indeed then truly *Lympheducts*, which carry that water that is ſeparated from the bloud in the Liver, towards the Meſentery, and from it to the common receptacle of the Chyle with which it mixes.

Beſides theſe Veſſels there are the numerous branches of the Gall-paſſage, of which we ſhall treat more fully in the next Chapter. And ſhall ſay no more here, but onely how one may diſtinguiſh betwixt the branches of the *Cava*, *Porta* and theſe of the Gall-paſſage, ſo as to know which are which. Thoſe of the *Cava* are clad but with one Coat, are white, thin and of a large cavity. Thoſe of the *Porta* have a double Coat, and ſo are thicker and ſtronger, and yet not ſo wide as thoſe of the *Cava*. Laſtly, the branches of the Gall-paſſage are of a duskiſh yellow, have a thicker Coat than either the *Cava* or *Porta*, and yet have the narroweſt channel. Theſe are included in a common caſe with thoſe of the *Porta*, which makes their outer Coat.

Its Uſe. Having in the beginning of this Chapter detected the errour of the Ancients in aſcribing Sanguification to the Liver in ſo eminent and large a ſenſe; we muſt however confeſs that it does ſomething towards the purifying of the Bloud, and that is, by ſeparating the Choler from it, as ſhall be fullier ſhewn in the next Chapter. In it alſo is a pretty quantity of ſerous or wheyiſh humour filtrated or ſtrained from the Bloud, which is ſent by the Lympheducts to the common receptacle of the Chyle as aforeſaid. In the third and laſt place it furthers the concoction of the Stomach by its kind and cheriſhing heat.

The *Sixth* Table ſheweth the Liver intire, and alſo its Veſſels freed from the *Parenchyma*.

Fig. I. Expreſſes the Liver taken out of the Body, and placed with its hollow ſide uppermoſt.

AAAA *The hollow ſide of the Liver cloathed with its Coat.*
B *The* Vena portæ *or Gate-vein, and its egreſs out of the hollow ſide of the Liver.*
C *The Trunk of* Vena cava *or hollow Vein alſo coming out of the Liver.*
D *The Gall or Choler-paſſage cut off cloſe to the Liver.*
E *An Artery which is branched to the Liver from the* ramus Cœliacus.
F *A Nerve of the ſixth pair (as commonly reckoned) alſo branching to the Liver.*
GG *The Edges of the Liver turned down and hanging over the hollow ſide of it.*
HHHH *The four Lobes or Scollops of the Liver.*

Fig. II.

Figure II

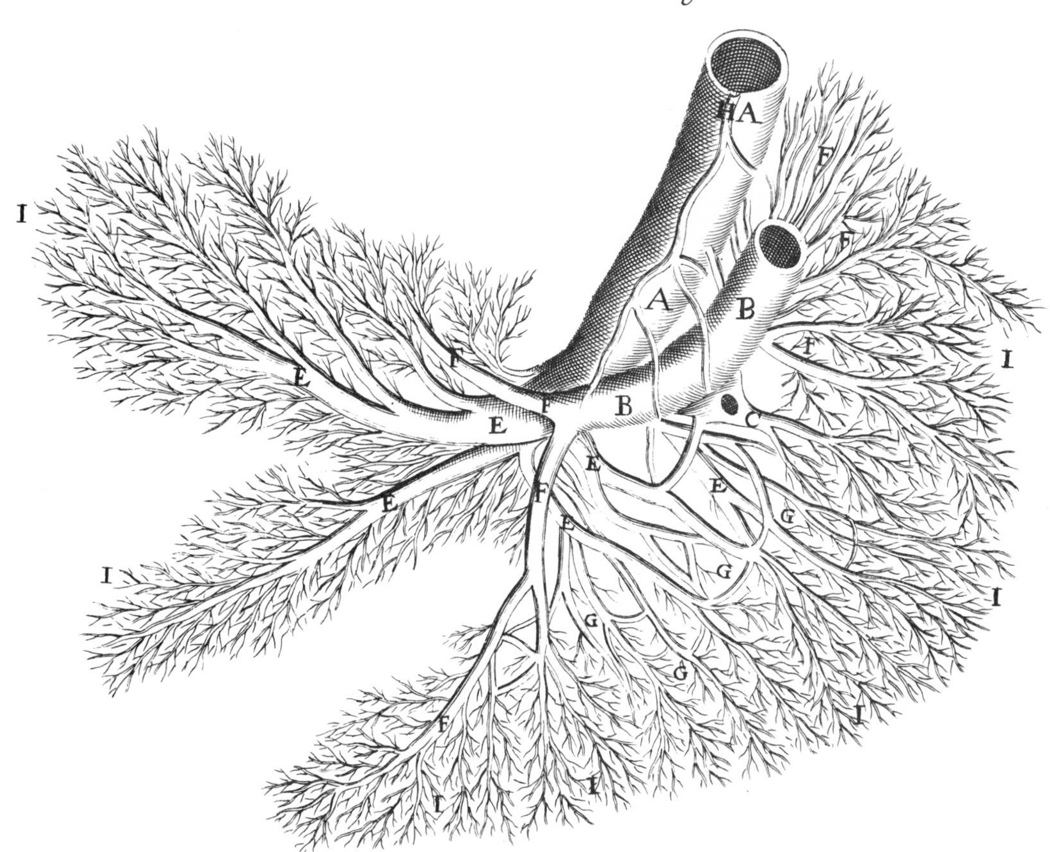

Figure. I.

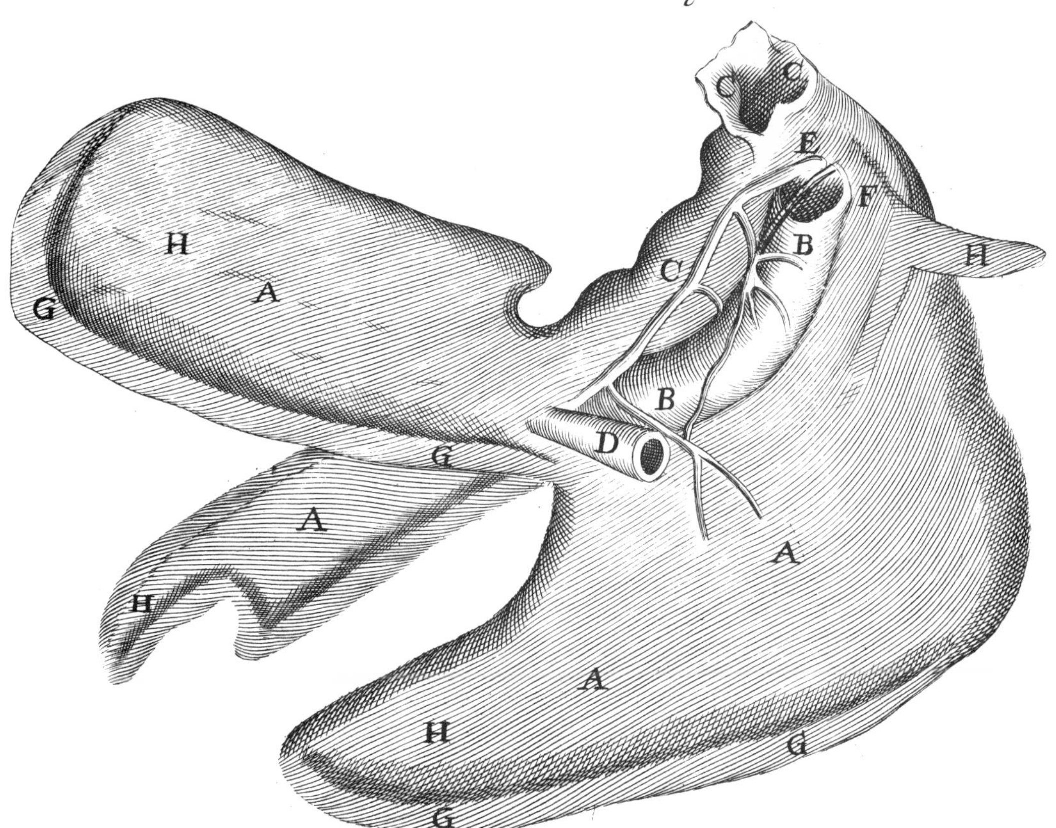

Fig. II. Represents the Vessels of the Liver freed from the *Parenchyma*, or fleshy substance thereof.

AA *A portion of* Vena cava.
BB *The Trunk of* Vena portæ *passing forth of the Liver.*
C *The Gall-passage cut off close by the Liver.*
EEEE *The Branches of* Vena portæ *dispersed through the Liver.*
FFFF *The Branches of the hollow Vein likewise distributed through the Liver.*
GGGG *The most remarkable Anastomoses or joinings together of the mouths of the* Cava *and* Porta.
HH *The Artery that is branched to the Liver from the Cœliack Artery.*
I *The Extremities or ends of the Veins, which for their smallness are called Capillary, or hair-like.*

CHAP. XV.

Of the Porus Bilarius, *or Gall-passage.*

IT is difficult to give a satisfactory account why most Creatures should have both a *Gall bladder*, for the collection of the Choler, and besides, a *Gall-passage*; and yet a Horse and all whole-hoofed Beasts, as also Harts, Fallow-deer and some few others, should onely have the *passage* without the *Bladder*. It would be worth the while for our *Virtuosi* to invent a probable reason of it, but for my own part I dare not pretend to be so sagacious. But much have those been mistaken that not finding any Bladder of Gall, have affirmed that an Horse hath no gall at all. And this, Dr. *Brown* reckons up amongst *vulgar Errors*.

Now the trunk of this *Gall-passage* enters the Liver very near the same place with the *Porta*, together with which it is enwrapped in one common Cover, which they both borrow from that skin wherewith the Liver is cloathed. I mean they begin to be so invested just at their entrance into the Liver, for before they have but each one single Coat. Its branches run along with those of the *Porta* through all parts of the Liver, and it has the same Artery and Nerve running through its Membrane. All these branches uniting into one trunk, it passes the directest way to the small Gut, into which it is inserted about a foot from the lower Orifice of the Stomach, where it discharges it self of the Choler. *Its branching in the Liver, and its tendency without it.*

Having described the Vessel, there remain two things to be enquired into, *first* how the Choler is separated in the Liver, and *secondly* of what use it is. As to the first, we must consider that there can be no such separation as this, without some sort of ferment to cause it. There comes indeed nothing to the Liver but under the form of bloud, but however it will be of use to examine from what parts that bloud comes: And amongst the rest we find that a considerable quantity comes from the Spleen by the splenick branch. Now every one that will taste it may discern that the bloud *Choler how separated from the Bloud, and its use.*

bloud that comes out of the Spleen by this branch has a kind of a sowrish harsh taste to what the rest of the mass of bloud has. This then mixing with the rest of the bloud and passing with it through the narrow Vessels in the Liver, causes it there to ferment (as a small piece of sowr Dough will I know not how much that is not leavened) and in that fermentation this yellow Choler is separated from the Bloud, much in the same manner as Yest from Beer in a Barrel, (which it partly resembles in colour.) And this fermentation is assisted by the proper nature and faculty of the Liver given by Nature to it; who hath also framed this liquor of Particles so differing from those of the Bloud, that though the Bloud pass out of the *Porta* into the *Cava*, yet the Choler stays behind and is received by the small mouths of the Choler-passage. Some affirm this separation is performed by the help of some Glands or little Kernels into which the ends of the several Vessels are inserted, but I have not been able to discern them. The use of the Gall is, Together with the Juice that is sent from the Sweet-bread, to make a ferment in the first Gut for the uses that are fully enough delivered in the eleventh Chapter: to which we shall onely add, that it serves by its acrimony to exstimulate the Guts to expell the Excrements contained in them. And seeing there is no bag or repository to store it up in, it passes continually to the Guts, whereby Horses come to dung oftener than most other Creatures: which as Dr. *Brown* notes, "was prudently contrived by Providence in this Animal, considering his plentifull feeding, the largeness of his Guts, and their various circumvolution. For, says he, Choler is the natural Glyster, or one excretion whereby Nature excludes another, *&c.*

CHAP. XVI.

Of the Spleen or Milt.

The substance of the Spleen. THE *Spleen* or *Milt* is of a soft, spongious *substance*, like thick, black and congealed Bloud, from which it is said to be generated; though some that of late have examined it more curiously with Magnifying Glasses, declare the greatest part of its substance, besides the Bloud-vessels, to consist of abundance of little Kernels inclosed in skinny Cells like Honey-combs, which in their own nature are of a white colour, and will appear such when the Bloud is washt from them. For my own part, I question whether there be any such Kernels in it, or if there be, they must be far different from those of any other part, and be of a much looser substance, seeing I have onely in River-water (after I had taken off the investing skin) washt off the parenchyma so clearly from the Vessels, that there has seem'd to be nothing else remaining. A figure of which Vessels so cleared of the parenchyma by washing, you have in the following Table.

Its situation and connexion. Its *situation* is under the short Ribs on the left side over against the Liver, between the Stomach and the short or bastard Ribs. It *cleaveth* oft-times to the Midriff by a skin or coat, which it hath from the Rim of the Belly. It is also fastned by a skin to the Stomach.

It is

Its Figure. It is of a triangular *ſhape*, yet long, and ſomething ſharp-pointed, as you may ſee in the Figure.

Its Colour. Its *Colour* is (in a ſound Horſe) reddiſh, inclining ſomewhat to black; but in an unſound Horſe it is more inclining to black, or of a leaden or aſhey colour: yet moſt times in an unſound Horſe it is of the colour of the Humour which offends.

Whether an Horſe can live without it. There are ſeveral Creatures that naturally have no Spleen, as all Inſects; and therefore that Proverb is not literally true, *That even a Fly has a Spleen*; Such alſo as have no Piſs-bladder, want the Milt, as the *Chameleon*, and many ſuch like: But now it is a great queſtion, whether ſuch Creatures as by Nature have Spleens, can have them taken out, and yet live. It is true indeed that other Parts that ſeem to be as conſiderable, have been taken even out of *Humane* Bodies, and yet the Parties have lived: So I have read of ſome Women that upon incurable diſtempers in the Part, have had their Womb cut out, and yet have liv'd in tolerable health afterwards (*Barthol.* Epiſt.) And it is a common thing to geld any ſort of Creature, though there be conſiderably large Veſſels that run to the Stones. But it is to be confeſs'd that theſe parts inſtanc'd in, ſeem to be wholly framed for the propagation of the ſeveral *kinds* of living Creatures, and not for the neceſſary ſervice of the *Individual* that has them. And therefore when they are taken away, though the end for which they were created, to wit *generation*, be fruſtrated by the loſs of them; yet may the Creature it ſelf that loſes them, live well enough without them. But now as for the Spleen, it does not at all ſerve for procreation, but is of uſe onely to that Body that has it. (What its *uſe* is, we ſhall ſhew towards the latter end of this Chapter.) Yet ſeveral have boaſted that they have taken it out of Dogs and Cats, and that they have lived in pretty good plight a conſiderable while after. The operation muſt needs be ſomewhat difficult, ſeeing the Spleen is ſeated on the inſide of the ſhort Ribs, nearer the Back than the Breaſt: nor can I believe that a Horſe could live any while if it were taken out of him; but leaſt of all could Man, in whom it is larger than in any other Creature, as *Bartholin* affirms. For the Veſſels that are inſerted into it are ſo many and large, that it would ſeem impoſſible to ſtanch the Bloud; beſides the neceſſary uſe that it ſeems to be of to the Body, of which by and by.

Its Membrane. The *skin* that it is covered with, is *thicker* than that of the Liver, both becauſe of the looſe and ſoft ſubſtance of the Spleen that required a ſtronger covering to defend it; and alſo that it might the better ſuſtain the ſtrong beatings of its Arteries that are pretty large and many. This skin it has from the *Peritonæum* or Rim of the Belly, to which it is commonly knit, as alſo to the left Kidney and the Midriff, and on its inſide to the Caul. Some late Anatomiſts have affirmed it to be clad with two Coats, the outer that which we have mentioned, and the inner ariſing from the Veſſels that enter the Spleen.

Veſſels. 1. Veins. All the *Veins* that it has, are from that branch of the *Porta* that is called the Splenick branch. For the *Porta* as ſoon as it comes out of the lower or hollow ſide of the Liver, ſends one notable Branch to the Spleen, which paſſing croſs the Body from the right to the left ſide under the Liver and Stomach, enters the Spleen and diſperſes it ſelf into innumerable Twigs all over it. A Twig of the ſplenick Artery opens into this Vein a little before it enters the Spleen: And from the lower end of the Spleen there

there go two or three Veſſels to the Stomach, which are called *Vaſa brevia* or ſhort Veſſels. The uſe of the ſplenick Vein is to bring from the Spleen all that arterial blood that is not ſpent on its nouriſhment; and beſides, that proper and peculiar juice that is made in the Spleen, of which preſently.

2. *Arteries.* Its *Arteries* are three or four times more in number than the Veins, and all of them ſpring from the left Cœliack branch that has the name of *Splenick*, from the Spleen, into which it is inſerted. Hereby it receives vital heat and nouriſhment, and matter out of which to make its proper juice. Before this Artery enter the Spleen, it ſends forth one twig that unites with and opens into the ſplenick Vein, as was noted before.

3. *Nerves.* Its *Nerves* are but ſmall yet pretty numerous. They ſpring from a meſenterick branch of the left Intercoſtal Nerve, and are diſperſed principally through the skin that covers it, though ſome few enter its ſubſtance.

4. *Lympheducts.* Laſtly, it has ſeveral *Lympheducts*, or Water-paſſages, which creeping all over its Coat, take their way along the Caul towards the common receptacle of the Chyle, into which they empty the liquor contained in them, as all thoſe that ariſe from the ſeveral parts of the lower Belly do. What theſe Lympheducts are, and what that liquor is which they contain, I have ſhown above in the 12th Chapter, *of the Meſentery.*

Its action and uſe. There is no part of the Body concerning whoſe uſe there has been greater diverſity of opinion. *Some* have made it the receptacle of black Choler (or of thick dreggy Bloud) ſeparated in the Liver and brought hither by the ſplenick branch. *Others* that thought this too ignoble and baſe an uſe for ſo conſiderable a part, eſteem'd it to be as it were a ſecond Liver: For as they believed that the thinner and more ſpirituous part of the Chyle paſſed to the Liver; ſo, that a thicker and more dreggy part went to the Spleen, of which was made a blacker and more earthy ſort of Bloud, partly for its own nouriſhment, and partly for the nouriſhment of the Stomach, Guts, Meſentery, &c. In anſwer to theſe two opinions it will be ſufficient to ſay, That the firſt is contrary to the circulation of the Bloud, nothing paſſing from the Liver to the Spleen, but contrarily from the Spleen to the Liver: and the latter, beſides that it is contrary to the ſaid circulation, is repugnant alſo to the true motion of the Chyle, none of which either paſſes to the Liver or Spleen, as we have more than once ſhown already. A *third* opinion is, That of the bloud that the Arteries bring to it in great plenty, is made a certain acid or ſowr Juice, which is ſent by the *vaſa brevia* or ſhort Veins to the Stomach, into which being diſcharged, it partly provokes appetite, and partly helps concoction: And this Opinion has had a great many Abettors, whereas its falſity may be demonſtrated by this, that if one open a Dog (or the like) alive, and tie theſe ſhort Veins with a thred, they will fill and ſwell betwixt the Stomach and Ligature, but will grow empty on that ſide toward the Spleen; which is a plain evidence that the Bloud or whatever other Humour that runs in theſe ſhort Veins, flows *from* the Stomach and not *to* it. However we will grant that the Spleen does indeed make ſuch a ſowr Juice, of part of the Arterial bloud that is imported into it by the ſplenick Artery; but then it paſſes not from thence to the Stomach, but to the Liver by the ſplenick branch of the *Porta*: for if one tie the ſaid branch, as was ſaid above of the *ſhort veins*, it will fill towards the Spleen and grow empty towards the Liver. And the uſe of this Juice ſeems to be

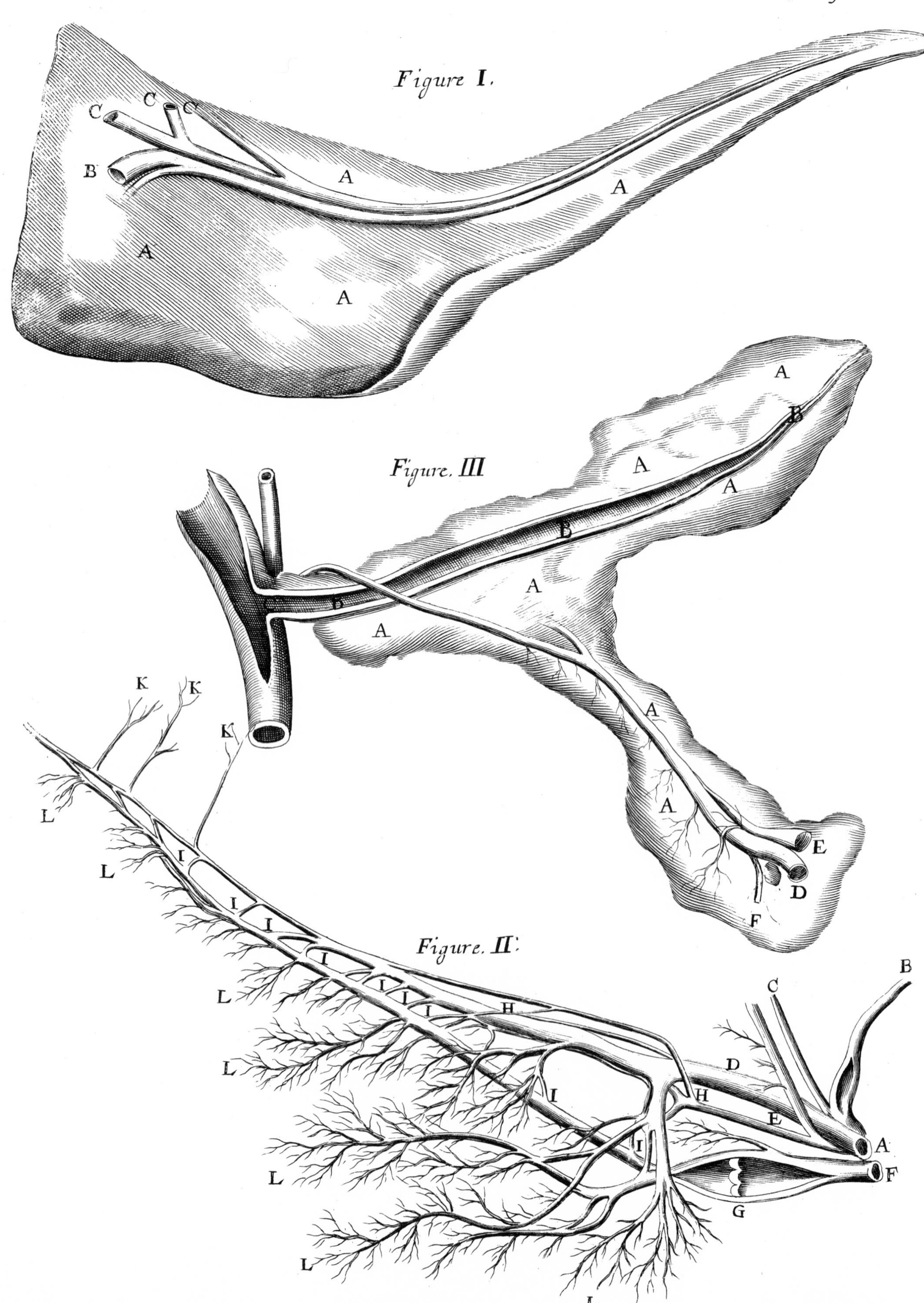
Figure I.
C
C
C
B
A
A
A
A
Figure. III
A
B
A
A
E
A
A
A
A
A
E
D
F
Figure. II.
K
K
K
L
L
I
I
I
I
I
I
I
H
L
L
I
H
D
E
I
L
L
L
C
B
A
F
G

be this, *viz.* That mixing in the trunk of the *Porta* with all the Bloud that is received by the branches thereof out of the ſeveral parts of the Lower Belly, eſpecially from the Guts, it enters with it into the Liver, where it cauſes the Bloud to ferment, whereby the Choler is ſeparated from it, for the uſes mentioned in the foregoing Chapter, where we have treated more at large of this ſeparation.

Another *uſe* of the Spleen is, by its warmth to cheriſh the left ſide of the Stomach, as the Liver does the right, to further the concoction thereof. And this it may be conceived to doe in a very conſiderable degree; for ſeeing it has ſo very many Arteries, it muſt needs be very warm.

There are many more Opinions concerning the uſe of the Spleen than theſe I have mentioned: but as it would be *tedious* to recite them, ſo it would be but *needleſs* to refute them, the new Doctrines of the circulation of the Bloud and the motion of the Chyle being improveable to a general confutation of them.

Table VII. Expreſſeth the Spleen intire with the Veſſels going in and out, and the ſame Veſſels alone freed from their *parenchyma*; as alſo the Sweet-bread intire with its Veſſels.

Fig. I Repreſenteth the Spleen intire, with the Veſſels going in and out.

A *Shews the body of the Spleen on the concave or hollow ſide which receives the Veſſels.*
B *The ſplenick Vein.*
C *The ſplenick Artery.*
D *Its Nerves proceeding from a Meſenterick branch of the left Intercoſtal Nerve.*

Fig. II. Repreſenteth the Veſſels of the Spleen deveſted of their parenchyma.

A *Shews the* Arteria Cœliaca, *cut cloſe off at the great Artery.*
B *Its* ramus dexter ſuperior, *or right-hand upper branch, producing the* gaſtrica dextra, *or right-hand Stomach-artery: it makes alſo the* cyſticæ gemellæ *that go to the Liver and Gall-paſſage.*
C *Its* ramus dexter inferior, *or right-hand lower branch, which goes to the Meſentery and Guts.*
D *Its* ramus ſiniſter, *or left-hand branch, called* Arteria Splenica *or ſplenick Artery, which brings the bloud to the Spleen.*
E *The Nerves of the Spleen coming from a meſenterick branch of the left Intercoſtal Nerve.*
F *The ſplenick branch of* Vena portæ *cut off cloſe by its trunk.*
G *The ſplenick Vein cut open to ſhew its Valves, which permit the Bloud to paſs from the Spleen to the Liver, but hinder any Bloud from returning from the Liver to the Spleen.*
HH *The Diſtribution of the Nerves through the ſubſtance of the Spleen, accompanying the Veins and Arteries.*
II &c. *Several (ſeeming) Anaſtomoſes or inoſculations of the Veins and Arteries.*
KKK *Veſſels going from the lower end of the Spleen to the Stomach, called* Vaſa brevia, *or ſhort Veſſels.*

LL &c. *The capillary branches of Veins, Arteries and Nerves diſperſed through the whole ſubſtance of the Spleen.*

Fig. III. Repreſenteth the *Pancreas* or Sweet-bread freed from its Membrane and part of its ſubſtance, the better to ſhew the courſe of the Veſſels in it, which come to it from the ſplenick Vein and Artery. It repreſenteth alſo the new *Wirtſungian* paſſage, ſo called from the late Inventer of it.

A *Shews the body of the* Pancreas *diſſected.*
B *The new paſſage called* ductus Wirtſungianus *or* pancreaticus.
C *The Orifice of the ſaid paſſage where it opens into the beginning of the ſmall Gut.*
D *The Artery of the Sweet-bread diſperſed through its ſubſtance.*
E *The Vein of the Sweet-bread diſperſed likewiſe through its ſubſtance.*
F *Its Nerves, being a branch of the Intercoſtal pair.*

CHAP. XVII.

Of the Kidneys, and Deputy-kidneys.

Their name. THE *Kidneys* are otherwiſe called *Reins* from their Latine name *Renes*, which is derived from a Greek word which ſignifieth *to flow*, becauſe the watery or wheyiſh part of the Bloud doth continually flow through them, and maketh the Urine.

Number, ſituation and connexion. They are in *number* two, that when one is ſtopt with a ſtone or gravel, or hurt by any accident, the Urine might be ſeparated in the other, or otherwiſe the Beaſt would die. They are *ſeated* in the Loins behind the Stomach and Guts, the right under the Liver and the left under the Spleen, on each ſide of the hollow Vein and great Artery, oppoſite to one another. They reſt upon the Muſcles of the Loins, and are included betwixt the Membranes of the *Peritonæum* which keeps them firm in their place. They are *knit* to the hollow Vein and great Artery by the Emulgent Veſſels, and to the Bladder by the Ureters which we ſhall deſcribe in the next Chapter.

Figure. They are ſeldom like to one another in *ſhape*; for the Right is in figure like a Heart, but ſomething flatter; whereas the left is like that of a Man, *viz.* of the ſhape of a Kidney-bean, as you may ſee them repreſented in the following Figure.

Membranes. They are covered with two *Membranes*, an *inner* which is *proper*, and an *outer* which is *common.* The *inner* Skin ſeems to ſpring from the outer Coat of thoſe Veſſels that enter into them: this cleaves ſo cloſe to them, that it can hardly be ſeparated, being very thin, and having ſmall threds of Nerves running along it from a twig of the Intercoſtal Nerve. The *outer* which is common, is borrowed from the Rim of the Belly, and is wrapped ſomewhat looſely about the Kidney. This Skin is bedaubed with fat, and is therefore called the *fatty Coat*; and into it are inſerted an Artery

tery and Vein, which have alſo the title of *fatty*, and ſpring from the great Artery and hollow Vein.

As to their *ſubſtance*, it has been always till of late held to be hard and compact fleſh; and indeed it handles pretty firm to the touch, and ſeems to be fleſhy to the bare eye. But ſeeing there is no ſeparation made of any thing from the Bloud in other Parts, but by the help of Glands or Kernels; (for ſo is the Slaver ſeparated in the Mouth, the Choler in the Liver, bad Humours in the Guts upon taking a purge, &c.) I ſay, for that cauſe it is reaſonable to give credit to thoſe curious Anatomiſts that by their Magnifying Glaſſes or Microſcopes have diſcovered the ſubſtance of the Kidneys to be for the greateſt part made up of ſuch Glands, by means of which the Urine is ſeparated from the Bloud, in ſuch manner as we ſhall ſhew by and by. *Subſtance.*

Their *Arteries* and *Veins* are called *Emulgents*, becauſe they do as it were *milk out* the Urine from the maſs of Bloud. Each Kidney has for the moſt part but one Artery and one Vein; yet ſometimes two or more of a ſort. But whether the Trunk be one or more, each as it enters the Kidneys is branched into ſeveral, and thoſe into more ſucceſſively, till they become as ſmall as hairs. The Emulgent *Arteries* ſpring from the Trunk of the great Artery, and the *Veins* from the hollow Vein: Both theſe as they enter the Kidney, are deveſted of their outer Coat, which makes the proper Coat of the Kidneys, as was obſerved above: but inſtead of that loſs they are inveſted in one common Caſe with the branches of the Ureter, even as we ſhewed in the fifteenth Chapter that the branches of the Gall-paſſage in the Liver are included in one common Coat or Caſe with thoſe of the *Porta*. The Arteries bring bloud for their nouriſhment, and moreover the watery humour that is ſeparated in them and makes the Urine. By the Veins the bloud circulates back again to the hollow Vein or *Cava*, and by it aſcends up to the Heart. *Veſſels, viz. Emulgent Arteries, and Veins.*

Beſides the innumerable little Kernels which we have ſhewn the ſubſtance of the Kidney to conſiſt of, there are about ten of a more conſiderable bigneſs in the middle or centre of it, placed at the entrance into the *pelvis* or Baſon, which are in Latin called *Carunculæ Papillares*, in Engliſh Papillary Caruncles, and by ſome they are called Teat-like Productions, both which names they have from the likeneſs they have to the Teats or Nipples of Women. They are ſomething harder than the reſt of the ſubſtance of the Kidney, and alſo of a fainter colour. They are in bigneſs as large as a ſmall Horſe-bean. They have each ſeveral ſmall holes or pores, through which the Urine deſtills out of the ſlender Urinary Pipes in the body of the Kidneys, into the cavity of the *pelvis*. *The Papillary Caruncles.*

Now this *pelvis* or Baſon is a membranous cell or cavity in the middle of the Kidney, and is nothing elſe but the head of the *Ureter* widened. There run out of it ſeveral large pipes to the aforeſaid Teat-like Kernels, (one pipe to each Kernel) by which the Urine drils into this cavity, and out of it into the *Ureter*. *The pelvis or Baſon.*

The *action* of the Kidneys, is to ſeparate the wheyiſh Humour from the Bloud, which they do in this manner and order. We find that an Horſe can no more live without drink than meat: Now the drink ſerves not onely to cool the Body, but much more is it of uſe to make the Chyle thin, that it may be able to paſs through the narrow ways of the milky Veins; ſo that the water which the Horſe drinks, paſſes along with the more oily Chyle into the maſs of Bloud, whither having con- *Their Action.*

ducted it, the water is now of no more use, and therefore the Emulgent Arteries above-described conveigh it to the Kidneys together with the Bloud, to cast it out: But the Bloud, being of a thicker body than the water, cannot enter through those narrow passages which the other destils through, and therefore what is more than serves for their nourishment, returns back from the Kidneys by the Emulgent Veins into the *Cava*, and so returns to the Heart again in its circulation. But the watery or wheyish part running out of the larger into the smaller branches of the Emulgent Arteries successively, and the said branches so often dividing themselves till at last they become as small as an hair and end in the little Kernels towards the outside of the Kidneys, this watery Humour is milked as it were through these Kernels into small urinary pipes, as slender almost as Fibres, by which it drills along to the Papillary Caruncles, and is again strained through them into the Bason, from whence it glides down the Ureters into the Bladder, where when it becomes troublesome either by its quantity or sharpness, &c. it provokes the Horse to stale, and is called Urine. But seeing the Piss is not of the same colour with the water that was drunk, but generally a great deal yellower, it is likely it gains that colour from a little quantity of Choler mixed with it: And as the Choler *either* retains it natural colour, to wit yellow, *or* is preternaturally of some other, as black, greenish, &c. the Urine will be tinctured accordingly; as any Man may observe in Horses that are distempered. So that in Horses as well as in Men, one may many times gain some knowledge of the Distemper from the Urine.

Deputy-kidneys, their name, situation, bigness and shape.

Over the Kidneys a little more outward, and about an inch from them, there stand two Kernels, which are known by several *Names*, from the several uses that Authors have ascribed to them. Some call them Deputy-kidneys, because of some resemblance they have to the true ones in their frame, and because they have been thought to assist them in separating the Urine. *Bartholine* calls them Black-choler Cases, from an Opinion that they receive black Choler from the Spleen. Others have impos'd other Names on them, which we shall not recite. It is not long since they were first found out. They are in an Horse about as *big* as a Garden-bean, and of that *shape* as they are represented in the Figure. They are covered with a single thin skin, which commonly sticks to the fatty skin that invests the Kidneys. They have a small cavity in them.

Their Vessels.

Their *Veins* and *Arteries* generally come from the *Emulgents*, but sometimes immediately from the great Artery and hollow Vein. The Arteries bring them bloud for nourishment, from which what remains, returns back by the Veins, as also does that Humour whatever it be that is concocted and separated in them, for there is no other vessel to do it. They have indeed some *Lympheducts*, but those are common to *them* with *other* parts, and have no peculiar use here. Their *Nerves* spring from that branch of the Intercostal pair that goes to the Stomach, to the Spleen, and to the inner or proper skin that cloaths the Kidneys.

Their Use.

In their Cavity there is commonly found a blackish Humour, which is made of part of the Arterial bloud that flows to them; but of what nature or use this Humour should be, is very uncertain. It has no way to go out of the Cavity but by the Veins, which deposite what is contained in them into the Emulgent Veins, or into the *Cava*, and so it must needs pass with the Venal bloud to the Heart. If there could be

found

found out any way whereby it could probably paſs to the Kidneys, then *Bartholine's* Opinion, that they make a ferment for the uſe of the Reins, for the better ſeparating of the wheyiſh Humour from the Bloud, were very plauſible; but till then, one muſt ſuſpend their belief of it. As for mine own part, ſeeing ſo many learned Anatomiſts as have treated of them, are at a loſs in diſcovering their true uſe, I will not be aſhamed to confeſs my own ignorance and unſatisfiedneſs therein alſo.

CHAP. XVIII.

Of the Ureters or Paſſages of Urine.

THE *Ureters* or Urine-pipes or Chanels are in number two, ſeated on each ſide of the hollow Vein and great Artery, at ſome diſtance from them. Their head or beginning is the Baſon of the Kidneys, at whoſe hollow ſide they come forth, and run in a crooked line like an ſ down to the Bladder, into whoſe back and lower part they are inſerted not far from the Sphincter, running for an inch between its two proper Coats, to prevent the return of the Urine back this way. For when the Bladder is ſqueezed, its Coats clap cloſe together, and ſo ſhut up the mouths of the Ureters. *The Ureters.*

They are in *ſubſtance* much like a Vein, onely whiter and thicker, and more nervous. They are commonly held to conſiſt of two Coats, an inner which is proper, and an outer which is borrowed from the Rim of the Belly. They have ſmall Veins and Arteries from the neighbouring Veſſels, and ſlips of Nerves in a conſiderable number from the Intercoſtals, whence proceeds that intolerable ſenſe of pain when a ſtone ſticks in them. *Their ſubſtance, and Veſſels.*

They are indifferent large, having a hollowneſs through them which is ſo wide, that they will admit of a large ſtraw in a dead Horſe, and therefore may be conceived in a living Horſe to be much wider. Through theſe paſſages or hollowneſſes, the Urine doth paſs from the Kidneys to the Bladder, and that is their ſole and true *uſe.* *Their cavity and uſe.*

CHAP.

CHAP. XIX.

Of the Piſs-bladder, or Bladder of Urine.

The ſituation and ſubſtance of the Bladder. THE Bladder of Urine is ſeated at the bottom of the Belly, in that hollowneſs that is formed of the *Os ſacrum*, Hips and the *Os pubis*, between the Coats of the Rim of the Belly; and is of a *ſubſtance* partly membranous, for ſtrength, extenſion and contraction; and partly fleſhy, for motion; for by its fleſhy Fibres are its Membranes contracted: and theſe fleſhy Fibres are wholly ſeated in its middle Coat, which is truly muſcular, as ſhall be ſhewed by and by.

Its Figure. It is of a round globous *figure*, in ſhape like a Pear, having within it a large cavity or hollowneſs, wherein to contain the Urine.

Membranes. It is compoſed of a treble *Coat* or Skin. The firſt and *outwardmoſt* of which it hath derived to it from the Rim of the Belly, which Skin is very ſtrong and cloſe. The *innermoſt* is thin, white and bright, of an exquiſite ſenſe, and is interwoven with all ſorts of Fibres, that it may the better bear inlarging and drawing up together, as need requireth. Within I have often found it covered with a mucous cruſt, which I take to be an Excrement of the third concoction of the Bladder, and to ſerve to defend it from being too much grated upon by the acrimony of the Urine. The *middle* betwixt theſe two, is as thick or thicker than them both, and is ſtuff with fleſhy Fibres, even as the ſame Coat of the Stomach and Womb are. Its Fibres run lengthways of the Bladder, and by contracting of themſelves ſqueeze out the Urine, forcing open the ſphincter Muſcle that encompaſſeth the neck of the Bladder.

Its perforations. It hath three *perforations* or holes, two on the hinder part a little below the neck to let in the Urine from the Ureters, and one in the neck to let the Urine out.

Its parts and connexion. The *parts* of the Bladder are two, its bottom and its neck. The bottom is its wider, more capacious part, and its neck, its narrower and more contracted. The bottom is faſt tied by a Membrane to the *Inteſtinum rectum* or Arſe-gut, and to the *Aorta* (a little before its diviſion) by the Umbilical Arteries, ſo that no violent motion can cauſe it to fall down upon its neck, which if it ſhould happen, would hinder the outgate of the Urine. The neck is narrower but longer in Horſes than in Mares, and in both it is fleſhy, being incompaſſed with a ſphincter Muſcle, which is woven with very many Fibres, ſome of which are ſtreight, and ſome overthwart, theſe laſt lying under the former. Now this ſphincter Muſcle ſeems to be nothing elſe but the middle Coat of the Bladder made thicker here than in any other part, by the acceſſion of the circular or overthwart Fibres. And its uſe is to purſe up the neck of the Bladder ſo, as no Urine can paſs out, till by its quantity or ſharpneſs it becomes ſo troubleſome to the Beaſt, as provokes him to force open the Sphincter by contracting the Muſcles of the Paunch, and the muſcular Coat of the Bladder. If this Sphincter happen to be overcooled, &c. the Horſe loſeth its uſe, and ſo for want of it his Water drops from him as faſt as it comes into the Bladder.

Its *Veins* and *Arteries* proceed from the hypogaſtrick branches of the hollow Vein and great Artery, and are implanted into its neck, on which, part of them is ſpent, and the remainder runs through the bottom. Its Nerves come partly from the Intercoſtals and partly from the Marrow of that Bone of the Back that is called *Os ſacrum*, that is next to the Crupper. *Its Veſſels.*

The uſe of the Bladder is to receive the Urine from the Kidneys by the Ureters, and to contain it, like a Chamber-pot, till it is ſo full as to become troubleſome and uneaſy to the Beaſt; for as ſoon as it becomes ſo, by the help of the Muſcles of the Belly and the middle muſcular Coat of the Bladder it is preſſed out of it by piſſing. *Its Uſe.*

CHAP. XX.

Of the Yard and Sheath.

BEcauſe the *Yard* of ſton'd Horſes beſides its principal uſe which is to copulate with the Mare, has alſo an inferiour uſe, *viz.* to diſcharge the Urine out of the Bladder; and becauſe this latter is the ſole uſe of it in Geldings, we will here treat of it next to the Bladder, in reſpect to the office it performs to *it*, and not defer it, as many Anatomiſts of Humane Bodies do, till we have diſcourſed of the parts that prepare, make and retain the Seed, to which it alſo miniſters.

The Yard of an Horſe lies hid for the moſt part within the Sheath, from which, when it is drawn, it borrows its covering, conſiſting of the Scarf-skin and true Skin, and the carnous Membrane, which are common to it with other parts of the Body: Its *Glans* has a proper Membrane that inveſts it, as the *Glans* of a Man's Yard has; and the whole conſiſts of two Nervous bodies (which make up the greateſt part of its bulk) a Partition-skin that goes betwixt them, the *Urethra* or Piſs-pipe, the *Glans*, four Muſcles and the Veſſels; of which in order. *The parts of the Yard.*

The two *Nervous bodies* are encompaſſed with a thick, firm and white skin, but their inner ſubſtance is very ſpongy and flaggy unleſs diſtended and filled with bloud and ſpirit, conſiſting for the greateſt part of nothing but Veſſels, to wit, Veins, Arteries and Nervous threads, which are wonderfully interwoven one with another. They ariſe from the lower part of the Share-bone at a ſmall diſtance one from the other, giving the Piſs-pipe room to go betwixt them, but in a little while they meet together, and ſo are extended one by the ſide of the other the whole length of the Yard to the *Glans*, onely a thin skin coming betwixt them. At their riſe they reſemble the letter Y. *Its Nervous bodies.*

The *Piſs-pipe* is ſeated betwixt theſe, or rather below them, and is of a ſubſtance much like them. On its inſide it is membranous and very ſenſible. It is continued from the neck of the Bladder, and is much of an equal width through its whole length. At its beginning where it is joined to the neck of the Bladder it has a membranous valve, that permits the Urine to come out, but hinders the Seed or any thing ſquirted into *The Piſs-pipe* into the Piſs-pipe to go in, unleſs it be forced open with a Probe or Catheter, or the like.

The Glans. Before the ends of the Nervous bodies there is prefixed the *Glans*, which is diſtinguiſhable from the reſt of the Yard by a round circle like a Crown going between them. This is of a more exquiſite ſenſe than the Nervous bodies, but of not much an unlike ſubſtance, though ſome ſay it is glandulous. When the Yard is drawn, it has no other covering, but one proper thin coat.

The Muſcles. The Yard has two *Muſcles* on each ſide at its root: The firſt pair are ſhort and thick, ſpringing from the knob of the Hip-bone, and are inſerted into the Nervous bodies near their beginning: they are called *Erectors*, becauſe they help the Yard to ſtand. The ſecond are longer and ſmaller, ariſing from the ſphincter Muſcle of the Arſe-hole, and paſſing along the ſides of the Piſs-pipe end about the middle of it, ſerving to open or widen it for the freer paſſage of the Seed and Urine, and are therefore called *Dilaters*.

The Veſſels. Its *Veins* and *Arteries* ſpring from the Hypogaſtricks, and enter it at the meeting of the Nervous bodies. Its *Nerves* come from the loweſt Vertebral.

Its Uſe. The principal and primary uſe of the Yard is for copulation, to convey the Seed into the Womb of the Female: but the ſecondary, and to ſuch Creatures as are gelt, the onely uſe of it, is to ſerve as a Tap to the Bladder, to let out the Urine when it becomes troubleſome; in which office the *Urethra* or Piſs-pipe is chiefly concerned.

The Sheath. Except when the Yard is diſtended with bloud and Spirits, (which is called its erection or ſtanding) it lies hid in its Repoſitory, the *Sheath*, of which little need to be ſaid, ſeeing it is onely a duplicature of the common coverings of the Body, and conſiſts onely of the ſcarf and true Skin, and the fleſhy Membrane, which is here but thin. It ſeems to anſwer to the prepuce or Fore-skin in Men: for as that in ſome Men, when the Yard is erect, turns back towards the root of the *Penis* and leaves the *Glans* wholly bare; ſo when a Horſe's Yard is drawn out to the full length, the Sheath is alſo drawn out or unfolded, and appears to be knit to the Yard a little behind the *Glans*, even as the prepuce is to a Man's *Penis* at the ſame place. I ſhall not need therefore to ſpeak any more of it.

Table VIII. Sheweth the deſcending Trunks of the hollow Vein and great Artery, the Emulgents, Kidneys, Deputy-kidneys, Ureters, Bladder, Yard, preparing Veſſels, Stones, deferent Veſſels, Seed-bladders and Proſtates.

A *Sheweth the deſcending Trunk of the hollow Vein.*
B *The deſcending Trunk of the great Artery.*
CC *The emulgent Veins ariſing out of the hollow Vein.*
DD *The emulgent Arteries ſpringing out of the great Artery.*
EE *The Kidneys.*
FF *The Deputy-kidneys, otherwiſe called the black Choler Boxes.*
GGGG *The Ureters.*
The Bladder.
H [illegible]*e Bladder cut open that its inſide may appear.*
I *Th*[illegible] *neck of the Bladder where it opens into the Piß-pipe of the Yard.*
K *The* [illegible] *Ligaments of the Bladder.*
kk *The*

L *The*

TAB VIII

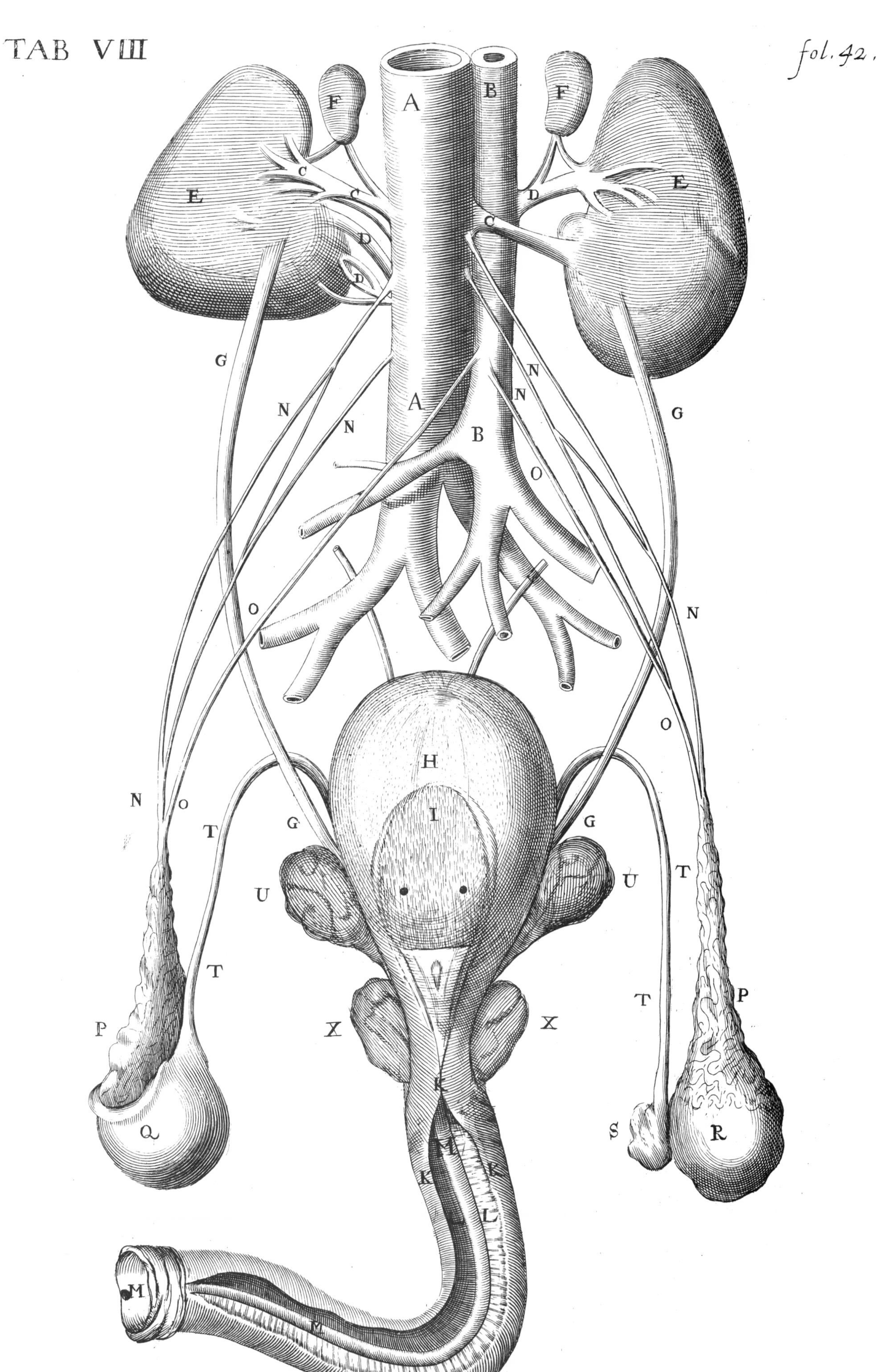
F
A
B
F
C
C
E
D
E
C
D
D
D
G
N
N
N
N
A
G
B
O
O
N
O
H
N
O
T
G
I
G
U
U
T
T
T
P
X
X
P
Q
K
S
R
M
K
K
L
M
M
K

L *The Nervous bodies of the Tard divided from its back down to the Piß-pipe.*
M *The* Urethra *or Piß-pipe.*
m *The end or thickest part of the Tard, called its* Glans.
NNNN *The Seed-preparing Veins.*
OO *The Seed-preparing Arteries.*
PP *The Pyramidal bodies, otherwise called* Corpora varicoſa, *or* Pampiniformia.
Q *The right Testicle with its inmost Coat on.*
R *The left Testicle divested of all its Coats.*
S *The* Epididymis *or* paraſtata *of the left Testicle.*
TT *The deferent Veſſels.*
UU *The Seed-bladders.*
XX *The Proſtates.*

CHAP. XXI.

Of the Parts miniſtring to Generation in Horſes, and First of the Preparing, Spermatick or Seed-veſſels.

HAVING ſhewed the Parts appointed for and ſubſervient to Chylification, and in ſome meaſure to *Nutrition* and Sanguification, I come in the next place to ſpeak to thoſe ſerving for *Generation.* And as the former, all except the Yard treated of in the laſt Chapter, are common to and alike in both Male and Female; ſo theſe latter differing conſiderably in the different Sexes, we muſt treat of them apart ; and ſhall begin with the Generative Parts of an *Horſe*, and afterwards treat of thoſe of a *Mare*.

The firſt in order are the *preparing* or *ſpermatick* Veſſels, *Arteries* and *Veins.* The Arteries carry bloud and vital ſpirit to the Stones to make Seed of, and the Veins bring back from thence ſo much of the bloud as remains ſuperfluous or unfit for that purpoſe. The Arteries ſpring out of the deſcending Trunk of the great Artery, almoſt two hands breadth below the Emulgents, one on each ſide : and the Veins out of the like Trunk of the hollow Vein, two on each ſide, a pretty deal higher up than the Arteries, as you may obſerve in the foregoing Figure. The left of theſe Veins in Humane Bodies commonly ſprings from the left Emulgent Vein, (and is but one) the reaſon whereof Anatomiſts give to be, leſt, if it ſhould have ſprung from the *Cava*, and thereby been neceſſitated to have marched over the great Artery, the return of the bloud from the Stones by it ſhould have been hindred by the continual beating of the Artery. But ſeeing Nature has not here made the like caution, where there was as great need of it, I cannot tell whether that be any ſatisfactory reaſon. Now theſe Arteries and Veins do at a little diſtance from their beginning meet with one another on their reſpective ſides, to wit the right Artery with the right Veins, and the left with the left, and at their meeting they acquire one common covering from the Rim of the belly, between whoſe two Membranes they deſcend down the Loins, *The preparing Veſſels.*

running over the Ureters, as the figure ſhews. As they deſcend, they beſtow little twigs upon the Rim of the Belly, and the Veins do divide themſelves into ſeveral, and by and by unite again; but the Arteries paſs along a great way by one Pipe onely, though variouſly twiſted and interwoven with the Veins, with which yet they do no where inoſculate, or unite into one body, as was generally affirmed they did before the circulation of the bloud was found out. For till then it was believed, that the Veins carried bloud to the Stones, and the Arteries vital Spirits, and that the Arteries opened into the Veins, and contrarily the Veins into the Arteries, for the mixing the bloud and vital ſpirits together, and thereby preparing matter for the Stones to make Seed of. But ſince the circulation of the bloud was fully underſtood, and it became certain that bloud and ſpirit flowed to the Stones by the Arteries onely; upon a ſtrict enquiry after theſe inoſculations, they were no where to be found, nor is there any thing like them, ſaving that both Veins and Arteries paſs along in one common Cover, which it is likely gave occaſion to the miſtake. When theſe Veſſels are arrived within little leſs than a quarter of a yard of the Stones, the Arteries then begin to branch themſelves into ſeveral, but the Veins into far more. And both of them paſs out of the Belly by the hole of the proceſs of the Rim into the Cod. The ſpace betwixt where theſe Veſſels begin ſo much to divide themſelves, and the Stones, is called the *Pyramidal body*, becauſe from the Stones upwards, it grows ſmaller and ſmaller like a Pyramid, as is repreſented in the Figure. It is alſo called *Corpus varicoſum*, becauſe the Veſſels ſo divided make a thicker body; and laſtly *plexus pampiniformis*, the tendril-like *plexus* or interweaving, becauſe the Veins and Arteries twine and claſp about one another like the tendrils of Vines. Both of theſe Veſſels enter the Stones by ſeveral branches, but the Veins by a far greater number than the Arteries, which was neceſſary, for that the bloud flows very quick to the Stones by the Arteries, but returns but ſlowly back again by the Veins, and therefore it was convenient it ſhould have more conducts or chanels to run in.

Their uſe. The *uſe* of theſe *Preparing Veſſels* may be ſufficiently learned by what we have already diſcourſed of them, by which it is alſo clear that the name of *Preparers* belongs onely properly to the Arteries that carry bloud and ſpirits to the Stones to nouriſh them and to make Seed of, and not at all to the Veins, which onely bring back that bloud that is not converted to thoſe uſes.

As for the *Nerves* and *Lympheducts* that run with the aforeſaid Veſſels to the Teſticles, becauſe the Teſticles are the parts for which they are deſigned, and they are onely in their paſſage thither while they accompany theſe Veins and Arteries, we ſhall ſay nothing further of them here, but ſhall ſhew their origine and uſe in the following Chapter.

CHAP. XXII.

Of the Teſticles or Stones, and the Paraſtatæ *or Attenders.*

THE Teſticles or Stones are called in Latin *Teſtes*, which otherwiſe ſignifies Witneſſes, becauſe they witneſs the ſtrength and courage of the Creature; or perhaps rather, as ſome think, becauſe no Man amongſt the Romans was admitted to be a Witneſs that had loſt his Stones. They are always according to Nature two, and therefore the Greeks call them by a word that ſignifies *Twins*. *Their name.*

They are of an oval *figure*, but ſomewhat flattiſh: and their *ſubſtance* has been formerly held to be glandulous, as if they were onely two great Kernels, not differing from other Kernels in other parts of the Body ſaving in bigneſs and uſe. But later Anatomiſts have diſcovered them to be of no ſuch ſolid ſubſtance as Glands are, but wholly to conſiſt of Veſſels that twiſt and twine this way and that way, and are kept in their order cloſe to one another by the inmoſt Skin that cloaths the Stones. When they are cut in two, they appear not red, but of that colour the Seed is of, becauſe the bloud as ſoon as it enters them, begins to loſe its colour and nature, and to be turned into Seed. And ſeeing I could never obſerve any bloud in the Stones, it is likely that the Veins reach no further than their Coats, ſeeing the Seed is not received into the Veins, but into peculiar Veſſels called *Deferent* or back-carrying, of which in the next Chapter. I ſay, I believe the Veins onely run through the Coats of the Stones, and have the ſuperfluous bloud tranſmitted into them from the Arteries, before ever they enter into the body of the Stones: And then thoſe Veſſels that the Teſticles conſiſt of, will onely be Arteries, run out into very fine and almoſt innumerable threads, for the elaborating of the Seed. *Their ſhape and ſubſtance.*

If this notion of mine be true, then I may ſay that both *Veins* and *Arteries* run through all the Coats wherewith the Teſticles are inveſted, but that they themſelves have no Bloud-veſſels but Arteries. And whether they have any other ſort of Veſſel, is uncertain. 'Tis true there are both *Nerves* and *Lympheducts* that come towards the Stones, as I obſerved in the foregoing Chapter; but I queſtion whether they reach any farther than their Coats any more than the Veins. As for the *Nerves*, they ſpring from a Vertebral pair according to ſome, from the Intercoſtal ſay others, and a third ſort think from both. But be their original where it will, I think they are moſtly if not altogether ſpent upon the ſuſpending Muſcles by which the Teſticles are ſuſtained, and upon the Coats ſo often mentioned. So far am I from thinking with ſome, that theſe Nerves contribute the greateſt or any conſiderable ſhare of matter for the making of the Seed. The *Lymphedučts* ſpring manifeſtly from amongſt the Coats of the Stones, and aſcend up into the Belly by the ſame hole, by which the preparing Veſſels came down, running ſo far till they reach and empty themſelves into the common Receptacle of the Chyle, deſcribed above *chap.* 10. and 12. *Their Veſſels.*

The Teſticles being ſenſible, tender and noble parts, are defended from the external cold or other Injuries by ſeveral *Coats*, of which ſome are *Their Coats.*

common to them with other parts of the Body, and ſome proper to themſelves onely. The *common* incompaſs both the Stones within one cavity, as in a Bag, and make that which we call the Cod. And theſe are two. The outer of them is the Skin with its Scarf-skin, and the inner the fleſhy Membrane. The outer is not divided as it is in Man, by a line that runs along the middle of it lengthways. The inner, as it ſticks pretty cloſe to this on one ſide; ſo to the next proper one ſomewhat looſely, by many membranous Fibres, on the other or inner ſide. The *proper* are alſo two, though by ſome they are reckoned to be three. The outmoſt is called *Vaginalis*, or the Sheath-like Coat, becauſe the Stone is included in it as in a Sheath. This is thick and ſtrong; ſmooth on the inſide, but rough on the outſide, by reaſon of many Fibres or Threads by which it is knit to the inner of the common Coats. It is full of Veins, and is a production of the Rim of the Belly: for as the preparing Veſſels deſcend over the Share-bone into the Cod, the Rim makes a Caſe for them for their defence and ſecurity, and reaches with them down to the Stone, encompaſſing *it* as well as *them*. Into this Coat is the Muſcle inſerted that ſuſpends the Stone, (which we ſhall deſcribe preſently.) Some make two Coats of this, the outmoſt of which retains the name of *ſheath-like* above-mentioned; and the inner they call the *red* Coat, from its colour; but indeed this latter is nothing elſe but the foreſaid Muſcle ſpreading it ſelf broad and thin on the Sheath-like Coat. The laſt and inmoſt, which immediately cloaths the Stone, (being the ſecond proper one) is called the *nervous*, and otherwiſe the *white*, Membrane, being thick and ſtrong, and of a whitiſh colour. It ſeems to ariſe from the outer Coat of the preparing Veſſels, and is rough on its inſide next the Stone, but ſmooth and ſlippery on its outſide.

Their Muſcles. Each Stone is ſuſpended or hangs by a Muſcle called *Cremaſter*, or the ſuſpender. Theſe Muſcles ariſe from the Ligament of the Share-bone, and deſcending by the proceſs of the Rim of the Belly (before ſpoken of) are inſerted into the Sheath-like Coat, which they ſtrengthen, the better to ſuſtain the weight of the Stones; and in the act of Copulation are ſaid to pull up the Stones, and thereby to ſhorten the ways the Seed has to paſs.

Paraſtatæ. On the top or back as it were of each Stone there lies a longiſh, whitiſh and ſomewhat round body, diſtinguiſhable very eaſily from them, though not of much an unlike ſubſtance; onely they are not ſo firm and compact as the Stones are. They are named *Paraſtatæ* or *Attenders*, becauſe they wait as it were on the Stones; and alſo *Epididymidæ*, becauſe they are placed *upon the didymi* or Twins, by which name the Stones are otherwiſe called. They conſiſt (as the Stones do) wholly of Veſſels running this way and that way, all which are united into one Thread or Chord, which is continued into the deferent Veſſel, of which in the next Chapter.

The uſe of the Stones and Paraſtatæ. From what has been already diſcourſed of theſe Parts, their *uſe* appears to be, to make and elaborate the Seed, for the propagation of the kind. Now the Matter out of which the Seed is made, ſeems to be onely the Arterial bloud, unleſs one ſhould admit ſome Animal ſpirits conveyed hither by the Nerves and mixed therewith. But ſeeing any inoſculations of the Nerves with the Arteries is a thing not yet diſcovered either in theſe or any other parts, I incline to believe that the Nerves onely contribute ſenſe to theſe parts, that the Animal may have the greater pleaſure in Copulation. A ſecondary uſe or rather effect of the Stones, is to cauſe courage and generoſity in the Horſe; for we obſerve that our Ston'd Horſes are generally much higher-ſpirited than Geldings.

CHAP. XXIII.

Of the Deferent or Ejaculatory Veſſels, the Seed-bladders and the Proſtates.

HAVING done with thoſe Parts that prepare and elaborate the Seed, we come next to thoſe that are the Store-houſes or Repoſitories of it, from whence it is ejected in Copulation. And of theſe the firſt are the *deferent* or back-carrying veſſels, otherwiſe called *Ejaculatory* or ſquirting, becauſe in thoſe Animals that have no Seed-bladders to ſtore up the Seed in (ſuch as Dogs and the like) it does immediately ſquirt through theſe Veſſels from the Stones in Copulation: though in others that have Seed-bladders (as Horſes have) it is continually a-paſſing by theſe Veſſels from the Stones to the Bladders by little and little as it is prepared.

Theſe *deferent Veſſels* are two, one on each ſide; they begin at the ſmaller end of the *paraſtatæ* (deſcribed in the former chapter) and are indeed but a continuation of them. They are whitiſh and pretty hard; not hollow like a Vein, but more like a Nerve, for their cavity is hardly diſcernable, unleſs the Seed-bladders be full of Seed, and ſo it regurgitate as it were into theſe Veſſels, as I have ſometimes obſerved. As ſoon as they are ariſen from the *Paraſtatæ*, they aſcend ſtreight out of the Cod into the Belly by the ſame proceſs of the Rim of the Belly by which the preparing Veſſels deſcended. Being entred the Belly, by and by they croſs over the Ureters from the outſide to the inſide of them, and taking a little compaſs they turn back again under the Bladder till they arrive almoſt at its neck, (towards which they grow wider than before) and there their ſides open into the Seed-bladders, into which they deſtill the Seed; notwithſtanding themſelves ſtill keep on their courſe as far as the Piſs-pipe between the Proſtates, but are grown much ſmaller before they reach them. Theſe Veſſels ſerve as Conduit-pipes for the Seed to drill along from the Stones to the ſeminal Bladders; and through their necks, that reach from the Bladders to the Piſs-pipe, does the Seed iſſue in the act of generation. *Deferent Veſſels.*

The place where the Seed is ſtored up and preſerved, is the *Seed-bladders*. Dr. *Wharton* affirms that in an Horſe "they conſiſt of *two* parts, "of which *one* is a mere membranous or ſkinny Bladder, the *other* glan-"dulous. The Bladder, he ſays, he has found ſix inches long and near "three broad, although it was empty and not opened; but it ſeem'd ca-"pable of being ſtretched out to a greater length and width, if it had "been filled. If one opened the bottom of this Bladder, and put a Probe "into it, the Probe paſſed obliquely towards the Piſs-pipe, and entred "into it through the ſame hole with the deferent Veſſel of the ſame ſide. *Seed-bladders.*

"The

" The *other* part of these Bladders, which we called glandulous, was " thicker, and broader on that side which joyned to the Piss-pipe; and " where the deferent Vessels were inserted, without descending towards " the bottom, it grew thinner and thinner like a wedge. The substance " of this glandule was not much unlike to that of the Stones, but of a " more clayie colour, and had holes within it so apparent that they would " admit an indifferent Probe: all which holes were united into one com- " mon duct, namely before they reach the *Urethra*. For putting a Probe " into any one of the said holes, it was driven easily and without any lett " into that common passage. But the passage it self did not quite pene- " trate the Piss-pipe, but was covered with the thin and spongie Mem- " brane of the *Urethra*. Through this Membrane is the spermatick Mat- " ter strained in Copulation. Thus far Dr. *Wharton* in his 30. chap. *of the Glands*. Now as for my self, I could never observe so great a diffe- rence of one part of the seminal Bladders from another, as that one should appear membranous and the other glandulous. And I would not imagine that so skilfull an Anatomist should mistake the Prostates for a part of the said Bladders, though these are the onely Parts that to me appear glandu- lous thereabouts. All the Seed-bladders that I have observed have been much of a like substance, though perhaps a little thicker in one place than another: they are whitish and very strong, being within all full of little Cells like Pomegranates. They have no communication the one with the other; for as their bottoms or thicker ends bunch out a little on each side of the Bladder (as you see in the Figure) so their smaller ends or mouths, that are nearest to one another, do each of them open apart into the deferent Vessel of their respective side, by whose neck they pour out their Seed in Copulation into the Piss-pipe. The Seed comes into them out of the deferent Vessels, and goes out of them again into the same Vessels, at one and the same passage or orifice. Dr. *Wharton* says, that the seminal Matter contained in them differs much from that which is made in the Stones: whence he concludes that the Seed-bladders receive not the *matter* which they contain, from the Testicles by the deferent Vessels, but do elaborate it in their own glandulous substance; and he calls it *Seed of a peculiar kind*. For my own part I have not discovered any difference, to speak of, betwixt this and that which I have some- times seen in the deferent Vessels, when the Bladders have been very full; nor is it probable they can be of a different kind or nature, seeing there is that manifest communication between the deferent Vessels and the Bladders, that these latter seem to contain or receive nothing, but what the former bring into them. Nor do I think that any Part does elabo- rate any Liquor that can with any propriety be called Seed, except the Testicles contained in the Cod, whose sole office and prerogative it is to make it.

Their use. The *use* of these Bladders (as hath been said) is to receive the Seed from the deferent Vessels, and to reserve it untill the time of Copulation. Now the Seed may (to satisfy the curiosity of the Ingenious Anatomist) be plainly seen, if you take the Bladders in your hand and squeeze them with your finger; for by such squeezing you shall force the seminal Mat- ter into the Pipe of the Yard, where you may by dissecting the Yard or opening that Pipe plainly see it. Or if you think it too much to take that pains, you may by dissecting the Bladders themselves see it; but then you lose the sight of one of the curious contrivances of Nature, which

which is a little Caruncle or Kernel that is placed at the mouth of the hole where the Seed distils into the Yard, which Caruncle is by Nature placed there, to prevent the issuing forth of the Seed when there was no need for it; for the continual gleeting of it, which would have happened but for this Caruncle, would be extremely prejudicial to the Creature. This Caruncle in Men being impaired or injured by the Venereal Distemper, or by their overstraining themselves in the act of Copulation, is generally by Physicians believed to be the cause of the running of the Reins. And this Disease Horses are not exempted from, although it doth not happen to them on the like occasions as to men it doth; for this Disease, which in Horses we call the mattering of the Yard, happens to them upon their catching suddain colds after hard riding: Likewise over-hard riding it self will bring it; and very often it is caused by weakness occasioned by great poverty and the like.

The Prostates. Their seat, bigness and shape. In the next place we come to the *Prostates*, which are so called from their *standing before* the Seed-bladders. They are Glandulous bodies, almost of the same nature and substance as other Glandules of the Body. They are situated at the root of the Yard above the sphincter Muscle of the Bladder, being in number two, on each side of the neck of the Bladder one; their quantity about the bigness of a small Burgamy Pear. They are of an oval figure, onely somewhat flat, and are covered with a very thick Coat to hinder the oily substance with which they are well stored, from issuing forth.

Their Vessels and Pores. They have Veins, Arteries, Nerves and Lympheducts; and besides, many Pores that open into the *Urethra*. In most Creatures, especially the lesser sort, these Pores are scarcely discernible in an healthfull state, but in an Horse they are very plain, and open into the upper part of the Piss-pipe about an inch distance from the insertion of the deferent Vessels into the same. Dr. *Wharton* has told twelve such little holes, before each of which as they open into the Piss-pipe, is placed a little Gland, about the bigness of a grain of Mustard-seed, which serve to hinder the entrance of the Urine into these holes, as it runs by them out of the Bladder.

Their use. The nature and *use* of the Liquor that is contained in these Prostates, and that issues out of them into the Piss-pipe, is somewhat difficult to determine. Some take them to be a kind of Testicles, and think that they make a sort of Seed, which though it be not of so noble a nature as that which is made in the Testicles contained in the Cod, yet is as necessary for generation: seeing such Men as are cut for the Stone become incapable of generation, if the Stone be so big and ragged as much to tear the Prostates in pulling of it out. But it is likely, such barrenness happens not so much from the tearing of these, as that the ends of the deferent Vessels are torn likewise, or it may be the Seed-bladders also: and so when the Wound is healed up again, the sides of these Vessels grow together, so that they can neither contain nor convey into the Piss-pipe any Seed. It is probable therefore that this oily clammy Humour that the Prostates discharge into the Piss-pipe, is of a nature far different from that of Seed, even as themselves are bodies of a far other nature than the Stones are. For, as was shewn above, the Stones are wholly vascular, that is, consist wholly of Vessels; whereas these are glandulous, or kernelly. So that I believe this Humour serves onely to make the *Urethra* supple and slippery, and to defend it from the acrimony or sharpness of the Urine.

And

And thus we have done with all the Parts that make or retain the Seed: as for the Yard, which ſome treat of in this place, becauſe it ſerves for injecting the Seed into the Womb; we deſcribed the Parts thereof above *chap.* 20. next to the Bladder, becauſe it ſerves as well for making water as for Copulation, and thither the Reader may pleaſe to turn back.

CHAP. XXIV.

Of the Parts miniſtring to Generation in Mares, and Firſt of the Preparing Veſſels, ſo called.

IT was *Galen*'s opinion, and from his authority, of many others, that the Parts ſerving for generation in the Female differed not from thoſe of the Male ſaving in ſituation; the Male's Genitals being without the Body, and the Females within. And this diverſity of ſituation they attributed to defect of heat in the Female, ſo that the Genitals could not be thruſt out of the Body as in the Male they are. But the truth is, they differ not onely in ſituation, but in number, bigneſs, figure, office and uſe, as will be apparent as well from the deſcription of them, as from their repreſentation in the Figures.

Preparing Veſſels. The firſt in order are the preparing Veſſels, Arteries and Veins. In theſe it was till of late believed that the bloud was prepared for the Stones the readilier to be turned by them into Seed. But as when we treated above of the preparing Veſſels of the Horſe, we ſhewed that the Veins could not properly be called *preparing* Veſſels, becauſe they carry nothing to the Stones, but bring bloud back again from them: ſo in Mares we cannot allow the name of *preparers* or *ſpermatick* to be proper even to the Arteries themſelves, ſeeing neither Mares nor any other Females have any true Seed. For their Stones are but improperly ſo called, being more truly Ovaries or Egg-beds, as we ſhall ſhew by and by in the next Chapter. However we ſhall retain the old name for diſtinction's ſake, and ſtill call both Veins and Arteries *preparing Veſſels.*

1. *Arteries.* The preparing Arteries of the Horſe we ſhewed to be onely two, one on each ſide; but in the Mare there are ſeveral, three or more on each ſide. All of them ariſe out of the great Artery, below the Emulgents, ſome higher, ſome lower. They paſs down along with the Veins of their reſpective ſides, with which they are very much interwoven, but no where open one into the other. Some branches of them go to the Teſticles, ſome to the Horns of the Womb, and ſome to its Sheath.

2. *Veins.* The preparing Veins in the Horſe were two of each ſide, though the Arteries were but one; yet in the Mare where the Arteries are ſeveral, the Veins are but one of each ſide. The reaſon whereof ſeems to be, That the Arteries in the Mare being not ſo much intended for the nouriſhment of her Genitals as of the Foal contained in her Womb, it was requiſite there ſhould be ſeveral Veſſels for the bringing the greater plenty of *nouriſhing juice* for it; all or the greateſt part of which being received by the Foal, there was not need of the like number of Veins to carry back

back the bloud that came along with it, that being very inconsiderable for its quantity to what was imported by the Arteries. But now all the bloud brought by the preparing Arteries of the Horse, serving for no other use but for the nourishment of the Genitals, and for the making of Seed: *As* a less quantity of bloud will suffice for these two uses, and so there is no need of a plurality of Arteries; *so* the bloud that is brought to the Genitals, is but a very small part of it spent in performing these two offices, and therefore more Veins were necessary to carry the surplusage back again, seeing the motion of the bloud in the Arteries is far quicker than of that in the Veins. These *two* preparing Veins then arise out of the *Cava* a little below the Emulgents, and neither of them from the Emulgent it self, any more than in the Horse, though in Men and Women the Left generally springs from the left Emulgent. They join in like manner with the Arteries as we shewed above that they did in Horses, and go to all those parts of the Genitals to which we just now shewed that the Arteries run.

When the Mare is not with Foal, the Arteries bring onely bloud for the nourishment of the several Parts into which they are inserted: but when she is with Foal, they bring besides the bloud a nutritious juice, (which is Chyle, impregnated with spirit, but not as yet perfectly changed into bloud) for its growth and nourishment, as we shall shew more afterwards when we come to speak how the Foal is nourished in the Womb. And whether she be with Foal or not, the Veins serve to carry back to the *Cava* and so to the Heart, the bloud that is superfluous. *Their use.*

CHAP. XXV.

Of the Testicles or Stones in Mares, otherwise called Ovaries; and of the Trumpets of the Womb.

THE *Testicles* in Mares do not agree in their description with those of Horses in any one particular thing, nor should I call them by that name, if the general mistake of so many Ages (in thinking the Female's Stones to have the same office with those of the Male) had not made it necessary to retain that appellation, if I would be understood by vulgar Readers of what part I am treating. For it has been an old Opinion, that the Male and Female's Seed being mixed in the Womb, doth make the Conception; and there are many that will not *yet* be beaten out of it. Whereas the Female hath no Seed at all, but their Testicles (so called) are as it were knots of Eggs, which being impregnated by the Male's Seed, one or more at a time, do each make a Conception. But of this more by and by. *The Testicles.*

The Mare's Testicles differ from the Horse's in these Particulars.

First, The Horse's Stones hang without the Body in the Cod, but the Mare's lie within the cavity of the Belly, a little distance from the horns of the Womb, to which they are knit by a strong Ligament. *Their situation.*

Bigness, and figure. Secondly, The Mare's Testicles are hardly half as big as the Horse's, nor are they of the same shape, but more flat and thin, having no *Parastatæ* upon them. And besides, they are somewhat uneven in their surface, whereas those of an Horse are smooth.

Coat. Thirdly, The Horses Testicles are covered with four Coats, two common, and two proper; but the Mare's are clad onely with one for about one half of them, and the other half with two; the outer of which they have immediately from the preparing Vessels that enter into them, but mediately from the Rim of the Belly.

Substance, and use. Fourthly and lastly, They differ very much from one another in their substance and use. For we shewed above in *chap.* 22. that the Horse's Stones did wholly consist of Seed-vessels turn'd and roll'd this way and that way: but the Mare's consist principally of numerous Membranes and small Fibres loosely united to one another; amongst which there are several little Bladders, about as big as a Pease, some bigger, some less, that are full of a very clear and thin liquor. Those that were of opinion that the Females made Seed as well as the Males, thought that these Bladders that are chiefly in the surface of the Testicle, answered to the Seed-bladders in the Male, and that the humour contained in them was true Seed. And whereas it might be objected that it is far more clear and watery than the Male's Seed, they thought it sufficient to answer, that that was from the colder and moister nature of the Female, that could not concoct it to that consistency as the Male's is of. But the truth is, it is not Seed; and if it were, there is no way whereby it could possibly arrive at the Womb. For that which was reputed to be the deferent Vessel, appears to be nothing else but a short and broad Ligament for fixing the Testicle in its place; for it has no cavity at all, but is of a solid, firm and close substance. These Bladders therefore must be concluded to be Eggs, answering to those of Fowl and other Creatures: which will be the more manifest if you boil them, for then, as those that have tried it do affirm, they will have the same colour, taste and consistency with the whites of Hens-eggs. Whence these Testicles may more properly be called *Ovaries* or Egg-beds, whose Eggs are nourished by the Bloud-vessels described in the foregoing Chapter; and when upon Copulation one (or more) of them is made fruitfull by the Male's Seed, it separates from the rest, and being received by the mouth of the Trumpet of the Womb, it descends by it into the Horn, and so to the bottom of the Womb, and there becomes a Conception. And whereas it has been thought a strong argument for the Female's having true Seed, and that these Testicles made it, in that when they are cut out of the Body in Bitches, Hogs, or any other Creature, such Creatures are always barren afterwards; this new Opinion shews that there is no strength or certainty at all in that argument. For granting, what is most certainly true, that Females that are gelt or spay'd, have never any Young after; yet it does not at all follow, that therefore their Stones make and conserve Seed; but onely that they contain something that is absolutely necessary for generation and conception: but whether that be Seed or somewhat else, is indifferent. And therefore that Argument will be as strong for the Opinion that the Testicles are *Ovaries*, seeing without the Eggs it is so far from possible that there should be a conception, that they are the very conception it self.

Of the *Bloud-vessels* that run through the Testicles we treated in the foregoing Chapter under the name of Preparing Vessels: As for their *Nerves*,

Nerves, they spring from the Intercostal pair, and from the Nerves of *Os sacrum*. *Bartholin* affirms that they have also *Lympheducts*.

There hath not been greater dispute about the matter of the Conception, than by what way any thing could go to the Womb or its Horns from the Testicles to make it. Some have pretended to the discovery of Vessels or Pipes for conveyance thereof, which others altogether as skilfull Anatomists could find no footsteps of. At last *Fallopius* assigned this office to two Ducts, which from their shape he called *Tubæ* or Trumpets; and from him (as being the first Inventer of them, or at least the first that ascribed this use to them) they are commonly known by the name of the Fallopian Trumpets. He says, "they are nervous and white, "arising from the Horns of the Womb, where they are very slender, but "at a small distance from it they grow wider, bending this way and that "way, till near their end, where ceasing their winding they grow pretty "large, and seem somewhat carnous.] Their ends next the Testicles are torn and jagged, and lie loose, being freed from the Membrane that sustains them the greatest part of their length. *The Trumpets of the Womb.*

Their *substance* seems rather membranous than nervous, (as *Fallopius* would have it.) And they consist of two *Membranes*; the *inner* is propagated from the inmost Tunicle of the Womb, and the *outer* from the outmost of the same. Where they are widest they will admit ones little finger, but towards the Horn of the Womb, they are not so thick as an ordinary straw, but yet are pervious; and where they open into the inside of the Horn, their Orifice looks like a little Teat. As to their length, it is something difficult to determine it exactly, because they run so to and again in their course; but I believe they are very near a quarter of a yard long. *Their substance, capacity and length.*

Their *use* is, *both* to serve as two Funnels whereby some subtile particles or steams may issue from the Seed, that is injected by the Male into the Womb, to the Testicles of the Female for the fecundating or making fruitfull the Eggs thereof, one or more, according to the different species of living Creatures; (but it is very rare, that there is above one so impregnated in a Mare, seeing it is so seldom that any brings forth twins:) *and also* when the Egg is fecundated by this means, and growing ripe as it were, drops off or separates from the Testicle, it is received by the jagged mouth of the Trumpet, along which it passes till it arrive in the Horn of the Womb, into which (as was said above) the Trumpet is inserted; and on this consideration the old name of *deferent Vessels* may still be granted them, from their conducting the Eggs from the Testicle to the Womb. Now seeing the wide ends of the Trumpets that first receive the Eggs lie loose, and are not fastened to the Testicle, it is probable that in Copulation these become turgid as well as all the other parts of the Genital, and with their jagged mouths clasp hold upon the *Testes* (as a Lamprey's mouth fastens upon a stone) and so convey to them a seminal air, and afterwards receive from them a fecundated Egg. *Their use.*

CHAP. XXVI.

Of the Womb and its Horns.

The shape and parts of the Womb. THE Womb of a Mare is shaped much like the Greek Letter Υ, in which the single stroak that is streight, answers to the *vagina* or Sheath, which receives the Horse's Yard in Copulation, and the two crooked stroaks that turn one the one way, and the other the other, are called *Horns*, because they in some sort resemble them; and that part of the Sheath where the Horns begin to separate, being somewhat wider than the rest, is the *fundus* or bottom of the Womb, where the Foal lies. For though in Dogs, Rabbets, &c. that have many young ones at one time, their burthen is contained wholly in the Horns of the Womb, as well as the Conception is first made there; yet in a Mare that commonly brings forth but one at a time, it is otherwise; for there is little or nothing that belongs to the Foal, contained in them, except some part of the Skins wherein the Foal is covered while it is in the Womb.

Its situation. The Womb is seated in the lowest part of the Lower Belly, in that wide Cavity that is formed out of and environed with the Hip-bones, the Share-bone, and the *os sacrum*. It is placed betwixt the Piss-bladder and the Arse-gut, and is firmly tied in its place by two pair of *Ligaments*.

Ligaments. The first *pair* arise from the Rim of the Belly, being shorter by much than the other, but broader, being for their shape resembled to Bat's wings. They are of a membranous, loose and soft substance, and are inserted into the Horns of the Womb, taking hold also of the Testicles, and tying them both fast to the Hip-bones, from whence they spring.

The second *pair* of Ligaments spring from the bottom of the Womb, and are called the round or worm-like Ligaments. They ascend on each side between the two Coats of the Rim of the Belly, towards the Share-bone, over which they pass slantingly, and then parting into many jags as it were, they end near the *clitoris*. This also serves to fasten the Womb the more firmly in its place.

Substance. It is of a nervous or rather membranous substance, more compact and close in Mares that are not with Foal, but more spongie in such as are. It consists of two Membranes, and a certain fleshy or fibrous parenchyma or substance between, unless one will make this a third Membrane. The outmost Membrane is borrowed from the Rim of the Belly, and therefore is truly double as that is, though we reckon it but for one. This is very strong. The inmost is not so strong nor firm as it, but seems to be somewhat porous. The middle substance betwixt these two is that which makes up the greatest part of its thickness at all times, but particularly when the Mare is with Foal, it imbibes so much of the nutritious Juice that flows plentifully hither at that time, that it is stuft up to almost an inch thickness.

Vessels.
1. Arteries. Its *Arteries* are branches partly of the Preparing Arteries and partly of the hypogastrick. These do inosculate or communicate by open mouths one with another, but not so with the Veins. They run along the Womb bending and winding, and not in a streight course, lest they should be broken

broken when the Womb is extended to that vast bulk as it is when the Mare is with Foal.

Its *Veins* spring also from the preparing and hypogastrick Veins, but are much fewer in number than the Arteries. For Nature having formed these Parts not so much for the benefit of the Individual, as for propagating the Kind; and the Foal while it is in the Womb receiving no nourishment but what is brought to it by the Arteries, it was necessary that they should be large and numerous for conveying the greater plenty of it: but seeing the greatest part of that which is brought by the Arteries is spent in the nourishment of the Young and the Parts in which it is contained, a fewer number of Veins are sufficient to convey back again what is not so spent. The Veins do inosculate with one another like as the Arteries did. *2. Veins.*

It has *Nerves* from the Intercostal pair, and from the Nerves of *os sacrum*. *3. Nerves.*

Some have also observed many *Lympheducts* creeping along its surface, which one after another meeting into one, empty themselves into the common receptacle of the Chyle and *Lympha*; and these *Lympheducts* some have mistaken for Milky-veins. *4. Lympheducts.*

Thus much of the *Womb* properly so called: and what we have said hereof, may be all applied to its *Horns* likewise as to their *substance* and *vessels*. As for their *figure*, you may view it in the following Cut. These Horns are less in Mares than in any other Creature that has them, in proportion to the bigness of their Bodies. From their first rise from the Womb to their end, they grow by degrees narrower and narrower, and about their middle are the Trumpets of the Womb inserted into them. They have a worm-like or successive motion as the Guts have, by which the Egg being received from the Trumpet is driven gently along till it come to the bottom of the Womb in Mares, and there becomes a Conception: but in such Creatures as bring forth many Young at one time, the Conceptions stay in the Horns till they are come to maturity, and never descend into the bottom of the Womb till they are about to be excluded. *Its Horns.*

By what has been said, it appears, that the *use* of the Womb is to receive the Seed of the Male, from which Seed a certain air or spirit steams through the Trumpets to the Testicles, where impregnating one or more Eggs, those that are so impregnated, are conveyed by the Trumpets into the Horns, and by these into the bottom of the Womb, where they become Conceptions, and stay (according to Nature) so long till all their Parts are finished, and they are become perfect Animals of their proper kind; and then the Womb being irritated by the motion and bigness of the Young, does by the help of the Muscles of the Belly, and the assistance of the Midriff exclude it. But having designed a particular discourse of the generation of Animals to be annexed to this Treatise, we shall pursue it no further here. *Its use.*

CHAP.

CHAP. XXVII.

Of the Vagina *or Sheath of the Womb, the Caruncles call'd* myrtiformes, *(of the ſhape of Myrtle-berries)* *the* Clitoris *and the external Privity.*

The Vagina *or Sheath.*

WE ſhall not need to enter upon the deſcription of the Veſſels running through the *Sheath* of the Womb, they being wholly the ſame that are diſperſed through the Womb it ſelf, and therefore the Reader may have recourſe to the former Chapter for them: nor is it neceſſary to ſpeak much of its ſubſtance, that being alſo much like to that of the Womb, though not ſo thick and ſtrong, but more ſoft, nervous and ſpongie. It is near half a yard long, being much of an equal width from one end to the other, but very uneven and wrinkled in its inner ſurface. Into its lower ſide (or that ſide next the Belly) a very little diſtance from the external Privity, is the neck of the Bladder inſerted; oppoſite to which in its upper ſide it is ſtrongly knit to the Sphincter Muſcle of the Arſe-gut. There is no ſuch neck to diſtinguiſh or ſeparate the Sheath from the bottom of the Womb, as Anatomiſts ſay there is in Women: but the Sheath it ſelf ſeems to be widened into what I call the bottom of the Womb.

The myrtiform Caruncles.

Whether there be any ſuch Membrane that goes croſs the *Vagina* in Mares that have never been cover'd, as Anatomiſts ſay there is in Maids, I never made any carefull examination, but believe there is none. But as for thoſe Caruncles or little kernelly knobs that are called *myrtiformes*, from their reſembling the Berries of the Myrtle in ſhape, they are to be found: yea they may be ſeen without diſſection, if one look near the Privity of a Mare when ſhe is luſtfull and deſires the Horſe; for as ſhe opens the Orifice of the *Vagina*, one may diſcern theſe Caruncles to ſtrut out. They are ſaid to be four in number, the largeſt of which ſtands juſt at the mouth of the Water-paſſage, which it helps, partly, to cloſe up. Their uſe ſeems to be, by their roughneſs and unevenneſs to cauſe the greater pleaſure to the Horſe in Copulation.

The Clitoris.

On the ſame ſide of the *Vagina* with the Bladder is placed a long ſpongie body called *Clitoris*, but lies a great deal farther within the *Vagina* than it is ſaid to doe in Women. For, that end of it which is next to the outward Privity is ſeven or eight fingers breadth from it, whereas in Women it is deſcribed to be within an inch. Thoſe that would make the generative Parts of the Male and Female exactly to reſemble one the other, ſay that this body in the Female, anſwers to the Yard in the Male. And indeed it is of not an unlike ſubſtance, but is not the twentieth part ſo big. It is ſoft and ſpongie, but it is likely when the Mare is luſtfull and deſires the Horſe, it plumps up and ſuffers a ſort of erection, being the principal ſeat of pleaſure in the Mare. It has two pair of Muſcles belonging to it, as well as the Yard of the Horſe. One pair is round, and ſprings from the Hip-bones: The other from the Sphincter of the Arſe-gut. Its *Veins* and *Arteries* ſpring from thoſe that are called *Pudendæ* (or *belonging to the Privity*) and its *Nerves*, (which are pretty large,

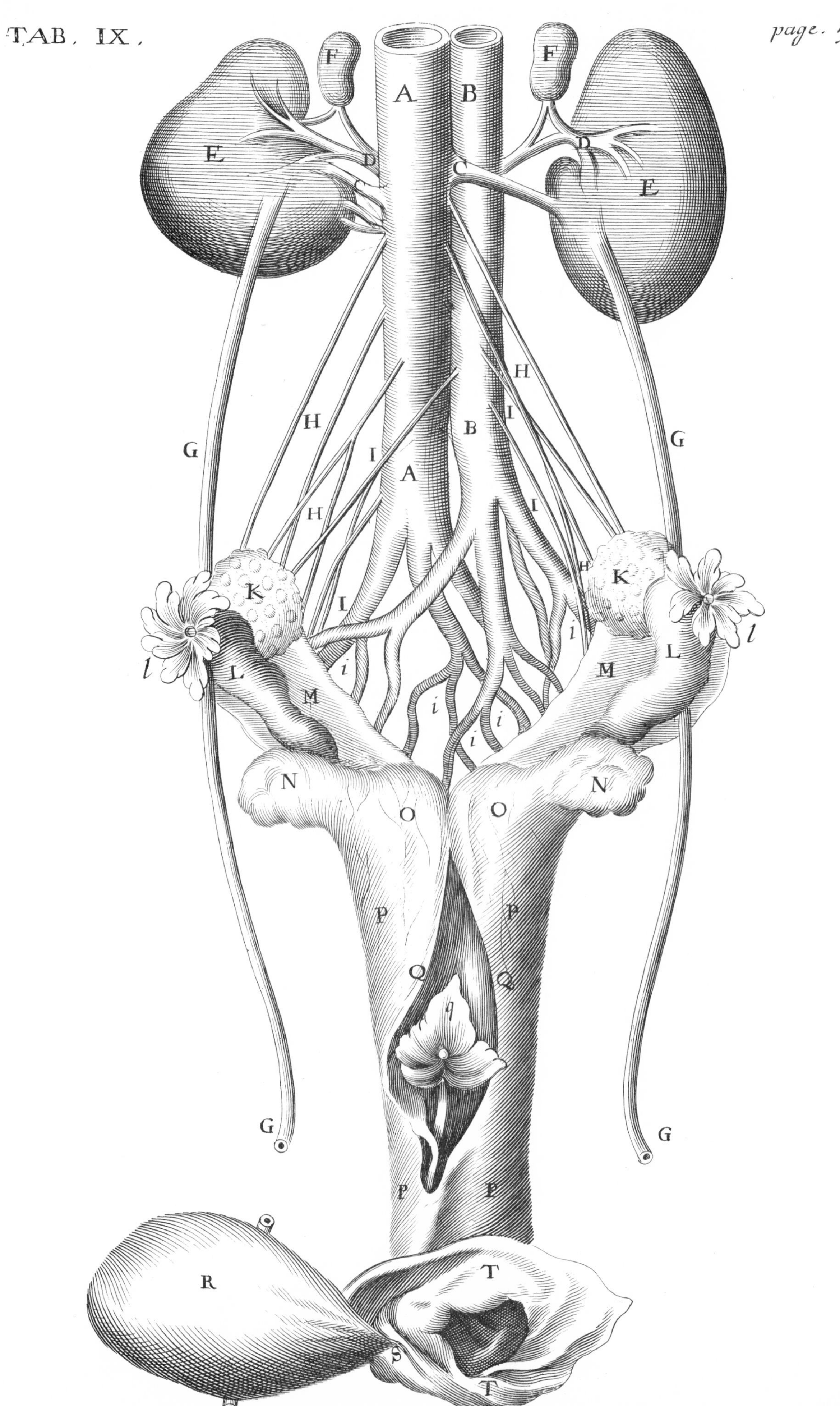
F
F
A
B
E
D
C
D
C
E
H
H
I
B
G
I
G
A
H
I
H
K
K
I
i
l
l
L
i
M
L
M
i
i
i
i
N
N
O
O
P
P
Q
Q
q
G
G
P
P
R
T
S
T

to make it the more ſenſible) ariſe from the ſame origine with thoſe that are diſperſed through the Sheath and Womb.

The outward Privity. The Lips. The Nymphs.

As to the outward Privity, the *Labia* or *Lips* are the firſt things that offer themſelves. Beſides the common Coverings, to wit the Skin and fleſhy Membrane, they are ſtuft with a little ſpongy Fat. They ſerve to cover the outer orifice of the Sheath for comelineſs ſake, and to defend it from the cold, and Inſects, or other injuries. The cloſing of theſe two makes that which is called the *fiſſure* or chink. If one draw the Lips a little aſide, then appear the *Nymphs*, ſo called becauſe they ſtand next to the Urine as it ſpouts out from the Bladder, and hinder it from wetting the Lips. They are two, on each ſide one, juſt within the Lips, beginning at the jointing or middle of the Share-bone, at the lower ſide of the Privity, from whence they aſcend cloſe by each other to a little above half the breadth of the orifice of the Sheath, and end each in a blunt corner. Their ſubſtance is partly fleſhy and partly membranous; they are ſoft and ſpongie and of a red colour, having the ſame Veſſels with the *Clitoris*. Beſides their uſe to keep off the Piſs from wetting the Lips, they ſerve, as well as the Lips, for cloſing up and covering the mouth of the *Vagina*, at leaſt ſo much of it as they reach unto.

And now we have done with all the Parts belonging to Generation, both in Male and Female.

Table IX. Repreſenteth the ***Cava*** and ***Aorta***, the Kidneys, &c. and all the Generative parts of a Mare.

A *Sheweth the hollow Vein.*
B *The great Artery.*
CC *The Emulgent Veins.*
DD *The Emulgent Arteries.*
EE *The Kidneys.*
FF *The Deputy-kidneys.*
GG *The Vreters cut off.*
HHH *&c. The Spermatick Veins.*
II *The Spermatick Arteries.*
ii *The Hypogaſtrick Veins.*
ιι *The Hypogaſtrick Arteries.*
KK *The Teſticles.*
LL *The Trumpets of the Womb.*
ll *Their jagged Orifices.*
MM *The broad Ligament that ſuſtains them, and alſo connects the Teſticles to the Horns, and both to the Hip-bones.*
NN *The Horns of the Womb.*
OO *The bottom of the Womb where the Foal lies.*
PP *The Sheath of the Womb.*
QQ *The Sheath cut open that the q* Clitoris *may appear.*
R *The Bladder of Vrine turned aſide.*
S *Its inſertion into the Sheath near its Orifice.*
TT *The outward Orifice of the Sheath.*

CHAP.

CHAP. XXVIII.

How the Foal is nouriſhed in the Womb; of the Membranes wherein it is wrapt, and the Liquors contained in them; and laſtly of the Navel-ſtring.

HAVING deſcribed all the Parts in Mares that do any ways ſerve for generation, and ſhewn their ſeveral uſes, I ſhould put an end to this Firſt Book, but that it may be convenient to ſpeak ſomewhat of the Young contained in the Womb, for the conceiving and generating of which all theſe Parts were formed. But this I ſhall not do largely in this place, but onely ſummarily and in ſhort, referring the Reader for his fuller information and ſatisfaction to the Treatiſe *of the generation of Animals* annexed to the latter end of this Volume; where by obſerving in what order and by what degrees the conceptions in other Creatures arrive to perfect Animals of their kind, he may by the rule of proportion conceive how they proceed in Mares alſo.

How the Young is nouriſhed. Now before we come to ſpeak of the Membranes that inveſt the Foal, *&c.* which will be the ſubject of this Chapter, it will be neceſſary to premiſe ſomething concerning the ways or Veſſels by which nouriſhment is conveyed to it, whereby it grows from no bigger than a Bee to ſo vaſt a bulk.

The firſt Opinion. It is not long ago till when it was the general opinion, that the Young was nouriſhed by the Dam's Bloud; namely, that the hypogaſtrick and ſome of the ſpermatick Veſſels of the Dam did inoſculate with or open into the branches of the umbilical or Navel-veſſels of the Young, and ſo the bloud run from one to the other in a ready courſe. And this Opinion had ſo far prevailed, and was taken for ſo certain a truth, that after the Young was excluded out of the Womb, and muſt needs receive its nouriſhment by the mouth, they believed that it was nouriſhed by Bloud ſtill: For they thought that Milk was firſt Bloud, onely it changed its colour, and its taſte partly, in the white Kernels of the Dugs. This was a ſtrange fancy, that Nature ſhould thus doe and undoe, firſt turn Chyle into Bloud, and then turn that Bloud again into a Liquor reſembling Chyle, and in truth differing very little from it. But this by the way. I ſay, the Dam's Veſſels were ſuppoſed to inoſculate with the Navel-veſſels of the Young; whereby Bloud was carried to it for its nouriſhment: but they never troubled their heads about making it out how the Young ſhould be nouriſhed before it had ever a Navel-veſſel, or before ever the Conception adhered to any part of the Womb. Now the Embryo or firſt draught (as I may call it) of the Young is formed in all Creatures before the Navel-veſſels, and it is grown to a pretty bulk before they are ſo well perfected as to be capable of receiving any Liquor into them. And when they are perfectly formed, and can perform their office, whatever it be; in ſome Creatures, as particularly in a Sow, they never reach further than the *Chorion* or outmoſt Membrane wherein the Pig is included, and therefore have no contact or communication with thoſe of the Sow, whoſe Veins and Arteries reach no further than the inmoſt Membrane of the

the Womb. And in the Creature we have now under consideration, namely a Mare, it is near six months before the *Chorion* adhere to the inmost Membrane of the Womb, (which how it does, we shall shew by and by.) Now these observations plainly demonstrate that the Young cannot be nourished by the Bloud of the Dam, seeing there is no way whereby the Bloud can be conveyed to it, in any Creature for a considerable time, and in some Creatures, at all.

Others sufficiently discovering the errours of this Opinion, and inclining to believe that the Young in the Womb was nourished with the same Liquor while it was there, as it is after it comes into the World, namely Chyle a little refined, and not finding any other convenient ways (as they thought) whereby the Chyle could be conveyed to the Womb, have fancied that they have found Lacteal or Milky-vessels going thither directly either from the great Kernel at the centre of the Mesentery, or from the common receptacle of the Chyle it self: but others that favour not this Opinion, suppose those Vessels that these have fancied to be Lacteals, to be onely Lympheducts, conveying the *Lympha* or superfluous Water from the Womb to the common Receptacle, whither the *Lympha* of all the other Parts contained in the Lower Belly is by the same Vessels likewise discharged. So that though this Opinion be very plausible for its inventing so ready a way for the Chyles coming to the Womb; yet it is very probable that these supposed Milky-veins are nothing but Lympheducts, and then the whole Supposition falls to the ground. *The second Opinion.*

But yet though this second Opinion be mistaken in the Vessels that bring the Liquor to the Womb whereby the Young is nourished, yet it seems to have hit right on the Liquor it self. For as it cannot be Bloud for the reasons I have before given, so there is no other Liquor in the Body but Chyle, that is capable of being turned into nourishment. For though they call that Juice, by which Bodies come to maturity are nourished, (and also the Young in the Womb) *nutritious Juice*, yet that name onely denotes its *office*, and does not suppose that a Liquor quite distinct in *nature* from Bloud or Chyle is understood by that denomination: but it does indeed partake of the nature both of the Bloud and Chyle; for it is Chyle a little exalted or impregnated with the spirit and life of the Bloud. Now this Juice arrives at the Womb by these ways. First the Chyle ascending from the common Receptacle by the thoracick Duct to the right Ventricle of the Heart, it is sent out from thence together with the Bloud into the Lungs, from whence they both return to the left ventricle of the Heart, out of which they are ejected into the *Aorta* or great Artery, by which means the Chyle runs confounded with the Bloud into all the Parts of the Body; but when the Dam is with Young we may conceive that a greater quantity of it may tend towards the Womb than to other parts: even as it is probable that more wheyish or watery Humour accompanies that Bloud that flows by the Emulgent Arteries to the Kidneys, than that which flows to other Parts, because Nature has appointed the Kidneys for the separating of it from the Bloud. I say it is also likely that more Chyle descends to the Womb by the spermatick and hypogastrick Arteries than to any other part, because a great quantity of it is to be separated from the Bloud here for the nourishment of the Young. Now these Arteries, as all others in the Body, do divide themselves so often, till they end in very small capillary or hair-like threads, which terminate in the inmost Membrane of the *The third and truest Opinion.*

Table X. Shews the *Fœtus* or Young lying covered in the Womb; the Stomach, Guts, *&c.* being removed.

AA *&c. The body of the Matrix.*
BB *The Horn of the Womb on the left ſide.*
DDD *The Liver.*
E *The Bladder.*
FF *The Ligaments of the Bladder.*
GG *The Ureters.*
HH *The Iliack Veſſels.*
II *The Hypogaſtrick Veſſels.*
MM *The Share-bone cut aſunder.*
N *The Privity or* Vulva.
O *The Dock.*
PP *The Midriff.*
Q *The neck of the Bladder joined with the ſheath of the Matrix.*
SS *The Veſſels called* pudendæ, *diſperſed into and about the Lips of the Privity.*

Womb. But all the branches of theſe Arteries about the Womb are much larger when the Female is with Young than at other times, which is an argument that nouriſhment is indeed brought by them. The greateſt difficulty is, how it can be diſcharged out of the Arteries into the Womb, and no Bloud go along with it. To ſolve this difficulty we muſt conſider, that the Particles of ſeveral Liquors are of different figures, as ſuppoſe ſome round, ſome corner'd, *&c.* Now we know that if two bodies of the *ſame* bulk be one round, and another fourſquare, the round will go through a hole which the fourſquare body will not, and on the contrary the fourſquare body will paſs through a hole that the round will not; accordingly as the hole is round or fourſquare. And this may be the reaſon that the Chyle can paſs out of the ſmall ends of the Arteries, and yet the Bloud cannot accompany it, but muſt return back by the Veins. And beſides the difference of figure, it is probable the Particles of that Chyle that ouzes into the Womb, are of much *ſmaller* bulk than thoſe of the Bloud, ſeeing it is a much thinner and watery body; and therefore may as eaſily be ſeparated from the Bloud into the Womb, as the Urine is by the Kidneys into the Ureters. And to further and aſſiſt this ſeparation ſome do believe there is a certain fermentation in the Womb, even as there is in other Parts of the Body, where other Juices are ſeparated from the Bloud, as Choler in the Liver, and according to ſome, Urine in the Kidneys. But be the ſeparation by what means it will, that there is ſuch a thing is moſt certain, and how the Young comes to partake of it for its nouriſhment we ſhall next ſhew.

The Membranes that the Foal is wrapt in.

While it was believed that a Conception was made of the Male and Female's Seed mixed together, it was ſomewhat difficult to imagine how ſuch a fluid ſubſtance ſhould ſo ſpeedily acquire ſo compact Membranes to include it, as we ſee it has in a few days. But now that it is believed that a Conception is nothing elſe but an Egg dropt off from the Teſticle and received into the Womb, that difficulty vaniſhes, for thoſe Membranes do originally inveſt the Egg, even as we ſee the like Membranes lie under the ſhells of the Eggs of Fowls, and encompaſſing the whole. Theſe Membranes are at the firſt but two, called *Amnios* and *Chorion*; but after a while there is a third commonly called *Allantoides*, or the Pudding-like Membrane.

That

TAB. X.

pag. 60.

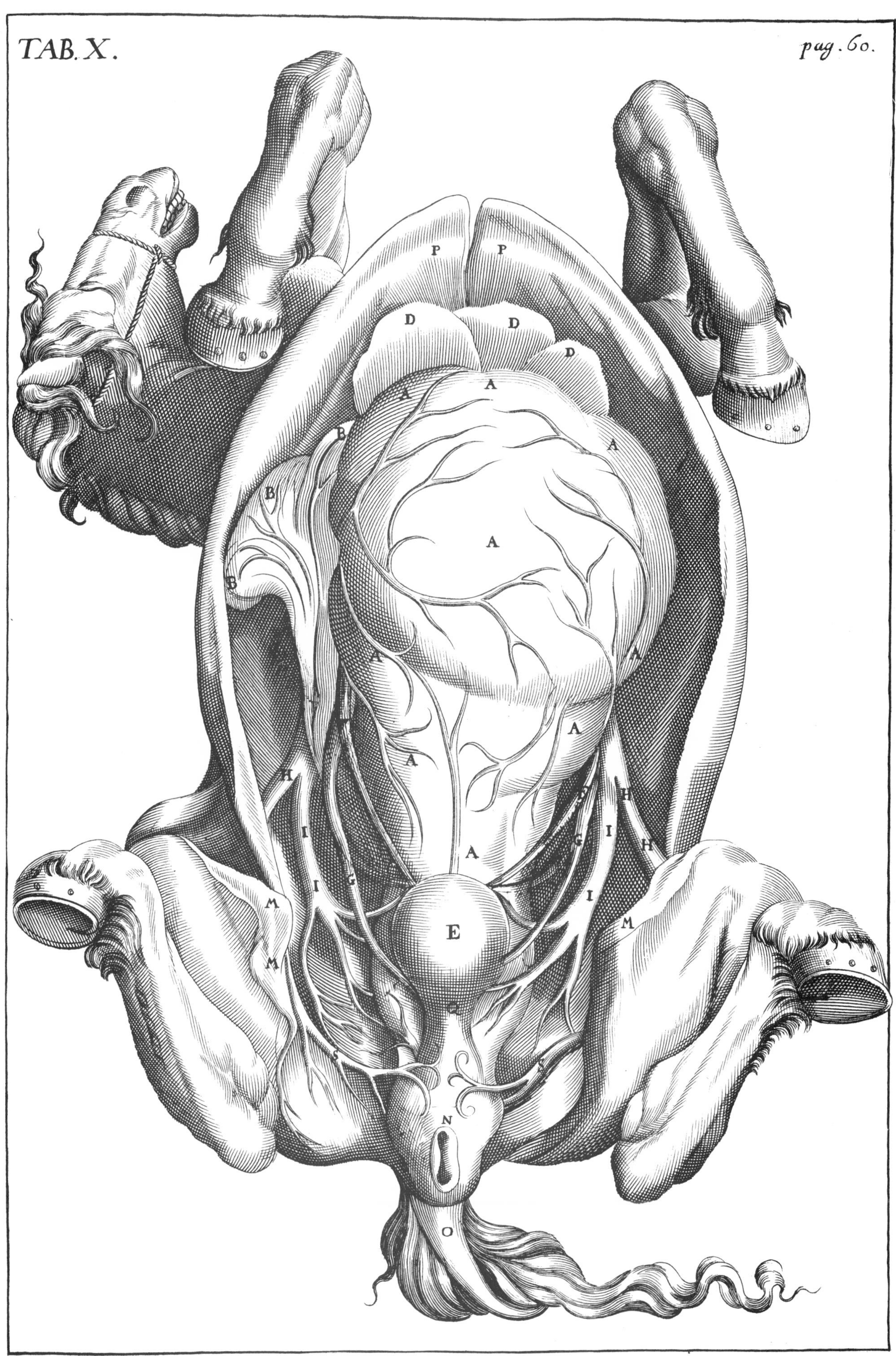

That Membrane or Skin that immediately infolds the Young is called *Amnios*. It is very thin, smooth and clear, and in it is contained that Liquor out of which the Young is first formed, and by which it is afterwards nourished. That Liquor out of which the Young is formed, is originally in it, even while the Conception is under the form of an Egg: but that by which the Young is nourished and its Parts increased, sweats into this Membrane immediately out of the *Chorion* or outmost Membrane for the first months, till the Navel-string is perfected, and that there grows a new Membrane betwixt these two, that contains a peculiar sort of Liquor, as we shall shew by and by. But the Juice that is in the *Amnios* from first to last (except that out of which the *Embryo* is *formed*) is Chyle, which at first sweats into it out of the *Chorion*, and afterwards is conveyed into it by the umbilical Arteries of the Young, who first received it by its umbilical Veins. For these Arteries send many branches into the *Amnios*, which discharge themselves into it, even as the hypogastrick and spermatick Arteries do into the Womb. Now this Liquor that is thus collected in this inmost Membrane, does at first nourish the *Embryo* or first rudiments of the Young by apposition, that is, those rudiments do attract to themselves such particles of the Liquor as are suitable for them, and thereby their bulk comes to be encreased by degrees: but as soon as the Young has its Mouth and Stomach perfected, it then sucks it up and drinks it in by its Mouth, and it passes by the same ways to the Heart as it does after the birth. *The* Amnios.

The second Membrane, that is originally in the Egg, and that invests the Young from first to last, is called the *Chorion*. This is somewhat thicker than the *Amnios*; it is smooth on its inside, but rough and unequal on its outside. This Membrane drinks up that nutritious Juice that is emptied into the Womb from the hypogastrick and spermatick Arteries, which Juice is again filtred as it were out of it into the *Amnios* for the nourishment of the Young. For the Liquor contained in this Membrane is altogether the same with that of the *Amnios*. Now this Membrane for several months (five or six) adheres not to the Womb in any part, but the Young that is clad with it, lies as loose in the Womb, as a Bladder in a Foot-ball that is not at all tied to the leather. (Thus I say it is in a Mare, though in most other Creatures this Membrane begin much sooner to be fasten'd to the Womb.) But at length first of all there begin to grow in the surface of it certain reddish specks or caruncles no bigger than a Vetch, and at the same time the Membrane grows thicker, and there appear innumerable Vessels in it. And these Caruncles as they become more in number, so they grow broader in dimension, insomuch as at last they are spread all over the *Chorion*, so that on its outside it seems to have lost the nature of a Membrane, and to have become a *placenta* or Womb-cake. At the same time that these Caruncles grow thus on this Membrane, the Navel-string penetrating the *Amnios* is inserted into it, and those numerous Vessels that are seen in the *Chorion*, are onely branches of the Navel-arteries and Veins dispersed through it. And now the *Chorion* by means of the Caruncles that grow upon it, adheres to the inner Membrane of the Womb, from whence the Navel-veins imbibe nutritious Juice and carry it to the Young for its sustenance, (as shall be further shewed presently, when we come to speak of the Navel-string.) But the Caruncles do not stick so fast to the Womb, but that they may be separated without tearing, much less are there any Anastomoses or Inoscula- *The* Chorion.

 tions

tions of the Veſſels that run through the *Chorion* with the hypogaſtrick or ſpermatick Veſſels of the Dam, as the Ancients believed. Nor is there in a Mare any of thoſe Glandules that are commonly called *Cotyledons* or Sawcers, ſticking to the inner Membrane of the Womb, into which the Caruncles of the *Chorion* are inſerted, like an Acorn into its cup, ſuch as are in Sheep and Goats : but the ſo often mentioned Caruncles ſtick immediately to the Membrane it ſelf, and ſeem to ſerve as Sponges to imbibe the nutritious Juice that plentifully bedews it ; which having done, the ſaid Juice is ſuckt up by the mouths of the Navel-vein, as was ſaid before. Part of this Membrane does on each ſide bag out into the Horns of the Womb.

Allantoides. As ſoon as the Navel-ſtring has penetrated the *Amnios*, there begins to appear a third Membrane betwixt theſe two already deſcribed, which contains a Liquor wholly different from what ſwims in *them* ; for *that* we have ſhewn to be *Chyle*, but *this* is the *Urine* of the Young, which, while the Young is in the Womb, is not emptied out of the Bladder the common way, but there is a Pipe called *Urachus* that paſſes from the bottom of the Bladder out at its Navel, and empties the Urine into this Membrane, in which it is collected to the quantity of many quarts. This Membrane is called *Allantoides* or Pudding-like, becauſe in many Creatures, as Cows, Sheep, *&c.* it is of that ſhape, and ſeems to be onely the *Urachus* a little widened. But it is of another figure in Mares (as it is alſo in Women) and is of the ſame dimenſion with the other two already deſcribed, incompaſſing the whole Young. It is more denſe than they, and may be eaſily diſtinguiſhed from them by this, that *they* are full of Veſſels, but *this* has not one, that one can diſcern. Although this Membrane appear not till the time aforeſaid, yet 'tis like it was originally in the Egg; and at its appearance the *Chorion* becomes empty, becauſe there is now no longer paſſage of any thing out of the *Chorion* into the *Amnios*, by reaſon of this Membrane and its Liquor interpoſing. Whence the *Chorion* claps pretty cloſe to the *Allantoides*, ſo that they cannot be eaſily ſeparated. In the Liquor contained in the *Allantoides* there ſwim ſeveral gobbets that look like as if they were fleſhy, but being pulled to pieces they appear skinny. They are ſuppoſed to be concretions of ſome part of the nutritious Juice that may come along with the Urine into this Membrane, wherein by its long ſtay it curdles into theſe kind of bodies. But there is one more notable one, that is ſaid to grow on the Forehead of the Colt, of the ſhape of a Tongue, and is called *hippomanes*, which, Tradition ſays, the Mare is wont to eat as ſoon as ſhe has foal'd ; which if ſhe do not, ſhe will never care for her Foal. This they were wont to dry and powder, and to put into drink for a Love-potion, as if there were ſome witchery in it. But ſuch things I can ſay nothing to, having never experimented them. This Membrane ſticking pretty cloſe to the *Chorion*, bags out on each ſide into the Horns of the Womb as well as it. The Liquor contained in it, is Urine, as was ſaid above, which daily increaſes in quantity, being imported into it by the *Urachus* from the Bladder of the Foal.

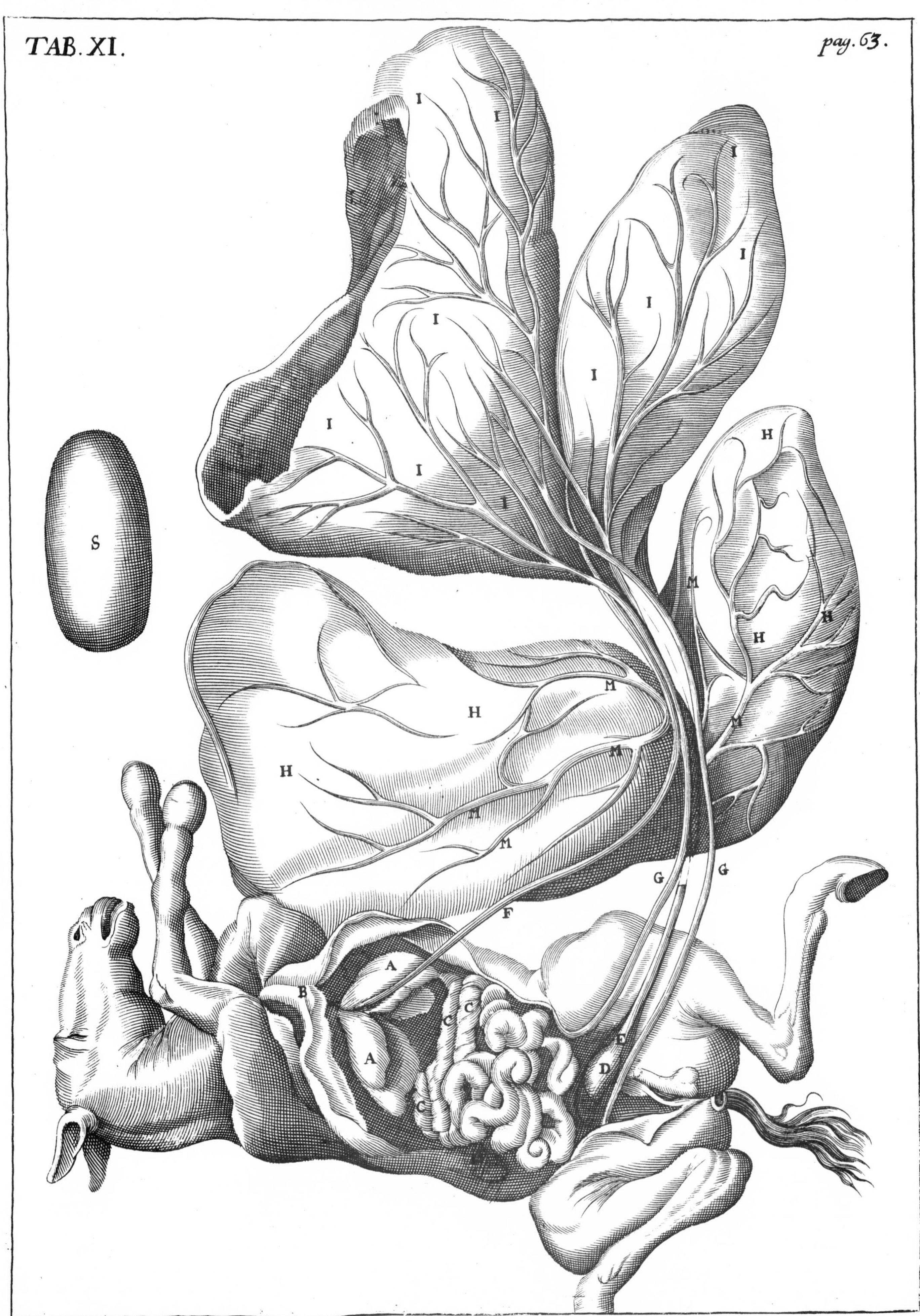
I
I
I
I
I
I
I
I
I
I
I
I
S
H
H
H
H
H
H
M
M
M
M
M
M
M
G
G
F
A
B
A
C
C
C
E
D

Table XI. Shews the Belly of the *Fœtus* opened, the better to ſhew the Umbilical Veſſels; as alſo two of the Membranes laid open, in which the *Fœtus* is included in the Wo..ıb, with the Veins and Arteries branching into them.

AA *The Liver.*
B *The* Sternum *or Breaſt-bone.*
CCC *The Gut* Colon.
D *The Bladder of Urine.*
E *The* Urachus *cut off ſhort, becauſe the* Allantoides, *into which it is inſerted, is not expreſſed.*
FF *The Umbilical Vein.*
GG *The Umbilical Arteries.*
HHH &c. *The Membrane* Amnios.
II &c. *The Membrane called* Chorion, *with the branches of the Umbilical Veins and Arteries diſperſed through it.*
MM &c. *The like branches running through the* Amnios.
S *The Caruncle called* Hippomanes, *which is ſaid to grow on the Foal's Forehead, but is indeed found in the middle Membrane called* Allantoides.

Laſtly, We are come to the Veſſels that make up the Navel-ſtring, and thoſe are four, one Vein, two Arteries, and the *Urachus*. Theſe are all infolded in a common Coat, and are wreathed one about another like a Rope. The greateſt part of its length is contained in the *Amnios*, the reſt in the *Allantoides*; for as ſoon as it has penetrated that, it is immediately and directly implanted into the *Chorion*. *The Navel-veſſels.*

The *Vein* is as big as both the Arteries, and ariſes out of the hollow or lower ſide of the Liver of the Young, and coming out ſingle with the reſt at the Navel, is immediately divided into two, which as they paſs through the *Amnios*, ſend ſome twigs to it, and from thence continue their march through the *Allantoides* to the *Chorion*, in which and the Caruncles that grow upon it they terminate, being divided into innumerable branches. Its uſe is to imbibe the nutritious Juice and alſo the Bloud that is ſuperfluous to the nouriſhing of theſe Parts, and to convey them to the Young. *One Vein.*

The *Arteries* being two, do ariſe on each ſide from the inner Iliacal Branches of the great Artery, (as is commonly held, but I have always obſerved them to ſpring from the *Aorta* it ſelf before the diviſion) and aſcending by the ſides of the Bladder, they meet the Vein at the Navel, and there begin to be wreathed with it. Their march and inſertions are the ſame with thoſe of the Vein, onely they ſend more twigs into the *Amnios* than the Vein doth. Their uſe is to carry vital heat and nouriſhment to the Parts that include the Young, to wit to the *Amnios*, *Chorion* and its Caruncles: and beſides, its branches that are diſperſed through the *Amnios* do diſtill into it ſome of that nutritious Juice which could not be turned into Bloud by once circulating through the Heart of the Young. Which Juice being collected in the cavity of the *Amnios*, is drunk in by the Young at its mouth, and ſo paſſes the ſame ways as it does after the birth. *Two Arteries.*

The Urachus. The fourth Veſſel included in the Navel-rope is called *Urachus*, from its office of conveying the Urine. It ſprings from the bottom of the Bladder, and paſſing out of the Navel with the Vein and Arteries, as ſoon as it has pierced the *Amnios* it opens it ſelf with a full mouth into the cavity of the *Allantoides*, ſerving as a Pipe to rack the Urine as it were out of the Bladder of the Young into this Membrane. For though the Young void no Excrements at the Fundament, while it is in the Womb, nor has any Repoſitory or Storehouſe for them ſaving its own Guts, (amongſt which the Gut *Cæcum* ſeems fitteſt for that office:) yet ſeeing it is nouriſhed altogether with Liquor that has a good quantity of wheyiſh humour mixed with it for its better conveyance through thoſe narrow ways by which it is to paſs, I ſay for this reaſon it is neceſſary there ſhould be ſome particular Repoſitory for it, ſeeing it cannot return to the Dam again, and the Bladder of the Young is not capable of containing a fifth (may be a tenth) part of it; and this Repoſitory is the Membrane *Allantoides*, into which it is poured out of the Bladder by the *Urachus*.

Theſe four Veſſels after they come out of the Navel are included in one common Coat, which conſiſts of a double Membrane, borrowed from the Rim of the Belly the inner of them, and the outer from the fleſhy Membrane or Pannicle deſcribed above *chap.* 4. After the birth of the Foal, theſe Veſſels loſing their original uſe, the two Arteries ſerve for Ligaments to keep the Bladder in its place, and the Vein performs the ſame office to the Liver; but the *Urachus* quite diſappears.

And thus much of the Membranes and Navel-veſſels, that are included in the Womb when the Mare is with Foal; and which at the Foaling make the After-birth or Cleaning as we call it: We might in this place further ſhew, what Parts of the Foal are firſt formed, and which ſooneſt perfected; alſo in what particulars a Foal in the Womb differs from it ſelf when foaled; and laſtly we might have been more full in ſhewing how it is nouriſhed in the Womb: but the diſcourſing of theſe things we purpoſely wave in this place, and refer the Reader to the Diſcourſe *of the generation of Animals* annexed to this Treatiſe of Anatomy, wherein we will endeavour to ſatisfy his curioſity to the uttermoſt.

Table XII. Shews the Foal taken out of the Matrix, both wrapt in the Membranes with which it was covered, and alſo quite cleared of them; and laſtly, the ſaid Membranes cut open, the Foal as yet remaining in them.

Fig. I. Shews the *Fœtus* taken out of the Matrix, remaining in the ſame poſture as in the Womb, and wrapt in its Membranes.

AA *The Membranes.*
CC *The hinder Legs of the Foal.*

Fig. II. Shews the *Fœtus* cleared of the Membranes, but continuing in the ſame poſture.

BBB *The Body of the Foal.*
SS *The common covering of the Umbilical Veſſels turned back, that the four Veſſels contained in it may appear.*
TT *The Umbilical Arteries.*

U *The*

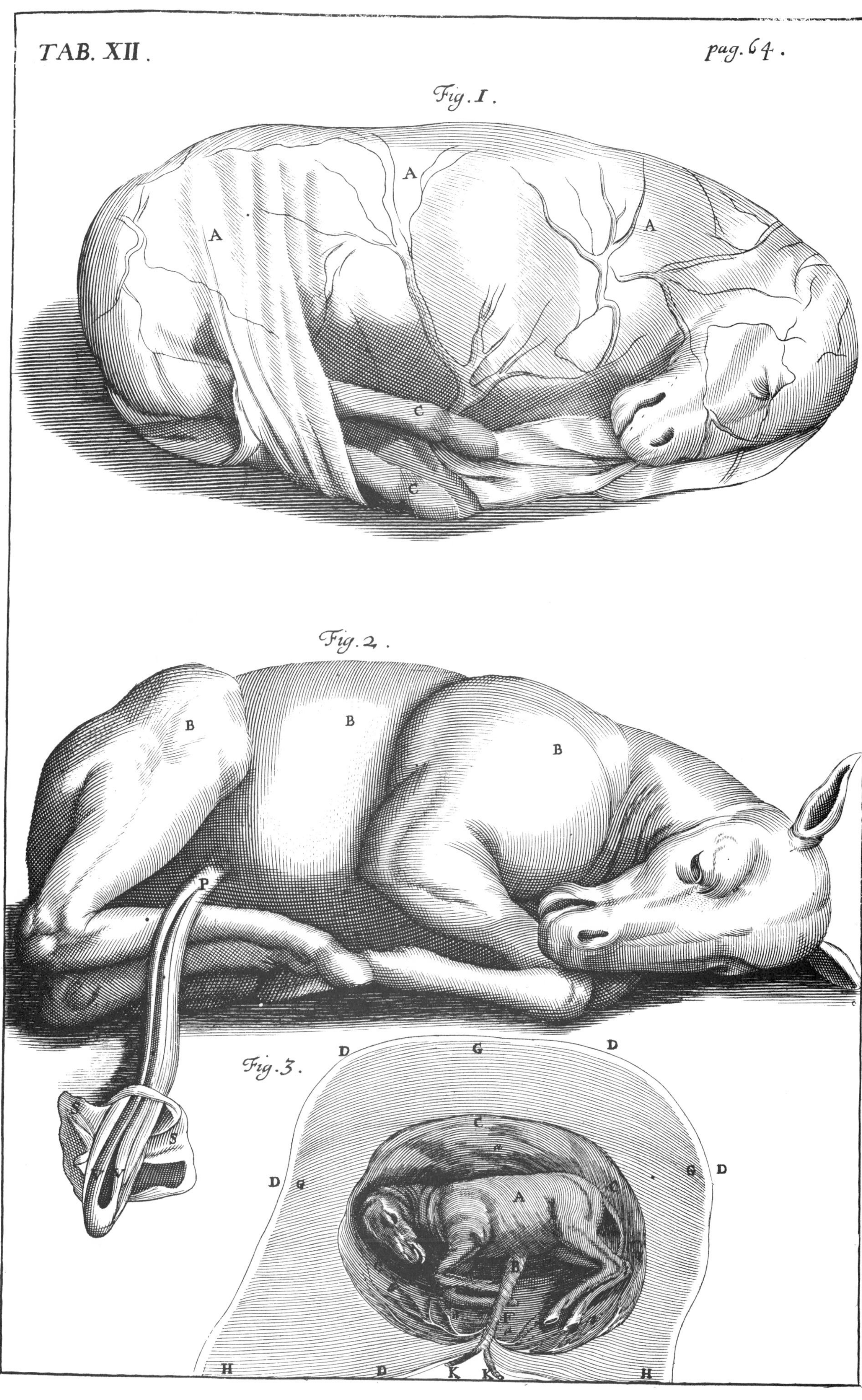
Fig. 1.
A
A
A
C
C
Fig. 2.
B
B
B
P
S
S
Fig. 3.
D
G
D
C
D G
G D
A
B
H
D
K K
H

U *The Umbilical Vein.*
X *The* Urachus.

Fig. III. Shews the Foal, and two of its Membranes, as repreſented by Dr. *Walt. Needham.*

A *The Foal lying within the Membranes.*
B *The Navel-rope whoſe production* E *paſſes through the cavity of the urinary Membrane toward the* Chorion.
CCC *The* Amnios.
DDDD *The place of the* Chorion *which naturally grows to the urinary Membrane, but is here removed, that the* Fœtus *may appear through the* Amnios *and urinary Membrane.*
E *The production of the Rope which at this place is divided into two, and ſo is cut off with the* Chorion.
F *The place in the Navel-rope, where the exit of the* Urachus *is deſign'd, between two blots. Which* Urachus *is not indeed a part of the Membrane* GG *or Urinary, but of* CC *or* Amnios. *and ſeems a duplicature of it turned back even to the Bladder.*
GGG *The urinary Membrane, (which here is not* Allantoides, *or of the ſhape of a Pudding) inveſting the whole* Fœtus *as well as the* Amnios; *which is common to it with a Man, Dog, Cat, Coney, and perhaps others that have Womb-cakes; although they differ from one another in ſeveral circumſtances.*
HH *The progreſs of this Membrane as alſo of the* Chorion *into the Horns of the Womb. Whereas all the whole* Fœtus *beſides,* &c. *lies in the bottom of the Womb, as a Child does in a Woman's.*
aaaa *The Bloud-veſſels diſperſed from the Rope into the* Amnios, *which the urinary Membrane wants wholly; for the reſt of the Rope is all ſpent on the* Chorion, *and is cut off with it.*

CHAP.

CHAP. XXIX.

Of the Udder.

THOUGH the Udder be an *external* Part of the Lower Belly, yet we have deferr'd the deſcription of it till this place, becauſe of the dependance that it has upon the Womb, and its office of yielding the ſame nouriſhment to the Foal when it is excluded out of the Womb, as it was nouriſh'd by while it remain'd in it.

It is ſeated at the bottom of the Paunch upon the lower ends of the ſtreight Muſcles; very ſmall, if compar'd to the bigneſs of a Mare's Body, and to its bulk in many other Creatures. When the Mare gives no ſuck, it almoſt diſappears.

Its ſubſtance. It conſiſts of the common coverings, Fat, a multitude of Veſſels, Glands or Kernels, and Pipes to convey the Milk to the Paps that is ſeparated from the Veſſels in the Glands.

Number. Now though when the Mare gives ſuck it ſeems to be but *one* roundiſh body, like a Breaſt with two Nipples, yet it truly conſiſts of *two* bodies, one being joined to the other onely by contiguity, for they have each their proper Veſſels, Pipes and Pap; and do indeed appear to the eye to be diſtinct when the Mare is neither with Foal nor ſuckles one.

Its Glands. The greateſt part of its bulk conſiſts of *Glands*, which are many in number, though they be ſo united to one another as to appear one continued body to an unwary obſerver, which they come to do from that Fat that fills up the ſpaces between them, and is much of the ſame colour with the Glands. There is one Gland greater than the reſt ſeated at the root of each Pap. By means of theſe Glands it is that the Milk is ſeparated from the Bloud, as ſhall be further ſhewn by and by.

The Paps. The *Paps* are round in ſhape and of a ſpongie ſubſtance, cloathed with a thinner Skin than the reſt of the Udder. At their head or end they have many little holes through which the Milk iſſues when the Foal ſucks.

The Veſſels belonging to the Udder. The Udder has all ſorts of *Veſſels*, Veins, Arteries, Nerves and Lympheducts; and beſides theſe it has peculiar Pipes for containing and conveying the Milk. The *Veins* and *Arteries* are branches of the *Hypogaſtricks*, which proceed from the *internal* Iliack branches of the *Cava* and *Aorta:* 'tis likely there come ſome twigs to it alſo from the *external* branches, which are called the *Epigaſtrick* Veſſels. Its *Nerves* I have not examin'd, but 'tis very probable they are the ſame with thoſe diſperſed into the Matrix and Sheath, which are twigs of the Intercoſtal pair and of ſome of the *Os ſacrum.* Its *Lympheducts* are pretty numerous, and tend, as all thoſe of the Lower Belly do, to the common Receptacle of the Chyle, at the centre of the Meſentery.

The milk-pipes. It has alſo a peculiar ſort of Veſſels, which may be called *Milk pipes*, being the Repoſitories or Store-houſes of the Milk. At the root of each Pap they are but one on each ſide, but a great many ſmaller ones coming from every part of the Udder diſcharge themſelves into this one, when the Pap is ſuckt by the Foal. But the Pipes belonging to one Pap have no communication with thoſe that belong to the other, but in reſpect of theſe

these Veſſels the two ſides of the Udder are as diſtinct Parts, as the Breaſts of a Woman are diſtinct one from another, as was noted before. Theſe Pipes have been miſtaken by ſome to be true Milky-veins, as if ſome of the Milky-veins of the Meſentery reached hither. But ſeeing there are no footſteps of them in the track betwixt the Meſentery and Udder, we may well deny them to be found in the Udder it ſelf.

The uſe of the Udder. The *uſe* of the Udder is to prepare and ſeparate the Milk for the nouriſhment of the Foal, which it does in this manner. The Chyle of the Mare being mixed with her Bloud in the Heart, flows from thence along with it by the Arteries into all Parts of the Body in the circulation, but moſt plentifully ('tis probable) towards the Udder, even as it does to the Womb while the Mare is with Foal. The Arteries that convey it immediately to the Udder are the hypogaſtrick Branches, which terminating in its Glands do ſquirt or ſtrain the Chyle through them into the Milk-pipes. And as for the Bloud that was mixed with the Chyle in the Arteries, that being of a thicker body, or conſiſting of Particles of another form, cannot enter the narrow pores of the Glands, and therefore is received by the ſmall mouths of the Veins that are likewiſe inſerted into them. So that it appears to be an erroneous Opinion, That Milk is made of Bloud, if we ſpeak of Bloud properly ſo called; yet ſeeing the Chyle, when it is confuſedly jumbled with the Bloud in the Arteries, is not eaſily diſtinguiſhable from it, but the whole Maſs ſeems to be homogeneal or of the ſame nature, in a large and leſs proper ſenſe we may affirm it to be ſo made. After that the Chyle is thus ſeparated by the Glands, it drills along the Milk-pipes, out of the ſmaller into the larger, in which it is reſerved for the uſe of the Foal.

The End of the First Book.

THE ANATOMY OF AN HORSE.

BOOK II.

Of the Middle Venter, *or Cheſt.*

CHAP. I.

Of the inveſting and circumſcribing Parts of the Cheſt.

HAVING finiſhed the Firſt Book, wherein I have abſolved or explained all the *Natural* Parts contained within the Lower *Venter*, as well nutritive as generative, and annexed a Diſcourſe of the Foal in the Matrix or Womb; order of diſſection requires that in the next place I come to treat of the Middle *Venter*, the *Thorax* or Cheſt, and the *Vital* Parts contained therein.

Where, in this one ſtep higher that I have climbed, I am methinks much delighted to ſee, how Nature in this place diſports her ſelf, having as in a curious Cabinet lockt up, as it were, her moſt exquiſite pieces of Workmanſhip, the *Vital* Inſtruments, by whoſe motion the life of the Creature is continued. Which motion is performed by ſo juſt a counterpoiſe, as no art of Man could ever with all their contrivances be able in the leaſt to imitate. Nay *Ariſtotle*, that wiſe Philoſopher, who was in his time thought to be the neareſt of counſel to Nature, was not able (notwithstanding his incomparable sagacity) to find out the true cause of the Vital motion, any more than he was, to find out the reciprocal Ebbing and Flowing of the Sea.

The Place wherein these Instruments are contained, is called the *Thorax* or Chest, which is composed of or environed with these Parts following.

By what parts the Thorax *is bounded.*

First it is bounded or circumscribed, above, by the Coller-bones, and below by the *Diaphragm* or Midriff; on the fore-part by the Breast-bone, and on the hinder part by the Spondyls or Back-bones; and on the two sides by the true and bastard Ribs and Intercostal Muscles. All which Parts are framed and composed by Nature for the benefit of the Creature, as well for the *defence* of the contained Parts from external Injuries, as for the use of *Respiration* or breathing: both which are very needfull; for without them the Creature cannot be preserved. Now that it might serve for these ends, it was necessary it should consist of sundry Parts; for should it have been made all bony, it could not have been contracted and dilated as occasion served, whereby the Lungs could not have had the liberty to play as now they have: And if it had been wholly fleshy, then would not the contained Parts have been sufficiently fenced. It is therefore made partly bony, partly gristly, and partly fleshy, that it might the better perform both the offices aforesaid.

In the next place I come to speak particularly to the *Investing* Parts of the Chest, some of which are *Common*, and others *Proper*.

Its common investing Parts.

The *Common investing* or *containing* Parts are the same as the Lower Belly hath, namely the Scarf-skin, the true Skin, the fleshy Pannicle, the Fat, and the common Membrane of the Muscles. Of all which having discoursed at large in the First Book, we shall say nothing of them here.

Its proper containing Parts.

The *Proper containing* Parts of the Chest are the Muscles, the Bones, the *Pleura* or Membrane that cloaths its inside, the Midriff and the *Mediastinum*, which is the Skin that goes across from the Breast to the Back, and parts the Lungs, called by some, the Partition-wall.

Its contained Parts.

The *contained* or *invested* Parts, are the Heart with the Heart-bag called the *Pericardium*, and by some the Purse of the Heart, the Lungs and part of the Weazand or Wind-pipe, by Anatomists called *Aspera Arteria*, or Rough-artery, and several Vessels, with the Trunks of *Vena cava* and *Arteria magna*, whose ascending branches are underpropped by the *Thymus*, or Kernel in the Throat.

CHAP.

CHAP. II.

Of the Muſcles of the Middle Venter *or Cheſt, called the Intercoſtal Muſcles.*

THERE are ſeveral pairs of *Muſcles* that lie upon the Cheſt on the outſide of the Ribs; but becauſe one may eaſily enough cut open the Cheſt for examining the Parts contained in it, without defacing any part of thoſe Muſcles, we ſhall omit to ſpeak of them in this place, referring the Reader to the Book of the Muſcles; and here onely deſcribe the *Intercoſtal*, which in laying open the Breaſt, whiles one breaks the griſtly ends of the Ribs, happen part of them to be defaced.

Theſe Muſcles are called *Intercoſtal* from their being placed *between the Ribs*, and filling up the ſpaces between them. Betwixt every two Ribs there are placed two of theſe Muſcles, the one lying upon the other; the uppermoſt being called the *External*, and the undermoſt the *Internal one.* *Intercoſtal Muſcles why ſo called.*

The *External* one takes his riſe from the lower part of the upper Ribs, and ends in the upper part of the lower. *The External.*

The *Internal* takes his riſe contrary to the former; for it ariſes or takes its original from the upper part of the lower Rib, and ends in the lower part of the upper. *The Internal.*

Now it is to be underſtood that thoſe are called the upper Ribs that are next to the Head, and thoſe the lower, that are next to the Paunch.

And as theſe Muſcles do differ as to their original and inſertion, ſo likewiſe in the courſe of their Fibres; for although they be both furniſhed with oblique or ſlanting Fibres, yet they run contrary ways, croſſing one the other, and making as it were a St. *Andrew*'s Croſs, or the letter X.

Theſe Muſcles are in number ſixty four, that is to ſay on each ſide thirty two, there being on each ſide of the Horſe ſeventeen Ribs, and between every Rib two Muſcles, as I have before intimated. *Their number.*

Now the *action* of theſe Muſcles is to aſſiſt Reſpiration by widening, and contracting the Cheſt. Firſt the *external* ones ſerve to raiſe the Ribs and draw them backward, whereby the Cavity of the Cheſt is enlarged, and thereby free room made for the Air to enter into the Lungs in *Inſpiration*, or taking in the breath. And on the contrary the *internal* pull in the Ribs by drawing them ſlanting downwards towards the Breaſt-bone, whereby the Cheſt is ſtraitned, and thereby the Air, wherewith the Lungs are puff'd up, expelled, which action is called *Expiration*, or breathing forth. But theſe Muſcles are not of themſelves alone ſufficient for theſe actions, but they aſſiſt towards them, being aided by the other that lie upon the Cheſt, by the Midriff, and by the Lungs themſelves. *Their action.*

CHAP. III.

Of the Pleura, *or Coat which invests or lines the Ribs on the Inside.*

THIS Coat or Skin called the *Pleura*, is the Skin which covereth all the Ribs on the inside of the Chest, being of the same nature and use here, as the *Peritonæum* or Rim of the Belly is in the Lower Belly. It is also of the same substance as the Rim of the Belly is, but much stronger and thicker, though *Riolanus* affirmeth the contrary as to Men.

It is as it were of a middle nature or temper, that is, neither too hard nor too soft; not too hard, lest it should not reach and yield in the act of Respiration, and so hinder the motion of the Chest; neither too soft, lest the motion of the Chest should violate it: but it is rather hard than soft, the better to defend the Vital Parts.

The original of the Pleura *or Rib-skin.* It is believed to take its *original* from the Coats of the Nerves of the Spinal Marrow, which come out of the Back-bones (or *vertebræ* of the Back) into the Chest, and is therefore thought to be continued with the Coats of the Brain: wherefore it is observed to be thicker upon the back part of the Chest than any where else, where it sticks so close to the Back-bones, that it can hardly be separated.

It is all over double, that the Intercostal-vessels might run without danger between its Membranes, and by it be preserved from the hardness of the Ribs, which would be apt to violate or break them.

The outward Skin of this Coat, namely that which is next to the Cavity of the Chest, is harder and thicker; and the inward (which is fastned to the Ribs) is softer and thinner. Now between these two Skins is bred that mortal Disease (in Men) called the Pleurisie, by which the never to be forgotten Doctor *Willis*, (for being in his time the honour of his University and Country) was notwithstanding the great pains he took in the inquiry into and finding out remedies against this Disease, (as his learned Works make appear, by which great benefit hath accrued to others) was, I say, himself by the tyranny of it taken from amongst the Living.

Its Perforations. This *Pleura* is perforated in many places, for the Ingate and Outgate of the Vessels. For above, it letteth out the Jugular and Axillary Arteries and Veins, and below, through the Midriff, the Trunks of the hollow Vein and great Artery. Besides where it receiveth in the Nerves of the wandring pair, the Windpipe, and both letteth in and out the Gullet.

Its Vessels. Its proper *Vessels* are, *Veins* from the *Vena sine pari*, or Vein without a pair, and from the upper Intercostal Vein. Its *Arteries* spring also from the upper Intercostals (as those from the Subclavian) which descend to about the seventh or eighth Rib: below which it receives twigs of Arteries from the back part of the descending great Artery. It has as many pairs of *Nerves* (wanting one) as there are Joints in the Backbone the whole length of the Chest: for betwixt each Joint there comes out a pair; but then the uppermost and lowest Joints being reckoned for the

the two extremes, (and not a pair of Nerves for either extreme) there muſt be one pair of Nerves leſs than there are Joints. The Joints therefore (or *vertebræ*) being ſeventeen, there muſt onely ſixteen pair of Nerves be reckoned to the Cheſt. Now theſe Nerves as ſoon as ever they come out of the Joint, are immediately divided into the *fore* and *hinder-branches*. Of which the *fore-branches* ſerve the Intercoſtal Muſcles and the *Pleura*; but the *hinder* are beſtowed on the Muſcles that lie upon the Back.

The *uſe* of it is much like that of the Rim of the Belly; for (as hath been ſaid) as the Rim of the Belly is ſtretched about all the Lower Belly, and furniſheth all the Bowels therein contained with Coats or Skins, (every Bowel with a particular Coat) ſo doth this *Pleura* the Bowels of the Middle *Venter*: for it is ſtretched about all the Cavity of the Cheſt, and giveth a Coat to every particular Part therein contained, (either mediately or immediately.) It covers alſo the Intercoſtal Muſcles, and makes the upper Membrane of the Midriff. Next to the Cavity of the Cheſt it is bedewed with a watery humour, that the Lungs which lie againſt it on their outſide, may move the more glibly, and not be offended by its roughneſs. *Its uſe.*

CHAP. IV.

Of the Midriff or Diaphragm.

THE *Diaphragm* (or *Midriff*) is ſo called from its office of diſtinguiſhing or ſeparating; becauſe it ſeparateth or diſtinguiſheth the Bowels of the *lower*, from the Inſtruments of Life and Reſpiration in the *middle* Belly. *The Diaphragm why ſo called.*

It is a Muſcle, long and round, ſeated at the lower part of the Cheſt, overthwart which it runs, ſloping a little lower towards the Paunch backward. It hath a figure and action different from all other Muſcles.

It is as broad as the Cheſt is wide: for its edges are knit to the lower part of the Breaſt-bone, and all round on each ſide to the Ribs, and to the loweſt vertebral Joint of the Cheſt.

It is ſaid to ariſe from its two long and fleſhy Productions, which ſpringing from the *vertebræ* of the Loins (to the muſcles whereof they are ſtrongly knit) do, as they go upwards, grow wider and wider, till they come to the loweſt *vertebræ* of the Cheſt, where they grow and unite together, and ſo ſpread themſelves into this Muſcle called the Midriff. Others, though they grant that theſe are part of its original, yet think that it does equally ariſe from its whole fleſhy circumference, by which it adheres to the ends of the loweſt Ribs. And a third opinion is, that its original is from its centre or middle where its Nerve is inſerted into it, from that common Maxim of *Galen*'s, That whereever the Nerve is inſerted, *there* is the head of the Muſcle. But as that Maxim does not hold in *all other* Muſcles, ſo *this* being a Muſcle of a peculiar ſhape and uſe, it may well be excepted therefrom, eſpecially ſeeing the centre of the Midriff is tendinous, *Its riſe.*

tendinous, which the origine of a Muscle does not use to be, but onely its end.

Its substance. As for its *substance*, it is partly fleshy, partly nervous and partly membranous. For Membranes, because it requireth great strength (it being in continual motion) it is furnished with two, and those very strong ones, the uppermost of which it hath from the *Pleura*, and the lowermost from the *Peritonæum* or Rim of the Belly. To the uppermost the lower part of the *Mediastinum* is knit, (and of the Heart-bag in Men, but not in Horses or other Brutes) and sometimes the lower tips or ends of the two great Lobes of the Lungs. Its circumference is fleshy, and its middle or centre nervous, in which part a wound is mortal, but one in the fleshy sometimes admits of cure.

Its Perforations. It hath in it several *perforations* or *holes*, some of which are little, and others bigger. The little ones are the *pores*, through which the Vapours are said to ascend from the lower Parts into the Chest; but besides that such ascent of impure Vapours from the Guts, *&c.* into the Chest, where the Vital Parts are seated, would be very inconvenient and prejudicial, I think the Midriff is so compact a body, and its Membranes so close, that we may either deny any *pores* at all, or however that they admit not any such steams. The *larger* holes (being those that ought to be reckon'd alone for such) are, *first*, that which is very near its middle or centre, but something towards the right side, which gives passage for the Trunk of the hollow Vein ascending from the Liver. The *second* is on the left side of the centre, being bigger than the former, and somewhat backwarder; and this serves for the letting forth of the Gullet and two Nerves which go to the Stomach. There is also a *third* hole more backwards by the *vertebræ*, for the through-fare of the great Artery, and the Vein without a fellow, and for the Nerve which Doctor *Willis* distinguishes from the wandring or eighth pair, by the name of the Intercostal.

Its Vessels. The Midriff hath *Vessels* of all sorts; for it hath *Veins* arising from the Trunk of the hollow Vein, which are called *Venæ phrenicæ*, and also some twigs branching to it from the *Vena adiposa*, or Fat-vein, so called because it is mostly bestowed on the fat Membrane that invests the Kidneys.

It hath *Arteries* from the Trunk of the great Artery, called also *Phrenicæ*.

Its *Nerves* are in number two, proceeding from the spinal Marrow at the third or fourth jointing of the Rack-bones or *vertebræ* of the Neck, from whence they descend through the cavity of the Chest, being in their course sustained and strengthened by the *Mediastinum*, lest by any violent motion they should be hurt. As soon as these Nerves reach the Midriff, they enter it in its centre, and thence disperse themselves into its whole substance, terminating in it. But besides these some have observed small twigs to be sent into it from the Nerves of the eighth pair, as they descend through it toward the Stomach.

The several uses of the Midriff. *1. It assists Respiration.* Various are the *Uses* that might be ascribed unto the Midriff, the chief are these that follow. *First*, It is the principal Muscle that assists the action of Respiration. Which action whether it be animal and voluntary, or natural and involuntary, has occasion'd great disputes. True it is, that it moves in breathing as well while we sleep, as when we are awake, so that our Will, which in sleep is dormant as well as the Body, seems not to be necessary to its motion: and yet we can hinder it from moving when we please by holding in our breath. We may therefore call its motion, a mixt motion, to wit, partly

voluntary

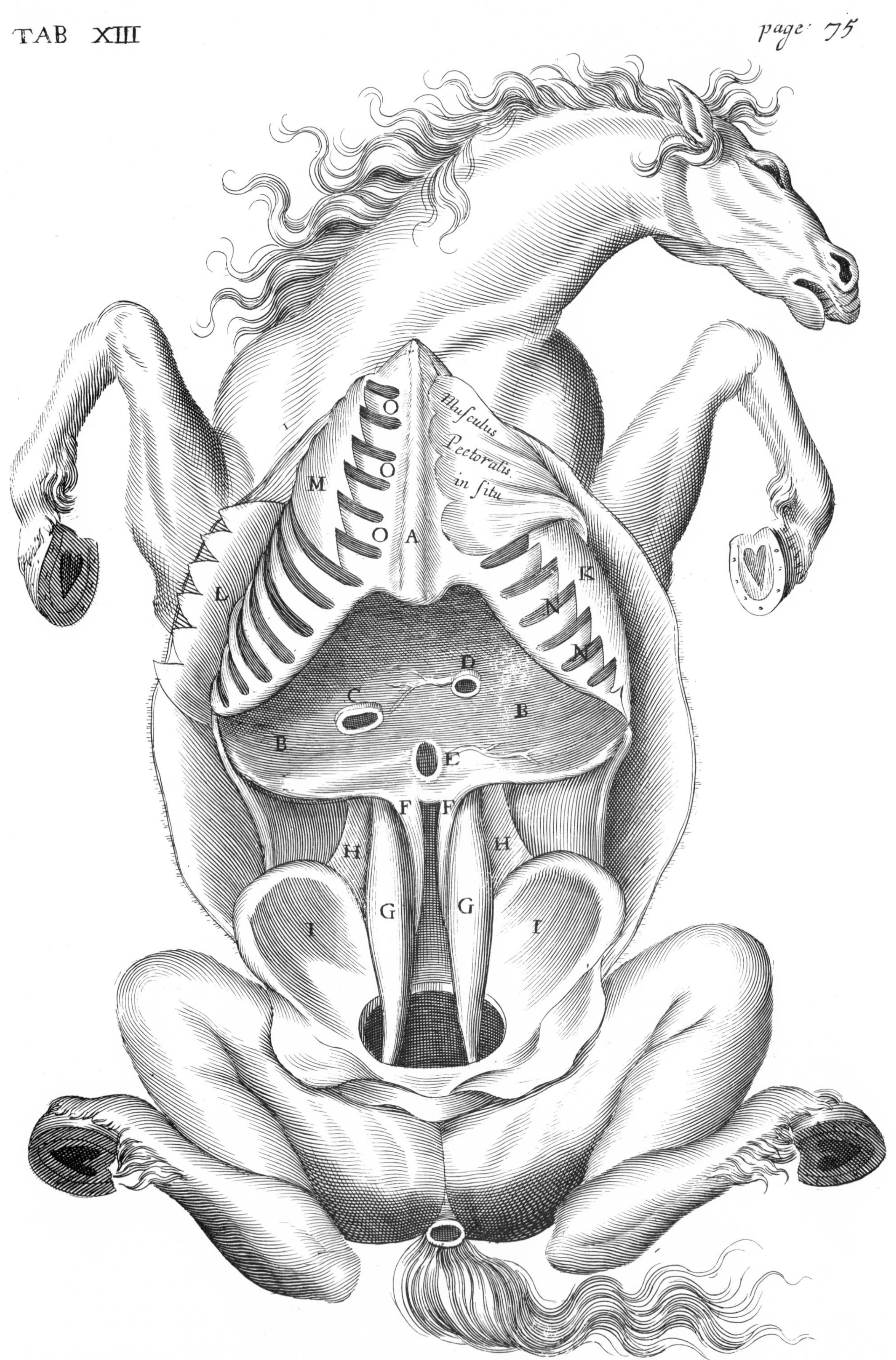
Musculus
Pectoralis
in situ
O
O
O
A
M
L
K
N
N
D
C
B
B
E
F F
H H
G G
I I

voluntary (or rather *spontaneous* in Beasts, because they have not properly any Will) and partly *natural.* Which motion is performed on this manner. In taking in ones breath it is stretched out and becomes plain and stiff, pressing down a little the Parts contained in the Lower Belly: but in letting out ones breath, it is relaxed and ascends somewhat up into the Chest, being partly driven up thither by the ascent of the Bowels of the Lower Belly, which in expiration is a little straitned by its Muscles, and therefore the Parts contained therein as they have less room breadthways, must have more lengthways. Now we must note, that onely one sort of motion agrees to one Muscle, to wit, that of contraction; for that of restitution or relaxation is owing to the opposite Muscle, as was shewed at large in the First Book, *chap.* 6. The proper motion of the Midriff therefore is onely in Inspiration or taking in ones breath, when all its Fibres being contracted quite round, it is stretched out plain, somewhat like the Parchment upon a Drum's head: but when it is relaxed and becomes flaggy in Expiration, that is onely a motion of restitution, and is not owing to it self, but to those Muscles that constringe or straiten the Chest, which are that called *sacrolumbus*, and the *triangularis* or three-corner'd one, which two lie on the outside of the Ribs as shall be shewn in the Book of the Muscles; and lastly, the internal Intercostals, described before in the second Chapter, to which some of the Muscles of the Lower Belly perhaps yield some assistance.

Secondly, By its ascending and descending, and so occasioning the Stomach, Guts, &c. to be always in a motion upwards and downwards, it assists them in driving forward the Liquors or whatever else contained in them, and so helps the distribution of the Chyle, which by the worm-like motion of the Guts alone could not so well be sent through those innumerable small Vessels through which it is to pass. And this I take to be a considerable use of it, though few Anatomists have taken any notice of it. *2. Its motion helps the distribution of the Chyle.*

A *third* use is to help forward the expulsion of the Excrements, and assist the Mare in the time of her foaling. For in both those offices the Midriff by holding in the breath is kept on the tenters as it were and pressed down upon the Parts contained in the Lower Belly that are next it, and those do successively bear hard upon others that are next them, whereby every Part contained therein is somewhat straitned, and so whatsoever is contained in any of them, be it the Dung, Urine or Foal, is squeezed out and expelled. *3. It helps to expel the Excrements, and in Mares the Foal.*

The *last* use is what was mentioned at the beginning of this Chapter, namely, to distinguish the Lower Belly with its natural Parts, from the Chest and its vital Parts; lest from the inferiour ignoble Parts noisom Vapours should ascend up to the more noble, such as are those contained in the Chest. *4. It serves to divide the* Abdomen *from the Chest.*

Table XIII. Represents the External proper Parts of the Chest, as likewise the natural situation of the Midriff.

A *The* Sternum.
B *The Midriff.*
C *The hole by which the hollow Vein ascends from the Liver towards the Heart.*
D *The hole whereby the Gullet passeth through the Midriff.*

E *The hole whereby the descendent Trunk of the great Artery passes through the Midriff.*

FF *The two Appendices or Productions of the Midriff.*

GG *The Muscles termed* Psoæ *in their natural situation.*

HH *The* Musculi Quadrati *or square Muscles of the Loyns.*

II *The Internal cavity of the Flank-bone.*

K *The Muscle called* Serratus major Anticus *in its proper place.*

L *The same Muscle removed out of its place and turned back, the better to shew the* Serratus minor *and other Parts underneath it.*

M *The* Serratus Anticus minor *or lesser foreside Saw-muscle in its place.*

NNN *Several of the External Intercostal Muscles.*

OOO *The Cartilaginous or gristly Parts of the Ribs fastened to the* sternum *or Breast-bone.*

CHAP. V.

Of the Partition-membrane called Mediastinum.

The Media-stinum *why so called.*

THIS Membrane is called by the Latins *Mediastinum,* from its office of partitioning or dividing, because it divides the Chest into two parts, standing across the *middle* of it.

Its rise and substance.

It is derived or hath its original from the *Pleura* or Rib-coat, of which we have already spoken in the third Chapter. For the *Pleura* springing from the Back-bone, keeps its way on each side of the cavity of the Chest (cloathing the inside of the Ribs) till it comes to the Breast-bone, where the two Membranes join together, but do *not* unite into one. From the Breast-bone these two Membranes hold a direct course back again towards the Back-bone through the middle of the Chest, but before they have gone an Inch, they begin to separate again, and that so far from one another by degrees, as to make a cavity wide enough for containing the Heart and the Heart-bag. But when they are arrived near the Back, they join together again. Note that the *Mediastinum* being composed of the doubling of the *Pleura,* must consist of four Membranes when united, (though onely of two where divided) seeing the *Pleura* it self consists of two. It is wholly membranous, as is the *Pleura* of which it is formed; smooth on the outside towards the Lungs, but rough on its inside towards the Heart, by reason that the Heart-bag adheres to it by several Fibres.

Its Vessels.

Between the duplicature of this Membrane there are many small Vessels of all sorts dispersed. For first there are *Veins* branching to it from the *Phrenica* or Midriff-vein and from the solitary Vein or *Vena sine pari*; it has likewise one proper Vein of its own from the subclavian branch, called after its own name, *Mediastina.* Secondly, its *Arteries* come from the *Phrenica* or Midriff-artery, which spring out of the descending Trunk of the great Artery. Thirdly, it hath *Nerves* from the Phrenick or Midriff twigs of those two branches of the eighth pair that descend through it to the upper orifice of the Stomach. *Bartholin* ascribes also *Lympheducts* unto it.

The

The use of the *Mediastinum* is first, to divide the Chest and Lungs into two parts, that if any hurtfull Accident should happen to one of the sides, the other notwithstanding might be preserved. And this hath been observed by Anatomists, who have found in dissections the one side or Lobe of the Lungs wasted and almost dryed away in Phthisical and Consumptive Persons, and at the same time the other hath been perfectly fresh and sound. And it hath been likewise seen and observed in wounds of the Chest, that if therewith one Lobe of the Lungs should happen to be hurt so much as to occasion the loss of the use of that Lobe, yet the other by performing his part hath preserved life. *Its uses.*

The next use of the *Mediastinum* is to permit the Heart in the Heart-bag to hang dangling in a free posture, that in its motion it might not strike against the bony sides of the Chest.

Again, it serves to sustain and preserve the Vessels running through it, and by its being knit to the Midriff, preserves *that* also from being drawn too much downwards by the weight of the Bowels of the Lower Belly, especially by the Liver, whose suspensory Ligament hangs by it.

CHAP. VI.

Of the Thymus *or great Kernel at the Throat; and of the Purse of the Heart called* Pericardium, *together with the water contained therein.*

THE *Thymus* (named the Sweet-bread by some) is a glandulous or kernelly body, soft and spongie, placed in the upper part of the Chest near the hole of the Throat, lying upon the ends of the Clavicles or Collar-bones. *What the* Thymus *is.*

It hath its name *Thymus* from the leaf of Time, which it very much resembleth in shape.

Its *use* is to serve as a Boulster or Pillow for the Veins and Arteries to pass over or lie upon, to keep them from the hardness of the Collar-bones, the sharpness of which would else be apt to break them or fret them asunder. *Its use.*

Now the Vessels which do cross over this *Thymus* are the hollow Vein and the great Artery, with the many divisions and branches of the same, which are in number many, dispersed from thence into most of the extreme Parts of the forepart of the Body, as some to the Shoulder-blades, and so down the Fore-legs; again, some to the Neck and Head, namely the internal and external Jugular Veins, and the Carotid Arteries; as also those branches which run all along the Belly, which are by us Farriers called the Liver-veins. This Kernel is bigger in Foals than it is in grown Hôrses in proportion to their Bodies; and in Calves it is pretty large, and is reckoned for a dainty delicate bit. *The Vessels which pass over it.*

Next come we to treat of the *Pericardium*, or Purse of the Heart, or Heart-bag, for by these several nominations or names it goes. This is that *What the* Pericardium *is.*

that Coat or Skin which compaſſeth the Heart, and in which the Heart hangeth, it being for that purpoſe made in figure like it.

From whence it takes its original.

It takes its original at the baſis or upper and broad end of the Heart, from the outer Coats which compaſs the Veſſels that enter into the Heart, which Coats do ſpring from the *Pleura.*

The ſubſtance of the Pericardium.

Its *ſubſtance* is thick and ſomething hard, though not ſo hard as to hurt the Lungs when it preſſeth againſt them, or they againſt it; neither is it too ſoft, leſt it ſhould it ſelf be hurt by the hardneſs of the Ribs, which in ſtrong pulſations of the Heart it beats againſt, the *Mediaſtinum* onely coming between: but being placed between two contraries, I mean, between the ſoft Lungs and hard Bones, it ought to have its ſubſtance of a middle nature between both. On the outſide it is rough and fibrous, adhering in many places to the *Mediaſtinum*; but within, it is ſmooth and ſlippery, that the Heart might move more freely in it.

Its Perforations.

It is perforated in *five* places; namely on the *right* ſide by the aſcending Trunk of the hollow Vein, which comes up from the Liver and enters the right Ventricle of the Heart; and by the Subclavian Vein which deſcends from the Channel-bones into the ſame Ventricle; and thirdly by the Pulmonary Artery which goes out of the right Ventricle into the Lungs. On its *left* ſide it is perforated by the Pulmonary Vein which comes from the Lungs and enters the left Ventricle of the Heart; and laſtly by the great Artery that paſſes out of the ſaid Ventricle.

Its Veſſels.

The *Veins* that it is furniſhed with, it receiveth at the lower part of it from the *Phrenick* or Midriff-vein, and at the upper part from the Axillaries; but the Veſſels from each place are mighty ſmall.

There are no Arteries derived to it from any place, that are viſible; and the reaſon ſuppoſed is, becauſe it is ſo near the Heart, that it is immediately ſupplied from it with vital heat and ſpirit. But ſeeing the Heart it ſelf is not without Arteries, though it be reckon'd the fountain of life, much leſs can any other part be ſuppoſed to be, and therefore neither this, though they are ſo ſlender as not to be diſcernible.

Thoſe ſmall *Nerves* it is furniſhed with, are branched to it from the left recurrent Nerves of the eighth or wandring pair.

To theſe Veſſels *Bartholin* adds *Lympheducts*, which ſerve to drink up part of the Liquor contained in the Heart-bag, to hinder its two great encreaſe.

Its uſe.

Next come we to the *uſe* of the Heart-bag, which is, to cover and preſerve the Heart, and to contain a certain moiſture or Humour in it for the uſes after-mentioned. Now concerning this Humour there are various diſcourſes and different opinions of Authours, I mean, as to the fountain from whence it proceeds; for ſome will have it, that it is fed by Liquors which we drink, of which opinion is the Learned *Hippocrates*, whence in his Book *de Corde* he ſaith, that the Heart dwelleth in a Bladder, becauſe of the reſemblance the Humour in the Heart-bag hath to that in the bladder of Urine; though at the ſame time he denies this Water or Humour to have any acrimony or brackiſhneſs, as the Water contained in the bladder of Urine hath.

Of the Water contained in the Pericardium.

And to confirm this Opinion of his, that this Humour contained in the Heart-bag doth proceed from Liquors taken in at the Mouth, he cites an Experiment to be tried on a Pigg, (though I ſuppoſe any other Creature may ſerve as well) which after it is kept faſting for ſome time ſhould have given it to drink Water or Milk mingled with Vermillion, and after

it

TAB. XIV

pag 79

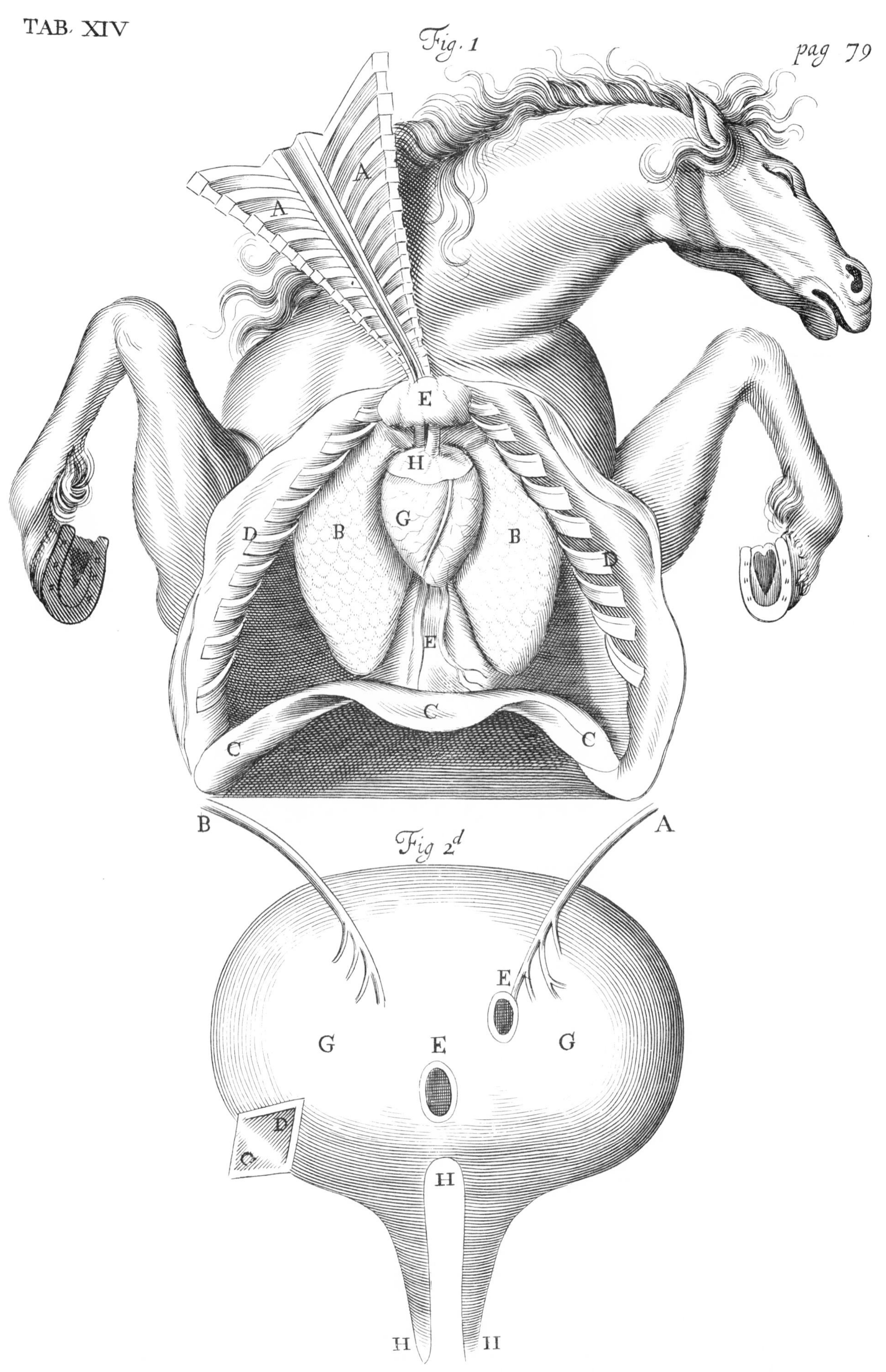

it hath drunk it, should immediately be killed, and as soon after as possible have his Wind-pipe opened, and also all or most of its branches, in which, saith my Authour, you will find along all its inside, the colour of the Liquor which it drank, even to the extremities or ends of the smallest Pipes; out of which Pipes (saith he) part of it is distilled into the Heart-bag. I confess this is no very probable Opinion, but I mention it for the great antiquity and fame of the Authour of it.

But other Authours are of opinions contrary to this, some saying that it proceeds from a moisture, slaver or spittle, which distils out of the Kernels under the Tongue into the Weazand, and from thence into the Arteries and Heart, and so into the Heart-bag. But this is as improbable as the former.

A late Learned Authour thinks that it issues out of certain Glands or Kernels seated at the basis of the Heart. And this is an Opinion that is somewhat likely, though I think the next is to be preferr'd before it.

Lastly, Others (amongst whom is *Bartholin*) conceive that it proceeds from moist Vapours and Exhalations forced out of the Humours of the Heart by the motion and heat thereof, which being stopt by the closeness of the Heart-bag, are by its respective coldness congealed into Water. *See* Bartholin, *lib.* 2. *chap.* 5.

The *use* of this Water or Humour is, in the first place, to keep the Heart moist and cool; for the Heart being a very hot Part, requires something of this nature to cool it, especially if that be true which some report of the left Ventricle, that it hath been found in live Dissections so hot, as almost to scald the Dissector's finger which he put into it. *The uses of the Water.*

By this Humour the Heart also becometh more easy in its motion, for by it, it is as it were born or buoy'd up, so that it swimmeth in a manner, whereby the sense or feeling of the weight of it is taken away.

Such a Humour as this before-spoken of is also found in the cavity of the Chest, onely something of a more ruddy colour, looking like Water and Bloud mingled together; and this I have never found wanting, but that there hath been some either little or much; with which moisture the Parts of the Chest are moistened and cooled, even as the Heart is by the moisture contained in the Heart-bag. *Of the Humour contained in the Chest.*

Table XIV.

Fig. I. Represents the *Sternum* or Breast-bone cut off, and lifted up or turned back, under which are to be seen the *Mediastinum*, Heart, Lungs and Midriff.

AA *Shew the inner surface or* superficies *of the Breast-bone, and the Gristles interwoven therein.*
BB *The Lungs in their natural situation.*
CC *A portion of the Midriff.*
DD *The ends of the Ribs where the Breast-bone was cut off.*
E *The glandulous body called the Sweet-bread or* Thymus.
F *The sides of the* Mediastinum *plucked off from the Breast-bone.*
G *The Heart in its natural situation.*
H *A portion of the Heart-bag.*

Fig. II.

Fig. II. Represents the Diaphragm and its Processes.

A *The left Nerve.*
B *The right Nerve.*
C *The upper Coat or Skin of the Diaphragm.*
D *The naked substance of the Midriff, or the Diaphragm laid bare.*
E *A hole for the Gullet to pass through.*
F *A hole for the hollow Vein to pass through.*
G *The membranous or nervous part of the Midriff, being its centre.*
HHH *The Processes or* Appendices *of the Midriff, betwixt which the Trunk of the great Artery doth descend.*

CHAP. VII.

Of the Heart.

The Heart a principal Part.

THERE is none can be so ignorant of the Parts of the Body, as not to know that the Heart is one of the *principal* Parts thereof: for as it is the fountain of the Vital faculty and power, it ought to be so styled. It is also the place of natural heat, the root of the Arteries from whence they all spring. It is moreover the Authour of the Pulse, and the first Bowel living (as I shall more at large declare in the following Chapter) and the last dying.

From whence it derives its name Cor. *Its situation.*

It is called in Latine *Cor, à currendo* from running, because of its continual motion.

It is onely one in number, *situated* in the midst of the cavity of the Chest, as well for its security, as for the equal ballancing of that part of the Body; in which place it is incompassed by the Lobes of the Lungs.

Yet notwithstanding the situation of it in the middle part of the Chest, it is to be understood that not the whole Heart but onely the basis or root of it is directly in the middle; for the point of it leans toward the left side, by reason of the smallness of the compass it hath to perform its motion in; for it would be apt to strike against the Midriff, should it not be so drawn to one side, which would not onely hinder its *own* motion, but also indanger the violating of the Midriff and hinder *its* motion; for *it* also is known to have a perpetual motion as well as the Heart.

Why the Pulse is felt on the left side and not the right.

And it is from the point of the Heart's inclining to the left side, that the motion of the Heart or its pulse is so plain to be felt on that side: which not being equally to be felt on the right, many, who have not taken the pains of looking or inspecting into Bodies to see the contrary, do conclude, that the Heart is situated altogether on the left side, and that it is not the point alone which they feel beat, but the whole Heart.

Another reason there is why it should incline to the left side, namely, because the ascendent Trunk of *Vena cava* lieth on the right side, so that were the point not drawn something to the other side, it would be apt

to

to lie upon or strike against that Vessel, and so hinder the ascent of the Bloud which is brought from the Liver by that Vein to the Heart.

The Heart has a double motion, Contraction called its *systole*, and Relaxation called its *diastole*. (Though this latter may rather be deemed a ceasing from motion, than a motion.) While it is relaxed or becomes flaggy and loose, it receives the Bloud into its Ventricles out of the hollow Vein and Lung vein; out of the former into its right Ventricle, and out of the latter into its left. And when it contracts it self, it expels or squirts out the Bloud out of its Ventricles into the Lung-artery and great Artery; out of the right Ventricle into the Lung-artery, and out of the left into the great Artery. *The motion of the Heart.*

As to the pulsation or beating of the Heart, it is very difficult, if not impossible to give any satisfactory reason of it. Some impute it to the flowing in of the Animal Spirits by the Nerves; others to the boiling and rarefaction of the Bloud in its Ventricles. 'Tis most certain that the muscular Fibres of the Heart are the immediate instruments of its motion, and that these receive their power to move, from the Animal Spirits conveyed by the Nerves: but what it is that puts these Fibres upon such a reciprocal motion of contraction and relaxation as the Heart observes, is the greatest difficulty to determine. The greatest Anatomists have confest their ignorance in this point: I shall not therefore pretend to give a reason of it, but admire the wisedom of the great Creator in framing such an Engine, so necessary for the conveying life, heat and nourishment to all the Parts of the Body. Waving this then, I shall proceed to the further description of the Heart. *The reason of the Pulse.*

The *figure* of the Heart is pyramidal or conick, that is, it is broad at the basis or bottom, and narrow at its summity or top. On the fore-side it is bossy or bunching, but on the hinder side more flat. It is sometimes longer and sometimes shorter, as thus: When in its motion it is contracted (at which time it pours out the Bloud) then is it shorter, but broader; and again when it is dilated, at which time it receives in the Bloud, then is it longer and narrower. *The figure of the Heart.*

Its *substance* is a solid, thick and compact flesh, that it might the better indure the perpetuity of the motion, and with more force drive the Bloud into the extreme or farthest Parts of the Body. It consisteth mostly of musculary or fleshy Fibres, a few of which run streight and are outmost, but the far greatest part run slanting or rather spiral-wise, especially towards its point, resembling somewhat the winding-rings of a Snail's shell. *Its substance.*

It is tied by the mediation of the Heart-bag to the *Mediastinum* and by its own Vessels to several Parts of the Body. *Its connexion.*

Its Parts are some *External* and some *Internal*. Those which be *External* or outward, are the Purse, the Coat, and the Fat; to which may be added some of its Vessels. *Its External Parts.*

As to the *Purse* or Heart-bag, we have treated of it in the foregoing Chapter. As to the *Vessels*, some of them encompass the Heart, as the Coronary Vein and Arteries; others reach into its Entrances and into the Ventricles, and those are the Ascendent and Descendent Trunks of the hollow Vein and Great Artery, also the Pulmonary Vessels. Of the Coronaries we shall speak by and by in this Chapter; but of the rest, in the next.

Its Coat. It hath a *Coat* proper to it ſelf, like the Coat of a Muſcle, for its greater firmneſs, which Coat ſticks ſo cloſe to it, that it is hard to be ſeparated or removed from it. It is the ſame with the outer Coat of the Great Artery, as that Skin which cloaths the inſide of its Ventricles is continued unto and conſtitutes the inmoſt Membrane of that Artery.

Its Fat. The Heart becauſe of its continual motion and great heat, is plentifully ſtored with *Fat*, to keep it from being over-dried, which Fat is moſt of it placed at the baſis or bottom of it; for its point hanging in the Humour contained in the Heart-bag is continually moiſtned with that, ſo that it ſtands not in need of being moiſtned or cooled any other way.

The difference between the Fat of the Heart and other Fat. Yet thus much notice is to be taken, as to this Fat which grows to the Heart, that it differs in conſiſtence from all or moſt of the other Fat of the whole Body, as being much harder: for ſhould the Heart, which is a very hot Part, have any ſuch ſoft Fat near it, it would certainly melt it. And as the Fat which grows or ſticks to the remoter Parts of the Body differs from this in nature, ſo hath it alſo a name different from this; for the former is called *pimele*, which ſignifies a kind of greaſie Fat; but the latter is called *Adeps*, which is to ſay Tallow, and is indeed as hard as Tallow, differing much from *pimele* or Greaſe.

The External Veſſels of the Heart. Next come we to the *Veſſels* of the Heart, and of theſe it is furniſhed with all ſorts; ſome of which do compaſs it round about at its baſis, like a Garland, which are one Vein and two Arteries.

One Vein. The *Vein*, from its encompaſſing or encircling it round, is called *Coronaria*, or the Crown-vein, which Vein ariſes from the Trunk of the hollow Vein a little before its entrance into the right Earlet of the Heart. Small branches do ſpring from this Coronary Vein, and are diſperſed or ſprinkled all down the ſurface or outſide of the Heart from the baſis to the point.

Two Arteries. Its *Arteries* are in number two, which are alſo called *Coronariæ* or Crown-arteries, from their encircling the Heart as the Vein does, where like it they diſperſe ſmall branches about all the external ſurface of the Heart, furniſhing it with arterial Bloud for its life and nouriſhment.

Their Valves. There is obſerved at the original of each of theſe Arteries, as is likewiſe in the Vein, a certain *Valve* which is to be ſeen if you diſſect either Veſſel, opening it a little before it paſſeth out of the Heart-bag; which Valve or Floud-gate in the Vein lets the Bloud into the Heart, but ſuffers none to come out again that way; and in the Artery it permits the Bloud to iſſue out of the Heart, but will let none return back out of it into the Heart.

Nerves. The Heart is alſo furniſhed with very many but very ſmall *Nerves*, ſpringing from branches of the eighth pair, which branches are thoſe that are ſent to the Heart-bag.

They branch into and enter the Heart in three ſeveral places; firſt, one enters into the Heart it ſelf, another into the Earlets of the Heart, and a third into its Veſſels.

Thus much of the Parts of the Heart which in ſome regard may be called *External*; in the next Chapter we ſhall proceed to thoſe that are more *Internal.*

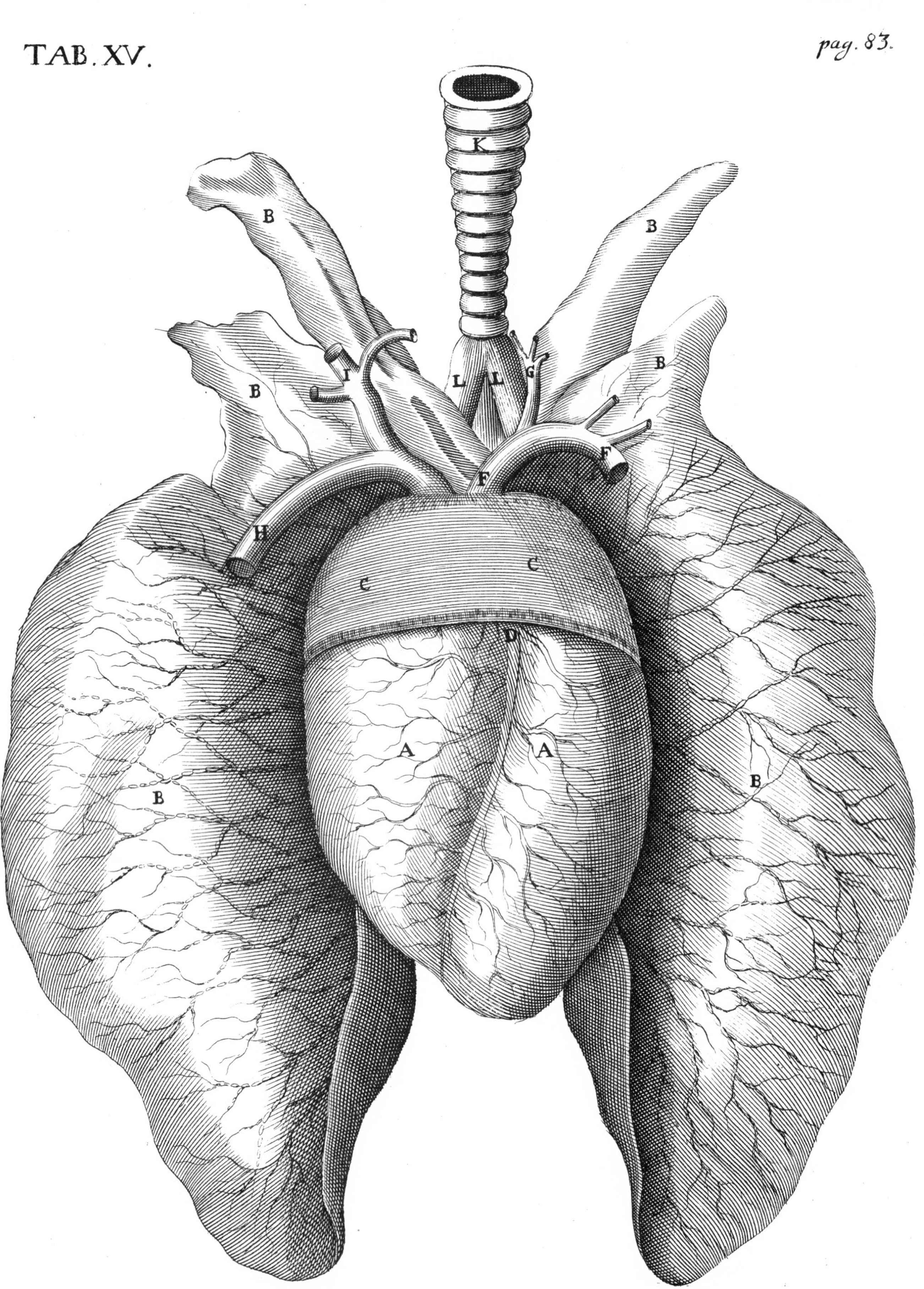
K
B
B
B
B
I
L
L
G
F
F
H
C
C
D
A
A
B
B

Table XV. Representeth the Heart and Lungs in their natural posture, but taken out of the Body.

AA *Shew the Heart in its Proper place.*
BB *The several Lobes of the Lungs.*
CC *The remaining part of the* Pericardium *or Heart-bag, a portion of it being cut off the better to shew the Heart.*
DD *The Coronary Vessels.*
E *The* Arteria magna *or* Aorta *going out of the Heart.*
F *Its descending Trunk.*
G *Its ascending Trunks.*
H *The* Vena cava descendens, *or the descending Trunk of the hollow Vein.*
I *The ascending Trunks of the same.*
K *A portion of the* Aspera Arteria *or Wind-pipe.*
L *Its division or branching into the Lungs.*

CHAP. VIII.

Of the Ventricles, internal Vessels, Valves and Earlets of the Heart.

WE will first speak of the Ventricles or *Sinus's* of the Heart, being in number two, on each side one, distinguished or divided by a fleshy partition into a right and a left.

The right (called the right *Sinus* or Ventricle, and by some the Cave or Chamber) is somewhat bigger than the left, because it receives as well that Bloud which is spent upon the nourishment of the Lungs, through which the Bloud passes from this Ventricle to the left, as that which actually is conveyed into the left, and from thence sent forth by the Arteries into all parts of the Body. But its larger capacity is onely in respect of its width, for the left is rather longer than it, as reaching nearer the tip of the Heart. *The right Ventricle.*

It is in *figure* not exactly round, but rather semicircular, or half-moon fashioned. *Its figure.*

The *substance* of its sides is not so hard and thick as is that of the left, nor is the surface of its inner cavity so uneven; nor has it so many and so strong fleshy Fibres reaching this way and that way, as the left hath. For it was not necessary it should be of so strong a composure as the left, seeing neither is the Bloud rarefied so much in it, nor does it send the Bloud out of it to any greater distance than the Lungs, whereas the left pours it into the remotest Parts of the Body, and therefore requires a stronger constitution to squirt it out. *Its substance.*

The *use* of this Ventricle is first to receive the Bloud out of the hollow Vein returning from the circulation, as also the Chyle and *Lympha* mingled with the Bloud, out of the axillar Vein, and then to attenuate, concoct and inspirit them for the nourishment of the Lungs, to which they *Its use.*

are carried under the form of Bloud by the Pulmonary Artery, otherwise called the Arterial vein. But it is but a very small portion of the Bloud that is spent upon the Lungs, the greatest part of it passing by the Pulmonary Vein to the left Ventricle, there to receive a greater perfection.

Why Fish have but one Ventricle. Now it is worth observation in this place, that such Creatures as live in the Water, as Fish in general, which have no Lungs, have but one Ventricle in their Heart. For the reason why Animals that live upon the Land have two Ventricles, being, that the Bloud as it passes from one to the other, should be conveyed through the Lungs, there to be ventilated and cooled by the Air drawn in in inspiration; and seeing Fish live in a cold Element, *viz.* the Water, which encompasses their whole Body, *that*, of it self, is sufficient to attemper the heat of the Bloud; therefore as it is impossible they should make any use of Lungs in the Water, so there seems to be no need of them, nor consequently of two Ventricles in the Heart, which are necessary for Land-animals that have Lungs, and breathe in the free Air. How far Water approaches to the nature of Air, or whether there be any truly airy particles contained in the pores of the Water; and if there be, whether there be any way imaginable whereby they can insinuate themselves into the Bloud and Hearts of Fishes, are Points too nice and philosophical for me to intermeddle with. But seeing Fish can live so brisk for very many years without respiration (at least properly so called, or that we can conceive of) one would suspect that some of our late Anatomists attribute too much virtue to the Air that we breathe in, as if it were *the All* that continues the Vital flame as they speak, and that the Vital heat and spirit are no otherwise owing to the Heart, than as like an Engine it keeps the Bloud in motion, and distributes it with the Spirits into all Parts of the Body by the Arteries. But this by the bye.

The left Ventricle. Its largeness. Next come we to the *left* Ventricle, which in magnitude doth not equal the former, it being much less, by reason it is to contain a less quantity of Bloud than the right Ventricle doth, part of that Bloud that comes out of the right, being spent upon the nourishment of the Lungs, before it reaches the left.

Its figure. This left Ventricle differs also in *figure* from the right: for as the right is observed to be semicircular, the left is almost round and longer, reaching almost down to the point of the Heart, which the other doth not.

Its sides are thicker, Likewise the flesh or *wall* of the left is much *thicker* than that of the other, and that partly because of the smallness of the cavity, which the narrower it is, must needs leave the sides so much the thicker. Onely the left side of this Ventricle near the lower end or tip of the Heart, is thinner than any part of the sides of the right.

and harder than those of the right. Also it is *harder* and more compact than the other, that the Vital Spirits might not exhale or evaporate, and that its constriction might be the stronger, so that the Bloud might with more force be thrown or pulst out and vented into the farthest parts of the Body.

Its use. Into this Ventricle is the Bloud received out of the Lungs by the Pulmonary Vein (otherwise called the veinous Artery.) Which Bloud when it is squirted out of this Ventricle into the great Artery, differs very much in colour from that which issues out of the right Ventricle into the Pulmonary Artery: for this latter is of a dark purple colour, but the former of a florid scarlet. But most think that this alteration of colour is not

so

ſo much owing to any ſupereminent virtue in this Ventricle above the right, as to the particles of Air that inſinuate themſelves into the Bloud in the Lungs whiles it paſſes out of the Pulmonary Artery into the Pulmonary Vein; for Dr. *Lower* affirmeth, that if in Live-diſſections one open the Pulmonary Vein in its paſſage from the Lungs to the left Ventricle, the Bloud will appear to be of the ſame ſcarlet colour as when it comes out of the ſaid Ventricle. Suppoſing this to be ſo (which I think we may do upon the teſtimony of ſo worthy and creditable an Authour) yet it cannot be denied but that the airy particles muſt be more intimately mixed with the Bloud by the great agitation it receives in the left Ventricle, ſo that we may ſtill conſent to the Ancients, that Vital Spirits (in which, Air ſeems to be a main Ingredient) are perfected and rectified to their height (as it were) in it more than in the right. The uſe therefore of the left Ventricle is to perfect the Vital Spirits, and to tranſmit them, together with the Bloud, by the Arteries over all the Body, for the preſervation of the Vital heat, and for the nouriſhment of each Part.

The inſides of the Ventricles. The inſides of both the Ventricles are unequal or uneven and rugged, being hollowed into many furrows diſtinguiſhed by fleſhy Fibres, that the Bloud which comes into the Heart might be the more agitated in them, and thereby more intimately mixed with the Chyle and Air that come along with it, the firſt into the right Ventricle, and both into the left. From theſe fleſhy Fibres are nervous ones extended to the Valves, of which we ſhall diſcourſe by and by. They are more numerous and ſtronger in the left Ventricle than in the right, becauſe a ſtronger conſtriction was neceſſary for the former than for the latter, ſeeing from the former Bloud is ſent to all Parts of the Body, but from the latter to no greater diſtance than the Lungs, as was obſerved before. Theſe Fibres, Furrows and Valves you may ſee very well expreſt in the following Figure.

The ſeptum. Theſe Ventricles are divided by a Wall called the *ſeptum* or partition, which is nothing elſe but the right wall of the left Ventricle; wherefore its right ſide is bunched, but the left hollow. On its left ſide it is furrowed and unequal as the reſt of the Ventricle is, but on the right it is well nigh ſmooth. It is a very ancient opinion, that there are a great many large pores or holes in this *ſeptum*, whereby the thinneſt and moſt ſpirituous part of the Bloud paſſes out of the right Ventricle into the left immediately, without taking that circuit through the Lungs that the reſt doth. *Its pores.* They are ſaid to be wider on its right ſide, and going ſlanting to grow narrower towards the left. There are many Modern as well as Ancient Vouchers of this opinion: amongſt whom is *Bartholin*, who having enumerated ſeveral Anatomiſts that have affirmed to have ſeen them themſelves, ſays that he himſelf has ſeen the *ſeptum* of a Hog's Heart ſlantingly pervious in ſeveral places with great and manifeſt pores, ſo large as to admit a pretty big Peaſe, and lying open without a Probe, which being put into any one of them on the right ſide paſſed to the left Ventricle, where a thin Membrane did hang before the mouth of the Pore like an Anaſtomoſis (as he calls it, I ſuppoſe he means a Valve) which hindred the putting in the Probe on that ſide, and conſequently muſt have hindred the return of the Bloud out of the left Ventricle into the right when the Animal was living. And he thinks that the *ſeptum* is nouriſhed by the Bloud that paſſes through theſe Pores, ſeeing the Coronary Veins (above-deſcribed) run onely through the ſurface or outſide of the Heart. And he will have not onely the more ſpirituous part of the Bloud, but the thinner part of the Chyle alſo to paſs through them. It would be *tedious* to recite all thoſe Authours that he quotes to ſecond him, as alſo his Apology for their often not-appearing in many dead Bodies, ſeeing there are many paſſages beſides theſe in Live-creatures, that there are no footſteps of after they are dead: for as it ſeems not likely that the *ſeptum* ſhould be nouriſhed by bloud that paſſes ſo rapidly through theſe ſuppoſed holes; ſo by the carefulleſt examination of other skilfull Anatomiſts there have been no ſuch holes to be found, unleſs they were firſt made by the Probe; though indeed there are ſeveral pits that look as if they went through, which I believe to be onely framed for the greater agitation of the bloud in the Ventricle.

The internal Veſſels of the Heart. In the foregoing Chapter we deſcribed thoſe Veſſels that may be called *external* from their running chiefly on the outſide of the Heart, (commonly named the Coronary) by which it is nouriſhed: but there are another ſort that may be termed *internal*, which are ſuch as open into and out of its Ventricles or inward *Sinus's*, but yield no nouriſhment to it. Theſe are four, the *Vena cava*, and pulmonary Artery; the pulmonary Vein, and great Artery.

Vena cava *and* vena Arterioſa *belong to the right Ventricle;* Of theſe, the *Vena cava* or hollow Vein, and the *Vena Arterioſa* or pulmonary Artery do belong to the right Ventricle; the hollow Vein filling it with venal bloud returning from all Parts of the Body, which it receives in when the Heart is relaxed, which ſtate is called its *diaſtole*; and the pulmonary Artery carrying forth the ſaid bloud into the Lungs when the Heart is contracted, which ſtate of the Heart is called its *ſyſtole*.

Arteria venoſa *and* Aorta *to the left.* To the left Ventricle do alſo belong two Veſſels, namely, *Arteria venoſa* or the pulmonary Vein, and *Aorta* or the great Artery. The pulmonary Vein within the ſubſtance of the Lungs doth receive the bloud from the pulmonary Artery, and pours it into the left Ventricle, there to kindle and ventilate the vital flame, and to perfect the arterial bloud and ſpirits. The great Artery is the trunk from which all other Arteries do branch, and through which the arterial bloud (after it is in this Ventricle perfected as aforeſaid) is diſperſed or thrown into all the Parts of the Body, for the life and nouriſhment thereof.

Three Valves to the Vena cava, *called* tricuſpides. Now to each of theſe four Veſſels do belong *Valves*, for the better performance of their offices before ſpoken of. And firſt to the hollow Vein do belong three, which are of a triangular figure, and are from that figure called *treble-pointed* Valves. They are placed at the baſis or bottom of the Heart at the entrance of the ſaid Vein into the Heart, and do look from without inward, that ſo they may admit of the bloud's paſſing through them into the Heart, but ſuffer none to paſs out again that way.

Three alſo to the vena Arterioſa, *called* ſigmoideæ. To the pulmonary Artery do alſo belong three Valves, which, contrary to the former, look from within outward, and from the reſemblance they have with the letter C, are called *Sigma*-faſhioned, the old Greek *Sigma* being of that ſhape. Theſe Valves as the former are placed at the baſis of the Heart, and at the entrance or rather outlet of the Ventricle. And their uſe is, to let the bloud, brought into this Ventricle by the hollow Vein, paſs again out of the ſaid Ventricle into the pulmonary Artery, to be carried by it into the Lungs; but they will not admit of any bloud to return from the Lungs into it.

To

To the pulmonary Vein do belong two Valves, which look from without inward, as the treble-pointed Valves do, and their use is to admit of the bloud brought out of the Lungs by the pulmonary Vein, into the left Ventricle, but they will suffer none to pass by that Vein back to the Lungs again. These, from the resemblance they are said to have with a Bishop's Mitre, are called Mitre-shaped Valves. *Two to the* Arteria venosa, *called* mitrales.

To the *Arteria magna* or great Artery do also belong three Valves, which go by the name of Semilunary or Half-moon-fashioned Valves. Their use is to hinder any bloud from returning into the left Ventricle out of the great Artery; but they permit the Bloud to pass by them out of the Heart into the said Artery, from whence it is sent by its several branches into all the Parts of the Body. *Three to the* Aorta, *called* semilunares.

Having spoken to the Ventricles, Vessels and Valves of the Heart, we are in the next place come to treat of the two Appendices or Processes which are placed at the bottom or basis of it, and are called the *Ears* or *Earlets* of the Heart, from some resemblance in shape which they have to the Ears of the Head. They are in number two, to each side of the Heart one, answerable to the number of the Ventricles. Of these, the right is larger, but softer; the left lesser, but harder. The right is larger, because the orifice of the hollow Vein belonging to the right Ventricle, is much bigger and larger than the orifice of the pulmonary Vein belonging to the left Ventricle. For it was not needfull that the Lung-vein should be so large as the hollow Vein, seeing the bloud that it conducts to the left Ventricle is neither so much as that which is brought by the *cava* to the right, and besides is thinner and more spirituous being impregnated with Air in the Lungs, and therefore passing more quickly needs the narrower channel. *The* auriculæ *of the Heart.*

The external part or *surface* of them, when full or extended, is smooth and bunching; but when empty, wrinkled. *Their surface.*

Their *substance* is peculiar, such as is to be found in no other part, thin and soft that they might be the easilier contracted, and yet nervous and strong, that they might endure that continual motion to which they are destin'd. Of the two, the left is the more compact, thick and fleshy. On their inside they have Fibres running from their basis where they are joined to the Heart, towards their top where the Veins enter them, (such as the Ventricles of the Heart themselves have) by help whereof they contract themselves in their *systole*, and squeeze the bloud contained in them, into the Ventricles. *Their substance.*

These Ears or Earlets have (as the Heart it self hath) two motions, first the *systole* or contractive, next the *diastole* or dilative motion. There is also betwixt these two motions (both in the Ears and Heart) a rest or pause, easy to be discerned in sick Horses, or Horses ready to die, but not so easy to be either discerned or felt in a sound or healthfull Horse; for in such, the motions are performed so swiftly, that there seems to be an immediate passage from one to the other, without any intermission or resting between. This pause or rest between the two motions, is called *perisystole*. *Their motion.*

The *systole* and *diastole* of both Earlets do happen at one and the same time; for when the right undergoes its *diastole*, then and at the very same instant the left undergoes the same. And they do the like in the *systole*. But though the Heart hath the same motions as these Earlets have, yet it doth not perform them when these do; for the *systole* of the Earlets happens at the same time with the *diastole* of the Ventricles; and on the

the contrary, the *ſyſtole* of the Ventricles, with the *diaſtole* of the Earlets.

Their uſe. Now the *uſe* of theſe Ears or Earlets is, to prevent the too violent ruſhing in of the bloud out of the *Cava* and Lung-vein into the Ventricles of the Heart, whereby both the Valves might have been violated, and the Vital faculty ſuffocated. For theſe receiving the bloud out of the ſaid Veins, do meaſure it as it were into the Heart, ſo much bloud diſtilling out of thoſe Veins into theſe Earlets in each of their *diaſtole's*, as can be conveniently rarefied and elaborated at one time in the Ventricles.

Table XVI.

Repreſenteth the Earlets, Ventricles and Valves of the Heart.

Figure I.

Shews the *Vena cava* with the right Ventricle diſſected, ſo as to ſhew the treble-pointed Valves.

A *Shews the orifice of the coronary Vein.*
B *The treble-pointed Valves, which admit of the bloud into the right Ventricle, but hinder its return back that way.*
CCC *The little Fibres which faſten the ends of the Valves to the ſubſtance of the Heart.*
D *The Ventricle cut long-ways, the better to ſhew the before-named Parts.*

Figure II.

Shews the right Ventricle of the Heart laid farther open, to ſhew the Valves of the pulmonary Artery.

A *Shews the Ventricle opened.*
BBB *The* Sigma-*faſhioned Valves of the pulmonary Artery, that let the bloud out of this Ventricle into the Lungs.*
CC *A Probe thruſt through the pulmonary Artery croſs the right Ventricle of the Heart.*

Figure III.

Shews the left Ventricle opened alſo long-ways to ſhew its Valves.

AA *The pulmonary Vein coming from the Lungs and bringing the bloud from thence, which it pours into the left Ventricle.*
BBB *The three Mitre-ſhaped Valves of the ſaid pulmonary Vein.*

Figure IV.

Fig. III.

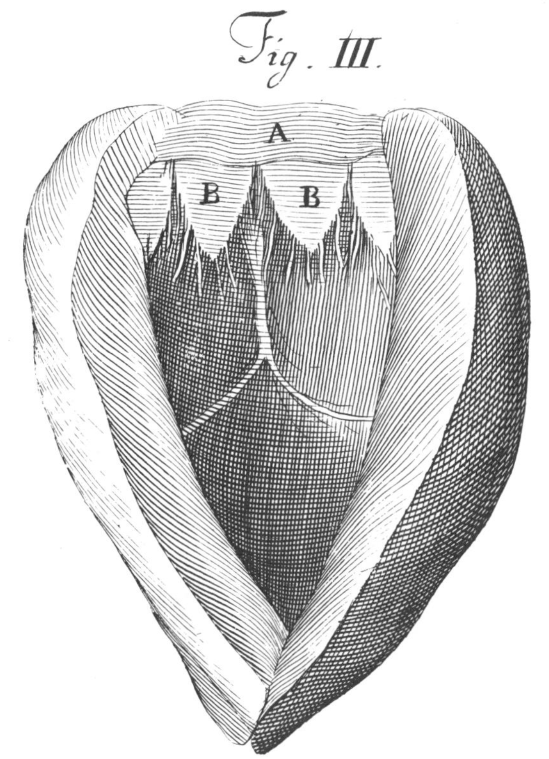

Fig. IIII.

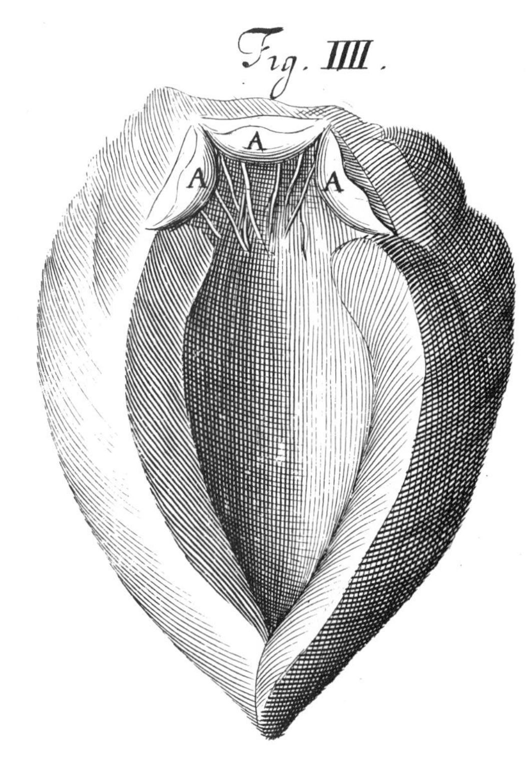

Fig. I.

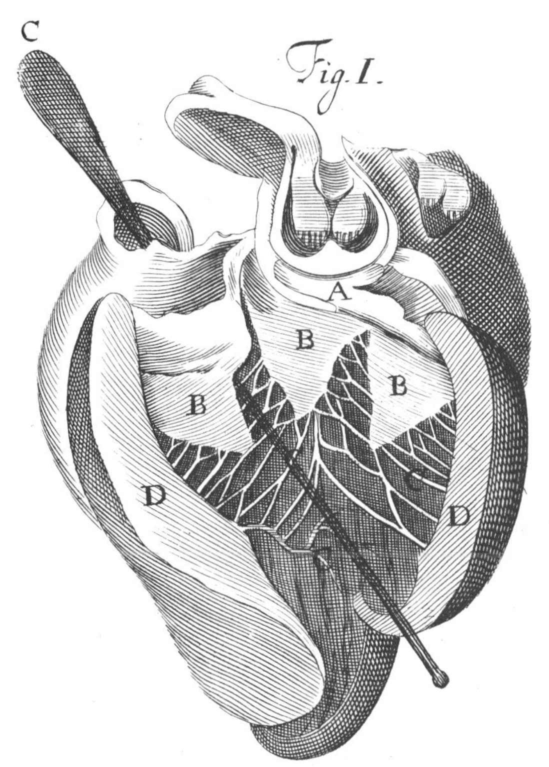

Fig. II.

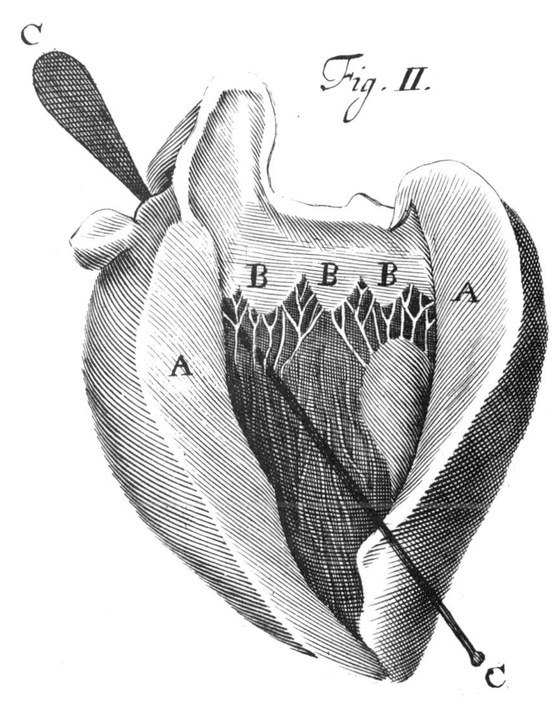

Figure IV.

Shews the great Artery cut asunder near the Heart to shew its Valves.

AAA *The said Valves of the* Aorta *or great Artery.*
BB *A Probe thrust through the pulmonary Vein into the left Ventricle of the Heart.*

CHAP. IX.

Of the Organs of Breathing, and their Use; viz. *of the Lungs, and Wind-pipe.*

THE *Lungs*, which are the chief Instruments of breathing or respiration, are called in Latin *Pulmones*, in Greek *Pneumones*, from their office of drawing in and blowing out the Breath or Air. *The names of the Lungs.*

Their *situation* is in the cavity or hollowness of the Chest, which cavity they almost fill up; especially when they are distended or filled with wind. They are divided into two equal parts called *Lobes*, one of which lies on the right side of the *Mediastinum*, or Partition-membrane of the Chest, and the other on the left. *Their situation and Lobes.*

Their *substance* hath hitherto been taken to be a *parenchyma* or fleshy substance; but by the diligent searching into Nature of some of our Modern Authors, especially of an Italian named *Malpighius*, they have been found of a contrary substance; for he affirms them to be excarnous or without flesh, and merely membranous, made up of the branches of the Wind-pipe and little bladders at the ends of them, likewise of the pulmonary Vessels, and the Skin that cloaths them. But the greatest part of their substance consists of the little bladders. *Their substance.*

This that worthy Man experienced by casting Water into the Lungs of some Creatures he dissected, while they were yet warm, so often till the whole frame of the Lungs appeared white; then squeezing the water clean out, he with a pair of Bellows or Pipe filled them by the Wind-pipe full of Air, and pent it in by tying the Windpipe; which done, he hung them up to dry; and when they were dried, he could discover (by holding them up to the light) the little bladders at the ends of each little branch of the Wind-pipe, as they are lively represented in Figures by that great Inquirer into Nature, the never to be forgotten Doctor *Willis*, justly styled the honour of his University and Country, in the second Part of his Book called *Pharmaceutice rationalis*. *See* Willis *Part* 2. *Sect.* 1. *cap.* 1. *of his* Pharmaceutice rationalis.

Again, saith the forementioned *Malpighius*, If you cut any part of the Lungs thus dried, you may very plainly see a great number of these bladders looking white. Moreover he affirms that by the help of a Microscope he could discern a certain wonderfull Net as it were, tying all these bladders to one another, which he conceived to be made up of the small branchings of the pulmonary Artery and Vein, which Vessels convey the bloud through the ſlender and winding ducts, and through the manifold bendings of the Pipes. And beſides theſe Veſſels which make this Net, Doctor *Willis* ſaith that there are another ſort to be perceived in living Diſſections, which are called *Lympheducts*, and are diſperſed all over the Lungs. Of what nature and uſe theſe Veſſels are, we have ſhewn above in the Firſt Book, chap. 12. and ſhall do further by and by. And *laſtly*, he ſays there are abundance of twigs of *Nerves* diſtributed every-where through them. Onely one thing further is to be noted concerning the Veſſels of the Lungs from the ſaid Doctor's obſervation, that the Bloud-veſſels thereof are not onely branches of the pulmonary Artery and Vein, but alſo ſome proceed from the *Aorta* it ſelf; which ſhould ſeem to intimate that the Lungs are truly nouriſhed by theſe laſt, as are all other Parts of the Body, and that the bloud that comes to the Lungs from the right Ventricle of the Heart by the pulmonary Artery, and returns to the left by the pulmonary Vein, paſſes not this way for the nouriſhment of the Lungs, but onely that it may be impregnated with Air, without which as it wants of its perfection, ſo is it unfit and unable to preſerve the vital heat of any Part, or to contribute any nouriſhment to it. But this onely by the bye.

Table XVII.

Repreſenteth the Wind-pipe deſcending into the Lungs, as alſo the whole ſtructure of the Lungs placed as they lie in the Body, to ſhew their ſeveral Lobes, as alſo the *Lympheducts*, after Doctor *Willis*.

Figure I.

AA *Shew the ſubſtance of the Lungs.*
BB *The ſeveral Lobes.*
CC *The* Lympheducts.
DD *A portion of the* Aſpera Arteria *or Wind-pipe.*

Figure II.

AA *Shew the upper part of the Wind-pipe cut off.*
B *The* Cartilago ſcutiformis.
C *The* Glottis.
DDD *The ſeveral Griſtles that make the Wind-pipe.*
EEE *The Membranes betwixt each Cartilage or Griſtle, which make the other part of the Wind-pipe.*

Now the ſeveral things here named, of which the Lungs are compoſed or framed, do plainly ſhew their ſubſtance is not carnous or fleſhy, but merely fiſtulous, being compacted of Pipes of ſeveral kinds and magnitude, and variouſly and intricately diſpoſed; which Pipes we will particularly ſpeak to in order, and firſt of the chief of them, which is the Wind-pipe, called *Aſpera Arteria* the rough Artery.

The Wind-pipe. The *Aſpera Arteria* is a Pipe or Chanel which deſcends down the Neck beginning in the Throat at the root of the Tongue, and reaches as far as the Lungs, in which it diſperſes it ſelf into innumerable branches great and ſmall, which branches reach to all the extreme parts of their ſubſtance,

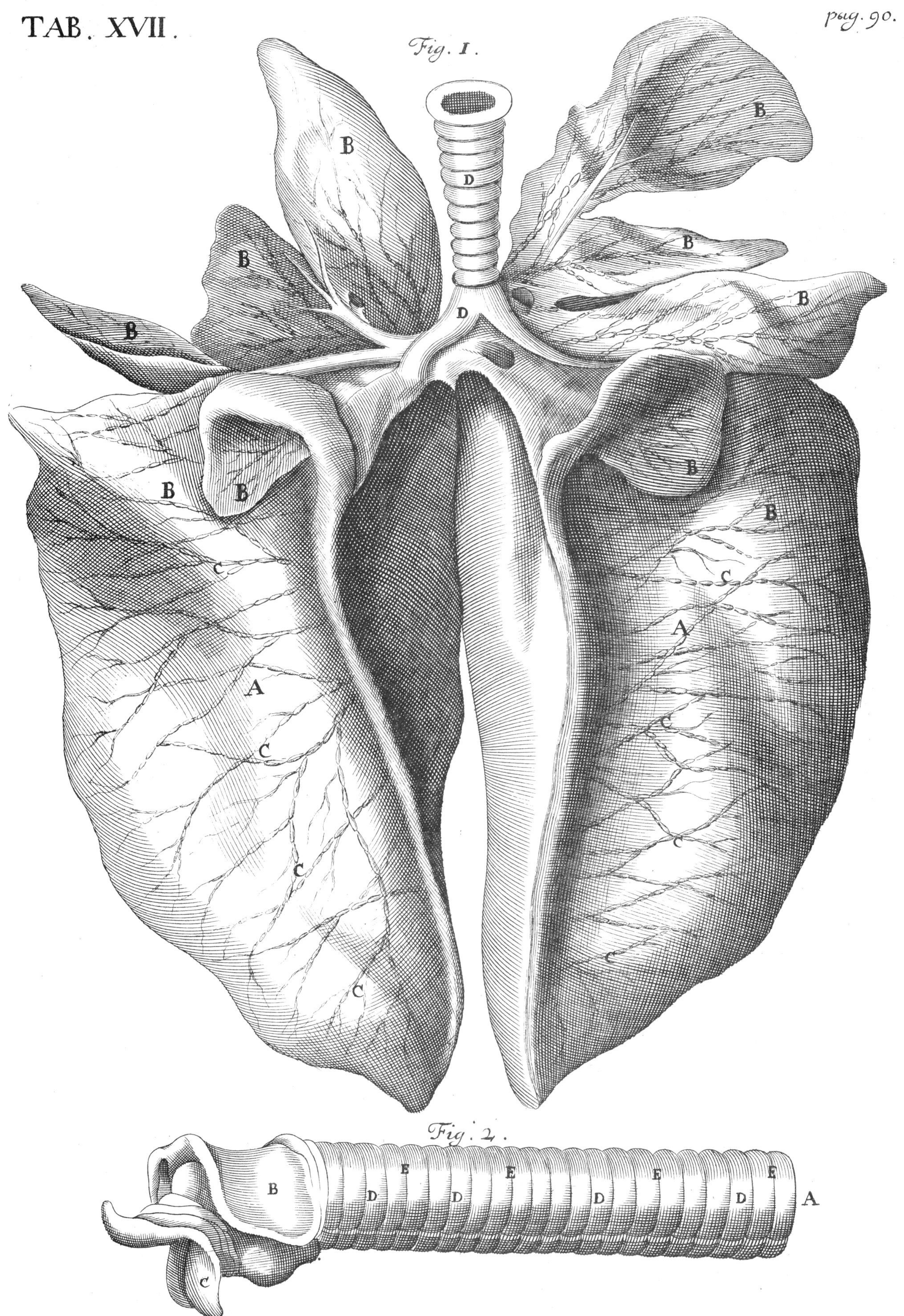
Fig. 1.
B
B
D
B
B
B
B
D
B
B
B
B
B
C
C
A
A
C
C
C
C
C
C
Fig. 2.
B
E
E
E
E
D
D
D
D
A
C

ſubſtance, and at laſt end in little bladders, each of them in reſemblance like a Grape, into which they conveigh the Air in inſpiration. Theſe Grape-like Bladders are lively repreſented by Doctor *Willis* in a Lobe of the Lungs of an Ox, as you may ſee in the firſt Figure of the third Table in his ſecond Part of the operation of Medicines; of which bladders you may there reade more at large.

Willis *Pharmaceut. Ration.* Part. 2. ſect. 1. cap. 1.

The fore-mentioned Wind-pipe is by Anatomiſts divided into three principal parts, *viz.* the *Larynx* or Throttle, which is the upper end of it (of which more afterwards.) The ſecond part between the *Larynx* and the Lungs, being a long Pipe, is called particularly *Trachea* or *aſpera Arteria*, the rough Artery; *rough*, to diſtinguiſh it from the *ſmooth* Arteries which contain the bloud and vital ſpirits; and an *Artery*, becauſe it *keeps* or contains *the Air* in reſpiration. The laſt part of the Wind-pipe is diſtinguiſh'd by the name of *bronchus* or *bronchia*, which includes the ramifications or branchings of it in the Lungs; though the name *bronchus* is ſometimes uſed to ſignify all of it.

The Parts of the Wind-pipe.

Now before we paſs on further to the deſcription of this Wind-pipe, it will not be amiſs to examine whether any part of the Liquors that an Horſe drinks paſs along it, or whether all go down the Gullet. That *part* of the drink glides down the Weazand was the opinion of the Ancient Phyſician *Hippocrates*, who experienced the ſame in an Hog newly killed, in whoſe Lungs was found a quantity of Liquor of the ſame colour with that which the Hog had drunk a little before. And *Bartholin* thinks that the ſame thing may be proved from an obſervation of *Julius Jaſolin* an Anatomiſt of the City of *Naples*, who ſeeking in the Body of a Noble Perſon the cauſe of his death, found his Heart-bag ſo filled with humour, that it being ſqueezed, ſome of the ſaid humour came out of his Mouth. But methinks it is an odd inference to conclude from hence, that therefore ſome part of the drink uſually paſſes down the Wind-pipe. For if one ſhould ſuppoſe that it did ſo paſs, it cannot eaſily be imagined by what ways it could paſs from thence to the Heart-bag; ſeeing all the branches of the Wind-pipe end in the Lungs, which are covered with a Membrane that never adheres to the Heart-bag, and very rarely if ever to the *Mediaſtinum* that comes between the Heart-bag and the Lungs. 'Tis true it ſeems ſomewhat ſtrange, that upon preſſing the Heart-bag, the liquor contained in it ſhould come up at the Mouth; but if the matter of fact be true, it muſt do ſo by ſome preternatural paſſage, ſeeing every one that is skilled in Anatomy knows, that there is no communication between the *Pericardium* and *aſpera Arteria*. Indeed as to the great quantity of humour in the Heart-bag, I have obſerved the ſame in Horſes, in which I have ſeen both it and the Cheſt extremely filled with liquor, but I dare not conclude from thence, that it came thither down the Wind-pipe; for ſeeing it has been onely in diſeaſed Horſes, that have been broken-winded and troubled with coughs, I am much rather inclined to think, that ſo great quantity of water proceeded from a Dropſie of the Cheſt, which is a diſeaſe not unfrequent in Mankind, in whom yet the beſt Anatomiſts deny that the leaſt drop of drink does naturally paſs down their Wind-pipe: of which any one may be pretty well ſatisfied, that has obſerved in himſelf or others, how when upon occaſion of laughing or the like in drinking, any of the drink paſſes down the wrong Throat as we ſay (which is down the Wind-pipe) the party falls preſently into a moſt violent cough. And as to *Hippocrates*'s obſervation, 'tis more likely the Hog's Lungs ſhould

Whether any part of the drink paſs by the Wind-pipe into the Lungs.

be tinctured by ſome preternatural and diſeaſed humour lodged in them, of a like colour to which his drink happened to be, than that they were tinctured by the drink it ſelf.

The coats of the Wind-pipe.

The Wind-pipe is covered with two coats or skins, one *outward* and the other *inward.*

The *outwardmoſt* is but of a reaſonable thickneſs, neither ſo thick nor ſo ſtrong as the other. It ſprings from the *pleura* or skin which inveſts the Ribs, and ſticks cloſe to the Ligaments of the Griſtles, yea does it ſelf ſerve to knit them more firmly one to another, and is a mean of connecting the whole Pipe more ſtrongly to its neighbouring Parts. It alſo uſhers along the Nerves of the Wind-pipe and Lungs.

The *innermoſt* is thicker and more ſolid than the former, in the Throttle eſpecially, whoſe inſide it covers, as alſo all the inſide of the Wind-pipe and its branches from thence to the bottom of the Lungs. It has two rows of Muſcular Fibres, the outer ſtreight, the inner ſlanting; the firſt ſerving to ſhorten the Wind-pipe, the latter to ſtraiten it. And one reaſon of the great ſtrength of this Membrane ſeems to be, that it might the better endure the violent motion of coughing without being injured. It is very ſenſible, and has its inſide beſmear'd uſually with a fattiſh or ſlimy humour, which likely is ſeparated in the Kernels of the Throat, and this ſerves to keep it moiſt and glib, that reſpiration may be performed with the greater eaſineſs and freedom.

The Griſtles which make the Wind-pipe.

Between theſe two coats or skins is the body or ſubſtance of the Wind-pipe, being partly of the nature of a Griſtle and partly of a Ligament; for it is made up of many round *Griſtles* like Rings, being pretty round on its fore-part, but on the back-part which is next to the Gullet a fourth part of the circle is wanting, in the room of which there is a thick, ſtrong and membranous ſubſtance, more ſoft than the Griſtles, that the Gullet which lies upon it on that ſide, might not be hurt by them.

Theſe Ring-faſhioned Griſtles are joined together by ſtrong Ligaments, which Ligaments do every-where keep the Griſtles at an equal diſtance one from the other.

Table XVIII.

Fig. I. Shews the lower part of the Wind-pipe with all its branches as they were ſpread through the Lungs, clearly ſeparated from all other Parts of the Lungs; to which branches are annexed all the bladders of Air, found out by *Malpighius* and here lively repreſented.

AA *Shew a portion of the* aſpera Arteria *or Wind-pipe.*
BBBB *Its diviſion into branches which run into the ſeveral Lobes of the Lungs.*
CCCC *The ſeveral extremities or ends of the ſaid branches.*
DDDDDD *The innumerable little bladders at the ends of thoſe branches.*
E *Shews where the Wind-pipe is cut off from the upper part of it.*
FFF *The ſeveral circular Griſtles which help to compoſe the Wind-pipe.*
GGG *The membranes or skins betwixt each Griſtle which are another part of the ſubſtance of the Wind-pipe.*

Fig. II.

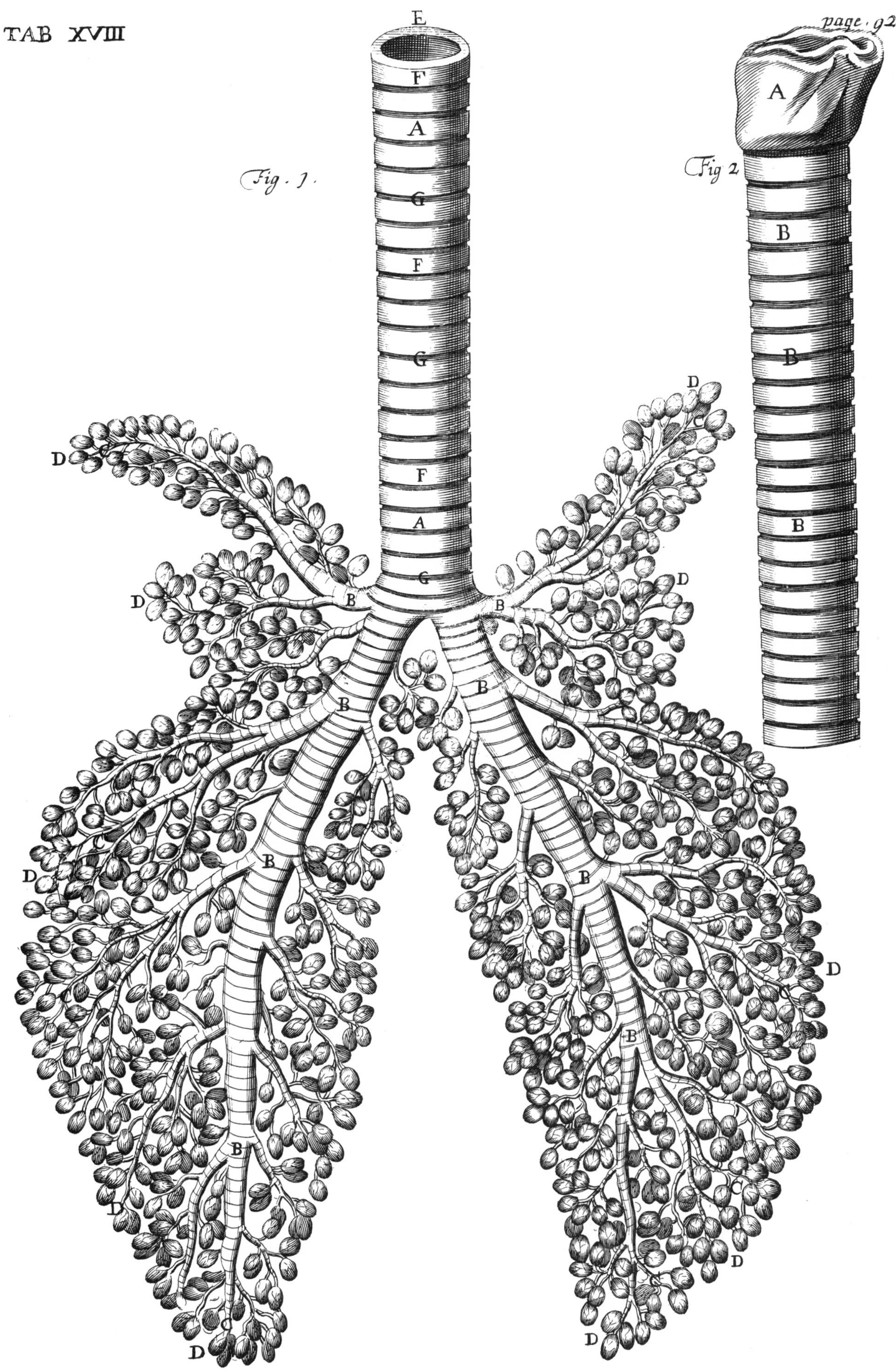
TAB XVIII
page. 92
Fig. 1.
Fig 2
E
F
A
G
B
C
D

Fig. II. Shews the upper part of the Wind-pipe cut off.

A *Shews the* cartilago scutiformis, *or Shield-fashioned Gristle.*
B *The several Gristles and Membranes that make up the body of the Wind-pipe.*

The Wind-pipe like other Parts hath *Vessels* of all sorts; first it hath *Veins* from the external Jugulars; *Arteries* from the *Carotides*; and *Nerves* from the recurrent Nerves of the wandring or eighth pair, (commonly reckoned for the sixth.) *Its Vessels.*

When it is descended about two hands-breadth into the Chest, it is divided into two trunks, one whereof goes into the right Lobe of the Lungs, and the other into the left. Into which as soon as they are entred, each is again subdivided, and those subdivisions still branch out into more, till they become very numerous and slender, and are dispersed among the pulmonary Bloud-vessels, but end into the little bladders above-described. *Its division.*

The *use* of the Wind-pipe is, first, to serve as a nozle to a pair of Bellows, to wit, that the Lungs by the Air entring in by it may be heaved up. Whence when the inside of it is flabby with too much flegmatick humour, or there happens to be any obstruction in it, or any of its branches in the Lungs, there follows a wheazing and shortness of breath, because the Air has not a free ingress into the Lungs. *Its uses.*

The next use of it is to let the Air out from the Lungs, and together with it smoaky vapours steaming through the pores of the Lungs out of the bloud. By help of it also, but especially of the Throttle or upper part, does the Horse neigh, or whinney as they call it in some Countrys, while the Air is driven forcibly out of it in expiration. And thus much as to the Wind-pipe.

A second sort of Vessel or Pipe dispersed through the Lungs, and composing a considerable part of their bulk, are the Bloud-vessels, which are partly a branch from the great Artery, but principally the pulmonary Artery and Vein, whose branches are spread to and fro in a great number through its whole substance, and there complicated and twisted with the branches of the Wind-pipe, the Artery running along the under side and the Vein the upper side of it, both cleaving so close to it that they are not easily to be separated. These Arteries and Veins have communication one with another in several places by *anastomoses*, the little twigs of the Arteries opening into those of the Veins, for the readier circulation of the bloud through the Lungs. Most admirable is the contexture of these Vessels about the Air-bladders; for their small thred-like twigs are interwoven one with another with the most curious artifice (somewhat resembling a Net) round about all of them; which most probably is so done, to the end that all the particles of the bloud may be impregnated with Air, while it passes through these fine Vessels that twine about the Air-bladders on all hands. *The Bloud-vessels of the Lungs.*

Table XIX.

Representeth the pneumonick or pulmonary Artery and Vein cut off from the right and left Ventricles of the Heart, and also freed or separated from the branches of the *bronchia* or Wind-pipe.

AA *Shew the pneumonick Artery cut off close by the right Ventricle of the Heart.*

BB *The pneumonick Vein cut off from the left Ventricle of the Heart.*

CCCC *Their several branches accompanying the branches of the Wind-pipe from which they were pulled or torn, which are dispersed through the whole substance of the Lungs.*

DDDD *The ends or extremities of all the said branches which do end in the extreme parts of the Lungs, and which for their smallness are called capillary or hairy.*

Their Lympheducts. A third sort of Vessel branching in the Lungs are the *Lympheducts*, so called from their office, which is to hold and convey a certain kind of water or humour called *Lympha.* These Vessels we described more fully in Book I. chap. 12. Here they wait on the Veins and Arteries through the whole surface of the Lungs, and receive the humour or water that they contain from them, being first separated by the Glands; which humour seems to be a superfluity of the bloud and it may be the nervous juice, which after they have received, they discharge into the thoracick duct, into which the greater branches of them are inserted. Though these Vessels be but slender, yet they are of great use and necessity; for as Doctor *Willis* affirms, if at any time any of the branches of them happen to be obstructed or broken, there follows thereupon in Man a Dropsie of the Lungs and Breast, oft-times accompanied with Coughs or Phthisicks: and this happens, because by their being obstructed or broken, the superfluous humour which they like so many chanels use to contain or let pass through them and carry off, is left behind, or distils into the Chest, which there breeds the fore-mentioned Distempers. Which opinion of his confirms me in my belief of the original of that watery humour in a Horse, which I have very often in a plentifull manner found in his *Thorax* in dissection, as I have above in this Chapter already said.

Their Nerves. To these three sorts of Vessels a fourth is also added, which are the *Nerves*, with which they are well stored, having innumerable branches of them dispersed through all their substance, accompanying the Bloud-vessels and Pipes of the Wind-pipe; which Nerves do branch to them from the recurrent Nerves of the wandring pair.

Their investing Membrane. Now the Lungs being thus interwoven with these four sorts of Vessels, are covered with a strong *skin*, or indeed two skins, for it is no hard matter to separate it into two.

These skins are furnished with very many pores or holes of an indifferent largeness, plain to be seen (saith *Bartholin*) if you blow up the Lungs with a pair of Bellows or Pipe. Which he doth not onely affirm that himself hath seen, but also quotes *Johannes Walæus*, who (saith he) hath observed them to be in Live-anatomies as large as to contain a pretty big Pease. Such pores, perhaps, there may be discernible in Live-anatomies, though whether so large as to receive a Pease I somewhat question.

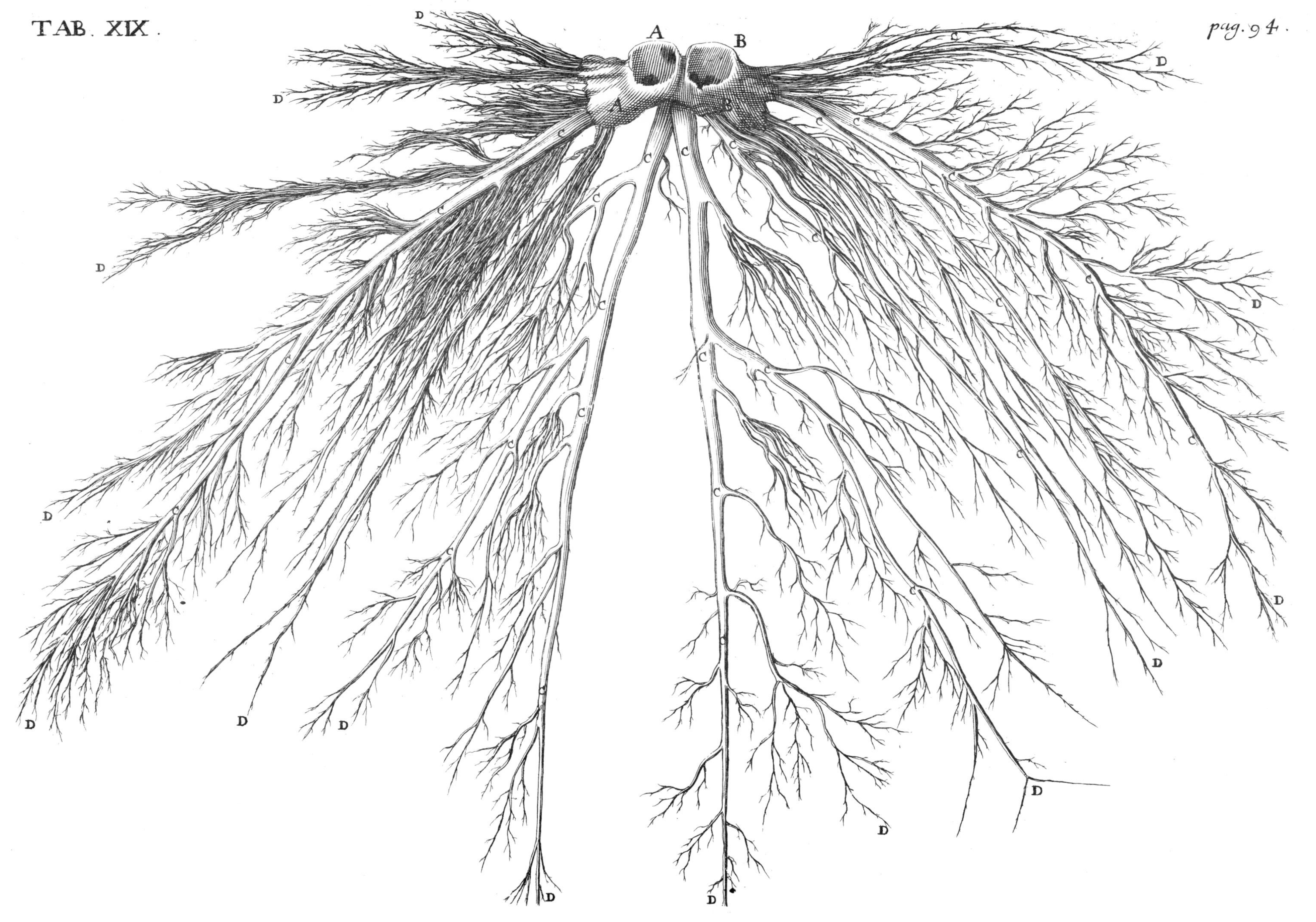
A
B
C
D

question. Indeed I had never my self the opportunity of observing the Lungs in Creatures yet alive, but as soon as they have been dead, though I have made never so great haste to take the Lungs out before they should be any thing cold, yet I could never see any of them, although I have blown the wind through the Wind-pipe with such violence, that I have broke some of the small branches of it, and with the said wind have raised little bladders in the outer skin of the Lungs; I say notwithstanding, I could never see or discern any of these little pores, that did let any of the said wind out, but the wind hath continued in those little bladders several days. Which experiment I alledge not with a design to disprove those worthy and learned Anatomists, that affirm to have seen them; but onely to shew that if any such there be, nothing passes through them out of the Lungs into the Chest. But now on the other hand, that something may be received by them out of the cavity of the Chest into the Lungs, is not improbable; seeing one cannot imagine how corrupt purulent matter collected in the Chest from an Imposthume breaking in it, or the like, should by any other way get into the Wind-pipe, so as to be cough'd up, which it often is as well in Horses as in Men. If the investing skins be removed in any part of the Lungs, and afterwards one blow into them through the Wind-pipe, then will the Air issue pretty strongly out at the Breach. The outer of the skins is smooth and thin, but the inner is pretty thick, and on its inside rough, appearing like an Honey-comb, by reason of the extremities of the Vessels, and of the bladders ending at it. Both growing close together as they do, make a very strong Membrane, which is very necessary; for otherwise in anhelation, or deep and violent inspiration, it would have been in danger of breaking when the Lungs are so much distended, to the great inconvenience if not certain death of the Creature to which it should so have happened.

Having finished the description of the several things of which the Lungs are compounded or framed, in the next place we proceed to speak of their *action* and *use*. *Their action and use.*

Their first *use* then is, (according to *Galen*) to serve as a soft Pillow or Bolster for the Heart to rest upon, that the hardness of the Parts behind them should not offend it in its pulsation.

Secondly, They are the instruments of respiration or breathing, which is their proper *action*. Now respiration is performed by two motions of the Lungs, *viz.* dilatation and contraction. When they are dilated, they receive in Air, and this is termed *inspiration*; but when they are contracted, they expel or drive forth the Air, which is called *expiration*.

While the Air is drawn in in inspiration, a double benefit accrews to the Beast: First his Heart and Bloud are thereby cooled; whence we see that the hotter he is, the more frequently he draws his breath, that the bloud may be the more fanned by the cool Air. Secondly, hereby the vital flame is continued; for as an ordinary Fire is extinguished by withdrawing the Air from it, so does the Animal die when it is denied Air to breathe in. To these benefits of inspiration may be added, that when the Lungs are heaved up by the Air drawn in, their substance is rarefied, so that there is granted a freer circulation of the bloud through them.

The Air having performed these offices, by its stay in the Lungs it becomes hot, and so can be of no further use for cooling the Heart and Bloud; and its nitrous particles are consumed by the vital flame that feeds upon them, and therefore it becomes necessary to expel it, that there may be be room for new and freſh Air to be drawn in for the uſes aforeſaid. So that this drawing in and expelling the Air ſucceed one another by turns, and anſwer to the *ſyſtole* and *diaſtole* of the Heart; onely this motion of the Lungs is partly voluntary and partly natural, but that of the Heart wholly natural.

But neither is *expiration* or breathing forth without its particular uſes; for by it are vented or voided the ſmoaky or ſooty ſteams or excrements of the Heart and arterial Bloud, (which excrements are brought from the Heart through the pneumonick Artery with the bloud:) alſo the thin and thick excrements of the Lungs gathered in the branches of the Wind-pipe are by this motion of expiration, (heighten'd into a cough) brought into the one great trunk thereof, through which as through a Reed it is driven by the force of the Air up to the Mouth and Noſe, to be by them voided.

Of what nature the motion of the Lungs is, and by what Muſcles of the Breaſt it is aſſiſted, the Reader may inform himſelf in the fourth Chapter of this Book that treats of the Midriff, whoſe motion correſponds to this of the Lungs.

CHAP. X.

Of the Neck.

HAVING now finiſhed my Diſcourſe of the two Lower *Venters*, order of Diſſection requires that I ſhould aſcend to the third and uppermoſt *Venter*, and treat of the Head and Animal Faculty; but I will firſt ſpeak to thoſe Parts which lead me thither, and thoſe are the Parts of the *Neck*.

The *Neck* is called in Latin *Collum, à colle*, from an hillock; for it ariſeth out of the Body as an hill doth out of the reſt of the Earth.

It comprehends the diſtance between the Head and Breaſt, and its Parts are *containing*, or *contained*: as for the former, they are ſuch as are found in the other Parts of the Body; but

The contained Parts of the Neck.

The Parts *contained* are peculiar to it ſelf, and are theſe: the Gullet, the Wind-pipe, the *Vertebræ*, or Joints of the Neck, and its Muſcles. Of theſe two latter we ſhall diſcourſe in the Fourth and Fifth Books; and of the two former, we treated of one in the Firſt Book, as belonging to the Stomach, and of the other in this as pertaining to the Lungs. But becauſe the uppermoſt parts of both theſe next to the Throat are diſtinguiſh'd from the reſt by peculiar names and have particular uſes, we ſhall treat of them in this Chapter. Now the top of the Wind-pipe is called *Larynx*, and of the Gullet, *Pharynx*.

Of the Larynx.

The *Larynx* or Throttle is ſituated, as hath been ſaid, at the upper part of the Neck, adjoining to the root of the Tongue. It is in Humane Bodies the inſtrument of the Voice, and in whatſoever other Creatures, of that noiſe which they make, by what name ſoever it be diſtinguiſhed, as particularly of the *neighing* of an Horſe.

Its

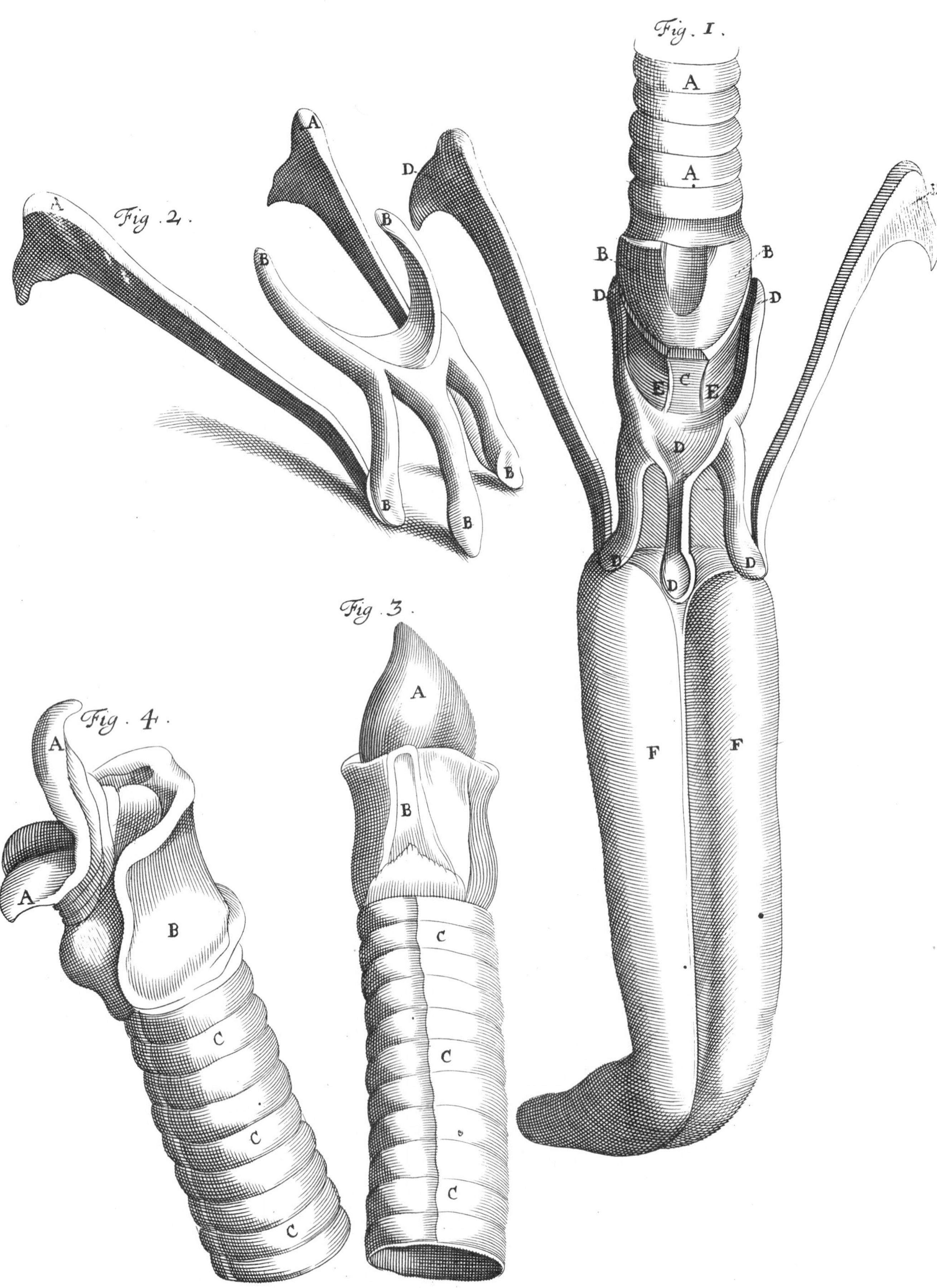
Fig. 1.
A
A
B
B
D
D
C
E
E
D
D
D
D
F
F
Fig. 2.
A
A
D.
B
B
B
B
B
Fig. 3.
A
B
C
C
C
Fig. 4.
A
A
B
C
C
C

Its *figure* is round and almost circular, onely bunching a little out on the foreside, and depressed as much on the back-part next to the Gullet, for the Gullets better and more secure passage, and that the meat in swallowing might not be hindred from descending by it. *Its figure.*

It is framed of five *Cartilages* or *Gristles*, the first of which is called *Scutiformis* or Buckler-like, because it resembles a Shield or Buckler, being hollow within and bunching without. In Humane Bodies (in Men more especially, for Women have it not so far sticking out as Men) this bunching out is by some Anatomists termed *Adam's* Apple, from an old Tradition that a part of the fatal Apple abode sticking in *Adam's* Throat in that place. *Its substance. Five* Cartilages.

The next or second Gristle of the *Larynx* is called *Annularis* from the resemblance it hath to a Turkish Ring, wherewith they arm their Thumb when they shoot. This Gristle is round, and incompasseth the whole *Larynx*.

The third and fourth, because as they are joined together they resemble the neck of an Ewer, are called *Guttales*. These two Gristles many times pass for one, because they have but one skin proper to them both, and untill that skin be removed they are not to be parted. These two form the *glottis* or little tongue, being a chink of that shape.

The fifth is termed *Epiglottis* because it is placed above the *glottis* or chink. The substance of this is soft, and its shape like an Ivy-leaf. Its use is to hinder the falling down of any thing that may be offensive to the Wind-pipe, when the Creature doth swallow either his meat or drink.

These Cartilages are moved by several pairs of *Muscles*, which shall be described in the Fourth Book.

Table XX.

Representeth the upper part of the Wind-pipe fastned to the *os Hyoides*, as also to the root of the Tongue; likewise the *os Hyoides* it self separated from all other parts; it containeth also two other figures of the upper part of the Wind-pipe, to shew its several Parts.

Figure I.

Shews the upper part of the Wind-pipe, and the Parts to which it is fasten'd.

AAAA *Shew the Cartilages or Gristles of the upper part of the Wind-pipe.*
BB *The head of the said Wind-pipe fastned to the* os Hyoides.
C *The Ligament that fastneth the head to the said bone.*
DDDD *The* os Hyoides.
EE *The bones that join with the* os Hyoides *at the bottom of the Head.*
FF *The Tongue.*

Figure II.

Shews the *os Hyoides* separated from the Wind-pipe and from the Tongue.

AA *Shew the two long bones joined to the* os Hyoides, *whose other ends are fastned (when in their places) to the bottom of the Head.*
BBB *The several cartilaginous bones that make up the* os Hyoides.

Figure III.

A *Shews the* Epiglottis *or Throat-flap turned more upon the upper side, the plainer to shew the back parts of it.*
B *The backside of the* Scutiformis.
CCC *The Cartilages or Gristles of the Wind-pipe.*

Figure IV.

Shews the upper part of the Wind-pipe with the Shield-fashioned Gristle and Throat-flap turned on one side to shew the sides of those Parts.

A *The* Epiglottis *or Throat-flap.*
B *The Shield-fashioned Gristle.*
C *A portion of the Wind-pipe.*

Its Vessels. The *Vessels* of the *Larynx* are of all sorts. *Veins* are derived to it from the external Jugulars; *Arteries* from the large branch of the *Carotides*; Its *Nerves* it hath from the recurrent Nerves of the (eighth, commonly reckoned for the) sixth pair, which are called in those Creatures which have voices, *vocales.*

Its Kernels. There are also *two* sorts of *Kernels* belonging to it. One pair is called *Tonsillæ,* which are placed at the sides of the *Uvula,* and at the upper part of the *Larynx.* These are those which in Humane Bodies are called the *Almonds of the Ears,* and are of this use, *viz.* to separate that flegmatick humour from the bloud that makes the slaver; which humour serves to moisten it, and also the Gullet, that by their glibness or slipperiness they may the better serve for their respective uses.

The other pair of Kernels are placed contrary to the former, namely at the lower end of the *Larynx,* in number two, one on each side of the Buckler-like Gristle. In Horses they are much larger than the former, and by them large branches of the external jugular Veins and Arteries do run. These are those Kernels under the Throat or between the Jaws of an Horse that one may plainly feel at any time, but more especially when an Horse has the Glanders, for in such they are much swelled.

The

The *Pharynx* (or top of the Gullet) is ſo called from a Greek word that ſignifies *to carry,* becauſe it conveys the meat and drink from the Mouth toward the Stomach. It is ſomewhat more fleſhy than the reſt of the Gullet, and reaches up, *behind,* to the *Uvula,* on the *ſides* to the *Tonſils,* and on the *fore-part* to the *Epiglottis.* It has ſeveral Muſcles by the help of which it performs its motion, of which we ſhall treat in the Fourth Book. Its uſe is to receive the meat when it is chewed, and graſping it on every ſide by contracting it ſelf, to ſqueeze it down the Gullet, by which it deſcends to the Stomach. *The Pharynx.*

Thus much of the Parts of the *Neck,* which brings me to

The End of the Second Book.

P THE

THE ANATOMY OF AN HORSE.

BOOK III.

Of the Head.

CHAP. I.

Of the Head and Animal Parts contained therein.

HAVING finiſhed the deſcription of the two Lower *Venters*, which are two of the principal Parts of the Body; I come now in the next place to betake my ſelf to the laſt principal Part which is the *Head*, being the ſeat of the Animal Faculty, as the two lower are of the Vital and Natural.

In diſſecting of this Part I ſhall follow the ſame method as in the two former, examining its Parts in order, as they offer themſelves to our ſight in diſſection, firſt dividing it into parts to that intent.

But before we begin to divide it, I think it will not be amiſs to ſpeak ſomething of its ſupereminency over all the other Parts; for in reſpect that it is the ſeat of the Senſes, it is lookt upon by Anatomiſts to be the chief Manſion-houſe of the Animal Soul; and Senſe is ſo neceſſary to every living Creature, that without it, it is not far from being without life. And as the Head in this regard is the moſt principal Part, ſo is it accordingly ſituated in the uppermoſt place, above all the other Parts of the

 Body,

Body, for this reaſon, *viz.* that the Animal ſpirits as from a fountain might ſpring from thence, and communicate ſenſe and motion down to all Parts of the Body: but for the Eyes ſake more eſpecially has it this high ſituation, for thereby two conveniencies accrue to the ſenſe of ſeeing; firſt, the Eyes being placed as in a Watch-tower, can diſcover things at the greater diſtance, and thereby prevent many dangers which might otherwiſe come unawares: and in the next place by being placed ſo near the fountain of Animal ſpirits, the optick Nerves, which are of a ſoft ſubſtance, and could not therefore endure a long paſſage, are ſecured from breaking.

As to the *figure* or ſhape of the Head, I will omit ſpeaking of that, ſince it is ſo viſible and ſo common to be ſeen. And though ſomething might be ſpoken as to the true and moſt natural ſhape of an Horſe's Head, yet that being already deſcribed by other Authours, and may by me (if God ſhall ſo long ſpare my life) be treated of more at large in another Book which I deſign to ſet forth of the ſeveral Cures performed by me, by ſuch means and methods as I have experimented ſince I came to underſtand Anatomy; I ſhall wave it at this time, and ſpeak no more of the Head in general, but proceed to treat of its Parts.

The *Parts* of the Head, (as of the other two *Venters* before diſcourſed of) may be diſtinguiſhed into Parts *containing* and *contained.* The *containing* are either *common* or *proper*; of which in order.

The common containing Parts of the Head.

Firſt then of its *common containing* Parts; the firſt of which is the Cuticle with its hairs, of which we have ſufficiently treated in the firſt Chapter of the Firſt Book; the next is the *cutis* or True skin, alſo the Fat and fleſhy Pannicle, of all which we have treated at large in the five firſt Chapters of the Firſt Book, whither the Reader may pleaſe to turn back for his better information.

The proper containing Parts.

The *proper containing* Parts of the Head are five, namely the Muſcles, the *Pericranium,* the *Perioſteum,* the Skull, and the Membranes or *Meninges* contained within it.

The Muſcles.

To the *Muſcles* we will ſpeak in the next Book which is of the Muſcles, as being the moſt proper place.

The Pericranium.

The fleſhy Pannicle or *membrana carnoſa* together with the other common inveſting Parts above it being removed, the *Pericranium* next appears, which is a thin, white and very ſenſible Membrane ſpread over the whole Skull, adhering immediately to the *Perioſteum* every-where, ſaving where the temporal Muſcles on each ſide come between them. There are many ſlender Fibres that paſs from this Membrane through the ſutures or ſeams of the Skull, which are knit to the *craſſa meninx* or outer skin, which cloaths the Brain on the inſide of the Scull; whence ſome are of opinion that the *Pericranium* has its riſe from it. Whether that be ſo or no, theſe Fibres however ſerve to ſtay the *dura mater* in its place, whereby it hinders the Brain which it inveſts from being claſh'd againſt the ruggid Skull in violent concuſſions of the Head.

The Perioſteum.

The next inveſting Part is the *Perioſteum,* which is a Skin of much alike ſubſtance with the *Pericranium,* onely thinner. It is of the ſame nature with that Membrane that inveſts all the Bones in the whole Body, excepting the Teeth which are bare. From this Membrane it is that the Skull as well as all other bones are ſenſible, for of themſelves they are ſenſleſs Parts. It ſticks very cloſe to the Skull, and it, as well as the *Pericranium,* has *Arteries* from the external *Carotides,* and *Veins* from the external Jugulars.

We

We ſhould in the next place ſpeak to the Bones of the Head, or the ſeveral Bones of the Skull diſtinguiſhed by ſeveral ſutures; but I omit them alſo here, and ſhall ſpeak to them in their proper place, (*viz.* in the Fifth Book) and proceed to the Parts within the Skull, the firſt of which is the *dura meninx*, that is, the hard Skin or Membrane, called likewiſe *craſſa meninx*, to diſtinguiſh it from the *thinner* that lies next under it, and immediately cloaths the Brain.

This hard or thick Membrane is called by many Authours *dura mater* or the hard mother, becauſe they conceive that moſt of the Skins of the whole Body do ſpring from it, and therefore it is eſteemed as their mother. Dura meninx.

Its *figure* and *amplitude* anſwer to the Bones of the Skull, by reaſon it inveſteth all its cavities. It is knit, and that very ſtrongly, to the bottom of the Skull, to its proceſſes, and to the circles of its holes, from whence it cannot eaſily be removed. It is ſuſpended alſo by the Fibres above-ſpoken of that come through the ſutures of the Skull from the *Pericranium*, as likewiſe by the Bloud-veſſels that penetrate the Skull and are inſerted into this Membrane. By which Veſſels it is in like manner faſtened to the Skin under it called the *pia mater*, and in ſeveral places to the Brain it ſelf. It conſiſts of two Skins, as the *Peritonæum* of the Loweſt *Venter*, and the *Pleura* of the middle do. In its upper part it is doubled, and its duplicature divides the Brain into two parts, the right and left. This duplicature being in the hinder part broad, and growing narrower ſtill as it inclines to the fore-part, I mean towards the Noſe, is by Phyſicians called *falx* or the ſickle, becauſe in a Man's Head which is pretty round, it makes almoſt an half circle, as a ſickle does. We may retain the ſame name for it in an Horſe, though leſs properly, as differing ſomewhat in ſhape. *Its connexion* *The* falx.

In this reduplication there are ſeveral cavities or hollowneſſes, commonly called by the Latin name *ſinus*, which are accounted receptacles of abounding bloud and ſpirits; by *Galen* they are called the Ventricles of the *dura mater*, by others ciſterns of bloud. The higheſt of theſe, and alſo the longeſt, doth run all along the top or upper part of the *falx* from the Noſe length-ways of the Head towards the Noll, where it is divided into ſeveral branches, two of which deſcend downwards to the bottom of the *occiput*, and a third runs to the *glandula pinealis*. *Its* Sinus's.

Into theſe hollowneſſes or *ſinus's* the mouths of the Veins and Arteries are ſaid to open, the Arteries pouring bloud into them, and the Veins receiving it from them again, as hath been obſerved in the diſſecting the Heads of living Creatures, for in the long or uppermoſt *ſinus* hath been ſeen a ſtrong beating or pulſe occaſioned by the bloud that is diſcharged into it by the Arteries.

The other Membrane or Skin which inveſts the Brain is called *tenuis meninx* from its thinneſs, and *pia mater* or tender mother from its immediate covering or cloſe ſticking to the Brain, imbracing it as a Mother does her Infant. It is ſpread over all the cortical or outer part of the Brain, inſinuating it ſelf into all its windings, as alſo into thoſe of the *cerebellum* and *medulla oblongata*, and ties all their proceſſes and parts to one another, that they cannot be diſplaced or bear hard upon one another. And whereever it goes, the Bloud-veſſels run along it, and are diſperſed out of it into the Parts that it cloaths. Tenuis meninx.

This Skin is very thin, and of a moſt exquiſite ſenſe, yea this and the *dura mater* ſeem to be the inſtruments of all ſenſation. For as ſenſe is commu-

communicated to every part immediately by the Nerves, so the nervous Fibres are more probably propagated from these Membranes that cloath the Nerves, than from the medullar Part it self of the Nerve which is derived from the *medulla oblongata* and spinal marrow, which of themselves have little or no sense, but onely by virtue of these Membranes that invest them.

Its Vessels. It is furnished with very many Arteries and Veins, most of which are exceeding small, but in number infinite, interwoven one with another in the manner of a Net. The Arteries do spring from the *Carotides* and Cervical Arteries, and the Veins from the jugular Veins.

The use of the Meninges. The use of these two Membranes that invest the Brain is to sustain the Vessels that enter into it, to cloath and defend it from the hardness of the Parts that environ it, to keep it in its due form and situation (for of it self it would run all about, it is of so soft a consistency) and lastly to afford a coat to all the Nerves, not onely to those that spring within the Skull, but to all those also that arise out of the Back-bone, for these two Membranes are propagated all along it, investing its pith, (called the spinal marrow) out of which those Nerves spring.

CHAP. II.

Of the Brain in general.

The excellency of the Brain. BEING come to treat of the *Brain*, it shall not be amiss, if before I speak of its several Parts, I say something as to its excellency, and the eminent offices it performs for the benefit of the Animal. All Authours agree that it is one of the most noble Parts of the whole Body, ranked for its dignity even with the Heart it self. And indeed, as I have intimated in the foregoing Chapter, its situation sheweth plainly as much, it being placed in the highest part of all the Body, and there fenced about as it were with strong walls on every side, to secure it from outward injuries. In it are contained the Animal Faculties, *viz.* those of Sense and Motion. The former of these two Faculties sits in it as in a Throne of Majesty, beholding the forms of all things under her feet, having all the Organs and Instruments of the Senses attending Her, at her command. For first the Eyes are placed near her, that as Spies or Centinels watching day and night they may discover the Enemy. The Ears also are seated near her, at her command to be turned this way or that way, to listen to any dangers that are approaching, that so they may be avoided. Likewise the Instruments of Smelling and Tasting are near her, that at her command those Foods that are profitable and necessary may be received, and that unpleasant or hurtfull Food may be rejected. And as the Faculty of Sensation hath the forementioned Ministers or Instruments placed near her for the execution of her offices; so hath the motive Faculty a dominion extended to the furthest limits of the Body, of which every Limb and Member is perfectly at her beck, to move this way or that way as she directs. I say, both these noble Faculties have their seat in the Brain;

for it is not a private or particular Organ of Senſe, but an univerſal one; nor doth the motive Faculty exert it ſelf in the Brain it ſelf, which is incapable of *voluntary* motion; but that motion which it has, is *natural*, and that not owing to it ſelf, but to the Arteries that are diſperſed in it, for the beating of theſe makes it ſeem to widen, and contract it ſelf, as hath been obſerved in Wounds of the Heads of both Men and Beaſts. This motion, I ſay, is communicated to it from the Arteries, and in its dilatation it receives arterial bloud by the Carotid Arteries, and in its contraction it forces that Bloud into the Veins, and the Animal Spirits into the Nerves, by which they are carried into all Parts of the Body, and with them the moving power is imparted; for without ſuch influence from the brain an Animal would be like a Log, it would be able neither to move nor feel, or rather it would ceaſe to be an Animal, and become a dead Carcaſe.

That an Horſe hath a Brain.

How abſurd and ridiculous a thing is it then for any Man that hath any Brain himſelf, to imagine a Horſe to have none? yet ſuch Men I have my ſelf met withall, yea I know ſeveral which to this day will not be convinced of that erroneous opinion by any arguments whatever. Neither will they take the pains to inſpect the Parts, to ſatisfy themſelves of the contrary, but will ſtill continue in their falſe-received opinion, merely taken from a ſilly obſervation they have made when they have ſeen Horſes and Oxen knocked on the Head, where they ſee the Skull broken and nothing under it, but a few hard and dry Bones, without any marrowy ſubſtance: I ſay from this obſervation they draw their concluſion, that a Horſe hath no Brain. I much wonder how any ſuch Dolt can have the confidence to take upon him the name of a Farrier, and pretend to cure he knows not what. Such Perſons I would deſire onely when they ſee another Horſe knockt on the Head, that they prevail with them that doe it, (or otherwiſe when any Horſe is dead) to ſtrike him a blow or two with the ſame force above the uſual place between the Ears or a very little lower, and they ſhall then be ſoon convinced that he hath a Brain, (though not ſo *large* by much as a Man hath, conſidering the different bulk of their Bodies.) And when they are convinced of that, I hope they will take pains to be ſatisfied in the other Parts of the Body by ſearching into them, as by theſe my Labours they are directed; ſo ſhall they improve themſelves in their profeſſions, and I have the wiſhed end of my pains, which I have taken to advance them.

CHAP.

CHAP. III.

Of the ſeveral Parts of the Brain, viz. *that which is ſtrictly called the Brain, the* Cerebellum *or After-brain, and the Spinal Marrow.*

The Parts of the Brain.

IF we take the *Brain* in a large ſignification, it comprehends all that marrowy ſubſtance that is found in the cavity of the Skull: yet for diſtinction's ſake it is by all Authours divided into three parts; firſt, the fore-part, being the largeſt, is called *the Brain*; ſecondly, the middle-part is called *Cerebellum,* the Brainlet or After-brain; and laſtly, the hindmoſt and lowermoſt is termed *Medulla oblongata,* being that part of the Spinal Marrow which is within the Skull.

The manner of ſawing the Skull aſunder.

Now to find out theſe ſeveral Parts we muſt divide the Skull with a Saw for that purpoſe, beginning almoſt as far back as the Noll-bone, or indeed quite as far, dividing the hole of the Noll-bone in the middle, and ſo go with your Saw firſt along one ſide of the Head a little above the auditory paſſage till you come to the Fore-head a little below the Eyes (or juſt even with them;) where being come, and having ſawed onely juſt through the Skull, (for you muſt have a care that your Saw do not pierce the Brain, for that will hinder your ſeeing the Parts of it) then croſs the Fore-head with your Saw and paſs along the other ſide till you come to the hole of the Noll-bone again: by doing which you will looſen the upper part of the Skull, which with care you muſt take off, that you break not the *dura mater* or Skin next under it, for that Skin is faſtened to it in ſeveral places. When you have removed that piece of the Skull, then remove the Skin alſo by parting it lengthways down the middle, whereby you ſhall plainly ſee the Brain with its convolutions or folds, alſo the After-brain with its wormlike proceſſes, *&c.* in ſuch manner as they are repreſented in the following Table.

Table XXI.

Fig. I. Shews the Skull of an Horſe ſawed aſunder in ſuch a manner as that the Parts of the Brain may be ſeen in their natural ſituation.

FF *Shew the ſubſtance of the Brain covered with the* pia mater *onely, the* dura mater *being removed for that purpoſe.*
HH *The* Cerebellum *or After-brain alſo in its natural ſituation.*
LL *The* proceſſus vermiformes *or worm-like Proceſſes.*
MM *A portion of the* medulla oblongata.
NN *The* dura mater *ſo far as it contains the* medulla oblonatag, *cut in ſunder and turned back.*
OO *The Noll-bone cut in ſunder.*

Fig. II.

TAI. XXB.

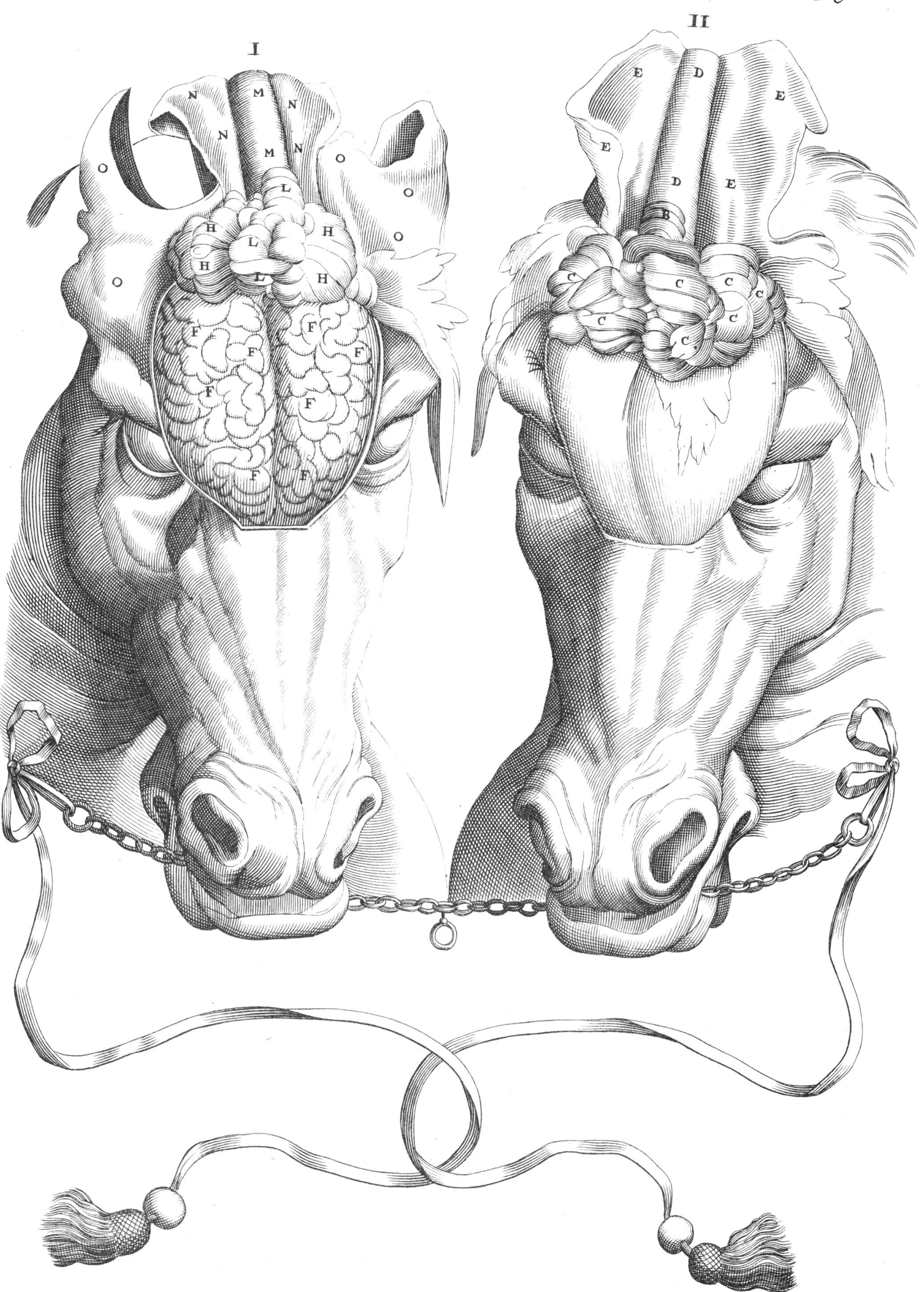

Fig. II. Shews the Brain removed and taken out, that the After-brain and its Worm-like Processes might be the plainer seen.

CCCC *The* Cerebellum *or After-brain turned a little downward, to shew its Parts more plain.*
B *The Wormlike Processes.*
D *The Spinal Marrow so much as is contained within the Skull.*
EE *That part of the* dura mater *which invests the Spinal Marrow within the Skull, opened and turned back.*

Of these several Parts of the Brain we shall speak in their order, and first of that which is strictly so called. It is of a marrowy substance, but not equally so, for the upper part of it uses to be called its *cortex* or bark, being of a more dusky colour; whereas the inner or lower part is more white, and is particularly called the marrow or pith of the Brain. It is divided into two parts, a right and a left, by a Membrane that runs length-ways of the Head, from the Fore-head to the Noll; but this division descends no deeper into the Brain than the Ash-coloured part of it reaches. The Skin which divides it, is called *falx* or the sickle, of which I have already spoken in the first Chapter. *The substance and division of the Brain, (strictly so called.)*

The *action* of the Brain is to elaborate the Animal Spirits, which from it are transmitted to the *Medulla oblongata*, and from thence into the Nerves, for the sensation and motion of the whole Body, as has been more fully shewn in the two foregoing Chapters. *Its action.*

The second part of the Brain, called the *After-brain*, is situated in the back-part of the Skull next the Noll-bone, onely parted from the Brain on its upper part by the *pia mater* or undermost Skin. *The* Cerebellum.

This differeth not much from the Brain either in colour or substance, but onely in its convolutions or foldings: for the Brain observeth no order in its winding, but the Brainlet doth, for all its folds are circular, being extended one over another like plates, and each is kept apart from other by the *pia mater* that invests each of them severally.

It is framed of four Parts, whereof two are lateral, (or on each side) the right and the left; and these are spherical, or round like a Globe: The other two are in the middle betwixt these, standing before and behind; and these are made up of several orbicular Portions in similitude like the Worms which are found in rotten Timber, and are from thence called Worm-like Processes. *Its Parts.*

The *use* of the Brainlet or After-brain is the same as of the Brain.

CHAP. IV.

Of the Spinal Marrow contained within and without the Skull.

The Spinal Marrow. Its substance. THAT part of the Spinal Marrow that is within the Brain, is termed particularly *medulla oblongata*, and is the third part of the Brain, being of an uniform, white and compact substance, something harder than either the Brain or After-brain.

Its rise. It *arises* out of the Brain and Brainlet, and that from six roots; two of which spring at the upper and fore-part of the Brain, and are called *corpora striata*, the streaked or chamfered Bodies, being onely the ends of its two Thighs; the other four arise lower and more backward, by which it adheres to the Brainlet, and are those protuberances or jettings out that are called *Nates* and *Testes*, its Buttocks and Testicles.

Its figure. Its *figure* (after its rise) is long and round, being thicker near its beginning than afterwards. Its length within the Skull is about two inches, beginning towards the fore-part of the Head, and reaching to the Noll, whence it is lengthned and continued down the Chine as far as the Dock. That part of it which is contained in the Chine, we commonly call in Horses the pith of the Back.

Its Membranes. Within the Skull it is clad onely with two *Membranes*; but without, it is covered with three. The first of which it hath from the inner Skin of the Brain or *pia mater*; this immediately covers it. The second it hath from the upper Skin of the Brain or *dura mater*; this is next to and covereth the former. And the third is said to spring from a strong Ligament which binds together the fore-part of the Rack-bones, covering both the former, and is very strong.

Its use. Now the *use* of the Spinal Marrow is to be the original of all the Nerves, which from it (as from a Fountain) like small Rivulets convey to all Parts of the Body the Animal Spirits. For although the Brain in common speech be accounted the original of the Nerves; that is to be understood in a large sense, when all the three Parts of the Brain are included in that one general appellation: But when the Brain comes to be divided into Parts, which are distinguish'd by particular names, then are both the Brain and Brainlet thrown out of the office of being the original of the Nerves. For ocular Inspection doth testify, that it is from that part of the Spinal Marrow contained within the Skull, from which all the Nerves of the Brain do spring; as likewise from that part of the Spinal Marrow without the Skull, called the Pith or Marrow of the Back, that all the other Nerves of the whole Body do arise. Which large and far distant origination of the Nerves is very necessary; for it would not have been safe (in consideration of the length of the way) that all the Nerves should be carried from the Brain to the inferior or lower Parts; and therefore it is wisely provided by Nature, that from the Marrow or Pith of the back those Nerves should spring which furnish the Parts so remote from the Brain.

As for the *number* of Nerves which spring from the Spinal Marrow without the Skull, they are in a Horse thirty seven pair, according to the number of Joints or *vertebræ* from the Noll-bone or the going out of the Marrow from the head, to the setting on of the tail; for out of the holes or perforations in every Bone do pass a pair of Nerves. Therefore there being so many Bones, there are so many pair of Nerves that spring from the Spinal Marrow. And from the *medulla oblongata* or that part of the Spinal Marrow that is within the Skull, there spring nine pair, as shall be further shewed hereafter. *The number of Nerves springing from it.*

CHAP. V.

Of the Parts of the Cerebrum, *or Brain properly so called, viz. the* Rete mirabile, Glandula pituitaria, Infundibulum, *the Ventricles of the Brain, the* Corpus callosum, plexus choroides, Nates, Testes, Penis *or* Glandula pinealis.

HAVING given a short description of the *Cerebrum*, (or Brain properly so called) the *Cerebellum*, and Spinal Marrow; we now return to the *Cerebrum*, to take a more exact view of its several Parts; and we shall begin with the *Rete mirabile* or wonderfull Net.

This Net is framed of innumerable twigs of Arteries which spring from the largest branches of the Carotid and Cervical Arteries, which pass into the Skull by proper holes in the Bones of the Temples. This Net is far more discernable in Oxen and Horses than in other lesser Animals. *The* Rete mirabile.

It is called *the wonderfull Net* by reason of its structure, the Arteries of which it is composed crossing one another like the threds of a Net, or rather as if several Nets were spread one over another. It is dispersed all over the bottom of the Brain both without and within the *dura mater*, some of the smallest shoots of it branching into the pituitary Glandule. *Why so called.*

The *use* of this Net is said to be for the preparing of the Bloud and Vital Spirits to make Animal Spirits of. For which purpose in the twinings and windings of these small Vessels they are a long time detained, for the better elaboration and preparation of them, and lest they might rush into the Brain in too full a stream, and thereby overflow and disturb the Animal Faculty. *Its use.*

To see this wonderfull Net, as also the other Parts of the bottom or under-side of the Brain, you must (after having sawn the Skull asunder, as is shewed in the foregoing Chapter) with a pair of sharp Pincers pinch off by little and little the sides of the remaining part of the Skull, all round, untill you come as near the bottom as you can; and you must then with as much care as possible lift up the Brain, beginning at the fore-part of it, where the Bone of the Fore-head a little separates it. After you have lifted it a little way up, there will come in sight the mammillary Processes together with their nervous Filaments or Threds that *The manner of taking out the Brain, and in what order the Parts appear.*

paſs through the Sieve-like Bone, hanging at them; which being looſened and the Brain farther pulled up, the next thing that appeareth are the branches of the Carotid Arteries, which having penetrated the Skull are carried to the Brain; which being cut off and the Brain yet a little farther turned up, the unition or coming together, and the going out of the Optick Nerves are to be ſeen; the Trunks of which if you likewiſe cut off, there are other Arteries (alſo branches of the *Carotides*) to be ſeen, coming in through the Bones of the Temples: which Arteries (as I have already ſhewed) are (with ſome ſmall Veins joined with them) thoſe Veſſels which make up the *Rete mirabile* or wonderfull Net, diſcourſed of at the beginning of this Chapter.

After you have cut in ſunder theſe Arteries alſo, then you may by liſting up the Brain ſtill a little higher, perceive the moving Nerves of the Eyes (for *they* come next to view) and after them the other pairs of Nerves follow in order, in ſuch ſort, that one pair of them being cut off and the Brain with its Appendices or Proceſſes more liſted up, the next is ſtill more plainly diſcerned by the carefull Anatomiſt. In which method and order all the Nerves, to which I ſhall particularly ſpeak in a convenient place, (I mean the Nerves ariſing within the Skull) and alſo the Arteries, as well the Carotid as Vertebral, being at length cut off, the whole frame of the Brain may be taken out of the Skull.

Table XXII.

Repreſenteth two Skulls, the one to ſhew the baſis or bottom of the Brain and the Head of the Spinal Marrow contained within the Skull, with the riſe of the Nerves from it; and the other ſhews the cavity of the Skull in which the Brain was ſeated, but now removed, the better to ſhew the *Glandula pituitaria* and other Parts that lie under the Brain.

Figure I.

Shews the bottom of the Brain and Spinal Marrow.

AA *Shew the Eyes.*
BB *The Optick Nerves.*
CC *The moving Nerves of the Eyes.*
DD *The fourth pair of Nerves, by Doctor* Willis *called the Pathetick Nerves, proper to one of the Muſcles of the Eyes onely, by which the Eye is chiefly moved in the Paſſions of Love, Anger,* &c.
EEEE *Several other Nerves ariſing from the Spinal Marrow within the Skull.*
FFFF *The bottom of the Brain.*
GG *The Spinal Marrow called here* medulla oblongata.
HH *The Spinal Marrow cut off at its going out of the Skull.*
IIII *The ſeveral barrs of the Palate of the Mouth.*
qq *The cavity or hollowneſs that goes from the Palate of the Mouth to the Noſe.*
RRRR *The ſeveral Teeth.*
SS *The* dura mater *cut inſunder and turned back.*
T *The* Glandula pituitaria.

Figure

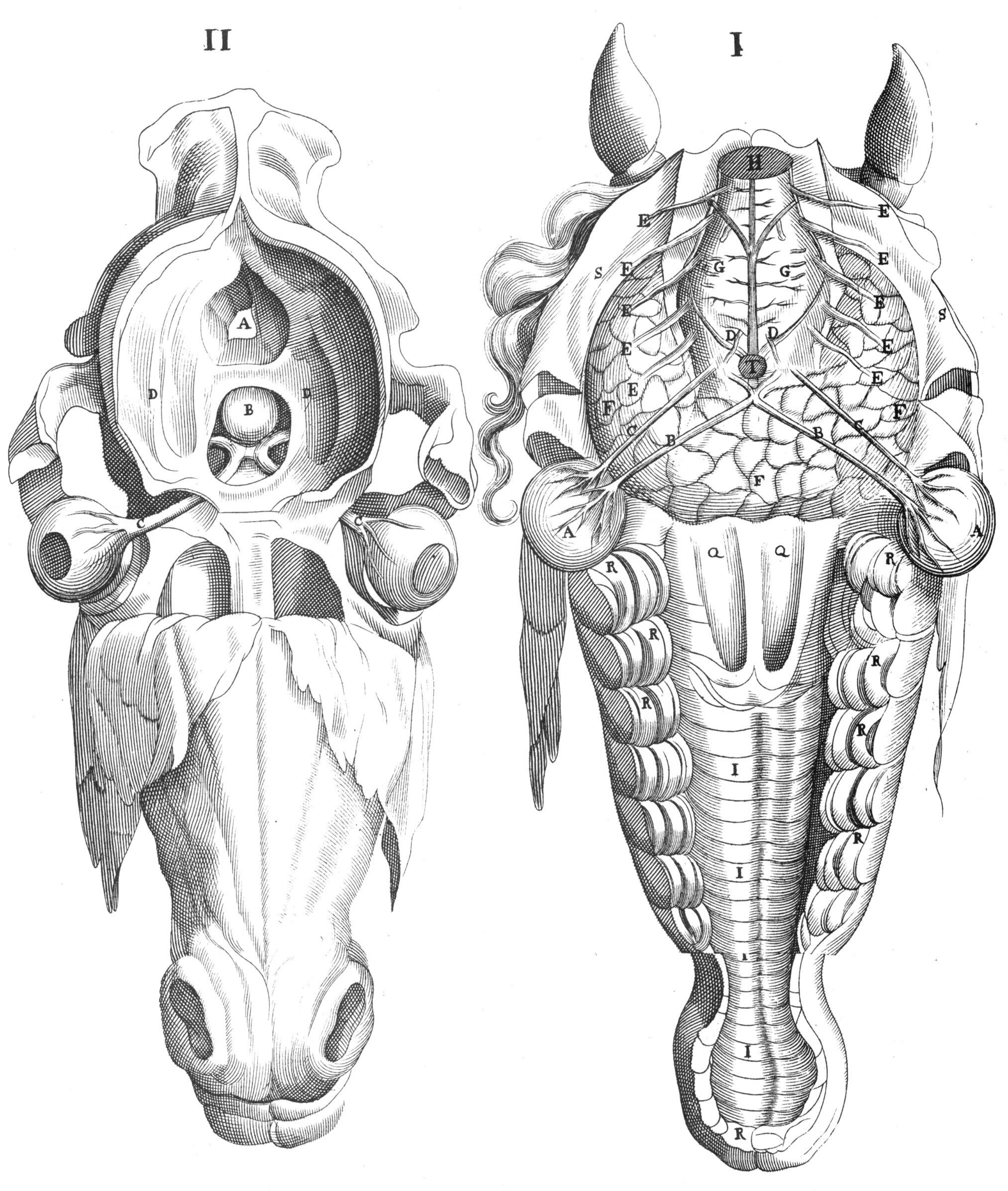
II
A
B
D
D
C
C
I
H
E
E
E
S
E
G
G
E
S
E
D
D
E
E
T
E
E
F
F
C
B
B
C
F
A
A
Q
Q
R
R
R
R
R
R
I
I
I
R

Figure II.

Shews the Skull with the Brain taken out of it.

A *Shews the hole where the Spinal Marrow passeth out of the Skull.*
B *The* Glandula pituitaria *or Flegm-gland.*
CC *The Optick Nerves.*
DD *The bottom of the Skull upon which the Brain did rest.*

After you have thus taken out the Brain and viewed all its Parts as they appear before you dissect it, you will at the very middle of its bottom, a little above the uniting of the Optick Nerves, within the hard Skin or *dura mater*, (for that is in the next place to be taken off and removed, otherwise it will hide all other Parts from you; but that Skin being removed in the place aforesaid, I say) you will find a small round Kernel, in compass about the bigness of a Groat, and something flat and round. Its seat is in a little hole made for that purpose at the very bottom of the Skull, in a Bone called the wedge-like Bone. This will be more plainly seen if you take the Brain out and leave the *dura mater* behind; for then you see it in its natural position, as the letter B in Fig. 2. of the foregoing Table shews it: but if you take the *dura mater* out, this comes out with it. This Kernel is called *Glandula pituitaria*, the snotty or flegmey Kernel, from its office, which is to receive the snotty Excrements of the Brain from the *Infundibulum* or Funnel, and afterward to transmit or convey them away, as some Authors say, into the Palate, from thence to be avoided by the Mouth or Nose. But others will have it, that it is sent into the Jugular Veins by two small ducts or passages, one on each side, being branches of one Trunk that begins at the bottom of the said Gland, and is divided into two, after it has penetrated the wedge-like Bone. Which passages they have found out by injecting Liquors of several colours with a syringe into them, for they have observed the said Liquors to pass into the Veins, but none to come to either the Palate or Nose. By which Experiment they conclude, that whatever *serum* or wheyish or flegmatick Humour issues out of the Ventricles of the Brain through the Funnel, distils not upon the Palate, but is poured again into the Bloud and mixed with it. Whence we may gather that the Rheum or Snot which issueth so plentifully out of the Noses of Horses that have great Colds, and also of glander'd Horses, falls not (as I have my self sometimes thought) from the Brain, but is separated out of the Arteries from the Bloud by the Glands or Kernels of the upper part and inside of the Nose. Which we may the rather believe, when we observe that other Glands are swell'd with Rheum at the same time, as particularly the Kernels under the Horse's Jaws; which is one of the certainest signs we have of a Horse's inclining to the Glanders. And this may serve to convict of errour all our ancient Authors who did hold, (and our Practitioners who at this day do hold) that the Glanders proceed from a defect and wasting in the Brain; and that all that snotty matter comes from thence which issues out of the Nose. Which were it so, all the Brain in the Horse's Head would not be sufficient to supply it with matter for three daies, according to the quantity that I have seen come from one in that time. It is therefore a very false opinion, taken up merely upon guess,

Glandula pituitaria.

From whence the Snot is separated in the Glanders.

gueſs, without inſpecting into the Parts, that our Practitioners do commonly entertain concerning this Diſeaſe.

No ſuch Diſeaſe as the mourning of the Chine.

Neither is there ſuch a Diſeaſe as the mourning of the Chine, as they do to this day hold; for it is impoſſible any Creature ſhould continue ſo long alive as till all his Brain be ſo far waſted by this Diſeaſe, that it comes to reach the Spinal Marrow without the Skull, which is that I ſuppoſe they call the Chine.

But this Diſeaſe, by them called the mourning of the Chine, is diſtinguiſhed into a different Diſeaſe from the former from the Matter's altering its colour; for it is generally obſerved that after the Horſe hath had this Diſeaſe running on him for ſome time, the corrupt Matter or Snot changes by degrees from an indifferent white to a more dull colour, inclining at firſt to a little reddiſh, but after a longer time, eſpecially when the Horſe begins to grow towards his end, it will be very black and very nauſeous both to ſee and ſmell.

From this alteration of the colour, as I have ſaid, I do believe they give the Diſeaſe this proper and diſtinguiſhing name of mourning of the Chine; whereas it is onely a greater degree of one and the ſame Diſeaſe, in which the Chine is not at all affected, at leaſt no more than any other Part of the Body, all of which languiſhes away by this inveterate Diſtemper. By what ſteps it proceeds, and how the Matter comes to alter its colour, I will give you my opinion.

The maſs of Bloud being depraved either by unwholſome Food, or by great Colds, or laſtly by infection from the Air and from other Horſes (for this Diſtemper is catching) this flegmatick Matter collected in it is ſpued out of the ends of the Arteries in the upper part of the Noſtrils, about the ſpongie Bones chiefly; for in an Horſe there is little of this Matter comes out of the Mouth, but it ſtill deſcends by the Noſtrils. This Humour, I ſay, diſtilling out of the Arteries by the ſpongie Bones continually, doth in proceſs of time ſo fill the ſaid Bones with filthy Matter, that like a Sink or Chanel being choaked up with filth, there is not ſo free a paſſage for the Humour, as when the Diſeaſe firſt began; ſo that the Matter by that means is there ſtayed, and by its continuance there it acquires ſo bad a quality that it corrodes and cankers thoſe Bones, and indeed ulcerates and gangrenes all the paſſages of the Noſtrils, till it have mortified and conſum'd them (as happens ſometimes to Venereal Perſons) and at length deſtroy'd the Beaſt: for indeed it is ſeldom or never curable when it is once come truly to be a Canker.

Now by the foulneſs of theſe Bones (as I have ſaid) that Matter or Snot which doth deſcend by theſe paſſages, (which indeed doth at length drivel down in a greater quantity than before, by reaſon of the paſſages being widened from the Parts being gnawn aſunder by the cankered Humour; I ſay that Matter or Snot which doth deſcend after this) is of a contrary colour to what it uſed to be, for it is become more black and wateriſh, mixed with a little Red, and hath a very ill ſmell: but this alteration happens not from the Matter's flowing from a new Part, but is cauſed by reaſon of the foulneſs of the Parts through which it paſſeth, for from thence it hath its dye in a great degree.

Not but that there is yet another cauſe of it, which is the greater foulneſs of the Bloud: for as the beginning of the Diſtemper did proceed from the corruption or depravation of the Bloud, which was become as it were degenerate from its ſpirituous, balſamick and volatiliſed condition, into a flat

flat and vappid ſtate, like to dead Wine; ſo in proceſs of time for want of the Spirits to quicken it, and cauſe the fermentations neceſſary in the proper places of the Body, where the excrementitious parts of the bloud ſhould be thrown off, (there being ſeveral Bowels of the Body appointed to ſeparate, and ſome that have Receptacles to receive the ſame) I ſay, for want of theſe Spirits to cauſe a fermentation whereby the excrementitious parts of the Bloud ſhould be thrown off, ſuch Excrements are collected every day in greater quantity, and acquire a greater degree of malignity, being hardly any part of them diſcharged any other way but this, which is preternatural, and moſt times becomes deſtructive to the Beaſt, after the Diſeaſe hath arrived to this height.

Thus have I given you my opinion concerning this Diſtemper, which though it be new, will I hope to the intelligent Reader appear to be truer than that of our Ancient or Modern Practitioners, few of whom (I may affirm without boaſting) have made ſo diligent an inquiry into this Diſtemper as I with great pains and charge have done; for if they had, they would with great eaſe ſee themſelves in an error, and no more believe that there is or can be ſuch a Diſeaſe as the mourning of the Chine. But enough of this, (though I hope it will not be deemed to be from the purpoſe:) I ſhall therefore return from whence I have digreſſed, and deſcribe the remaining Parts of the Brain.

Having examined ſufficiently the *Rete mirabile* or wonderfull Net, as alſo the Pituitary Gland, if you then remove the *dura mater* quite from the Brain at the baſis or bottom of it, there will appear the head of the Spinal Marrow, ſo much as is contained within the Skull, of which we have treated in a foregoing Chapter. There may be alſo plainly ſeen the riſe of the ſeveral conjugations or pairs of Nerves, of which we will treat at large in a convenient place; alſo the bottom of the Cerebel or After-brain, as the next Table doth demonſtrate to you.

The Infundibulum *or Funnel.*

After theſe you may take a plain view of the end of the *Infundibulum* or Funnel, (a cavity ſo called) which end reaches (before diſſection) to the Pituitary Gland, upon which it pours the flegmatick Excrements of the Brain, as hath been already ſhewed.

This Funnel is ſo called from its ſhape; for above, the head thereof is large; but the lower part, is a long and ſtrait Pipe. By ſome Authors it is called *Pelvis* the Baſin. Its beginning is ſaid to be on the fore-part of the *third* Ventricle, by ſome ſo called, but I could never in a Horſe ſee more than two that I could properly call Ventricles, between which two this Funnel is ſeated, and into which they do empty themſelves, diſcharging their ſerous or wateriſh moiſture into it. This Funnel I have often found near filled with a thickiſh Flegm; and Doctor *Willis* ſays that in an Horſe's Brain he has obſerved it wider than a Gooſe-quill, and full of a clear Water.

Corpora ſtriata, Nates, *and* Teſtes.

Next come we to ſpeak to thoſe Parts of the Brain that lie hid, and cannot well be ſeen without diſſecting of it; and firſt of the *Buttocks* and *Stones*. Theſe are four orbicular Prominences or round Bodies jetting out of the *medulla oblongata* (or head of the Spinal Marrow) of which the two firſt, namely the Buttocks, are largeſt, and the latter (*viz.* the Stones) ſeem to be onely accreſcences to them. The Buttocks ſtand lowermoſt, and adhere to the Brainlet; (as do alſo the Stones.) They are larger than in a Man, and look of a fleſhy colour while they are cloathed with the *pia mater*; but that being removed, they appear yellowiſh,

yellowish, and of a different colour from the rest of the Marrow. But of these we discoursed before at the beginning of the fourth Chapter; as also of the *corpora striata* or utmost ends of the *medulla oblongata*, that adhere to the Brain properly so called.

These four Prominences are by Doctor *Willis* compared to Mole-hills, and are therefore by him so called. They may be plainly seen if you but lift up the hinder part of the Brain after you have separated it from the After-brain, turning it as far back as you can without breaking it.

The Pine-apple Gland. Between these four Prominences, or rather between the two lower of them, to wit the Buttocks, there is placed a certain Glandule or Kernel, which goes by the name of *glandula pinealis*, or Pine-kernel Glandule, from the resemblance it is said to have with the Kernel of a Pine-apple. It is also called the Yard or Prick of the Brain, from its being placed so near the Buttocks and Stones, as also because it resembleth a Man's Yard. This Gland as also the Buttocks and Testicles before-spoken of are represented in the next Table.

Its use. Concerning the *use* of this Glandule there are great disputes among the Learned; but I subscribe to *Bartholin's* opinion, who believeth its use to be the same with that of other Kernels, which is to separate the *Lympha* from the Arterial Bloud.

There is as it were a chink between the Buttocks near this Glandule, which I think fit to mention, because most Authours speak of it. Some give it the name of *Anus* or Arse, others call it *Vulva*; but why they have imposed such names as these upon these Parts, I cannot judge, nor is it worth the while to inquire, seeing they have no other foundation but fancy: however, since they are known by these names, I did think it fit not to pass them by, finding them as plainly to be seen and as easie to be found in Horses as Anatomists find them in Humane Brains.

The Ventricles. I come in the next place to speak to the *Ventricles* of the Brain, which are by some accounted four, by others three; but if dissection be made by beginning from beneath, there will appear onely two: and indeed I could never find more; for that which is called the third, I cannot think to be one, but rather a portion of the other two joined together. Nay, some Authours will have it that there is but one, being onely divided at the beginning, but at the end they unite into and become one common Cavity, as any one that will diligently trace them may observe.

The manner of discovering them. To see these Ventricles you must cut the whole substance of the Brain insunder in or as near the middle as you can guess, dividing the upper from the lower side, whereby you will discover them in the middle of the Brain of that shape as the first Figure of the following Table represents them in: for there they are represented to the life, as much of them I mean, as can be seen without farther dissection; and appear to be of a semicircular or Half-moon shape. But if you cut the Brain further, and so follow their Cavities lightly with a Probe *forwards* down towards the Nose (for there they sink deep into the callous body, or white inner part of the Brain) you will trace them as far as the mammillary Processes; and if *backwards*, you will find them to descend as far as the basis or bottom of the Brain; and then if you will take a view of them when you have laid them so far bare both ways, you will find them to resemble in shape an Horse-shoe.

Their uses. Now the *uses* of these Ventricles according to the divers opinions of Authours are many, but I will follow the most Modern in this point.

First

II

I

First then they are framed for the more easie passage of the Bloud; for along their sides do pass many branches of the Bloud-carrying Vessels, which could not so conveniently be conveyed through the substance of the Brain, lest being compressed by the great weight of it, the passage of the Bloud should have been obstructed, whereas now it hath a free passage.

Another use of them is, to serve for the reception of the serous or wheyie excrement of the Bloud that is separated from it by the glandulous Skin that invests them, and by the *glandula pituitaria*; which serous Humour issuing out of the Arteries, is suckt up again by branches of the Jugular Veins, and is by them returned with the Bloud to the Heart.

In the Membrane that cloaths these Ventricles there is a contexture of small Vessels of both Veins and Arteries, which is called *plexus Choroides*. The Vessels that make up this *plexus*, are little branches of the Carotid Arteries, and some of the internal Jugular Veins interwoven with them. The Skin wherein these Vessels are so interwoven has a great many small Kernels sticking in it, which as I have already said, separate the serous Matter from the Bloud.

In the Anatomical Discourses of Humane Brains there are several other Parts of the Brain considered, as the *fornix*, the *corpus callosum*, the *septum lucidum* and the like, all which are as discernible in the Brains of Horses as in Men, and might therefore as largely be discoursed of: but it being not very material to treat of them, I will for brevity sake but in a manner name them.

First then, that which is called the *corpus callosum*, is the white substance of the Brain, plainly seen when you cut the Brain asunder in the middle to see its Ventricles; for then you may view its white substance which makes the middle part of the Brain; the outside of it being of an Ash-colour, and going by the name of *cortex*, or *the bark*.

The *septum lucidum* is onely the Partition that divides the two Ventricles above-described, some taking it to be a reduplication of the *pia mater*, and others a portion of the Brain.

The *Fornix* or Vault is a kind of an Arch that stands between the Brain and the *medulla oblongata*. It is of a substance like the *corpus callosum*, and is of a triangular figure. Its use is to bear up the upper part of the Brain, that its weight may not press upon the subjacent Parts.

Table XXIII.

Fig. I. Representeth the Ventricles of the Brain with the *plexus Choroides*.

AA *Shew the two Ventricles of the Brain.*
BB *The* corpus callosum *or white substance of the Brain, being the middle part of it.*
CCC *The* Cerebellum *or After-brain.*
DD *The* plexus Choroides *seated in the Ventricles of the Brain.*

Fig. II. Represents the protuberances of the *medulla oblongata* called *Nates* and *Testes*, and also the *Glandula Pinealis.*

D *The* Glandula Pinealis *or Pine-kernel Glandule.*
GG *Those two bunchings out of the* medulla oblongata *called* Testes *or Stones.*
HH *Its other two protuberances called* Nates *or Buttocks.*
II *A Ventricle between the Brainlet and roots of the* medulla oblongata, *by some Authours called the fourth.*
MM *The* Processus Vermiformes *or Worm-like Processes.*
NNN *The other Parts of the After-brain.*
OOO *Part of the* Cerebrum *or Brain to be seen under the After-brain.*

CHAP. VI.

Of the Action of the Brain, and the exercises of the Animal Faculty by the Nerves and Fibres.

HAVING hitherto spoken of the structure of the Brain, and discoursed of all its Parts; I come in the next place to speak of its *Action*, in general, and to shew, according to the opinion of our most Learned and Modern Authours, how the Animal Faculty exerts it self.

The action of the Brain. It is generally agreed that the proper *action* of the Brain (taken in a large sense) is the elaborating of Animal Spirits; which Spirits are conveyed from it by the Nerves into the several Parts of the Body for the performing of the Animal actions or motions; for all voluntary motions are performed by the help of these Spirits.

What the Animal Spirits are made of. These Spirits are made out of the Vital Spirits and Arterial Bloud, as out of their proper matter. And the place wherein, or the principal instrument that elaborates them, is not the Vessels, but the very substance of the Brain, into whose parenchyma or marrowy substance the Bloud and Vital Spirits are extravasated.

Now concerning the manner how this Work is performed there are great controversies amongst the Learned, and many arguments urged by each, which will be too tedious here to recite: I will therefore give you onely the opinion of a late Worthy Authour as delivered in his own words.

How the Animal Spirits enter into the Nerves; "The Heart, says he, is like the *primum mobile* of the Body, to "which the motion of all the Humours that have once past it, is owing. "This by its *systole* impells the Bloud as into all other Parts, so into the "Brain, by the several branches of the *Carotides*, whose innumerable "twigs run partly through the outer *cortex* or greyish part of the Brain, "and partly into the inner medullar or white substance of it. These "twigs of Arteries spring partly from the *Plexus Choroides* and *Rete mi-* "*rabile*, and partly from the *Carotides* themselves immediately. The "superfluous *serum* of the Bloud is separated by the Glands before de- "scribed;

" ſcribed; and that Bloud which is not elaborated into Animal Spirits, is " returned again to the Heart by the Veins. But thoſe particles that are " fit and proper to be converted into them, are extravaſated into the very parenchyma of the Brain, or at leaſt are diſtributed through it by " inviſible capillaries, in which being perfected into Spirits, theſe by the " help of the Fibres or Filaments which the inner part or ſubſtance of the " Brain chiefly conſiſts of, are conveyed into the *Corpora ſtriata* (or " other Proceſſes of the *medulla oblongata* that adhere to the Brain) which " conſiſt of the like Filaments, and by them to the Nerves, whoſe inner " ſubſtance is fibrous like the *medulla* from whence they ſpring. And " the reaſon of this ſucceſſive motion from one to another, is the pulſe of " the Heart, whereby that which comes behind always drives forward " what is before. Whence (ſays my Authour) the true cauſe of an Apo-" plexy (wherein motion and ſenſe are almoſt quite aboliſhed) is from " the obſtruction or compreſſion of the Arteries of the Brain: whereby " both little Bloud and Vital Spirits can be conveyed thither to make " Animal Spirit of; and alſo when it is made, it is not impelled out of " the Brain along the Fibres into the Nerves, to enable them to perform " their functions. Theſe are the words of that worthy Authour concerning this Work.

It remains now to inquire how theſe Spirits, after they are thus elaborated, do perpetually flow from the Brain through the paſſages of the Nerves, and how they enter and fill the ſeveral ſorts of Fibres of which the moving and ſenſitive Parts conſiſt.

And how into the Fibres.

That the Brain and Cerebel are the firſt fountain of the Animal Spirits I have in my foregoing Diſcourſe already ſhewed; from whence they flow along the Nerves as by ſo many rivulets unto differing and diſtant Parts; till at length they paſs out of the moſt capillary Nerves into the ſmall Fibres interwoven in the Membranes, the muſculous Fleſh, and other Parts, and laſt of all into the tendons of the Muſcles, making them the organs of Senſe and Motion: in which Parts becoming more fixed, they are called the *implanted* Spirits, attending their office whenſoever the Nerves with their *influent* Spirits bring from the Brain the inſtinct for performing the ſame.

Whence the Fibres ariſe.

Now concerning theſe *nervous Fibres* in their ſeveral Parts, which are the immediate inſtruments of the Animal Faculty, we ought to inquire from whence they have their riſe: It is plain they do not ariſe immediately from the Head, or any of its marrowy Parts; neither can we reaſonably judge them to ſpring from the Nerves, becauſe the Fibres in moſt Parts do much exceed the bulk or bigneſs of the Nerve that is brought to them, as may be eaſily ſeen by the tendon of every Muſcle, which being made up of united Fibres, is obſerved to be far greater than the Nerve that is inſerted into the Muſcle: ſo that it is unlikely they ſhould be onely continued portions of the Nerves divided or jagged into fine threds, as ſome have imagined; and it is more probable that they are ſpermatick and primigenial Parts, that is, that the rudiments of them were drawn in the firſt formation of the Parts of the Embryo in the Womb, as well and as ſoon as the Nerves themſelves; unleſs one would with Doctor *Willis* except the Fibres of the ſanguineous Parts, which he thinks to be bred ſecondarily of the Bloud and nervous Juice flowing into thoſe Parts.

They can move by the Spirit implanted in them.

One thing further we must note concerning these Fibres, that they are enabled to perform their motion, not onely from the Animal Spirits that flow by the Nerves at the instant of such motion, but also from the Spirits that are stored up in the Fibres themselves; of which any one may satisfy himself in observing an Animal newly killed when its Skin is taken off; for when life is perished, and all the force of the Spirits flowing in through the Nerves hath quite ceased, yet the Spirits implanted in these Fibres breaking forth from the Muscles still move and shake them, and force them into several convulsions and trembling motions. This I have not onely seen my self in several Horses I have caused to be killed on purpose to dissect, but have also shewed it to several Spectators who have been very much pleased at the observation, and at the variety of their motions.

CHAP. VII.

Of the several pair of Nerves arising from within the Skull, particularly of the first, second and third pair.

HAVING sufficiently treated of the Brain and Animal Faculty or Spirits, it is fit that in the next place I should come to speak of the Nerves, beginning according to the order of dissection with those that arise immediately from the Brain, which I find to be of the same number in Horses as Dr. *Willis* hath observed them to be in Humane Bodies, *viz.* nine pair. I will therefore observe the same method, and begin as the said Learned Doctor hath done, with the *smelling Nerves* first, because they are the foremost, and therefore do first appear in dissection.

The first pair of Nerves, viz. the Smelling.

These Nerves are called the *mammillary Processes*, because they are round at their end like a Pap. They take their rise from the shanks of the *medulla oblongata* betwixt the *corpora striata* or chamfered Bodies, and the chambers of the Optick Nerves; from whence running under the bottom of the Brain they do in their course by degrees increase, and become broader and larger, and at length reach as far as the Sieve-like Bone that is seated at the top of the Nostrils. During all which way they are soft and marrowy, (being hollow within and pretty full of moisture) but being arrived at this Bone, they receive a new covering or coat from the *dura mater*, (being clad before onely with the *pia mater*) with which they are divided into many little Fibres or Filaments like little strings, which do many of them pass through the holes of the Sieve-like Bone into the cavities of the Nostrils, where they are distributed on every side, entring into the Membranes that cover those Parts. These Fibres or Filaments which do thus proceed from the before-named Processes, are believed to be the true organs of Smelling, and of Sensation also. From whence it is that those Persons that do not accustom themselves to draw snush up their Noses, are upon the least scent of it provoked to sneeze: which is occasioned by the Powder's ascending up the Nose and resting upon the tender Membranes thereof, wherein the little Fibres of the smelling

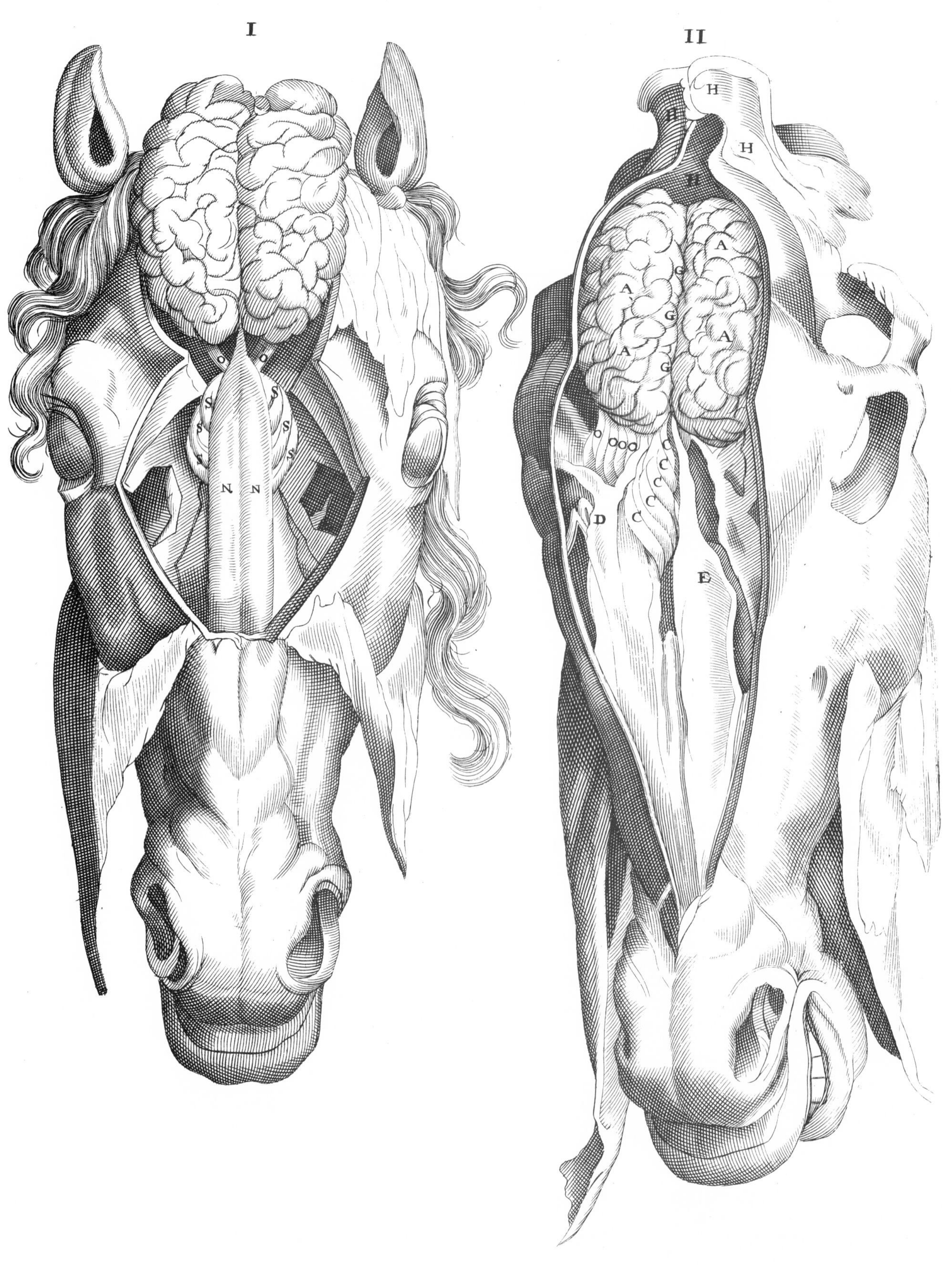
I
II
O
O
S
S
S
S
S
S
N
N
H
H
H
H
A
A
A
A
G
G
G
O
O
O
O
C
C
C
C
C
C
D
E

ling Nerves being diſperſed, are immediatly irritated or provoked into a convulſive motion, which is that we call ſneezing. It was an old opinion that the Snivel was milked as it were out of the Ventricles of the Brain by theſe Proceſſes; but having above in the fifth Chapter ſhewn other Veſſels which diſcharge that flegmatick matter into the Noſe, namely the Arteries, it ſeems more probable that theſe Mammillary Proceſſes have a nobler uſe, namely *that* we have aſcribed unto them, to be the inſtruments of ſmelling. And therefore they are larger in Horſes and all ſorts of Cattle than in Men, becauſe it was neceſſary their Smell ſhould be very exquiſite, ſeeing they can diſtinguiſh of the wholſomneſs or hurtfulneſs of their Food by that Senſe onely.

Table XXIV.

Fig. I. Shews the Mammillary Proceſſes, and the Bones at the upper part of the Noſtrils.

NN *Shew the Cartilaginous or griſtly Bones of the Noſtrils.*
OO *The Mammillary Proceſſes or Smelling Nerves.*
SSSS *The Sieve-like Bone through whoſe holes the Fibres of the Smelling Nerves are branched.*

Fig. II. Shews the Brain in its natural ſituation, and the Parts aforeſaid, &c.

AAAA *Shew the Brain in its natural ſituation covered with the* pia mater.
CCCC *The ſpongy Bones laid bare.*
D E *The griſtly Bones of the Noſtrils.*
GGG *The Partition which divides the upper part of the Brain into two parts, a right and a left.*
HHH *The* os occipitis *or Noll-bone.*
OOOO *The Sieve-like Bone, upon which the Mammillary Proceſſes do reſt.*

Next come we to the ſecond conjugation or pair of Nerves, and thoſe are the *Optick* or Seeing *Nerves*; ſo called, either becauſe they carry the viſive Spirits to the Eyes, or becauſe they convey the repreſentations of viſible things from the Eyes to the Brain. *The ſecond pair, or Optick Nerves.*

Theſe ariſe a little behind the former out of the *medulla oblongata*, and having proceeded a while with a certain compaſs, they are united above the ſaddle of *os ſphenoides*, and that with a total confuſion and mingling of their ſubſtances, as far as by the naked Eye I could ever diſcern in all Horſes that I have diſſected; though ſome Authours ſay that in Humane Bodies they do unite indeed, but that it is onely by contact, without confounding their Fibres with one another.

Theſe Nerves after they are thus united, do ſoon after again ſeparate, and go out of the Skull into the centre of the Eyes, three of whoſe coats are made out of the ſubſtance of theſe Nerves being dilated.

At

At their riſe and a pretty way in their progreſs they are very ſoft, being covered onely with the *pia mater*; but as ſoon as they reach the *dura mater*, they are covered with *it* alſo, and thereby become ſtronger and harder. This outmoſt Membrane it is which doth conſtitute that coat of the Eye called the horney Coat or *ſclerotica*; and from the inner or *pia mater* doth proceed the next Coat or Skin of the Eye called *uvea* or Grape-like, from its colour; and laſtly the marrowy ſubſtance of the Nerve doth make the third Coat called *Retina* or Net-like.

The Senſe of *Seeing* like that of *Smelling* is by Doctor *Willis* ſaid to be performed not ſo much by the help of the Nerve, as of the Fibres which are interwoven with the Organ; namely, ſaith he, the little Fibres in the Coats of the Eyes, and eſpecially thoſe that are inſerted into the *cornea* or ſclerotick Coat, and diſpoſed after the manner of a Net, do receive the impreſſion of the viſible ſpecies, and by repreſenting the image of the thing ſo as it is offered without, cauſe ſight: but it is the office of the Nerve it ſelf to tranſmit inwardly, as it were by the paſſage of an Optick Tube, that image or ſenſible ſpecies, and to carry it to the common ſenſory.

The third pair, or Eye-movers.

The next pair are the *Eye-movers*, which are by Ancient Authours accounted the *ſecond* pair, but do by our Modern Authours go for the *third* pair.

Theſe take their beginning from the baſis or bottom of the *medulla oblongata* behind the *Funnel*, from whence they proceed forwards by the ſides of the Optick Nerves. At their riſe they are united, whence is a reaſon drawn that when one Eye is moved toward any object, the other is directed alſo towards the ſame.

They are ſmaller, yet much harder than the former, and as was ſaid, run along by their ſides untill they come to the *os cuneiforme* or Wedge-like Bone; where, as the Optick Nerves paſſed through the firſt, ſo theſe paſs through the ſecond hole of that Bone, and ſo on untill they come to the Muſcles of the Eyes, into ſeveral if not all of which they ſend a twig or ſmall branch, which is in each Muſcle ſubdivided into innumerable other ſmaller ones, by which the Animal Spirits are conveyed into the Fibres of the Muſcles, and by conſequence the ſeveral motions of the Eye come to be performed, as ſhall be ſhewed at large in a more convenient place, when I come to treat of the Muſcles of the Eyes in the next Book.

CHAP.

CHAP. VIII.

Of the fourth and fifth pair of Nerves that arise within the Skull.

THE *fourth* pair of Nerves do ariſe contrary to all other: for whereas the reſt do take their riſe from the bottom or ſides of the oblong Marrow, theſe have their beginning at the top of it, behind thoſe round bunchings out of the Brain called *Nates* and *Teſtes*, (of which we have already treated where we deſcribed the Parts of the Brain.) From whence bending a little forwards by the ſides of the ſaid oblong Marrow, they are immediately hid by the *dura mater*, under which they run for ſome time, untill they come to that hole of the Skull, where the other Nerves deſigned for the Eyes do paſs out, which theſe accompany, but do not unite with, and at length terminate in the Trochlear Muſcles of the Eyes. *The fourth pair called Pathetick.*

This pair of Nerves are by Doctor *Willis* called the *Pathetick Nerves*, becauſe, ſays he, their office is to move the Eyes *pathetically*, according to the force of the *paſſions* and *inſtincts of Nature*, delivered and remanded from the Brain to the After-brain, and on the contrary from this to that, through the *Nates* and *Teſtes* and their Medullar Proceſſes. For, ſaith that Learned Anatomiſt, ſeeing that by the diverſe impulſe and undulation of the Animal Spirit's dwelling in this by-path, there happen certain mutual commerces between the Brain and *Præcordia* (the Cerebel mediating between either, from whoſe Ring-like Proceſs he will have the Nerves of the *Præcordia* to ariſe;) it is neceſſary that theſe Nerves that are rooted in the middle way, ſhould be ſtruck upon by every march or remove of the Spirits going this way or that way, whereby the motions of the Eyes muſt needs follow the affections of thoſe Parts. With theſe Nerves, (ſaith he) all perfect Animals are furniſhed, there being none but are obnoxious to anger, love, hatred, and other Affections, as may be diſcovered in every little Creature, but much more in this which we are a-diſcourſing of, there being none the aſpect and geſture of whoſe Eyes do ſhew them more than a Horſe's do.

Next come we to treat of the fifth pair, concerning the riſe of which there are ſeveral diſputes amongſt Authours, (Doctor *Willis*, particularly, affirming that they ſpring from the Ring-like Proceſs of the Cerebel:) but if their original be ſtrictly inquired into, I cannot find, in an Horſe, (however it may be in Humane Brains) but that they do take their beginning as the others do, I mean from the oblong Marrow, onely a little below the former pair. *The fifth pair.*

Theſe conſiſt of very many Fibres gathered together, ſome of which are ſoft, and ſome hard; ſo that they ſeem not to be ſo much one ſingle pair of Nerves, as a collection of many ſmall Nerves into one bundle, ſome of which are deſigned for one uſe and ſome for another, being for that purpoſe diſtributed into ſeveral Parts remote one from another; in which they ſerve, in ſome for motion, in others for ſenſe: from whence it is, ſaith Doctor *Willis*, that there is that ſympathy and conſent of actions

actions in thoſe ſeveral Parts to which theſe Nerves are diſtributed. As for inſtance, ſeeing ſome twigs go to the Eyes, others to the Palate of the Mouth, Noſe, *&c.* therefore when we ſee or ſmell what pleaſes our Palate, our Mouth waters, as we commonly phraſe it.

But that it may be better underſtood what and how many Parts have conſent by means of theſe Nerves, it will be convenient to diſcover their diviſion, progreſs and different inſertion. Their Trunks, beginning or ariſing out of the oblong Marrow, as hath been ſhewed, are divided each of them into two notable branches, the firſt whereof tending ſtreight *downwards*, and going out of the Skull by their proper holes, are in their deſcent towards the lower Jaw, (for whoſe Parts, ſaith my Authour, they are chiefly deſign'd) divided into many leſſer branches, which provide for the Temporal Muſcles, as alſo for the Muſcles of the Face and Cheeks. From theſe branches alſo there go twigs or little ſhoots into the Lips, Gums, roots of the Teeth, Jaws, Throat, and to the farther end of the Palate, and alſo to the Tongue.

The other branches of this pair of Nerves are called the *ſuperiour* or uppermoſt branches, being larger than the other, and do thus run their courſe. After their diviſion from the former they go ſtreight forward for a little ſpace under the *dura mater* nigh the ſide of the Bone called the Turkey chair, and over againſt the *glandula pituitaria* ſend little twigs to the Trunk of the *Carotides*, that makes the *wonderfull Net:* then they are inoculated into the Nerves of the ſixth pair, and from thence ſend back ſometimes one, ſometimes two ſhoots a-piece, which being united with two other ſlips turned back from the Nerves of the ſixth pair, do conſtitute the root or firſt trunk of the intercoſtal pair of Nerves, reckoned for the ninth pair, of which more ſhall be ſpoken by and by in the tenth Chapter.

After they have ſent out the ſlips for the root of the Intercoſtal Nerve, theſe ſame great branches of the fifth pair are again divided each into two notable branches; the *leſſer* and upper of which tends towards the globe of the Eye, and being again divided ſends forth two other, the *firſt* of which is parted into two more, that go, one, to the Noſe, and the other to the Eye-lids; and the *ſecond* into four or five ſlips, that are moſtly ſpent on the Eye-lids, but partly on the Coats of the Eye and its Glands.

The ſecond or *greater* branch of the ſecond diviſion of theſe Nerves, being carried towards the orbit of the Eye, is again divided into two new branches: the *lower* of theſe being bent downwards, and cleaving it ſelf into many ſhoots, is beſtowed on the Palate and upper region of the Jaws; the other, being the *higher*, is carried beyond the orbit of the Eye, and paſſeth through a proper hole of the upper Jaw with the Vein and Artery which it twiſts about, and ſends many ſlips to the Muſcles of the Cheeks, Lips, Noſe, and roots of the upper Teeth.

The reaſon of bluſhing.

From this pair of Nerves being diſtributed to ſo many Parts, I ſay, may the conſent of thoſe Parts one with another be learned: and particularly this is worthy obſervation, That ſeeing they twiſt about the Bloud-veſſels that go to the Cheeks, *&c.* hence it is, that when in Men and Women the Animal Spirits are diſturbed by the imagination of ſome uncomely thing; as if they took care to hide the Face, they enter theſe Nerves diſorderly, whereby their twigs that embrace the Bloud-veſſels do compreſs and pull them, ſo that the Bloud comes to flow too impetuouſly into the Cheeks, *&c.* by the Arteries, and is detained there for ſome time

by

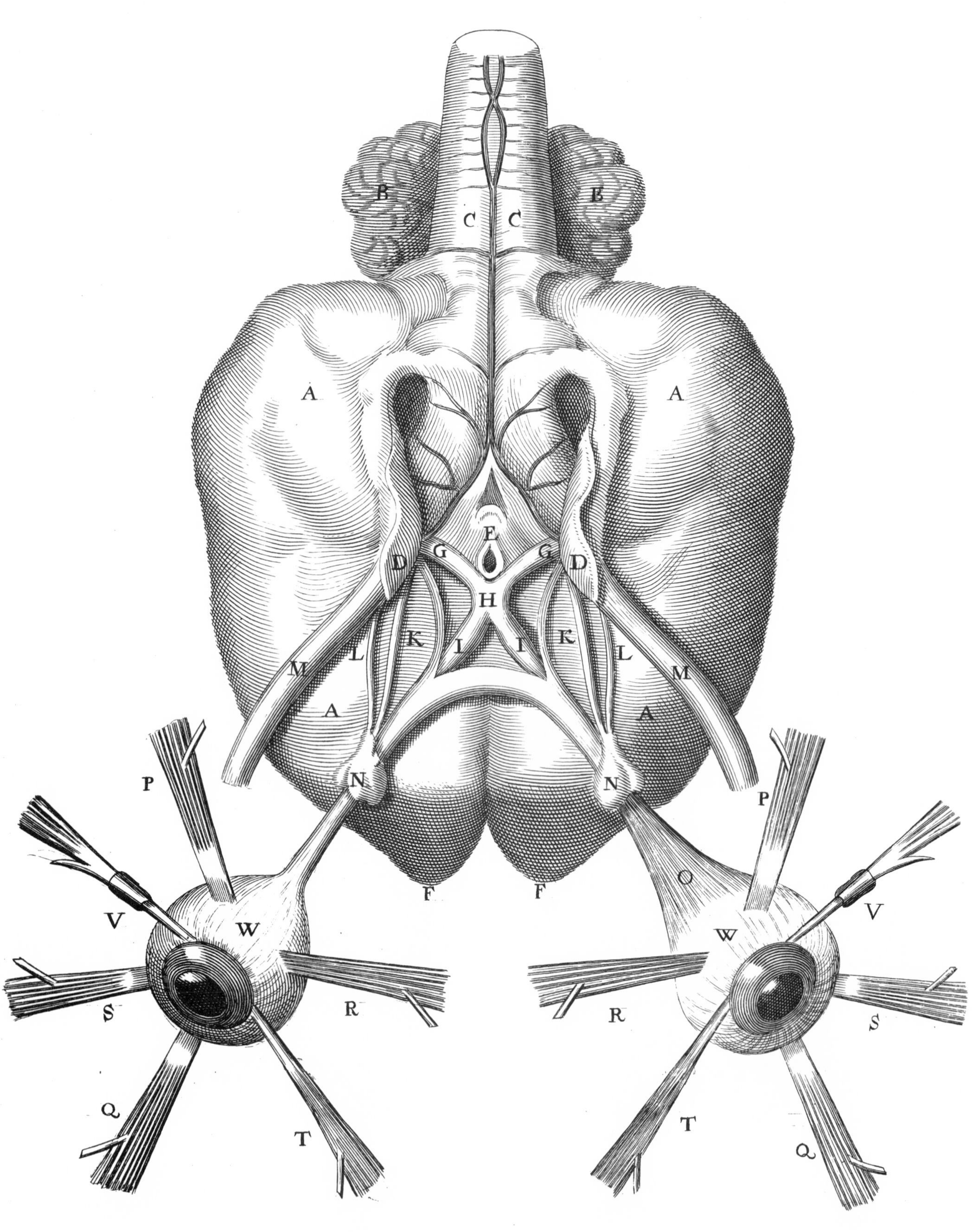
B
B
C
C
A
A
E
G
G
D
D
H
K
K
I
I
L
L
M
M
A
A
P
P
N
N
O
F
F
V
V
W
W
S
R
R
S
Q
T
T
Q

by ſtraitning the Veins. But ſuch obſervations belong more to an Anatomiſt of Humane Bodies to which they are proper, and therefore I ſhall return from this digreſſion, which yet, I hope, will not be unpleaſant to the inquiſitive Reader.

Table XXV.

Repreſents the Brain of an Horſe taken out of the Skull, with the Optick, Eye-moving, and Pathetick Nerves; as alſo the Eyes with their Muſcles faſtned to them, having been taken out of the Skull without tearing or breaking of them.

AAAA *Shew all the bottom of the Brain covered with the* dura mater.
BB *The* Cerebellum *or After-brain.*
CC *Part of the* medulla oblongata, *or head of the Spinal Marrow.*
DD *The* Glandula pituitaria *cut in two in the middle, and turned back to each ſide with the* dura mater, *the better to ſhew the Chink or Funnel.*
E *The Chink called* Vulva.
FF *The Mammillary Proceſſes covered with the* dura mater, *otherwiſe called the Smelling Nerves or the firſt pair.*
GG *The riſe of the Optick Nerves, or ſecond pair.*
H *The uniting of the Optick Nerves.*
II *Their ſeparating again, and their courſe down to the Eyes.*
KK *The moving Nerves of the Eyes or the third pair.*
LL *The Pathetick Nerves reckoned by Doctor* Willis *for the fourth pair.*
MM *Doctor* Willis *his fifth pair of Nerves.*
NN *The heads of the Muſcles of the Eyes, from whence they were all of them cut, to be ſeparated and placed as in the Figure.*
OO *The orbicular Muſcle of the Eye in its natural ſituation in this Eye, but in the other Eye it is quite removed, the plainer to ſhew the courſe of the Optick Nerve to the Eye.*
PP *The Muſcle that pulls up the Eye, called* Attollens, *or* ſuperbus, *the proud Muſcle.*
QQ *The humble Muſcle or puller-down of the Eye, called* humilis.
RR *The Muſcle that brings the Eye inwards to the Noſe, called* Adducens, *or* bibitorius, *the drinking Muſcle.*
SS *The Muſcle that pulls the Eye outward, called* Abducens, *or* indignatorius, *the angry Muſcle.*
TT *The Muſcle that brings the Eye towards its inner corner obliquely, and from that office is called* obliquus inferior.
VV *The* obliquus ſuperior cum trochlea, *whoſe office is to bring the Eye obliquely to its outward corner.*
WW *The horney Tunicle or Coat of the Eye, with the* pupilla *or ſight.*

CHAP. IX.

Of the sixth and seventh pair of Nerves arising within the Skull.

The sixth pair.

THOSE Nerves which are by Doctor *Willis* reckoned for the *sixth* pair, are in the next place to be spoken to. These take their beginning just by the fifth, and being for a little time hid under the *dura mater*, go at length out of the same hole of the Skull with the before-named fourth and fifth pairs, and are carried each with a single Trunk nigh to the Sockets of the Eyes; but so, that near the side of the Turky-chair-bone they are inoculated with the second or greater branches of the fifth pair. Whence they send back sometimes one, sometimes two twigs, which being united with the first or recurring branches of the fifth pair, as was noted in the foregoing Chapter, do constitute the beginning of the Intercostal Nerves. Afterward going a little forwards, each of them near the Orbit or Socket of the Eye, is divided into two branches; one of which is inserted into the Abducent Muscle of the Eye (or the Muscle that draws the Eye outward) which is seated in its outer corner; and the other being split into very many Fibres is bestowed on the seventh Muscle of the Eye, which is said to be proper onely to Brutes. Whether Men do wholly want them, let others examine; however, in the Animal we are treating of, they are very conspicuous and most easie to be found, concerning whose use I will speak when I come to a proper place for that purpose.

The seventh pair, or Auditory Nerves.

Next are the *seventh* pair to be examined, which by the Ancients (and by all untill Dr. *Willis* altered the account) were reckoned for the fifth pair. These are employed about the Sense of *Hearing*, and are therefore called the *Auditory* Nerves. They take their rise in Humane Bodies (according to Doctor *Willis*) out of the lower side of the Annular or ringy protuberance of the Cerebel; but I am sure they do not so in Horses, in whom I have always found them to arise from the sides of the oblong Marrow.

They have each of them two *Processes*, one soft and the other harder; which distinction of them makes many be of the opinion that they are indeed two pair of Nerves, though usually they are accounted but for one.

The *softest* of these two Processes is properly called the *Auditory Nerve*, the which is carried through an hole of *os Petrosum* (or the craggy Bone) into the Cells of the Ear, which it cloaths with a most thin Membrane, and by which the sounds are conveyed to the common Sensory.

The *harder* part or process of the Nerve is said to conduce more to Motion than Sense; which passing out also through its proper hole in the aforesaid Bone doth immediately receive a twig from the eighth or wandring pair; after which it is streight divided into two branches; the first of which tending downward is bestowed on the Muscles of the Tongue and the Bone *Hyoides*; the other winding about the auditory passage and bending more upwards, is divided into *three* Shoots; the *first* of which answering to the Nerve of the former division, bestows certain ſlips on the Muſcles of the Lips, Mouth, Face and Noſe, and ſo actuates ſome of the outward organs of the Voice, as the former doth ſome of the inner. The *ſecond* of theſe Shoots being divided into many other leſſer, is ſent into the Muſcles of the Forehead, as alſo to the Eye-lids. And the *third* or laſt of them doth run towards and ſpreads it ſelf into the Muſcles of the Ears. Whence upon any unuſual and aſtoniſhing ſound the Ear is by a natural inſtinct prickt up, to liſten to it the more attentively, and at the ſame time the Spirits flowing by other branches of this Nerve into the Muſcles of the Eye-lids, cauſe them to be drawn as far aſunder as is poſſible, that the Beaſt may have the clearer view of any threatning danger; which poſture of the Eyes we call *ſtaring*.

CHAP. X.

Of the eighth and ninth pair of Nerves.

THE next pair of Nerves we are to treat of are the *eighth*, (commonly reckoned for the *ſixth*) otherwiſe called the *wandring pair*, from their being diſtributed into many Parts, wandring as it were not onely through the Head and Neck, but through many of the inferiour Parts of the Body both in the Cheſt and Paunch, furniſhing them with Nerves branching from them. *The eighth or wandring pair.*

Theſe Nerves do alſo ariſe out of the oblong Marrow a little below the Auditory Nerves. Their root or beginning conſiſts of many Fibres, ſome of which are ſmaller and ſome thicker, to which is added a notable Fibre or rather Nerve, much greater than the reſt, coming from the Spinal Marrow of the Neck, which is joined with them and wrapped about with one and the ſame Coat taken from the *dura mater*, as if they were but one Nerve. They continue to be thus united till they have paſt without the Skull, after which they are diſperſed to ſeveral Parts. The Acceſſory Nerve is diſtributed to the Muſcles of the Neck and Shoulders: and one notable Fibre of the eighth pair joins it ſelf on each ſide to the harder Proceſs of the Auditory or ſeventh pair, as alſo two others run to the Muſcles of the Gullet and Neck. But the reſt of the Fibres of the wandring pair continue together, going forward in one Trunk; and inſtead of the other companion lately parted from them (I mean the Spinal or Acceſſory Nerve) they entertain a new one, which is the Intercoſtal, or Nerve of the ninth pair.

In this place where the ſaid Intercoſtal Nerve is united with this Nerve of the eighth pair, there is made a notable *Plexus*, (that is, the Trunk of the Nerve in that place ſwells into a kind of tumour, reſembling the joint or knot of a Cane.) For as the Intercoſtal Nerve is received *into* it, ſo *out* of it there ſprings a conſiderable branch, which being carried towards the Throttle is divided into three twigs; the *firſt* of which is ſtretched out into the ſphincter of the Gullet; the *ſecond* being hid under the Shield-faſhioned Griſtle, diſtributes its Shoots to the upper Muſcles of the Throttle, and particularly to the Muſcle by which the Chink of the

Throttle is ſhut up. The *third* of theſe ſhoots or twigs going alſo under the Shield-faſhioned Griſtle, meets the top of the Recurring Nerve and is united with the ſame.

Below the aforeſaid inoculating of the Intercoſtal with the wandring pair, which makes that *Plexus* before-named, the Trunk of this latter goes ſtreight down by the ſides of the aſcending Carotid Artery, on which it beſtows ſome ſlips, and at the bottom of the Neck it ſends out another twig into the Recurrent Nerve, but this it does onely on the left ſide.

From hence the Trunk of the wandring pair deſcends without any noted branchings till it comes over againſt the firſt or ſecond Rib, where out of a ſecond *Plexus* many ſhoots and numerous Fibres are ſent forth towards the Heart and its appendages, but not altogether in the ſame manner on both ſides. Doctor *Willis* ſays, many more branches are ſent from this pair towards the Heart in Beaſts than in Men; for in theſe latter there are a great many twigs ſent thereto from the Intercoſtal pair, whereas there are very few in Brutes; ſo that in both, the plenty of the one ſupplies the defect of the other.

There is (ſaith the ſame Authour) one notable difference worthy of note, of the two Recurrent Nerves that ſpring out of the Trunk of this eighth pair, *viz.* that that on the right ſide ariſes out of it higher, and winds about the Axillar Artery; whereas that on the left ſprings much lower therefrom, and twiſting about the deſcending Trunk of the *Aorta*, returns back from thence, and aſcends upwards where in its progreſs it ſends forth ſhoots to divers Parts.

And that obſervation of the ſaid Doctor is worthy to be taken notice of, *viz.* That the Nerves that paſs towards the Heart of Brutes are much fewer in number than thoſe in Men, of which (as alſo of their proceeding chiefly from the wandring pair) he gives this ingenious reaſon; That ſeeing Beaſts want prudence, and are not much liable to various and divers paſſions, it was not therefore neceſſary that there ſhould be two ways of deriving the Spirits from the Brain to the *Præcordia*, namely one to bring Spirits to maintain the exerciſe of the vital function, and the other to miniſter to the impreſſions of the affections; but it is ſufficient that all the Spirits, for whatſoever office they are deſtin'd, ſhould be conveyed thither by one and the ſame path.

Over againſt the Heart, the *Trunk* of the wandring pair ſends forth many notable branches on either hand, which paſſing to the Lungs, are diſtributed through their whole ſubſtance along with the Bloud-veſſels and branches of the Wind-pipe, which they climb upon and twiſt about: and as it deſcends by the ſides of the Wind-pipe, it diſtributes alſo many ſlips into the Coats of the Gullet. After theſe branches have grown out of theſe Nerves, then is each Trunk, as it deſcends by the Gullet, divided into an *outer* and *inner* branch: but preſently the outer branches unite with the outer, and the inner with the inner; and being ſo united, the *former* deſcends by the outſide of the orifice of the Stomach to its bottom, where it diſperſes it ſelf; and the *latter* deſcending by the inſide of the orifice of the Stomach, turns back there, and creeps along its upper part. To what other Parts the twigs of this eighth or wandring pair are extended, the Reader may learn in the deſcription of the Parts themſelves, in treating of which we have conſtantly obſerv'd to ſhew from whence their Nerves were derived.

After the *wandring* or *eighth* pair, by order of diſſection the *ninth* and laſt pair of Nerves that ſpring from within the Skull are to be ſpoken to. Concerning the riſe of which pair, there are various opinions; for ſome there be that will have them onely branches of the wandring pair, and that they take their beginning from them: but that opinion is rejected, ſince it is now made very apparent that they have another original, of which the often before-cited Doctor *Willis* was the firſt diſcoverer, whom I may be bold to follow, ſince none have given, nor 'tis probable can give a better account of them than that Learned man, who ſaith that the beginnings, (as alſo the different Trunks in the progreſs) of theſe Intercoſtal Nerves are eaſily diſtinguiſhed from the former, notwithſtanding they do often communicate or join together by branches ſent forth from one to the other.

The ninth or intercoſtal pair.

But though they owe not their original to the wandring pair, and much leſs are to be reputed as branches of them, yet have they no proper root of their own, but do borrow their original from two or three recurring branches of the fifth and ſixth pairs near their origine, growing out of them as a Shrub upon another Tree or Shrub.

Theſe Nerves thus conſtituted do afterward run out of the Skull by their proper holes, and preſently on each ſide form a *Plexus* near that of the wandring pair, into which two Nervous Proceſſes out of the firſt vertebral pair are inſerted, and out of which there goes one twig or ſlip into the Sphincter of the Gullet, and another into the *Plexus* aforeſaid of the wandring pair. Whence deſcending by the *vertebræ* of the Neck,by that time they arrive at its middle, they have each another greater *Plexus*, into which a large Nerve from a neighbouring vertebral pair is inſerted,and from which proceed ſome twigs that uniting with others of the wandring pair are diſtributed all about the *Præcordia*, (that is, to the Heart and Lungs) as alſo one ſingle one a little lower. 'Tis true, Doctor *Willis* affirms that this *Plexus* laſt ſpoken of is *proper to Man onely*; but ſince I find ſo little difference in the other Parts between a Man and the Animal I am treating of, I ſuſpend my belief whether this *Plexus* may not be found in him alſo, though I have not been yet ſo diligent as to make any exact inquiry into it.

This *Plexus* is called the *Plexus cervicalis*, becauſe it is formed in the Neck; whence the Trunks of this Intercoſtal pair deſcending by the *Claviculæ* or Chanel-bones into the Cheſt, as ſoon as they have arrived at the ſecond Rib, each of them receives three or four branches from the Vertebral Nerves next above, whereby is made another notable *Plexus*, commonly called the Intercoſtal. From whence as its Trunks paſs down by the roots of the Ribs, in every one of their Interſtices, and even as low as the *Os ſacrum* from every jointing of the *Vertebræ* each Trunk receives a Vertebral Nerve.

As ſoon as they are deſcended out of the Cavity of the Cheſt, and are come over againſt the bottom of the Stomach, they ſend forth on each ſide a notable branch, each of which tending towards the Meſentery makes its chief *Plexus's*, being in number ſeven, *viz.* five large ones which are *upper*, and two leſs that are *lower*. For each branch is preſently divided into two other, and every one forms one *Plexus*, which make four; and the fifth is in the middle of theſe, being the largeſt: and theſe are the five *upper*.

The

The two *lower Plexus* are framed of two branches that ſpring from the Trunks deſcended as far as the lower part of the Loyns, and are diſtinguiſhed by the names of *Plexus infimus,* and *minimus,* (*i. e.* the loweſt, and the leaſt) which two *Plexus* do furniſh ſeveral Parts of the Lower Belly with Nerves.

Laſtly, When this Intercoſtal pair have deſcended as low as the *Os ſacrum,* and have furniſhed in their courſe the ſeveral Parts of the Lower Belly with Nerves, they bend towards one another and ſeem to be knit together by two or three Proceſſes, and at length each of them ends in ſmall Fibres which are diſtributed into the Sphincter Muſcle of the Arſe.

Thus have I given a deſcription of the ſeveral pairs of Nerves ariſing within the Skull, in deſcribing of which I muſt own my ſelf obliged to ſeveral worthy Authours, whoſe Doctrine I have been forced much to follow and relie on in this particular, having not as yet made a thorow inſpection into theſe moſt curious Inſtruments of the Animal Faculty my ſelf: the chiefeſt of which Authours and whom I have moſt followed, is that accurate Tracer of them, Doctor *Willis,* to whom all that have treated of theſe Parts ſince him, have been ſo much beholding. But onely where he aſſigns ſome differences betwixt the courſe of the Nerves in Men, and *all* Brutes *in general,* I cannot eaſily acquieſce in his opinion in relation to a Horſe, the frame of whoſe Body comes almoſt in all reſpects ſo near to that of a Man's; however, till I have made a more exact ſcrutiny, I ſhall forbear contradiction.

Table XXVI.

Shews the baſis or bottom of the Brain of an Horſe taken out of the Skull, having the *dura mater* removed, the better to ſhew the riſe of all the Nerves, and the other Parts of the bottom of the Brain.

AAAA *Shew the ſubſtance of the baſis or bottom of the Brain.*

BB *The Cerebel or After-brain placed in the hinder part of the Head.*

CC *The Oblong Marrow.*

DD *The Smelling Nerves, being the firſt pair.*

EE *The Optick Nerves, being the ſecond pair.*

FF *The third pair of Nerves, which move the Eyes.*

GG *The fourth pair of Nerves, by Doctor* Willis *called the* Pathetick Nerves.

HH *The fifth pair.*

II *The ſixth pair.*

KK *Doctor* Willis *his ſeventh pair, being the Auditory Nerves, which went formerly for the fifth pair.*

LLlll *The eighth pair of Nerves, called otherwiſe the wandring pair, which before Doctor* Willis *were reckoned for the ſixth pair.*

MM *The Spinal Nerves, or Acceſſory pair, that unite with the wandring pair.*

NN *The ninth pair.*

OO *The tenth pair (or rather the firſt of the Neck) ariſing from the further or hinder part of the Oblong Marrow near its going out of the Skull.*

PP *The Trunk of the Carotid Artery cut off where it is divided into the fore and hinder part.*

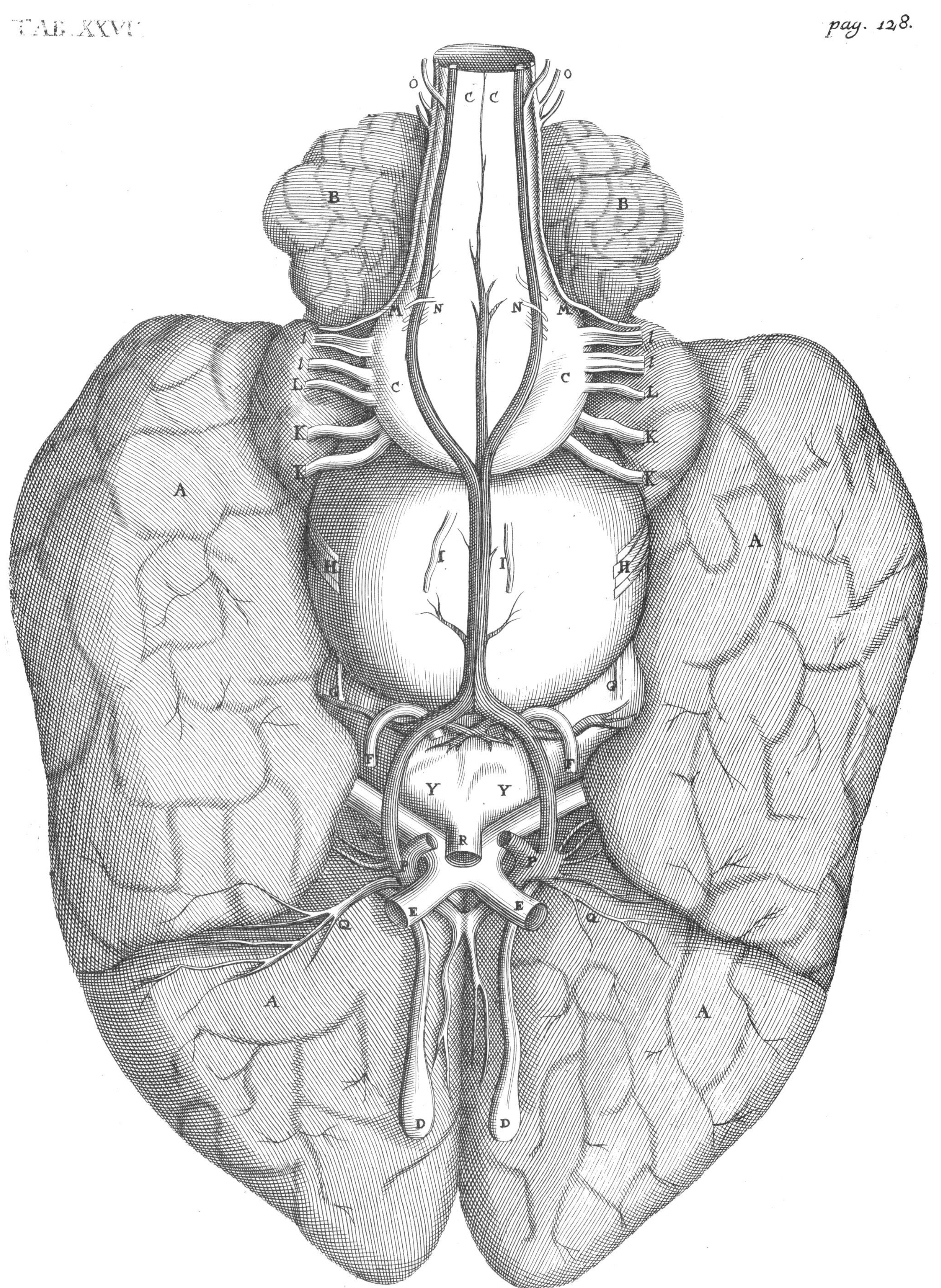
O
C C
O
B
B
M N
N M
C
C
L
L
K
K
K
K
A
A
H
I
I
H
G
G
F
F
Y
Y
R
P
P
E
E
Q
Q
A
A
D
D

QQ *A branch of it going into the ſubſtance of the Brain.*
R *The* Infundibulum *or Funnel.*
SS *Two Glands or Kernels placed behind the Funnel.*

CHAP. XI.

Of the Nerves ariſing from the Spinal Marrow, while it is in the Vertebræ *of the Neck.*

HAVING treated of the ſeveral Conjugations or Pairs of Nerves which take their beginning from that part of the Spinal Marrow contained *within* the Skull, the uſual and moſt natural method requires me next to proceed to thoſe that ſpring from that part of it that is contained in the *Vertebræ* of the Neck and Chine without the Skull.

We obſerved in a Chapter above, that in its whole progreſs from the Skull to the Rump-bones there ſpring from it thirty ſeven pair of Nerves. Particularly, while it is in the Neck, there ariſe out of it ſeven pair; while it is in the Back, ſeventeen pair; while it is in the Loyns, ſeven pair; and while it is in the *Os ſacrum*, ſix pair: for as was noted before, ſuch is the number of the Joints in the Rack-bone, betwixt every of which a pair of Nerves iſſues. Of all which we will treat briefly in order. *Thirty ſeven pair of Nerves ſpring out of the Spinal Marrow.*

The *firſt* pair of the *Neck*, though it be commonly reckoned among the pairs of the Spine or Rack-bone, becauſe it comes out from between the firſt *Vertebra* and the Skull; yet if we conſider its riſe, it ought rather to be reputed the *tenth* pair of the Brain; for it riſes with many Fibres from the Spinal Marrow while it is yet within the Skull, but preſently after its riſe tends backwards or downwards (whereas all the reſt that ariſe within the Skull go forwards.) This pair is chiefly beſtowed on the Muſcles of the Neck. *The firſt pair of the Neck.*

The *ſecond* pair comes out between the firſt and ſecond *Vertebræ* of the Neck, and is beſtowed upon the Neck, Head and Face. *The ſecond.*

The *third* and *fourth* pair come forth of the holes that are between the ſecond and third, and the third and fourth *Vertebræ*, and are ſpread into the Muſcles of the Cheeks, as alſo into the Muſcles that are common to the Head and Neck. *The third and fourth.*

The *fifth* ſpringeth forth between the fourth and fifth *Vertebræ*. A twig from each Nerve of this pair, being joined with the like twigs of the fourth and ſixth, do make that remarkable Nerve that goes to the Midriff, and is called *Nervus Phrenicus.* The other branches of this fifth pair are diſtributed ſome of them backward and ſome forward into ſeveral Muſcles; ſome of which do bow the Head; other twigs run toward the Fore-legs, and are diſtributed into ſeveral Muſcles about the Shoulders. *The fifth.*

The *ſixth* pair cometh out under the fifth *Vertebra*, and hath, as the reſt, ſeveral branches; ſome of which go to the Muſcles of the Fore-legs, and ſome to the Muſcles of the Neck; but one particular twig helps to make *The ſixth.*

make up the Trunk of the *Nervus Phrenicus,* joining it ſelf with the aforeſaid twigs of the fourth and fifth pairs.

The ſeventh. The *ſeventh* pair cometh out of the hole common to the ſixth and ſeventh *Vertebræ,* which joining with the foregoing pair, *viz.* the ſixth of the Neck, and likewiſe with the two following, *viz.* the two firſt of the Cheſt, is diſperſed into ſeveral Muſcles of both the Shoulders, alſo to the Neck and Cheeks.

The Acceſſory Nerve, that aſcends to the Brain, and unites with the wandring pair. About where this ſeventh pair of Nerves ariſes, there ſprings another, found out by Doctor *Willis,* and by him called *Nervus ad par vagum acceſſorius,* which aſcends up by the ſides of the Spinal Marrow (growing in its courſe thicker and thicker) untill it reach up to the Skull, during which way it continues in one body without ſending any branches to any Part. When it has entred the Skull, it then joins it ſelf with the Fibres of the eighth pair of the Brain called the wandring pair, with which it takes its progreſs out of the Skull, but preſently after ſeparates from them, and is diſperſed into the Muſcles of the Neck and Shoulders, as was ſhewed before in the foregoing Chapter, while we diſcourſed of the wandring pair.

CHAP. XII.

Of thoſe Nerves that ariſe out of the Spinal Marrow whilſt it is in the Vertebræ *of the Back, Loyns, and* Os ſacrum.

FROM the Marrow of the Back proceed ſeventeen pair of Nerves, there being in an Horſe ſo many Spondyls or Back-bones; which number exceeds that of the Joints of the Back in Humane Bodies, there being in *them* but twelve, and ſo accordingly they have no more than twelve pair of Nerves from the Marrow within the Back.

The firſt pair of the Back. The *firſt* of theſe pairs ſpringeth out of the hole which is common to the laſt *Vertebra* of the Neck and the firſt of the Cheſt: Each of them (as are likewiſe all the following) is preſently divided into two branches, of which the *formore* is larger than the *hinder.* The *formore* joineth it ſelf with the two laſt of the Neck, and ſo goeth the greateſt part of it to the Fore-legs; onely one little twig that ariſeth out of it before ſuch conjunction, is beſtowed upon ſome of the Muſcles of the Breaſt and Neck; and the ſmaller which is the *hinder,* is beſtowed upon the Muſcles ſeated on the Back.

The ſecond pair. The *ſecond* pair ſprings out between the firſt and ſecond *Vertebræ* of the Cheſt, whoſe *formore* branch being united with the firſt of the Cheſt, together with it is joined with the ſixth and ſeventh of the Neck, which all together make one *Plexus,* out of which proceed moſt of the Nerves that are inſerted into the Muſcles of the Shoulders and Fore-legs. But before the aforeſaid formore branch unite with the foregoing, it ſends forth a twig to the Intercoſtal Nerve (or Nerve of the ninth pair) deſ-

cending

cending down the *Thorax* or Cheſt, as alſo do all the reſt of the remaining fifteen pair.

That branch of this pair which is called the *hinder* branch, hath the ſame diſtribution with the hinder of the foregoing pair, and therefore I will omit ſpeaking particularly of it: Neither do I think it neceſſary to treat of every particular of the remaining pairs that proceed from the Marrow of the Back; firſt, becauſe my deſign is to be as brief as poſſible both in theſe and all other Parts, that I may not make my Volume ſwell too big; and in the next place, the remaining pairs coming out of the ſeveral holes betwixt the jointings of the other Bones of the Back as theſe already ſpoken of do out of the former, it would be but repeating almoſt the ſame things over again ſo to deſcribe particularly every pair. I will therefore onely ſpeak thus much of them in general, that after they are come out of their ſeveral holes of the *Vertebræ*, they do each of them immediately divide themſelves into two branches, whereof the *formore* (being, as hath been ſaid, the larger) ſends one twig to the Intercoſtal Nerve, and the remainder of it is beſtowed on the Muſcles between the Ribs, called the Intercoſtal Muſcles, both external and internal, and a few twigs alſo upon the other Muſcles of the Cheſt that lie upon the Ribs; and laſtly, a twig or two on the obliquely deſcending Muſcles of the Lower Belly. The *hinder* and leſſer branches preſently upon the diviſion bend backward to the Spine, and are ſpent upon the Muſcles and Skin of the Back. *The remaining fifteen pair.*

Next come we to ſpeak to thoſe Nerves that ſpring from that part of the Spinal Marrow that is contained within the *Vertebræ* of the *Loyns*, which are in number ſeven pair according to the number of Bones in that Part. The *firſt* of which cometh out between the firſt *Vertebra* of the Loyns and the laſt of the Back. Each of them, like thoſe of the Back, is preſently divided into two branches; the *formore* of which is beſtowed upon the fleſhy part of the Midriff, eſpecially its two Proceſſes, and partly on the Muſcle *Pſoas*; and the *hinder* of them is inſerted into the *Muſculus longiſſimus* or longeſt Muſcle of the Back. *The firſt pair of the Loyns.*

The *ſecond* pair come out between the firſt and ſecond *Vertebræ* of the Loyns under the Muſcle *Pſoas*; the *formore* of whoſe branches is beſtowed upon the Muſcle that fills up the Cavity of *Os Ileum* or Haunch-bone (which Muſcle is the ſecond bender of the Thigh) alſo a twig of it is ſent to the *Muſculus faſcialis*, and to other neighbouring Parts. The *hinder* branch paſſeth into the Buttock Muſcles, and doth loſe it ſelf in the bodies of thoſe Muſcles. *The ſecond pair.*

The *third* pair of theſe Nerves of the Loyns come forth between the ſecond and third *Vertebræ* of the Loyns, from under the Muſcle *Pſoas*, as the former did. The *fore* branch is diſperſed down the hinder Leg to the Cambrel or Hock, furniſhing ſeveral Muſcles about thoſe Parts with Nerves. The *hinder* branch is bent back and diſperſed through the Muſcles of the Loyns, ſupplying them with Nerves. *The third pair.*

The other four pair of theſe Nerves of the Loyns, like the former, come forth from between the other four *Vertebræ* of the Loyns. Their *fore* branches are diſperſed into moſt of the Muſcles of the Buttocks and hinder legs; alſo ſome twigs are ſent from them to the Muſcles that raiſe the Yard, ſome others to the neck of the Bladder; and in Mares ſome twigs are ſent to the *Matrix* or Womb. And the *hinder* branches are carried backward, and are beſtowed upon ſeveral Muſcles of the Back. *The remaining four pair.*

In the next place I come to treat of the remaining Conjugations or pairs of Nerves that ſpring from the Spinal Marrow, which are thoſe that come forth of the holes of *Os ſacrum*, and are in number ſix pair, there being in the ſaid Bone ſix *Vertebræ*, with pretty wide holes for the coming forth of the Nerves.

The firſt pair of Os ſacrum. The *firſt* of theſe pair iſſueth out between the laſt *Vertebra* of the Loyns and the firſt of *Os ſacrum* in the ſame manner as thoſe that ſpring out of the *Vertebræ* of the Loyns, and like them is divided into two branches; the *foremoſt* of which is a great part of it mixed with thoſe other of the *Loyns*, and with them runs down to the hinder Legs, ſupplying ſeveral Muſcles of thoſe Parts with Nerves. And the *hinder* furniſheth the biggeſt Buttock-muſcle and other Parts thereabouts with Nerves.

The remaining five pair. This pair of Nerves, as I have ſaid, come out ſide-ways like the Nerves of the Loyns, and are divided like them afterwards into a *fore* and a *hinder* branch; but the other five pair come out before and behind; but before they go out of the Bone, they are on each ſide double, and on each ſide one Nerve goes into the fore-parts and the other into the hinder. Thoſe that go into the hinder-parts are diſperſed as thoſe of the Loyns were, that is, into the Muſcles that lie upon the *Os ſacrum*, and *Ileum*; but thoſe that go into the fore-parts are diſperſed into ſome Muſcles on the fore-part of the Thigh; alſo ſome twigs of them are ſent to the Cods, the Bladder, and to the Muſcles of the Fundament.

Table XXVII.

Repreſents all the Nerves of the whole Body, as well thoſe that ariſe from the Oblong Marrow within the Skull, as thoſe that ſpring from the Spinal Marrow without the Skull, (taken out of a French Authour.)

AAAAAA *Moſt of the Nerves that ſpring from the Oblong Marrow within the Skull.*

B *The ſaid Oblong Marrow.*

CC *The Eyes with the optick and moving Nerves branched to them, the one making their Coats, and the other ſerving to move them.*

DD *Doctor* Willis *his eighth pair or the wandring pair of Nerves, with their courſe through the Middle and Lower Belly.*

From the Figure or Cipher 1 *to* 7. *are ſhewn the Nerves that ſpring from the Spinal Marrow while it is in the* Vertebræ *of the Neck.*

From the Figure 1 *to* 17. *are ſhewn thoſe that ſpring from it while it is in the* Vertebræ *of the Back.*

From the Cipher 1 *to* 7. *are ſhewn thoſe that ariſe out of it while it is contained within the* Vertebræ *of the Loyns.*

From the Cipher 1 *to* 6. *are ſhewn thoſe that ariſe out of it while it is in the* Os ſacrum, *which Nerves are branched into all the hinder Parts and down the hinder Legs, imparting to them both Senſe and Motion.*

Thus have I given a brief deſcription of the ſeveral Conjugations or Pairs of Nerves that ſpring from the Spinal Marrow, ſhewing where they ariſe, which way they paſs, and to what Parts they run; which may

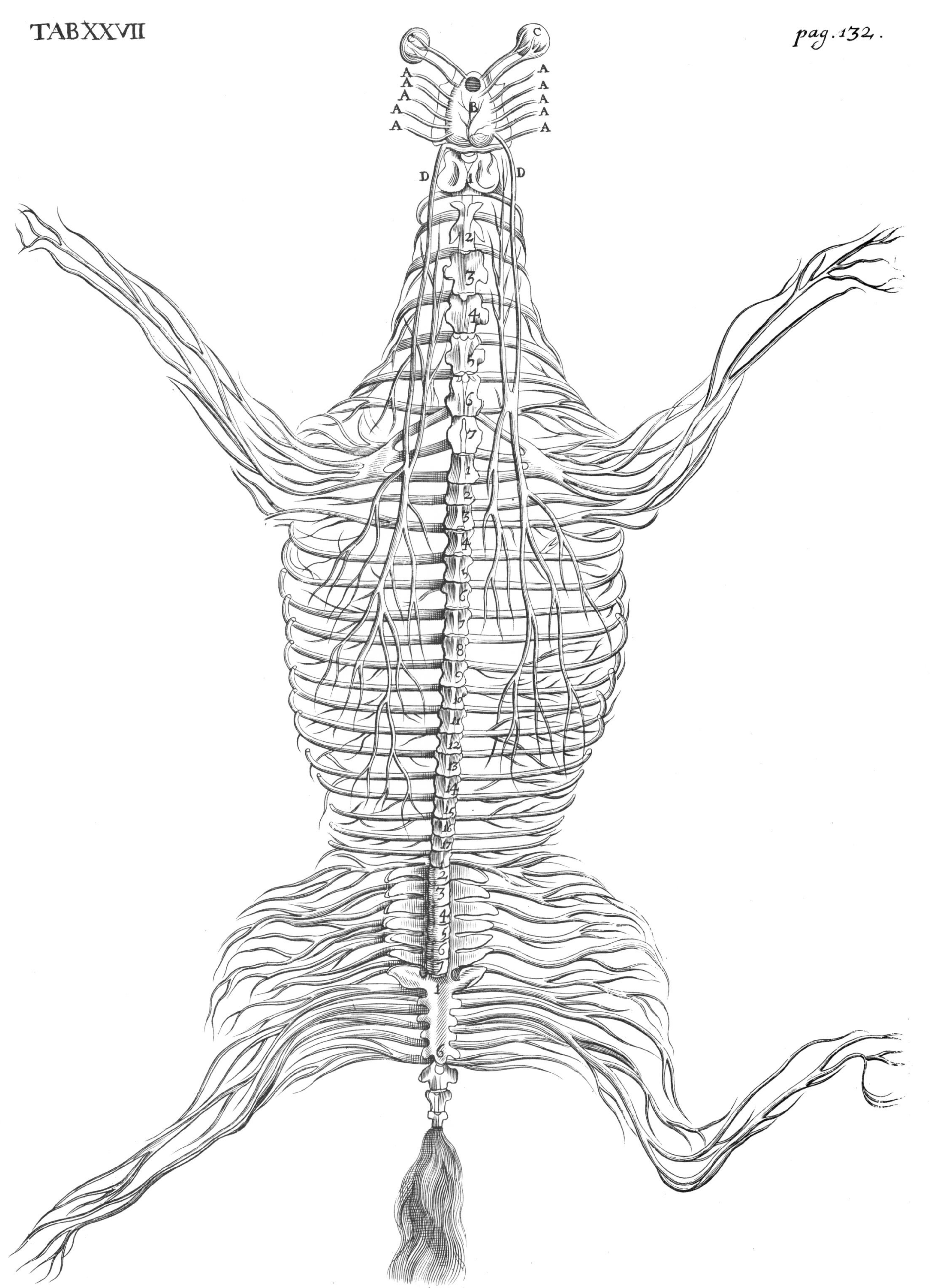
C
C
A
A
A
A
A
A
A
A
A
A
B
D
D

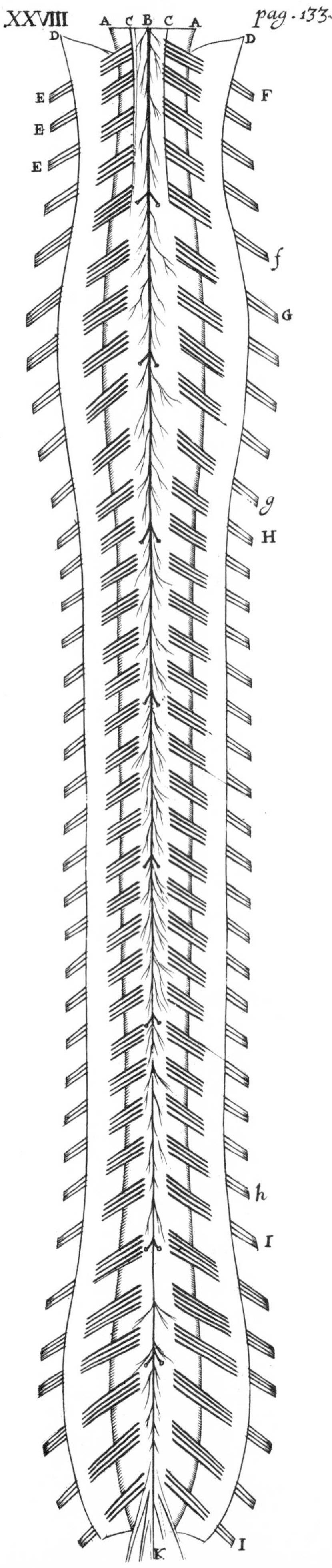
A C B C A
D
D
E
E
E
F
f
G
g
H
h
I
E
I
K

may be of great uſe to our Practitioners, if they will but take the pains to inquire into this part of Anatomy; for by underſtanding the beginning or riſe of the Nerve that furniſheth an affected Part, one may learn where to apply the Remedy. As for inſtance; When from any outward cauſe, as from a fall, ſtroke, bruiſe or any other accident, any Part hath loſt either Senſe or Motion or both; or from any inward cauſe a Palſie happens, by which the uſe of ſome particular Limb is taken away; it would conduce very much to the cure if the riſe of the Nerves of ſuch Part were known by the undertaker of the cure of thoſe Affections; for the Medicine is to be applied always to the beginning or riſe of that Nerve that paſſes to that Part, or as near to it as is poſſible.

I ſhould here put an end to this diſcourſe of the Spinal Nerves, if it were not convenient to add a word of the manner how they ariſe out of the Marrow, which is very accurately deſcribed thus by Doctor *Willis.*

How the Nerves ſpring out of the Spinal Marrow.

"On each ſide of the Spinal Marrow, near its outer edge four or five "Fibres ariſe in its upper ſide, and as many in its lower: both which "companies penetrate firſt the *pia mater* or inmoſt Coat of the Spinal "Marrow, and then the *dura mater* or middle Coat, (which is as it were "a common caſe to them all) with *diſtinct* Fibres: but afterwards as "both companies of Fibres are to paſs through the third Membrane (for "the Spinal Marrow has three) they meet together, and being inveſted "with the Coat they borrowed from the ſecond Membrane, they become "as it were one Trunk: which Trunk paſſing out of the jointing of the "*Vertebræ,* is again divided into ſeveral Nerves deſign'd for ſundry Parts. "After this manner in the whole tract of the Spinal Marrow have the "ſeveral vertebral Nerves their origine; and in thoſe places where the "brachial (*or fore-leg*) and crural Nerves paſs out, the Spinal Marrow "encreaſes both in thickneſs and breadth, and the nervous Fibres are lar-"ger. All which that it may be the better apprehended, I have thought good to annex the following Figure from Him, onely encreaſing the number of the pairs of Nerves as they are found to be in an Horſe.

Table XXVIII.

Shews the Spinal Marrow taken whole out of the Rack-bone, where the Membrane that cloatheth it is diſſected and turned back on each ſide, the better to ſhew the beginnings and productions of all the vertebral Nerves, (from Doctor *Willis.*)

AA *Shew the top of the Spinal Marrow, where it is cut off from the Oblong Marrow.*

B *The Spinal Artery ſeeming to deſcend through the whole Marrow, which however is made up of Arteries brought into it from between the ſeveral jointings of the* Vertebræ.

CC *The Spinal Nerve coming from the fifth or ſixth* Vertebra *of the Neck to the beginning of the wandring pair.*

DD *Portions of the Membrane cloathing the Marrow diſſected and turned back.*

EEEE *The Spinal Nerves ſent out of the upper margin of the Marrow by bands, with which the like bundles ſpringing from the lower margin alſo meet, and join together all into one Trunk* within *the junc-*

tures of the Vertebræ, *then being separated again* without *them, they are carried into their respective provinces.*

Ff *Nerves springing within the region of the Neck.*

Gg *Nerves destinated for the Shoulders and Fore-legs, where both the Marrow is thicker in bulk, and the Nerves greater.*

Hh *Nerves going out about the Back and Loyns, where both the body of the Marrow is again become smaller, and the Nerves are somewhat slenderer.*

Ii *Nerves destinated for the Buttocks and hinder Legs, where both the Medullar body and the Nerves are again larger.*

K *Nerves going out of* Os sacrum.

CHAP. XIII.

Of the Eye-lids, Eyes and their several Parts, viz. *their Coats and Humours.*

The Eyes, their name. THE *Eyes* are termed in Latin *Oculi*, from the word *occludo* to shut, or from *occulto* to hide, because they are hid by the shutting of the Eye-lids. They are the Organs or Instruments of Sight, consisting of many Parts, *viz.* of Humours, Membranes, &c.

Their number. Their *number* is by all People known to be two, and that for the security and perfection of sight; that if one be defective, or should by accident be lost, the other may supply its place and office, though not altogether so perfectly.

Their figure. The Eye alone, when its Muscles, and the Nerves and Bloud-vessels that enter into it, are removed, is of a round figure, both that it might move the better, and also that it might the better receive the visible Rays.

Their Parts. Adjoining unto the Eyes are the *Eye-lids*, which contain them as it were, and serve as a safeguard or cover to preserve them from external injuries: United with them are the Fat and Muscles: and lastly the Parts that constitute the Eye it self are the Membranes, Humours, and Vessels.

The Eye-lids. The *Eye-lids* do serve as Curtains to the Eyes, by which dust, Flies, or any thing else that might annoy them, is kept out. They are made up of the Skin, the *membrana Carnosa* or fleshy Pannicle, and Muscles; but both the Muscles and fleshy Pannicle are in these Parts very thin. On the inside next the Eye they are lined with a Membrane that is propagated from the *Pericranium*, which is very smooth, that it may move glibly upon the Eye. The extremities or edges of the Eye-lids are hard and gristly, partly to strengthen them, and partly that they may meet the more exactly, and not fall one over the other. And thus much shall suffice for the outward or containing Parts of the Eyes, *viz.* the Eye-lids.

As for the *Muscles*, we shall defer speaking of them till the next Book. And as to the *Fat*, it differs not from that which is intermixed among the Muscles in other Parts, and serves here to keep the hinder-part of the Eye and parts adjoining moist, that the Eye may move the more glibly in its Socket.

We

We ſhall therefore next proceed to the Eye it ſelf, and deſcribe the Parts of which it conſiſts, and firſt its Tunicles or Coats, the firſt or outmoſt of which is a *common* Coat, ariſing from the *Pericranium*, and is ſpread over all the white of the Eye. By this is the Eye kept firmly within its Socket or Orbit. It is of exquiſite ſenſe, and hath many ſmall Arteries and Veins creeping through it, which are very diſcernible when there is any inflammation in that Part. It is called *Adnata*. *The Tunicles of the Eyes.* 1. Adnata.

This *Adnata* being removed, the *proper* Tunicles or Coats do appear, being in number three; the firſt of which from its hardneſs is called *ſclerotica*. This ariſes from the *dura mater*, or (which is all one) from the outmoſt Coat of the Optick Nerve. It is ſomewhat hard, and opaque on its backſide; but on its fore-part, becauſe it is tranſparent like an Horn, it loſes its name of *ſclerotica* which it had from its hardneſs, and is called *tunica cornea* or horney Coat from its clearneſs. 2. Sclerotica.

The *ſecond* proper Coat lieth next under this, and goeth by the name of *Choroides*, becauſe it reſembles that Membrane that inwraps the Foal in the Womb, called *Chorion*. As the former did ariſe from the *dura mater*, ſo doth this from the *pia mater*, (or if you will, from the inner Coat of the Optick Nerve.) All over the back-part of the Eye, this Coat on its inſide is blackiſh, that the Idea's received in might appear the more illuſtrious. 3. Choroides.

This Coat is perforated before as wide as the *pupilla* or ſight of the Eye is in compaſs, to permit the rays of viſible Species to paſs in to the cryſtalline Humour. Which fore-part, becauſe ſo much of it as is from under the white is ſomewhat of the colour of a Grape, is called *uvea*: by which name the fore-part of this Coat is diſtinguiſhed from its hinder-part, as the former was by the name of *cornea*, from *ſclerotica*; which I thought fit to take notice of in this place, that the Reader might not take the four names for four ſeveral Coats, when they are but two, and ſo might go about to find what indeed there is not.

From the circumference of the *uvea*, where its duplicated Membrane bends it ſelf back to the cryſtalline Humour, there is formed a Ligament called *ligamentum Ciliare*, becauſe it conſiſts of ſlender Filaments or Fibres like the hairs that grow upon the Eye-lids in Humane Bodies, running like ſo many black lines from the circumference of the *uvea* to the ſides of the cryſtalline Humour; which Humour they encompaſs, and widen or conſtringe it as there is occaſion, by contracting or opening the perforation of the *uvea*.

The *third* or inmoſt proper Tunicle of the Eye is called *Retina* or the Net-faſhioned Coat, becauſe it encompaſſes the vitreous or glaſſey Humour like a Net. 4. Retina.

This Coat is made of the medullar ſubſtance of the Optick Nerve, being very thin, and rather of a dark than lightſom colour, mixed with an obſcure redneſs. Its figure is ſemicircular, round on its outſide, and hollow within, containing in it the vitreous Humour, and receiving into its boſom the cryſtalline Humour alſo, having its Fibres extended as far as the *ligamentum Ciliare*, to which theſe Fibres afford animal Spirits for the continuance of its motion. It is obſerved that if this Coat be taken and put into warm Water, ſhaking it a little to waſh off the mucous or ſnotty matter that cleaves to it, and then be held up to the light, the Fibres or Filaments will appear very numerous like the threads of the fineſt Lawn.

Having

The Humours of the Eyes. Having done with the *Tunicles* or Coats of the Eyes, I come next to ſpeak of the *Humours* contained within thoſe Coats, which are in number three, that is the *Aqueus* or watery, the *Vitreus* or glaſſey, and the Cryſtalline: of which the laſt for its uſe is the moſt noble, and is placed almoſt in the centre of the Eyes.

The watery Humour. Of theſe Humours the *Aqueus* or *watery* is outermoſt, being thin and fluxive like Water, from whence it hath its name. It fills up that ſpace that is betwixt the horney or outmoſt Coat and the cryſtalline Humour in the fore-part of the Eye. It is obſerved in Men, that if any clotted and coloured bits or motes ſwim in this Humour, the ſhapes of ſeveral Inſects, as Gnats, Flies, Spiders and the like, will ſeem to be flying before their Eyes, as hath been oft declared by Men who have had this Affection. I am therefore apt to believe that many Horſes are not without ſuch kind of congealed bits floating in this Humour, that without any evident or external cauſe to occaſion it, are much given to ſtart, eſpecially with their Head; the repreſentation of the aforeſaid Inſects moving before the cryſtalline Humour, which makes them fear ſomething or other is ſtill flying into their Eye.

Yea it is in Humane Bodies farther obſerved, that oft times ſeveral of theſe coloured Particles in the watery Humour do gather together, and unite ſo cloſe, that they grow as it were into a skin or film, ſpreading before the ſight of the Eye, which cauſes an abſolute blindneſs, and is that Diſeaſe which Phyſicians call a *Cataract*; which Diſeaſe the Animal we are treating of is much ſubject to, though we have not ſo proper a term for it as this is.

The Cryſtalline. The next Humour is the *Cryſtalline*, which is ſo called from its exceeding bright and ſhining colour, being as tranſparent as Cryſtal; It is it ſelf of no diſtinguiſhable colour, that it might receive the Idea's of all colours.

It is placed betwixt the watery and glaſſey Humours, but not exactly in the middle or centre of the Eye, but rather towards its fore-part. It is incloſed in the boſom, as it were, of the glaſſey Humour, and is flattiſh on the fore-ſide, but rounder behind.

This Humour is believed to be the primary or chief inſtrument of the ſight, becauſe it collects or receives the rayes of viſible things; though the *tunica Retina* doth afterwards ſtop them by its dark body, and communicate them to the common Senſory by the Optick Nerve.

The Glaſſey. The third and laſt of the Humours of the Eye is the *Vitreus* or *glaſſey*, ſo called becauſe in colour it is like to molten glaſs. This is not of ſo thick a conſiſtence as the cryſtalline; but it much exceeds both it and the watery in quantity. It is round in its hinder part but plane before, onely it has a little hollowneſs in the middle wherein the cryſtalline Humour is placed as in a mold or caſe. It fills up all the hinder part of the globe of the Eye, as alſo ſome part of the ſides.

The *uſes* of this Humour are ſaid to be, firſt, to nouriſh the cryſtalline Humour, as *Galen* conceived; next, that the viſible ſpecies received into the cryſtalline Humour might not be reflected, or return defiled by dark and coloured tinctures, whereby the ſight ſhould be diſturbed; but that they might have a free paſſage through it to the *Retina*.

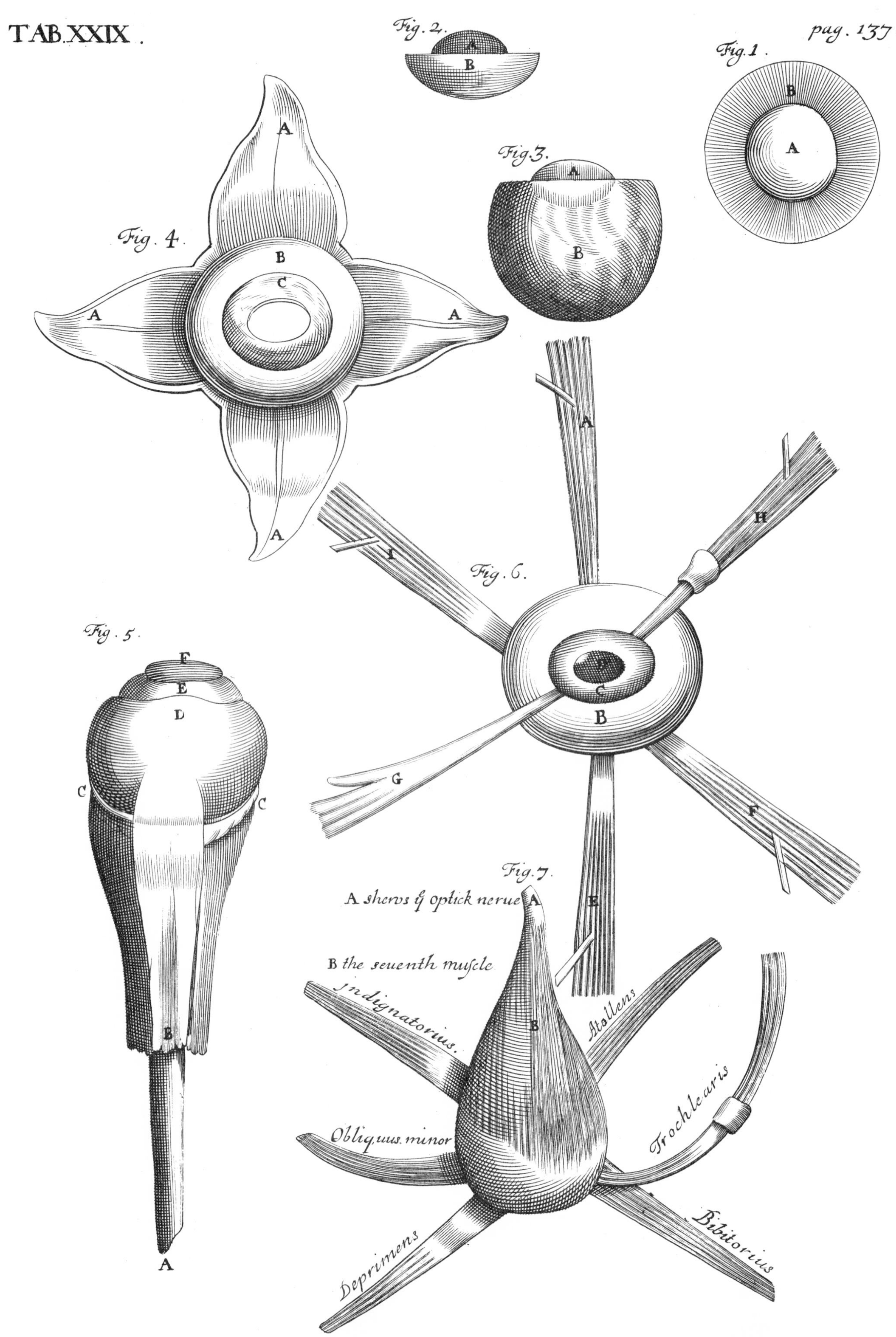
TAB. XXIX.
pag. 137.
Fig. 1.
Fig. 2.
Fig. 3.
Fig. 4.
Fig. 5.
Fig. 6.
Fig. 7.
A shews y^e optick nerue
B the seuenth muscle
Indignatorius.
Atollens
Obliquus minor
Trochlearis
Deprimens
Bibitorius

Table XXIX.

Represents the ſeveral Coats, Humours and Muſcles of the Eyes.

Figure I.

A *Shews the cryſtalline Humour.*
B *The* Iris *or circle about the ſight of the Eye.*

Figure II.

A *The cryſtalline Humour.*
B *The watery Humour encompaſſing the cryſtalline on its fore-ſide.*

Figure III.

A *The back-ſide of the cryſtalline Humour.*
B *The vitreous or glaſſey Humour receiving the cryſtalline into its boſom.*

Figure IV.

AAAA *The common Coat of the Eye or* Adnata, *cut aſunder and thrown back.*
B *The* Cornea *or horney Coat.*
C *The* Choroides, *whoſe fore-part is called* uvea *by reaſon it is of the colour of a Grape.*

Figure V.

Shews the Eye taken out of the Head with its Muſcles *in ſitu,* not being looſened from either their riſe or termination.

A *The Optick Nerve cut off near the Brain.*
B *The riſe of the Muſcles.*
CC *Their ſeveral terminations or endings into the Coats of the Eye.*
D *The common Coat of the Eye called* Adnata *or* Conjunctiva.
E *The* Cornea *or horney Coat.*
F *The Apple of the Eye.*

Figure VI.

Shews the fore-part of the Eye with its Muſcles removed from their originals, and placed round the Eye according to the motions they perform.

AAAA *The right Muſcle that lifts up the Eye, called* Attollens.
B *The* Adnata *Tunicle.*
C *The* Tunica cornea *or horney Coat.*
D *The* Pupilla *or Apple of the Eye.*
E *The right Muſcle that draws down the Eye, called* Deprimens.
F *The Muſcle that draweth the Eye from the Noſe towards the outer corner, called* Indignatorius.
G *The Muſcle called* Bibitorius, *which brings the Eye inwards towards the Noſe.*
H *The ſuperiour oblique Muſcle called* Trochlearis, *which carries the Eye ſlantingly to its outward angle.*
I *The inferiour oblique Muſcle, that moves the Eye ſlantingly to its inward angle.*

CHAP. XIV.

Of the Ears and their ſeveral Parts.

THE *Ears* (which according to order we come now to ſpeak to) are the inſtruments of Hearing, framed by Nature with no leſs Art than the Eyes; yea ſo full of intricate Meanders they are, and conſiſt of ſo many Parts, that they will be very hard to be deciphered. Notwithſtanding I will endeavour to give what ſatisfaction I can, by what I have learned by Inſpection, as well as by the Writings of the moſt accurate Anatomiſts.

The Auricle. Firſt then the Parts of the Ear are either *Outward* or *Inward.* The *outward* part is called *Auricula,* which is onely an adjuvant or aſſiſting inſtrument of Hearing, collecting in its hollowneſs ſome part of the Air that is the vehicle of the ſound, as it is paſſing by.

Its Parts. The Parts whereof the outward Ear is framed, are either *proper,* or *common.* The *common* are the Scarf-skin, the true Skin, and *membrana nervea,* or nervous Membrane. The *proper* are the Muſcles, Veins, Arteries, Nerves, and the Griſtle. Of the *Muſcles* we ſhall ſpeak in their proper place, *viz.* in the next Book that treats of the Muſcles. The *Veins* of the Ear are branched to it from the external Jugular Vein; the *Arteries* from the Carotid Arteries; and the Nerves from the ſecond pair of the Neck being joined with the harder Proceſs of the ſeventh pair. As to the *Griſtle* of which for the greateſt part it conſiſts, that is a ſubſtance that is fitteſt for this place; for if it had been bony, the Ear would both have been immoveable,

moveable, and ſo could not have turned it ſelf toward the ſound, as we ſee the Horſe can now move it; and alſo it would have been in continual danger of being broken off: and if it had been fleſhy or membranous onely, the Horſe's Ears would have flap'd down like Hounds Ears, which would have been a great deformity.

The *uſes* of this outward Ear are, firſt, to ſerve for an ornament to the Head; ſecondly to receive, or at leaſt to help to receive the ſounds; for firſt, it gathereth them being diſperſed in the Air; ſecondly, it doth moderate the fierceneſs of their motion, ſo that they come gently to the *Tympanum*, or Drum, and beat moderately againſt it. *Its uſe.*

The internal or inward Ear hath alſo ſundry Parts, contained *in* the *Os petroſum*, as the outward Ear is faſten'd *upon* it. *The inward Ear.*

Theſe Parts are firſt the Drum with its Cord and Muſcles; ſecondly, four little Bones; thirdly, its Cavities with the implanted Air; and laſtly, its Veſſels. *Its Parts.*

The *Drum*, called *Tympanum*, is a nervous, round and tranſparent Membrane, of moſt exquiſite ſenſe, ariſing from the ſofter proceſs of the Auditory Nerve expanded. It is exceeding dry, that it might give the better Echo to the ſound. It is alſo ſtrong, that it ſhould the better endure outward harms or injuries. It hath a *Cord* behind it for ſtrengthning and ſtretching of it, even as the Military Drum hath. As for its *Muſcles*, we ſhall deſcribe them in the next Book. *The Drum.*

Within the Membrane of this *Tympanum* or Drum there is an internal Cavity, called *Concha*, in which are ſeveral little dry Bones, which have in them no Marrow, nor are covered with any Membrane or *perioſteum*: yet at their ends where they are joined together, they are bound with a ſmall Ligament, proceeding from the before mentioned Cord of the Drum. *Four little Bones.*

Theſe little Bones are four in number; the *firſt* of which is called *malleolus*, that is, a little Hammer. This Hammer hath a round head, which by a looſe Ligament is jointed into the Cavity of the ſecond little Bone that is called the Anvil; which head is continued into a ſmall neck, that reacheth beyond the middle of the Drum and adhereth to it. About its middle it hath two Proceſſes, the one of which, being ſhorter, hath the tendon of the internal Muſcle inſerted into it; and the other, being longer, hath the tendon of the external, the Drum intervening. *The Hammer.*

The next of theſe little Bones is by Anatomiſts called *Incus*, the *Anvil*, having one head and two feet, being therefore more like to one of the grinding Double-teeth than to an Anvil. *The Anvil.*

The head of this is indifferent thick, having in the top of it a little ſmooth hollowneſs, which receives the knob or head of the Hammer. The ſmaller foot of the Anvil is tied to the top of the Stirrop by a looſe but firm Ligament, but the thicker foot reſteth upon the *Os ſquamoſum*, or ſcaly Bone.

The third is called the *Stirrop*, having a perforation in the middle, and is fixed before or rather round that paſſage that is called the oval Window, by which ſounds paſs out of the firſt Cavity into the ſecond called the Labyrinth. Which Cavities are wrought by Nature in the Rocky-bone, and contain in them the inbred Air. Now as the cryſtalline Humour of the Eye is the chief inſtrument of the Sight, in reſpect of the reception of viſible Images or Forms; ſo is this inbred Air of the Ear, the chief inſtrument which receiveth the forms of Sounds, although there be another more noble Organ which judgeth of them, as ſhall be ſhewn by and by. *The Stirrop.*

The figure of this Bone is in Horſes triangular, very like the Greek Letter Δ, (but in Men it is repreſented to be of ſomewhat another ſhape) which Letter is like ſuch a Stirrop as we often ſee in old Hangings (not ſuch Stirrops as are uſed now-a-daies) from its ſimilitude unto which I ſuppoſe it hath its name.

The upper part of this Stirrop is ſmall, as you may ſee by the figure of it, upon which the longeſt foot of the Anvil ſtands.

The orbicular Bone. The fourth and laſt of theſe little Bones of the Ear was not long ſince found out by a diligent Anatomiſt, named *Franc. Sylvius*, till whoſe time there were but three Bones of the Ear reckoned.

This Bone from its round ſhape is called *orbiculare*. It is tied by a ſlender Ligament to the ſide of the Stirrop, in that part where the Stirrop is faſtned to the Anvil.

The uſe of theſe Bones. The *uſe* of theſe four Bones is not, that by hitting one againſt another they ſhould produce a ſound, but firſt, to defend the Membrane of the *Tympanum* or Drum, leſt it ſhould be torn and beat inwards by the violent ſhaking of the outward Air againſt it, in loud ſounds, ſuch as Thunder, or the noiſe of great Guns and the like.

Secondly, They are aſſiſting to the Senſe of Hearing on this manner: The external Air beats againſt the Drum, which is driven againſt the Hammer, and this ſtrikes upon the Anvil, as the Anvil bears againſt the Stirrop; which as it does, more ſtrongly or weakly, ſo does the Stirrop open the oval Window more or leſs, and proportionably the ſound appears to the common Senſory, louder, or lower.

The Cavities of the Ear. We come in the next place to ſpeak of the Caverns or *Cavities*, by ſome called Dens, which are formed in the midſt of the *Os petroſum* or Rockey-bone where it bunches out moſt, and are three in number.

Concha. The *firſt* of them is to be ſeen as ſoon as the Membrane of the Drum is taken away, and is called *Concha*, from its reſemblance to the ſhell of a Taber. Others call it the Baſin, and ſome the Den. It has its firſt denomination, (which is that which it is moſt commonly known by) not ſo much from its ſhape, as from its uſe; for when the Membrane is ſtruck upon by any outward ſound, the Echo is made in this Cavity, even as it is in the hollow of a Taber, or in our common Drum when the Parchment is beat upon; for in all theſe the ſound is principally occaſion'd by the Air included in the Cavity.

Nature hath placed in this Cavity divers Inſtruments; as firſt, ſome ſerving for pulſation, ſuch are the four Bones, the Cord and the Muſcles, (of all which before.) Secondly, others for conduction into the other Cavities; ſuch are two *perforations* or little holes, commonly called Windows. And laſtly, a third ſort for Expurgation; ſuch are the paſſages which lead, one into the Palate, and another into the Noſtrils, by the help of which the pituitous Matter which is collected in this Cavity is diſcharged.

Feneſtra ovalis. The firſt of the *perforations* being the upper and larger, has added to it the Epithet *Oval*, alluding to its figure. This opens inwards or backwards, and that with a pretty wide mouth, into the Labyrinth; but is kept ſhut next the *Concha* by the baſis of the Stirrop, when ſound ceaſes. The other being the leſs and lower, is of a round ſhape (and therefore

Feneſtra rotunda. ſtyled *Rotunda.*) This is always open having no covering, and is divided by the *Os ſquamoſum* into two Pipes, one of which tends to the *Cochlea*, the other into the Labyrinth.

The

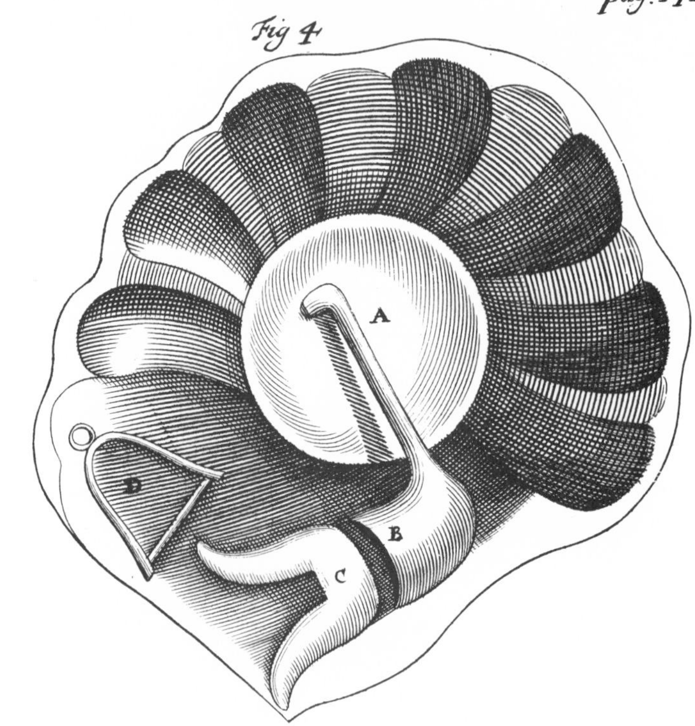
Fig 4
A
B
C
D

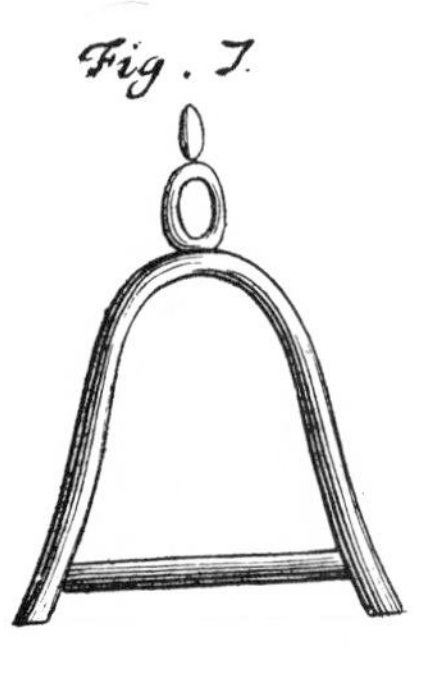
Fig. 7.

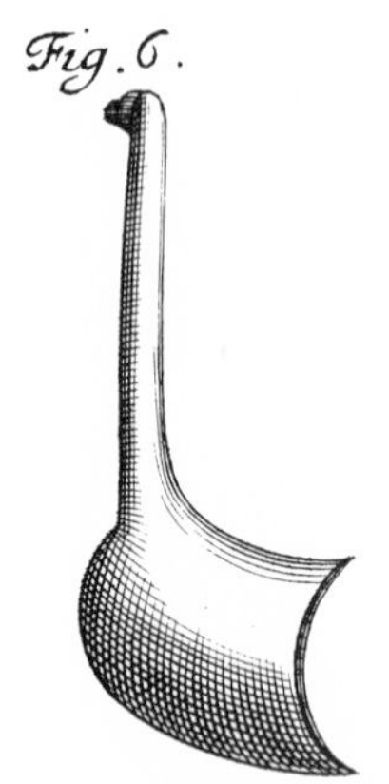
Fig. 6.

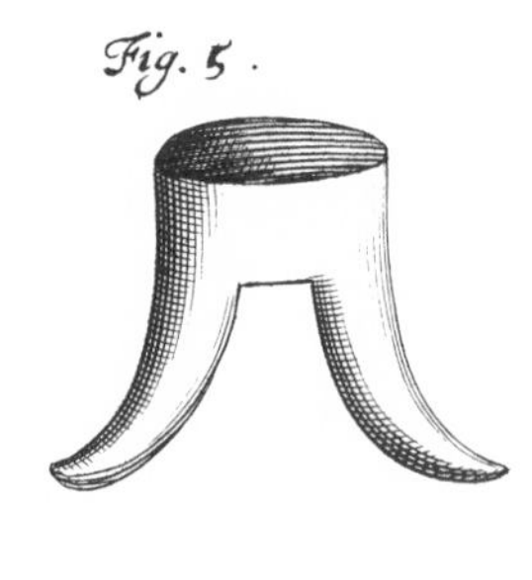
Fig. 5.

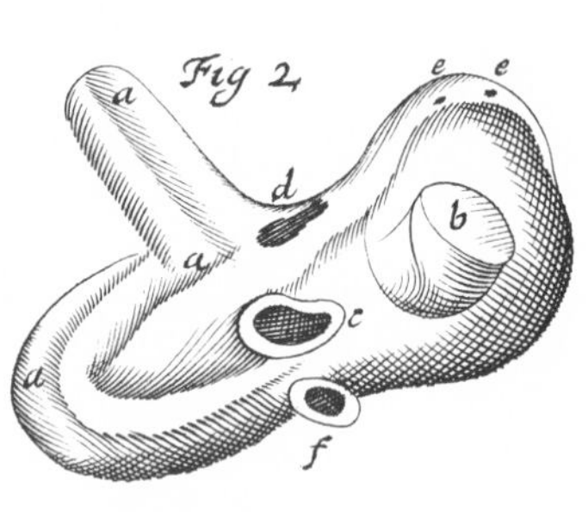
Fig 2
a
a
a
b
c
d
e e
f

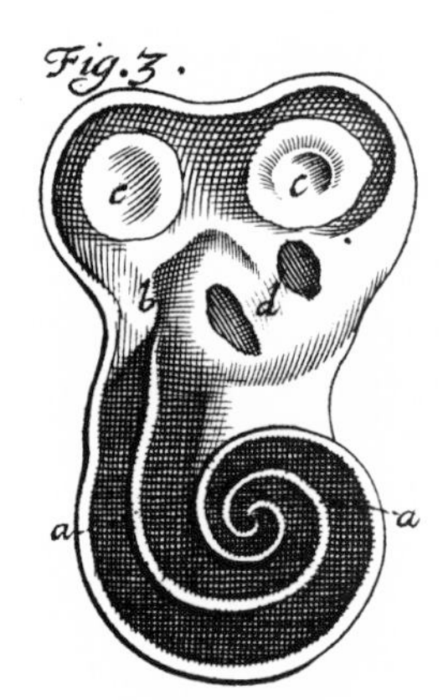
Fig. 3.
c
c
b
d
a
a

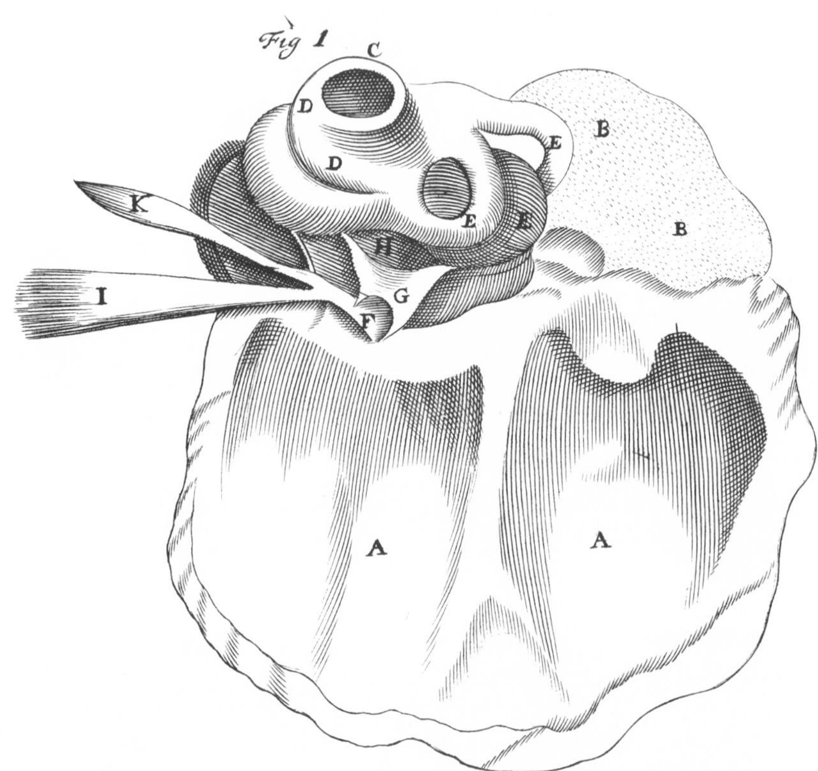
Fig 1
C
D
D
E
B
B
E E
K
H
I
G
F
A
A

The *second* of these Cavities of the inward Ear is (from its windings and turnings) called *Labyrinthus*, the Labyrinth. If one consider it in its whole dimension it is round, and much less than the former. Its windings are circular, yet the circles run not quite round the Cavity, but come as much short of an intire circle as the Gristles of the Wind-pipe in the Throat do, or rather more, so that they are commonly termed semicircular. Their use is to modulate the sounds so as they may be leisurely communicated to the Auditory Nerve which is dispersed through the Membrane that invests this Cavity, or rather makes it. It has three pretty wide holes, two opening *into* it, and one *out of* it. The two that open *into* it, are the oval and round holes, mentioned in the foregoing Paragraph. By these the internal agitated Air passes out of the *Concha* into the Labyrinth. That which opens *out of* it is that which passes towards the third Cavity called *Cochlea,* into which the aforesaid Air passes further by it out of the Labyrinth. Besides these there are four other very small holes for the ingress of the nervous Fibres that are inserted into the Membrane that cloaths this Cavity. **The Labyrinth.**

The *third* and last inner Cavity is called *Cochlea* or the Snail-shell, from the resemblance it hath with that Shell, especially in its Spiral winding; which, if you take off the upper part of the Bone, will plainly appear. **Cochlea.**

This Cavity is far less than the former two, being indifferent long but crooked. Into this endeth one Pipe from the round hole of the first Cavity, and another from the second, just now mentioned.

It is invested, as the other Cavities are, with a soft and thin Membrane (after the same manner as the sockets of the Teeth are) into which (as into that of the Labyrinth) the slender Fibres of the Auditory Nerve do enter, and that through three or four several holes which are all very small.

It is filled with the internal inbred Air as well as the former, by which the Echo is made to the impulse of the external Air upon the *Tympanum* that is the vehicle of the sound: And the Auditory Nerve being inserted into the Membrane that cloaths the Cavities, is affected therewith, whereby it comes to be communicated to the original of the Nerves where the common Sensory is seated, that judgeth and distinguisheth of them.

Into these three Cavities that make up the Internal Ear, are the same Bloud-vessels distributed as to the External: The Nerves are also from the same conjugation, namely the seventh pair; onely whereas the harder Process of the Nerve goes to the External Ear, it is the softer that comes to the Internal.

Table XXX.

Represents the inner structure of the Ear or Organ of Hearing, with the Auditory Bones as well lesser as bigger.

Figure I.

AA *The inside of the Temple-bone, or* Os temporis.
BB *The spongy Bone, or* Os spongiosum.
C *The hole into which the Auditory Nerve is inserted.*
D *The greater winding of the* Cochlea *or Snail-shell.*

E *The three bony half-circles that form the Labyrinth.*
F *The* Malleus *or Hammer in its situation.*
G *The* Incus *or Anvil.*
H *The* Stapes *or Stirrop.*
I *The External Muscle of the Ear.*
K *The Internal Muscle.*

Figure II.

aaa *Shew the Labyrinth.*
b *The* Cochlea *or Snail-shell.*
c *The oval hole before which the Stirrop is seated.*
d *The Aqueduct found out by* Fallopius.
ee *Little holes to let out the Veins and Arteries.*
f *The* Fenestra rotunda, *or round Window.*

Figure III.

Shews the *Cochlea* and Labyrinth dissected.

aa *The intermediate space dividing the* Cochlea *into two wreaths.*
b *The round hole that makes the passage out of the* Concha, *into the lower wreath of the* Cochlea.
c *The windings or circumvolutions of the Labyrinth opened.*
d *The* Fenestra ovalis, *or oval Window.*

Figure IV.

Shews the *Os petrosum* cut through the middle, the plainer to shew the round circle over which the Drum is placed.

A *The round circle covered with the* Tympanum *or Drum.*
B *The* Malleus *or Hammer in its natural situation.*
C *The* Incus *or Anvil in the like.*
D *The* Stapes *or Stirrop also* in situ.

Figure V.

Shews the *Incus* or Anvil taken out and freed from the Hammer.

Figure VI.

Is the Hammer taken out also and freed from the other Parts.

Figure VII.

Is the Stirrop out of its place.

CHAP.

CHAP. XV.

Of the Nose, Lips and Mouth.

HAVING described all the Organs of *Seeing* and *Hearing*, we come in the next place to the third outward Sense which is the *Smelling*, of which the Nose being the Instrument, we are now to enter upon its description.

As therefore the Ear is divided into an External or outward, and an Internal or inward part; so will we divide the Nose, it being made of the like parts.

The *External* Parts are the Skin, the Muscles and Gristles, Vessels of all sorts, as also many Bones, and those distinguished or divided by several Sutures. *The external Parts of the Nose.*

The *Skin* wherewith the Nose is covered is thin, and without any fat under it, for beauty sake; for if there had been any fat naturally in this place, it might have been collected to that quantity or bulk, as to have become a great deformity to the Creature: for which reason Nature hath so ordered it, that in this place the Skin sticketh so fast to the Muscles and Gristles, that it is not easie to part it from them without renting. *The Skin.*

The *Bones* which make the Cavities of the Nose are some proper, and some common: of which hereafter in the Fifth Book *of the Bones.* The *Gristles* are five in number, of which we shall also discourse in the same Book. *Bones and Gristles.*

The *Vessels* of the Nose are, *Veins* from the Jugular Veins, and *Arteries* from the *Carotides*; also *Nerves* from the third pair of the Brain, which send to each side of the Nose one branch, (besides the olfactory Nerves or first pair, called the Mammillary Processes.) *Vessels.*

As to the *Internal* Parts of the Nose, we shall begin first with the *Coat* or Skin which compasseth the whole capacity of the Nostrils. This Coat is said to arise from that Skin of the Brain which is called the *dura mater*; and is not peculiar to this Part alone, but is as well common to the Mouth, Palate, Tongue, Larynx, &c. as to the Nostrils; onely in the Nostrils it is thinner and of exquisite sense; for any thing blown up the Nose that is of a biting nature, so irritates it, as immediately to cause the Horse to sneeze. This Skin hath on its back-side abundance of little Glands or Kernels, in which the Rheum is separated that runs out by the Nose. *The internal Parts. The nervous Membrane.*

There is also another Skin belonging to the inside of the Nose called the *muscular Membrane*, which is said to draw together or contract the Nostrils. *The muscular Membrane.*

In the upper part of the Nostrils there is a red *fleshy spongious substance*, with which the spongy Bones are filled up. *Spongy Flesh.*

There are also seated at the upper end of the Nose next to the Brain over both Nostrils a Bone which from its likeness to a Sieve, (by reason of the innumerable little perforations or holes that are in it) is called *Os cribriforme* or Sieve-like Bone. In the inside of this Bone are seated those two productions of the Brain called *processus mammillares*, which are the *Sieve-like Bone.*

true

true Instruments of Smelling, and are therefore better called the Smelling-nerves. There pass from them through the holes of this Sieve-like Bone many little Strings or Fibres, which are dispersed into all the inward capacity of the Nose, serving there to be the immediate Organs of Smelling, but the Scents are communicated to the common Sensory of the Brain by the aforesaid Mammillary Processes.

The uses of the Nose. The principal *use* of the Nose is for Smelling, which is performed in this manner. The Nostrils are adjuvant Instruments of Smelling even as the External Ear is of Hearing. For as the Ear gathereth the sounds that fly in the Air; so when smells exhale out of odoriferous Bodies into the Air, the Horse by taking in his breath at his Nose, (which he for the most part does, and not in at his Mouth as we often do) the scents accompanying the Air ascend up the Nostrils to the top of their Cavity, and so to the before-named Sieve-like Bone, where affecting the little Fibres of the Olfactory Nerves that come, as hath been said, from the Mammillary Processes through those little holes, those Fibres communicate their sensation to the Processes, and these convey it to the original of the Nerves or common Sensory, by which it is distinguished.

Inferiour uses of the Nose are, first, to take in the breath by; and next, to serve as a common Shore or Sink for the discharge and evacuation of the superfluous flegmatick Humours of the Bloud.

The Lips. Their substance. In the next place we come to treat of the *Lips* (or the external Parts of the Mouth) which are two in number, one upper and the other lower. These are framed of a soft fleshy fungous substance, as also of some proper Muscles covered with the hairy Skin on the outside of them, but on the inside they are covered with a Membrane common to the Mouth and Stomach.

Their use. The *uses* of the Lips are first to gather the Hay or Oats or other Food into the Mouth; secondly to retain, or help to retain it, while it is chewing; thirdly, they serve to keep the Gums and Teeth from external Injuries.

The Mouth. Within the Lips is the *Mouth*, whose Parts are either *containing* or *contained*, that is, either those that make the Mouth, or such as are contained in it.

The Parts containing. The Parts whereof the Mouth is made, are of two sorts, some fleshy, others bony. The *fleshy* Parts are the Lips, of which we have already spoken; also the Muscles of the Cheeks and lower Jaw. The *bony* are the upper and nether Jaws, with the Teeth fixed in them.

All these Parts (as also the whole inward capacity of the Mouth) except the Teeth, are lined with a thick Membrane or Skin, which in the Palate is rugged and knotty as it were, by reason of the many little Glands on the back-side of it, by which part of the Slaver is separated into the Mouth; and this Membrane reduplicated maketh the *Uvula*, as some think; though others more probably hold, that it is of a peculiar substance.

The Parts contained. The Parts *contained* within the Mouth are divers. As first the Teeth and the Bone *Hyoides* at the root of the Tongue; of both which we shall treat in the Book of the Bones.

Besides these there are the Gums, the Palate, the *Uvula*, the Almonds, the Tongue, and the Muscles that serve to move it.

The Gums. The *Gums* being in number two, are made up of a hard fleshy substance, destitute of motion, that so the Teeth might be better fastned in their Sockets.

The

The *Palate* is the upper part of the Mouth, and is called by that name, from its being as it were fenced or *paled* in with Teeth. It extends from the back-part of the Mouth to the Fore-teeth, but is not ſo much hollowed in an Horſe as in Humane Skulls. It hath in it ſome eighteen ſteps or bars which reach from the inſide of the Fore-teeth to the very farther end of the Mouth. It conſiſts of Bones, of a peculiar glandulous Fleſh, and a thick Coat; which Coat is full of little perforations or holes for the Slaver that is ſeparated in the little Glands (above-mentioned) to diſtill through into the Mouth. *The Palate.*

The *Uvula* is a red, fungous and longiſh kind of a Kernel ſeated in the inward or backer-part of the Palate, where the Noſtrils open into the Mouth, hanging directly downward with a ſmall but bluntiſh end juſt over the chink of the *Larynx*. *The Uvula.*

The *uſe* of this *Uvula* is ſaid to be, firſt, to moderate the coldneſs of the Air drawn in by the Lungs. This is *Bartholin*'s opinion, who ſays further, that from this uſe of it it comes to paſs, that ſuch Perſons as want it, die Phthiſical. Whether that be ſo or no I cannot tell: but the main uſe of it in an Horſe I take to be, ſecondly, to hinder the Water, when he drinks, from paſſing out of his Mouth into his Noſtrils. *Its uſe.*

This Kernel is very neceſſary to be known by all profeſſed Farriers, for ſuch knowledge might have contributed to the preſervation of many Horſes which for want of it have been loſt. Such are thoſe which by reaſon of Humours too much flowing to this Kernel have had it ſo much diſtended, that it hath hung down into the Throat to that degree, that the Horſe hath not been able to ſwallow, there being no paſſage left for the Meat to go down; but when he has chew'd it and endeavours to ſwallow it, inſtead of its going down the Gullet into his Stomach, it comes out at his Noſe; whereby it comes to paſs that although the Horſe have never ſo good a Stomach, yet for all that he comes to ſtarve to death with hunger. *The falling of it a Diſtemper incident to Horſes as well as Men.*

This my ſelf have been ſometimes an Eye-witneſs of, and have oftener heard of it by others; but could never ſee nor hear of any of them, that had any help for this Diſtemper; their endeavours proving ſtill unſucceſsfull by their not well underſtanding either the Diſtemper, or the Part affected.

This ſwelling of the *Uvula* in Men is called by Phyſicians *Caſus Uvulæ*; and by the Vulgar, the falling down of the Palate of the Mouth. It is a Diſtemper that commonly comes upon taking ſome great cold; but is very ordinarily cured not by Phyſicians onely, but by every old Woman, who knows that by holding Pepper or Ginger or the like againſt it, the Rheum is thereby drained out of it, and it contracts it ſelf to its due and natural bulk, whereby the Party is ſpeedily relieved. How far ſuch Medicines might contribute to the cure in Horſes, I ſhall forbear in this place to give my opinion, becauſe as I have already ſaid, I do by God's aſſiſtance deſign to publiſh a Book of Cures by it ſelf, but was willing in the firſt place to teach my Practitioner the frame and uſe of the Parts, and to hint ſome of thoſe Diſeaſes they are incident to, which we have leaſt underſtood: and by that time the Ingenious Student is come to underſtand them, I ſhall I hope be ready to publiſh a new and certainer way of curing them than has hitherto been practiſed.

Next we come to ſpeak of the *Tongue* and its Parts. It is called in Latin, *Lingua, à lingendo*, from Licking. It is in figure long, broad and *The Tongue.*

thick,

Its Membranes. thick, especially towards the root. It is covered with two Skins; the *outward*, cloathing onely its upper part, which in an Horse is almost as smooth as in Men, though it is much rougher in Oxen, and the like. This Membrane is very porous.

The *inward* Skin covers the whole Tongue, the lower side as well as the upper, and is thin and soft, having many Teat-like Protuberances bunching out of it, which are inserted into the pores or holes of the outward Coat.

Its substance. Concerning the *substance* of the Tongue there is diversity of opinions; for some would have it of a glandulous, others a musculous substance; and some, that it has a peculiar substance: to which opinion I most incline, because I do not find in any Part of the Body a substance like it.

Its Vessels. It hath *Vessels* of all sorts; *Veins* from an inward branch of the external Jugular; *Arteries* from the Carotid Arteries; and *Nerves* of two kinds, one from the fifth and another from the eighth pair of the Brain.

The Tongue hath at its root several *Muscles*, by which all its motions are performed, of which we will speak in the next Book. And besides the Muscles, there is also at the root of the Tongue a considerable quantity of Fat, with which the Muscles are interlarded as it were.

Its uses. The *uses* of the Tongue are, first, to taste the Food that is offered, whereby (as well as by the smell) the Horse distinguisheth whether it be good and wholsom for him or not; and in the next place it helpeth the chewing of the Meat, by tossing it to and fro, and after it is chewed, it assisteth in turning it down to the Stomach.

The salival Ducts. There is to be found out by dissection underneath the root of the Tongue a large Kernel, from whence two Pipes, called salival Ducts, do spring, one from the fore, and the other from the hinder-part of it: These two at a small distance from the Gland unite into one, which runs pretty streight forward under the Tongue toward the Chin: but in the middle way, as Doctor *Wharton* affirms, there are other pretty remarkable Glands (in an Horse) that stand on each side this Duct, and discharge themselves into it. When it is come near the Chin at the Bridle of the Tongue, it ends into other small Glands, through which it pours into the Mouth part of the Slaver that keeps it continually moist.

Besides this Duct there are two others of the same use, which do arise out of the Kernels below the root of the Ear, (called *Parotides*) and run on the outside of the Jaw-bone to the middle of that Muscle of the Cheek that is called *Buccinator*, where they open into the Cavity of the Mouth, into which they discharge the before-named Liquor, which in these and the other Glands of the Mouth is separated from the Bloud.

The use of the Slaver. Now we must understand, this Slaver (or *Saliva*) is not merely an Humour excrementitious, as that is which is separated in several Kernels in other Parts of the Body, as particularly in the Guts; for this is of great use, not onely in that it continually moistens the Mouth, as also the Hay and Oats whilst they are in chewing; but being swallow'd down with the Meats, it doth further the fermentation and concoction of them in the Stomach, whither part of this Juice also goes with every morsel. It is of the same nature with that which in Men we call the Spittle, and of the same use.

And here it may not be amiss to recite a story I have read of a Person that had one of these external salival Ducts wounded, because I have observed (the last Spring at *Greenwich*) the same accident happen to an Horse, with the same symptom. The Story is thus: A Noble-man being

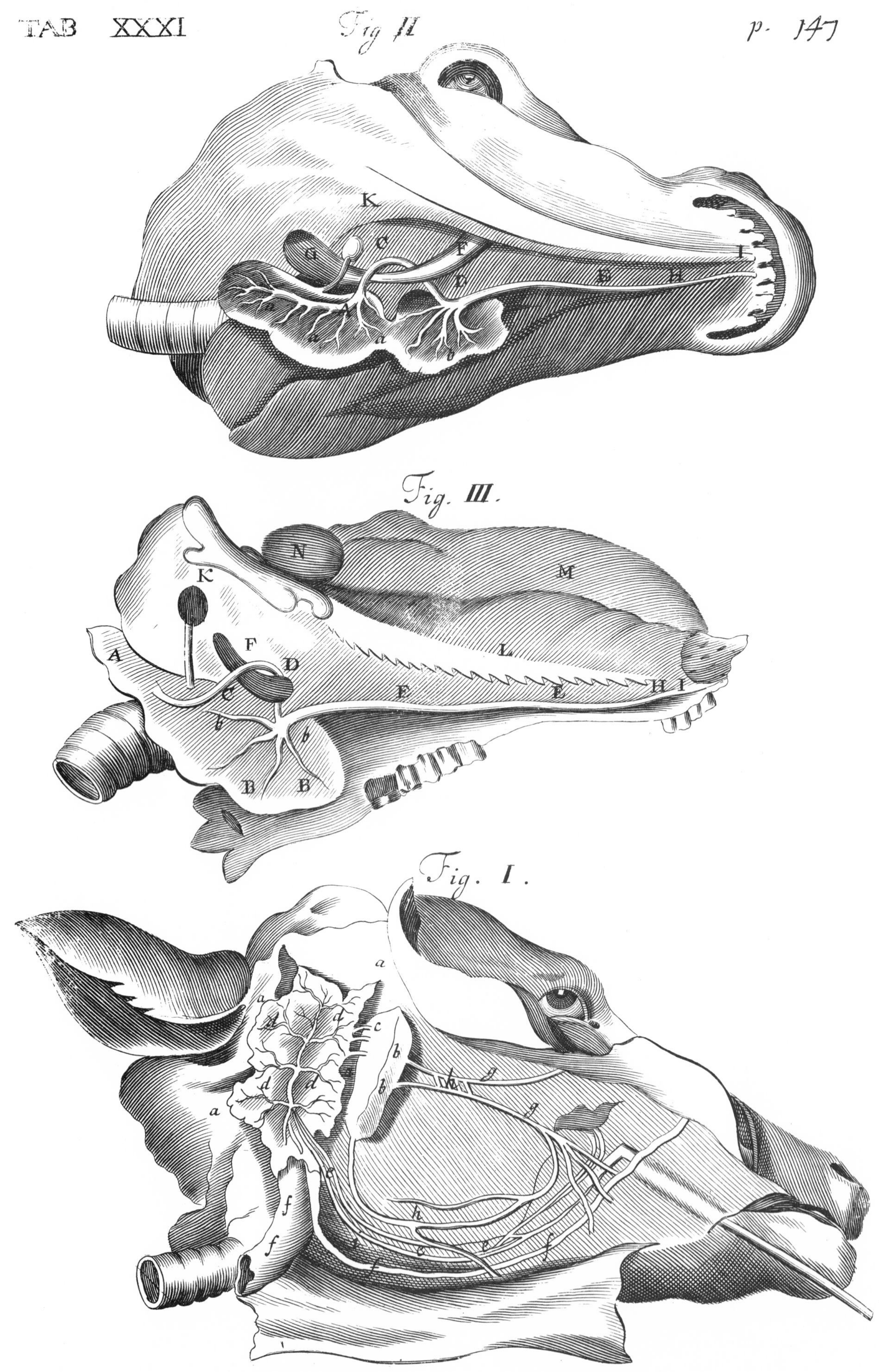
Fig II
K
G C F
D E H I
A
a a a b
Fig. III.
N
K M
A F D L
C E E H I
b b
B B
Fig. I.
a
a d d c
b
a d d a b h g
g
e
h
f f e e e f

wounded in the middle of the Cheek with having a Glaſs thrown at him; the Wound was quickly *almoſt* cloſed, but in the middle of it, through a little hole, there leiſurely diſtilled out of it for a long time a watery and clear Liquor, which for all that ever the Surgeon could doe, hindred the intire cloſing up of the Wound for almoſt two years. This Liquor did diſtill out of the ſalival Duct, which was not then found out; but at laſt an actual Cautery being applied to the end of the Duct, the Liquor was by that means ſtopt, and the Wound preſently healed. The Horſe that I ſaw had a clear watery Humour running in like manner out of the ſide of his Cheek, but in that quantity, that in a few hours time (eſpecially in the time next after his drinking) it would make his Manger all a float. A Farrier had him under cure there, and my opinion being ask'd, I adviſ'd to ſear it, but he that had him in hand not knowing the occaſion of this flux of Humour, thought rowelling of him would ſerve; but what he did to him, I had no opportunity ſince to inform my ſelf.

Now ſeeing a like caſe to this may happen, that my Practitioner may underſtand where to apply his Cautery (or red-hot Iron) for the ſtanching of the Liquor, I have thought it convenient to annex a Scheme of each of theſe ſalival Ducts; *that* under the Tongue being found out by Doctor *Wharton*, and the *other* ariſing from the *Parotides* and running on the outſide the Gums, by one *Steno*, a Dane.

Table XXXI.

Fig. I. Shews the ſalival Duct that ſprings from the Glands under the Ear called *Parotides*, (in a Calves Head.)

aaaa *The conglomerate* Parotis.
bb *The conglobate* Parotis.
c *The lymphatick Veſſel tending downwards from the conglobate Gland.*
dddd *The roots of the ſalival Duct.*
eee *The Trunk of the ſaid Duct.*
ffff *The outer branches of the Jugular Vein.*
ggg *The Nerves, which as they are inoculated one with another within the Gland and the head, ſo without theſe places as in* h.
ii *The twigs of Nerves accompanying the ſalival Duct.*

Fig. II. and III. Shew the Gland under the Tongue (called the maxillar Gland) with the Duct that ſprings from it, (from Dr. *Wharton.*)

A *The hinder part of the Gland.*
aaa *The hinder roots of the ſalival Duct.*
B *The fore-part of the Gland.*
bb *The fore-roots of the ſaid Duct.*
C *The hinder Trunk of the ſame Duct, climbing upon the Tendon of the double-belly'd Muſcle.*
D *The return of the ſame and its union with the Fore-duct.*
E *The common Trunk of the ſalival Duct.*
FG *The double-belly'd Muſcle.*
H *The progreſs of the ſaid Trunk towards the Fore-teeth of the lower Jaw.*

I *The opening of the salival Duct under the tip of the Tongue near the Foreteeth of the said Jaw.*

K *The round Gland that lies by the Maxillar.*

L *A row or rank of asperities (or roughnesses) under the side of the Tongue.*

M *The Tongue thrust to one side out of its place, that the exit of the Vessel may be seen.*

N *The Tonsil or Almond of the Ear.*

Having now gone through the first division of the Body, which is into three Venters or Regions, wherein I have principally treated of the Parts contained in them; it now remains that I examine the Parts wherewith the Venters themselves are made up, laying each apart by themselves, that their natures, differences and figures may better appear. The Parts of this nature are the Flesh and Bones, of which two it will be most proper to begin with the Flesh, both because it maketh the greatest part of the bulk of the Body, and also because of its quick tendency towards putrefaction, whereas the Bones are of a durable nature, and so no inconvenience will happen upon deferring the examination of them to the last.

The End of the Third Book.

THE

THE ANATOMY OF AN HORSE.

BOOK IV.

Of the Muscles.

CHAP. I.

Containeth a description of the several sorts of Flesh, and an Apology for not expressing the Muscles so particularly in Figures as I have done other Parts of the Body.

IN the First Book Chap. 6. treating of the Muscles of the Belly, I affirmed that all the *fleshy* Parts of the Body are *muscular*; which must be understood not of all *Flesh* in *general*, but onely of Flesh *properly* so called. For there are four kinds of Flesh: First, that which is properly so called, such as is that of the *Muscles*; secondly, that of the Bowels, as of the Liver and Spleen, and the like; thirdly, that of the Glands or Kernels; and fourthly, membranous Flesh, such as is that of the Stomach, Guts, &c.

The Flesh of the *Muscles* is soft and ruddy, consisting of Fibres and coagulated or curdled Bloud, called a *Parenchyma*. For the Bloud in its circulation as it passeth out of the Arteries into the Veins, is extravasated out of the Arteries into the very fleshy substance, out of which it is not ſo clearly imbibed or drunk up by the Veins, but that ſome particles of it adhere to the fleſhy Fibres, and fill up their interſtices, that is, the empty ſpaces between one and another: which Bloud congealing and fixing there, does, I ſay, together with the Fibres conſtitute that ſubſtance which we properly call Fleſh.

As to the other Parts that ſerve to conſtitute a Muſcle, as alſo of its uſe, and the reaſon of their ſundry denominations, I diſcourſed ſo fully in the above-mentioned ſixth Chapter of the Firſt Book, that I ſhall not need to add any thing to the ſame purpoſe here: onely I think my ſelf in this place obliged to give the Reader the reaſons, why I have not repreſented the Muſcles in Figures particularly, as I have done other Parts of the Body, nor dare be ſo confident of my exactneſs in the deſcription of them; for

Firſt, The Muſcles are ſo numerous, that to have expreſt them all in Figures would have made this Volume at leaſt half as dear again as it is; as may be gueſt by the number of Copper-plates (in Folio) that Mr. *Brown* has repreſented the Muſcles of an Humane Body upon; for they are near fourty, and theſe of an Horſe muſt have required rather more than fewer.

Secondly, Though ſome knowledge of the Muſcles, eſpecially the external ones, is neceſſary that one may know in Tumours which way to make inciſion (that is, lengthways of the Muſcle and not acroſs, for fear of rendring it uſeleſs by cutting its nervous Fibres aſunder) yet to be ſo very exact in the knowledg of all of them, is matter rather of commendable curioſity than real uſefulneſs.

But thirdly, The chief reaſon is (for I will confeſs it) that I have not had the opportunity my ſelf to raiſe and inſpect every particular Muſcle, ſo that I muſt have delineated ſeveral of them by gueſs and upon truſt, whereby I ſhould both have betrayed my own importune vanity, and have led my Reader 'tis like into ſeveral Errours. Neither probably may my verbal deſcription of them be *truly exact* as to thoſe which I have not my ſelf viewed: though ſeeing in thoſe that I *have* inſpected, I have found ſo great a ſimilitude between the Muſcles of an Horſe and thoſe of a Man, I hope I ſhall not be much wide of the truth, if I preſume of the ſame Analogy or likeneſs in thoſe that I have *not* inſpected.

Now as to the likeneſs of a Man's and an Horſe's Muſcles the Reader may be pretty well ſatisfied if he compare thoſe of an Horſe's Belly (delineated with the autopſie or ſelf-view of the Graver) expreſt at the end of the ſixth Chapter of the Firſt Book, with thoſe of a Man's: or take but a proſpect of the next following Figure which repreſents an Horſe, ſeveral of whoſe Muſcles I have preſerved, and after having raiſed them, placed them in their ſeveral places again, the Horſe ſtanding up in a Preſs with them on, juſt in the ſame poſture as he appears in the Figure.

To theſe reaſons I might add the impoſſibility that moſt of my Profeſſion ſhould ever attain to an exact knowledge of them; ſo that this Book being principally deſigned for their uſe, I ſhould have been at a great deal of coſt and more pains to no great purpoſe. Now the difficulty lies in this, That moſt of the names of the Muſcles being originally Greek, and ſeveral of them ſuch as can no way aptly or intelligibly be rendred into Engliſh; and conſidering the mean education of moſt Farriers, that few of them underſtand ſo much as Latin; I ſay conſidering theſe things, 'tis impoſſible to deſcribe them to their capacity, and therefore I have contented my

ſelf

ſelf with a more ſuperficial and ſuccinct deſcription of them. And though for my own part I may without vain-glory pretend to a more liberal education than moſt of my Profeſſion, ſo that the Cramp-names (as we call them) of the Muſcles are no ſuch hindrance nor diſcouragement to me as they will be I fear to moſt others; yet I hope no curious and ingenious Anatomiſt, that knows how much time and pains is neceſſary to be ſpent upon the exact examination of any one Part, will think me ſluggiſh and ſupine, that I have not in thoſe few years that I have applied my ſelf to this ſtudy, attained as yet to the full knowledge of all the Parts of this Beaſt that I anatomize. And as on the one hand I hope I may my ſelf attain to greater skill in this Art than I have yet arrived at; ſo on the other hand I would not be guilty of the vanity of thinking to monopolize it, but ſhall both deſire and hope that others will make up what I ſhall leave imperfect. But thus much I hope may ſerve for mine Apology with all ingenuous Men, I ſhall therefore return from whence I have digreſſed.

A ſecond ſort of Fleſh is that of the *Bowels*, as of the Liver, Spleen and Kidneys, whoſe ſubſtance hath been held to be for the greateſt part parenchymous, or to conſiſt of an affuſion of Bloud congealed about the Veſſels; though latter Anatomiſts do affirm them to be for the greateſt part glandulous. And to theſe hath uſed to be reckoned the Heart; but that is of a ſubſtance far different from theſe, as being truly muſcular, and may therefore more properly be ranked with the Muſcles, though it be of a more hard and compact frame than them alſo.

A third kind of Fleſh is that of the *Glands*, ſuch as the *Thymus*, which by ſome is called the Sweet-bread, and is ſituated near the Collar-bone juſt within the Cheſt, of which we have already treated in the Second Book. Of this ſort of glandulous Fleſh likewiſe are the *Parotides* or Kernels below the Ears, alſo the Tonſils (commonly called the Almonds of the Ears) very many Glands in the Meſentery and other Parts of the Body; to which may be added the *Pancreas* ſeated in the Lower Belly, which is commonly known by the name of the Sweet-bread.

Now the Glands being ſpermatical Parts, their parenchyma or fleſhy ſubſtance is not ſanguineous or bloudy, as that of the two former kinds of Fleſh; but ſpermatical, compoſed out of the very firſt rudiments of the embryo or conception. And though the Glands are many times encreaſed in bulk, as particularly in Humane Bodies affected with the King's-Evil, and in Horſes which upon taking great Colds have the Tonſils or Almonds of the Ears, and alſo the *Parotides* or Kernels below the Ears, ſo ſwelled and ſore, that the Horſe will not be able to ſwallow his Drink, or at leaſt not to hold down his Head to take it, but muſt be forced to have it given him in a Pail held up as high as the Manger; yet I ſay, the encreaſe of theſe Kernels happens not upon any extraordinary afflux of Bloud flowing to thoſe Parts, but by a flegmatick Humour falling upon them, and when the Diſtemper is cured they return again to their former ſmallneſs, being according to Nature incapable of that growth that is natural and proper to the Parts called ſanguineous. To this ſort of Fleſh (ſay ſome Authours) may the Brain be reduced.

The laſt ſort of Fleſh is that which is called *Membranous*, ſuch is that of the middle Coat of the Gullet, Stomach, Guts, Womb and Bladder. For though the inmoſt and outermoſt Coats be purely nervous or membranous, yet the middle conſiſts of two ranks of Fibres and a Parenchyma

chyma that adheres to them, which is diſcoverable particularly in the Guts, when they are ſcraped by Men that make ſtrings for muſical Inſtruments, for then you may perceive a great deal of ſlimy ſtuff to be ſcraped off them, which is this Parenchyma: For that they loſe no part of their membranous or fibrous ſubſtance is evident, in that their ſtrength is rather increaſed than diminiſhed by ſuch ſcraping. This Coat notwithſtanding it is muſcular, yet its Parenchyma differs in many regards from that of the ſanguineous Muſcles, particularly in that it is ſpermatical as was ſaid before of the Glands.

Now the Parts that conſiſt of theſe three latter ſorts of Fleſh are all deſcribed in their proper places; but thoſe that conſiſt of the firſt ſort, which as I have ſaid, is moſt properly ſo called, I intend to treat of in this Book which containeth the Doctrine of the Muſcles.

CHAP. II.

Of the Muſcles of the Eye-lids.

HAving in the ſixth Chapter of the Firſt Book ſpoken of the ſeveral Parts of which a Muſcle is compounded, and alſo of the differences and actions of them; as likewiſe of what uſe they are in general; (to which Chapter I refer the Reader) My propoſed method requires that I ſhould now come to ſpeak to every particular of them, beginning with thoſe of the Lower Belly: but having in the before-cited Chapter of the Firſt Book treated particularly of *them*, I will in this place paſs them by, deſiring the Reader to conſult the ſaid Chapter for his ſatisfaction; for I love not to be tedious with repetitions.

The Eye-lids have three pair of Muſcles.

The next Muſcles then that we come to ſpeak to according to order, are the Muſcles of the *Eye-lids*, which are in number three to each Eye.

One pair to open them; and

The firſt of theſe is called *Rectus* or *Aperiens*, from its office, which is to lift up or open the Eye-lid.

This is ſeated in the upper part of the orbit of the Eye, and ſpringeth with a ſlender but fleſhy beginning from the ſame place as the *Elevator* of the Eye doth, (which is at the hole which the Optick Nerve paſſes through into the orbit) and holds the ſame courſe with it, being of the ſame figure and ſubſtance, that is, fleſhy; till at laſt parting from it, with a pretty broad but thin Tendon, it is inſerted into the Griſtle at the edge of the upper Eye-lid, where it ſerves (as hath been ſaid) to open the Eye-lid by lifting it up.

Two to ſhut them.

The two other Muſcles of the Eye-lid are called *Shutters*, and otherwiſe *ſemicircular*, becauſe each runs the length of one Eye-lid: though there are ſome that call them *circular* or *orbicular*, ſuppoſing them to be but one Muſcle which compaſſes the Eye-lid round as with a circle. But in Bodies that are very muſculous or fleſhy, they have by curious Anatomiſts been plainly diſcovered to be two, and that the rather, becauſe each receives diſtinct Nerves from different places. They lie betwixt the carnous Membrane and the inner ſmooth Skin that lines the Eye-lids.

That

That which draweth down or ſhutteth the upper Lid is larger, and ariſeth from the inner corner of the Eye, from whence it paſſeth acroſs, though with a kind of an oblique line, towards the outward corner, growing preſently fleſhy and broad, ſo that it filleth up all the ſpace betwixt the Eye-brow and the loweſt edge of the Eye-lid, and ſo at laſt is inſerted into the outward corner of the Eye.

The leſſer of theſe two is that which moveth the lower Lid in order to ſhut it. This is rather membranous than fleſhy at its origin, (being alſo very thin) and takes its riſe at the inner corner of the Eye with a ſharp beginning as the former did: whence being carried overthwart, it proceeds to the middle of the Eye-lid, where it becomes ſomething fleſhy, and continues its courſe to the outward corner, which it turns about, and aſcending a little to the upper Eye-lid, is with an indifferent broad end inſerted into it.

The Fore-head Muſcles.

There is another pair of Muſcles which though not belonging properly to the Eye-lids, yet ſeem to contribute ſomething to their motion upward or opening, which therefore may reaſonably be deſcribed in this place, and thoſe are the *muſculi frontales*, or Fore-head Muſcles. Theſe ariſe from the Skull near the coronal Suture, and deſcend with ſtreight Fibres to the Eye-brows, where they terminate. By the help of theſe Muſcles the Skin of the Fore-head to which they cloſely ſtick is contracted or wrinkled, and ſo by conſequence the upper Eye-lid's a little drawn upward.

CHAP. III.

Of the Muſcles of the Eye.

The Eyes have ſeven pair of Muſcles.

TO the moving of each Eye of an Horſe do belong ſeven Muſcles; though in Humane Bodies there are accounted but ſix, becauſe the circular or ſuſpending Muſcle is ſaid in them to be wanting.

Of theſe ſeven, four are ſtreight, two oblique or ſlanting, and the other circular or round. The ſtreight ſerve to move the Eyes upwards and downwards, to the right hand and to the left. The oblique move them obliquely; and the circular or round one keeps the Eye ſuſpended up in its place.

Their riſe and inſertion.

Theſe Muſcles have all their riſe from one and the ſame place; they have alſo the ſame progreſs and ſtructure, and their termination is alike: for they do all ariſe from the Membrane that inveſts the Orbit of the Eye near the hole where the Optick Nerve paſſeth from the Brain into the ſaid Orbit, touching one another at their beginning; but they immediately ſeparate, and in their courſe become ſtill more and more bulky and fleſhy till their middle, which is round and buncheth out with a kind of a belly; but as they grow toward their ends or terminations they degenerate from their fleſhy into a thin membranous ſubſtance, which is inſerted into the horney Coat of the Eye, encompaſſing it as far as it is white.

Whence they have their names. Attollens *and* Deprimens. These Muſcles have their ſeveral appellations or names from the ſeveral motions they perform; as firſt, The firſt of the *ſtreight* Muſcles, from its office of pulling up the Eye, is called *Attollens:* The ſecond is called *Deprimens,* becauſe it is an Antagoniſt to the former, for as that pulls the Eye up, ſo this by a contrary motion pulls it down again. From which offices they have alſo in Men other two names given them by Anatomiſts: the firſt is called *the proud,* becauſe when the Eye is pulled up, a Perſon looks high and lofty or proud: and on the contrary when the Eye is pulled down by the other Muſcle, he looks with a contrary countenance, ſubmiſſive and humble, for which reaſon this ſecond Muſcle is called *humilis* or *the humble* Muſcle.

Adducens. The next, being the third ſtreight Muſcle, is called *Adducens,* becauſe it pulleth the Eye towards the Noſe. It is otherwiſe called *Bibitorius,* becauſe it performs that motion of drawing the Eye to the Noſe when we drink, for then we commonly look into the Pot or Glaſs that is before our Noſe.

Abducens. The fourth ſtreight Muſcle is called *Abducens* or *Indignatorius,* from its office of drawing the Eye to the outer corner, which turn or aſpect of the Eye betokens anger or ſcorn.

Now theſe four Muſcles have theſe four ſeveral motions, when they work ſeverally; but when they all four work together, they have but one action, which is to keep the Eye ſteady and fixt, which Phyſicians call a tonick motion: but in Beaſts that have the ſuſpending Muſcle, the tonick motion is performed mainly, if not altogether, by that Muſcle. You have theſe four, as alſo the three other lively repreſented to you in the twenty fifth Table of the Third Book, *p.* 123.

The upper oblique Muſcle. The next are the *oblique* Muſcles, being as hath been ſaid, in number two pair, which from their rolling the Eye about are called *circumagentes.* The *firſt* of them is called *obliquus major vel ſuperior* (or the uppermoſt and largeſt oblique Muſcle) being longer than the other, but rather ſlenderer. It ſpringeth from the upper but inner part of the Orbit of the Eye by the hole where the Optick Nerve comes through, (as do all the reſt.) From hence it paſſeth ſtreight to the upper part of the inner corner of the Eye, where it endeth in a ſmall round Tendon, which paſſeth through a tranſverſe Cartilage or Griſtle there placed, called *Trochlea* (or the Pully) and thence continueth its courſe ſlantingly along the upper part of the Eye, till at laſt it is inſerted into the outmoſt Skin of the Eye between the Tendons of the Muſcles *Attollens* and *Abducens.* This rolleth the Eye towards its inner corner.

The lower oblique Muſcle. The *ſecond oblique* Muſcle is called *obliquus minor ſive inferior,* or the leſs and lower oblique Muſcle, being ſhorter than the other, though rather thicker. This ſpringeth from a chink which is in the lower part of the Orbit of the Eye, beginning with a fleſhy head, from whence it aſcends with a ſlanting courſe towards the outward corner of the Eye, about which it turns, and then ends in a ſhort roundiſh and nervous Tendon, which meets with the Tendon of the other oblique Muſcle, and ſeeming to unite with it, is inſerted in the ſame place. This rolls the Eye towards its outer corner.

The orbicular Muſcle. The ſeventh Muſcle is called the *orbicular* or *round*; likewiſe *Muſculus ſuſpenſorius,* the ſuſpenſory Muſcle; and laſtly, becauſe it is onely found in Brutes, it hath the name given it of *ſeptimus Brutorum,* the Brute's ſeventh Muſcle. It is ſhort and fleſhy, encompaſſing the Optick Nerve,

and

and is inserted into the hinder part of the *Cornea*. You have the figure of it in the afore-mentioned twenty fifth Table of the Third Book, wherein it is removed from one Eye, but in the other it is plainly represented *in situ*. The use of this Muscle, as hath been said, is to sustain the Eye, lest by looking continually down toward the ground, it should hang too much outward; and by it also the tonick motion is performed.

Having discoursed of these several Muscles and of their several actions and uses, I think it very necessary to set down the manner of raising them, that he that will take the pains to examine them in the Creature it self, may the better find them, without violating of them unawares, whereby he will lose his labour, and miss of satisfaction in the inquiry after them.

The manner of raising the Muscles of the Eye.

You must then, after the taking the Eye and all its appurtenances clear out of the Orbit (if you will make your dissection that way; but if you will take the pains to remove the Bones of the Orbit and not cut the Eye out, it will be much better, for then you are sure to see the Muscles in their natural situation: but whether you remove the Bones, or take the Eye out, you must I say) make your dissection on this manner: First, you must with a pair of Scissers cut off the Fat and the Skins before you raise any of the Muscles, making them as clean as you can. Then begin with them in order thus: first raise the larger or upper oblique Muscle, then the lesser or lower oblique; then the four streight Muscles: but you must onely raise the larger oblique Muscle and not remove it, untill you have seen and removed the other five; for when the others are removed, you will the plainer perceive how the Tendon of the said Muscle passeth through the Pully, that is seated in the inner corner of the Eye.

After you have had a full view of these Muscles before-named, then mind the last and seventh Muscle, which still encompasseth the Optick Nerve, reaching from the place where the other Muscles had their rise, quite down to the hinder hemisphere of the Eye.

CHAP. IV.

Of the Muscles of the Nose.

THE *Nose* of an Horse so far as it is gristly, is moved several ways, which motions are performed by these following Muscles. First it is drawn together to shut the Nostrils by the *Adducent* or *Claudent* Muscles: and secondly it is drawn asunder to open the Nostrils by the *Abducent* or *Aperient* Muscles. And to the performing each motion there belong two pair of Muscles; so that in all there are eight Muscles that belong to the Nose. I shall describe the two latter pair first, whereof

The first pair of Abducent Muscles.

The first pair arises from the upper Jaw-bone, near the first proper pair of the Lips, and is inserted partly into the lower part of the *Alæ*, or gristly circumference of the Nostrils, and partly into the upper part of the upper Lip.

The second pair. The other pair begins at the top of the Nose near the Eye, with an acute and fleshy beginning, whence descending somewhat slantingly, and in its passage lying upon each side of the Nose, it doth at last end at the *Alæ*, as the other pair did, but with a broader and fleshier end. Each of these Muscles being narrow at the beginning, and ending broad, is in shape triangular or three-square, like the Greek Letter Δ *delta*, from whence it is called by some *deltoides*. The use of this pair, as also of the former, is to draw the gristly circumference or wings of the Nostrils upwards, and so to widen and open them.

The first pair of Adducent *Muscles.* The other two pair are called the *Adducent* or closing Muscles; the first pair of which is *external*, arising about the root of the Gristle, and ascending cross-ways to the ridg or tip of the Nose, into which it is inserted. This pair is more fleshy than the other, though indeed there is not much Flesh in any of the Muscles of the Nose, and therefore it will require a very accurate Anatomist to raise any of them, and to distinguish them.

The second pair. The second pair of the closing Muscles are *internal*, and are hid in the Cavity of the Nostrils under the inner Coat that cloaths them. These are not so fleshy as the former. They arise from the end of the Bone of the Nose, and spreading into a kind of membranous substance, they descend to the gristly circumference of the Nostrils where they terminate.

The first pair of these Muscles being contracted depress the *Alæ* or Gristles of the Nose, and the latter pair draw them inwards, and so close the Nostrils; to which motion the orbicular or round Muscle of the upper Lip is assistant, for by its drawing the upper Lip downwards, it doth at the same time constringe or straiten the Nostrils.

CHAP. V.

Of the Muscles of the Lips and Cheeks.

TO the *Lips* do belong several pair of Muscles, some of which are *proper* to the *Lips* alone, and others are *common* both to the *Cheeks* and *Lips*.

The first common Muscle, called the foursquare *Muscle.* The *common* are on each side of the Face two. The first of which is called *detrahens quadratus*, or the four-square drawers aside of the Cheeks and Lips. This shews more like a Skin than a Muscle, being broad and thin, onely it is interlaced with fleshy Fibres, which makes it to be accounted a Muscle.

It arises from one of the Vertebres of the Neck on its outside, as also from the Shoulder-blade, the Collar-bone and Breast-bone, from whence it ascends with oblique or slanting Fibres up to the Chin, Lips, and root of the Nose; which Parts it draws downwards with a slanting motion.

The second common Muscle, called the Trumpeter. The second *common* Muscle of the Cheeks and Lips, is called in Humane Bodies *Buccinator* the Trumpeter, because in blowing a Trumpet the main stress lies upon this Muscle; though others derive that name from *Bucca* the Cheek, because it is the most considerable Muscle of it, and

and on this account it may retain the ſame name in an Horſe: or it may be called the *Contracter*, from its action, which is to contract the Cheek.

It ſprings from almoſt the whole length of the *upper* Jaw-bone, and is inſerted into the whole length of the *lower*, at the root of the Gums. It is thin and membranous, and interlaced with divers Fibres running ſundry ways; and hath the inner Coat of the Mouth ſo cloſely and firmly adhering to it, that it is ſcarce ſeparable from it. This Muſcle is ſeated under the upper part of the former, and is ſpread over the whole dimenſion of the Cheek.

Its *uſe* in Horſes and other Brutes is to be as a Hand to help the Mouth in its chewing motion; for as the Meat in chewing falls on the outſide of the Teeth, betwixt them and the Cheek, this Muſcle helps to turn it over the Teeth again, that it may be ſufficiently broken and ground, and made thereby the readier for concoction when it is turned down to the Stomach.

Beſides this office of aſſiſting in chewing, it doth ſerve alſo at other times upon any occaſion to move the Cheeks and Lips.

The firſt proper pair of Muſcles of the Lips, called par Attollens.

Next come we to the Muſcles that are *proper* to the *Lips* onely, and thoſe are by Anatomiſts accounted five pair and one odd one. The firſt of them is called *par Attollens*, or Lifters up of the Lip. This pair ſpring from the upper Jaw, where it makes the hollow of the Cheek. At their riſe they are broad and fleſhy, from thence paſſing down obliquely along the Cheeks, each of them is inſerted into its own ſide of the upper Lip, near the Noſe. The *uſe* of theſe Muſcles, if they both of them act together, is to draw the upper Lip directly upwards and outwards; but if onely one acts, then is but one ſide of the Lip drawn upward obliquely. You may plainly ſee theſe Muſcles work, if you take notice of a Ston'd Horſe after he hath ſmelt to a Mare; for then he will moſt times hold up his Head in the Air, and turn up his upper Lip till he hath almoſt turned it inſide outwards. And the like you may ſee many Horſes doe, if you onely let them ſmell to another Horſe's Dung.

The ſecond pair, called par Abducens.

The *ſecond* pair is called *Abducens*, the Drawers of the Lip on one ſide. This ariſes at the Cavity that is under the *Os jugale* with a fleſhy and round beginning, which is cover'd with ſome Fat, eſpecially in fat Horſes; from whence they run down on each ſide to the middle of the upper Lip, into which they are inſerted with a ſtrong round Tendon. Theſe jointly move the Lips upwards and outwards as the former did, aſſiſting them in their motion; and when either of them acts ſingly, then it aſſiſts the action of one of the former that is on its own ſide, and helps to draw the Lip upwards of one ſide.

The third pair, called Zugomaticum.

The *third* pair is called by *Riolanus*, *Zugomaticum* or *Jugale*, from its riſe, which is outwardly from the proceſs of the *Os jugale*. At their beginning they are fleſhy and ſomewhat round, and running downward a little overthwart the Cheeks they reach at laſt to the ſides of the upper Lip, where they are inſerted near the corner of the Mouth. The *uſe* of this pair is to draw the Lip upwards ſideways.

The fourth pair, called Deprimens.

The *fourth* pair is called *Deprimens*, or the Drawers down of the lower Lip. Theſe ariſe fleſhy and broad from the lowermoſt and outwardmoſt part of the Lower Mandible; from whence each marches obliquely to the under Lip, into which they are inſerted about the middle of it. The uſe of this pair is to draw the under Lip downwards and ſomewhat outwards. So that it joineth in the same action with the first pair of the common Muscles called *Detrahens quadratus*.

The fifth pair, called Obliquè detrahens.

The *fifth* pair is called *Obliquè detrahens*, from their office, which is to draw the lower Lip obliquely downwards and outwards. They take their beginning from the sides of the lower Jaw, where they rise with a fleshy and broad head; from whence they ascend upwards, growing in their passage something narrower, and are each inserted into the corners of the lower Lip. The *use* of this pair is, as hath been said, to draw the lower Lip obliquely downwards and outwards.

The odd Muscle, called Orbicularis.

In the next place we come to the odd Muscle, called *Orbicularis*, or orbicular, because it goes round the circuit of both the Lips. It is also called *Constringens*, because it serves as it were for a Sphincter Muscle to purse up or contract the Lips. Besides these names it has in Men that of *Osculatorius*, the Kissing Muscle, because it contracts or draws the Lips together in kissing. It sticks very close to the Skin of the Lips, and makes up the greatest part of their substance.

CHAP. VI.

Of the Muscles of the lower Jaw.

THE *upper Jaw* being immoveable hath no Muscles, there being no occasion for them where there is no motion, which is their onely use. But the *lower Jaw* which hath motions of divers sorts, doth require divers sorts of Muscles to perform them. Now these Muscles are in number five pair.

The first pair of Muscles called the Temporal.

The *first* pair of these Muscles is called the *Temporal*, because they are seated upon the Temples. They spring on each side from the Bones of the Brow or Fore-head, the *Synciput*, Temples and Wedge-like Bone. They are the strongest and largest of all the five pair. Their beginning is fleshy, large and semicircular, their inside lying upon the *Periosteum*, and their outside covered with the *Pericranium*. They descend under the *Os jugale* to the acute Process of the lower Jaw, into which they are inserted by a short but very strong Tendon. These Muscles with great force pull up the lower Jaw, and so shut the Mouth.

The second pair, called Deprimens.

The *second* pair hath the name of *Deprimens*, because they pull down the Jaw. They are also from their shape, having as it were two bellies, called *biventre*. These being assisted by the *quadrati*, which were described in the foregoing Chapter (being one of the pairs that are common to the Cheeks and Lips) pull down the Jaw, and so open the Mouth. They arise with a broad and nervous beginning from the Process of the Temple-bone called *Styloides*, and suddenly becoming round, fleshy and small, they pass downwards, and in their middle where they come to the flexure of the lower Jaw-bone, they lose their fleshy substance and degenerate into a nervous and round Tendon, and then becoming fleshy again they are inserted into the inner side of the lower Jaw at the middle or fore-part of it.

The

The *third* pair is called *Maſſeteres*, becauſe they are very aſſiſtant in the office of *chewing*, by moving the Jaw to the right and left ſide. Each hath two beginnings: the firſt is large, ſtrong and nervous, ariſing from that Suture where the fourth and firſt Bone of the upper Jaw are joined; the other beginning is fleſhy, ſpringing from the *Os jugale*. They are firmly and largely inſerted into the outſide of the lower Jaw. Theſe Muſcles, by reaſon of their diverſity of Fibres, move the nether Jaw both forwards, backwards and to the ſides, and ſo in a manner circularly. *The third pair, called* Maſſeteres.

The *fourth* pair are called *Pterygoideum externum*, as if they reſembled a pair of *Wings*. Theſe like the former have alſo a double beginning, partly nervous, and partly fleſhy. They ſpring partly from the upper and outward ſide of the Wing-like Proceſs of the Wedge-like Bone, and partly from the rough and ſharp line of the ſame Bone, from whence they march down with ſtreight Fibres, becoming in their courſe larger and thicker, till they come to the lateral part of the lower Jaw, into whoſe inſide they are inſerted with a ſtrong Tendon. The *uſe* of this pair of Muſcles is to open the Jaw and move it forward, which appeareth when the Teeth of the lower Jaw are ſtretched farther out than thoſe of the upper. *The fourth pair, called* Pterygoideum externum.

The *fifth* and laſt pair of Muſcles of the lower Jaw are called *Pterygoideum internum*. Theſe ariſe with a nervous beginning from the inner ſide or cavity of the Wedge-like Bone, at its wing-like Proceſs; then becoming fleſhy, large and thick, they march down with a ſtreight paſſage to the inner and hinder part of the lower Jaw, where they are inſerted by a nervous, broad and ſtrong Tendon. The *uſe* of theſe Muſcles is to draw the Jaw towards its head or backwards; and alſo to help the Temporal Muſcle to draw the Jaw up. *The fifth pair, called* Pterygoideum internum.

CHAP. VII.

Of the Muſcles of the Ear.

THE Muſcles of the *Ears* in Brutes (eſpecially ſuch as have large Ears, as Horſes, Aſſes, Oxen, Hares, *&c.*) differ much in magnitude from thoſe of Men, in whom they are ſo very ſmall, that *Galen* calls them, the lineaments of Muſcles. The reaſon of which is, that in Man the Ears are moſt commonly immoveable, (though there have been ſome that could move them) and therefore to have large Muſcles were needleſs; and yet to have none at all, would look like a defect in the moſt perfect of all Animals. But though Man cannot move his Ears, yet is that no prejudice to his hearing; for the want of that motion is recompenced by the eaſie and ſpeedy motions of his Head, whereby he can turn it on every ſide to receive the ſounds; whereas four-footed Beaſts, that have the motions of their Heads not ſo nimble, have need to have their Ears always moveable every way, to receive the ſounds from every ſide: and their moveableneſs has alſo a further uſe, to wit, to drive away Flies

Flies and other Insects that are troublesome to the Beast, which Men can doe with their Hands.

The External Ear hath four Muscles. The Ear we divided, in the former Book, into the *Outward* and *Inward*. The *Outward* (of which we have been discoursing thus far in this Chapter) has four Muscles; and these are those which are so much larger in Brutes than Men. The *Inward* Ear has two, which are of a proportionable largeness in both.

1. The lifter up of the Ear. The first of these we come to treat of is the *first* of the *Outward* Ear, which goes by the name of *Attollens Aurem*, the lifter or puller up of the Ear. This arises at the outside of the Frontal or Forehead Muscle, and at its rise is thin and membranous; from whence being carried over the Temporal Muscle, and growing in its course something narrower, it doth at last insert it self into the upper part of the Ear, moving it upwards and forwards.

2. The puller back of the Ear. The *second* is called *Detrahens Aurem*, or the puller back of the Ear. This Muscle arises from the Mammillary Process with a fleshy, broad and fibrous head; and so growing narrower in its progress is at length inserted into the root of the Gristle of the Ear, sometimes by two, sometimes by three Tendons. The *use* of this Muscle is to draw the Ear backwards and somewhat upwards.

3. Adducens Aurem. The *third* is called *Adducens Aurem*, by which the Ear is drawn forwards and somewhat downwards. This is said to be but a part of the *musculus quadratus* before spoken of in the fifth Chapter of this Book, being one of the common Muscles of the Cheeks and Lips. This Muscle ascending with its Fibres is implanted into the lower side of the root of the Ear.

4. Abducens Aurem. The *fourth* is called *Abducens Aurem*, because it draws or pulls the Ear backwards. This takes its beginning at the *Occiput* or back-part of the Head from the Coat that cloaths those Muscles that belong to that part, where it is at first something narrow, but afterward waxing broader it is carried transversly to the hinder part of the Ear, into which it is inserted. This assists the second in its action, having sometimes two, and sometimes three Tendons as that has.

The Inward Ear hath two. *1. The External.* The next are the two Muscles of the *Inner* Ear (called *Auris*, as the *Outward* Ear is called *Auricula*) the first of which is called *Externus Tympani Auris*, or the external Muscle of the Drum of the Ear, because it moves the Membrane of the Ear so called upwards and outwards. This is thin but broad at its rise, which is from the upper part of the passage of the Ear; then becoming narrower it grows into a very fine and small Tendon, which is carried on the outside of the *Tympanum* till it arrive at its centre or middle into which it is inserted, where on the inside of this *Tympanum* the little Bone called the Hammer sticketh, which with the Membrane or *Tympanum* this Muscle draweth a little outward and upward. This Muscle as also the next are very small, there being scarce any in the whole Body again so small as they are; and therefore it will require great skill to raise them without violating of them. To prevent which the undertaker is to open with great care the *Os petrosum* which is to be done on that side which is next to the Temples, taking out the pieces of Bones by degrees that these Muscles may receive no prejudice. It is left to the discretion of the Dissector whether he will remove the Bones with a Chissel, or Saw, or by filing, so he doe it carefully.

The

The ſecond is called *Internus*, and hath its origination from the bottom of the *Os cuneiforme* or Wedge-like Bone, there where it is joined with the *Proceſſus petroſus*. It is ſeated inwardly in the Cavity of the *Os petroſum*, being fleſhy at its beginning, yet thin and ſmall: at its middle it is divided into two very ſmall and very thin Tendons, whereof one is inſerted into the upper Proceſs of the *Malleus* or Hammer, and the other into the neck of it. The *uſe* of this Muſcle, alone, is to draw the head of the Hammer obliquely forwards, and alſo to draw it ſomewhat inwards: but when theſe two act both together, they move the *Tympanum* with its ſmall Bones upwards and downwards, which is done when the Horſe would carefully liſten or harken to any approaching noiſe. *2. The Internal.*

CHAP. VIII.

Of the Muſcles of the Tongue.

THE *Tongue* in Brutes hath but two principal uſes, *viz.* to taſte the Food, and to rowl it up and down the Mouth: but in Men it has a third uſe, which is to be the main inſtrument of Speech. Yet notwithſtanding there are as many Muſcles that belong to it in Brutes as there do in Men; for in ſome regard it has a further uſe in them than in Men, ſeeing it does not onely taſte and rowl about the Meat, but it ſerves alſo to gather it into the Mouth; for *that* they doe with their Tongue, becauſe they have not the help of Hands as we have. Wherefore that the Tongue might perform all theſe offices, it was neceſſary it ſhould be furniſhed with variety of Muſcles, to make it capable of being moved every way, outward and inward, upward and downward, and ſideways. And leſt in undergoing theſe motions it ſhould be made to reach farther than is neceſſary, Nature hath reſtrained it with a ſtrong Ligament underneath, which in Men is called the *Frænum* or Bridle of the Tongue.

The *Tongue* therefore hath five pair of Muſcles *proper* to it ſelf, beſides thoſe that are *common* to it and the *Os hyoides*, of which in the following Chapter. *The Tongue hath five pair of proper Muſcles.*

The *firſt* pair *proper* to it is called *Genioglossum* (or the Chin-tongue pair) ſo called becauſe their riſe is from the Chin, and their inſertion into the Tongue. This name is proper enough in Men who have Chins, but agrees not ſo well with them in Horſes (or other Brutes) in whom we call all that part below the Teeth, *the lower Jaw*, not diſtinguiſhing any part of it by the name of *the Chin.* But notwithſtanding I ſhall deſcribe them by that name, becauſe it would be too tedious and too bold an undertaking for me to invent new names for this as well as for others that are in Brutes as improperly called by ſuch names as this pair is; leaving ſuch an attempt to thoſe that have both more leiſure, and that make a greater figure in the Anatomical Province. *1. Genioglossum.*

This pair ariſe from the ruggedneſs which is in the middle of the lower Jaw before, in the inner and lower part of it. In their progreſs they are ſaid to have ſeveral ſuch inſcriptions as the ſtreight Muſcles of the Paunch

Paunch have, as if each consisted of several Muscles; however that be, they reach to the middle of the Tongue where they are inserted into its lower side. Their *use* is to move the Tongue forwards, towards the Fore-teeth, and many times out of the Mouth, that is, when the Beast gathers in his Meat.

2. Hypsiloglossum. The *second* pair is called *Hypsiloglossum*, (which word should be writ without an H, seeing they have this name because they rise from the bottom of the *Os hyoides*, which is otherwise called *Ypsiloides*,) from its resembling in shape the Greek Letter υ (*Ypsilon.*) They end in the middle of the Tongue, and have an action contrary to the former; for as those mov'd the Tongue outward, so these move it streight inward or backward.

3. Myloglossum. The *third* pair is called *Myloglossum*, from the places of its rise and insertion; for they arise from the inner part of the lower Jaw, at the roots of the farthest *grinding Teeth*, and are inserted into the Ligament by which the *Tongue* is tied to the *fauces* or Jaws. If this pair work together, they draw the Tongue downwards; but if onely one of them work, then it draws the Tongue obliquely to its own side.

4. Ceratoglossum. The *fourth* pair is called *Ceratoglossum*, because they arise from the *horns* of the *Os hyoides*, and reaching from thence to the sides of the *Tongue* are there inserted into it. If one of these work alone, it draws the Tongue aslant to either the right or left side; but if both work together, they draw the Tongue downwards and inwards.

5. Styloglossum. The *fifth* and last pair of Muscles *proper* to the Tongue are called *Styloglossum*, because they arise from the *Styloides* (or Pen-like) Process of the Temple-bones, being fleshy at their beginning, though very small and sharp; but afterwards becoming broader and thicker, they run to the sides of the Tongue, into which they are inserted about the middle of its length. If either of these Muscles move singly, the Tongue is drawn to the right, or left side; but if both act together, they pull the Tongue upwards and inwards.

CHAP.

CHAP. IX.

Of the Muscles of the Bone of the Tongue, called Os hyoides.

THE Muscles of the Cheeks and Tongue serving to toss the Meat to and again in the Mouth, and those of the lower Jaw helping to chew or grind it; after it is sufficiently minced, it wants afterward to be swallowed and to be transmitted into the Stomach. Now none of the foresaid Muscles contribute any thing thereto, therefore it was necessary there should be others appropriated thereto, which by moving diversly the root of the Tongue might make way for the morsel to descend into the Gullet. Such are those that are common to the Tongue and the Bone called *hyoides* that is fasten'd to its root or basis, which are in number four pair. *The* Os hyoides *hath four pair.*

The *first* pair is called *Sternohyoideum*, because they spring from the upper but inner part of the *Sternum* or Breast-bone (with a broad and fleshy beginning) and ascending under the Skin of the Neck by the Wind-pipe (still keeping the same largeness and substance) are at length inserted into the root or bottom of the *Os hyoides*, which they move downward and backward. 1. Sternohyoideum.

The *second* pair is opposite to the former, and is called *Geniohyoideum.* These are large, short and fleshy all over, and arise with Fibres of a divers course, from the inside of the fore-part of the lower Jaw (called in Men the *Chin*) and are inserted into the middle part of the Bone *hyoides*, which they draw streight upwards and a little forwards. 2. Geniohyoideum.

The *third* pair is called *Coracohyoideum.* These are slender, but strong, and long; yea considering the slenderness of them, they are the longest Muscles of the whole Body. They arise out of the Process called *Coracoides* at the upper end of the Shoulder-blade near the Neck, and run obliquely upward under the first pair of Muscles of the Head called *Mastoideum*, where they lose their fleshy substance, as giving way to the other that are more worthy and considerable than themselves, and degenerate each into a nervous and round Tendon for some time; but so soon as they are past these Muscles, they become musculous again, and so continue till they reach to the *Os hyoides*, into whose horns they are inserted. These because of their two bellies are by some called Digastricks. Their *use* is to pull the *Os hyoides* obliquely downwards. 3. Coracohyoideum.

The *fourth* and last pair of Muscles of the *Os hyoides* is called *Stylocceratohyoideum.* These arise from the root of the Appendix or Process called *Styloides*, and end in the *horns* of *Os hyoides.* They move the Bone obliquely upwards. 4. Styloceratohyoideum.

I hope the English Reader will pardon me for not translating the names of these Muscles, for it is impossible for any Man to doe it, seeing our English Tongue is not capable of such compositions as the Greek admits of, from whence these names are borrowed: but he will see the reasons of the names, if he observe but the parts from whence the Muscles are said to rise, and into which they are inserted, in the description of them.

CHAP. X.

Of the Muscles of the Larynx *or* Throttle.

The Larynx *hath two pair of* common *Muscles, viz.*

THE *Larynx* in Mankind is the main instrument in modulating or forming the Voice, so as to make the tone high or low, &c. And though few Beasts can alter their tones with that variety that a Man can, yet have they the same number of Muscles to move the several Gristles whereof the *Larynx* is composed. Now its Muscles are either *proper*, or *common*. The *common* are those that are implanted into the *Larynx*, but arise not therefrom; and the *proper* are those that both arise and end in the *Larynx*. The *common* are four, and the *proper* nine.

1. Sternothyreoideum.

The *first* of the *common* pair is called *Sternothyreoideum*, and by some *Bronchium*, or the Weazand-muscles. These arise with a fleshy and broad beginning from the upper and inner part of the *Sternum* or Breast-bone at the very Throat, ascending with right or streight Fibres up by the sides of the Wind-pipe, continuing the same largeness and substance till they reach to the *Cartilago thyreoides*, or Shield fashioned Gristle, into which they are inserted. Their *use* is to draw down the said Gristle, and so to widen the Chink as some Authours think; though others are of opinion that such drawing of it down, serves to straiten the Chink.

2. Hyothyreoideum.

The *second* pair is called *Hyothyreoideum*. These arise from the lower side of the Bone *hyoides*, having a broad and fleshy beginning; from whence descending with streight Fibres they are inserted into the *Cartilago thyreoides*; by lifting which upwards they are said to straiten the Chink of the *Larynx*; though some on the contrary affirm that they widen it.

and four pair proper *ones and an odd one, viz.*

1. Cricothyreoideum.

Next come we to the *proper* Muscles of the *Larynx*, the *first* pair of which is called *Cricothyreoideum anticum*, because they take their beginning from the *fore-part* of the Ring-fashioned Gristle called *Cricoides*, and proceed obliquely to the Shield-fashioned Gristle or *Thyreoides*, into whose sides they are implanted. The *use* of this pair of Muscles is to move the Shield-fashioned Gristle or *Thyreoides* obliquely downwards, and by that means to open the *glottis* or Chink of the *Larynx*.

2. Cricoarytænoideum posticum.

The *second* of the *proper* pairs of Muscles of the *Larynx* are called *Cricoarytænoideum posticum*. These contrary to the former arise from the lower and *back-part* of the Ring-fashioned Gristle, and running upward with streight Fibres are inserted with a nervous end into the lower side of the *Arytænoides* or Ewer-like Gristle, which it pulls upward and backward, and thereby opens and widens the *Larynx*.

3. Cricoarytænoideum laterale.

The *third* pair is called *Cricoarytænoideum laterale*, because they are seated at the *sides* of the former pair. They arise from the sides of the Anulary or Ring-fashioned Cartilage somewhat slender; from whence proceeding directly upwards, and becoming more large and fleshy, they come to the *Arytænoides*, into the sides of which they are implanted in that part that the foregoing pair did not cover. The *use* of this pair is to open the *Larynx* by drawing the Gristles obliquely aside.

The *fourth* pair is called *Thyreoarytænoideum.* These are the largest and strongest of all the proper Muscles of the *Larynx*, yea almost equal to all the rest put together. They arise close one to the other from the inner hollow and middle part of the *Thyreoides* or Shield-fashioned Gristle, whose inner Cavity they fill through the whole length of it, and with oblique Fibres they ascend upward, growing narrower in their ascent, till they come to their insertion into the sides of the Ewer-like Gristle. These are the Muscles that are principally affected in Humane Bodies when they are in the greatest danger from that Disease called the Squinancy or Quinsie. For when these Muscles are inflamed, they swell inwards into the Throttle, and make the Cavity thereof so strait, that the Patient cannot fetch his breath, but is strangled. 4. Thyreoarytænoideum.

The *fifth* and last is reckoned but for one single Muscle, and is called *Arytænoides*, also *Claudens secundum*, or the second Shutting-muscle. They take their rise from the hinder line of the Ewer-like Gristle or *Arytænoides* from whence it hath its name. It is very small but fleshy, and running with transverse Fibres, it is inserted into the sides of the same Gristle, which it helps to constringe or draw both its sides together, and so straitens the Throttle. 5. *The Muscle* Arytænoides.

The *Epiglottis* or Throat-flap, that covers the Chink of the *Larynx* has no discernible Muscles in Man, nor I believe in an Horse: but in Cattle, Sheep, &c. that chew the Cud, it is said to have evident ones; some of which spring from the *Os hyoides*, and are inserted into the basis of the *Epiglottis*, which they lift up; and others are placed between the Coat and Gristle of the *Epiglottis*, helping it to shut the *Larynx*.

CHAP. XI.

Of the Muscles of the Uvula *and Throat.*

THE *Uvula* is said to have two Muscles to hold it up, *one* of which is called *Pterygostaphilinus externus.* This springeth from the upper Jaw a little beyond the furthermost Grinder, and is inserted into the *Uvula*. *The* Uvula *hath two Muscles.* 1. Pterygostaphilinus externus.

The *second* is called *Pterygostaphilinus internus.* This proceeds from the lower part of the inner Wing of the Process *Pterygoides* (or Wing-like) and is inserted in like manner as the former into the *Uvula*. 2. Pterygostaphilinus internus.

This is the description that Anatomists commonly give of these two Muscles; but it may be question'd whether they are any more than imaginary ones; for seeing the *Uvula* has no apparent voluntary motion, it seems to have no occasion for any Muscles.

Next to the Muscles of the *Uvula* come those of the *Throat* (or the beginning of the Gullet called *Pharynx*) to be treated of, to which belong seven Muscles, that is, three pair and a Sphincter. The *first* of the pairs is called *Sphenopharyngæum.* These arise thin and nervous from the Appendix of the Wedgelike-bone, descending by the inward Cavity of its *The* Pharynx *hath seven Muscles.* 1. *Par* Sphenopharyngæum.

Wing-like Processes, and are inserted into the lateral parts of the Palate and *Pharynx*, which they widen in swallowing.

2. Cephalopharyngæum. The *next* pair is called *Cephalopharyngæum*. These spring from that part where the *Head* is joined to the first *Vertebra* of the Neck, from whence they descend to the *Pharynx*, into which they are spread with a large *plexus* of Fibres, which seemeth to make its Membrane. The action of this pair is contrary to the former; for as those widen the *Pharynx* to let the nourishment descend into the Gullet, so these straiten it when the Food is past by it, and thereby squeeze the Food down the Gullet.

3. Stylopharyngæum. The *third* pair is called *Stylopharyngæum*. These arise with a small beginning from the inner part of the *Styloides* Process of the Temple-bone, and descending with a thin body are inserted into the sides of the *Pharynx* which they dilate or widen.

4. *The Muscle* Oesophagiæus. The *last* of these Muscles is that which hath no fellow, and is called *Oesophagiæus*, or the Sphincter of the Gullet. This arises at one side of the *Thyreoides*, or Shield-fashioned Gristle, and is inserted into the other side of the same, wholly encompassing in its course both the fore and back part of the Gullet, in the same manner as the Sphincters of the *Anus* and Bladder do those Parts, serving here for the same use, *viz.* to draw or purse in the mouth of the Gullet, as those do the Arse and Bladder. Now though I have the warrant of several Authours in describing of this Muscle last of the seven, yet there be others that treat first of it, and reckon it the first Muscle of the Throat, saying, that if you first raise this, the two next before-mentioned pairs, namely, the *Stylopharyngæum* and the *Cephalopharyngæum*, may be the better found.

Two pair of Muscles lately found out by Doctor Croune, *viz.* Having done with the Muscles of the *Uvula* and Throat, as also with all the Muscles of the inward and outward Parts of the Mouth and Chaps, according as they are treated of by the Ancient and Modern Anatomizers of these Parts; it remains now that I should descend to the Muscles of the Head and Neck, and so to the inferiour Parts; but before I depart quite from hence, I think it necessary to give the Reader an account of two pair of Muscles more, which belong to the Palate of the Mouth, never treated of by any Anatomist yet, save Mr. *Brown*, who in his Book of the Muscles lately set forth, gives the first account of them, at the desire of the discoverer of them, which was the most ingenious Doctor *Croune* now living, and at this time Lecturer at Chirurgeons Hall in *London*.

This worthy and learned Discoverer hath given them these names following; the first he calls *Musculi Pterygo-palatini*, and the other *Spheno-palatini*.

Pterygo-palatini, *and* This description hath he also given of them, *viz.* The first or *Pterygo-palatini* are seated in the lower part of the Cavity of the Wing-like Processes of the Wedge-like Bone, and terminate about the *Glandula palati* with their Tendons, which run upon part of the fore-mentioned Processes, as on two *Trochleæ* or Pullies. The *use* of this pair is to depress the before-named Gland of the Palate and the *Uvula*.

Spheno-palatini. The latter of them, which he calls *Spheno-palatini*, have an use contrary to the former, *viz.* to lift up the fore-mentioned Gland and *Uvula*. Their rise is from the *Os sphenoides* or Wedge-like Bone, and their insertion (with a broader Tendon than the former) into the sides of the before-mentioned Gland and *Uvula*. It is believed from the situation and action of this last pair of Muscles, that when the Rheum that had swelled the

Gland and relaxt the *Uvula*, is drained away, these Muscles help to reduce the *Uvula* to its proper and natural situation; though to me it seems, that its own contracting of it self is sufficient.

CHAP. XII.

Of the Muscles of the Head.

THE Muscles of the *Head* are either *proper* or *common*. The *common* are those which primarily move the Neck, and the Head onely secondarily, of which in the next Chapter; for according to order the *proper* are first to be spoken to, and these are they that move the Head onely, the Neck at that time remaining unmoved, the number of which are sixteen, or eight pair. *The Head hath eight pair of proper Muscles.*

The *first* pair is called *Mastoideum* (which pair some Authours indeed reckon for the eighth or last pair, and the *Splenium* for the first; but being willing to follow the more modern Writers I will begin with the *Mastoideum* and reckon them for the first pair.) 1. Mastoideum.

These are seated in the fore-part of the Neck, having each a double beginning; one of which is from the Breast-bone, being altogether nervous, and the other from the Collar-bone, which is fleshy. From these originals they ascend obliquely upwards by the Neck, till they come to the hinder part of the Head, *viz.* to the Mammillary Process of the Temple-bone, into which each is inserted by a round and fleshy Tendon. If both these Muscles work together, then they bend the Head right forward or downward; but if one onely works, then that draws the Head a little to one side. Of all the eight pair there are onely this that bend the Head streight forward, and that are placed in the fore-part of the Neck; for all the rest are seated behind towards the Mane, and do either pull the Head back, or else to one side.

The *second* pair (or first pullers back of the Head) is called *Splenium*. These are long and thick, arising from the five uppermost *Vertebræ* of the Chest and five lowermost of the Neck, with a nervous beginning; from whence ascending to the hinder part of the Head, they there end with a broad and fleshy Tendon. The use of these, if both of them act together, is to draw the Head directly backward; but if either of them act singly, then it draws the Head a little to one side. 2. Splenium.

The *third* pair, (being the second puller back of the Head) is called *Complexum* or *Trigeminum*, because each Muscle seems to consist of three, for it arises with three heads; one of which is from the transverse Process of the fourth and fifth *Vertebræ* of the Chest; the second from the first and second of the same, and the third from the ridge of the seventh *Vertebra* of the Neck: all which uniting into one body, the Muscles ascend upward as far as to the *Occiput* or Noll-bone, (in their course becoming fleshy and broad) and are inserted into the said Noll-bone, at the root of the Mammillary Process, sometimes by one, and sometimes by a triple Tendon. 3. Complexum.

The

4. Parvum & crassum. The third puller back of the Head, or *fourth* pair, is called *parvum & crassum*, because they are small and thick. These are situated under the former, arising from the transverse Processes of the six uppermost *Vertebræ* of the Neck, with a nervous beginning; but afterward becoming fleshy, they are carried obliquely upward, and are inserted into the hindermost root of the *Processus Mammillaris*. Their *use* is, if they act both together, to bring the Head lightly backwards; and if but one act, then to bring it backward to one side.

5. Rectum majus. The *fifth* pair is called *Rectum majus* or the greater right pair, being small, fleshy and slender, and arising from the tip of the Spine or ridge of the second *Vertebra* of the Neck, where they touch one another; but presently part, and ascending both upward, end with a round Tendon in the middle of the Noll-bone or *Occiput*. The action of this pair is the same as of the former.

6. Rectum minus. The *sixth* pair (being the fifth of the pullers back) is called *Rectum minus*, or the lesser right pair. Their situation is just under the former pair, as it were concealed, and are of the like substance, form and progress. They arise close together from the back-part of the first *Vertebra* of the Neck where the Bone should have ended in a Spine, but that Spine is wanting because it would have offended the former pair of Muscles that spring from the second *Vertebra* and march over this. Presently after their original they part, and ascend upwards, and on either side are implanted into the Noll-bone. The *use* of these is to assist the motion of the two foregoing pair. Now the reason why there are so many Muscles appointed to move the Head backward, and but one pair forward, is because the Head by reason of its great bulk and weight, is prone enough of it self to incline forward or downward; but it requireth a great force to move it upward or backward.

7. Obliquum superius. The *seventh* pair is called *Obliquum superius*, or the upper Oblique pair. These are seated under the right or streight pairs, and are like them in form and substance. They are small, arising out of the middle of the *Occiput* at the outside of the streight pairs, from whence they descend downwards, and are inserted into the tips of the transverse Processes of the first *Vertebra* of the Neck, the right-hand Muscle into the right Process, and the left into the left. The *use* of these, if they both act together, is to nodd the Head gently directly backwards.

8. Obliquum inferius. The *eighth* pair is called *Obliquum inferius*, or the lower Oblique pair. These arise from the Spine or ridge of the second *Vertebra* of the Neck, from whence running obliquely upwards, they end at the transverse Processes of the first *Vertebra* of the Neck. They are longish, round and fleshy; and make (as do also the former) a Triangle of equal sides.

The *use* of this pair is to move the Head as it were semicircularly, (for it cannot be moved quite round) the first *Vertebra* turning upon the Tooth-like Process of the second: but this motion is performed, when one of them onely acts at a time; for if both of them move or act together, then they either keep the Head steady (as some Authours conceive) or else draw it a very little backwards.

CHAP

CHAP. XIII.

Of the Muſcles of the Neck.

THE Head is not onely moved by its *proper* Muſcles mentioned in the laſt Chapter, primarily; but ſecondarily alſo by other Muſcles belonging to the *Neck*, which are in number eight, on each ſide four, by the help of which the Neck is ſometimes bent forward, other times extended backward; it is alſo ſometimes drawn to one ſide, and ſometimes to the other: but there are more Muſcles to draw it backwards than either forwards or to one ſide, becauſe the labour is greater by reaſon of the weight of the Head and Neck (as was ſaid in the former Chapter.) There are therefore two pair of Muſcles to bend the Neck backward, namely the firſt and ſecond, which do alſo draw it a little obliquely; and the third and fourth pair draw it both forward and to one ſide, as both act together, or but one of each pair at a time. *The Muſcles common to the Head and Neck are four pair.*

The *firſt* pair of theſe is called *Spinatum*, becauſe they are ſeated amongſt the Spines of the *Vertebræ*. They ariſe from the roots of the Spines of the ſeven uppermoſt *Vertebræ* of the Cheſt, and five lowermoſt of the Neck, being ſeparated from one another onely by the tips of the Spines, and are inſerted into the whole lower ſide of the Spine of the ſecond *Vertebra* of the Neck. They bend the Neck backward, or a little obliquely. Some think that they have no original from the Spines of the Neck, but that they onely adhere to them in their paſſage. 1. Spinatum.

The *next* pair is called *Tranſverſale*, becauſe they both riſe from and are inſerted into the tranſverſe Proceſſes of the *Vertebræ*. They take their beginning from the roots of the tranſverſe Proceſſes of the ſix uppermoſt *Vertebræ* of the Cheſt; from whence aſcending by degrees they become ſtronger and thicker, and are inſerted into the outſides of all the tranſverſe Proceſſes of the Neck-bones. The *uſe* of this pair, as alſo of the former, is as hath been ſaid, to pull or draw the Neck directly backwards; but if one Muſcle of either pair work alone, it pulls the Neck with an oblique motion. 2. Tranſverſale.

The *third* is called *Longum*, or the Long pair. Theſe lie hid under the *Oeſophagus* or Gullet, wherefore they are by ſome called the Under-gullet-lurkers. They ariſe with a thin and ſharp but fleſhy beginning from the body of the fifth and ſixth *Vertebræ* of the Back, and as they aſcend upwards, are knit to the ſides of all the *Vertebræ*, till they come to the firſt or higheſt of the Neck, where each touching other they are both inſerted into its Proceſs. The uſe of this pair, when they work together, is to bend the Neck directly forward, and withall to incline the Head; but if one of them act alone, then is the Neck drawn towards that ſide on which the Muſcle moveth. 3. Longum.

The *fourth* and laſt pair of the Muſcles of the Neck is called *Scalenum* or *Triangulare*. Theſe by ſome Authours are accounted as the eighth pair of the Cheſt. They are ſeated on the ſides of the Neck inclining rather to the fore than hinder part of it. They take their beginning from the firſt Rib, ariſing fleſhy and large, and are inſerted into the inſide of all 4. Scalenum.

the

the transverse Processes of the *Vertebræ* of the Neck. Their *use* is the same with the foregoing pair. They are observed to be perforated or to have holes through them, by which Veins, Arteries and Nerves do pass out of the Body into the Fore-legs.

Table XXXII.

Representeth an Horse standing with his Face towards us, that one may have the fuller view of some of the Muscles of the Head and Neck. It sheweth also several other Muscles, less perfectly.

AA *Shew the* par Mastoideum.
BB *The Muscles of the Shoulder-blade.*
CC *The* par Trigeminum *or* Complexum.
DD *That pair of Muscles of the Neck called* Scalenum *or* Triangulare.
E *The Wind-pipe in its natural situation.*
FF *That pair of Muscles of the Neck called* Longum, *removed from under the Gullet.*
GG *The pair of the Nose called* Philtrum.
HH *The Adducent or closing Muscles of the Nostrils.*
II *The Muscles of the Eye-lids.*
KK *The Temporal Muscles.*
LL *The Muscles of the Ears.*
M *The Frontal or Fore-head Muscle.*
N *The* Cucullaris *or Monk's hood.*
O *The* Deltoides *of the Shoulder.*
P *The* Serratus major Anticus *(shrunk up, for naturally their Teeth reach to those of the obliquely descending pair of the* Abdomen.)
QQ *The* Pectorales.
R *The* Obliquè descendens *of the* Abdomen, *a little shrunk up from the* Serratus major.
S *The* Deltoides *of the Thigh, (which I presume to call so, for it is just of the same figure with that of the Shoulder.)*
T *The* Serratus posticus.
VVV *The external Intercostal Muscles.*
W X Y *The three Buttock Muscles.*
Z *The* Vastus externus.
a *The* Sacrolumbus.
b *The* Longissimus dorsi.
c *The* Semispinatus.

CHAP.

TAB XXXII
p. 170.

CHAP. XIV.

Of the Muscles of the Breast.

HAving dispatched the Muscles of the Head and Neck, we come in the next place to speak to those of the Chest or *Thorax*, in which are contained the principal Instruments of Life, the Heart and Lungs. Now the Lungs being the principal organs of Respiration, and wanting Muscles whereby to dilate or contract themselves, it was necessary they should receive assistance from the Chest in which they are included, by the dilatation or contraction whereof, they might be also dilated and contracted. To which end the Chest is furnished with several Muscles, some of which contract it in Expiration, that is, when the Horse lets forth his breath, and others dilate it in Inspiration, when he receives in his breath.

Of the Dilaters or those that widen the Chest there are four pair, besides the sixteen pair of the External Intercostals, there being (as is already said in Chap. 2. of the Second Book where I largely treated of them) between each Rib two Muscles, an External and an Internal one. Now there being in number seventeen Ribs, reckoning a Rib for the extreme part both toward the Neck and toward the Flank, there must be one pair of Muscles fewer than there are Ribs, of which those that are seated externally, serve all as one Muscle to assist in the widening or dilating the Chest, and those that are seated internally (lying under the former) assist in the contraction of it. For a more full description of these Muscles you may please to turn back to the afore-cited Chapter. *There are four pair of Muscles that widen the Chest.*

The *first* pair of the dilating or widening Muscles is called *Subclavium*, from their situation, which is under the Collar-bone called *Clavicula*, for they fill up that space that is between the Clavicle and the first Rib. These arise fleshy from the inner and lower part of the Clavicle or Collar-bone, which is next to the Rib, and running obliquely or slanting forward, are implanted into the first Rib near the Breast-bone with a fleshy end. The action of this pair of Muscles is to draw the first Rib upwards and outwards, by which motion the cavity of the Chest is widened. 1. Subclavium.

The next or *second* pair of the Dilaters is called *Serratum majus Anticum*, or the greater and foremost Saw-like pair, so called partly from their situation and magnitude, and partly from the figure of their Tendons which resemble the teeth of a Saw. They arise from the inside of the Shoulder-blade and the two upper Ribs, and are inserted into the lower five True-ribs and two upper bastard or Short-ribs, before they end into Gristles; so that its breadth takes up a great part of the side of the Chest, and it is also very fleshy. The *use* of this pair of Muscles is to draw the Ribs outwards and upwards, and so to dilate or widen the Chest, which it doth more especially in great and violent strainings. 2. Serratum majus Anticum.

The *third proper* pair of the Muscles of the Chest is called the upper backward Saw-pair, or *Serratum posticum superius*. They are seated on the Back under the Muscle called *Rhomboides* or the fourth Muscle of the Shoulder-blade, betwixt both the Blades, and above the first pair of the 3. Serratum posticum superius.

Head. They ſpring membranous from the Spines of the three lower Rack-bones of the Neck and the firſt of the Back, and are inſerted into the Interſtices of three or four of the upper Ribs. Their *uſe* is the ſame as of the former, *viz.* to draw the Ribs upward, whereby the Cheſt is dilated, and the inner Cavity thereof inlarged.

4. Serratum poſticum inferius. The *fourth* is called *Serratum poſticum inferius*, the lower backward Saw-pair. Theſe are ſeated almoſt in the middle of the Back, under the broad Muſcle that is the firſt of the Depreſſors of the Shoulder. They ariſe from the Spines of the three loweſt *Vertebræ* of the Back and of the firſt of the Loins, with a membranous, nervous and broad beginning; afterwards they paſs with an overthwart line croſs the Muſcles of the Back, and being increaſed with fleſhy Fibres are inſerted into three or four of the lower ſhort Ribs before they turn into Griſtles. Their *uſe* is to draw the three or four loweſt Ribs outwards, and ſo to dilate or widen the lower part of the Cheſt.

Beſides the four pair already named there is yet another Muſcle that aſſiſts theſe in the motion of widening the Cheſt in Inſpiration, which is the *Diaphragma* or Midriff, of which I have already ſpoken in its proper place, namely in the fourth Chapter of the Second Book; I ſhall therefore omit ſpeaking of it any farther here.

Two pair that contract the Breaſt. Next come we to treat of the Muſcles that *contract* or ſtraiten the Cheſt in Expiration or letting forth the breath. The firſt pair of theſe is called *par Triangulare*, or triangled pair, though they make not a perfect triangle, becauſe they conſiſt of two long ſides and one ſhort one.

1. Par Triangulare. Theſe ariſe from the middle line of the Breaſt-bone on the inſide of it, (for their ſeat is within the Cavity of the Cheſt, under the Breaſt-bone) being little and ſlender, and are inſerted into the bony ends of the third, fourth, fifth and ſixth True-ribs (where they are faſtned to the Griſtles.) The uſe of this pair is to draw the Ribs toward the Breaſt-bone, and thereby to ſtraiten the Cheſt in Expiration.

2. Sacrolumbum. The next is called *Sacrolumbum* from their riſe, which is from the *Os ſacrum* and from the Spine or ridge of the *Lumbi* or Loins. They are ſeated under the *Serratum poſticum inferius*, and creeping upwards mix themſelves with the long Muſcle of the Back, and alſo faſten themſelves to the tranſverſe Proceſſes of the Racks of the Loins as far as to the loweſt Rack of the Cheſt, from whence aſcending up to the Ribs, they are inſerted into the lower ſide of them all by a particular Tendon about three or four fingers breadth from the ridge of the Back. The *uſe* of this pair according to *Veſlingius*, is to contract the Cheſt; but *Spigelius* and alſo *Bartholinus* do believe that becauſe it grows out of the ſame beginning with the long Muſcle of the Back, therefore it extends and raiſes up the Cheſt as that doth.

Cervicale deſcendens. There is another pair oppoſite to this deſcribed by *Diemerbroeck*, a diligent Anatomiſt, who hath given them the name of *Cervicale deſcendens*. Theſe, ſays he, do ſpring from the third, fourth, fifth, ſixth and ſeventh *Vertebræ* of the Neck, and are inſerted into the upper ſide of each Rib, as the *Sacrolumbum* is into the Lower; and ſays, that this pair by pulling the Ribs upwards in Inſpiration widen the Cheſt, as the other by drawing them down in Expiration ſtraiten it.

To the Muſcles already ſpoken of, which do contract the Cheſt, do belong the ſixteen *Internal Intercoſtal* Muſcles: For as the *External* ones aſſiſt the Wideners or Dilaters of the Cheſt in their motions, ſo do the

Internal

Internal alſo aſſiſt theſe contracting Muſcles in the drawing together of the Cheſt, and do all act together as one Muſcle, as the others do; for they paſs obliquely from the lower to the upper Ribs, as the others did from the upper to the lower, their Fibres running contrary to or acroſs the former. All theſe Muſcles are ſaid, ſecondarily, to be aſſiſted in their motion by the Abdominal Muſcles, as alſo by the Muſcles of the Shoulder-blade and Fore-legs.

CHAP. XV.

Of the Muſcles of the Back and Loins.

THE Muſcles of the *Back*, as alſo of the whole Spine, are ſo diverſly and intricately intermixed and knit together, that ſome Anatomiſts have divided them into more, others into fewer, and that by reaſon of the infinite originals of the Fibres and the multitude of their inſertions, all which the admirable wiſedom of Nature thought fit to mingle and knit one within another, that they might the better and with the more ſtrength ſuſtain and accompliſh thoſe ſtrong and violent actions to which they are deſign'd, and alſo with more eaſe and ſafety bear ſuch extraordinary heavy weights, as this noble Animal, the ſubject of my Diſcourſe, doth continually undergo. For if *power united be the ſtronger*, (as the common ſaying is) then certainly if many Muſcles conſpire together unto one motion, they will be better able to perform it.

The Muſcles of the Back have but one motion.

Now that there are not more than one apparent motion performed by the Muſcles of the Back of an Horſe is plain, which motion is by the help of the Back-bones to raiſe up and ſuſpend as it were the whole bulk of the Body, and to bear alſo great weights many times upon it: I ſay this is the main, if not the onely motion performed by theſe Muſcles; for the Bodies of Horſes cannot be turned backwards and forwards, to the ſides, and almoſt ſemicircularly, as the Backs of Men are, as may be ſeen in Dancers, Tumblers and the like.

Again, theſe Muſcles though they are by later Anatomiſts divided into ſeveral pairs, yet the Ancients (as *Galen* for one) were of opinion, that ſeeing they cannot be by any means truly ſeparated, either there muſt be ſo many pair as there are Rack-bones, or elſe (which is more likely) that there is but one onely pair, offering tendinous diſtributions to all the *Vertebræ* of the Back. And ſays *Galen*, If one of this pair work alone, the Spine is inclined towards that ſide, be it the right or left; but if they both work together, the Spine is bended to neither hand, but pulled ſtreight backward, or rather the Spines are held in their ſeveral proper places. And, adds he, whereas almoſt all Muſcles have their Antagoniſts, that are the Authours of a contrary action to theirs, yet theſe Muſcles of the Spine (if you except the bending Muſcles of the Neck) have no Antagoniſts or Oppoſites.

Four pair of the Back and Loins.

Neither are theſe Muſcles of the Back proper to the Back alone, but common to the *Loins* alſo, being reckoned their ſecond pair, of which I

 will

will first treat though it be contrary to the custom of Anatomists to doe so. This pair then goes by the name of *Musculi longissimi*, so called from their extraordinary length, as being the longest Muscles (and also the strongest) in the whole Body: For they arise from the *Os sacrum*, and *Ileum* or Haunch-bone, and passing along by the Spine or ridge of the Loins, Back and Neck, they reach as far as to the *Processus Mammillares*, or Mammillary Processes of the Temple-bones. They are almost confounded with the *Sacrolumbum* and *Semispinatum* in their march through the Loins, whence by some those are taken to be parts of this pair: but as soon as this pair arrives at the Back, it parts with those, and appears to be distinct from them. Their *use* is (if they act together) directly to extend the Back and Loins; but if one onely work, then is the Spine inclined on one side, for their Fibres are oblique or slanting.

1. Musculi longissimi.

2. Par Quadratum.

The next pair goes by the name of *Quadratum* or the Square pair, from their Figure; for whilst they are in their natural situation they both of them together make a four-square figure, though when they are separated they are each of a triangular shape. They arise broad, thick and fleshy from the backward and upper Cavity of the Haunch-bone, and from the inner and upper side of *Os sacrum*, and remaining fleshy in their whole course, they are inserted into all the transverse Processes of the *Vertebræ* of the Loins as far as the lowest Rib. Their *use* is to bend the Racks of the Loins with a right motion forward or downward; but if one of them work alone, it draws the Loins to one side a little downward.

3. Sacri.

The next are the Muscles called *Sacri*, or holy Muscles, from their rise, which is from the *Os sacrum*. They spring with an acute original from that part of the said Bone where the Spine is fastned to the Haunch-bones. After their original they grow broad by degrees, and though they end not till they come to the Spine of the lowest *Vertebra* of the *Thorax*, yet in their progress they are inserted into several of the Spines and oblique Processes of the *Vertebræ* of the Loins, their Fibres running obliquely or with a slanting line upwards and inwards. The *use* of this pair, if one work alone, is to pull the Body a little on one side, but if both act or work together, they extend that part of the Spine to which they are fastned.

4. Par Semispinatum.

The last pair is called *Semispinatum*. These arise with a nervous original or beginning from all the Spines or Ridges of the *Os sacrum* and the Loins, and are inserted into the transverse Processes of the *Vertebræ* of the Loins and some of the lowermost of the Chest. These with the former pair do fill up the distances between the Spines, where they touch one another, nothing coming between them to separate them from one another, but a membranous Ligament issuing from the upper Spine. The *use* of this pair is to join the Spines together, and to extend or erect that part of the Back to which they grow. Now if all these Muscles of the Back and Loins work together, the whole Back is extended, or in a manner drawn backwards: but if the Muscles of one side work alone, the Body is inclined to that side.

The distemper called a sway'd Back is oftner an affection of these Muscles,

These Muscles are apt to have their tone and strength violated by several accidents, as by over-great Loads, by a sudden Cold taken by pulling off the Saddle after hard riding before the Horse be quite cold, and the like; whereby the Muscles become benumbed and relaxed, and so are in a manner deprived of both sense and motion; by which means the Horse

Horſe becomes uſeleſs, being ſo far from being able to carry Burthens or to perform any other ſervice for his Maſter, that when he is up he can hardly ſerve himſelf, I mean, ſtand to eat his Meat; or if down, not able to riſe without help. This alſo often happens to old and lean Horſes, in whom by reaſon of the weakneſs of their Bodies, as alſo becauſe they abound with flegmatick Humours, theſe Muſcles are ſo relaxt that they are ſcarce able to ſupport the weight of their own Bodies, much leſs other Burthens. And in this caſe I think nothing more proper than good ſtore of ſtrengthening Food, to ſupport and nouriſh their inſide, whereby they may gain ſtrength, and withall to [illegible]ly ſome ſtrengthening Plaſter to the outſide at the ſame time.

than any diſlocation in the Vertebræ.

But to recover thoſe that come by this affection by great Colds taken as is above-mentioned, it will be the beſt way to give them warm, ſtrengthening and comfortable Medicines inwardly, and alſo to apply firſt ſome warm Sheep-skins pretty often renewed, and at the ſame time to anoint the Loins with ſome ſovereign Ointments or Oyles outwardly; or if this will not doe, then to ſweat him in a Dunghill, and after he comes out, to apply to the Loins a ſtrengthening Charge or Plaſter.

I thought my ſelf a little obliged in this place to inlarge upon this account, to undeceive many of our Profeſſors, who take all Diſtempers in this kind to be as one, concluding ſtill that all Horſes thus affected, are either ſtrained in the Kidneys or ſwayed, as we call it, in the Back; when indeed theſe Muſcles are either benumbed by cold as aforeſaid, or by ſtrains gotten by carrying over-great weights or burthens, they are diſtended to that degree, that for ſome time they loſe the ſtrength and vigor they uſed to perform their motions with; this, I ſay, is often the true cauſe of the debility and weakneſs of the Back.

Not that I will deny that there is any ſuch malady as a ſwayed Back, for I have my ſelf by diſſection ſeen in a Horſe that was knocked on the Head, (being not curable of this Diſtemper) not onely all the muſcular Parts as it were bruiſed, and many of their interſpaces filled with a kind of a congealed Humour or Matter, but alſo found a kind of diſlocation in that part where the *Os ſacrum* or loweſt *Vertebra* of the Loins are joined, and a deal of congealed Matter ſettled about thoſe Parts. But ſuch a ſtrain is ſeldom curable, or if ever, not without great charge and long keeping. What I have therefore ſaid upon this account is to let our Profeſſors know, that moſt of thoſe affections which they call ſway'd Backs are onely diſtempers of the Muſcles, and therefore eaſily cured if ſoon taken in hand: but thoſe which have broken Backs, (which we commonly underſtand by ſwayed Backs) are ſeldom curable. And thus much ſhall ſuffice as to this ſort of diſcourſe in this place; it remains now that I return to my former diſcourſe, and deſcribe the remaining part of the Muſcles, of which thoſe of the *Anus*, Bladder, and Genitals both in Horſes and Mares come next to be ſpoken to.

CHAP.

CHAP. XVI.

Of the Muscles of the Fundament, the Bladder, the Testicles, Yard and Clitoris.

A Horse being a Creature made for service, it was fit that he should void his Excrements at his own conveniency and choice, and not perpetually; As therefore Nature hath provided Muscles about the Mouth and Chaps for the receiving, chewing and swallowing of the Food, so at the end of the Guts and at the outlet of the Urine there are Muscles set as Porters to interclude the passage, that nothing might go out but by the Horse's own accord; whereas were it not for these Muscles, his Excrements would come from him continually and involuntarily, as I have seen to happen in such Horses whose Sphincter Muscle hath by some accident or extraordinary weakness been violated. Neither hath Nature onely provided Muscles for the keeping of the Excrements in, I mean till such time as it is necessary they should be let forth; but others also as instruments to assist in the voiding or letting of them forth. For the former purpose is appointed one Muscle at the *Anus* called the Sphincter, and for the latter, two, called Levators.

The Sphincter *Muscle of the* Anus. The *Sphincter* is a fleshy Muscle seated at the very end of the Arse-gut, the which it incompasseth round like a Ring, to which it may fitly be resembled. It is rather knit to than arises from the lower *Vertebræ* of the *Os sacrum*, being round and broad, and furnished with transverse or overthwart Fibres, or indeed orbicular ones. This Muscle is much thicker above or inwards, than below or at the Fundament, where it adheres so firmly to the Skin, that it is not easie to separate it from it. Its *use* we have mentioned in the former Paragraph.

Two Levators. The other two are called the *Levators* or lifters up of the Fundament. These are small, broad and nervous, arising from the Ligaments of the Hip-bones and *Os sacrum*, from whence passing by the sides of the streight or Arse-gut they adhere to it, and are inserted into the upper part of the Sphincter. A portion of them also grows to the root of the Yard, and in Mares to the neck of the Matrix. Their *use* is to assist the Abdominal Muscles in the expulsion of the Excrements, which they doe by lifting up the Fundament. They also help to keep the Fundament from falling out, which sometimes happens when they are too much relaxt.

The Sphincter *of the Bladder.* To the *Bladder* doth also belong a Muscle called a *Sphincter*, which is seated in the beginning of its neck, the which it compasseth round. It is furnished with orbicular Fibres as the Sphincter of the Fundament is, and is of the same use; for it constringes or purses up the neck of the Bladder (as that doth the *Anus*) that the Urine may not pass out without a spontaneous relaxing of this Muscle. In Mares it is seated at the very end of the Bladder, *viz.* at the hole where the neck of the Bladder opens into the *Vagina*.

The Muscles of the *Yard* are in number four (or two pair) of which we have already treated in the First Book at Chapter 20. of which the first pair are called the *Erectores* or Lifters up of the Yard, and the other

Dilatantes,

Dilatantes, Wideners, and by ſome they are called *Acceleratores* or Haſtners. I thought fit in this place onely to name them, referring the Reader to the above-named Chapter for his farther ſatisfaction; as alſo to the ſaid Book at Chap. 22. for the deſcription of the Muſcles of the *Teſticles* called the *Cremaſter* Muſcles, by which the Teſticles are ſuſpended. The Reader may alſo be ſatisfied in the ſame Book at Chap. 27. concerning the Muſcles of the *Clitoris* in Mares, which are two pair, as the Yard of a Horſe, to which it is reſembled, hath; for I ſhall not inſiſt upon *them* in this place neither.

CHAP. XVII.

Of the Muſcles of the Scapula *or Shoulder-blade.*

HAving ſufficiently treated of the Muſcles of the three *Venters*, it remains that I deſcend now to treat of thoſe of the *Limbs*, beginning firſt with the formoſt of them, the firſt of which ſhall be thoſe that move the *Shoulder-blade.*

The Shoulder-blade hath four pair.

The *Shoulder-blade* is obſerved to have four motions, *viz.* forward, backward, upward and downward, which motions are performed by four pair of proper Muſcles. The *firſt* pair are ſeated betwixt the two Shoulder-blades, covering the top of the Withers. They are called *Cucullares* from the reſemblance they have with a Monk's Hood or Cowl. **1. Cucullares.** Their firſt original is fleſhy and thin, which they take from the *Occiput* or hinder part of the Head; but as they deſcend down the Neck they have other membranous beginnings from five of the Spines thereof, yea and from eight or nine of the uppermoſt of the Cheſt: but they preſently begin to be ſtraitned as they deſcend towards the Shoulder-blades, into whoſe whole ſpine or ridge they are implanted, as likewiſe into the Shoulder-bone and broader part of the Collar-bone. This pair of Muſcles, becauſe of their divers originals, from whence they have ſeveral ſorts of Fibres, are ſaid to perform ſeveral motions; as when the upper part of the Muſcle that ariſes from the *Occiput* is contracted, then is the Shoulder-blade lifted obliquely upward, that part being furniſhed with oblique Fibres; and when that part which ſprings from the Withers is contracted, then it is pull'd ſtreight thitherward.

2. Levatores. The *ſecond* pair are called *Levatores*, the Lifters or Heavers; and by ſome (in Men) *Patientiæ Muſculi.* Theſe are ſituated above the Collar-bone, taking their beginning from the tranſverſe Proceſſes of the firſt, ſecond, third and fourth *Vertebræ* of the Neck; which beginnings being united in the middle (or thereabouts) of the length of the Muſcles, they are at laſt inſerted into the Shoulder-blades at their fore corner. The *uſe* of theſe Muſcles is to draw the Blades upward and forward.

3. Serratum minus Anticum. The *third* pair is called *Serratum minus Anticum* or the leſſer fore Saw-pair. Theſe lie under the Pectoral Muſcles, and ſpring from the four uppermoſt Ribs before they become griſtly, by four fleſhy portions repreſenting the

the teeth of a Saw; from whence they paſs ſomewhat ſlantingly to the Shoulder-blade, into whoſe Proceſs (called its Anchor-like Proceſs) it is inſerted with a broad (partly fleſhy and partly nervous) Tendon. The *uſe* of this pair is to move the Shoulder-blades forward to the Cheſt.

4. Rhomboides. The *fourth* and laſt pair is called *Rhomboides.* Theſe are ſeated under the *Cucullares*, being thin, broad and four-ſquare. They ſpring fleſhy from the hinder Proceſſes or Spines of the three loweſt Rack-bones of the Neck, and as many of the uppermoſt of the Cheſt, and continuing fleſhy to their very inſertion they are implanted into the baſis of the Blades. Their *uſe* is to draw the Blade ſomewhat upward and backward, couching it to the Back.

Note, that ſeeing a Horſe and all four-footed Beaſts go prone, whereas Man walks erect or upright, the motions of the Muſcles might, and ought in ſtrictneſs, to be explained diverſly in *them* from what they are in *him*: As for example, Thoſe which are ſaid in Man to move the Part upward, *viz.* toward the Head, ought in a four-footed Beaſt to be ſaid to move it forward; and thoſe which move it backward in Man, move it upward in the other, becauſe of the different poſture of their Bodies: and the ſame might be ſaid as to their motions forward and backward. But ſeeing many of the Muſcles have their names from their offices in *Men*, it would make but a confuſion and a great impropriety in their appellations to explain their motions by other termes in Brutes. And therefore the Reader is deſired to obſerve, That when we ſay a Part is moved upward, we mean towards the Head; when downward, toward the Tail; when backward, toward the Back; and when forward, we underſtand it toward the Breaſt or Belly.

CHAP. XVIII.

Of the Muſcles of the Shoulder.

THAT which I call the *Shoulder* is that Part or Bone that reaches from the top or pitch of the Shoulder (and is joynted into the Shoulder-blade) to the next Joint which we call the Elbow; which it is neceſſary to intimate for diſtinction ſake, becauſe the Shoulder-blade and this part are commonly both underſtood by the name of the Shoulder. Having advertiſed this, paſs we now to its Muſcles.

Each Shoulder hath nine Muſcles, viz. *firſt, two Erectors.* The motions of the Shoulders are five, *viz.* backwards, forwards, upwards, downwards and circularly. To perform which each hath nine Muſcles, of which there are two that move it upward, namely the *Deltoides* and *Supraſpinatus*; and of theſe we ſhall treat in the firſt place.

Deltoides. The *firſt* is called *Deltoides* from its figure, which reſembles the ſhape of the Greek Letter Δ *delta.* It is fleſhy and (as you may ſee) triangular, ariſing from the midſt of the Clavicle or Collar-bone, the top of the Shoulder, and the whole ridge of the Shoulder-blade, and is extended as far as to the middle of the Shoulder-bone, where it is inſerted. This Muſcle is obſerved to have divers ſorts of Fibres; ſome of which run obliquely

liquely downwards, such are those on the fore-part; others run obliquely forward, which are those on the back-part of it; and a third sort, which are placed in the middle, run directly toward the Fore-leg: Wherefore (says my Authour) when the Fibres of the fore-part are contracted, the Shoulder is lifted upward and forward towards the Horse's Nose; if the middle Fibres be contracted, the Shoulder is lifted directly towards his Back; and if the hinder Fibres be contracted, then is the Shoulder carried obliquely backward: so that this Muscle is said not onely to raise up the Shoulder (which is indeed its chiefest use) but helps also to perform other motions as well as that.

The *second Erector* or Lifter up of the Shoulder is called *Supraspinatus* by some, but by others *Superscapularis superior*, or the upper Blade-rider, because it is seated uppermost upon the Shoulder-blade, and filleth up all that cavity which is between its spine and upper edge. It arises from the spine of the Blade with a long and fleshy beginning, and passing over the jointing of the *Scapula* with the Shoulder-bone by a broad and strong Tendon, is inserted into the neck of the said Shoulder-bone. This Muscle is by some Authours thought not onely to lift up the Shoulder (which is its principal use, as being one of the Erectors) but also to help to turn it a little round. **Supraspinatus.**

The *Depressors* or Pullers down of the Shoulder are also two, namely *Latissimus* and *Rotundus major*. The *Latissimus* is so called from its breadth and largeness, for with its fellow it covereth almost the whole Back. It goeth also by the name of *Ani-scalptor*, or Scratch-arse Muscle (in Men.) It rises with a membranous and broad beginning from the tops of all the spines of the Rack-bones that are betwixt the sixth *Vertebra* of the Chest and the middle of *Os sacrum*, as also from the upper part of *Os ileum* or Haunch-bone: from thence ascending upward untill it come to that part of the Back where the Ribs begin to bend backward, there it becomes more fleshy, and is carried over the lower or hinder corner of the Shoulder-blade, at which place it begins to grow narrower but continues fleshy: and at length by a broad and strong Tendon it is inserted below the upper head of the Shoulder-bone lengthways, on the inside, betwixt the Pectoral and Round Muscles, there being a space left betwixt them for that purpose. This draws the Shoulder downward or toward the Tail, though a little obliquely backward. ***Secondly, two Depressors.*** **Latissimus.**

The *second* Puller down of the Shoulder (or its fourth Muscle) is called *Rotundus major*, or the greater Round Muscle. It takes its beginning from the whole lower *Costa* or Rib of the Shoulder-blade, and is inserted into the upper and inner part of the Shoulder-bone with a short but broad, strong and nervous Tendon. The *use* of this is the same with the former, *viz.* to pull the Shoulder downward. **Rotundus major.**

The two pair of Muscles that pull the Shoulder *forward* are called, the one by the name of *Pectoralis*, and the other *Coracoideus*. The *Pectoralis* is so called from its situation, which is upon the fore-side of the *Breast*. It hath a very large and for the greatest part membranous beginning, which it takes from divers parts: for its upper part arises from the middle of the Collar-bone on that side next the Breast; its middle, from the whole length of the Breast-bone and the ends of the Gristles of the Ribs that end in it; and its lower part springs from the Gristles of the sixth, seventh and eighth Ribs. After it hath taken these beginnings, it presently becomes fleshy and thick, and running towards the Shoulder is at ***Thirdly, two Pullers forward.*** **Pectoralis.**

length inſerted into the Shoulder-bone with a ſhort, but broad, ſinewy and ſtrong Tendon a little below its head, betwixt the Muſcle *Deltoides*, and that which is called *Biceps.* The office of this Muſcle is, when it contracteth it ſelf equally, to move the Shoulder equally and directly forward or toward the Breaſt, inclining to neither hand: but if all its Fibres be not equally contracted, (for by reaſon of its divers beginnings it hath alſo divers ſorts of Fibres, ſome running with a ſlanting line from above downwards, others with the like ſlanting line from below upward, and thoſe betwixt theſe running ſtreight; wherefore I ſay, if all theſe Fibres be not equally contracted, but ſome work, and others not) then are other motions performed by this Muſcle, as the Shoulder drawn more upward or downward, as the different Fibres work.

Coracoideus. *Coracoideus* is by *Bartholin* accounted the ninth Muſcle of the Shoulder (which, ſays he, was firſt obſerved by *Arantius* and *Placentinus*) but we do after the more modern Authours reckon it for the ſixth, and ſecond drawer forward of it. It hath its name *Coracoideus* from its beginning, which is from the *Proceſſus Coracoides* of the *Scapula*; from whence it reaches to the middle of the Shoulder-bone where it terminates. Its *uſe* is (as ſay the diſcoverers of it) to draw the Shoulder to the Proceſs of the Blade-bone, or forward upon the Breaſt.

Fourthly, three Pullers backward. The Shoulder is moved alſo *backward* by three Muſcles, which are *Infraſpinatus*, *Subſcapularis* or *Immerſus*, and *Rotundus minor.*

Infraſpinatus. That which is reckoned the firſt of theſe, is the *Infraſpinatus*, by ſome called *Supraſcapularis inferior.* It is ſeated upon the Shoulder-blade and fills up all that ſpace which is betwixt the ridge or ſpine of the *Scapula* and its lower edge, even as the *Supraſcapularis ſuperior* fills up the upper ſpace. It ariſes fleſhy from the baſis of the Blade below the ridge of it, becoming narrower in its progreſs as the Blade-bone grows narrower, and is inſerted by a broad and ſhort Tendon into the fourth Ligament of the Shoulder-bone.

Subſcapularis. The ſecond Puller or Drawer back of the Shoulder is the *Subſcapularis*, the Under-blade-lurker, or *Immerſus* the drowned Muſcle, becauſe it is ſeated under the Blade-bone betwixt the Ribs and it. Very fleſhy it is, ariſing ſo from the inner part of the baſis of the Blade; in figure it is triangular, like the Bone, growing narrower or ſtraiter by degrees as it deſcends, and is inſerted into one of the Ligaments of the Shoulder.

Rotundus minor. The next being the third and laſt of the Drawers back of the Shoulder is called *Rotundus minor*, the leſſer Round Muſcle, from its figure. It ariſes from the loweſt corner of the *Scapula*, and is implanted into the neck of the Shoulder-bone.

As for the *circular* motion of the Shoulder, *that* is not performed by any one Muſcle, but by ſeveral of theſe already named, acting ſucceſſively one after another.

CHAP. XIX.

Of the Muscles that move the Fore-leg and Foot.

How far the Fore-leg of an Horse answers in its Parts to the Arm of a Man.

THAT part of the Leg which reaches from the Elbow to that which we call the Knee, answers to that part in Humane Bodies which reaches from the Elbow to the Wrist. Onely in an Horse there is but one Bone in this space (which we shall call the Cubit-bone) whereas in Men there are two going by two distinct names, one of which being the greater is called *Cubitus* or the Cubit, and the other *Ulna* or the Ell. But as for that part which we call the Knee, it agrees more exactly with the Wrist in Men, and might more properly be called so: For examining the Part to see of what it is compounded, I find it made up of two ranges of little Bones as the Wrist of a Man is, and not like the Knee of a Man, which consists of one little round Bone (called the Knee-pan) fastned between the Jointings of the lower head of the Thigh-bone and the heads of the *tibia* and *fibula*: for that Bone is exactly found in the Hind-leg of a Horse in that Joint we call the Stifle, which is indeed the Knee, as shall be proved in a convenient place. And as the Knee of a Horse is like the Wrist of a Man, so is that Bone below it, (or indeed three Bones, for the Bone which we call the Shank or Shin, hath two small Bones fastned to it running by its sides down almost all its length till within two or three inches of the great Pastern; I say that as the Knee is that part which is the Wrist in Man, so is this part between the Knee and great Pastern) answerable to the *Metacarpium*, that is, to that space which reaches from the Wrist to the setting on of the Fingers. Onely in Man there are five Bones, and in an Horse but three. So likewise does the great Pastern correspond to the first Joint of the Finger; the little Pastern to the second Joint; and the Coffin-joint on which the Hoof grows, to that Joint of the Finger on which the Nail grows.

By this you may see that these Parts of an Horse come very near the like Parts of a Man, the number of Bones and Muscles of the Fingers onely excepted. For a Horse is *solidipes*, or whole-footed, so that the whole of it is necessarily moved at one time, and therefore has no need of that variety of Muscles that a Man's Hand is endowed withall. An Horse's Fore-feet are of no other use than to go upon, any more than his Hinder-feet; whereas the Hand of a Man is ordained for other uses, and is therefore accordingly shaped, and divided into more Parts, to wit four Fingers and a Thumb, all which have their peculiar Muscles to enable them to perform those motions to which they are designed. Whence the number of the Muscles come to differ greatly. Now we shall take no notice of those that a Man has more than an Horse, but shall onely treat of those that are to be found to move the Joints of an Horse already mentioned, *viz.* the Cubit-bone, the Shank, the two Pasterns, and the Coffin-joint.

Two Muscles bend the Cubit.

1. Biceps.

First, the *Cubit* is either *bended*, or *extended*. Of the *Benders* there are two; the *first* of which is called *Biceps*, from its double beginning; for it hath two heads, the first being outward, tendinous and round, ariſeth from the upper brim of the hollowneſs of the Shoulder-blade; the ſecond head is broader, and is framed partly of a Tendon and partly of Fleſh: this ariſes from the *Proceſſus Anchoriformis* or Anchor-like Proceſs of the *Scapula*; then deſcending by the inner head of the Shoulder-bone, it meeteth with the former head, and becometh a ſtrong fleſhy Muſcle, running down the inſide of the Cubit-bone to the Knee, where it is inſerted. This bends the Cubit forwards and ſomewhat inwards.

2. Brachiæus internus. The *ſecond Bender* is from its ſituation in Humane Bodies (being placed as the former is, upon the inſide of the Arm in them, and of the Leg in Horſes; I ſay from its ſituation it is) called *Brachiæus Internus.* This lies inwardly under the *Biceps*, and is ſomething ſhorter than it, but of a fleſhy ſubſtance like it. It takes its beginning near the end of that Muſcle of the Shoulder called *Deltoides*, about the middle of the Shoulder-bone, to which it is firmly faſtned: after which it runs its courſe as the former, and is inſerted into the foreſide of the Cubit-bone a little above the Knee, aſſiſting the motion of the former.

Two alſo extend it. 1. Longus. There are alſo two Muſcles to *extend* the Cubit, which lie on its outer and hinder ſide. The firſt of them from its length is called *Longus.* This ariſes with a ſtrong and broad original, partly nervous and partly fleſhy (which ſome make to be two heads) from the lower Rib of the Blade-bone, after which it deſcends on the hinder ſide of the Shoulder-bone, and alſo of the Cubit-bone, and is inſerted into its outſide juſt at the Knee. This draws the Cubit backwards and ſomewhat outwards, and thereby extends it or ſtretches it out ſtreight.

2. Brevis. The *ſecond Extender* of the Cubit is called *Brevis* from its ſhortneſs. It ariſes from the hinder-part of the neck of the Shoulder-bone, and holding the ſame courſe as the former, is inſerted into the lower end of the Cubit-bone at the ſame place with the former, and aſſiſts its motion.

Beſides theſe there are ſaid by ſome Anatomiſts to be two more *Extending* Muſcles, *viz.* one called *Brachiæus Externus* from its being placed on the *outſide* of the Arm in Men. But this is by *Spigelius* looked upon to be the ſecond head of the *Long* Muſcle, becauſe it grows into one Muſcle with it, and has the ſame inſertion with both it and the *Short* one.

The other is called *Anconæus*, being a ſmall-bodied Muſcle, ariſing from the lower and back-part of the Shoulder-bone, and is inſerted into the Cubit an inch or two below the Elbow. But ſome make this to be but a part of the *Short* Muſcle.

As for the other Bone of this Joint in Men, called *Radius*, *that* alſo has its Muſcles, which ſerve to turn the Arm and Hand round: But ſeeing there is no ſuch Bone in an Horſe, as neither any ſuch motion of an Horſe's Leg, it cannot be expected there ſhould be found any Muſcles in *him* anſwerable to the other, as to this part.

Paſs we on therefore to the next Joint commonly called the Shank, but which truly anſwers to the Metacarp, or back of the hand in Men. And this like the Cubit is either *bended* or *extended.*

Two Muſcles bend the Shank. 1. Cubitæus internus. To *bend* it there are two Muſcles; of which the *firſt* is called *Cubitæus internus.* This ariſeth from the inner knob of the Shoulder-bone, and deſcending along the inſide of the Cubit, is implanted into the inner and hinder ſides of the top of the Shank.

2. Radiæus internus, The *ſecond* is called *Radiæus internus* in Men, though very improperly in an Horſe, ſeeing he has no *Radius.* This has the ſame riſe, progreſs and inſertion with the former.

There

TAB XXXIII
p. 187.

There are alſo two Muſcles to *extend* it; the firſt of which is called *Cubitæus externus*. This ſprings from the outer knob of the Shoulder-bone, and deſcending down the Cubit, is inſerted into the outer and fore-ſide of the head of the Shank. *Two alſo extend it.* 1. Cubitæus externus.

The *ſecond* of the *Extenders* is called *Radiæus externus* (improperly as to an Horſe, as was noted before.) This has the ſame riſe, progreſs and inſertion with its fellow. 2. Radiæus externus.

The next Joint is the *great Paſtern* which anſwers to the firſt Joint of the Finger in a Man's Hand, as the *little Paſtern* anſwers to the ſecond Joint, and the *Coffin-joint* to the laſt on which the Nail grows. All theſe are either bended or extended as the former Joints were. But before we deſcribe thoſe Muſcles that perform theſe actions, there is one other to be treated of that is called in Man *Palmaris,* from its being ſpread over the Palm of the Hand; but in an Horſe its Tendon is ſpread over the Sole of the Foot, whence the name of *Plantaris* would better agree to it. This ſprings fleſhy from the inner knob of the Shoulder-bone, but preſently grows into a ſlender Tendon which deſcends to the Sole of the Foot as aforeſaid.

The *Paſterns* and *Coffin-joint* are bended by two Muſcles; the *firſt* of which is called *Sublimis,* (I ſuppoſe becauſe it riſes *high* up.) It ſprings from the inner knob of the Shoulder-bone, and is inſerted into the Paſterns. *The Paſterns and Coffin-joint are bended by two Muſcles.* 1. Sublimis.

The *ſecond* is named *Profundus*. This ariſes from the upper part of the Cubit-bone, and is inſerted into the Coffin-joint. 2. Profundus.

They are extended by *one* very conſiderable Muſcle, called *Extenſor magnus*. This ſprings from the outer knob of the Shoulder-bone, and its Tendon is inſerted into the fore and outer ſide of the Paſterns and Coffin-joint. Some reckon this to be two Muſcles. *They are extended by one, viz.* Extenſor magnus.

There are ſeveral other proper Muſcles that belong to the Fingers in Men, ſome to one and ſome to another, as alſo others that move them laterally, or to and from one another, which it were from our purpoſe here to mention, as not being to be found in an Horſe. Though I dare not affirm poſitively that there are no more than I have here deſcribed; for I am apt to ſuſpect the contrary from the multitude of Tendons that deſcend into the Coffin-joint: however theſe that I have mention'd are the moſt conſiderable and plainly diſcoverable; and rather than encreaſe their number at a *venture,* I will be content that this Chapter be reputed imperfect.

Table XXXIII.

Repreſents an Horſe with the Side towards you, that you may have a ſight of as many of his Muſcles at one view as is poſſible.

AA *Shew the oblique deſcendent Muſcle of the* Abdomen *or Paunch.*
B *The oblique aſcendent Muſcle of the ſame part, at its original from the Hip-bone.*
C *Its membranous Tendon reaching to the White-line.*
D *The tranſverſe Muſcle of the Paunch.*
E *The right or ſtreight Muſcle of the ſame part.*
F *The Pectoral Muſcle.*
G *The* Serratus major Anticus.
H *The* Deltoides *of the Shoulder.*

II *The*

II *The* Serratus Posticus.
K *The* Cucullaris.
L *The* Sacrolumbus.
M *The* Longissimus Dorsi.
N *The* Semispinatus.
OOOOO *The Intercostal Muscles.*
PPP *The Ribs laid bare.*
Q *The end or gristly part of the Shoulder-blade.*
R Glutæus minor *or lesser Buttock-muscle.*
S Glutæus medius *or middle Buttock-muscle.*
T Glutæus major *or greater Buttock-muscle.*
V *The* Deltoides *of the Thigh, having its Tendon broken off it.*
XX *The* Musculus Biceps.
Y *The* Vastus Externus.
Z *The* Musculus Rectus.

a *One of the proper Muscles of the Cheek called* Lateralis.
b *A Muscle of the Nostrils called* Philtrum.
c *The external Adducent Muscle or closing Muscle of the Nose.*
d *The* orbicularis *or* constringens, *which draws the Lips together, being common to both Lips.*
e *The Muscles of the Eye-lids.*
f *The Temporal Muscle.*
g *The* Buccinator *or Trumpeter.*
h *One of the Muscles of the Neck called* Longus, *seated under the Gullet, but to be seen in this Figure by reason of the posture of it.*
ii *One of the proper Muscles of the Head called* Mastoides.
k *The Muscle of the Head called* Splenius *or* Triangularis.
l *The Frontal or Fore-head Muscle.*
m *The* Spinatus, *being one of the Muscles that move the Neck.*
n *The* Complexus *or* Trigeminus *so called from its threefold beginning.*
o *The* Subclavius *pulled a little outward from under the other Muscles.*
p *The* Infraspinatus *or* Subscapularis inferior.
q *The* Supraspinatus *or* Superscapularis superior.
r *The* Scalenus.
s *The* Rotundus major *or* Humerum deprimens *a little out of its place at its lower end.*
t Musculus Biceps.
u Longus.
w Brachiæus externus.
x Cubitæus externus.
y Radiæus externus.
z Extensor magnus.
α Radiæus internus.
β Cubitæus internus.

11 *The* Gastrocnemius internus *of both the Hind-legs.*
22 *The* Gastrocnemius externus *of the like.*
3 *The Tendon of the Muscle* Plantaris *coming out as out of a Pully.*
4 *The* Tibiæus Anticus.
55 *The* Extensor tertii internodii digitorum aut Longus, *so called by* Mr. Brown.

CHAP.

CHAP. XX.

Of the Muscles of the Thigh.

BY the *Thigh* we mean that part which is betwixt the Joint of the *Huckle* or *Whirle*-bone, and that which is called the *Stifle*; which consisteth of one large and long Bone, going by the name of the Thigh-bone, or *Femur*. This Bone hath a round head which is jointed into the round Cavity of the Hip-bone, so that it admits of all kinds of motions, whence it hath a multitude of Muscles to perform these motions; some of which move the Thigh forwards, whereby it is bended; some move it backwards, and thereby extend it: a third sort bend it inward, as when a Horse rubs the contrary Leg with his Foot, which is often seen upon any itching or pricking humour affecting that Part: a fourth sort move it outwards; and a fifth obliquely about. But first of the *Benders forwards*, which are accounted to be three in number.

The Benders of the Thigh are three. 1. *Psoas.* The *first* of which is called *Psoas* or *Lumbaris*. This is almost round, thick and livid, and lieth in the inner part of the *Abdomen*, upon the *Vertebræ* of the Loins. It arises fleshy from the transverse Processes of the two lowest *Vertebræ* of the Chest and two or three uppermost of the Loins; from whence descending by the inside of *Os ileum*, at length it ends in a strong and round Tendon, which is inserted on the foreside of the upper part of the lesser head of the Thigh-bone. The *use* of this is, strongly to draw the Thigh upward, and somewhat inward. Upon this Muscle the Kidneys are placed, near that part of it where its Nerve enters into it; which in Men is the cause of that stupor or numbness that is felt in the Thigh by those that are troubled with the Stone in the Kidneys, on that side that the Stone is on.

2. *Iliacus internus.* The *second Bender forward* is called *Iliacus internus*, or the inward Haunch Muscle. It springeth with a slender and fleshy beginning from the inside of the Haunch-bone, and being joined by its Tendon to the former Muscle, is inserted with a round Tendon into the lesser head or *Rotator* of the Thigh-bone. The *use* of this is the same with the first, which is, to lift the Thigh up and so to bend it forward; yet it doth not move it so much inward as the *Psoas* doth.

3. *Pectineus.* The *third* is called *Pectineus*, arising broad and fleshy from the line of the Share-bone near its Gristle, and is implanted into the inside of the lower end of the Thigh-bone with a broad and large Tendon. Its *use* is to draw the Thigh upward and inward. This is the Muscle that in Men helps to lay one Thigh over the other in sitting.

Note, that both this last foregoing, and all the following Muscles save the two last, are inserted at the lower end of the Thigh-bone, just above the Stifle; whereas in Men they are most of them if not all inserted into its upper part, *viz.* either into its neck, or into one or other of the two knobs jetting out at the lower end of the neck, (called the great and little Trochanters.) What may be the reason of this different insertion is not easie to guess, unless it be the shortness of the Thigh-bone, which in an Horse is not half so long as it is in a tall Man; so that an Horse's Muscles being so plump and bulky upon his Buttocks, it was necessary they should have some considerable space to grow slenderer in and to become tendinous; and therefore they are extended as far as the *Stifle* which answers to the *Knee* in Man.

The Extenders are also three. 1. Glutæus major. Next come we to the Muscles that bend *back* and so *extend* the Thigh, (as when an Horse stretches himself) which motion is also performed by three Muscles. The *first* of which is called *Glutæus externus*, or the outwardmost Buttock Muscle; in Men it is also called *Glutæus major*, the greatest Buttock Muscle; but in an Horse it is not so, for in them the middlemost is the largest. This springeth with a very fleshy beginning from the Crupper, from the Spine or ridge of the Haunch-bone, and from the *Os sacrum*. Afterward descending a little obliquely and riding over the Joint of the Huckle-bone, it at length grows narrower and more slender, and so endeth into a strong and broad Tendon, which is inserted into the inner part of the Thigh-bone just above the Stifle, yea it seems to reach as far as to the top of the *Tibia*. Its *use* is to draw the Thigh backward and so to extend it, as also to enable the Horse to go backward.

2. Glutæus medius. The next or *second* is called *Glutæus medius*, or the middle Buttock Muscle. This in Man (because of his going erect) lieth quite under the former, and is so hid by it, that unless the former be first removed, it cannot be seen. But in Horses it is larger than the former, and lieth side by side with it, as doth the next also, and they are both to be seen without removing the first, as may be plainly observed by the following Figure. It arises with a fleshy and broad beginning, a little higher than the first, from the Spine of the Haunch-bone on the fore-part of it, and from thence descends somewhat obliquely over the Joint of the Hip as far as to the lower end of the Thigh-bone, into the outer side of which it is inserted with a broad, strong and membranous Tendon. Its *use* is to extend the Thigh and to draw it outward and backward, as when the Horse stands to stale.

3. Glutæus minor. The *third* and last of the *Extenders* is called *Glutæus minor*, or lesser Buttock Muscle. This in a Horse arises equal in height with the former at the Spine of the Haunch-bone. At its beginning it is round, sharp and fleshy; but in its course it becomes more broad, descending with an oblique line by the side of the second Muscle, and is inserted at the lower end of the Thigh-bone, rather towards its fore-side. This assists the action of the former, drawing the Thigh outward and backward.

One Mover of the Thigh inward, viz. Triceps *or* Quadriceps. The Thigh is drawn to the *inside* by the Muscle *Triceps*, or *Quadriceps*, for it goes by both names, because some affirm it to have four, and others but three beginnings. This Muscle is looked upon to be the thickest of all the Muscles of the whole Body, being furnished with great variety of Fibres.

The first of its beginnings is from the upper part of the Share-bone, where it arises with a nervous head, and descending is inserted into the inside of the lower end of the Thigh-bone.

The second part of it arises from the lower side of the same Bone, being fleshy and broad, and is inserted into the inside of the Thigh-bone, a little higher up than the former.

The third head of this Muscle arises with a fleshy and sometimes nervous beginning from the whole lower part of the *Coxendix*, round about the circumference of its wide hole; and is inserted near the last.

The fourth head ſprings with a nervous and fleſhy beginning from the tip of the *Coxendix*, and afterward running along the inſide of the Thigh, endeth into a round Tendon, which joining with the Tendon of the firſt part of this Muſcle is inſerted into the lower end of the Thigh-bone with it.

The Thigh is alſo turned *outward*, which motion is performed by four ſmall Muſcles called *Quadrigemini*, all which are placed one by another upon the outſide of the articulation of the Thigh. The firſt of them is from its ſituation called *Iliacus externus*, and from its figure, *Pyriformis* or Pear-like Muſcle. This is longer than any of the reſt of them, ariſing round from the lower and outer part of *Os ſacrum*; thence it runneth downward upon the backſide of the great *Rotator*, and is implanted into the outſide of the lower end of the Thigh-bone. *Four Muſcles move the Thigh outward, called* Quadrigemini.

The ſecond and third of theſe Muſcles do want particular names; but both of them ariſe from the knob of *Os iſchium*, near one another, and are inſerted with the firſt.

The fourth and laſt is called *Quadrigeminus quadratus*. It is more fleſhy and broad than the reſt, ariſing from the inner part of the knob of the *Iſchium*, lying ſome two or three inches diſtant from the third, and endeth with the former.

To theſe muſt be added that Muſcle which we have named the *Deltoides* of the Thigh, not finding any in Humane Bodies to anſwer to it, ſo as to borrow a name from thence. It ſprings (as you may ſee plain in the foregoing Figure) from the outſide of the tip of the *Ileum*, with a ſharp beginning; but preſently enlarging it ſelf, becomes three-ſquare, and is inſerted with a broad membranous Tendon into the outſide of the Thigh-bone, from which inſertion it appears torn off in the Figure. By its ſituation it ſeems to aſſiſt the action of the *Quadrigemini*. *Alſo the* Deltoides *of the Thigh.*

The Thigh is turned about obliquely by two Muſcles called *Obturatores*, or Stoppers, becauſe they fill up the wide hole between the *Os pubis* and Hip-bone. The firſt is called *Obturator internus*. This ariſeth from the inner circumference of the hole before ſpoken of, and paſſing overthwart the end of the Hip-bone, is inſerted into the Cavity of the great *Rotator*. *The Thigh is turned a little about by two Muſcles, viz.* 1. Obturator internus.

The other is called *Obturator externus*, the outward Filler. This ariſes out of the external circumference of the above-named hole with a fleſhy and broad beginning, and winding about the neck of the Thigh-bone turneth into a ſtrong and large Tendon which is implanted into the Cavity of the great *Rotator* with the former. 2. Obturator externus.

And thus much for the Muſcles of the *Thigh*, which for order ſake I have according to the cuſtom of Anatomiſts firſt treated of; but it is neceſſary that we make our diſſection in the Leg firſt, to remove thoſe Muſcles; for we cannot ſo eaſily nor conveniently raiſe nor ſhew theſe of the Thigh, untill thoſe of the Leg be removed, becauſe the heads of ſome of them lie upon the Muſcles of the Thigh.

CHAP. XXI.

Of the Muſcles of the Tibia *or Leg.*

THE Muſcles of the *Tibia* or Leg are of the ſame number in Horſes as in Men, (like as the Muſcles of moſt other Parts are) the inſertion of ſome of them onely excepted. Which difference ſprings from hence, that this Bone of the Leg which in a Horſe is but one main Bone ſupported on each ſide with another ſlender immoveable one for ſtrength, as alſo for the ſafer paſſage of the Tendons of the Muſcles between them, (which I ſuppoſe to be the onely uſe of them, as not being moveable; I ſay this Bone which in a Horſe is but one) is in a Man two, going by two different names, *viz.* the one by that of *Tibia*, and the other, by that of *Fibula*, and ſome of the Tendons of the Muſcles are inſerted into one of them, and ſome into the other. But otherwiſe ſo far as I have had opportunity to examine them, I have found them to have the ſame original, ſubſtance, figure and courſe in a Horſe as in Man; and therefore I ſhall proceed to treat of them after the ſame method as I have done of all the reſt, forbearing to ſpeak any further of the difference (in a Man and an Horſe) between the Parts that are moved by the Muſcles to be treated of in this and the following Chapter, untill I come to the Book of the Bones, where I ſhall ſhew at large the ſimilitude between them, and that the difference is not ſo much as it may be believed to be.

The Leg is extended by five Muſcles. 1. Membranoſus. The *Leg* hath three motions allowed it, *viz.* bended, extended, and moved obliquely outwards. All the *Extenders* are placed on the fore-part of the Thigh, of which the firſt is called *Membranoſus*. This Muſcle is by *Bartholin* called the *Abductor*, as if its uſe were to move the Leg obliquely outwards; but that office is by other Anatomiſts ſince him aſcribed to the *Poplitæus*, and this ſaid to extend the Leg. It ariſeth fleſhy from the upper part of *Os ileum* on the outſide, and near the great Proceſs of the Thigh-bone it becomes broad and nervouſly membranous, wherefore it is called *Faſcia lata*, the broad Swadling-band, for it enwrappeth almoſt all the Muſcles of the Thigh within it ſelf; and being come as low as the Knee in Humane Bodies, and that Joint we call the Stifle in Horſes, (which exactly anſwers to the other, even as far as to the little round Bone between the two Bones of the *Femur* and *Tibia*, called the *Patella* or Knee-pan) I ſay when it is come as low as the Stifle (over which it croſſes) it is at laſt inſerted into the *fore-ſide* of the *Tibia* or Bone of the Leg. Its *uſe* is, as hath been ſaid, to extend the Leg directly; or as ſome Authours will have it, ſomewhat to abduce it or draw it obliquely outwards.

2. Longus. The *ſecond Extender* is called *Longus*, and *Sartorius* or *Sutorius*, from its uſe in thoſe Men that ſit croſs-legg'd at work, as *Shoomakers* and *Tailors*. It ariſes ſharp and nervous from the upper and fore-part of the appendix of *Os ileum*, and as it paſſes obliquely down the inſide of the Thigh, it becomes more fleſhy and broad, continuing ſo till it come to the inſide of the Leg a little below the Stifle, where it ends in a broad Tendon, and is inſerted into the Bone of the Leg or *Tibia*. The *uſe* of this Muſcle

Muſcle is not onely to extend the Leg, but alſo to draw it inwards, wherefore it is by ſome Authours reckoned for one of the *Benders* of the Leg.

The *third*, from its *ſtreight* courſe, is called *Rectus*, the Streight Muſcle. This takes its beginning from the lower brim of the Haunch-bone, and paſſing with a fleſhy and round belly ſtreight down the fore-ſide of the Thigh untill it come to the Stifle, it there turns into a ſtrong and broad Tendon, which adhering to the *Patella* deſcends over it, and is implanted into the fore-ſide of the upper part of the Shank. 3. Rectus.

The *fourth* is called *Vaſtus externus*, becauſe of its *great* fleſhy *bulk*, and becauſe it deſcends on the *outſide* of the Streight Muſcle. It ariſes broad and nervous from the root of the great *Rotator* or *Trochanter*, cleaving cloſe to the outward part of the Thigh-bone all along its courſe, untill it come to the Stifle, where it becomes membranous and broad, and uniting with the Tendon of the Streight Muſcle or *Rectus*, is inſerted into the ſame place with it, but on its outſide. 4. Vaſtus externus.

The *fifth* is called *Vaſtus internus*, running on the *inſide* of the *Rectus*. It ariſes from the root of the leſſer *Trochanter* and from the neck of the Thigh-bone with a nervous beginning, and afterwards growing fleſhy deſcends down the Thigh-bone, ſticking cloſe to it, till it come to the Stifle, over which it paſſeth, and afterward unites its ſelf with the former two, and takes its inſertion in the ſame place of the *Tibia* as they do. 5. Vaſtus internus.

It is worth the Diſſectour's taking notice of theſe three laſt Muſcles, how they be joined all in one juſt at their croſſing the Stifle, where they make one broad and very ſtrong Tendon, which ſpreads over and involves the *Patella* or little Bone of the Stifle, and ties it ſo faſt in its place upon the jointing of the Thigh-bone with the *Tibia*, that it is very ſeldom diſplaced, or indeed never. For although by diſtentions or ſtrains we often have this Part affected; yet never did I ſee an abſolute diſlocation in it. The *Patella* indeed may be (and often is) wrenched either to one ſide or the other as the accident may happen, but it is immediately reduced to its place again by this compound ligamentous Tendon, which like a *Spring* retracts it ſelf into its former Station, and the Bone to which it is knit, alſo. So that, that malady which is commonly taken for a diſlocation of this Bone, ſeems rather to be from Bloud extravaſated out of the Capillary Veſſels, which by great diſtentions many times may be broken; which Bloud lieth congealing and putrifying in the ſpaces between the Membranes and Muſcles, affecting the ſenſible neighbouring Parts, which puts the Horſe to that great pain we obſerve him to have on ſuch accidents. Now the means we uſe to remove this pain is by chafing the Part with penetrating Oils, which commonly effect the cure, if they be uſed preſently before the Bloud be too much congealed: But if the pain be not removed by this means, we are fain to open the Skin by way of an Iſſue, blowing in wind to ſeparate the ſeveral Skins one from another, and ſo make way for the congealed Matter the better to come forth; which done, the pain is removed, and the affection quite taken away, and the Horſe moſt times goes again as well as ever. Whereas ſhould this Bone be diſplac'd, as it is by many Farriers thought to be, this way of proceeding ſeems ſo far from contributing to the cure, that by laying the Skins open there is rather given more liberty for the Bone to remove out of its place, than any aſſiſtance afforded toward the reſtoring it again. But so much by way of digression to inform our Professours in this point; I shall now proceed to describe the remaining Muscles, the next of which are the *Benders* of the Leg.

Four Muscles bend the Leg. 1. Biceps. These are in number four; the first of which (according to *Bartholin*) is called *Biceps*, though by other Authours it is reckoned the last and fifth, supposing that there are five of these Muscles. It arises sharp and nervous from the appendix of the *Coxendix*, and being carried on the outside of the Thigh, it doth about its middle become fleshy, as if it begun there with a second head; from whence descending it groweth in its course more thick and outwardly nervous, untill it becomes a strong Tendon, which is inserted into the outer side, (but somewhat backward) of the appendix of the *Tibia*. The *use* of this Muscle is to bend the Leg by pulling it backward.

2. Semimembranosus. The *next*, according to the before-named *Bartholin*, is the *Semimembranosus*, which by others is reputed the fourth Bender. It takes its beginning from the knob of the *Coxendix* as the former doth, with a small, membranous head, from whence it runneth down the back-part of the Thigh, till it come to the Leg-bone, into which it is inserted with a round Tendon behind, in that place which in Man is called the Ham.

3. Seminervosus. The *third* (according to the same Authour) is the *Seminervosus*, so called from its substance, it being partly nervous and partly fleshy, as the former was partly fleshy and partly membranous. This arises small and nervous from the same knob of the *Coxendix* as the former two did; from whence descending obliquely by the back and inner part of the Thigh (in which course it becomes fleshy) its Tendon reaches towards the middle of the Leg-bone, into whose inner and backer part it is inserted.

4. Gracilis. The *fourth* is called *Gracilis*, the slender Muscle. This by some Authours is accounted for the *second* Bender of the Leg, but I shall after the method of the before-named Authour rank it for the fourth and last. It arises with a large and nervous beginning from the middle of the Share-bone just at its jointing, from whence it runs down the inside of the Thigh untill it comes to the *Tibia* or Leg-bone, into whose inside it is inserted with a round Tendon near the former.

Note, that some of these Muscles being placed more outward and others more inward; if they all work together, they draw the Leg directly backward; but if one be contracted alone, then it doth bend the Leg a little either to this or that side, according as the Muscle is placed, as well as draw it backward.

One moves it obliquely, viz. Poplitæus. There is another Muscle whose use is to move the Leg *obliquely*; its name is *Poplitæus*. It takes its rise broad and nervous from the outer head of the Thigh-bone, and afterward becoming fleshy runs with a flanting line down the Thigh to the back and inward part of the upper knob of the *Tibia*, where it is inserted.

CHAP.

CHAP. XXII.

Of the Muſcles that move the lower part of the Leg, and the Foot.

BY the *lower part* of the Leg is to be underſtood that Bone which is below the Hock or Hough, reaching from thence to the great Paſtern; which Bone anſwers to thoſe five in Humane Bodies that make the Inſtep. Likewiſe the great Paſtern and little Paſtern anſwer to the firſt and ſecond Joints of the Toes in Men; and laſtly that which is called the Coffin-joint on which the Hoof grows, is anſwerable to the laſt joint of the Toes on which the Nails are placed. Onely the difference is, that a Man becauſe of his going upright, treadeth upon the whole ſpace from the Heel to the Toes; and his Foot is alſo divided into five Toes, each conſiſting of ſeveral Joints, that by ſpreading themſelves and graſping cloſely on what he treads upon, they may keep him the more firmly erect. Whereas a Horſe and other four-footed Beaſts having four Feet upon the ground, have no need of ſo broad nor large a Foot, and do therefore go as it were upon Tip-toes, their Heels reaching as high up the Leg as to the Hock, which indeed is the Heel of the Horſe, as a very eminent and learned Phyſician who did me the honour to take a view of my Skeleton, intimated to me. For make but any Quadruped, as a Dog or the like, ſtand upright, lifting up his Fore-feet, and you may obſerve all that part of his *Leg* from the Hough downwards to lie upon the ground as a Man's Foot does; yea ſome, as Coneys, *&c.* in their ordinary gate tread upon all that ſpace: onely ſuch Creatures have their Feet cleft into Toes, whereas a Horſe is whole-footed, and thence ariſes a difference as to the number of the Muſcles of the Foot.

Note, that the Muſcles which move each Bone have onely their *Inſertions* into that Bone they are to move, and that they take their *riſe* from the Bone or ſome other Part (immediately or mediately) above it, as may be obſerved by the foregoing diſcourſe of the Muſcles of the Thigh and Leg. Thus thoſe Muſcles that move the Thigh, take their original from either the Hip-bone, Share-bone, or *Os ſacrum*, all of which are above it; likewiſe thoſe that move the Leg, ariſe from the Hip or Share-bones, or elſe from the Head or ſome other part of the Thigh-bone which is the Joint above it; and thus laſtly do the Muſcles that are to move all that part of the Leg or Foot which is below the Hock, ſpring from and lie upon the Parts above the Hock, ſave the *Flexor brevis* and *Tenſor brevis*, and the *Plantaris* which is at the Sole of the Foot (which cannot properly be called a Muſcle neither, for it is very little or not at all carnous, but rather ligamentous) for otherwiſe onely the Tendons of the Muſcles reach hither, and are inſerted ſome into one Joint, ſome into another.

The Inſtep-bone is bended by two Muſcles.

The *Foot* is bended, extended, and moved (a little) to either ſide, according to the motion of the *Inſtep-bone* (for ſo we ſhall call it for diſtinctions ſake.) Firſt, it is *bended* when it is drawn upwards and forward. To perform which motion there are two Muſcles aſſiſting: the firſt of which is called *Tibiæus anticus* or the forward Leg-muſcle, ſo named

1. Tibiæus anticus.

named from the situation of it, which is upon the fore-part of the Leg-bone towards its outer side. It arises sharp and fleshy from the upper appendix of the Leg-bone, cleaving close to it all along as it descends, and towards the bottom of it, it turneth by degrees to a Tendon, which passing under the Gristle that compasseth about the next Joint or Hock, is divided into two or more Tendons that are inserted into the foreside of the Instep-bone, which (together with the rest of the Foot) it moves forward and upward.

2. Peronæus anticus. The next is called *Peronæus anticus*, because it arises in Man from that Bone of the Leg that is called *Perone* or *Fibula*, and therefore it is improperly so called in an Horse that wants that Bone, and in whom it springs from the upper appendix of the *Tibia*, and descending downwards with a fleshy body till it come almost to the bottom of this Bone, it turneth into a Tendon as the former did, which Tendon passeth down by the outside of the Hock, and is inserted into the outside of the Instep-bone, which with the rest of the Foot it moves forward and somewhat outward.

It is extended by three. The Foot is also *Extended*, that is, when the Instep-bone is drawn backwards, which motion is performed by three Muscles: of which the

1. Gastrocnemius externus. first is called *Gemellus externus*, or *Gastrocnemius externus*. This in Men makes the greatest part of the Calf of the Leg. It takes its rise broad and fleshy from the inner head of the Thigh-bone at the lower end of it, and also from the outward head of the same Bone, for it hath a double beginning; which two heads descending for a while apart, they begin to be united into one about the middle of the Leg-bone, after which they both turn into one entire, broad, strong and nervous Tendon, which unites with the Tendon of the following Muscle called *Gastrocnemius internus*, and both are inserted into the Heel-bone.

2. Gastrocnemius internus. The *second Extender* of the Foot is called *Gastrocnemius internus*. This Muscle lyeth something under the former, arising from the hinder-part of the upper end of the Leg-bone with a strong, nervous beginning, and growing tendinous toward the lower end of the Bone unites with the Tendon of the foregoing, and is inserted into the Heel-bone with it as aforesaid.

3. Plantaris. The *third* and last is called *Plantaris*, or the Muscle of the Soal or Tread. This arises fleshy, round and slender between the former two, taking its beginning from the back-part of the lower head of the Thigh-bone. After it hath descended a little way down the Leg-bone it becomes a slender round Tendon, which running between the Tendons of the former two and joining very closely with them descends down to the Heel-bone, where it leaves them and proceeds along the back-part of the Instep-bone and the two Pasterns, and terminates within the Foot, spreading all about the bottom of it, making that Part which is called the Soal of the Foot in Men, and in Horses that Part that lieth next under the Soal, and is plain to be seen when we have drawn the Soal of the Foot out.

The Tendons of these three Muscles make the magna Chorda. It is the Tendons of these three Muscles that make that strong and thick Tendon by which Butchers hang up their Meat, which by reason of its greatness and singular strength is called *Chorda magna*. It is also this Tendon running down the back-part of the Leg, which we call the back Sinew, which being affected either by a strain or bruise or other accident, causes so great a pain, by reason of the sensibleness of the Tendon. When it is hurt, the Horse many times falls exceeding lame, though such acci-

TAB XXXIV
p.193
M P R S T
K Q A
A
D
D
L
O B
N
F
E
C
G
H
D
E
V
H
E
H
W
I
X Y W

accidents are not so dangerous to life in Horses as they are said to be in Men; for we make no difficulty in curing them, especially if presently taken in hand, but Chirurgeons do most times conclude Wounds of this Part in Men to be very dangerous by reason of their frequent falling into convulsions thereupon.

The Foot is also moved somewhat sideways, *viz.* inward and outward, by two Muscles. The *first* of which is called *Tibialis posticus.* This springeth from the upper end of the Leg-bone, from whence it descends among the before-named hinder Muscles till it come to the Instep-joint, where it becomes tendinous, and from thence runs down the inner side of the Instep-bone and Pasterns, till it come to the Soal of the Foot, into which it is inserted. Its *use* is to move the Foot obliquely inward.

It is moved sideways by two.
1. Tibialis posticus.

The *second* is called *Peronæus posticus* (improperly in an Horse.) It arises from the upper and hinder-part of the Leg-bone by a nervous and strong beginning, from whence it descends all along the outside of the Bone cleaving firmly to it, untill it reach its middle, where it becomes tendinous, and descends with the Tendon of the *Peronæus anticus* on the outside of the Instep-joint or Hock, but is not joined with it; for it continues its course further untill it reach the Foot, into the bottom of which it is implanted. This moves the Foot contrary to the former, *viz.* obliquely outward.

2. Peronæus posticus.

The Pasterns and Coffin-joint are likewise *bended,* or *extended* by their proper Muscles. The *Benders* are two, of which the *first* is called *Flexor longus,* or the Long Bender. This arises from the upper and hinder-part of the Leg-bone, about the middle whereof it becometh tendinous, and descends on the inner side of the Hough down the Instep-bone and Pasterns into the Coffin-joint.

The Pasterns and Coffin-joint are bended by two Muscles.
1. Flexor longus.

The *second* is called *Flexor brevis,* the Short Bender. It springs from the inside of the Heel-bone a little below the Hock, and has the same insertion with the former. These bend the Pasterns and Coffin-joint by drawing them backward.

2. Flexor brevis.

The *Extenders* are also two. The *first* is called *Longus Tensor,* or the Long Extender. It arises from the fore and inner side of the Shank just under the Stifle, and descends on the fore-side of that Bone, the Instep-bone and the Pasterns, and is inserted into the fore and upper part of the Coffin-joint.

They are extended also by two.
1. Extensor longus.

The *second* ariseth from the fore-part of the annular Ligament that binds about the Instep-joint, and descending under the former has the same insertion. These two extend the Pasterns and Coffin-joint by drawing them forward.

2. Extensor brevis.

Thus I am come to the end of the Treatise of the Muscles, in describing of any of which if I have erred, I hope the Apology with which I prefaced this fourth Book will obtain my excuse with all ingenuous Men: and as for the morose and carping, I shall take it as a favour from them, if instead of railing at random, they will take the pains to demonstrate my mistakes.

Table XXXIV.

Represents an Horse with his hinder-part toward you, that the Muscles of his Buttocks, &c. may be the plainer seen.

AA *Shew the* Cucullaris *or Monk's Hood.*
B *The edge of the* Deltoides *of the Thigh.*

C *The*

C *The* Glutæus minor *or lesser Buttock Muscle.*
DDD *The* Glutæus medius *or middle Buttock Muscle.*
EE *The* Glutæus major *or greater Buttock Muscle.*
F *The* Biceps.
GG *The* Seminervosus *of both Legs.*
HHH *The* Lividus *or* Pectinalis *of both Hind-legs.*
I *The* Semimembranosus.
K *The* Orbicularis *or orbicular Muscle of the Lips.*
L *A portion of the* Longissimus dorsi.
M *The circular Muscle of the Nose.*
N *The sphincter Muscle of the Fundament.*
O *The* Mastoides *on the other side the Neck.*
P *The* Musculus lateralis *or* Mansorius, *being one of the Muscles of the Cheeks.*
Q *The* Musculus scalenus *or* Triangularis.
R *The* Complexus *or* Trigeminus.
S *The* Transversalis Colli *or transverse Muscle of the Neck.*
T *The* Spinatus Colli *being one of the Extenders of the Neck.*
V Vastus externus.
WW Gastrocnemius externus.
X Peronæus anticus.
Y Peronæus posticus.

The End of the Fourth Book.

THE

THE ANATOMY OF AN HORSE.

BOOK V.

Of the Bones.

CHAP. I.

Of the nature, definition, differences and parts of Bones.

THE *Bones* are by a learned and ancient Philoſopher compared to the Carkaſe of a Ship, to which the reſt of the Parts are faſtned and whereupon they are ſuſtained. Theſe afford ſtability, ſtreightneſs and form to each Part and to the whole. The knowledge of them is moſt neceſſary; for without it we muſt needs be ignorant of the originals and inſertions of the Muſcles; and upon fractures or diſlocations of them, it were very unlikely that any ſhould ſet them right again without the knowledge of their ſhapes, and the manner of their jointing one with another.

A *Bone* is ſaid to be a *ſimilar Part, the drieſt and coldeſt of all the reſt, made of the moſt earthy and tartareous part of the Seed in the Womb,* (*i. e.* of the Humour in the *Ovum* or Conception) and is nouriſhed with the like particles of Bloud after the birth, and moiſtned with the Marrow contained in it. *The definition of a Bone.*

The material and efficient causes of a Bone.

In which description the word [*Seed*] is to be interpreted as we have intimated, and not of the Male and Female's Seed mixed together in the Womb, as the Ancients conceived; for it is certain that the Female hath no true Seed, and that the Male's being onely an active principle of generation, affords nothing of matter to the Parts of the *Fœtus*, but onely impregnates the *Ovum*, as shall be shewed more at large when I come to speak to the *Generation of Animals.* Thus the Male's Seed is no material cause at all of the Bones, but onely a *remote* efficient cause of them as it is of other Parts of the Body; of all which the plastick or formative power that is seated in the *Ovum* it self, is the *immediate* efficient.

Their differences.

As to the *differences* of Bones, they are many, as being divided or distinguished several ways. And first from their hardness, or softness: thus the lower parts of the Temple-bones are called *Petrosa*, stony Bones, and such are also the Bones of the Teeth. Others are in respect to these, soft; such are the spongy Bones of the Nose, and those which are called *appendices* to any Bone. And lastly of a mean substance between these may be reckoned all the rest of the Bones.

They are again divided or distinguished by their magnitude; thus some are esteemed great, some little, and some of a moderate size betwixt both.

Also they are divided by their figure; some being plain, some round; some have three sides, others four; some are like a Boat, some a Cup; some like a Hammer, an Anvil, or a Stirrop, such are the Auditory Bones.

They are also distinguished from their situation, connexion, cavity, sense, and upon several other considerations, which it would be tedious further to prosecute.

Their Parts.

Again, the Bones are many of them divided into three *parts*; first, that part whereof the body of the Bone consisteth; secondly, the part that groweth to the Bone; thirdly, the bunching part of the Bone: of which the first hath no proper name belonging to it, but is called by the name of the whole Bone; the second being that part that groweth to the Bone is properly called *Epiphysis*, the Appendage; and that part that bunches out beyond the plain surface, is called *Apophysis*, or the Process.

How many Bones of the Head.

In relation to this discourse of the Bones we shall divide the Body into three Parts, *viz.* the Head, the Trunk and the Limbs. By the *Head* is implied both Head and Neck. The first and uppermost Part of the Head is the Skull, called *Cranium*, because it is as it were *Cranos* an Helmet to the Brain. It is compounded of several Bones to the number of fifteen or seventeen in Humane Bodies, say most Anatomists, that is, in all, as well little as big; for of the large ones there are but nine, three of which are common to the Skull with the upper Jaw-bone, which are the Wedge-like Bone or *cuneiforme*, the Yoke-bone, and *spongiosum*, the spongy or Sieve-like Bone. The other six are proper Bones and make up the Skull it self; and those are the Fore-head Bone, the Noll-bone, the two Bones of the *Syncipút*, and the two Temple-bones, in which last are contained (in each of them) three small Bones, of which we have already treated where we spoke of the Parts of the Ear in the third Book at Chap. 14. namely the Hammer, the Anvil and the Stirrup, all which make up the said number of fifteen Bones of the Skull; to which if we add the lately found-out Bone of the Ear, called the orbicular Bone, there will be seventeen. Now the larger Bones are divided or distinguished by

several

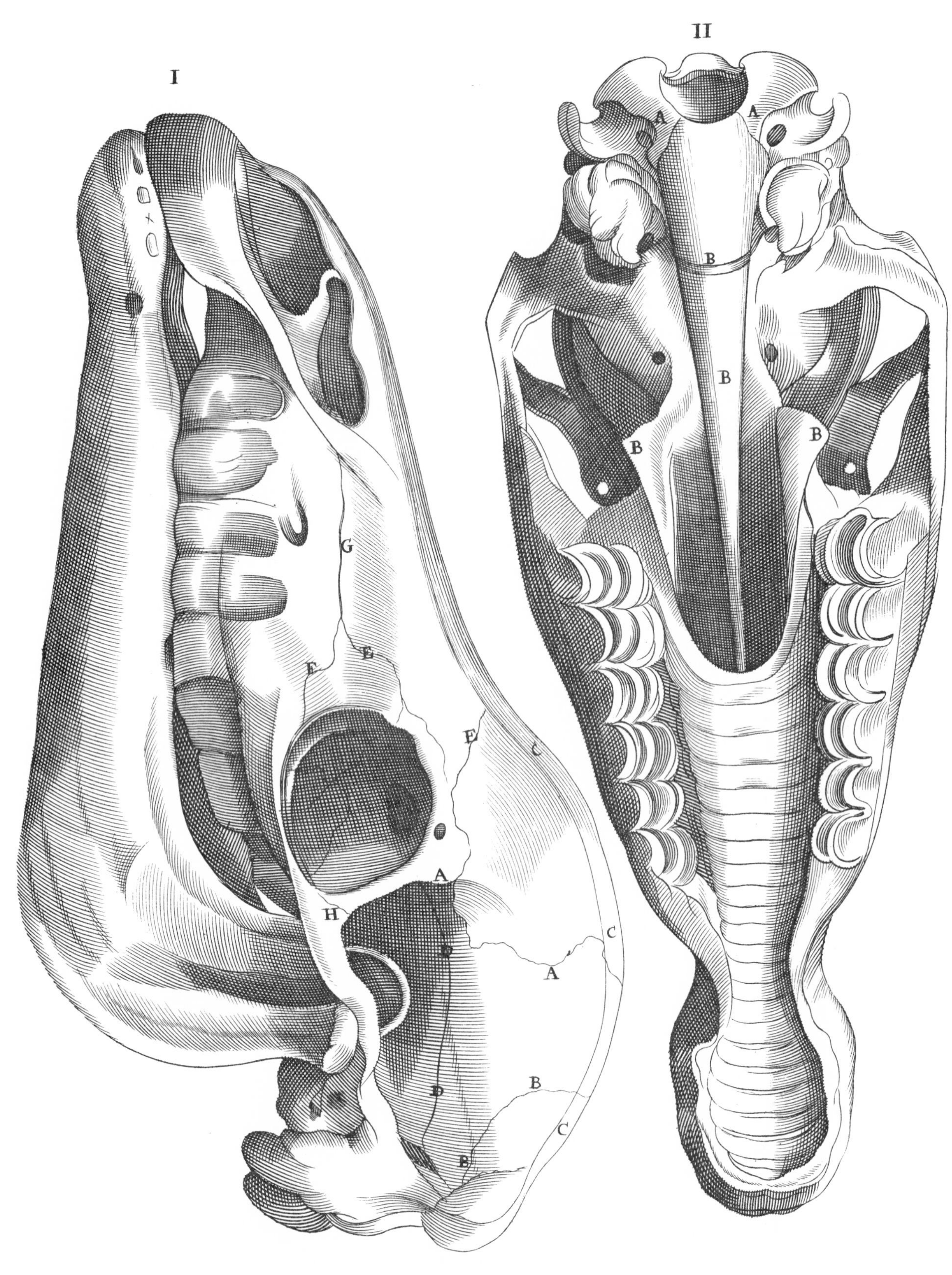
I
II
A
A
B
B
B
B
G
E
E
E
C
A
H
D
C
A
D
B
C
B

ſeveral Seams called Sutures, and both Bones and Sutures are of the ſame number in this Animal we are treating of as in Men, as may be ſeen by the following Figure.

Table XXXV.

Repreſents the Sutures or Seams of the Skull of a young Foal newly foaled, which in a grown Horſe are not ſo diſcernible.

Figure I.

Shews the Sutures of the top and ſides of the Skull.

AAA *The firſt Suture called* Coronalis, *or the Coronal Suture.*
BB *The ſecond proper Suture called the Lambdoidal or* Lambdoides.
CCC *The third proper and true Suture called the Sagittal or* Sagittalis.
DD *The firſt counterfeit proper Suture, ſo called becauſe it is not Saw-like as the other three are; it is alſo called* Squamoſa.
EE *The firſt common Suture by which the lower Proceſs of* Os frontis *is joined with the firſt Bone of the upper Jaw.*
F *The ſecond common Suture by which the Wedge-like Bone is joined with the ſaid firſt Bone of the upper Jaw. This is called* Cuneiformis.
G *The third common Suture called* Cribroſa, *which is common to the Wedge-like Bone and the* ſeptum *of the Noſe.*
H *The common Suture that divides the* Os jugale *into two, or by which it is joined together.*

Figure II.

Shews the Sutures of the bottom of the Skull.

AA *The common Suture that joins the bottom of* Os occipitis *to the* Os ſphenoides.
BBBB *Some other Sutures that belong to the bottom of the Skull.*

CHAP. II.

Of the Sutures or Seams of the Head.

A Suture what, and of how many kinds.

A *Suture* is the connexion of one Bone of the Head to another, of which there are two ſorts: the one is plain and linear, like two boards glewed or ſtones cemented together; the other indented like the teeth of two Saws put tooth within tooth.

The Sutures are proper or common. The proper are true or falſe.

Of theſe Sutures ſome are *proper* to the Skull alone, and ſome are *common* to it with the upper Jaw. The *proper* Sutures are again double, that is to ſay, *true* or *falſe*. Of the former ſort are thoſe Saw-like ones before-named, which are three in number, *viz.* Coronal, Lambdoidal and Sagittal; and of the latter are the plain ones, which ſome reckon to be more, ſome fewer.

True Sutures are 1. The Coronal.

The *firſt* of the Saw-like ones is called in Humane Skulls *Coronalis* or the Crown-Suture, becauſe the Ancients were wont to wear their Crowns or Garlands in that place. This Suture, as in Men, ſo likewiſe in a Horſe runs overthwart the Skull above the Fore-head, reaching from the Temple-bone of one ſide to the Temple-bone on the other, joining the *Os frontis* or Fore-head-bone to the *Synciput* or Bone of the fore-part of the Head.

2. The Lambdoidal.

The *ſecond* is called *Lambdoides* or Lambdoidal Suture, as reſembling in its dimenſion the Greek letter Λ *lambda*. This is ſeated on the back-part of the Head, being oppoſite to the former, beginning at the bottom of the *Occiput*, from whence it aſcends obliquely to either Ear in Men, but in a Horſe ſomething above the Ear, running with a more ſlanting line. It joins the Bone of the *Occiput* to the Bones of the *Synciput* and Temples.

3. The Sagittal.

The *third* runs not overthwart the Head as the two former, but lengthways of it, reaching in Humane Skulls from the top or middle of the Lambdoidal to the middle of the Coronal Suture onely; but in Horſes it reaches further (as it does in Children) croſſing the Coronal Suture, and runs afterward down the Fore-head-bone to the Noſe. This is not ſo Saw-like in Horſes Skulls as the other two are, as may be ſeen by the foregoing Figure. It is the laſt of the true or Saw-like Sutures, and hath the name of Sagittal, from its ſtreightneſs, its courſe being ſtreight like an *Arrow*.

The falſe Sutures are two.

Next come we to the *falſe*, counterfeit or baſtard proper Sutures, which are thoſe that reſemble a Line onely, and are not Saw-like at all. Theſe are in number two; the firſt of which paſſeth from the Root of the *Proceſſus mammillaris* upwards with a circular Duct, and paſſeth downwards again towards the bottom of the Ear, after it hath compaſſed in the Temple-bone. By this Seam are the Bones of the *Synciput*, *Occiput* and *Sphenoides* joined with the Temple-bones.

The ſecond of the baſtard proper Sutures runs obliquely downwards, ariſing from the ſide or rather top of the former, and runs down toward the Socket of the Eye, to the beginning of the firſt common Suture.

The

The *common* Sutures are thoſe that belong not to the Skull alone, but are common to it with the Wedge-like Bone and the upper Jaw. Of which theſe that follow are the moſt remarkable. *The common Sutures are*

Firſt, the *Frontalis*, by which the outer Proceſs of the Fore-head-bone is joined with the firſt Bone of the upper Jaw. 1. Frontalis.

The *ſecond* is that which is called *Cuneiformis* or Wedge-like, by which the Wedge-like-bone is joined with the firſt Bone of the upper Jaw. 2. Cuneiformis.

The *third* is called *Cribroſa*, which is common to the Wedge-like-bone, and the *ſeptum* or partition of the Noſe. 3. Cribroſa.

Now the *uſes* of theſe Sutures or Seams are, firſt, to be vents of the Brain, through which the impure and ſooty excrements might exhale or evaporate; ſecondly, to help to ſtay the Brain from tottering, and its parts from being miſplaced in violent motions, by giving way to the Fibres that paſs through them from the *Dura mater* within, to the *Pericranium* without the Skull, by which Fibres the ſaid *dura mater* and alſo the Brain it ſelf (which is wrapt within it) is kept ſuſpended as it were, that ſo the hardneſs of the Skull might not offend it by preſſing againſt it, nor the Brains own weight bear too hard upon the bottom of the Skull, which it would be apt to do were it not for its being thus born up or ſuſpended by theſe Fibres that tie the *Dura mater* to the outſide of the Skull. *The uſe of the Sutures.*

Theſe Sutures were alſo made for the ingreſs and egreſs of the Veſſels, for the life and nouriſhment of the Parts contained within the Skull.

Laſtly, that if at any time the Head ſhould happen to be broken, the fracture might not run through the whole Skull, but ſtay at the end of the fractured Bone; whereas were it not for theſe Seams, it would like an earthen Pot with one knock or fall be in danger of being ſhivered all in pieces, which it is not now ſo apt to do, for the crack will not ſo eaſily paſs over a Seam as it would run along an intire bone.

CHAP. III.

Of the proper Bones of the Skull.

THE Bones of the Skull are of two ſorts, *proper* and *common*. Of the firſt in this Chapter; and of the latter in the next. *The Bones of the Skull are proper or common.*

The *proper* are in number ſix; one of the Fore-head, another of the hinder-part of the Head or *Occiput*, two of the Crown, and two of the Temples, all which are divided or diſtinguiſhed from one another by the before-named Sutures. *The proper are ſix.*

The Fore-head-bone, called *Os frontis*, is ſeated before, and maketh the fore-part of the Skull, both above and a little below the Orbit of the Eyes. It is bounded before by the Coronal and firſt common Suture, on the ſides by the Temporal Bones, and on the inſide by the ſpongy Bones. 1. *The Fore-head-bone.*

Betwixt

Its Cavities. Betwixt the *Laminæ* or Scales of this Bone at the top of the Noſe there is a large (or rather double) *Cavity*, from whence two holes paſs to the Noſtrils, diſtinguiſhed by many bony Fibres and ſmall Scales, which are encompaſſed with a green Membrane, and contain a ſoft medullar, or as it were an oylie body.

The *uſes* aſcribed to theſe Cavities are various: as firſt, to prepare the air that is drawn in by the Noſtrils, for the generation of animal Spirits; ſecondly, to keep for ſome time the odoriferous air whereby ſmells may be more leiſurably perceived; thirdly, ſome think that they ſerve for the collection of flegmatick Excrements; and others, laſtly, that they aſſiſt or promote the ſhrilneſs or echo of the Voice. I will not determine of the truth of any of theſe opinions; but ſhall onely obſerve this further, that theſe Cavities are much larger in an Horſe than they are in a Man, even the difference of the bulk of their Bodies conſidered.

Beſides theſe Cavities there is alſo a Den or *Sinus* made of a double Scale; one of which being outermoſt maketh the upper (inward) part of the Orbit of the Eye, and is plain; the other maketh the Cavity above the Eyes on either ſide, and is not plain, but hath inſcriptions anſwerable to the winding convolutions of the Brain, whoſe bunching-out portions it receives.

Its Holes. This Fore-head-bone hath alſo two *Holes* in the middle part of the Eye-brow, which go to the Orbit of the Eye, by which the firſt branch of the Nerve of the fifth conjugation of the Brain goeth to the Muſcle of the Fore-head.

Its Proceſſes. It hath alſo four *Proceſſes*, two of which are ſeated at the greater corner of the Eye, and other two at its leſſer, all helping to make the upper part of the Orbit.

The Bones of the Synciput. *Their connexion.* Next come we to the Bones of the *Synciput* or fore-part of the Head, which are in number two, being joined before with the Bone of the Fore-head by the Coronal Suture, with the *Os occipitis* behind, by the Lambdoidal Suture, on each ſide to the Temple-bones by the ſcaly Sutures, and to the Wedge-like-bone by one of the common Sutures. They are alſo joyned together, or one to another, in the middle or top of the Head (lengthways) by a Suture common to them both, called the Sagittal Suture.

Their ſhape, ſubſtance, ſurface and holes. Their *figure* is almoſt four-ſquare; their *ſubſtance* thinner than that of the other Bones, yet conſiſt of two plates, ſave in their lower edges, where they are joined to the Temple-bones. On the outſide they are ſmooth, but on the inſide uneven, having ſeveral ſhallow Cavities or Dens by the ſides of the Sagittal Suture, to which the *Dura mater* firmly grows; as alſo many long and winding inſcriptions or furrows for the Veſſels which run from the internal Jugulars through the ſaid *Dura mater* to the Brain. They have likewiſe ſeveral perforations or little *holes*, ſome of which indeed penetrate but one Plate, which are for the entrance and exit of the Veſſels that run between the Plates; but moſt run quite through them, and are made for ſmall Veins and Arteries to paſs both from within outwards, and from without inwards.

The Os occipitis. Next is the *Os occipitis*, or Noll-bone, which makes the hinder and lower part of the Head, and the middle part alſo of the baſis of the Skull. It is of a very hard ſubſtance, harder than any Bone of the Skull beſides, (except the *Os petroſum* of the Temple-bones) being thicker at the bottom where it is without fleſh, and where the two *Sinus* of the *Dura*

mater

mater are joined. At the ſides of the great perforation (through which the Spinal Marrow deſcends) it is ſomewhat thin and without any Cavities or ſmall Dens in it; but that its thinneſs here might be no prejudice to it, from the edge of this perforation there aſcends on the inſide a large Proceſs or Prominence running along to its top, to ſtrengthen it and arm it againſt any accidents that might happen by blows, *&c.* This Prominence it is that diſtinguiſhes the two Protuberances of the *Cerebellum.*

This Bone is in ſhape five-corner'd, by two of which corners it is joined in its upper part to the Bones of the *Syncipu*t by the Lambdoidal Suture; by two other in its fore-ſides to the Temple-bones by one of the counterfeit Sutures; and by its fifth corner to the *Os cuneiforme*, or Wedge-like Bone. *Its ſhape and connexion.*

It hath in it ſeveral *Sinus's* or Chanels, of which ſome are on the inſide, and others on the outſide of it. Of thoſe on the *inſide* there are two which are pretty large, ordained for the receiving the protuberances or bunchings out of the *Cerebellum* or After-brain. The others on the inſide are ſome to receive the protuberances of the Brain it ſelf; others to receive the two *Sinus's* of the *Dura mater*, that they might not be compreſſed by the Bones of the Skull; and the reſt are for the like uſes. The two that are on the *outſide* of this Bone, are in its lower part by the ſides of the great perforation, of a ſemicircular ſhape. *Its* Sinus.

This Bone hath alſo ſeveral *Proceſſes*, four of which being clad with a glib Griſtle are received into ſo many *Sinus's* of the firſt *Vertebra* of the Neck. But that is the moſt conſiderable which I mentioned before, and ſerves to ſtrengthen the Bone. It has *Holes* to the number of five; the firſt is in the midſt of the bottom of the Noll, which is the largeſt of all the inward holes of the Head, being in ſhape round and ſomewhat long, through which the *Medulla oblongata* or Spinal Marrow paſſeth out of the Skull into the Cavity of the *Vertebræ* of the Neck. The other four are leſs by far, and are made for the tranſition of ſeveral Veſſels. *Its Proceſſes and Holes.*

The *Temple-bones* come next to be treated of, which are ſeated on the ſides of the Skull and reach to the bottom of the Ears. They are joyned on their upper part to the outſide of the Bones of the Crown by the Suture called *Squamoſa*, or Scale-like. In their fore-part they are joined to the firſt Bone of the upper Jaw, by its firſt Proceſs; and their hinder-part is joined to the *Os occipitis*, by one of the counterfeit Sutures. *The Temple-bones. Their connexion.*

The *figure* of the Temple-bone is in its upper part ample, equal and ſemicircular; but below, it is very ſhapeleſs, like to a rude, rugged and unequal Rock, from whence as alſo from its hardneſs it hath its name of *Petroſum*, or the Rocky-bone. *Their figure.*

The *ſubſtance* of this Bone is alſo full of variety; for at its bottom it is thick and rugged; but as it aſcends, by degrees it grows much thinner, and at its top is ſo thin that it is almoſt tranſparent, (eſpecially where it gives way to the Temporal Muſcle) and like a Scale lies upon the lower edge of the Bone of the *Synciput*, which Bone in its deſcent under the Temple-bone is alſo attenuated. *Their ſubſtance.*

The Temple-bones have each of them two *Sinus* or Cavities. The *outer* of theſe is much larger than the other, being lined with a Cartilage or Griſtle, ſeated betwixt the Auditory paſſage and the Proceſs of the Yoke-bone. It is of an indifferent length, running as it were tranſverſly or overthwart, and has the longer Proceſs or the head of the lower Jaw inſerted or articulated into it. The other Cavity is *inward* at the back-ſide *Their* Sinus.

ſide of the Proceſs of the Yoke-bone, and is common to the Temple-bone with the Noll-bone.

By theſe *Sinus* or Cavities there ſtands a ſharp and longiſh, and (in Horſes) pretty thick (but in Men far more long and ſlender) Appendix, from its ſhape in Humane Bodies called *Os ſtyloides*, the Pen-like Bone. Beſides which there are alſo three *Proceſſes*; two of which are external, and one internal.

Their Proceſſes.

The *firſt external* is blunt, thick and ſhort; (ſaid to be ſomewhat hollow within) tending downwards, in ſhape ſomething like to the Nipple of a Cow, from whence it is called *Mammillaris*.

The *ſecond* of the *outward* Proceſſes runs forward from the hole of the Ear to the Proceſs of the firſt Bone of the upper Jaw, both of them framing the *Os jugale*, or Yoke-bone. For theſe two Proceſſes, one of the Temple-bone and the other of the firſt Bone of the upper Jaw, being joined by an oblong Suture do make the faſhion (as it were) of a Bridge, or of an Oxes Yoke, from whence that Bone hath its name, and of which we ſhall treat further in the next Chapter.

Os petroſum. *Its Holes, and Cavities.*

The *third* Proceſs, which is *internal*, is that which is called the Rocky-bone. It is pretty long, jetting out to the inſide of the bottom of the Skull, within which it hath two *holes*, through one of which an Artery, and through the other the Auditory Nerve paſs to the inner *Cavities* of the Ear, which are three in number, namely the *Tympanum* or Drum, the *Labyrinthus* or Labyrinth, and the *Cochlea*, or Snail-ſhell. On the outſide of the Skull this Proceſs has three perforations or holes. The firſt and largeſt of which is called *meatus Auditorius*, or the hole of hearing. The ſecond is narrow, ſhort and oblique, near to the firſt, by the firſt hole of the Wedge-like Bone. Through this the Jugular Vein enters into the inner Cavities of the Skull. The third hole is ſeated betwixt the *Proceſſus mammillaris* and the *Styloides* or Pen-like *Appendix*, ending into that paſſage that goes from the Ear to the Mouth. As to the little Bones that lie hid in the Cavities of this Proceſs, by ancient Anatomiſts they were reckoned to be but three, but there is by modern Authours added a fourth; and they are commonly known by theſe following names, *viz. Incus, Malleus, Stapes*, and *Os orbiculare*, of all which I have already treated in the fourteenth Chapter of the Third Book, where they are alſo lively repreſented in Figures, to which place I refer the Reader for his further ſatisfaction; having not mentioned them in this place, but that they make up the number of the *proper* Bones of the Skull.

Table

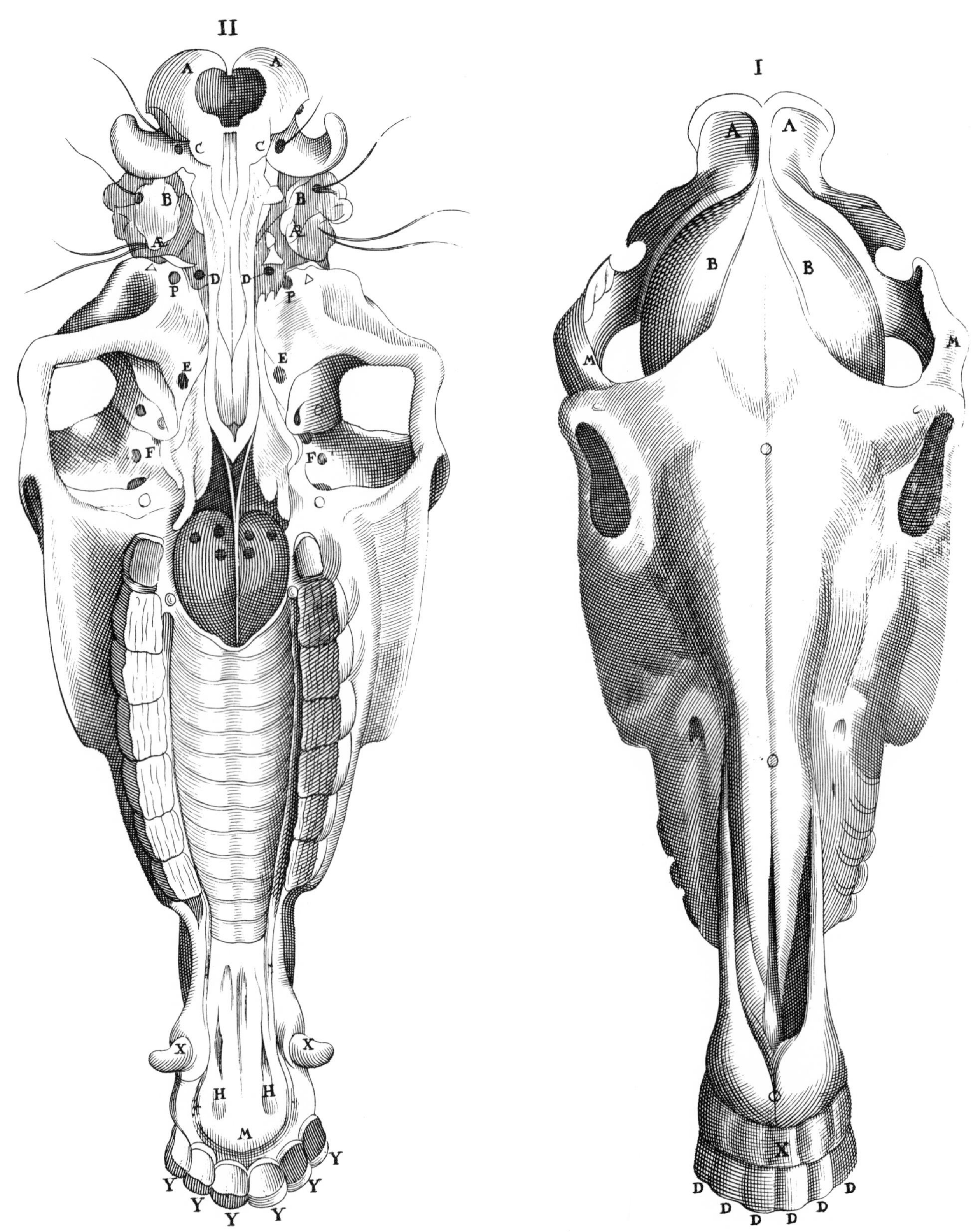
II
A
A
C
C
B
B
Æ
Æ
D
D
P
P
E
E
F
F
X
X
H
H
M
Y
Y
Y
Y
Y
Y
I
A
A
B
B
M
M
X
D
D
D
D
D
D

Table XXXVI.

Shews the ſeveral Bones of the Skull both proper and common, together with the ſeveral perforations for the outgate and ingate of the Veſſels, as many as can be ſhewed in two Figures, one ſhewing the top and the other the bottom of the Skull.

Figure I.

Shews the uppermoſt Bones of the Skull, of the Noſe, and of the upper Jaw.

AA *The Bones of the* Synciput *or fore-part of the Head.*
BB *The Temple-bones, on which the Temporal Muſcles reſt.*
MM *The* Os jugale.
OO *The common Suture that joins the Fore-head-bone and the Bones of the upper Jaw together.*
DDD *The ſix Fore-teeth of the upper Jaw.*
X *A hole a little above the upper Gumm, through which do paſs the Palate-vein and Artery, which branch afterward about the upper Lip.*

Figure II.

Shews the hinder and lower Bones of the Head, with their perforations.

AA *The* Os occipitis *or Noll-bone.*
BB *The holes through which the ſixth pair of Nerves (formerly ſo reckoned) do paſs out of the Skull.*
CC *The two holes through which the ſeventh conjugation of Nerves (of the ſame reckoning) do paſs out of the Skull.*
DD *The holes through which the taſting Nerves do paſs, which are diſperſed about the Tongue, the Muſcles of the* Os hyoides *and ſeveral other parts within the Mouth.*
EE *The holes by which the external Jugular Veins and Arteries paſs into the Skull.*
FF *A hole in the Proceſs of the Wedge-like Bone called* Pterygoides, *ſeated at the bottom of the Skull.*
HH *Two holes in the Bones of the Palate.*
M *The hole of the Palate through which the Palate-vein and Artery paſs out of the Mouth to the upper Lip.*
OO *The holes through which do paſs the Veins, Arteries and Nerves to the roots of all the Teeth.*
PP *The holes through which the Optick Nerves do paſs to the Orbit of the Eyes.*
YY *The Six Fore-teeth or Shearing-teeth of the upper Jaw.*
XX *The Tuſhes, or Dog-teeth.*
ÆÆ *The holes through which the fifth pair of Nerves do paſs forth of the Skull.*

CHAP. IV.

Of the Bones common to the Skull and upper Jaw.

HAving hitherto treated of the Bones *proper* to the Skull onely, I come now to treat of those which are *common* to it with the upper Jaw; and these are in number three, namely, the *Os sphenoides* or *cuneiforme*, the *Os cribriforme*, and the *Os jugale*.

The Wedge-like Bone. Its situation. The first of these is the *Sphenoides*, or Wedge-like Bone, so called from its situation, which is betwixt the Bones of the Skull and the upper Jaw, and not from the likeness of its figure to that of a Wedge, as some do believe. It is joined before to the Fore-head-bone, and behind to the *Os occipitis*. At the sides it doth a good part of it join to the *Os petrosum*. Above, it is joined to the first, fourth and sixth Bones of the upper Jaw; and below, to the Bones of the Palate of the Mouth.

Its Processes. It hath several *Processes*, of which some are external, and some internal. The *internal* are four, standing out like four feet of a Table or Chair, which (taking in the space between them) form the *Sella Turcica*. The *external* are also four, of which the two *formost* are contiguous to the upper Jaw, and are called the Wing-like Processes, from the resemblance they have to Bats-wings; for they are thick in some places, and yet end into a notable thinness, almost as thin and sharp as the edge of a Knife. The two *hinder* are stretched out toward the *Styloides* Processes of the Temple-bones.

Its Cavities. This Bone hath several *Cavities* or hollownesses; two of which are common with it and the Temple-bones, and the Bones of the *Synciput*.

Its Holes. It hath also many perforations or little *Holes* to the number of seven on each side. One of which being round gives a passage to the Optick Nerve toward the Eye. The rest are penetrated some by one, some by several pairs of Nerves; others by the Carotid Arteries and Jugular Veins; and others again by both Nerves and Bloud-vessels.

The Sieve-like Bone. Its situation and connexion. The next common Bone of the Head and upper Jaw is the *Os cribriforme*, so called from the several or indeed innumerable little holes in it, which make it like a *Sieve*, through which holes the smells do pass to the Mammillary Processes, or Olfactory Nerves. It is situated in the fore-part of the Skull, between or a little below the Sockets of the Eyes, under the middle basis of the Fore-head-bone, and at the upper part of the Nostrils. It is joined by a plain or simple line to the Fore-head-bone, the second Bone of the upper Jaw, and to the *Os cuneiforme*.

Its Parts. This Bone is by some divided into *four parts*; of which the *first* is a Process in the upper and middle part of it, which is long and triangular, ending in a sharp point, whence it is called *Crista galli*, or the Cock's Comb. This runs in betwixt the Mammillary Processes dividing them one from the other. To its sharp point the *Sinus* of the *Falx* adhereth.

The *second* part of this Bone is that which most properly is called *Os cribriforme*, being perforated all over like a Sieve, some of which holes are streight and some oblique. They are observed to be much larger in

Dogs

Dogs than in any other Animal (allowing for the proportion of their Bodies) which is supposed the reason why their smell is more exquisite than that of any other Creature.

The *third* part is a Process in its lower or under side opposite to the upper Process; which part divideth the upper part of the Nose into two Nostrils, whence it is called *septum Nasi*, the Partition-bone of the Nose.

The *fourth* and last part of this Bone is compared to a Sponge or Pumice-stone, being porous and full of small cavities, which are filled with a spongie flesh; and from this part the whole Bone is by some called *Os spongiosum*. For the names of *cribriforme* and *spongiosum* are confounded one with the other, being either of them given indifferently to the whole Bone. But if we will consider the *spongiosum* onely as a part of the *cribriforme*, then we must say, that it is that part of it that is seated just at the top of the Nostrils. Some make two Bones of it, affixing one at the top of each Nostril, and call them in the plural number *Ossa spongiosa*.

The *use* ascribed to the *Os cribriforme* by most Anatomists hath been to discharge through its pores or holes flegmatick excrements from the Brain into the Nose, but he that shall examine them, will find that its holes are so filled either with the spongie flesh before-named, or else with the Fibres of the smelling Nerves passing through them to the inside of the Nostrils, that there is no passage left for any humour by them. What we therefore account their true use to be, the Reader may be informed, if he please to turn back to the fifteenth Chapter of the Third Book, where we treated of the Nose, and described its uses: adding to what is there said of it, that it makes up the inner corner of the Orbit of the Eye. *Its Use.*

The *third* and last Bone common to the Skull and upper Jaw is called *Os jugale*, or the Yoke-bone. This is seated on each side of the Horse's Face between the *meatus* of the Ear or Auditory passage, and the first Bone of the upper Jaw; being framed of two Bones, one of which is a Process of the Temple-bone that is carried from the *meatus Auditorius*, and is the hinder of them; and the other Bone being the foremore is a Process of the first Bone of the upper Jaw, and which maketh the lower side of the lesser or outer corner of the Eye. These two are joined by a slanting or oblique Suture, and being so joined do constitute this Bone called *Os jugale*. Over this Bone runs the Tendon of the Temporal-muscle, and also the Tendon of the *Masseter* or Chewing-muscle, as they pass to the lower Jaw. **Os jugale.**

Some make but two common Bones of the Skull and upper Jaw, not reckoning this for any particular Bone, seeing (as has been said) it is formed onely of the two Processes of the Temple and upper Jaw-bone. But seeing it is distinguished from the others by a particular name (though not of any peculiar substance) I thought it not absurd to reckon it for a *third* common Bone.

CHAP. V.

Of the Jaw-bones and their Parts.

THE Bones of the *upper* and *lower Jaws* come next to be ſpoken to, with the firſt of which we will begin.

The Bones of the upper Jaw. This Jaw hath Bones of two ſorts, the one proper to it ſelf, and the other common to it and the Skull. The *common* Bones are the Wedge-like and Sieve-like Bones, and the *Os jugale,* of which we have already treated in the foregoing Chapter. I ſhall therefore proceed to treat of the Bones *proper* to the upper Jaw onely, which make the lower ſide of the Orbit of the Eye, the Noſe, Cheeks and Roof of the Mouth.

1. Zygomaticum. The Bones that conſtitute all theſe Parts are twelve in number, on each ſide of the Face ſix; the *firſt* of which is called *Zygomaticum,* becauſe by its Proceſs it makes up the greateſt part of the *Os jugale.* This is ſeated at, and maketh, the lower part of the outer corner of the Eye.

2. Lachrymale. The *next* is a round, little, brittle and thin Bone, ſeated in the inner corner of the Eye, called *Os lachrymale,* becauſe it has a hole in it through which the ſerous humour that makes the tears in Men doth iſſue. Upon this hole the little Kernel called *caruncula Lachrymalis* reſteth, that hindreth the continual gleeting of the foreſaid humour. There is alſo in the lower part of this Bone another hole which goes to the cavity of the Noſtril, through which doth paſs a branch of the fifth pair of Nerves to the inner Skin of the Noſe.

3. Innominatum. The *third* is ſeated in the inner ſide of the Eye, and within is continued with the fungous Bones of the Noſtrils. It is broad, and ſomewhat quadrangular or four-corner'd, alſo thin and tranſparent, like the Scale of a Fiſh. On its outſide it is ſmooth, but within rugged and unequal, becauſe of the Scales that cleave unto it. It is joined to four Bones, *viz.* to the Fore-head-bone, to the Wedge-like Bone, to the ſecond Bone of the Jaw, (*viz.* the next foregoing) and alſo to the fourth, or next following. It is not known by any peculiar name; I have therefore made bold to call it *Os innominatum.*

4. Os malæ, *or Cheek-bone.* The *fourth* Bone is called *Os malæ,* the Cheek-bone, becauſe it maketh up the greateſt part of the *Cheek,* as alſo of the Palate. It likewiſe con-*Its connexion.* tains the upper Teeth in its cavities or caverns. It is much larger than any other Bone of the upper Jaw, and is circumſcribed with many Sutures; for not to mention the Teeth that are inarticulated into it, it abutteth upon or is joined to ſeveral Bones. In the firſt place it is joined above, on the ſide next the Noſe, to the Bone of the Fore-head; below, to the Wedge-like Bone, and the Bone of the Palate of the Mouth; before, to the *Os lachrymale,* and to the fifth Bone that makes the upper part of the Noſe, (which is next to be deſcribed;) and laſtly to its own companion, *viz.* the Cheek-bone of one ſide to that of the other.

Its Holes. This Bone hath three perforations or *holes,* two of which are under the Orbit of the Eye; that is, on each ſide one, running from the lower part of the Eye outward. Their *uſe* is to tranſmit or let paſs two branches of the fifth pair of Nerves out of the Orbit of the Eye to the Face, on the Parts whereof they are beſtowed.

The

The *third* of these holes is in the Palate, at the backside of the Grinding-teeth where both Bones of the Jaw meet. It is presently divided into two, one of which runneth on one side of the *septum* of the Nose, and the other on the other, to the Nostrils, to which there pass through these holes a small Vein and a small Artery.

It hath also a den or cavity on each side, by the side of the Nose under the Orbit of the Eye, which is covered with a very fine Membrane. This is often full of a mucous or slimy phlegm.

The *fifth* Bone of the upper Jaw doth with his companion make the bony prominence of the Nose. It is a small Bone, in figure almost four-square. It is hard, solid, and reasonable thick, having sundry small perforations in it. It is joined above to the Fore-head-bone, *viz.* to its internal Process. In the sides above it is joined to the first Bone, and a little lower to the fourth Bone of this Jaw. In the middle it is joined to its companion, and below to the Gristles that make the lower part of the Nose. *5. The Nose-bone.* *Its connexion.*

The *sixth* is that which makes up the Roof of the Mouth, with its companion; for you must reckon every one of these Bones double, one on one side of the Face, and another on the other. It is a broad Bone, thin and solid, and in the end, where it is rough, it resembleth a semicircle. It is joined behind to the Wing-like Processes of the Wedge-like Bone, and on the inside, to the Partition-bone of the Nostrils. It is likewise joined to the fourth Bone of this Jaw or Cheek-bone, and lastly to his companion or fellow in its back-part. *6. The Palate-bone.*

This Bone hath also two perforations, on either side one, running upward and backward to two of the holes of the Wedge-like Bone.

The *lower* Jaw comes next to be treated of, which makes the lower part of the capacity of the Mouth. This differs from the former in that it is moveable, whereas the upper is not. In shape it is long and prominent. At both the ends of it, there are two *Processes*, which are by some called *Horns*. The *foremost* of them runs upward, and from a broad basis grows sharp, ending into a cone or point. This point receives the Tendon of the Temporal Muscle, which Tendon compasseth it round about, and is strongly implanted into it: from whence it is that a luxation of the lower Jaw, because of the distention of this Tendon that happens thereupon, is very dangerous, and hard to cure. *The lower Jaw-bone. Its Processes and Sinus's.*

The other being the *backward* Process, is called *Articularis*, because it serves for articulation. This hath a neck and a longish head, (called *Condylus*) that is covered with a Cartilage for its easier motion: By this head it is articulated into the *Sinus* of *Os petrosum*, that is also lined with a Cartilage, and is knit thereto strongly by a membranous Ligament. At the sides and roots of these Processes it hath shallow Sinus's or Cavities in its surface, but they are deeper on the inside than on the outside. The principal use of both seemeth to be for the passage or insertion of the Muscles.

This Bone of the lower Jaw is very hard, and for the most part very solid, to make it the stronger. Yet on each side (more backward than in Men) it hath a Cavity within it, which contains a marrowy juice for its nourishment. It hath also four perforations or holes, of which two are at the roots of the Processes, by which a branch of the fifth pair of Nerves, as also a Vein and Artery do pass to the Teeth. The two other *Its Cavities and Holes.*

holes are in its fore-part by the ſides of the Chin, through which two twigs of the ſaid fifth branch of Nerves do paſs out again to the lower Lip, and its Muſcles and Skin.

The Sockets of the Teeth. This lower Jaw as well as the upper hath Sockets for the Teeth to ſtand in, in number equall to the Teeth, which Sockets are called by the Latins *Alveoli* or little Pits. Theſe are digged deep, that the Teeth like ſo many Nails might be the firmlier faſtned in them. When any of the Teeth fall out of them, (as the Foal-teeth, *&c.*) in a ſhort time they are obliterated, the Jaw becoming ſmooth without any pit in it in that place.

Table XXXVII.

Repreſents an Horſe's Head and Jaws as much of them as can be ſeen by the Head ſtanding with one ſide towards us; and ſhews thoſe Bones which could not ſo well be ſeen in the foregoing Table, where the Head is repreſented in one Figure with the top, and in the other, with the bottom of it towards us.

Figure I.

A *The Temple-bone on which the Temporal Muſcle is placed.*

B *A hole in the Skull through which doth paſs forth from the Brain a ſmall Nerve, which is diſperſed about the top of the Skull.*

DD *The Bones which make the top of the Noſe.*

HH *The* Os jugale.

F *The hole through which doth paſs a branch of the Nerve of the fifth conjugation, which furniſheth the Muſcles of the upper Lip and alſo the Muſcles of the Noſtrils with Nerves.*

L *The round production of the upper Jaw, which production is called* cervix.

M *The Auditory Paſſage or hole of the Ear.*

N *The Mammillary Proceſs of the Temple-bone.*

OOO *The lower Jaw-bone.*

P *The hole where the Nerve of the fifth pair comes forth, which Nerve furniſheth the Muſcles of the lower Lips with twigs from it.*

Q *The Production of the lower Jaw, which doth articulate into the upper.*

K *The Noll-bone.*

Figure II.

Repreſents the Skull and upper Jaw onely, the lower Jaw being removed, the better to ſhew the ſeveral perforations in the ſide of the bottom of the Skull, which perforations or holes in the other Figure are hid by the articulation of the lower Jaw.

A *The hole by which the Nerve paſſes from the Brain to the upper Jaw.*

E *A hole whereby a ſmall Nerve doth paſs from the Brain, which is diſtributed upon the bottom of the* Occiput, *and other Parts at the bottom of the Skull.*

F A

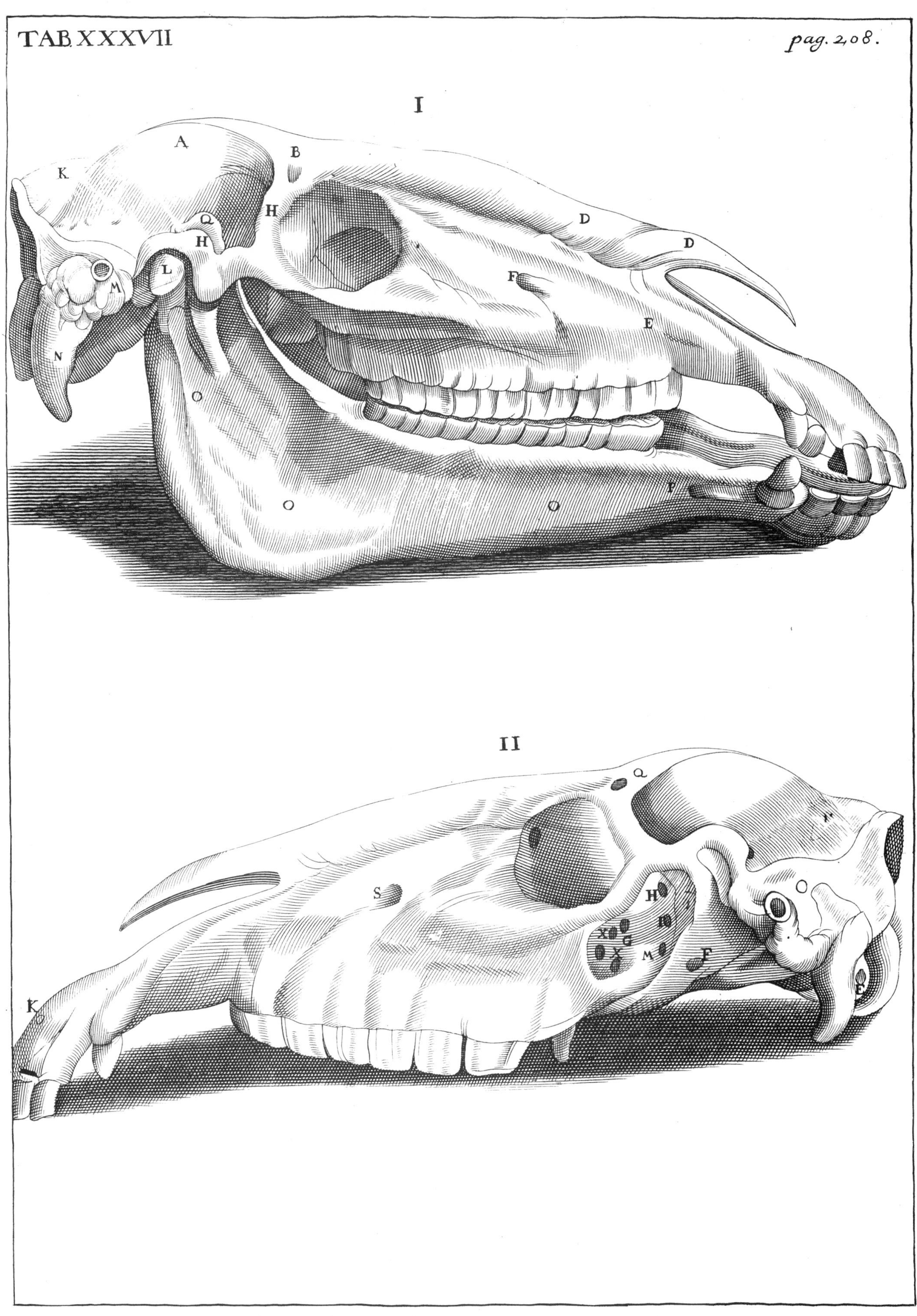
TAB. XXXVII
pag. 208.
I
A
B
K
Q
H
H
L
M
N
O
O
O
D
D
F
E
II
Q
S
H
X
G
X
M
F
K
E

F *A hole by which a branch of the external Jugular Vein and Artery doth paſs to the Brain.*

G *A hole through which do paſs the ſixth pair of Nerves, according to Doctor* Willis.

H *The hole through which the Optick Nerves do paſs from the Brain to the Eyes.*

I *A hole through which do paſs another pair of Nerves, which branch into the Muſcles of the Tongue, and alſo ſend twigs to the Muſcles of the Ears.*

K *The hole where the Palate-vein comes forth.*

M *Another hole through which doth paſs a ſmall twig of the external Jugular Vein and Artery up to the Brain.*

O *The Auditory Paſſage.*

Q *A hole through which a ſmall Nerve doth paſs from the Brain to be diſtributed about the top of the Skull.*

S *The hole where the Nerve of the fifth pair comes forth of the upper Jaw after it hath furniſhed the roots of the Grinding-teeth with Nerves, from whence it marches towards the lower Lip, where it is diſperſed amongſt the Muſcles thereof.*

XX *Two other holes in the bottom of the Skull through which do paſs other conjugations of Nerves, which are diſperſed about the Head, Face and Mouth.*

CHAP. VI.

Of the Figure, Magnitude, Number and Articulation of the Teeth.

THE *Teeth* are called in Latin *Dentes, quaſi Edentes,* from *eating.* They are of a very hard ſubſtance, yea, harder than any of the other Bones in the whole Body. That part of them that ſtands out above the Gumm, is ſmooth and free from any covering; but that part that is within the Sockets of the Jaws is more rough and covered with a thin Membrane or *Perioſteum,* which Membrane is of exquiſite ſenſe. Thoſe ſort of them which we call the Grinding-teeth, have a manifeſt Cavity within, but the *Inciſores* (or Fore-teeth) and Dog-teeth have but very obſcure ones. Into theſe Cavities by the very ſmall holes that are in the roots of the Teeth, are received (into each Tooth) a Capillary Artery from the *Carotides,* alſo a ſmall Vein from the Jugulars, and a twig of a Nerve from the fifth pair; which Nerve being expanded through the thin Membrane that inveſts the ſaid Cavity, gives it a moſt acute ſenſe; whereas the bony part of the Tooth is of it ſelf inſenſible. Theſe Veſſels before-mentioned, namely, the Vein, Artery and Nerve, are united together and cloathed with a common Coat when they enter the Jaw, within which they have a proper chanel to run along in under the roots of the Teeth, to each of which roots they ſend ſmall twigs as they paſs by, as aforeſaid.

The Teeth. Their ſubſtance and Veſſels.

Three ſorts of them.
1. Inciſores.

As in Men, ſo in Horſes, there are three kinds of Teeth, namely, *Inciſores, Canini* and *Molares*. The *Inciſores*, Cutters or Shredders are thoſe we call the Fore-teeth from their being ſeated in the fore-part of the Jaw. They are ſharp-edged like a Knife, and broad alſo, that they may the better bite off or crop the Graſs, &c. They are in number twelve, that is to ſay, in each Jaw ſix. They have each but one root or phang, though that root is indifferent large, moſt times larger than any one of the phangs of the great or Grinding-teeth.

2. Canini.

The next to theſe are thoſe which in Horſes we call the *Tuſhes*, but in Men they are called the Dog-teeth or *Canini*, not onely becauſe in figure they are like the Teeth of a Dog, and ſtand out of the Gumms as Dog's-teeth do; but from their uſe alſo, which is to gnaw upon and break (with their ſharp points) what is too hard for the Fore-teeth to cut or ſhear in ſunder. The roots of theſe as of the former are ſingle, having but one phang.

3. Molares.

Thoſe of the third rank, are the double Teeth, which are called *Molares*, or Grinders, becauſe the Meat is broken or ground by them, even as Corn is ground by the Mill-ſtone. Theſe are in Horſes twenty four in number, in each Jaw twelve. Their ſeat is in the inner part of the Mouth, being environed in their outſide by the Cheeks, leſt the broken or ſhredded Meat, being rowled by the Tongue upon the Teeth, ſhould ſlip over them out of the Mouth, before it be ſufficiently ground.

How to know the age of an Horſe by his Teeth.

The two foremoſt of theſe Teeth, ſtanding next to the Dog-teeth or Tuſhes, are thoſe by which the age of an Horſe is known till after ſeven years old, and that by their unevenneſs at the top, having ſeveral little thin ſhells or ſcales as it were ſticking up round the outſide of the top of them, whereby their middle part is made to appear hollow; which hollowneſs where it is found, is a certain ſign of the Horſe's being under ſeven years of age. And it is alſo to be obſerved, that the nearer the Horſe comes to that age, the more doth that hollowneſs grow out by degrees: ſo that when he comes to be full ſeven years old it is quite obliterated, and ſo the Horſe's age to be no more known by that ſign, being paſt the mark in the Mouth as we ſay: for by the perpetual uſe that the Horſe makes of his Teeth, the before-mentioned Shells at the top of them, which cauſe their hollowneſs, are worn down even with the other parts of the Teeth, ſo that the whole top of the Tooth becomes even, ſmooth and plain.

Neither are the reſt of the Grinding-teeth without ſome hollowneſs or at leaſt roughneſs in their tops; but this is of a different nature from the other: which roughneſs or unevenneſs is very neceſſary, for by it they are made more fit for the comminution of the Meat: For as Millers when their Millſtones are grown ſmooth, do pick them anew, to make them grind the better; ſo hath Nature made the upper part of theſe Grinding-teeth, elegantly to imitate the rough ſuperficies of a Milſtone, having here and there formed little pits in them. We ſhall not need to ſhew the uſes of theſe, or of either the foregoing ſorts of Teeth, that being intimated ſufficiently in the deſcription of them.

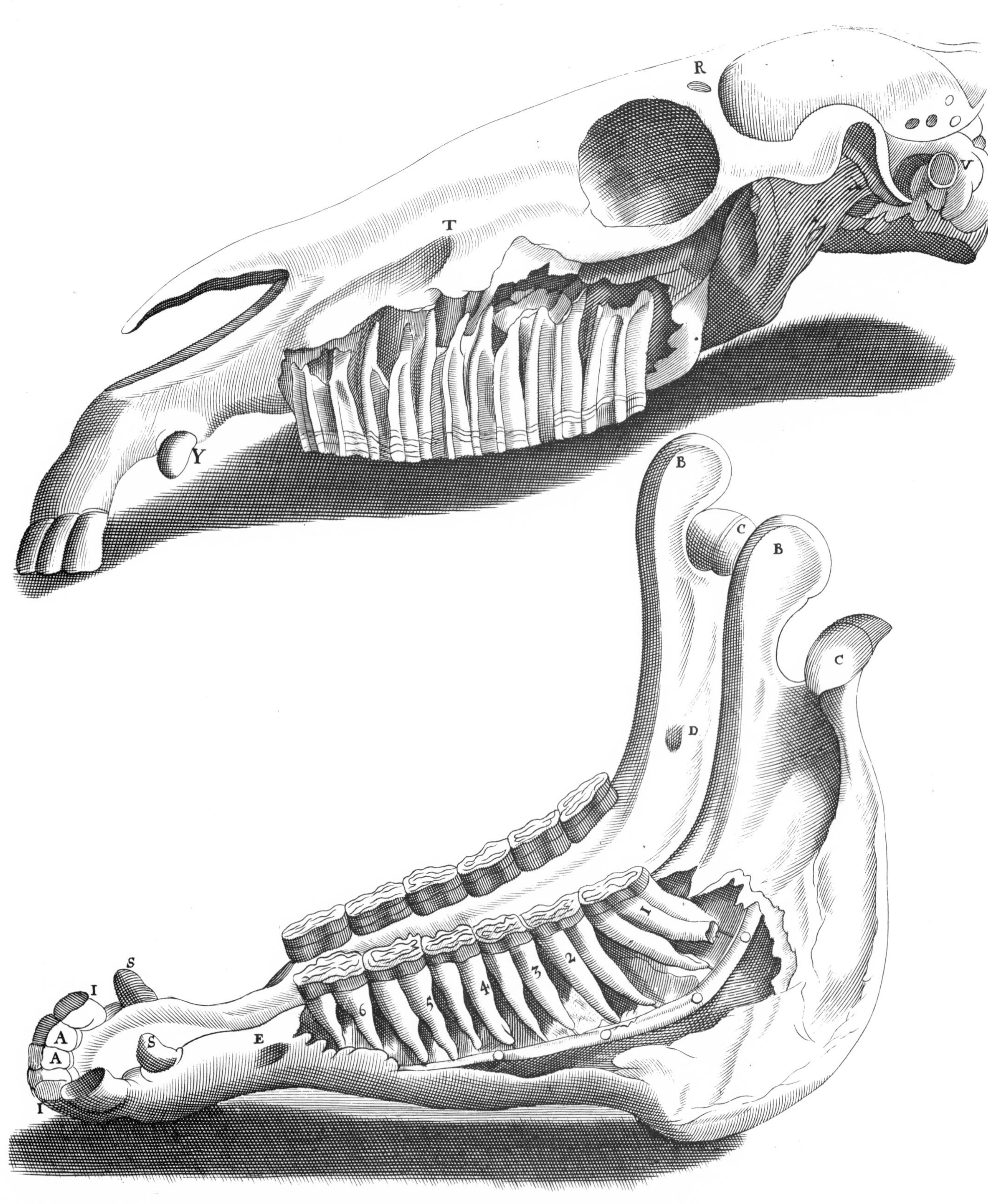
R
V
T
Y
B
C
B
C
D
I
S
I
A
A
S
E
I
6
5
4
3
2
1

Table XXXVIII.

Shews the upper and lower Jaw ſeparated from one another and placed ſideways, with ſo much of each Jaw broken off as till one come to the roots of the Teeth, to ſhew how the Nerves branch into the ends of the roots of each Tooth.

Figure I.

AA *The Shearers or Fore-teeth.*
BB *The two Productions of the lower Jaw which articulate into the upper Jaw.*
CC *The Proceſs into which the Temporal Muſcle is inſerted.*
D *A hole through which doth paſs a branch of the external Jugular Vein and Artery.*
E *A hole through which doth paſs the Nerve that furniſheth the Teeth with twigs from it as it paſſeth along, (being a branch of the fifth pair which trunk doth afterwards loſe it ſelf about the Lips, furniſhing all the Muſcles of the Lips and Noſe with Nerves.*
☞ (*Note that this Nerve in the upper Lip is that which Farriers do improperly (and by a miſtake) call* the Cord, *which they many times take up with a Cornet and cut inſunder to prevent a Horſe from ſtumbling; believing that the ſaid Cord reaches from the tip of the Noſe where they cut it, down to the Fore-legs and ſo to the Feet, by which they imagine that the Horſe's Head is ſo bound down, that he cannot have the freedom of it, which cauſes him to ſtumble. This fancy how ridiculous ſoever, is common amongſt Farriers, and is owing merely to their ignorance of the Parts; for it reaches no farther than from the Brain to the Lips: ſo that the cutting of it is likelier to hinder the motion of the Lips than to remedy ſtumbling.*)
R *A little hole through which doth paſs a Nerve from the Brain to the* Pericranium.
T *The ſame hole in the upper Jaw, as the letter* E *points to in the lower, through which the Nerve which they call the Cord, doth paſs to the Lips.*
S *The Tuſhes or Dog-teeth of the lower Jaw.*
V *The Auditory Paſſage or hole of the Ear.*
Y *One of the Tuſhes of the upper Jaw.*
1 2 3 4 5 6 *The Grinding-teeth.*
OOOO *The Nerve that ſends twigs to the roots of the Teeth of the lower Jaw, being the firſt branch of Doctour* Willis *his fifth pair.*

CHAP. VII.

Of the Bone of the Tongue called Os hyoides.

Os hyoides. *Its figure and parts.*

THAT Bone which is called *Os hyoides*, is of the ſhape of a Greek υ (*ypſilon*) and is ſeated under (or at the root of) the Tongue, being as it were the foundation and ſupporter of it. It is compounded of three Bones, *viz.* one in the middle, (being larger than the other two) which is gibbous forwards (or outwards) and ſomewhat hollowed inwards; by its gibbous ſide it is joined to the baſis or bottom of the Tongue: The other two Bones are lateral, and are called *Cornua*, or Horns. To the firſt Bone there are affixed two Griſtles, and to each of theſe one. They are all tied to the adjacent parts, partly by a fleſhy, partly by a nervous ſubſtance. It hath three *Sinus* or Cavities; above, a tranſverſe depreſſed *Sinus*, to admit the ſecond pair of Muſcles proper to it; and in the ſides of this *Sinus* there are two other, which give way unto the firſt pair of Muſcles that are implanted into the ſides of this Bone.

Its Uſe.

The *uſe* of this Bone (although it be but a little one) is very great; for moſt if not all the Muſcles that move the Tongue either are inſerted into it or ariſe from it. It ſerves alſo to keep the Throat open, admitting the *Epiglottis* or Throat-flap into its boſom, when it is lifted up in breathing. And laſtly ſome of the Muſcles of the *Larynx* or Throttle ariſe from it.

CHAP. VIII.

Of the Bones of the Neck.

HAving treated of the Bones of the *Head*, we come in the next place to ſpeak to thoſe of the *Neck*, which, in dividing the Body into three Parts at the beginning of this Fifth Book, (*viz.* the Head, Trunk and Limbs) we conſidered as annext to the Head. Its Bones are of two ſorts, *viz.* the Collar or Chanel-bones, and the *Vertebræ*. But firſt of the *Collar-bones*.

The Collar-bones, their ſubſtance and uſe.

Theſe are in number two, one on each ſide. They are called *Claviculæ*, either from their reſembling the ſhape of old-faſhioned Keys, which were of the ſhape of an Italick *ſ*; or becauſe they lock up as it were and cloſe the Cheſt; for by ſome they are accounted as belonging to *it*. Their ſubſtance is ſpongy and thick, eſpecially about their heads; but in their middle they are thin and flat. By one end they are joined to the top of the Breaſt-bone, and by the other to the firſt Rack-bone of the Back, wherein they differ from thoſe in Man, which are jointed into the

the Proceſs of the Shoulder-bone. Their *uſe* is to uphold the Shoulder-blades, that they ſhould not ſlide down upon the Breaſt together with the Shoulder-bone, which upon a diſlocation or fracture of theſe Collar-bones doth often come to paſs.

The Vertebræ of the Neck, their number and holes.

The number of the *Vertebræ* or Rack-bones of the *Neck* is ſeven, and they are reckoned from the Head downward; that next the Head being the firſt. They have in each of them a large Cavity as thoſe of the Back and Loins have, to give way to the Spinal Marrow to deſcend by. Beſides this large hole which is common to theſe with thoſe others, they have alſo each of them two other ſmaller holes in their tranſverſe Proceſſes, through which the Cervical Veins and Arteries do paſs to the Head. And betwixt their jointing one with another there is a third hole, or rather half of one, for one half is formed out of the lower ſide of the upper, and the other out of the upper ſide of the lower *Vertebra*: By theſe the Nerves paſs out from the Spinal Marrow.

The firſt deſcribed.

The *firſt* of theſe Bones is called *Atlas*, becauſe in Men the Head ſtands upon it like the Globe of the World, as the Poets feigned *Atlas* to bear the Celeſtial Globe upon his Shoulders. The body of this Bone is more ſlender, but ſolider than the reſt, and it wanteth its hinder Proceſs or Spine, having onely a kind of a ſemicircular knob jetting out inſtead of it: the reaſon of which ſeems to be, leſt the greater ſtreight pair of Muſcles of the Head that ſpring from the ſecond *Vertebra* of the Neck, and march over the back-ſide of this, ſhould be hurt in bending the Head forwards. But it has all its other Proceſſes, *viz.* aſcending, deſcending and tranſverſe. Within on the fore-ſide of its great *Foramen*, it has a *Sinus*, in ſhape ſemicircular, which is lined with a Cartilage or Griſtle, and which receiveth the Tooth-like Proceſs of the ſecond *Vertebra*.

The ſecond, &c. deſcribed.

The *ſecond Vertebra* is called *Dentata*, becauſe out of its upper ſide, between its two aſcending Proceſſes, there ſprings an Appendix or Proceſs, round and long, like the Dog-tooth in Man (or Tuſh in a Horſe.) This Tooth is covered with a Cartilage, and is jointed into the foreſaid *Sinus* of the firſt *Vertebra*, and upon it, as upon an Axle-tree, the head turns round, from whence the whole Bone is called by ſome *Axis*. That part of the Tooth which enters not into the ſaid *Sinus* (*viz.* its baſis) is encompaſſed with a Ligament, which knits it to the *Occiput*. This and the four following have Spines or hinder Proceſſes, each of which are divided into two for the better connexion of the Ligaments and Muſcles to them. We ſhall not need to deſcribe particularly any more of them, ſeeing they are in all things like to the ſecond, ſaving that their lateral Proceſſes are larger, and divided into two as well as the hinder: yea the ſeventh it ſelf differs not from the reſt, though in Man it do.

The bodies of theſe *Vertebræ* of the Neck are longer than thoſe of the Back or Loins; for though the Neck of an Horſe be of ſo conſiderable length, yet as hath been ſaid its *Vertebræ* are but ſeven (as they are in Man) whereas thoſe of the Back and Loins are twenty four in all, which ſpace notwithſtanding is not ſo long again as the Neck is; whereas were the *Vertebræ* of a proportionable length, it ſhould be more than three times the length.

Table XXXIX.

Represents the seven *Vertebræ* of the Neck all joined together in one Figure. They are placed so, as that the first Figure shews their sides, the second their back-parts, and the third their fore-parts.

Figure I.

A *Shews a hole through which a branch of the internal Jugular Vein and Carotid Artery comes forth of the first* Vertebra, *having entred the same* Vertebra *at the hole marked with the letter* F.

B *A hole in the said* Vertebra *out of which doth pass the first Nerve from the Spinal Marrow without the Skull, which Nerve marches streight to the beforesaid Vein and Artery and joins it self with them, and runs their course both up to the Head and down to the Body, there being an ascending and a descending branch of it for that purpose.*

C D E *The ends of the said Vein, Artery and Nerve where they were cut off with the seventh* Vertebra *from the Trunk of the Body.*

F *The hole in the first* Vertebra *by which the Vein and Artery entred the said Bone, and come out again at the letter* A.

P *The hole betwixt the first and second* Vertebra *through which doth pass the second pair of Nerves of the Spinal Marrow.*

HH Q R S T *The rest of the holes in the other six* Vertebræ *through which the Jugular Vein and Artery, and the Spinal Nerves do pass in and out.*

1. 2. 3. 4. 5. 6. 7. *The seven* Vertebræ *of the Neck.*

Figure II. Shews the back-side, and Figure III. the fore-side of the said *Vertebræ*.

CHAP.

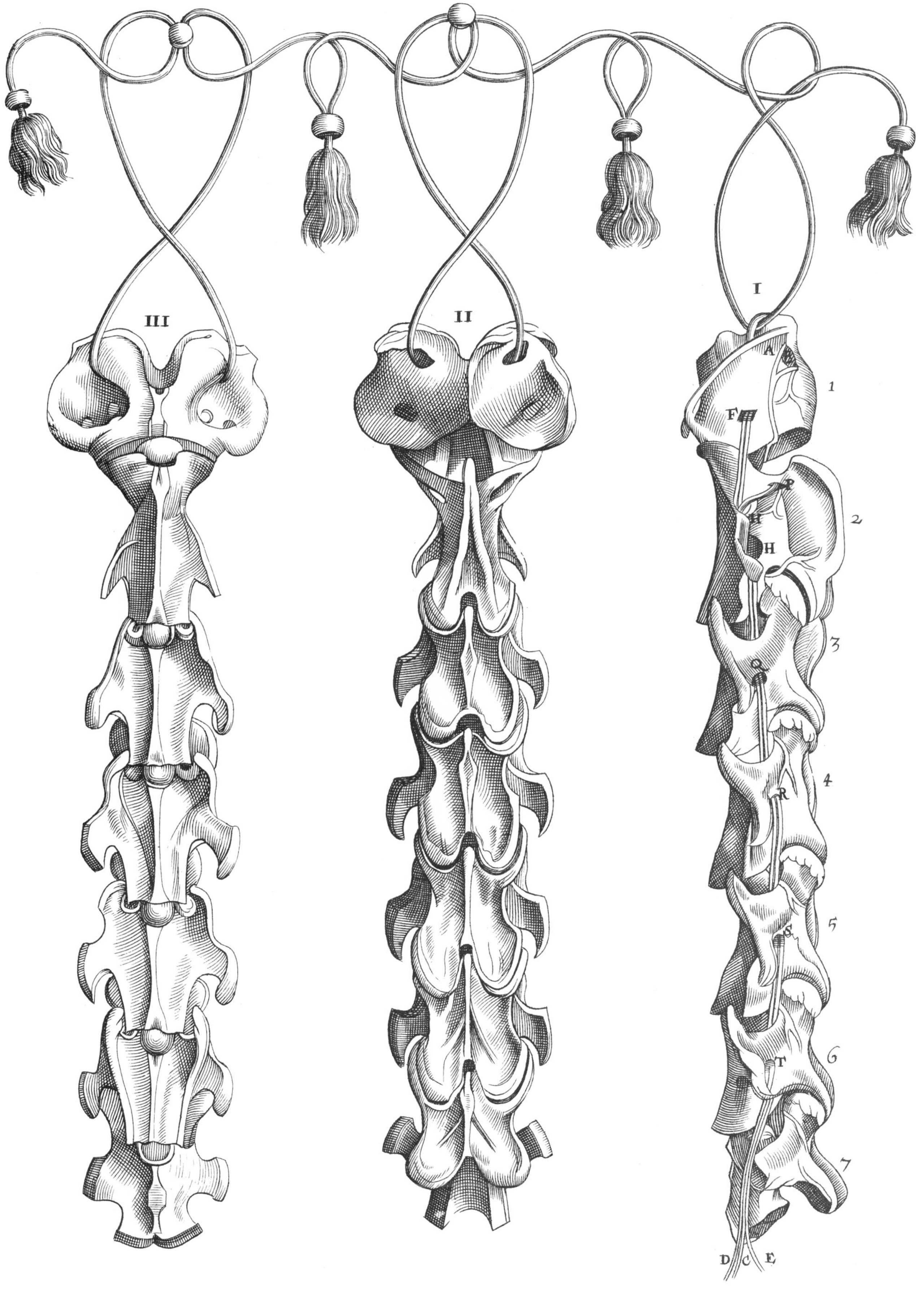
III
II
I
A
B
1
F
P
2
H
H
3
O
4
R
5
S
6
T
7
D C E

CHAP. IX.

Of the Vertebræ *of the Back and Loins; and of the Ribs.*

THE *Back* conſiſteth of ſeventeen *Vertebræ* or Rack-bones, juſt ſo many as there be Ribs on a ſide, for on each ſide of every Rack-bone is there a Rib articulated. But ſeeing, as we have ſaid, the Collar-bone is inſerted into the firſt *Vertebra* of the Back, it will ſo fall out that the laſt Rib will be articulated into that *Vertebra* which we reckon for the firſt of the Loins: into which the Rib indeed is ſo jointed, that it is not eaſy to ſay whether it be into the top of this, or into the lower end of the ſeventeenth of the Back. The *Bodies* of the Racks as well as their *Proceſſes* do differ ſomewhat from the *Bodies* and *Proceſſes* of the Racks of the Neck; for the *Bodies* of the Racks of the Neck are longer than theſe, and more flat on their inſide, that the Gullet might reſt the more ſecurely on them: and as for their *Proceſſes,* the hinder are not cleft into two as thoſe of the Neck are, and the tranſverſe ones are more ſhort and blunt, having (inſtead of the holes that are in thoſe of the Neck) each a ſhallow *Sinus,* into which the Ribs are partly articulated. But the *Proceſſes* are in both of an equal number, namely four oblique ones, (that is, two tending obliquely upwards, and two obliquely downwards) two tranſverſe or lateral ones, and one acute or hinder one, which is called the Spine.

The Back hath ſeventeen Vertebræ.

Their Bodies and Proceſſes deſcribed.

The *Bodies* of theſe *Vertebræ* are not ſo ſolid as thoſe of the Neck, but they are more bulky or thicker about, and are full of ſmall perforations for the admiſſion of the Bloud-veſſels to the Spinal Marrow, and beſides have two at each Joint for the egreſs of the Nerves from the Spinal Marrow. They have each of them on each ſide a *Sinus* or Cavity for the inarticulation of the head of the Rib, which *Sinus* thoſe of the Neck want, as having no Bones to joint into them.

Note that the tranſverſe Proceſſes of two or three of the loweſt of theſe Racks begin to grow ſhorter and ſhorter, and their Spines are more blunt, and ſtand evener out, declining not ſo much downwards as thoſe before-going. As for the great Cavity or Perforation in the middle of the Bodies, it is proportionable to the Marrow which it contains.

Next to the Bones of the *Neck* we come to thoſe of the *Loins,* which make the third part of the Spine. They are in number ſeven, and are bigger than any of the fore-going either of the Neck or Back. Their hinder Proceſſes or Spines are ſhorter, but broader and thicker than thoſe of the Back, ſomewhat bending upwards as moſt of thoſe decline downwards; but as for the lateral or tranſverſe Proceſſes, they exceed thoſe of the Back in length. Theſe *Vertebræ* are joined one to another by a clammy Griſtle, and likewiſe the uppermoſt of them to the laſt of the Back, and the loweſt to the firſt of *Os ſacrum* in like manner.

The Loins have ſeven. Their Bodies, Proceſſes and connexion.

Beſides their lateral Perforations betwixt their jointings for the tranſmiſſion or letting forth of the Nerves, they have alſo ſeveral other little holes for the intromiſſion of the Bloud-veſſels. As for their middle Perforation, nothing need be ſaid particularly of it, ſeeing it differs not from that of those of the Back, being of capacity equal to the thickness of the Marrow that it contains.

The Ribs are seventeen. The *Ribs* (in Latin *Costæ*) are in number thirty four, that is to say, on each side seventeen. Their substance is partly bony, and partly cartilaginous or gristly; the first serving for firmness, and the latter for articulation, that upon occasion they might yield a little without breaking. They are divided into two sorts, the one called *true*, and the other the *Bastard*-ribs. *Nine true.* The *true* are the nine uppermost, so called because each with its fellow makes a compleat circle, being joined together by the mediation of the Spondyls of the Back behind, and the Breast-bone before. I say the Ribs are articulated into the Back-bones behind, something of a cartilaginous substance coming between: (the manner whereof is well exprest in the following Figure.) At this articulation into the *Vertebræ* each Rib has two knobs, one of which is received into the *Sinus* of the Body of the *Vertebra*, and the other which is less, into that of the transverse Process. And they are joined before to the Breast-bone by way of articulation also; for their Cartilages end into little heads which are received into the smooth *Sinus's* of the Breast-bone.

Eight bastard. The *Bastard*-ribs are the eight lower, being of a more soft and gristly substance than the other; because being articulated onely at one end, it was necessary they should be of a more yielding and pliable nature, otherwise they would have been very apt to break. Yea their yielding is not onely a security to themselves, but very convenient in respect to the parts that are contained under or within them. For seeing the Stomach lies in this region which uses to be distended with Meat or Water, these Ribs ought to give way to it when it or the intermediate parts, as the Liver and Spleen, bear against them.

Their figure. The *figure* of the Ribs is (as you may also see in the following Figure) semicircular, like a Bow when it is drawn; which Nature hath so ordered to make the Chest stronger and more capacious.

Their surface. They are on the outside rough and unequal, especially near the *Vertebræ*, that the Ligaments might take the firmer hold on them, by which they are tied to the Rack-bones: but on their inside they are smoother (being covered with the *Pleura*) lest they should hurt the Lungs and other Parts that bear against them. They are all of them narrower and roundish toward the Back, and broader and flatter toward the Breast. In their lower and inner part they have a furrow that runs along them, in which a Nerve and the Bloud-vessels are conducted.

Their uses. The *uses* of the Ribs are, first, to be a defence to the Bowels within the Breast, and to the Stomach, Liver and Spleen in the Lower Belly; and secondly, to support the Muscles which serve for respiration, and to be moved by them: for which cause the Breast ought not to consist of one Bone, for then it would have been immoveable; whereas now it easily admits of dilatation and contraction.

CHAP.

CHAP. X.

Of the Sternum *or Breaſt-bone, and of the* Scapula *or Shoulder-blade.*

THE Breaſt-bone in an Horſe is not flat on the outſide as it is in Men, but ſtands out with a ridge, and is ſomething like the keel or bottom of a Boat, jetting out with its middle on the outſide, and is hollow on the inſide. It is of a ſpongy ſubſtance, neither ſo ſolid nor ſo white as moſt of the other Bones of the Body. In Foals it is rather griſtly than bony, and does then conſiſt of more parts than it does in grown Horſes; for as by age the Griſtles grow into a bony ſubſtance, ſo they do unite ſo one to another in time, that no footſteps are left of their firſt diviſion. *The* Sternum, *its figure and ſubſtance.*

In its upper part towards the Throat it is rather pointed and ſharp, than horned as it is in Men; however on the inſide it is hollowed, for the more convenient deſcent of the Wind-pipe. Without on each ſide of its upper end there is a little *Sinus* into which the heads of the Collar-bones are received or articulated. Betwixt which articulation of the Collar-bones into it, and its lower end, there are ſeveral *Sinus* on each ſide of it, to the number of nine, into which the griſtly ends of ſo many true Ribs are jointed. Its lower end terminates in a Griſtle even in old Horſes, whoſe end is of a more obtuſe or blunt ſhape than in Men, in whom it is called *Cartilago enſiformis*, or the Sword-point-like Griſtle. *What parts articulate into it.*

Its *uſe* is for the articulation of one end of the Collar-bones and true Ribs into it, and to ſerve as a Breaſt-plate for the ſafeguard and defence of the noble Bowels (*viz.* the Heart and Lungs) that are lodged within it. *Its Uſe.*

The *Shoulder-blade* is called in Latin *Scapula.* There are two of them (*viz.* on each ſide of the upper part of the Cheſt one) as there are of all the ſorts of Bones in the fore and alſo in the hinder Legs; but we ſhall for brevity's ſake ſpeak of the Bones onely of one Leg before and another behind, becauſe the other two are in all things like unto theſe, wherefore it is not any way neceſſary to repeat the deſcription of them, nor yet to ſpeak of them in the plural number.

The *Shoulder-blade* is ſeated upon the ſide of the true Ribs, (like a Target) reaching from the *Vertebræ* of the Back almoſt to the bottom of the Collar-bone. It is in figure after a ſort triangular, on the inſide concave or hollow, and on the outſide prominent or arched. It is jointed to no Bone but by its lower end to the Shoulder-bone; but yet it is knit to ſeveral Parts by the Muſcles that are inſerted into it, or riſe from it; as to the hinder-part of the Head by the Cucullar Muſcles, being the firſt of its movers; alſo to the *Vertebræ* of the Neck by its ſecond pair; and to the Back by the Muſcle *Rhomboides*, &c. *The* Scapula, *its ſituation, figure and connexion.*

It hath three *Proceſſes.* The *firſt* being the ſhorteſt, is called its *Neck*, which neck ends into a ſinuated or hollow cup or head, which receiveth the head of the Shoulder-bone, and its brim is compaſſed with a thick Griſtle, *Its Proceſſes.*

Griſtle, whereby its Cavity is made the deeper that the head of the Shoulder-bone that is jointed into it ſhould not ſo eaſily ſlip out. The *ſecond* Proceſs, which by ſome is accounted the firſt, is extended along its middle on the outſide, and is called its *Spine*; and that end of this Spine that by a ſhallow Sinus receives one of the Heads of the Shoulder-bone, is called *Acromium*, that is to ſay, its point or tip. The third and laſt of theſe Proceſſes is toward the lower and inſide of the Bone, and from the likeneſs it hath with an Anchor is called *Ancyroides*, Anchor-like; ſome alſo who compare it to a Crows Bill, do give it the name of *Coracoides*: This Proceſs doth ſomewhat help to hold the Shoulder-bone in its place, entring a little into a ſhallow *Sinus* of the ſaid Bone.

Its Appendixes. It hath five Appendixes about its Neck, three of which do afford an original to ſome Muſcles, and from the other two do ſpring Ligaments which join the Shoulder-bone to the head of the Blade.

Its Cavities. By means of the ſecond Proceſs that runs like a Ridge or Spine along the middle of its back there are formed on its outſide two long Furrows or *Cavities*, in which ſeveral Muſcles lie, eſpecially the *Supraſcapularis* and *Subſcapularis*, which are otherwiſe called *Supraſpinatus* and *Infraſpinatus*, from their being placed the firſt above this Spine or on that ſide next the Neck, and the latter below it or on that ſide next the Ribs.

Table XL.

Repreſents all the Bones of the Cheſt, the *Vertebræ* of the Back and the Shoulder-blades.

Figure I.

A B *Shew the length of the Breaſt-bone, (the Bones of the Cheſt being placed in a ſupine poſture.)*
CC *The upper end of the ſame Bone.*
DD *That Griſtle which in Men is called* Cartilago enſiformis *or the Sword-faſhioned Griſtle, at its lower end.*
1. *The Collar-bone, (imitating a Rib.)*
2. 3. 4. 5. 6. 7. 8. 9. 10. 11. 12. 13. 14. 15. 16. 17. 18. *The ſeventeen Ribs.*
EEE *The ſeveral* Vertebræ *of the* Thorax *into which the Ribs are articulated.*
FFFF *The cartilaginous or griſtly part of the Ribs.*

Figure II.

Shews the ſeventeen *Vertebræ* of the *Thorax* or Cheſt on one ſide, the better to ſhew how the Ribs are articulated into the ſides of the ſaid *Vertebræ*.

AAB *The two Productions of the firſt* Vertebra *of the Cheſt, which were articulated into or with the ſeventh* Vertebra *of the Neck.*
CCCC *Several of the ſmall Ligaments which did bind in the heads of the Ribs into the articulations of the* Vertebræ.
I. II. III. IV. V. VI. VII. VIII. *to* XVII. *The ſeventeen backward Proceſſes or Spines of the Spondyls or Rack-bones of the Cheſt.*

Figure

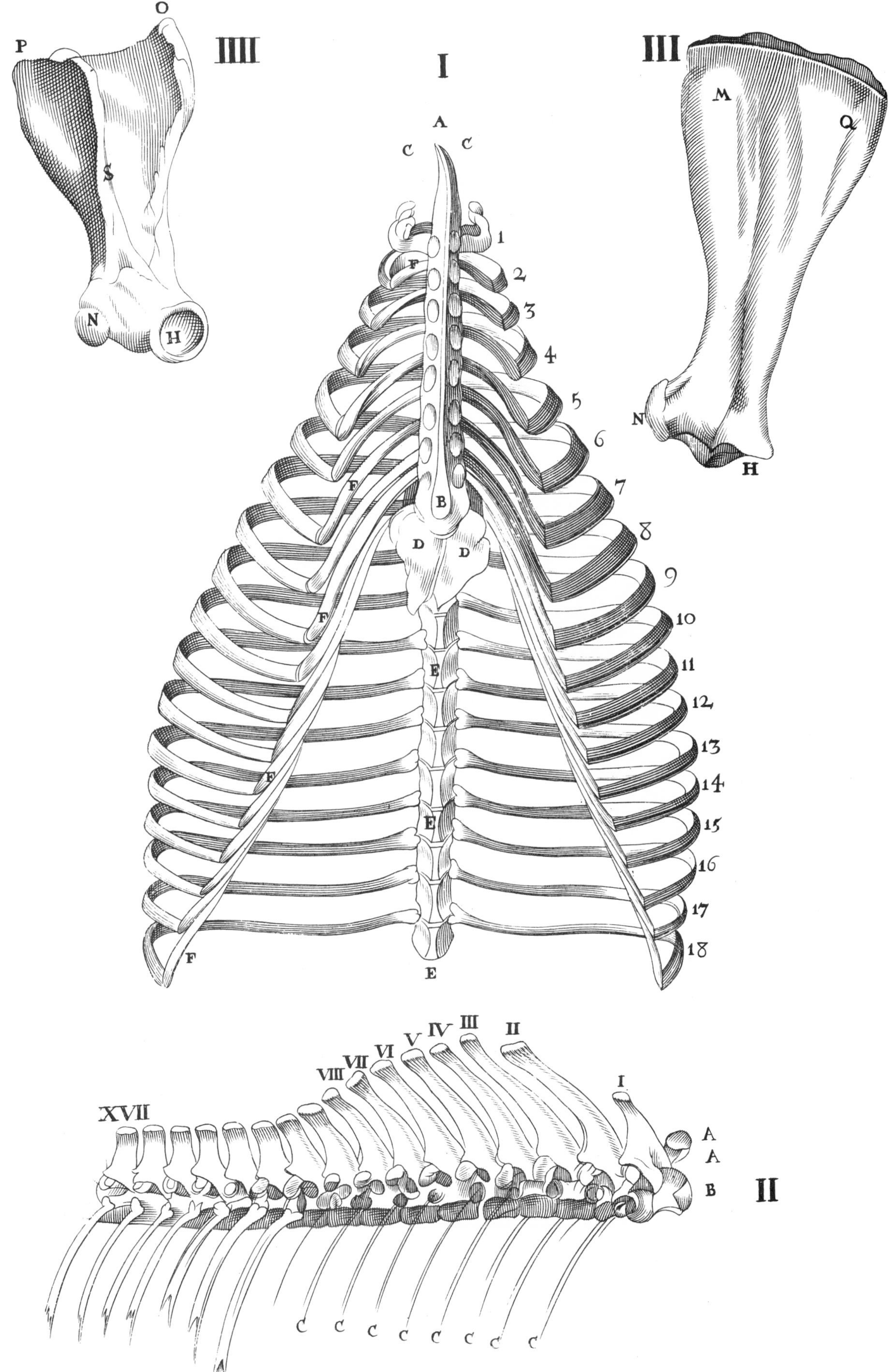
IIII
P
O
S
N
H
I
A
C
C
1
2
3
4
5
6
7
8
9
10
11
12
13
14
15
16
17
18
F
F
F
F
F
B
D
D
E
E
E
III
M
Q
N
H
II
XVII
VIII
VII
VI
V
IV
III
II
I
A
A
B
C
C
C
C
C
C
C
C

Figure III.

Shews the *Scapula* or Shoulder-blade with that ſide that is next the Body outermoſt.

H *The Cup into which the great round head of the Shoulder-bone is articulated.*
N *The Proceſs which is inſerted into the Shoulder-bone.*
M Q *The under-ſide of the Blade-bone.*

Figure IV.

Shews the *Scapula* with its outer or right ſide uppermoſt.

H *The Cavity or Cup into which the Shoulder-bone is articulated.*
N *The Proceſs which is inſerted into the Shoulder-bone.*
O P *The upper end of the* Scapula, *its Cartilage being taken off.*
S *That Proceſs of the* Scapula *which is called its Spine or Ridge.*

CHAP. XI.

Of the Os humeri *or Shoulder-bone, and the next Bone under it called the Cubit.*

THE Bones of the *Fore-leg* under the *Scapula* or Shoulder-blade are the Shoulder-bone, the Cubit-bone, the Seven Oſſelets or little Bones that make the Knee, anſwering to the eight little Bones that make the *Carpus* or Wriſt in Humane Bodies, the Shank-bone anſwering to the Bones of the *Metacarpus* or back of the Hand, the great Paſtern anſwering to the firſt Joint of the Fingers, the little Paſtern to the ſecond Joint, and the Coffin-bone to the laſt Joint, on which the Nail grows, as doth the Hoof of the Horſe on the Coffin-bone. Of the ſimilitude there is betwixt theſe ſeveral Joints in a Horſe's Fore-leg, and thoſe in the Arm and Hand of a Man, I have already diſcourſed pretty fully in the Book of the Muſcles, where I treated of the Muſcles of theſe Parts : wherefore I ſhall in this place ſpeak no more of that, but proceed to the deſcription of the before-named Bones in their order. *The Bones of the Fore-leg.*

The *Shoulder-bone* is that which reaches from the Shoulder-blade to the Elbow. Both its ends are called Heads, being thicker than the reſt of the Bone, the upper of which that is inſerted into the cup of the Blade-bone, is naturally an appendix to the Bone, but in time grows to be a part or proceſs of the Bone it ſelf. *The Shoulder-bone.*

This Head is large and orbicular, covered over with a Griſtle, that it might be turned more glibly within the cavity of the Cup of the Blade. On the outſide of this Head there bunch out two rough and uneven Proceſſes, into which two Ligaments are inſerted for the ſtrengthning of the Joint; (one of which is like a ſecond Head, and is articulated into the ſhallow cavity of the *acromium*, or end of the Spine of the Shoulder-bone;) and betwixt theſe two Proceſſes there is a long and round chink *What Bones it articulates with.*

through which the nervous Head of the Muſcle *Biceps* doth paſs. There is alſo on the inſide another round Cavity in the ſide of the Head, out of which the ſtrong Ligament ſprings that ties this Head in the cup of the *Scapula.*

The lower Head of this Bone which in Men is articulated with two Bones, *viz.* the *Vlna* and *Radius*, in a Horſe is jointed but with one, (which I call the Cubit-bone) yet is ſo jointed to that one, that it receives it and is received by it, having three Proceſſes, and two *Sinus* betwixt them, much like the ſame Proceſſes and *Sinus* in the ſame Bone of a Man.

Beſides theſe Proceſſes already mentioned, it hath on its inſide another notable one, from which ariſe the Muſcles that lie on the inſide of the Leg upon the Cubit-bone: and on its outſide it hath yet another Proceſs, but ſomething leſs than the former, from whence do ariſe the Muſcles that lie on the outſide of the Leg upon the Cubit-bone. About the middle of this Bone, on its inſide, may be perceived a hole, through which both Veins and Arteries paſs to the Marrow contained in this Bone, for its nouriſhment.

The Cubit-bone, its Articulations.

The next part of the Leg is called the *Cubit*, conſiſting, as hath been ſaid, in Men of two Bones, but in a Horſe onely of one: The two Bones in Men reach from the Elbow to the Wriſt; and this one in Horſes from the Elbow to that Joint commonly called the Knee, but which might properly enough have the ſame name as in Men, ſeeing it is of a like fabrick. This Cubit-bone in its hinder and upper part hath a notable Proceſs, long and round, onely ſomething flattiſh, which entreth into the larger *Sinus* or Cavity of the lower Head of the Shoulder-bone, and maketh that bunching-out which we call the Elbow. This Proceſs is ſomething rough and uneven, partly that the Ligaments might be the more ſtrongly knit to it that encompaſs the Joint; and partly for the inſertion of ſome Muſcles of the Cubit, as alſo to give original unto the Muſcles that bend the lower part of the Leg and Foot; for which cauſe alſo the Bone it ſelf is rough at the root of the Proceſs. The circumference of the *Sinus* into which it is inſerted, is alſo rough, that from thence Ligaments might iſſue. Its leſſer and inner Proceſs is received by the leſſer *Sinus* of the Head of the Shoulder-bone. There are three cavities in this upper Head, for the reception of as many Proceſſes of the lower end of the Shoulder-bone. Its lower end articulates with the three upper little Bones of the Knee (that make the firſt range) as ſhall be ſhewed in the next Chapter.

CHAP.

CHAP. XII.

Of the ſeven Oſſeletts or little Bones of the Knee, of the Shank-bones which reach from the Knee to the great Paſtern, and alſo of the two Paſtern-bones and the Coffin-bone.

BEtween the Cubit-bone and the Shank-bone there are two ranges of little Bones, one above another, being in number ſeven, that is to ſay, three in the firſt and four in the ſecond range: all which are joined one to another ſo firmly, that they are not eaſily to be ſeparated. The upper range are articulated with the lower end of the Cubit-bone, and the lower range with the upper end of the Shank-bone. *The number of the little Bones of the Knee.*

Theſe Bones do differ one from another in their magnitude, form and ſituation, and are ſaid in their firſt generation to be all Griſtles and not Bones, but in proceſs of time they become hard and grow bony. Their ſubſtance is ſpongy, as are all the reſt of the Bones which of Griſtles become bony, of which kind are all the Appendices of Bones, the Bones of the Breaſt and ſuch like. They are all covered over with both a membranous and griſtly Ligament, whereby they are ſo compacted together, that without dividing the ſaid Ligaments, and ſeparating the Membranes or Skins, it is a hard matter to diſtinguiſh them one from another, ſo that at the firſt view they may be thought to be all of them but one Bone.

They have a double *Superficies*, one outer, which is gibbous or bunching, and another inward which is concavous or hollow; and in their upper part where they join to the Cubit-bone, they are ſmooth and cruſted over with the before-mentioned Griſtle.

Theſe Bones I will not undertake to give proper names to, but ſhall diſtinguiſh them by their order and number, calling that the *firſt* that is placed on the inſide of the *upper* rank. This is ſomething longiſh and curved inward, articulated with the Cubit-bone above, and below with the ſecond Bone of the lower rank, yea it toucheth both the third and fourth of the ſame rank. Its inſide joineth cloſely to the inſide of the ſecond Bone of its own rank. *The upper rank.*

The *ſecond* of theſe Bones is cloſe knit to the former, being ſomething leſs than it. It is joined to the Cubit-bone in its upper part, which part is hollowed to receive the Appendix of the ſaid Bone. It is alſo joined with the firſt Bone by one ſide, and by the other or rather hinder part to the third Bone, and laſtly by its bottom to the ſeventh Bone or fourth of the lower rank.

The *third* is alſo joined above with a plain Superficies to the Cubit-bone, by its inſide to the ſecond Bone of its own rank, and by its lower part to the fourth Bone of the next rank.

The *fourth* Bone or *firſt* of the *lower* rank, is ſomething ſmaller than any of the before-mentioned three, and is in ſhape almoſt round. It is ſmooth, not being hollow nor protuberated as the reſt are. It is joined *The lower.*

above to the outside of the lower-part of the first Bone, below to the Shank-bone, and on its inside to the fifth Bone or second of its own rank.

The fifth (or *second* of the lower rank) hath several little *Sinus's*; It hath one notable one above into which the first Bone of the upper rank is articulated, and another below for the reception of part of the Head of the Shank-bone.

The sixth (or *third* of the lower rank) is joined with a plain Superficies on each side to the seventh (or *fourth*) and to the foregoing; above, to the second, and below to the Shank-bone.

The seventh (or *fourth* of the lower rank) is not much unlike the former, on its inside being joined to the foregoing, on its upper side to the third of the upper rank, and on its lower to the head or top of the Shank-bone.

The Shank-bone, its Articulation.

The next part of the Leg which answers to the *After-wrist* or back of the Hand in a Man, is made of three Bones, one of which is long and round and much larger than the other two. It reaches from the Knee to the great Pastern, being articulated above with every one of the lower rank of the little Bones of the Knee; and below it is joined to the great Pastern by a mutual articulation, having two round heads and three small Cavities at that end of it for that purpose. This we call the *Shank-bone.*

The Splent-bones.

To each side of this Bone is fastned another long thin Bone, in figure something like a Bodkin, being somewhat thick and round at their upper part, and from thence as they run down towards the Foot, becoming thinner and sharper, till at last they end in a sharp point, a little above the joining of the Shank-bone with the great Pastern. Between these two Bones do run the Tendons of the Muscles that move the Foot, as they descend down the Shank-bone. These two we may call the *Splent-bones,* standing on each side of the Shank-bone like two Splents, such as Bone-setters use for broken Bones.

The next is the Bone which answereth to the first joint of the Fingers in Man, in whom they are five in number, by the wonderfull wisedom of the Creator so ordained as was fittest for that variety of motions to which they are design'd. But an Horse being *Solidipes* or a whole-footed Creature, hath all his Foot necessarily moved together, and the Bones thereof in each Joint being single, answer but to the Bones of one Finger.

The great Pastern.

The form of this Bone, which is called the *great Pastern,* is gibbous and crooked. At its top, where it is articulated with the Shank-bone, it has three small Processes and two Cavities betwixt them: also two small triangular Bones fastned to its back-part. Its outside is plain and smooth, and without any roughness at all. Its lower end consists of two heads which are round and bunching and are articulated into the *Sinus* of the *lesser Pastern* which is under it.

The little Pastern.

The next is the *little Pastern,* answering to the second Joint of the Fingers. This is not much unlike the former, onely it differs in the length, for it is not much above half so long. Its upper end (as was said) is articulated with the great Pastern, and its lower end is received by the Coffin-bone in the same manner as it self received the lower end of the great Pastern by its own upper end.

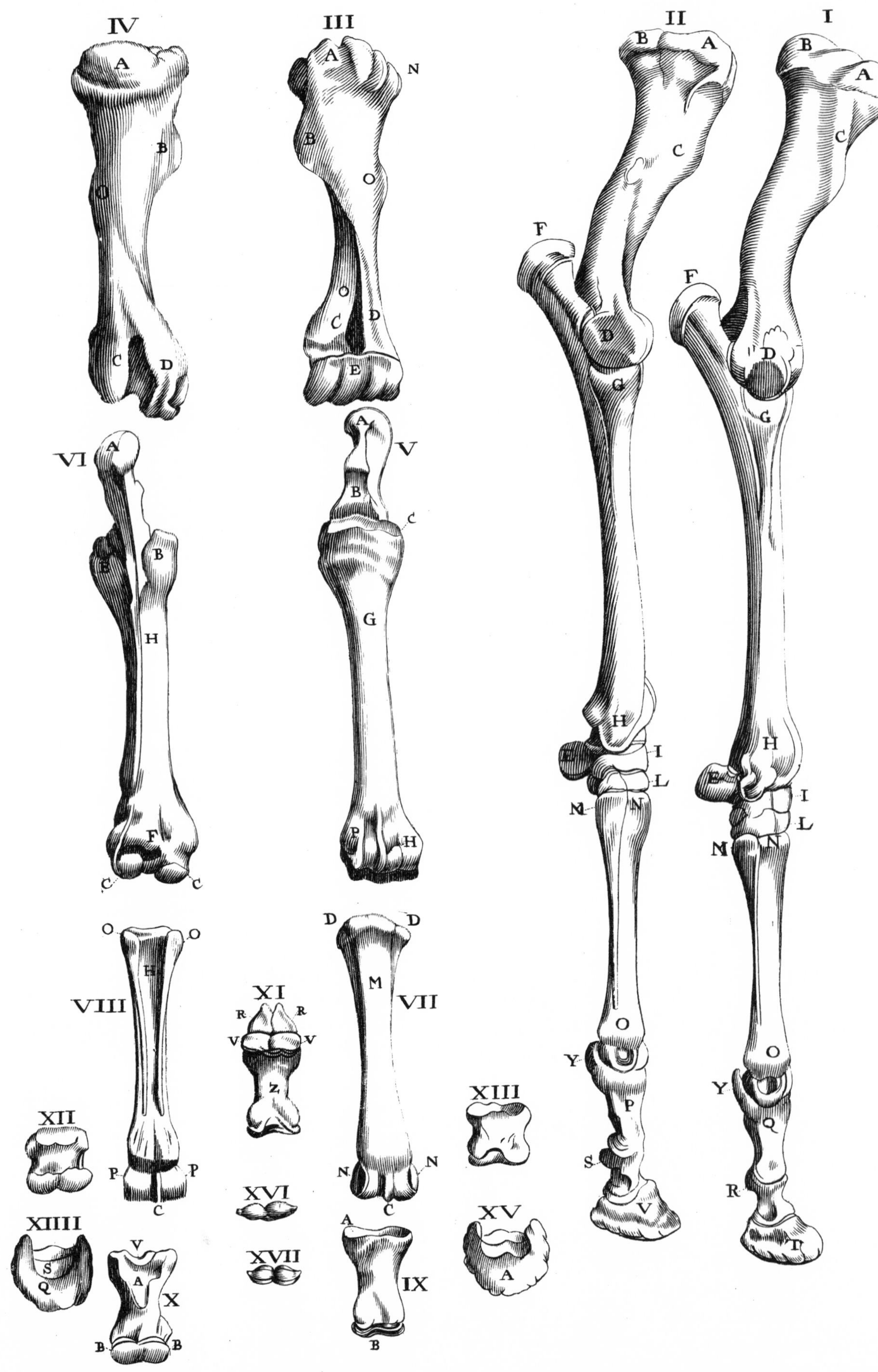
IV
A
B
C
D
III
A
N
B
O
C
D
E
II
B
A
C
F
D
G
H
I
L
N
O
Y
P
S
V
I
B
A
C
F
D
G
H
E
I
L
N
O
Y
Q
R
T
VI
A
B
H
F
C
V
A
B
C
G
P
H
VIII
O
O
P
P
C
XI
R
R
V
V
Z
VII
D
D
M
N
N
C
XII
XIII
XIIII
S
Q
X
V
A
B
B
XVI
XVII
IX
A
B
XV
A

The next and last Bone of the Foot is the *Coffin-bone*, so called (I suppose) from its hollowness on its under-side. Its *figure* is semilunary or Half-moon-fashioned. It is thick at its top, (where it has cavities to receive the heads of the lower end of the little Pastern) but thin and broad at its bottom and toward its edges, for its more firm fixing upon the ground. Its *substance* is fungous or spongy, having innumerable little holes piercing through its sides for the passage of the Vessels; as also very many small *Sinus's* whereinto are implanted the ends of the Tendons of the Muscles that move the lower part of the Leg, and the Foot: whose Fibres being at any time affected either by bruises, ill shooing, or by standing in the water after hard riding whilst the Horse is hot, or but by standing still in the Stable for several days without having the Feet stopt up, and the like; I say the tendinous Fibres being affected by these or other means, cause the Horse to have such great pain in his Feet, that he can scarce endure to tread upon them; which lameness we call a *Founder*. Now this distemper is so much the harder to cure by reason these Fibres lie so far out of reach, most of them running on the upper side of the Bone (betwixt it and the Hoof) and not to its bottom; so that the Hoof growing upon the sides as the Soal doth at the bottom, there is great hazard but we shall miss of effecting a cure, if we onely pull the Soal out, and do not cut part of the Hoof off also. This is not my bare opinion, but the experience of those that have had good success in curing foundred Horses, who by rasing the Hoof from the Coronet or top of it to the very bottom, in five or six places, untill they have made the Bloud come, and then applying their remedies to those places, have made those Horses sound, whom the drawing out of their Soals would not cure.

The Coffin-bone. Its figure, substance and Sinus's.

The cause and cure of a Founder.

Table XLI.

Represents all the Bones of the Fore-legs as well joined one to another as separate.

Figure I.

Shews the Bones of the near Leg before, all joined together, (the Blade-bone being taken off.)

A B *The heads of the Shoulder-bone which were articulated into the cavities of the Shoulder-blade.*

C *A production in the side of the said Bone, from whence some Muscles of the Leg do take their rise.*

D *Its lower head which is jointed with the top of the Cubit-bone.*

E *The outer part of the first Osselet or little Bone of the upper range or rank that make the Knee.*

F *The Process of the Cubit-bone called the Elbow.*

G *The top of the Cubit-bone joined with the lower end of the* Humerus *or Shoulder-bone.*

H *The bottom of the said Bone.*

I *The first range of Osselets or little Bones of the Knee.*

L *The second range or rank of the said Bones.*

M *The*

M *The little Bodkin-like (or Splent-) Bones on each ſide of the Shank-bone.*

N *The top of the Shank-bone, where it is articulated into the ſecond range of the little Bones of the Knee.*

O *The bottom or lower end of the ſaid Shank-bone.*

Q *The great Paſtern.*

Y *The two little triangular Bones which are joined to the back-part of the great Paſtern near the top of it.*

R *The little Paſtern.*

T *The Coffin-bone.*

Figure II.

Shews the Bones of the Off-leg or right Leg, all of them *in ſitu.*

A B *The heads of the Shoulder-bone that articulate with the* Scapula.

C *The production in the ſide of the ſaid Bone.*

D *Its lower head with which the Cubit-bone is articulated.*

E *The firſt Oſſelet of the firſt range of the Knee.*

F *The production of the Cubit-bone called the Elbow.*

G *The top or head of the Cubit-bone.*

H *The bottom or lower end of the ſaid Bone.*

I *The firſt range of the little Bones of the Knee.*

L *The ſecond range of the ſaid Bones.*

M *The Bodkin-like (or Splent-) bone that is on the ſide of the Shank-bone.*

N *The top of the Shank-bone.*

O *The lower end of the ſaid Bone.*

P *The great Paſtern.*

S *The little Paſtern.*

Y *The two little triangular Bones faſtned to the top of the great Paſtern-bone.*

V *The Coffin-bone.*

Figure III.

Shews the fore-part of the Shoulder-bone ſeparated from the other Bones.

A N *The heads of the Shoulder-bone that are articulated with the* Scapula.

B *The production in the ſide of the ſame Bone.*

E *The heads at the bottom of the ſaid Bone, which are articulated into the cavities of the upper end of the Cubit-bone.*

D *The cavity into which the long production of the Cubit-bone is articulated.*

OO *The body of the Shoulder-bone.*

Figure

Figure IV.

Shews the hinder-part of the Shoulder-bone by it ſelf.

A *The great round head at the top of the Shoulder-bone.*
B *The great production of the ſame Bone.*
C D *The diviſion of the head at the lower end of the Shoulder-bone.*
O *The little eminence in the ſide of the ſaid Bone.*

Figure V.

Shews the fore-ſide of the Cubit-bone.

A *The top of the long production at the upper end of the Cubit-bone, called the Elbow.*
B *The middle of the ſaid production.*
C *The cavities at the upper end of the Cubit-bone, into which the lower heads of the Shoulder-bone are articulated.*
G *The body of the Cubit-bone.*
P H *The round heads at the bottom of the Cubit-bone.*

Figure VI.

Shews the back-ſide of the Cubit-bone.

A *The top of the long production of the Cubit-bone.*
BB *The upper heads of the ſaid Bone which are articulated with the lower end of the Shoulder-bone.*
CC *The lower heads of the ſaid Bone which do articulate with the upper range of little Bones of the Knee.*
F *A cavity of the lower end of the ſaid Bone, into which one of the little Bones of the upper range doth articulate.*
H *The body of the ſaid Bone.*

Figure VII.

Shews the fore-ſide of the Shank-bone.

DD *The upper head of the ſaid Bone, as alſo of the two Bodkin-like Bones on each ſide of it, where they were articulated with the lower range of the little Bones of the Knee.*
C *The two lower heads of the ſaid Bone, whereby it was articulated into the cavities of the upper part of the great Paſtern.*
M *The body of the ſaid Bone.*
NN *The two cavities or dens at the ſides of the lower heads of this Bone, into which cavities the heads of the great Paſtern were implanted or articulated.*

Figure VIII.

Shews the back-side or hinder-part of the Shank-bone, on which the back Sinews lie.

OO *The heads of the Shank-bone and of the two Bodkin-like Bones on each side of it.*
PP *The two heads at the lower end of this Bone which were articulated with the great Pastern.*
C *The cavity between these two heads, in which is articulated a Process of the upper end of the great Pastern.*

Figure IX.

Shews the fore-part of the great Pastern.

A *The dens or cavities in its upper part which receive the heads of the lower end of the Shank-bone.*
B *The heads at the lower end of this Bone which were articulated into the* Sinus *or cavities of the upper end of the little Pastern.*

Figure X.

Shews the back-part of the great Pastern.

A *The* Sinus *or cavity into which the heads of the two little triangular Bones were articulated.*
BB *The two heads at the lower end of the great Pastern, which were joined with the little Pastern.*
V *The cavities at the upper end of this Bone which did receive the heads of the lower end of the Shank-bone.*

Figure XI.

Shews the fore-part of the great Pastern with the two triangular Bones fastned to the back-part of it.

RR *The two triangular little Bones.*
VV *The cavities into which the two heads of the lower end of the Shank-bone were articulated.*
Z *The body of the great Pastern.*

Figure XII.

Shews the little Pastern on its fore-side.

Figure XIII.

Shews the back-side of the little Pastern.

Figure XIV.

Shews the bottom of the Coffin-bone.

Q *The circumference of the ſaid Bone which gives the round ſhape to the Foot.*
S *The cavities or hollowneſſes whereinto the heads of the little Paſtern were articulated.*

Figure XV.

Shews the ſides and top of the Coffin-bone.

A *Shews all the outſide of the ſaid Bone.*

Figure XVI.

Shews the fore-ſide of the two little triangular Bones ſeparated from the upper part of the great Paſtern-bone.

Figure XVII.

Shews the back-ſide of the ſaid Bones.

CHAP. XIII.

Of the Os ſacrum *or holy Bone, together with the* Coccyges *or Rump-bones, otherwiſe called the Bones of the Dock or Tail.*

THE *Os ſacrum* or holy Bone, is ſeated at the lower end of the Back, at the end of the *Vertebræ* of the Loins, to the laſt of which one end of it is articulated, and the other end to the firſt of the Bones of the Dock or Rump-bones. It is much the broadeſt and largeſt of all the Bones of the Back. Its *figure* is almoſt triangular, having a broad beginning, and ending by degrees into a narrowneſs. On the inſide it is ſmooth and hollow, but ſomething unequal; behind or on its outſide it is gibbous and alſo rough, becauſe of the Muſcles of the Back and their Ligaments cleaving unto it. Its *acute* Proceſſes or Spines are very ſmall; and the *tranſverſe* ones but obſcure: as for the *oblique,* there is no appearance of *them,* ſave in the firſt *Vertebra.* On its outer ſide near its edges there are certain *Sinus's* or hollowneſſes, to which the Haunch-bones do cleave firmly by an intervening Cartilage. Os ſacrum, *its ſeat, connexion, figure and ſurface.*

Its *Vertebræ* are in number ſix, whoſe Spines are much leſs than the Spines of the *Vertebræ* of the Loins, and the lower or nearer to the Rump-bones, the leſſer they are ſtill. *Its* Vertebræ.

This holy Bone is perforated in ſeveral places; as firſt, quite through its length it hath a large hole or cavity to receive the Spinal Marrow; out from which there go many other leſſer for the egreſs of the Nerves; *Its Holes.*

and theſe are not in the ſides of the *Vertebræ* as thoſe are that be in the *Vertebræ* of the Neck, Back and Loins, but on the inſide and outſide or and above, of which thoſe below are much the larger.

The Rump-bones. To this Bone at its lower end are joined the *Rump-bones*, which in this Animal we are treating of are in number eighteen. Theſe are joined to each other by a Cartilage or Griſtle, but ſo looſely, that the Horſe can bend his Rump which way he will. Thoſe of theſe Bones that are next to the holy Bone, are ſomething thicker and broader, than thoſe further from it; for as they deſcend down, they each grow leſs and leſs, ſo that the loweſt grows into a cartilaginous or griſtly point, as you may ſee in the figure of the Skeleton, where they are all lively repreſented *in ſitu.* Theſe Bones are not ſo hard as moſt of the other Bones are, but more ſoft and ſpongy; neither have they any Proceſs, or any hollowneſs, except the firſt of them, which hath a ſmall cavity or den to receive the laſt *Vertebra* of the *Os ſacrum,* which *Vertebra,* is the furtheſt part whither the Spinal Marrow reaches.

Table XLII.

Repreſents the *Os ſacrum* and Rump-bones joined together; alſo the *Os ſacrum* joined with the *Vertebræ* of the Loins; and ſeveral other figures of theſe Bones.

Figure IV. and V.

Shew the *Vertebræ* of the Loins joined with the upper end of *Os ſacrum.*

1. 2. 3. 4. 5. 6. 7. *Shew the ſeven Spines or backward Proceſſes of the* Vertebræ *of the Loins.*
1. 2. 3. 4. 5. 6. *The ſix Spines of the holy Bone.*
1. 2. 3. 4. 5. *Holes in the* Os ſacrum *for the egreſs of the Nerves from the Spinal Marrow out of that Bone.*
G *The hole of* Os ſacrum *which contains the Spinal Marrow.*
DDD *The long and flat Productions or tranſverſe Proceſſes at the ſides of the* Vertebræ *of the Loins.*
VVV *The little Productions in the ſides of the* Vertebræ *of the Loins whereby they are articulated into each other.*

Figure VI.

Shews the laſt *Vertebra* of the Loins removed from the reſt and turned on one ſide.

Figure VII.

Shews the laſt *Vertebra* of the Loins with that ſide forwards whereby it was join'd with the laſt but one, in which *Vertebra* is to be ſeen the hole where the Spinal Marrow did paſs through it.

Figure VIII.

Shews the ſame Bone with that ſide uppermoſt that reſpects the cavity of the Body.

Figure

TAB XLII

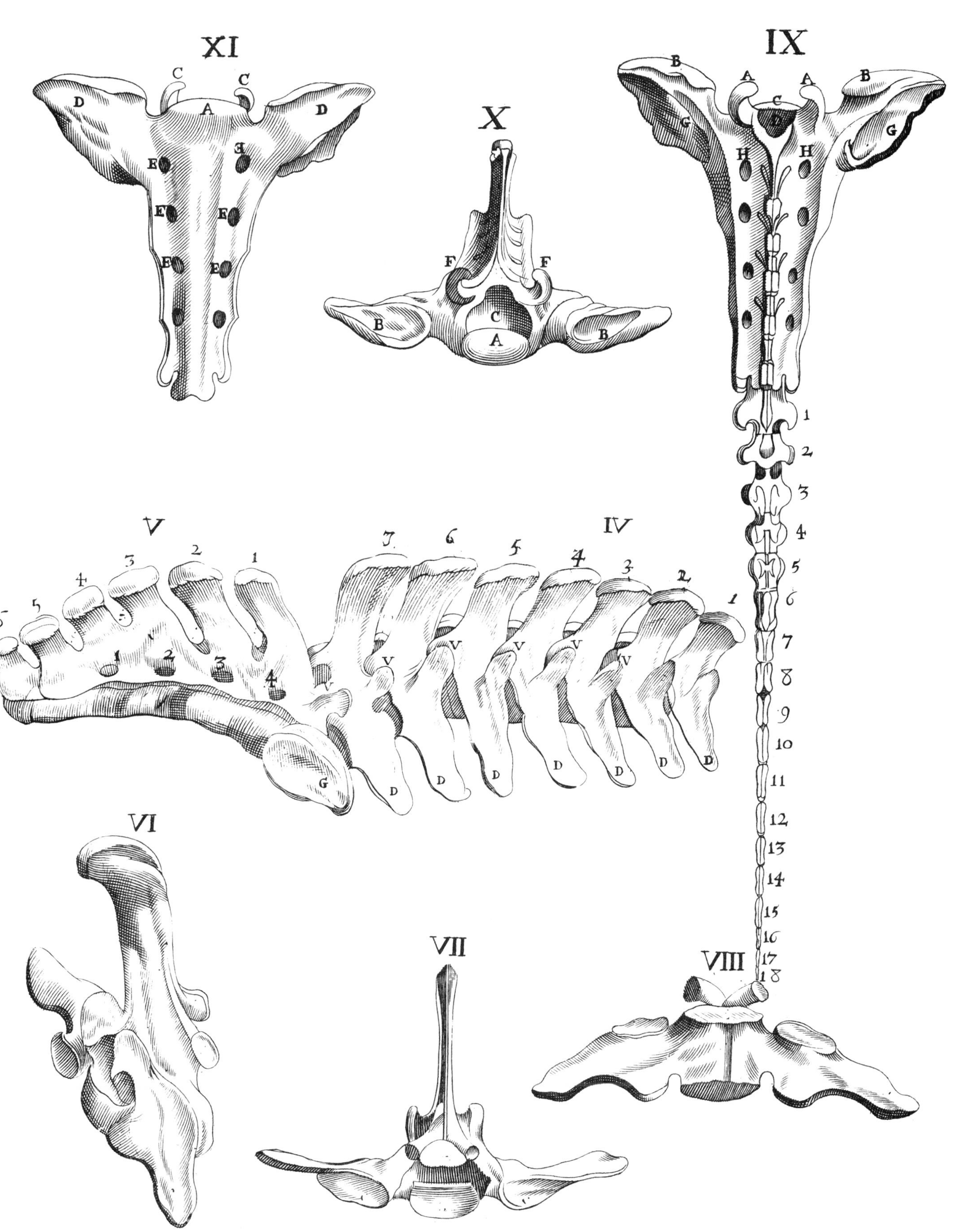

Figure IX.

Shews the lower side or inside of *Os sacrum*, as also the Rump-bones joined to it.

AA *The foremost Productions of the said Bone, which were articulated with the last Bone of the Loins.*
BB *The two long and wide Productions of the* Os sacrum, *which were joined with the Haunch-bone or* Os ilium.
C *A cavity at the upper end of* Os sacrum *which did receive the head of the last* Vertebra *of the Loins, and was articulated with it.*
D *The hole in which the Spinal Marrow was contained.*
GG *Other Productions of the* Os sacrum *which were articulated with the* Os pubis.
HH *The holes in the* Os sacrum *out of which did pass the conjugations or pairs of Nerves that are distributed about all the hinder parts.*
1.2.3.4.5.6.7.8.9.10.11.12.13.14.15.16.17.18. *The eighteen Rump-bones or Bones of the Tail.*

Figure X.

Represents the upper part of *Os sacrum* that joins to the Loins, as also partly its inside turned upward.

A *The round cavity into which the head of the last* Vertebra *is articulated.*
BB *The lower side of the broad Productions of the* Os sacrum, *which join with the* Os ilium.
C *The cavity in the said Bone wherein the Spinal Marrow is contained.*
FF *The two little foremost Productions with which the hindmost of the last* Vertebra *of the Loins are articulated.*

Figure XI.

Shews that side of the *Os sacrum* which looks to within the Body, as also its several perforations through which the Nerves do issue forth from the Spinal Marrow.

A *The cavity that receives the round head of the last* Vertebra *of the Loins.*
CC *The two Productions that are articulated with the hinder ones of the lowest* Vertebra *of the Loins.*
DD *The lower side of the two broad Productions of the said* Os sacrum.
EEE *Its holes through which the Nerves do pass from the Spinal Marrow contained in it.*

CHAP. XIV.

Of the nameless Bone, commonly divided into the Hip, Haunch and Share-bones.

Os innominatum, *or nameless Bone.*

THE *Hip-bone* (commonly so called) is by Anatomists divided in to three parts. First, *Os ilium,* so named because the Gut *Ilium* lieth under it. The next is called *Os coxendicis,* or *Ischium,* which is the lower and outer part of the nameless Bone, (or *Os innominatum*) which is the name of these three Bones as joined all together, for they are truly but one Bone in old Horses, though in Colts they are divided one from another by Cartilages, from whence this distinction is made, and they come to be discoursed of by three several names. The third part of this Bone is called *Os pubis,* also *Pectinis,* or the Share-bone.

Os ilium *or Haunch-bone.*

That part that is called *Os ilium,* is the uppermost and broadest, which is joined to the holy Bone. In figure it is semicircular, and its semicircular circumference is called its Spine. On its outside it is something arched, but within hollow; the arched part is called *dorsum,* its Back, the hollow part *costa,* or its Rib.

Its Spine.

That part which is called its *Spine,* is in many places unequal, that some Muscles might take their original from it, *viz.* the Oblique ascendent Muscle of the *Abdomen* or Paunch, the *Deltoides* of the Thigh, the first Extender of the Leg called *Membranosus,* &c. And on the back of this Bone there are unequal inscriptions or lines for the rise of the three Muscles of the Thigh that help to make the Buttocks (called *Glutæi;*) and also for other Muscles that lie under these.

Coxendix *or Hip-bone.*

The second of the parts of this nameless Bone is called *Os coxendicis.* This is the lower and outer part of it, in which there is a great *Sinus,* called *Acetabulum,* the Cup or Sawcer, into which the head of the Thigh-bone is exceeding strongly articulated. This Cup has its edges environed with a Gristle, called *Supercilium,* its brow; in whose circumference there are observed three *Sinus,* two Protuberations and an acute Process, and lastly an Appendix that is very thick: all which were ordained for the production partly of Ligaments and partly of Muscles.

Os pubis *or Share-bone.*

The third and last part of this nameless Bone is called *Os pubis,* or the Share-bone. This is originally two Bones, parted one from another in the middle with a Gristle, but in continuance of time the Gristle it self becomes bony, and so unites them into one Bone. It is placed at the bottom of the Paunch, betwixt the two hinder Legs as the Horse stands. On its outside it has on each side a *Sinus* for the descent of the crural Vessels. On the same side also it is rough to give the firmer original to the streight Muscles of the *Abdomen* and to the second Bender of the Leg. It is but a thin Bone, being hollow within, and perforated with the greatest hole of any such-like Bone in the whole Body. On its hinder and inner side it has two Processes, from whence the nervous bodies of the Yard, and some Muscles take their original.

Pelvis *or the Bason.*

These Bones with the holy Bone do make that cavity which is called *the Bason,* which is the place wherein are contained part of the Guts, and the Bladder in a Horse; and in a Mare part of the Guts, the Bladder and the Womb.

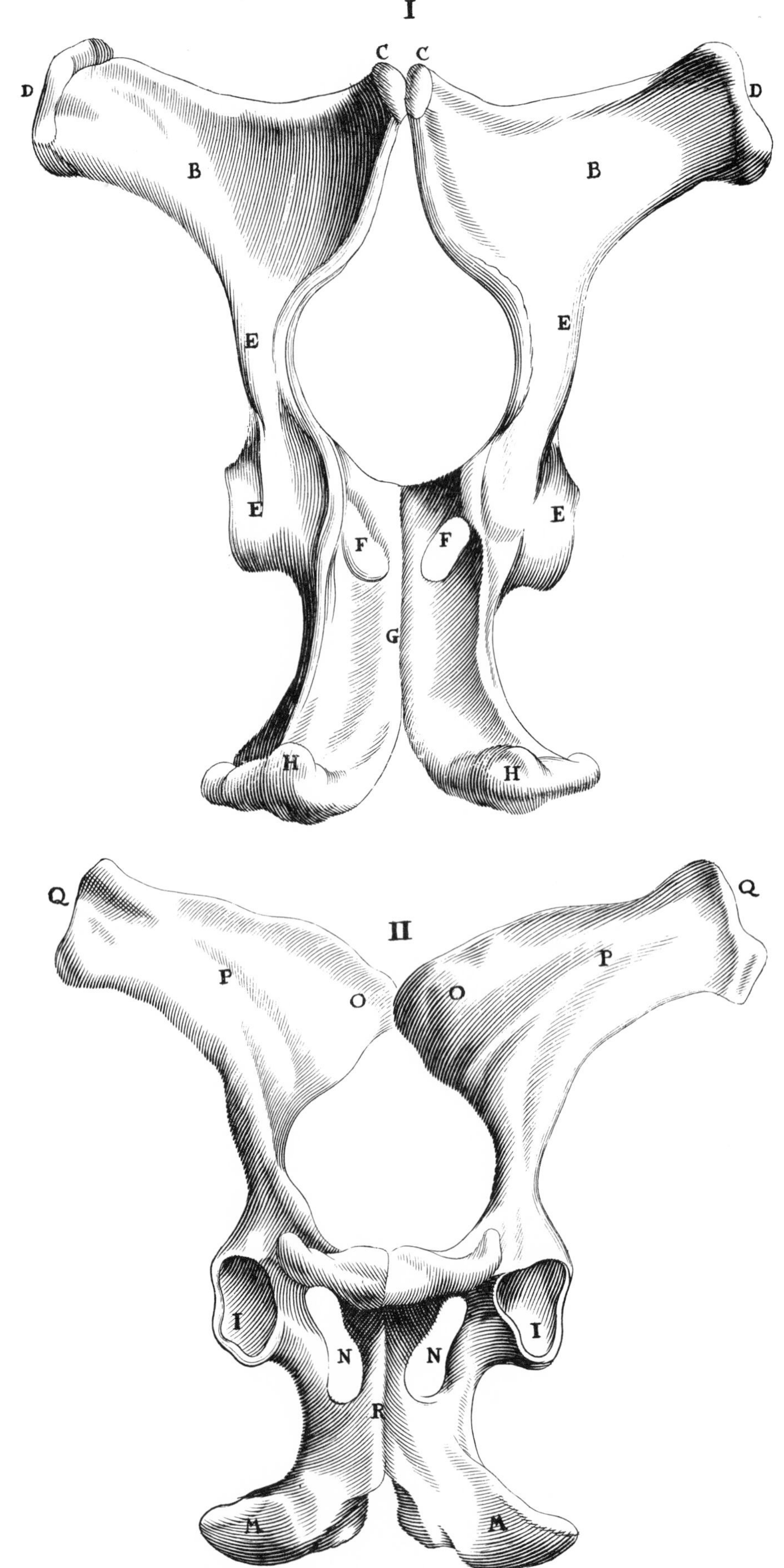
I
C
C
D
D
B
B
E
E
E
E
F
F
G
H
H
Q
Q
II
P
P
O
O
I
I
N
N
R
M
M

Table XLIII.

Reprefents the three Bones that make the *Os innominatum* or nameleſs Bone.

Figure I.

Shews the ſaid Bone with the right ſide upward.

BB *Shew the upper part of* Os ilium.
CC *The two Productions of the ſaid Bone which are faſtened by very ſtrong Ligaments to the Proceſſes of* Os ſacrum.
DD *The Spines or Ridges of the ſaid Bone.*
EEEE *The* Os coxendicis *or lower and outer part of the nameleſs Bone.*
FF *The two holes in the* Os pubis *or Share-bone made for the ingate and outgate of Veſſels.*
G *The Seam which divides the Share-bone in the middle.*
HH *The extremities or ends of the ſaid Bone.*

Figure II.

Shews the *Os innominatum* turned the upſide downward.

II *Shew the Cup of the* Os coxendicis, *into which the head of the Thigh-bone is inſerted.*
MM *The extremities or ends of the Share-bone.*
NN *The two large holes in the bottom of the ſaid Bone.*
OO PP *The inſide of* Os ilium.
QQ *The Spines or Ridges of the ſaid Bone.*
R *The Seam of the Share-bone which divides it into two parts.*

CHAP. XV.

Of the Thigh-bone and Patella *or little Bone of the Stifle.*

THE *Thigh* is called by the Latins *Femur à ferendo* to bear, becauſe the Creature is born up or ſuſtained by it. This Bone (like the Bone of the Shoulder) is but one, reaching from the Hip-bone to the Stifle. The *figure* of it is long, round and ſtreight, except where its Heads and Protuberances bunch out; of which it hath, above, one Head, one Neck, and two Proceſſes; and below, it determins into a Head which hath two Productions and a Cavity between them. *The Thigh-bone.*

The *upper Head* is an orbicular Appendix ſtanding upon the Neck, and is the thickeſt and largeſt Head of any Bone in the whole Body. It is round and long the better to enter into the Cup of the Hip-bone, which is not onely deep of it ſelf, but rendred deeper by a large Griſtle that compaſſeth the edges thereof. For it was neceſſary that a very firm articulation ſhould be in this place, becauſe of the huge weight which the Thigh was to ſuſtain. And beſides, to ſtrengthen it the more, and to faſten the *Its upper Head.*

two

two Bones the firmer together, there ariſeth out of the Cup of the Hip-bone an exceeding ſtrong and round Ligament, which is implanted into a little *Sinus* that is in the Head of the Thigh-bone. This Head is ſmooth and cruſted over with a Griſtle, that it might move the more glibly within the Cup.

Its Neck. The ſlender part under this Head is called the *Neck* of the Thigh-bone. This is pretty long and oblique, reaching upward but inclining inward, and is a Proceſs of the Bone. At its lower end, where the Bone grows broader, do ariſe two other Proceſſes, called Trochanters or *Rotatores*, from the Muſcles of that name that are inſerted into them. The upper of theſe Proceſſes is greater than the lower, nay greater indeed than any Proceſs in the whole Body which is not joined to another Bone; It bends upward and outward; but the other which is much leſs than this, bendeth backward and ſomewhat inward.

Its lower Head is divided into two. The Thigh-bone below its middle becometh thicker, and its lower end terminateth into an ample and broad Head; out of the backſide of which are produced two Proceſſes, as it were two other Heads, betwixt which there is a large ſpace left about two inches wide, which receiveth a protuberation or ſwelling of the Head of the Leg-bone.

Theſe two Heads at the lower end of the Thigh-bone are on their outſides rough, but their inſides are covered with a Griſtle, and thereby are made ſmooth and ſlippery for the more eaſiy motion of the Joint. One of theſe Heads is thicker, and is ſeated inward; the other is thinner but broader, and is ſeated outward. From them do ſome of the Muſcles that move the Leg ariſe; and into them are ſome that move the Thigh inſerted. The ſides of theſe Heads are full of little holes, out of which do iſſue the roots of the Ligaments which ſtrengthen the Stifle-joint.

Their Cavities. Theſe Heads have alſo four *Cavities*, two of which are in the middle between the two Heads, and one on the outſide of either of them. One of the middle Cavities, being the foremoſt, is made to receive the protuberation of the *Patella* or Pan, and is therefore cruſted over with a Griſtle for that purpoſe. The ſecond of the middle Cavities being more backward, is deeper than the other, alſo rough and unequal, made to receive the protuberation of the Leg-bone. The third is at the outſide of the outer head, and the fourth at the outſide of the inner, through both which the Tendons of ſeveral Muſcles of the Leg deſcend.

The Patella. At the lower end of this Thigh-bone, betwixt it and the Head of the Leg-bone, on the fore-ſide, is placed a ſmall roundiſh Bone, (called the *Patella* or Stifle-pan) about three inches broad, being plain without, but within bunching, bored through with many ſmall holes. It is covered over on its inſide with a Griſtle, and is made firm in its place by the broad Tendons of the ſecond, third and fourth Muſcles that extend the Leg, to which the *Patella* is very firmly knit. This Bone ſtrengtheneth the jointing of the Thigh-bone with the Leg-bone, and hindreth their diſlocation forwards.

CHAP. XVI.

Of the Leg-bone and Ranges of Osselets which make that part we call the Hock, answering to the Heel of a Man.

THERE is the same difference between the hinder Legs of an Horse and a Man's Legs, as we shew'd above to be between the Fore-legs of an Horse and a Man's Arm. For as in Man there are two Bones which reach from the Elbow to the Wrist, and but one Bone in that Joint of an Horse's Fore-leg that answers to this (reaching from his Elbow to that Joint we commonly call the Knee;) so whereas in a Man's Leg there are two Bones, called *Tibia* and *Fibula*; in the same Joint of an Horse that reaches from the Stifle to the Heel, there is but one, which we shall call by the name of *Tibia*, or the Shin or Shank-bone, because the Bone of a Man's Leg that goes by that name, is the more considerable of the two. *The Shank-bone is but one.*

The *figure* of this Bone is long, and *round* in an Horse, but in a Man it is three-square. The upper part of it which joins with the Thigh-bone, is broader and thicker than the lower. *Its figure.*

Its *upper Head* in which are two cavities and a prominence betwixt them, is crusted over with a Gristle, and both receives and is received by the two Heads and cavity of the Thigh-bone; which Gristle is fastned to it by Ligaments. This Gristle is slippery and smooth, and the cavities which it lines are full of an unctuous or oily matter or humour, which serves to further the motion of the Joint by rendring it moist and slippery. *Its upper Head.*

The lower part of this Bone, or its lower Head, is round and likewise covered with a Gristle, with which it is made something broad, but notwithstanding equals not the largeness of the upper Head. *Its lower Head.*

This Bone hath several *Sinus's* and *Appendices*, as well as the Thigh-bone hath; the former for conveniency of the Tendons of some Muscles to descend by, and the latter for the rise or original of other Muscles which are to move the Foot. *Its Sinus's and Appendices.*

This Bone as well as the Thigh-bone (and most other Bones) is notably hollowed within, having its cavity filled with Marrow. It is also perforated in several places, admitting through its perforations several Vessels to the said Marrow. *Its Cavity.*

Next come we to the little Bones of the *Hock*, which Joint answereth to the Instep and Heel of a Man. These are of the same number as those of the Knee in the Fore-legs were, and do also lie in two ranges, the one above the other, *viz.* three in the upper, and four in the lower. These Bones, as those in the Knee, are so closely articulated one with another, and so closely wrapt up and bound together with membranous Ligaments, that it is not easie for the Dissector to discover where all of them are divided: so that without diligent inspection they may be taken to be not above half the number they are truly of. *The seven little Bones of the Hock.*

To treat of every particular Bone of them and of their connexion one with another, or lastly of their jointing with the Shank-bone above, or with the three Bones of the *Metatarsus* below, would be in a manner the repeating

repeating of the same description over again that we gave above of the seven little Bones of the Knee. Onely that which is the hindmost and largest of them deserves to have particular notice taken of it, and that is it which is truly, and ought to be called the Heel-bone, whose shape and posture you may see in the following Figure. Into this Bone it is that several of the Tendons of the Muscles that bend the Leg are inserted. On its inside it has a large *Sinus* by which the Tendons of those Muscles that move the lower Parts of the Foot do descend, as also the larger Vessels thereof.

The Instep-bones.

The next Bones to these are the three that answer to those five that make that part of the Foot in Humane Bodies which is called the *Metatarsus* or Instep. These I say are but three in a Horse, though in a Man they are five, to answer to the number of the five Toes. They reach from the lower range of the little Bones of the Hock before-mentioned, down to the great Pastern. One of them is a large, long and round Bone; the other two are much more slender, and shorter, being the one of them placed on the inside and the other on the outside of it, adhering so closely thereunto, that they are not easily to be separated from it. These little Bones answer in all things to the like Bones which run down by the sides of the Shank-bone of the Fore-legs, which from their shape I called the Bodkin-like Bones, (as likewise the Splent-bones, because they stand by the sides of the middle great Bone, like the Splents that Bone-setters make use of for strengthning broken Bones till they are knit again;) I say these are like those, and therefore may be called by the same names.

The Pastern-bones and Coffin-bone.

The remaining part of the Bones of the hinder Leg and Foot are the great Pastern (with the two little triangular Bones adhering to the top of it,) the little Pastern, and the Coffin-bone; of all which having already treated where I described the Bones of the Fore-legs, (with which these of the Hinder-legs agree in every particular) I shall for brevitie's sake omit speaking particularly of them, and here conclude my discourse of the Bones.

Table XLIV.

Represents the Skeleton of an Horse, (drawn exactly by one that I keep standing in a Press.)

AA *The Shoulder-blade.*
B *The Breast-bone.*
CC *The Shoulder-bone.*
DDDD *The Leg-bones both before and behind.*
EEEE *The little Bones that make the Knee and the Hock.*
FF *The Shank-bones.*
ff *The Instep-bones.*
GGGG *The Bodkin-like or Splent-bones.*
HHHH *The great Pasterns.*
IIII *The little Pasterns.*
KKKK *The Coffin-bones.*
LLLL *The little triangular Bones that cleave to the upper end of the great Pastern.*
MM *The* Os ilium *or Haunch-bone.*

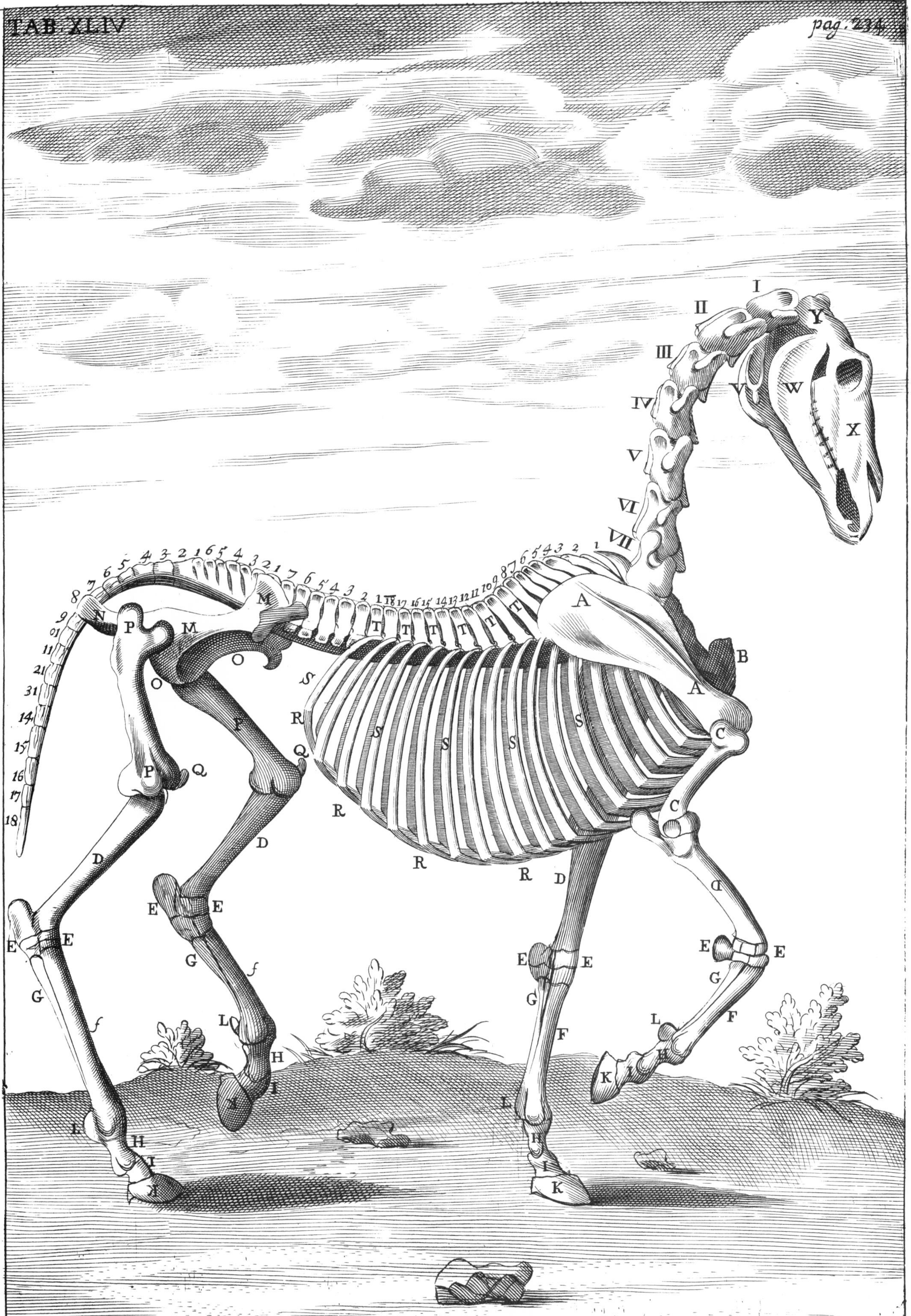
I
II
Y
III
V
W
IV
X
V
VI
VII
A
B
A
C
C
D
E
E
G
F
L
H
I
K
M
N
P
M
O
O
S
R
F
Q
P
Q
R
D
R
R
D
E
E
D
E
E
G
f
G
f
L
H
I
K
L
H
I
K
S
S
S
S
T

N *The* Os coxendicis *or Hip-bone.*
OO *The* Os pubis *or Share-bone.*
PP *The Thigh-bones.*
QQ *The little Bone of the Stifle, called* Patella.
RRRRRR *The Cartilages at the end of the Ribs.*
SSSSSS *The seventeen Ribs.*
TTTTTT *The upper end of the Ribs where they are articulated into the* Vertebræ *of the Chest.*
V *The* Os hyoides, in situ.
W *The lower Jaw.*
X *The upper Jaw.*
Y *The* Os occipitis *or Noll-bone.*
1.2.3.4.5.6.7.8.9.10.11.12.13.14.15.16.17. *Are the seventeen* Vertebræ *of the Chest.*
1.2.3.4.5.6.7. *The seven* Vertebræ *of the Loins.*
1.2.3.4.5.6. *The six upper Productions or Processes of the holy Bone.*
From the Cypher 1. *to* 18. *are represented the eighteen Bones of the Rump or Dock.*
I.II.III.IV.V.VI.VII. *Shew the seven* Vertebræ *or Rack-bones of the Neck.*

CHAP. XVII.

Of the Hoofs of an Horse answering to the Nails of a Man's Fingers or Toes.

CONcerning the Nails of a Man's Fingers and Toes (to which the Hoofs of Horses bear a resemblance) learned Men are divided into several opinions about their generation. *Hippocrates* is affirmed to be of opinion, that they are made of a glutinous matter or moisture parched and dried by heat, and driven to the extreme parts. *Empedocles* thinks them to be made of the extremities of the Nerves, calling them *Nervorum clausulas summas*, the utmost terminations or boundaries of the Nerves; and that therefore when these fall off, it is a sign of great weakness. *Aristotle* in lib. 2. cap. 6. *de generatione Animal.* saith, that the Nails, Hairs, Beaks of Birds, Hoofs of Beasts, and such like, are ingendred of *adventitious* aliment. And lastly, *Columbus* thinks they take their original partly from the Skin, and partly from the Tendons of the Muscles which move the Fingers and Toes, and that they are encreased like the Teeth by an apposition of aliment to their root.

How the Hoofs are nourished, and how fastened upon the Foot.

As for the *Hoofs* of Horses, whatever be their original matter, out of which they are formed, their growth seems to be (according to the opinion of the last mentioned Authour) from the addition of new particles to their roots, which drive down successively those before them. They are of a middle substance betwixt Bones and Gristles: not so hard as Bones, for then they would be apt to splinter and break; nor so soft as Gristles, for if they were, they could not support so great a bulk as the Body of an Horſe, much leſs endure to travel amongſt ſtones, &c. But they are of a horney ſubſtance, without ſenſe, growing pretty firmly to the parts included within them, and faſtened to the Coffin-bone by a Ligament that proceeds from their top or root, which root the Skin alſo ſomewhat encompaſſeth.

Under them lie many twigs of Nerves, and Tendons of Muſcles, which run even to the very bottom of the Hoof or Soal of the Foot, upon pricking of which with a Nail or the like, or when they are but bruiſed with riding in hard way, the Horſe preſently bemoans himſelf, as was more at large ſhewed before in the twelfth Chapter of this Book.

CHAP. XVIII.

Of a Cartilage or Griſtle.

AS an Appendix to the hiſtory or doctrine of the Bones, it will not be unneceſſary to ſpeak ſomewhat of the *Cartilages* or *Griſtles*: eſpecially ſeeing through the whole diſcourſe of this Fifth Book we have had occaſion ever and anon to mention them, but have not as yet given any particular account of them; as neither of a *Ligament*, which we have alſo often mentioned: but of this latter in the next Chapter, and onely of the *Griſtles* in this, becauſe they come neareſt to the nature of Bones.

A Griſtle what. A *Cartilage* is a *ſimilar part, cold and dry, made* (as ſome Authours affirm) *out of the moſt glutinous part of the Seed.* They are flexible and without ſenſe, and are much ſofter than a Bone, though the nature of the one is not ſo much diſtant from the other, but that ſeveral Griſtles in tract of time, and as the Creatures grow old, harden into Bones.

Their uſes. The *uſes* of the *Griſtles* are many. For *firſt* they help the motion of the Bones at their jointings one with another. For which end in the Joints that are ſubject to great motions, the edges of the *Sinus*, or Cups and Cavities of the Bones that articulate one with another, are generally lined with a Griſtle, to make the motion more glib and ſecure; ſuch are the articulation of the Shoulder-bone with the Shoulder-blade, of the Thigh-bone with the Hip-bone, and ſeveral others.

A *ſecond* uſe of the Griſtles is by *yielding*, a little to give way to the violence of outward injuries; whereas if Bones had been in their places, they would have been in danger of breaking, from their hardneſs and ſtiffneſs: for which end the ends of many Bones which are expoſed to external injuries are furniſhed with Griſtles, as the Noſe and Ears, and the like.

Another uſe of the Griſtles is, that by their mediation, as it were by a glue, ſome Bones might be conjoined; as the Share-bones in particular are by this means united to one another.

There are many other *peculiar* uſes of particular Griſtles, ſome belonging to the Sight, ſome to the Hearing, ſome to Smelling, ſome to Reſpiration or breathing, and the like; all which have their ſeveral denominations:

nations: But of these we have already treated as they fell in our way when we discoursed of the parts to which each did belong. I shall not therefore need to inlarge any further upon them in this place.

CHAP. XIX.

Of a Ligament.

AS the lubricity or slipperiness of Gristles makes the motion of the Bones more easie and glib; so the *Ligaments* do secure that motion by strengthning the articulation of one Bone with another.

A *Ligament* is a *similar part, cold and dry, of a middle nature betwixt a Gristle and a Membrane*; harder than Membranes, lest in vehement motions they should be broken; and softer than Gristles, that they might the more easily follow and obey the Muscles which move the Bones. Those that tie one Bone to another are generally insensible, as well because they receive no Nerves into them, as also lest being perpetually moved they should breed perpetual pain. But such as tie other parts, as the Ligaments of the Liver, of the Womb, the bridle of the Tongue, &c. these are endued with sense. **A Ligament what.**

The *differences* of Ligaments are many, being taken first from their *substance*, whence some are said to be hard, others soft, the former of which are called cartilaginous, and the latter membranous Ligaments. The epithet of *membranous* is likewise given to some from their breadth, in opposition whereto others are called *nervous*, because they are round like Nerves. **Their differences.**

They are also distinguished from their *original* and *insertion*; for some *arise* from Bones, some from Gristles, and some from Membranes; and are accordingly diversly *inserted*. And lastly they are differenced from their *strength* and *figure*. To give particular instances of all which, would be a needless curiosity: I shall therefore break off when I have added a word of their *use*.

The *uses* of the Ligaments, as well as Gristles, are many: for *first* they confirm and strengthen the articulations of the Bones: they *also* bind and fasten the Bones to one another where there is no true articulation. *Thirdly*, they serve as an outward garment to the Tendons of the Muscles, many of which are throughout their whole length covered with Ligaments and Membranes. *Fourthly*, they interpose like a Pillow betwixt the Bones and the Tendons of the Muscles. *Fifthly* and lastly, some of them do serve to suspend the Bowels, that they should not fall with their great weight, such are the Ligaments of the Liver, &c. **Their uses.**

The End of the Fifth Book.

COMMENTARY

DEDICATION

SNAPE dedicates his book to King Charles II (who himself had quite a tumultuous career); Charles II died in 1685, prior to the second printing of *The Anatomy of An Horse.* Of note is that Snape's family served as farriers to the Crown for over two hundred years. Snape assigns to his book the lofty purpose of improving the knowledge of farriers so as to help in treating the problems of "the Generous Animal, which yields your Majesty and your Subjects that great service both in peace and War."

INTRODUCTION

THE introduction is intended to show Snape's approach to anatomy and suggest the reasons that he undertook the work. There are some good bits of philosophy in the introduction as well.

FIRST PAGE. "There is nothing that gives a greater check to the progress of an Art, than to believe it is already perfected by those that have gone before us."

You could say the same thing today. You should never be satisfied by what you think you know.

Snape asserts that it is the rare farrier indeed that knows something of anatomy and that *Horse–Doctor* frequently becomes a term of derision. Can you imagine trying to treat horses with no knowledge of their anatomy?

SECOND PAGE. One of the questions most frequently asked of veterinarians is, "Don't you wish your patients could talk?" (The answer is, "Sometimes, but at least we don't have to listen to any complaints.") Snape points out that a (human) doctor's job is made easier by the "complaints and relations" of the patients themselves.

Snape rightly observes that a knowledge of anatomy is important for the treatment of disease. The term *distemper* is noteworthy (and is still in use today).

Snape asserts that he is a true pioneer in equine anatomy and that, "none have gone before me or shew'd me the way." This just isn't correct; almost half of Snape's illustrations are direct (but reversed) copies of those found in *Anatomia del Cavallo,* by Carlo Ruini, published almost a hundred years prior to this book.

THIRD PAGE. Snape mentions that his drawings are from dissections but that they don't show every part, so that the book won't be too big and expensive. It is something of a disingenuous disclaimer. Many of the drawings are plagiarized. Some of the other drawings don't even appear to be from a horse! He also asserts that the knowledge of anatomy must be gained from dissection and that you can't just rely on a book. Truer words were never spoken.

FOURTH AND FIFTH PAGES. Snape tries to categorize everything (a tendency that has characterized anatomists through the ages). He tries to place the body components into "spermatical and solid" and "sanguineous" (that is, from blood) as well as "simple or similar" and "compound or dissimilar." These categories really aren't of any use to the modern anatomist, but it's interesting to see how he tries to place some sort of order on the body that he's studying.

SIXTH PAGE. Snape closes the introduction and introduces the first of the five books.

BOOK ONE

Of the Lowest Belly or Paunch

SNAPE appears to have been very interested in what happens inside the horse's abdomen. The abdomen is home to many mysterious organs. It's also home to all of the digestive processes. The book is filled with a number of wonderful and fanciful discussions as Snape tries to explain what's going on in this large cavity of the horse.

The chapter begins with an illustration of the horse with a poem underneath.

CHAPTER 1, PAGES 1–2

Snape begins his dissection of the abdomen with a discussion of the skin and hairs. This is really great stuff. In these two pages you will find an imaginative discussion of what hair actually is (it is not considered part of the body) and how it is produced. Hair is just "excrement" of the body's humors! Furthermore, you'll find out why horses are always dusty (the dust comes from the inside) and why they shed. Finally, you'll find that the horse's color is a direct reflection of his temperament (his humors). The humors are:

1. *Choler* is derived from the ancient Greek. Choler relates to bile, the substance produced by the liver as a by-product of its metabolic functions. Bile is yellow. *Choleric* refers to a bitter or angry temperament. According to Snape, chestnut or sorrel horses have a predominance of choler (the word *sorrel* is from a Middle French word meaning "reddish brown").
2. *Melancholy* (also known as black choler) is supposed to be a thick, black, and acrid fluid that was secreted by the glands of the kidneys. A predominance of this humor resulted in the characteristic melancholic temperament. Iron-gray or mouse-dun horses had this humor predominating.
3. *Phlegm* is a cold, whitish or grayish, moist humor. When it predominates, it causes apathy or indolence. Phlegm gave milk-white or yellow-dun horses their color.
4. *Blood* is a warm, red fluid. Blood is the supposed seat of emotion and passion (think of some of the phrases using blood—"his blood is up," "hot-blooded," "her blood ran cold"). Bright bay or roan horses had blood as their primary humor. Even today, a brightly colored bay horse is also known as a "blood bay"!

CHAPTER 2, PAGE 3

Snape breaks down the skin into two parts, sensible and insensible, which is not unlike the skin as we know it today. He deviates quite a bit from modern physiology, however, when he talks about noxious vapors getting trapped between the two layers of the skin—but that's the seventeenth century for you.

At the end of the page he talks about the skin diseases "Grease in the Heels" or "Scratchets." Both terms are used today, although the latter term is now usually referred to as "scratches." It is interesting to see how old these terms really are.

CHAPTER 3, PAGE 4

Snape's impressions of the cutis, what he describes as the "true skin" that lies under the "scarf-skin," don't bear much relation to reality. Of special interest is his concept of how sweat is produced and how the cutis helps keep in the internal heat when it's cold outside.

CHAPTER 4, PAGE 5

When referring to the "pannicle," Snape appears to be referring to the large, thin muscle that is called the *panniculus,* the muscle that causes the skin to twitch when flies land on it. "Some very curious anatomists deny that man has any such membrane at all." Very curious and very correct; humans do not have a panniculus muscle.

It's also interesting to see the concept of internal heat (see the Introduction) brought up here (it will be mentioned repeatedly). Snape says that were it not for the pannicle, the fat under the skin would be melted by the heat from the muscles. (That's some heat!)

CHAPTER 5, PAGES 5–7

Snape's thoughts as to what fat is and how it gets under the skin are fascinating but inaccurate.

CHAPTER 6, PAGES 7–11

Snape's anatomy of the abdominal muscles really isn't bad. The illustration on page 11 is also nicely done (even though it's plagiarized) and gives a remarkably contemporary look at the horse as it is.

Of course, many of his ideas are off-base when compared to current thinking. For example, blood isn't used up by the muscles; the muscles merely draw oxygen from the blood. The blood is returned to the heart via the veins so that it can reload with more oxygen (in the lungs).

The name *muscle* is indeed derived from the Latin for "mouse." The name doesn't, however, appear to come from the resemblance of the tissue to a "flayed" mouse, but from the fact that many muscles appear to have a mouselike shape—narrow at the beginning and end and wide in the middle.

Snape notes that external muscles of the abdomen join at the "white line (so called even today)."

Toward the end of the chapter, there's a fanciful discourse on circulation in the abdominal muscles.

CHAPTER 7, PAGES 12–13

The name *peritoneum* is indeed derived from the Greek word for "stretching over." The peritoneum is a tough membrane that lines the abdominal cavity. Snape does a nice job of describing it. He also presents a wonderful description of hernias (a hernia is an abnormal opening) through the peritoneum. As usual, his description of the function of the peritoneum contains some elements of fancy and some of truth.

CHAPTER 8, PAGES 13–15

The *omentum* is a filmy membrane (it's part of the peritoneum) that attaches the stomach to other abdominal organs such as the liver and spleen. Its name is straight from Latin and doesn't appear to have anything to do with omens or foretelling the future, as Snape states (too bad—it's a nice story).

Snape again shows the creative side of his physiology when he ascribes to the omentum functions such as to lick up the "superfluities" of the belly and to "cherish and heat" the bottom of the stomach. To Snape, the omentum is part of the blanket that covers the baby's stomach. It helps keep the stomach warm and moist! He thinks it is the cause of barrenness in women (it slips down and compresses the mouth of the womb; it doesn't do that) but not in horses.

The omentum is streaked with fat. How this fat gets in the omentum is a puzzle for Snape. His discussion of how it gets to be like that (condensation of oily vapors from the arteries) is nonsense (at least by today's standards), but it is an explanation that appears again later, in his discussion of the mesentery.

The lovely illustration on page 15 is reversed from the actual anatomy. It's a direct (though backward) copy of Ruini's plate of the same area.

CHAPTER 9, PAGES 15–19

According to Snape, the *stomach* is "the kitchen of the body and the receptacle of meat and drink." From that colorful introduction, Snape enters into some of the more creative bits of speculation to be found in the book.

Early in the chapter, Snape describes little glands that "separate a flegmatic humour to keep the inside [of the gullet] moist and glib." He must be describing the thyroid glands. However, they don't have any such function. (That function belongs to the saliva, which comes from glands higher up in the throat.)

According to Snape, the opening of the stomach is surrounded by muscle fibers that act like the lid of a pot (not true). This is to keep in the vapors (Snape's physiology is full of humors, spirits, and vapors) that assist in digestion. Furthermore, if those vapors were allowed to ascend into the brain, they might cause all sorts of diseases and distempers!

At the base of the stomach is the *pylorus* (the entry into the small intestines). It does not open and close, as Snape suggests.

The circulation to the stomach comes under considerable scrutiny. Snape refers to Harvey's seminal work on the circulation (William Harvey, 1578–1657, an

English physician and anatomist who is credited as being the true discoverer of the circulation of blood) and dismisses the old ideas that the veins of the stomach nourished the stomach. He hasn't got the true function of the circulation quite right, either.

A wonderful discussion of why and how drink is refreshing (which was apparently the source of some controversy at the time) is found toward the end of the chapter. In this discussion, you are also introduced to the word *chyle.*

Chyle comes from the Greek for "juice of plants." In Snape's day, chyle was the fluid to which the ingested food was reduced by the body's digestive processes. In modern physiology, the term *chyle* is reserved for a milky fluid that is taken up from the intestines during digestion. It will be described in more detail later.

Accordingly, *chylification* was the process deemed responsible for breaking down food and providing nourishment to the body. Briefly described, food was passed into the stomach where it was mixed with saliva and various stomach juices. The juices, aided by the heat of the stomach, caused the whole mass of food to ferment and become chyle. As the chyle passed down the intestines, the "milky veins" removed the nutritive part of it and took it to the common receptacle of the back. There, the chyle ascended to the subclavian vein near the heart, where it became completely mixed with the blood, so that it could never be seen or separated. (Incidentally, the propulsive movements of the bowel provided the impetus to move the chyle up the milky veins, kind of like hydraulics.) The excrement that passed out the back was thus the non-nutritive remnants of the food that was initially ingested. Snape introduces all the elements of this process (which does not bear any resemblance to actual digestive physiology) in the succeeding chapters of this book.

Even though Snape's description of the stomach's functions is surprisingly accurate, his description of the digestive process is more amusing than accurate. He tries to describe this process as coming from the heat supplied by the arteries, "slaver" (saliva) from the mouth, and a mysterious "vigour" from "steams" evaporating from the arteries. What a cauldron he must have thought the stomach to be!

The illustration of the stomach facing page 19 does not bear much relationship to that of the actual horse (and it's not plagiarized from Ruini). In fact, it must have been drawn from a man or a dog. The horse's stomach has a remarkable appearance and there's no way that even a casual observer could have made such an inaccurate rendering. Also, Snape shows the pancreatic and bile ducts entering at two different places when in fact there's only one entrance.

CHAPTER 10, PAGES 20–21

As Snape says, the word *intestines* is derived from the Latin for "inner." As usual, he takes great pains to describe why things are the way they are. And, as usual, his reasoning is quite colorful. In this chapter, Snape describes his understanding of the structure of the intestines in general. Some salient differences between Snape's anatomy and what actually exists are:

1. There are four layers to the intestines, not three.
2. Milky veins, "found out by one Asellius" (Gaspare Asellio, 1581–1626, an Italian anatomist, whose name is given to a group of glands in the abdomen), are what are currently known as lacteals. The lacteals are vessels that carry fat from the intestines. They are part of the body's lymphatic system (a specialized circulatory system that carries a type of non-blood fluid throughout the body). Snape describes the course of these vessels correctly.
3. Snape makes the first mention of the horse's collarbone. It's an error that will be repeated many times. Horses don't have collarbones.
4. When describing the nerves of the area, Snape refers to Dr. Willis. This is Thomas Willis, 1621–1675, an English anatomist and physician who made a number of important discoveries, especially concerning the anatomy of the nervous system. An important figure in seventeenth-century medical history, Snape refers to him often.

CHAPTER 11, PAGES 21–24

In talking about the intestines in particular, Snape begins with the small intestines. He doesn't break the small intestines down into three parts as we do today (although he acknowledges that, in humans, different parts of the small intestines are talked about). He notes that there are fluids contributed to the digestive process by the liver and pancreas (but they don't cause the ingesta to ferment like beer or ale).

His discussion of cecum is wonderful. Interestingly, Snape notes that "only in a rabbit it [the cecum] bears much the same proportion with the rest of the guts, as it does in an horse." That's true; the two animals have very similar digestive processes (incidentally, so does a rhinoceros). The discussion of the "whys" of the cecum is must reading.

Snape divides the colons of the horse into three segments; modern anatomists make four divisions. His explanation of why there aren't very many milky veins in the colon as compared to the small bowel is interesting.

A lovely illustration of the horse's guts (from Ruini; it's also reversed) can be found facing page 24.

CHAPTER 12, PAGES 25–26

The *mesentery* is a fold of peritoneum that attaches the small intestines to the body wall. Its name is, as Snape states, derived from the Greek for "middle."

There is no "third" layer of mesentery, an opinion subscribed to by Thomas Wharton, 1614–1673, an English physician and anatomist.

Here's where you'll find the first mention of the lymph vessels and glands. Snape credits Danish anatomist Thomas Bartholin, 1616–1680 (to whom Snape will refer repeatedly throughout the book), for their discovery. It's obvious that Snape is not clear on what the lymph vessels are but his experiment showing that lymph is a different kind of fluid from blood is fascinating.

It's interesting to note that Snape describes lymph vessels as similar to the milky veins and running to the same spot but doesn't make the connection that they are actually vessels of the same system. To Snape, the milky vessels are for the chyle; the lymph vessels are for the lympha.

CHAPTER 13, PAGES 26–27

The name *pancreas* does derive from "all flesh," as Snape asserts. The other name for this gland, *sweetbread,* refers to its use as a food. (It was called sweetbread by the Greeks.) It provides a digestive juice (as Snape notes; in dogs he even notes that it has a saltish and sourish taste). Of course, the pancreas also makes insulin, which is needed to regulate blood sugar levels, but that function wasn't known until the beginning of the twentieth century.

CHAPTER 14, PAGES 28–31

As a matter of historical interest, Snape begins by going over the old (incorrect) theory of the function of the liver before going on to his own (mostly incorrect) theories.

Snape's anatomy of the liver is mostly correct, but the description of the circulation is a bit muddled. This is undoubtedly unavoidable since the circulation to the liver is quite complex and can't be figured out with the naked eye. Suffice it to say that the portal vein (as properly described by Snape) collects blood coming from the guts, spleen, and stomach. This portal blood does not, however, nourish the liver (that blood comes from the hepatic artery, which Snape also describes). The blood from both of these vessels is collected by the vena cava, which takes it back to the heart. At the end of the chapter, Snape does a remarkable job of describing the differences in the various vessels that occur in the liver.

A full and proper discussion of all of the functions of the liver is beyond the scope of this book and was certainly not known in Snape's day. The liver, as Snape suspected, has something to do with the "purification" of the blood. However, it does not have anything to do with heating up the stomach.

There's a nice illustration following page 30 to close this chapter.

CHAPTER 15, PAGES 31–32

Horses don't have a gallbladder, and this "vulgar Error" is perplexing to Snape and he can't begin to explain it (who could?).

He gives an imaginative explanation for how the gall (choler) is produced by the liver. There's also an explanation of why horses defecate so often; gall is a natural *glyster* (an archaic term for a stimulant for the bowels), and since it can't be stored (there's no gallbladder), it's secreted continuously, thus stimulating frequent defecation!

CHAPTER 16, PAGES 32–36

Milt is an outdated term for the spleen and refers to its supposed digestive functions (of which it has none).

Snape makes some rough observations as to the structure of the spleen and relates the color of the spleen to its composition. In unsound horses he says it becomes the color of the offending humor!

He notes that some men have "boasted" that they have taken the spleen out of dogs and cats and that these animals have lived; he doubts if that would be possible in humans or horses. It is in fact possible in both species, although it's a difficult procedure in horses and requires the removal of a rib (it's an operation that has been done almost exclusively for experimental reasons).

Snape states that, "There is no part of the Body concerning whose use there has been greater diversity of opinion" than the spleen. The opinions he goes on to give are inventive to say the least, but the discussions concerning each are terrific. (Actually, the spleen isn't all that interesting an organ. In the horse, it serves mostly as a storage site for blood cells and has other functions related to the blood and to the immune system. It is not an organ that is essential for life.)

There is a nice three-part illustration facing page 35, which depicts the spleen and its vessels and also the pancreas with capillary branches of veins and arteries.

CHAPTER 17, PAGES 36–39

Contrary to Snape's etymology, the word *reins* (an archaic term for the kidney) is not derived from Latin or Greek. Rather, it's an adaptation of an Old French word for the kidney. His description of the external shape and internal anatomy of the kidneys is reasonably accurate.

The function of the kidneys is to filter the blood and remove waste products. The by-product of this filtration is urine. Snape's description of how the kidneys work bears little relation to reality, but it is fascinating. His explanations of the function of water and how urine is separated from the blood are especially engaging. His explanation of urine color and his thoughts as to how the urine can be used to gain some knowledge of the body's distempers are also interesting.

The "deputy-kidneys" mentioned in this chapter are today known as the adrenal glands. Snape confesses his ignorance as to their function and it's clear that they were a considerable source of consternation to anatomists of Snape's day (perhaps they were a source of black choler!). In fact, they are the source of several important hormones.

CHAPTER 18, PAGE 39

Snape's description of the ureters, the tubes that connect the kidneys to the urinary bladder, is largely accurate.

CHAPTER 19, PAGES 40–41

The urinary bladder is another structure that's anatomically simple but the source of some more wonderful physiology. Of particular interest are Snape's descriptions of:

1. A mucous "crust" in the bladder (to protect it from the "acrimony of the Urine") that doesn't exist.
2. The functions of the ligaments of the bladder.
3. The stimulus for urination.

CHAPTER 20, PAGES 41–43

Snape's description of the "yard" *(penis)* and associated structures is reasonably accurate. It's accompanied by a nice illustration facing page 42. Note that the "sheath" around the penis (properly called the *prepuce*) is another term that's still in use today.

CHAPTER 21, PAGES 43–44

This chapter is the first of nine chapters devoted to the reproductive organs and accessory structures. These are among the most interesting chapters in the book. It's obvious that the whole concept of generation of animals was poorly understood at the time. Yet it was a subject of intensive investigation. Snape's thoughts (also contained in the appendix that follows the original version of the book) are up-to-date for the period. However, his observations do not appear to have been made entirely on horses, as you will see.

Snape begins by discussing the parts proper to the male horse. He points out that times have changed; previously it was thought that arteries brought blood and veins brought vital spirits to the "stones" *(testicles);* the "current" thought is that the arteries bring both blood and spirits and the veins carry away what wasn't used! (As you may know, arteries bring blood with oxygen in it to the tissues; veins take the blood back to the heart so it can get refilled with oxygen; as for vital spirits, modern physiologists seem to have lost a bit of faith in them.)

CHAPTER 22, PAGES 45–47

Snape's analysis of the origins of the word *testes* ("witness") is certainly interesting, but it is disputed by some authorities. Some suggest a connection with the Latin word for "pot" or "shell."

Blood does not enter into the testes and get turned into seed, as Snape states. Nor is his discussion of the circulation to the testes correct. It's clear fiom Snape's discussion that in his day there was a lot of interest in how the seed was generated.

Snape states that there's no midline division on the scrotum as there is in man. There most certainly is! In fact, it's hard to see how he could have missed it. However, when discussing the coverings, muscles, and associated structures of the stones, Snape is pretty accurate. The discussion of the function of the nerves to the area is entertaining.

At the close of this chapter, Snape discusses the two uses of the stones. First, they make seed. Second, they cause "courage and generosity in the Horse; for we observe that our Ston'd Horses are generally much higher spirited than Geldings." So it is.

CHAPTER 23, PAGES 47–50

The horse has three distinct accessory glands that supply fluid to the sperm that is produced in the testicles. The resulting ejaculate, a mixture of this fluid and the sperm cells, is called *semen.* Males of various mammalian species have some or all of these three glands.

Anatomists of Snape's day apparently had a difficult time figuring out what these glands were. The "seed bladders" described by Snape (and Dr. Wharton, whom Snape has previously referenced) are today called the *seminal vesicles.* They do not, as Snape asserts, "store up and preserve" the seed. In fact, Dr. Wharton's assertion that the seed bladders produce a "seed of a peculiar kind" is more accurate than Snape's musings on the subject.

Snape then discusses "running of the Reins" (in man) or "mattering of the Yard" (in horses). This appears to be some sort of incontinence or inability to control bladder function (a very rare condition in horses).

Next, Snape describes the prostate gland and the fluid that's within it. Again, the "true nature" of the fluid in the prostate gland is a source of controversy among seventeenth-century anatomists and Snape discusses a variety of opinions. Snape feels that the prostatic fluid serves to make the urethra "supple and slippery, and to defend it from the acrimony or sharpness of the urine."

The third accessory gland, known as the *Cowper's* or *bulbourethral gland,* isn't mentioned or discussed at all. It's probably just as well.

CHAPTER 24, PAGES 50–51

Snape presents Galen's ideas that the sex glands of the male and female differ only in location and then discounts them. In fact, although there are significant differences, in the fetus the sex glands in both the male and female start out at the same point in the body.

Snape's thoughts as to the comparative blood circulation to the ovaries and testicles is inventive and well worth reading. Also, note that according to Snape the function of the blood in the vessels of the mare changes depending on whether or not she is in foal (it doesn't really).

CHAPTER 25, PAGES 51–53

The history of how a conceptus is formed is absolutely fascinating, as is Snape's discussion about how the mare's "stones" differ from the horse's. Snape attempts to show that the mare has eggs, not seed. (He says that the eggs are pinched off from the inside of the ovary. Although this is not an accurate description of what happens, the ovaries certainly produce eggs.) Furthermore, according to Snape, if you boil the mare's ovaries, they'll turn out just like hen's eggs (the author has no idea if this is true or not).

Snape further notes that if you take out an ovary, the female will be barren. To Snape, this only proves that the ovary makes something critical, not that the ovary produces seed.

He describes the "Fallopian trumpets" (described by the Italian anatomist Fallopius, 1523–1563, and today called the *Fallopian tubes*) that, as is known today, convey the egg to the womb. However, Snape says that the trumpets funnel seed to the egg! Then the egg, which has been fertilized in the ovary, is conveyed back through the trumpets to the womb. In fact, the egg is fertilized in the womb and the Fallopian tube is just an inlet for the egg to get there from the ovary.

CHAPTER 26, PAGES 54–55

In discussing the womb and its horns, Snape describes them accurately enough. He errs, however, when he asserts that the foal is not carried in the horns of the mare; it certainly can be.

Snape states that the womb needs lots of arteries but not so many veins. This is because the foal uses up the blood and nourishing fluids brought by the arteries, and there's not much left to bring back. That's just a flight of fancy. His assertion that the horns of the womb move in a manner similar to the guts isn't right either.

You shouldn't miss the discussion of the use of the womb, found at the bottom of page 55.

CHAPTER 27, PAGES 56–57

In describing the vagina and external genitalia of the mare, Snape's imagination takes off. At times, you have to wonder if he's embarrassed to talk about them. For example:

1. He's not sure if there's a "Membrane that goes cross the Vagina in Mares that have never been cover'd, as Anatomists say there is in Maids," but he believes there is none. There is, and it's called the *hymen* (as it is in Maids).
2. The "myrtiform bodies" that he says give the horse pleasure just don't exist.
3. The *clitoris* is said to be an analog of the yard in the male (which it is), but it's pretty hard to imagine it as "the principle seat of pleasure in the mare." (As a matter of fact, it's hard to imagine that a mare thinks breeding with a male horse is anything but a chore.)
4. The *labia* (of the vulva) are there "for comeliness sake."
5. The "nymphs" that keep the urine from wetting the lips aren't there at all!

Facing page 57, there's a lavish illustration of the urogenital tract of the mare that shouldn't be missed. Although there are some things about the drawing that are accurate, the delicately (and surprisingly floral) structures described as the clitoris and "jagged orifices" of the trumpets of the woumb do not appear in twentieth-century horses (nor, one suspects, would they have been there in Snape's day).

CHAPTER 28, PAGES 58–65

It should come as no surprise to anyone that the generation of a newborn was the subject of anxious and intense investigation in the seventeenth century. The wonder and mystery of life is still nothing short of a miracle for those who are lucky enough to experience it; how this miracle happens is still a stimulating question to scientists. This chapter is a treasure trove of history and exploration and is must reading (although to properly understand the development of the fetal membranes—and to correct Snape—probably requires a bit of medical training).

At the beginning of the chapter Snape refers the reader to the appendix on the generation of animals. Although that appendix is not included in this facsimile edition, the thoughts contained therein are all presented in this chapter (most of the appendix is about rabbits anyway).

Snape begins by discussing several opinions as to how the foal is nourished in the womb. The first opinion is that there is a direct link between the mare's blood and the fetus (not true, although the fetus is certainly nourished by the nutrients in the mare's blood that's conveyed via the placenta). Snape mentions that the mare's milk was thought to be blood also but changed in color by the "white kernels of the dugs." *Dugs* is an obscure term for the mammary glands. Snape smugly discounts the idea of blood nourishment as impossible since the foal couldn't have gotten blood nourishment before the navel vessels were established.

The fetus does in fact receive nourishment from the mare's blood. As for blood nourishment in the early embryo stage, the fetus supplies its own nutrition via a structure called the *yolk sac* until the attachments with the circulatory system of the mother are formed.

Having discounted the first opinion of fetal nutrition, Snape gives us a second opinion that involves chyle and milky veins. This doesn't work for him either, since in his opinion, the milky veins are actually just lymph vessels.

Snape's third "and truest" opinion is that the fetal fluid itself supplies the nourishment to the fetus. Snape goes on to eloquently describe the filtration system by which this nutritious fluid is formed (it is the ever-present chyle). Of course this is just nonsense—albeit clever nonsense.

There's a dramatic illustration of a dissection of a pregnant mare facing page 60.

Next, Snape discusses the membranes that surround the fetus. In Snape's opinion, they have been there all along as part of the covering of the egg (in the strictest sense this may be true since all parts of the fetus and the fetal membranes develop from the fertilized egg. However, the membranes are not just the expanded outer covering of the fertilized egg).

The development of the fetal membranes is a complex process and a discussion of it is certainly beyond the scope of this book. Suffice it to say that Snape's explanations for their development are yet another valiant attempt to make sense out of something that he didn't really have the tools to explain. Some points of interest in the pages that follow are:

1. The allantoic membrane *(allantois)* is indeed derived from the ancient Greek for "sausage." Pudding is an English term for sausage, and when Snape calls the allantois the "Pudding-like membrane," he is undoubtedly referring to its shape.
2. The chorion does not lay loose inside the womb for six months "as a bladder in a Foot-ball."
3. The allantois is important for the storage of urine in the eggs of birds and reptiles, but not in mammals. (Snape was apparently familiar with work done on embryonic chickens by both W. Croune [1633–1684] and William Harvey [1578–1657.])
4. Note Snape's mention of the *hippomanes.* This curious object that's expelled at the time of birth is still the subject of some lore today (it's just made up of cellular debris).
5. When speaking of the fetal vessels, Snape is absolutely right when he states that the arteries become the ligaments of the bladder, the veins become the ligaments of the liver, and the urachus disappears.

Make sure you look at the illustrations facing pages 63 (Table XI) and 64 (Table XII). They are nothing short of spectacular.

CHAPTER 29, PAGES 66–67

The anatomy of the udder is pretty straightforward. But, Snape has trouble figuring out what milk is and how it's produced. He falls back on its being the ubiquitous chyle and states that the glands of the udder separate the milk from the blood by filtration. The milk is also stored in the "milk pipes" (which are in actuality just the large veins that run along the mare's abdomen).

BOOK TWO

Of the Middle Venter, or Chest

ANOTHER of Snape's chief areas of interest is the circulation. The idea that the blood circulates through the body was still relatively new, having first been described by William Harvey. This discovery stood the medical world on its head. (Prior to Harvey's work, Galen's medical dogma was that the blood ebbed and flowed through the arteries and veins like the tides.)

In the seventeenth century, the heart was the seat of life and, along with the brain, the most "noble" organ in the body. It's no wonder that this book goes into such great detail on the anatomy of the heart and takes such pains to describe the goings-on that make the mysterious force of life possible.

CHAPTER 1, PAGES 69–70

Snape speaks of the chest in general terms and lays out the parts that he's going to describe in subsequent chapters. He notes that even Aristotle couldn't figure out why life's forces existed. As usual, he also gives credit to Nature for the perfect construction of all the body parts. At the end of the chapter, the word *weazand* is found. It's an archaic term for esophagus, gullet, or windpipe.

CHAPTER 2, PAGE 71

Snape accurately describes the muscles of the chest wall. The action of the chest wall muscles is not quite as simple as Snape describes, however. Furthermore, the lungs themselves have no active function in respiration, as suggested at the end of the chapter. (They're just pulled open by the action of the muscles of respiration, kind of like an accordion.)

CHAPTER 3, PAGES 72–73

The lining of the chest cavity, the *pleura,* is accurately described here. At the beginning of the chapter, Snape refers to Riolanus (Jean Riolan, 1580–1657, French physician and physiologist), whose name has been given to a couple of structures in the human abdomen. Contrary to Snape's beliefs, the pleura does not originate from the spinal nerves.

Snape accurately refers to "that mortal Disease (in Men) called the Pleurisie" as occurring between the inside of the chest wall and the pleura (and it killed Dr. Willis!). Pleuritis (or shipping fever, as it's frequently called today) can be a big problem in horses.

The "nerves of the wandring pair" should be recognized by anatomy students as the vagus nerves.

The "watery humour" noted at the end of the chapter is the pleural fluid that exists between the lungs and the chest wall. Snape's description of its function is, as usual, imaginative. (The fluid actually helps keep the lungs sucked up against the inside of the chest wall. You get the same effect when you put a thin layer of water between two pieces of glass—try to pull them apart!)

CHAPTER 4, PAGES 73–76

The diaphragm was apparently a structure of some controversy in Snape's day. He talks of several opinions as to its structure and origin, and asserts that it has an action different from all other muscles. It doesn't really; like all muscles, it just contracts and relaxes. In an interesting side note, Snape also discusses the results of wounds to the diaphragm.

Snape describes the holes in the diaphragm that allow the passage of vessels, nerves, and the gullet. He follows with a discussion of whether or not there are pores in the diaphragm to admit "vapours" from the lower parts (there aren't; there aren't any vapors, either).

Next, Snape addresses the uses of the diaphragm. His discussion of whether the motion of the diaphragm is voluntary or involuntary is an entertaining bit of reasoning (it's actually both; you have to breathe and the body does so automatically, but you can also take a breath if you want to). He also goes to some lengths to try to describe how the rest of the body's muscles assist in respiration. Frankly, he shouldn't have bothered. Snape correctly notes that the diaphragm is used to help expel excrement and in mares to deliver foals as well; uses such as assisting in the distribution of chyle and protecting the chest from the vapors that arise from the ignoble parts of the abdomen are thought to be somewhat less important in the physiology texts of our era.

There's a nice (though highly schematic) drawing facing page 75.

CHAPTER 5, PAGES 76–77

In addressing the *mediastinum,* which is (correctly) described as a membrane that roughly divides the chest down the midline, Snape asserts that it serves as a barrier so that one side of the chest can be unaffected if the other becomes sick or wounded. While this is true in most mammalian species, in the horse the mediastinum is not a complete division. It's also not rough in some areas and smooth in others.

CHAPTER 6, PAGES 77–80

The thymus is given a bit of attention at the start of this chapter. Unfortunately, most of the information is way off-base. In fact, the four paragraphs addressing the gland are almost wholly inaccurate. One wonders what Snape was looking at. The name of the gland has nothing to do with a leaf of thyme (it's derived from a Greek word for "warty growth"), it certainly isn't a "pillow" for veins and arteries (it has immune system functions), and it isn't near the collarbone (since horses don't have collarbones). Furthermore, it disappears entirely in adult horses! Snape is right, however, that the thymus from calves is considered by some people to be a "dainty delicate bit."

Snape's discussion of the pericardium (heart sack) and the "watery humour" contained within it is a delight. Once again, he takes great pains to describe why it's there, fitting his observations to the greater design scheme that he is sure exists. Apparently there was some discussion in Snape's day as to whether or not there are any blood vessels in the pericardium; he correctly infers that there must be.

The section on the uses of the pericardium is engrossing. Snape gives several opinions as to where the fluid comes from (all wrong). He begins with Hippocrates, the famous Greek physician who is generally regarded as the father of medicine and who thought it was the same fluid as urine. Snape also describes an "experiment" that Aristotle did to show where the fluid comes from. Snape comes down on the side of those who feel that the heart sack contains congealed vapors from the heart itself.

Equally fascinating are two paragraphs devoted to the use of the fluid in the pericardium. The idea that the heart is the engine of the body, generating tremendous heat, is introduced here (and expanded upon in the next chapter). According to Snape, the blood in the heart is so hot that it will scald your finger! Thus, the pericardial fluid is considered to be some sort of coolant, just like the antifreeze in your car. Needless to say, that's not so. The fluid doesn't make the heart buoyant in the heart sack, either.

Another highly schematic illustration is to be found facing page 79.

CHAPTER 7, PAGES 80–83

The heart deserves special mention in Snape's anatomy. After all, it is "the fountain of the Vital faculty and power," "the place of natural heat," "the Author of the Pulse," and the "first Bowel living . . . and the last dying." What organ could be more important?!

Cor (as in coronary) does not come from "running" as Snape states. Rather, it refers to the fact that the vessels of the heart (the coronary vessels) encircle the heart like a crown (*corona* is the Latin word for "crown").

Snape's description of the heart's position in the chest is correct. However, as with all of Snape's teleology, the "reasons" that it was put in its position are entertaining.

His description of the motion of the heart is correct, but he admits to having some difficulty giving a reason for why it beats (of course, there's no real reason; it's part of the mystery of life). Perhaps it's best to, like Snape, "admire the wisdom of the great Creator in forming such an Engine."

The "heat" of the heart is again brought up later in the chapter. According to Snape, it's the reason that there's a different kind of fat in the heart (to keep the heart from drying out requires a fat that's less likely to melt). He even asserts that there are two types of fat: "adeps" (from the Latin word for fluid fat, or grease) and "pimele" (from the Greek word for fat). Frankly, in the body, fat is fat.

The chapter ends with a flowery description of the valves that occur in blood vessels. Valves were only first discovered about a hundred years earlier by the Italian anatomist Fabricius (1537–1619). The only problem with Snape's description is that there are no valves on *venae cavae,* the large veins that enter the right side of the heart. Because of the absence of valves there, when the horse lowers his head, you can frequently see blood pulsing back up the jugular vein.

There is an illustration of the heart and lungs facing page 83. Unlike those of most mammals, a horse's lungs don't really have lobes, as the illustration shows.

CHAPTER 8, PAGES 83–89

Snape continues his fascinating description of the heart and its vessels in this chapter. He begins by describing the differences between the two sides of the heart, paying special attention to the right ventricle, which pumps blood to the lungs.

Snape makes a remarkable digression on fish. It is must reading. He notes that fish have only one ventricle, and states that since water cools their blood, they don't have or need lungs. He goes on to muse that for fish, water must somehow approach the nature of air. Given that the chemical makeup of water wasn't known at the time, his thoughts that fish got something out of water that helped them breathe is really something! He then lets his observation get the best of him by inferring that since fish can live for years without breathing (at least as we know it), too much importance is attributed to air in its perpetuation of the "vital flame" of life.

Snape moves on to the left side of the heart. He correctly notes that the wall of the left ventricle is thicker (even today, most physiologists would presume this is because it has to work harder pushing the blood throughout the whole body than does the right ventricle, which just shoots blood through the lungs). He correctly notes that the blood coming into the left ventricle is "florid scarlet" due to "the particles of air that insinuate themselves into the Bloud in the lungs."

Snape refers to dissections by Dr. Lower (Richard Lower, 1631–1691, an English anatomist, who first described the fibrous rings around the openings in the heart) and defers to his observations. He notes that the left side of the heart is the primary location for the mixing of the vital spirits (whatever those may be).

The insides of the ventricles are supposed to be rough to help the mixing of the blood and chyle (in fact, they are quite uneven, but that's not the reason). Snape then discusses a controversy as to whether there are pores in the wall (septum) that divides the two ventricles. (There aren't any, but it's fun reading.)

Snape describes the vessels of the heart nicely. However, when it comes to the heart valves, Snape is a bit off-base. There are indeed four valves in the heart. Snape correctly states that valves are found where the pulmonary artery (which takes blood from the right side of the heart to the lungs for oxygen) leaves the right ventricle and where the aorta (the large artery that leaves the heart and begins the distribution of blood to the body) leaves the left ventricle.

There are no valves at the vena cava and pulmonary vein as Snape states. The three-part tricuspid valve is on the right side of the heart; the two-part bicuspid valve (or *mitral,* from, as Snape notes, its resemblance to the bishop's pointed hat, called a *miter*) is on the left. The actual location of these heart valves is between the atria (the chambers that receive the blood) and the ventricles (the chambers that pump the blood).

Frankly, it gets a bit confusing when Snape starts talking about the auricles ("earlets") of the heart. In Snape's day, *auricle* was used instead of *atrium.* Today, both terms are used. The atrium is the chamber of the heart that receives the venous blood (there are, of course, two of them). The auricle is a very small appendage attached to the atrium that has no apparent function. Horses have a small auricle attached to the right atrium only. His description of the function of the "earlets" is sheer imagination.

In describing the heart's motion, Snape makes a big mistake. He says *systole* (contraction) and *diastole* (relaxation) of the chambers of the heart occur in opposition to each other, that is, that the earlets contract when the ventricles relax and vice versa. All four chambers of the heart relax and contract at the same time! (By the way, in modern physiology, there is no "perisystole." *Presystole,* a period just prior to the heart's muscular contraction, is described, however.)

There are illustrations of various views of the heart facing page 88. The locations of the valves are quite inaccurate; they actually occur much lower in the heart.

CHAPTER 9, PAGES 89–96

The word *pulmones* is from the Latin, as Snape notes, but it is just the Latin for "lung." The Greek word *pneuma* refers to the spirit or soul. These roots are still used in making words associated with lung function (pneumonia, for example). The length of the chapter attests to the importance that Snape attributed to these organs.

Snape opens by referring to Malpigius (Marcello Malpighi, 1628–1694, an Italian anatomist who first described blood capillaries and the lung "bladders" noted by Snape; the bladders are called alveoli today). He goes into some detail regarding Malpighi's observations which, given that they were the first ones described, are quite remarkable. He also notes (correctly) that the blood vessels that nourish the lungs are separate from those that bring the air in and out.

There's a nice drawing of the lungs and trachea facing page 90. Again, you have to wonder what Snape was drawing from (maybe a dog), since horses don't have lung lobes as shown in the drawing.

The windpipe is up next for treatment. The anatomy of the windpipe is pretty straightforward and so is Snape's description of it.

The physiology of the windpipe is another matter. Snape devotes a good bit of time to discussing whether or not any of the liquid that a horse drinks goes down the windpipe. It doesn't, but learned scholars from Hippocrates to Bartholin and Jassolin (Giulio Jasolino, 1538–1622, an Italian anatomist who, among other things, was a teacher of Bartholin) thought it did, especially in instances where there was fluid accumulation in the "heart sack" (pericardium). To Snape's credit, he doesn't see how there could be any fluid coming into the lungs from the "gullet" and observes, as everyone knows, that if you get fluid in your windpipe, you cough (or drown!).

Snape ascribes the accumulation of heart sack fluid to "Dropsie." *Dropsy* (as it's spelled today) is an archaic medical term referring to an accumulation of fluid in the body cavities (it's derived from *hydrops,* the Latin for "water").

The discussion of the windpipe's two membranes doesn't require much attention, but Snape's assertion that the "kernels of the throat" (the thyroid glands) provide lubrication to keep the inner membrane "moist and glib" is entertaining (though wrong). He describes the rings of the trachea eloquently.

There's a nice drawing of the lung with it's "little bladders" facing page 92, along with more detail of the trachea. It's highly schematic but not altogether inaccurate.

On the page following the drawing, Snape closes his treatment of this area by describing, in his usual florid style, the functions of the windpipe.

Snape describes the blood vessels flowing to the lungs and correctly notes that they intertwine around the air bladders to allow for the air to get into the blood. It's curious that he refers to "anastomoses" between the arteries and veins. Malpighi had already described blood capillaries as being the connection between the veins and arteries (capillaries are the minute microscopic connections between the larger vessels). Thus, given his relatively up-to-date knowledge (he'd obviously read Malpighi's work), it's a bit surprising that the information about capillaries apparently escaped Snape and he instead relied on the older (and incorrect) ideas about how arteries and veins connect.

Facing page 94 is an illustration of the "pneumonick" vein and artery. The branching of the vessels of the lungs looks just like a piece of dill (for those of you who cook).

In discussing the lymph vessels of the chest, Snape (again quoting Willis) credits them (incorrectly) for the "watery humour" of the chest. Rupture of these vessels is supposed to be responsible for "Dropsie," a condition accompanied by "Coughs and Phthisicks" (*phthisick,* pronounced thí-zick, is an old medical term that was used to describe both asthma and tuberculosis). Rupture of the lymphatic vessels of the chest can occur, but it's mostly seen in dogs and cats and rarely in horses.

Toward the end of the chapter he begins a lively discussion as to whether or not the surface of the lungs has pores. Both Caspar Bartholin (1585–1629, Danish anatomist and the father of Thomas) and Johannes Waleus (1604–1649, Dutch anatomist and a contemporary of Harvey's who did extensive work on blood circulation) asserted that pores existed on the surface of the lungs (they don't). To his credit, Snape looked for these pores with an experiment of his own design. In spite of the imposing anatomic credentials of these men, Snape almost disagrees with them (he doesn't want to offend anyone). He does opine that if there are pores on the surface of the lungs, they act like a one-way valve, possibly letting air in from the chest but certainly not from the lungs to the chest (unless there is some sort of rupture of the surface membrane).

The account of the physiology of the lungs makes for wonderful reading. According to Snape, the lungs are a pillow on which the heart rests and are vital for cooling that old hot engine that is the heart, as well as for continuing the vital flame of life. They also expel the various "smoaky or sooty streams or excrements" of the heart and lungs. (One must admit that the physiology of Snape's day makes for better reading than the more accurate but drier physiology of today.)

CHAPTER 10, PAGES 96–99

Snape's etymology strikes again when talking of the neck. *Collum* is Latin for "neck," but the word *neck* is derived from obscure German origins and has nothing to do with Latin.

The larynx (the top of the windpipe) is correctly identified as the origin of the horse's neighing. It's quite a complex structure, and although a full dissection is beyond the scope of this commentary, Snape's discussion is engaging and gives some fun history, such as the origin of the term *Adam's apple.* There's an illustration of the larynx, the tongue, the bones, and the cartilages facing page 97 that's nicely rendered, though highly schematic.

Toward the end of the chapter, Snape introduces the uvula. When you look in the back of a person's mouth, there's this little bit of tissue dangling there called the *uvula* (you've probably seen it emphasized in cartoons of people with open mouths). Snape will talk about the uvula quite a bit in later chapters. The only problem is, horses don't have one.

At the bottom of the page, Snape describes what can only be the thyroid glands. These do not swell up when a horse has glanders. *Glanders* is a severe respiratory condition caused by bacteria. It is usually fatal. In writings of the time, glanders is often confused with what most people today call *strangles,* another, much milder and rarely fatal bacterial respiratory infection.

BOOK THREE

Of the Head

THERE'S no doubt that the brain and other structures of the head were an area of great interest to Andrew Snape. After all, the head was considered "the seat of the Animal Faculty," that is, the part of the body from which life itself springs.

In this book he goes into the anatomy of the brain in considerable detail. He largely follows the lead of the English anatomist and physician Thomas Willis (although he does differ from him with regard to the origin of the fifth and seventh cranial nerves). Snape considers that there are nine pairs of nerves that originate from the brain; today the number is twelve. The interested student of anatomy can easily see where the discrepancies are (mostly, nerves that are now considered separate nerves were then considered as part of the same nerve trunk).

The discussion of the nerves is confined to the brain and the nerves arising from the spine; the nerves to the extremities (which, frankly, are of utmost interest to people who work on horses today) are not discussed at all.

Toward the end of the book, considerable attention is paid to the eye and the ear. This part of the book is not original (those areas having been previously and thoroughly dissected by other anatomists) but the accompanying illustrations are wonderful.

CHAPTER 1, PAGES 101–104

This chapter is largely an overview of Book Three. Snape begins by giving the head an exalted place in the anatomy of the horse, asserting its "supremacy over all other parts," and calling it "the seat of the Senses" and "the chief Mansion house of the Animal Soul." Given its many attributes, it's no wonder that such an illustrious structure as the head is given such attention! His explanations of why the head is on top of the body and the location of the eyes are teleology at its finest.

In the chapter, Snape mentions a book of cures that he was preparing to write. Sadly, there is no record of this book ever having been written.

As with other areas of the body, Snape tries to separate the head into two categories: parts contained in something and parts containing something (these are, admittedly, not particularly useful distinctions). He launches right into a lengthy description of an important structure called the *pericranium.* There is a pericranium, but it's a term that is applied to the outer covering of the bones (the *periosteum*) of the skull in human anatomy. There is no membrane passing from one side of the skull to the other to suspend the dura mater of the brain (which does exist and is described with reasonable accuracy).

The discussion of the other membranes of the head and brain is reasonably good. However, Snape later comes to the remarkable conclusion that the membranes contain all of the sensing functions of the nerve fibers and that the rest of the cord has "little or no sense." (That's just wrong.)

The ventricles of the brain (Snape also calls them sinuses) are actually one continuous little cavity. They do contain a fluid but they do not contain any blood. (Think of the brain as a jelly donut; the donut is the brain, the hole for the jelly is the ventricle, and the jelly is the fluid.) The ventricles certainly don't have any arteries or veins opening into them.

CHAPTER 2, PAGES 104–105

You have to read these two pages. The chapter opens with what can only be described as a testimonial to the brain. It's wonderful reading. Snape also gives his opinion as to how the animal spirits are moved around the body from arterial pressure. This may seem a bit silly until you realize that for most of history nerves were thought to be hollow vessels through which the "animal spirits" moved in the same manner that water flows through a pipe.

At the end of the chapter, Snape excoriates those people who think that a horse doesn't have a brain. "I much wonder how any such Dolt can have the confidence to take upon him the name of a Farrier, and pretend to cure he knows not what." As easy as it is to laugh at the idea that horses don't have a brain, remember, ideas do change as people actually look at firmly held and long-established beliefs (for example, compare human dietary recommendations today with those of the 1960s). Ideas that are held dear today may be the "horse has no brain" of tomorrow.

CHAPTER 3, PAGES 106–107

If you want to learn how to open up a horse's skull so that you can see the brain, this is your chapter. There's a gorgeous illustration facing page 106 of an open skull with the brain exposed. The legends for the illustrations are pretty accurate and things like the "wormlike" processes are still called that today.

It should come as no surprise that in Snape's day the functions of various portions of the brain weren't known. Thus, the cerebellum (or "after-brain" as it was known) is said to have the same use as the brain. In fact, it has some specialized functions.

CHAPTER 4, PAGES 108–109

The *medulla oblongata* is the "stem" of the brain from which the spinal cord begins. Snape's anatomy here is fairly good, although his mention of a "third" membrane arising from the "Rack-bones" is a bit hard to figure out. You're also introduced to the word *chine.* This term was used to refer to the backbone or spinal cord (and it is a word that will reoccur later in this book).

Snape looks at the brain as sort of a miniature body. Considering that the brain controls the whole body, perhaps it shouldn't be surprising that anatomists once considered the brain to have parts analogous to the areas of the body that those parts control. Thus, there are references to the thighs, buttocks, and testicles of the brain. This sort of phraseology is no longer used today.

Snape correctly notes that there are nerves that arise from the "pith or marrow" of the spinal cord. Snape alleges that this is for safety's sake (presumably in case of an accident; given the distance that nerves have to travel, you wouldn't want to have all of the nerves affected). There are indeed nerves that arise from the spinal cord, but they are not in any way isolated from the rest of the body's nerve supply. Snape says that there are thirty-seven spinal nerves; in fact, there are forty-two.

CHAPTER 5, PAGES 109–116

This chapter is devoted to a detailed study of the cerebrum, the largest part of the horse's brain (the cerebrum is the part of the brain that you normally associate with its shape). The chapter begins by describing the "wonderful net" of blood vessels around the brain. The term is still in use today, although it's not applied to the brain (there's a rete mirabile in the kidneys, for example). Modern-day anatomists have also been unable to find any evidence that the blood vessels around the brain actually elaborate animal spirits. He follows this discussion with instructions on how to get the brain out of the skull.

Facing page 110, there's yet another beautiful illustration of the skull and its contents.

The pituitary gland is a small gland (Snape says it's the size of a Groat, which was an old English coin about the size of your thumb from the last joint forward) found at the base of the brain. Today, the pituitary gland is known to be a hormone factory. Of course, hormones were unknown in Snape's day, so some function had to be invented. In the case of the pituitary gland, the function was, according to some authors, to drain excrement from the brain.

In the middle of the chapter, there are two pages essentially completely devoted to nasal discharge. It is fascinating reading. Apparently many doctors felt that discharge from the horse's nose came directly from the brain or spinal cord. "Mourning of the chine" was a term used to describe this process. Evidently, this "disease" caused the brain and/or spinal cord to melt and discharge from the nose. (One would imagine that this was a fatal condition once the brains ran out.)

Snape disparages this line of thinking by pointing out that there's not enough brain and spinal cord tissue to provide all the discharge that you see in conditions like glanders ("all the Brain in the Horse's Head would not be sufficient to supply it with matter for three daies [days]"). He also points to experiments that show that the ventricles of the brain (which carry the brain's discharge, according to Snape) end in the pituitary gland (which they don't) and (correctly) don't connect with the palate (where the excrements could be blown out of the nose). He therefore concludes that there cannot be such a disease as mourning of the chine (this is a perfect example of coming up with the right answer with the wrong reasons).

Having disproved the idea that the brain melts away to cause nasal discharge, Snape goes off on his own almost equally fanciful explanation for the stuff. In his mind, nasal discharge is a combination of two things. First, there are the rotting bones of the nose (the bones are corroded and "cankered"—*canker* is an ancient medical term referring to an eroding process like a sore or ulcer; today it is used primarily to describe a disease process of the horse's foot). Second, there is "corruption or depravation [deprivation] of the Bloud [blood]." This results in a "flegmatic humour" that is spilled out from the blood by the arteries in the upper part of the nostrils and is "destructive to the Beast." He considers this condition incurable (as it certainly would have been in his day).

Following his discourse on nasal discharge, Snape returns to the brain with a discussion of various parts, such as the infundibulum (a channel in the brain that does in fact exist) and the yard, buttocks, testicles, and "arse" of the brain. One can't help but agree with Snape that all of these names "have no other foundation but fancy." He also mentions the pineal gland, known today to be a hormone factory but thought then to be just another "Kernel."

The brain's ventricles come up for discussion again here. Today, it is accepted that there are four ventricles in the brain (thus, the solution to Snape's dilemma as to how many there are). The ventricles have no apparent purpose, but that doesn't stop Snape from giving them several.

Snape concludes this chapter by mentioning several of the brain's internal structures such as the corpus callosum and septum lucidum; these exist, but they are of interest only to the serious neuroanatomist.

Don't miss the illustration facing page 115.

CHAPTER 6, PAGES 116–118

This chapter is devoted to trying to explain how the brain and the nervous system work. Frankly, even with the advent of modern science, such a question is never going to be answered exactly. One thing is certain; today's answers are not nearly as creative as Snape's.

The chapter is a wonderful summary and historical record of what must have been the current thoughts of the day in regard to the elaboration of the "animal spirits" and their transmission through the nerves.

Snape also gives his reasons for the occurrence of apoplexy (today, apoplexy is described as an impairment of the nervous system caused by a disorder of the circulation to the brain). Understandably, he has trouble comprehending nerve distribution in the tissues and impulse transmission; a reasonable understanding of this had to wait another four hundred years.

Snape concludes with an interesting observation that some animal spirits must be stored in the nervous fibers of the tissue. As proof of this, he notes that the hide of a dead horse will twitch as it is being removed, thus releasing the animal spirits. Well, why not?

CHAPTER 7, PAGES 118–120

This chapter begins Snape's discourse on the cranial nerves that are seen to arise directly from the brain. There are twelve cranial nerves, although Snape, quoting Willis, says that there are nine (he combines nerves that are now considered separate). The important nerves of smelling, sight, and eye movement are considered in this chapter.

Snape addresses the nerves of smelling first. He gives his understanding of why sneezes happen (irritation or convulsive motion of nerve fibers) and refutes the assertion that "snivel" was milked out of the brain via the "mammillary processes" (they are no longer called that) of the first cranial nerve.

Next come the nerves of sight (the second cranial nerve). He incorrectly states that the coats of the eye are formed from the nerve and agrees with Willis that the nerves themselves aren't responsible for sight so much as are nerves that are interwoven into the eye (Willis was wrong, too). The retina, at the back of the eye, was not yet given proper credit for its function of interpreting the visual stimuli that come through the eye.

The third pair of nerves (known today as the *oculomotor nerves*) were thought to take animal spirits to the eyes, which considering that these nerves cause movement of some of the eye muscles, isn't that far off-base.

Check out the illustrations of the brain facing page 119.

CHAPTER 8, PAGES 121–123

The fourth and fifth cranial nerves are addressed here. Snape correctly identifies the fourth nerve as going to the trochlear muscles of the eye. In modern usage it's called the trochlear nerve. (The term *trochlear* means "like a pulley"). Apparently, these nerves really get a lot of animal spirits. Snape also notes how sensitive and expressive the eyes of the horse are.

The important fifth nerve is a bit confusing to Snape, but to be fair, the nerve does have many functions. It's called the *trigeminal nerve,* providing sensation to the face, teeth, and mouth and supplying the nerve impulses responsible for chewing movements. Snape's anatomy here is really pretty good. The chapter has a couple of engaging discussions on why your mouth waters when you see food and why people's cheeks blush; they really shouldn't be missed.

The illustration facing page 123 is highly schematic but does give the proper basic positions for the various structures listed.

CHAPTER 9, PAGES 124–125

Snape's sixth and seventh nerves are addressed in this chapter. The sixth nerve (today called the *abducens nerve*) is a small nerve with a fairly simple function. It supplies the "Abducent Muscle" of the eye (to abduce means to "draw away or out").

Snape's seventh nerve actually combines three nerves (he notes that some people at the time felt that it was two nerves; it's actually three). He correctly notes that the nerve arises from a different place in horses than in humans. He describes the nerve as having a hard and a soft part; anatomists don't mention textural differences today but it's a wonderful observation. The "soft" part is the eighth cranial nerve, responsible for hearing. The "hard" part is the seventh nerve, responsible mainly for moving the muscles that cause facial expression (Snape correctly notes that its function is "more to Motion than Sense"; today nerves are described as having motor function and sensory function, or both). The "twig" from the "wandring pair" of nerves is what in today's anatomy is the ninth cranial nerve.

Toward the end of the chapter, Snape explains the "Staring" reflex that makes a horse open his eyes wide when he hears an unexpected sound. (This reflex doesn't exist.)

CHAPTER 10, PAGES 125–129

Snape's eighth nerve (the "wandring pair") is today considered the tenth cranial nerve. It's called the *vagus* nerve (from the Latin word for "wandering" or "straying"). The term is apt because the nerve's course wanders throughout the whole body and supplies most of the internal organs. Snape combines today's eleventh cranial nerve with the "wandring pair." His origin of the ninth nerve (our twelfth nerve) is also a bit muddled.

Honestly, this chapter is difficult reading, at least partly because the vagus nerve itself is quite large and its anatomy is quite complicated.

This commentary is not the place to try to address the proper anatomy. Still, there are some interesting observations:

1. Dr. Willis noted that, "Nerves that pass towards the Heart of Brutes are much fewer in number than those in Men" (in reality, they aren't). That's because "Beasts want prudence, and are not much liable to various and divers passions," so apparently they don't need as many nerves to the heart!
2. It seems apparent that, when talking about the ninth nerve, Snape is describing something he's never seen. He appears to be following the course of the vagus nerve and a few of the spinal nerves. Mostly he just makes a big mess out of the actual anatomy.
3. It's clear that Snape has relied mostly on Willis for the preceding chapters—and he acknowledges it. Still, Snape does differ from Willis in that he's inclined to think that the neuroanatomy of the horse is pretty much the same as in humans (although he reserves judgment until he actually gets to do a thorough inspection).

The illustration of the brain facing page 128 is just lovely (and fairly accurate).

CHAPTER 11, PAGES 129–130

Snape now begins to take on the formidable task of describing the nerves that arise from the spine. He starts with the nerves of the neck vertebrae. This is fairly dry and inaccurate reading, and again Snape appears to not have actually looked at a horse in preparing his book. Specifically:

1. There are forty-two pairs of spinal nerves, not thirty-seven. This breaks down as eight cervical, eighteen thoracic, six lumbar, five sacral, and five caudal, or coccygeal. (The coccygeal vertebrae are not noted at all by Snape.)
2. The first spinal nerves of the neck don't come from the brain.
3. The origin of the phrenic nerve as described is that of a human, not a horse.
4. The "accessory nerve" that ascends to the brain doesn't exist.

CHAPTER 12, PAGES 130–134

More fairly dry anatomy is found here. Of note:

1. There are eighteen pairs of thoracic nerves, not seventeen.
2. Snape correctly identifies the big nerve plexus of the forearm (called the brachial plexus).
3. He rightly (and happily) notes that there's no reason to discuss all of the thoracic nerves.

Snape concludes that knowing something of the anatomy of the nervous system should be of use to someone practicing medicine. According to him, in the case of various bruises, accidents, or "Palsie," by knowing the locations of the nerves the practitioner should have a better idea on which part he should place his "cures." It's a good thought, but not one that's important in today's medicine.

Two illustrations conclude this chapter. The drawing facing page 132 is taken from the famous French farrier J. L. de Solleysel (who's first book was published in the 1660s). The drawing facing page 133 is from the oft-cited Dr. Willis. Neither drawing is of much actual value (and the drawing on page 132 looks like something that could have been sculpted by Deborah Butterfield).

CHAPTER 13, PAGES 134–138

In beginning his discussion of the eye, Snape's etymology gets in the way again. The word *eye* comes from an old Aryan root and the word *ocular* comes from the Latin word for eye (and has nothing to do with the word *occlude*). However, in case you've wondered why there are two eyes or why the eyes are round, Snape has your answer. Snape also says that the inner lining of the eyelids comes from the (nonexistent) pericranium and that the fat that exists behind the eye is there for lubrication.

Equally as curious as these conclusions is a significant omission. There's no mention of the prominent third eyelid! This is especially significant since the third eyelid (known as the "haw") was frequently removed by farriers of the day, who feared that it would become inflamed and enlarged and obstruct the horse's vision. It must have been a barbaric operation.

Snape's discussion of the "coats" of the eye is rarely accurate as to function and origin, but it is fairly descriptive of the actual anatomy. There are a couple of interesting asides giving the origins of the terms *uvea* and *retina.* Curiously, there's no mention of the *tapetum,* a reflective coat on the back inner surface of the eye that reflects light and helps horses see in the dark. (It's also the reason that horse eyes shine green in the dark when a light is pointed at them.)

Snape next addresses the "humours" of the eye itself. He's figured out that horses shy or startle easily because of floating bits in the humor that look like insects. (It's an explanation that has apparently lost some credence over the years.) He also mentions that cataracts come from a growing together of these particles (they don't).

Snape's "crytalline Humour" is easily seen to be the lens of the eye. His description of its function is basically correct (as is his description of the function of the retina). However, the third humor, the vitreous, doesn't nourish the lens.

The lavish illustration facing page 137 is a useful reference in understanding this chapter, even if it misses a lot of anatomy. As previously noted, the third eyelid isn't shown and the tapetum isn't mentioned. Also, the pupil is shaped wrong (normally it's rectangular) and there's no notice of the very obvious corpus nigricans (the balls of pigment that you see along the top edge of the pupil in the horse's eye).

Note also, in Figure V, the "apple" of the eye. The "apple" refers to the pupil. It was called the apple in the early days of medicine because the pupil was supposed to be a globular, solid body (of course, it's not; it's just a hole in the iris). This particular illustration is pretty poor; the pupil is covered by the cornea and is inside the eye, not outside of it as shown here. Those interested in anatomy will enjoy the old names of the muscles of the eye.

CHAPTER 14, PAGES 138–142

This chapter, on the ear, opens with a lovely (and not entirely inaccurate) description of the function of the ear, "collecting in its hollowness some part of the Air that is the vehicle of the sound, as it passes by." It also gives a lively description of why the ear tissue is not too hard or too soft (presumably, it's just right).

Snape's description of the inner parts of the ear is actually rather nicely done, although the information presented was not new for the time. In fact, the only significant error that he makes is attributing "implanted air" to the inner cavities of the ear. There's no implanted air; in fact, this air comes from the pharynx via the eustachian tube and allows for pressure on the ear to be equalized (that's why you can pop your ears while under water or on an airplane as it descends).

The uses of the little bones inside the ear are engaging reading. Actually, as Snape suggests, the bones of the inner ear are modulators of sound, though they don't exactly function in the manner that Snape describes.

Some other points of interest include:

1. The "stirrop" (it's stirrup today) is not really shaped like a triangle.
2. The "orbicular" bone (discovered by Franciscus Sylvius de la Boe, 1614–1672, a Dutch anatomist who described various aspects of brain and heart anatomy in humans) is today called the lenticular bone.
3. The concha (so-called today) does resemble the shell of a tabor (a tabor is a type of drum). It does not normally collect any "pituous matter" (phlegm).
4. What Snape refers to as the rotunda is today commonly called the round window. It is covered by a membrane (he says it has no covering).

5. His description of where the nerves go is accurate but he's describing two nerves, not one.
6. It's hard to see how he could have missed the guttural pouches in talking about the head and ear of the horse. These structures (there are two, one on each side) are large mucous sacs that occur on the course of the tube that runs from the inner ear to the pharynx. Among domesticated animals, they are unique to horses and they're quite large. Who knows—perhaps he was in a hurry.

The illustration facing page 141 is terrifically stylized (the bones only vaguely look anything like the way that they are drawn) but pretty to look at.

CHAPTER 15, PAGES 143–148

In the opening paragraphs of this chapter, Snape tells you why horses don't have any fat on their muzzle—just in case you've wondered. He describes the vessels and nerves accurately enough but then makes the remarkable (and inaccurate) assertion that the lining of the nostrils originates from the dura mater of the brain!

Snape refers to the kernels that separate the "Rheum." *Rheum* is from the Greek, meaning "to flow" (and also gives rise to words like *rheumatism*). In Snape's day, the term was used to refer to any of the various secretions from the mucous glands of the body, such as are seen in the nose, eyes, or mouth. When there was disease, the rheum would become abnormal.

Snape's muscular membrane, which he says contracts the nostrils, doesn't exist. The "red fleshy spongious substance" does exist and is called the *turbinate bone* today. Snape concludes his discussion of the nose by describing its uses, including evacuation of the "superfluous flegmatick Humours of the Bloud" that cause disease.

After the nose, Snape addresses the lips and mouth. His description of the palate isn't too far off except for the fact that there aren't any holes in it for the "slaver" to "distill through into the mouth."

In the middle of the chapter is a lengthy description of the uvula. As previously mentioned, the uvula is the funny little fleshy projection that hangs at the back of your mouth. The whole discussion is all well and good and even quite interesting (and the distemper of the uvula is cured in a manner that is known by "every old Woman"). In fact, the only problem with it is that horses don't happen to have a uvula.

The discussion of the tongue begins with more inaccurate etymology (*lingua* is just the Latin word for "tongue"). It's interesting that Snape thinks that the tongue is some sort of a unique structure. In his mind there's nothing else in the body like it. In fact, the tongue is just another big muscle. His uses of the tongue are pretty much right on the mark.

Snape does a good job both in describing the location of the ducts and uses of the saliva. He refers to Thomas Wharton, 1614–1673, the English physician and anatomist who ended up with the salivary duct (known as the sublingual duct for its position under the tongue) in question being named after him.

Snape follows with an interesting story about a nobleman whose salivary duct was cut by glass and how it was ultimately healed. Snape suggests that "roweling" might help cure the problem if it occurred in horses. (A rowel was a crude surgical instrument, often made of leather, that was inserted between the flesh and skin of a horse. It was intended to cause a discharge or release of humors.) Actually, salivary ducts, when cut, often go on and heal by themselves.

At the close of the chapter, Snape refers to the other large salivary gland, the parotid, as having been discovered by "Steno" (Neils Stensen [1638–1686], a Danish priest, physician, anatomist, physiologist, and theologian). Like Wharton, Stensen also gave his name to a salivary duct.

Facing page 147 is an illustration of the salivary glands and ducts, shown (for some reason) on the head of a calf.

The drawings are rather well done.

BOOK FOUR

Of the Muscles

FRANKLY, Snape just doesn't seem all that interested in the muscles of the horse. Perhaps it's because muscles have a very limited function (they contract and relax) that's not very mysterious. Or, perhaps it's because, relative to other structures, not many problems affect the horse's muscles. It would seem that Book Four might be a good place to address the large tendons and ligaments of the horse's lower limb; in fact, these areas are not addressed anywhere in *The Anatomy of An Horse* (a curious omission, given the importance of the structures to a horse's soundness).

Perhaps inevitably, a listing of muscles, such as the ones in this book, can make for some fairly dry reading. Still, the chapter does contain a great number of amusing and interesting observations and is well worth perusing. As usual, the illustrations found in the various chapters are remarkable (although, regrettably, there are only a few of them).

CHAPTER 1, PAGES 149–152

Snape begins this chapter with a discussion of the "four kinds of Flesh" that he feels make up the body, beginning with the muscle. Of course, this sort of distinction is not particularly useful and it's not made today. However, it does show how medical people of the time (just like those of today) were trying to place some sort of order on the body.

The composition of muscle is "called a Parenchyma." *Parenchyma* is a general term used in medicine today to refer to the tissue that is characteristic of any particular organ, such as the heart, liver, or lungs (as opposed to the supporting or connective tissue that's found around an organ). The word *parenchyma* is derived from the Greek for "something poured in beside." It was apparently coined by the ancient Greek physician Erasistratus, who supposed that the substance of parenchymous tissues was formed of blood strained through blood vessels and coagulated. A couple of thousand years later, Andrew Snape hadn't come up with any better explanation.

Snape follows with an apology of why his section on muscles isn't as lavishly illustrated as the previous sections and why his description of the muscles isn't as exact as it could be. It's basically an admission that this part of the book isn't very accurate, but the reasons that he gives are:

1. More illustrations would have made the book too expensive.
2. Knowing the names of all of the muscles is more a matter of curiosity than real usefulness (one tends to agree, but it's kind of a poor excuse—this is an anatomy book after all). He does make the very accurate observation that you should know which way the muscle fibers run, so that when you remove something (like a "Tumour"), you try to cut with the fibers rather than across them (and thus not disrupt the fibers any more than necessary).
3. He hasn't had the time to study them. He also presumes that the anatomy of the muscles in a horse is just like that of a human, a remarkable leap of faith indeed.
4. The names are usually in Greek and frequently can't be "rendered into English." Since most farriers couldn't understand the names anyway (given their "mean education"), he figures there's no point in bringing them up at all.

Snape's lengthy apology concludes with the hope that no one will think him "sluggish and supine" for not actually getting around to describing all of the muscles. Additionally, he promises that he will try to get better at this part of the horse.

The flesh of the bowels is thought largely to be a parenchyma (though a different sort) and the heart a muscle. Glands are considered a completely different sort of flesh (not from blood). "Spermatical" flesh, according to the authorities of the day, arises from the "first rudiments of the embryo or conception"; like the formation of parenchyma, this idea is actually just another bit of ancient physiology that had hung around for a couple of thousand years.

Toward the end of the chapter, Snape discusses swelling of glandular tissue and notes correctly that glands swell when they're affected (by a "flegmatick Humour" falling upon them) rather than grow (due to an influx of blood). He suggests that elevating the horse's head to drink and eat may help with the swelling from "great Colds."

Snape also notes an interesting human condition called "King's Evil." This condition, also known as *scrofula,* was a swelling of the glands (mostly the glands of the neck) that, at least in some cases, was caused by the bacteria that cause tuberculosis. In the England and France of Snape's day, this condition was supposedly cured by a touch from the king (or queen)! Accordingly, days were set aside on which people could come from all around to get touched (and cured!) by the king. Reportedly, King Louis XVI of France touched more than 1,600 people in a single day!

To close the chapter, Snape discusses "membranous" flesh, a type of flesh that, in addition to being somewhat different from the other types of flesh, is useful for making strings for musical instruments.

CHAPTER 2, PAGES 152–153

Snape correctly notes that there are three pairs of muscles around the eyelids, but he doesn't get their actual uses right. The "two" muscles that shut the eyelids are actually one muscle (the orbicularis oculi muscle); those who "suppose them to be but one Muscle which compasses the Eye-lid round as with a circle" are right!

CHAPTER 3, PAGES 153–155

Snape correctly describes the seven pairs of eye muscles and gets their functions pretty much right. His only serious mistake is that the "circular or round" muscle that he credits with suspending the eye in its place is actually the muscle that pulls the eye back into the socket when the horse is threatened (it's a muscle that people don't have).

Snape then begins a series of wonderful descriptions of the eye muscles, using names that are much more colorful than those in use today (regrettably, muscles aren't described as "proud" or "humble" anymore).

The actual movements of the eyeball aren't nearly as simple as Snape makes them out to be. Virtually all of the movements come from the organized actions of several muscles. These actions are very complex and almost impossible to analyze. He concludes with some suggestions on how to properly dissect the eye muscles.

CHAPTER 4, PAGES 155–156

Here, Snape accurately describes the four pairs of muscles of the nose. The names are archaic and it should be noted that horses don't have any muscles with which to shut their nostrils.

CHAPTER 5, PAGES 156–158

The chapter begins with a description of a muscle that doesn't exist (the "detrahens quadratus") but moves on well enough from there. Snape describes the *buccinator muscle* of the cheeks as the "Trumpeter" because it is strained by blowing a trumpet (remember Dizzy Gillespie). The rest of the muscles described are those of the lips, being "five pair and one odd one." The five pairs are described with largely archaic names but their location and function descriptions are fairly accurate. Don't miss the lively description of the "Atollens" muscle that is, among other reasons, used by the "Ston'd Horse after he hath smelt to a Mare." The "odd one" is the orbicularis muscle (it's still called that) that closes the lips (and is the muscle that lets you pucker up for a kiss).

CHAPTER 6, PAGES 158–159

The lower jaw has six pairs of muscles (not five, as Snape states). The muscles here are fairly accurately described, although there's no such thing as a pericranium covering the outside of the muscles.

CHAPTER 7, PAGES 159–161

This chapter begins with a wonderful description of why animals can move their ears and why humans don't need to ("though there have been some that could move them"). Reasonably enough, Snape divides the ear muscles into internal and external groups. He notes only four groups of external ear muscles (there are eleven). Many of these are the same muscles that Snape is describing; Snape combined what are, in fact, separate muscles to make his four pairs.

The internal muscles described are those of the little bones inside the ear. Snape correctly notes that you have to be very careful in your dissection if you intend to see them.

CHAPTER 8, PAGES 161–162

Snape begins this chapter by describing the uses of the tongue. Curiously, he also states that "Brutes" use the tongue to gather food into their mouth, which is true of cattle but not of horses. Horses gather the food with their teeth. The names of the muscles described in this chapter are not in use today and the function of the various muscles is largely incorrect. Muscular function used to move the tongue is actually quite complex and not well described here.

CHAPTER 9, PAGE 163

The large muscles that assist in swallowing are discussed in this chapter. The muscles described are mostly a confusion of various muscles, and it's pretty clear that Snape never actually looked at them. At the end of the chapter, however, he correctly notes that the names of the muscles in this area come from observing where the muscles arise and attach; that's still the case today. (Also, it's still impossible for anyone to translate the Greek names to English!)

CHAPTER 10, PAGES 164–165

An accurate account of the complex and small muscles of the horse's larynx is beyond the scope of this book; Snape's rendering is not in accord with the anatomy of today and is made even more difficult to understand by the lack of drawings.

Toward the end of the chapter, Snape discusses "Squinancy or Quinsie" in humans. Contrary to Snape's assertion, this condition is not an inflammation of any muscles. Rather, it refers to an abscess that occurs next to a tonsil (in people; horses don't have tonsils).

Referring to the epiglottis (a little tongue of tissue in the back of the mouth that is located just in front of the entrance to the windpipe and the esophagus), Snape notes that it doesn't have any muscles in humans and horses but it does in cattle, sheep, and cud chewers (in fact, these animals don't have a muscular epiglottis, either).

CHAPTER 11, PAGES 165–167

Since horses don't have a uvula, it's kind of hard to accurately discuss the muscles of the structure. That doesn't stop Snape from doing so. Clearly, he's borrowing from human anatomy for this chapter.

CHAPTER 12, PAGES, 167–168

Snape describes eight pairs of muscles as being proper to the head; in fact, there are many more pairs of muscles than eight. As is the case with most of Book Four, the descriptions are a bit arcane and difficult to follow. (The idea of an anatomy book on muscles without reference illustrations is a bit droll.)

Snape says that there are lots of muscles to move the head up and back but only one to move it forward and down. This is because the head is so heavy that it tends to go down by itself! (This is incorrect.) As previously noted, there are many muscles responsible for the movement of the head. Like the eye, muscle action resulting in head movements is very complex and not the result of the simple action of one of Snape's muscle pairs.

CHAPTER 13, PAGES 169–170

This chapter on the muscles of the neck is much like the previous chapter, with fanciful descriptions and old names that bear little relation to the anatomy of today.

However, you are treated to a beautiful illustration facing page 170 that finally gives you some idea of what Snape is talking about.

CHAPTER 14, PAGES 171–173

This chapter, on the muscles of the chest, is reasonably descriptive but provides relatively few insights. Snape launches right into a description of the first pair of rib muscles and says that they arise from the collarbone, which, as you remember, doesn't exist in the horse. He correctly mentions that "serratum" (there is a muscle of the horse named the *serratus ventralis*) is so called because the tendons resemble "the teeth of a Saw" (which they do).

Several anatomists of Snape's era are referenced in this chapter, including:

1. Johann Vesling, 1598–1649, a German anatomist and botanist, who was the first to see the thoracic duct of the human chest.
2. Bartholin. See page 342.
3. Adriaan van der Spieghel (Spigelius), 1578–1625, a Flemish anatomist whose name has been given to a part of the human brain.
4. Isbrand van Diemerbroeck, 1609–1674, an obscure Dutch anatomist whose book on the anatomy of the human body appears to be the last anatomy

textbook written in which the soul is part of a routine description of the human body.

CHAPTER 15, PAGES 173–175

The muscles of the back and loins of the horse are, as Snape correctly notes, all intertwined and quite massive. There was apparently some controversy in Snape's day as to whether the muscles of the back should be identified as a few large groups or many small ones. The anatomists of today have come down firmly on the side of giving names to more groups (anatomists are like that).

The actions of the back muscles are quite complex. Snape states that they have only one motion (unlike in humans). While it's true that muscles can only do two things, contract and relax, the horse can move his back in many different directions as a result of a combination of muscle actions. The horse is not as nimble as a dancer of course, but not so stiff as to only be able to move in one direction, either.

Snape asserts that according to Galen the muscles of the back have no muscles to oppose their actions. Today, we say that the muscles of the abdomen perform that exact function.

The description of the muscles is reasonably good. One curiosity is the name *sacrum,* which is indeed derived from the Latin for "holy" (the word *sacred* comes from the same root). This bone was apparently used in ancient sacrifices, hence it's name.

The chapter contains a wonderful discourse on back problems in the horse and it deserves careful reading. You will see that the same sorts of things said about problems with the horse's back today were mentioned in the seventeenth century! The treatments are a bit different, though. As a veterinarian, the author is glad that to treat a horse's sore back; it's no longer advised to "sweat him in a Dunghill" followed by a "strengthening Charge or Plaster."

Snape further tries to "undeceive many of our Professors" about back problems in the horse. Just like today, the kidneys got credit for back problems in the horse. (In fact, kidney problems can cause back soreness in people but appear to rarely, if ever, do so in horses).

Snape also refers to horses "swayed" in the back. It's interesting to see how old this term really is. Of course, a "sway-backed" horse refers to a horse with a curvature of the spine that goes downward toward the ground. The word itself apparently has Scandinavian origins and refers to a twig or wooden switch; presumably the term *swayed* refers to the curve of a switch or twig. Snape credits various "congealed Humours" as the cause of swayed back and says that it is difficult (though possible!) to cure (unless the back is actually broken, in which case it's incurable). Interestingly, he asserts that he had seen a horse with a dislocated sacrum; while this condition can occur in the horse, it's very rare and can be difficult to resolve.

CHAPTER 16, PAGES 176–177

This chapter, which addresses the muscles of the genitalia and the anus, doesn't have a lot of useful or accurate information in it. However, the reasons and purposes for the various muscles are, as usual, entertaining and worth a look.

CHAPTER 17, PAGES 177–178

The names of the muscles described as being on the shoulder blade have been mostly changed today, although there are still muscles referred to as "serratus" and "rhomboideus."

Of most interest is the end of the chapter and Snape's description of the direction of the movement of body parts relative to the body. In order to discuss muscle movement intelligently, a generally accepted terminology must be used. Terms such as *upward* and *downward* are no longer used today. Instead, to describe bending, anatomists refer to *flexion* (moving closer together) and *extension* (moving farther apart) of muscle groups or limbs. Movement away from or toward the trunk of the body is today referred to as *adduction* or *abduction,* respectively.

CHAPTER 18, PAGES 178–180

This chapter on the muscles of the shoulder provides few insights but does give the origin of names, such as *deltoid* and *latissimus* (which, it must be noted, was called the "Scratch-arse Muscle" in humans). In his description of the "coracoideus" (today, called the *coracobrachialis muscle*), Snape refers to the oft-cited Bartolin, as well as Arantius (Julius Caesar Aranzi, 1530–1589, an Italian anatomist and physician whose name graces a number of structures in the human body) and Placentius (Johannes Placentius, ca. 1500–1550, an obscure German anatomist who has virtually disappeared from the historical record).

Finally, Snape discusses the "circular" motion of the shoulder. In horses, this sort of motion is possible but uncommon. It's performed by a complex series of muscular actions.

CHAPTER 19, PAGES 181–184

This chapter opens with a delightful (and fairly accurate) comparison of the horse's limbs to the limbs of humans. For those of you who wonder which area of the horse is analogous to the same area of a person, this page is colorful reading (and, frankly, a lot less dry than most other comparisons that you'll ever see).

The description of the muscles of the horse's forelimb that follows is a bit confused and not very accurate. (Snape concludes the chapter by admitting that he "will be content that this Chapter is reputed imperfect.") Virtually none of the names of the muscles given are used today.

Curiously, Snape asserts that the horse has no radius bone (he calls it the "cubit bone"). Actually, there are two bones between the horse's knee (carpus) and the elbow. However, the two bones (the radius and ulna) are fused. This prevents the horse from rotating his forearm, like a person can. Still, the two fused bones are certainly there. The name of the larger of the two bones, the radius, is used to describe the large fused bone today.

Note that "pastern" and "coffin-joint" are terms that were in use in the seventeenth century. *Pastern* comes from the Old French for "pasture," and most likely refers to the fact that if a horse was turned out into a pasture in hobbles (there being fewer fences in those days), the hobbles were placed around the part of the lower limb called the pastern. Apparently, "pasture" evolved into "pastern."

"Coffin" was and is used to refer to the joint of the foot as well as the bone of the limb that's closest to the ground. An eighteenth-century veterinary text states that "the Coffin Bone is that which lies within the Hoof as in a Coffin."

The illustration facing page 183 and the accompanying legends are marvelous, though inaccurate.

CHAPTER 20, PAGES 185–187

This chapter, on the muscles of the thigh, opens with a reference to the "Huckle or Whirle-bone." *Huckle* is an old word referring to the haunch or hip. Although it's not a term that you hear much today, some people, especially those involved with Standardbred racehorses, still refer to the *whirlbone.*

Whirlbone is an obscure word that comes from Old English. It refers to the round head of a bone turning in the socket of another bone (such as happens in the hip). The term has also been used to describe the kneecap (patella) and the greater trochanter of the femur (which is a big bony projection that can be felt in the hip area of the horse). In Old German, the word *werbelvein* refers to the vertebrae. This term also may have something to do with the origin of the English word *whirlbone.*

The term "stifle" is also mentioned; this area of the horse is analogous to the human knee. No one is sure where *stifle* came from, but it's very old (it shows up in books printed in the 1300s). A connection with the word *stiff* is commonly assumed (but most etymologists think it's doubtful). There are also some thoughts that it comes to English from an Old French word for "pipe" or "leg" or possibly from the Latin word for "stick."

Snape mentions the psoas muscle (a little muscle on the inner part of the hip) and relates it to kidney problems and the resulting back pain. Many horse people think that horses get sore backs from kidney problems; this is rarely, if ever, the case.

The rest of the chapter is devoted to various muscles of the thigh and their actions. As with the other chapters, the names and muscle functions are not accurate.

CHAPTER 21, PAGES 188–190

The opening paragraph of this chapter on the muscles of the tibia is a bit confusing. Horses, like people, have a tibia and fibula, but the fibula is very small and has no apparent function. Snape doesn't do a good job of explaining the anatomy of this area. A discussion of archaic muscle names and functions follows.

Snape next undertakes an interesting discussion of the muscles associated with the patella (kneecap). His anatomy here is clearly wrong; the muscles do not "make one broad and very strong Tendon." In fact, the muscles end in three separate ligaments that run over the top of the patella and tie it down onto the tibia. Snape's anatomy is that of a human.

Snape feels that because of the strong tendon attachment it's not possible for the kneecap to displace. He says that what is said to be a dislocation is actually "Bloud extravasated out of the Capillary Vessels" that "lieth congealing and putrifying in the spaces between the Membranes and Muscles." His treatment for this condition is to rub on "penetrating Oils," and if that fails, to open up the skin, "blowing in wind" to "make way for the congealed Matter the better to come forth." Pity the poor horses that received this "treatment."

A temporary and intermittent dislocation of the kneecap can occur in horses (it's called upward fixation of the patella), though fortunately, the condition is rare. It's often treated by cutting the innermost of the three ligaments of the kneecap. The surgery is not only reserved for therapeutic purposes, however. Some people routinely cut this ligament in a misguided attempt to "free up" the horse's hind leg.

The chapter concludes with the usual discussions of the location and function of various muscle groups.

CHAPTER 22, PAGES 191–194

Snape addresses the muscles of the lower leg and foot in this chapter. He begins by addressing the "Hock or Hough."

Hough is an older term, coming from the Scottish. The ending letter *k* (in hock) is an anglicization that makes the word easier to pronounce. The word comes from the Old English for "heel"; the horse's hock is the analogous structure to the human heel.

The first part of the chapter includes a fun discussion of why horses stand "tip toe" (as it were). Snape also has some thoughts on the comparative anatomy of dogs and "Coneys" (rabbits).

The remainder of the chapter is devoted to the discussion of various muscle groups, with the usual archaic names (for example, you'll recognize the "Chorda magna" as the Achilles tendon) and less-than-accurate descriptions of muscle location and function.

All in all, you have to at least respect Snape for recognizing the limitations of his book on muscles. He knows it's not perfect. In fact, he concludes this chapter by apologizing for any errors, "and as for the morose and carping, I shall take it as a favour from them, if instead of railing at random, they will take the pains to demonstrate my mistakes."

BOOK FIVE

Of the Bones

THE final book in Snape's *Anatomy of An Horse* addresses the bones. It's a good deal more engaging than the previous book and contains numerous bits of interest. It's certainly not a complete description of the limbs of the horse, however. Curiously, the navicular bone, which is the subject of so much attention in horses of today, isn't even mentioned in Snape's book (nor does it appear in any of the illustrations).

CHAPTER 1, PAGES 195–197

Snape begins by correctly comparing the bones to the "Carkase of a Ship." He spends some time trying to discern the origin of bone and, as usual, tries to distinguish various types of bones according to their shape, size, and hardness (some bones can be distinguished by their hardness; however, the other distinctions are not made today). The "three parts" of a bone mentioned by Snape are also not entirely accurate. The term *epiphysis* refers to the end of a bone from which the bone grows; Snape's use of *apophysis* reflects the same meaning that the word has today.

The chapter ends with Snape listing the bones of the head. The term *cranium* does come from Greek, but the Greek word that it comes from just means "skull" not "helmet."

The fine illustration facing page 197 is an accurate and lovely presentation of the skull of a foal.

CHAPTER 2, PAGES 198–199

The "sutures" of the skull are the little lines that divide the separate bones of the skull. The skull bones grow as the animal increases in size and the sutures eventually grow together, leaving only a line to indicate where separate bones had once been. Snape divides sutures into categories of true and false; in fact, a suture's a suture. The description at the end of the chapter of the uses of the sutures is inventive, pretty much completely inaccurate, and quite amusing (vents for the brain?).

CHAPTER 3, PAGES 199–203

The "proper" bones of the skull (as opposed to the bones that are "common" to the skull and jaw) are nicely described in this chapter. However, at the top of page 200, Snape is immediately confounded by a large "cavity" (the frontal sinus). Snape's musings on the purpose of this cavity are worth a read.

The word *noll,* as in "Noll-bone" (today, it's called the occipital bone), is an obscure variant of the word *knoll,* meaning "a little hill." The word actually describes the shape of the bone quite nicely!

The remainder of the chapter describes the various bones, holes, and projections that occur in the horse's skull. The ornate illustration that ends the chapter, facing page 203, is helpful to refer to when you are reading the chapter. Of interest in Figure II is letter *X,* the "Tushes, or Dog teeth." The teeth in question are called the canine teeth; "tush" is an obscure variant of the word *tusk;* tusks are really long (and frequently sharp) canine teeth that occur in a number of mammalian species.

CHAPTER 4, PAGES 204–205

There's some fairly dry discussion of the bones of the head and jaw in this chapter. Of historical note is Snape's mention of the sella turcica (a bony process that still goes by that name) as well as Snape's discussion of the use of the cribriform plate.

Snape concludes by discussing the "os jugale." There's no bone by this name in the horse's head today (it is, rather, a part of a bone called the temporal bone).

CHAPTER 5, PAGES 206–209

In discussing the jawbones, Snape is fairly accurate as to the location, even though some of the names have changed. He notes the "caruncula Lachrymalia" (the little pink thing that's in the corner of the horse's eye) and even gives it an important function (to hinder the continual "gleeting" of the tears)! He has "made bold" to give the bone on the inside of the eye the name of "os innominatum" (unnamed bone); in reality it's just a part of the lacrimal bone that makes up the skull in the area.

Snape describes luxation of the jaw (the jawbone moving out of its socket) as "very dangerous and hard to cure"; he's undoubtedly right. Fortunately such a problem is virtually unknown in the horse. The chapter closes with observations about the alveoli (the "little pits" in which the teeth lie). His observations are accurate and impressive, particularly as they came so long ago.

The beautifully rendered illustrations facing page 208 are a big help in understanding what Snape is talking about in this chapter.

CHAPTER 6, PAGES 209–211

If you own a horse, you undoubtedly give his mouth some attention. This chapter gives a wonderful historic perspective as to how the horse's mouth was looked at four hundred years ago.

Of immediate interest is that to Snape teeth were just another type of bone (albeit a really hard type of bone). His description of the anatomy of a tooth is pretty good. Snape asserts that there are three types of teeth. In fact, there are four. Snape mentions the tushes (canine teeth; he also gives them an important function—gnawing—which they don't have), incisors (the teeth in the front of the mouth), and molars (known commonly as the cheek teeth; the word *molar* is Latin for "grinding"). He doesn't refer to the premolars, however. It's an understandable omission, given that the premolars of the horse (the first three cheek teeth) have the same shape and function as the three molars that come behind. The only difference is semantic; the premolars are permanent teeth that replace the baby teeth of that area as the horse matures. (There's no mention of the "wolf teeth," either; these tiny premolars that sit next to the first large cheek tooth don't occur in every horse, however).

Snape gives his method for describing the age of a horse by looking at the first cheek tooth. This method, which involves looking at "their unevenness at the top," is only useful for horses up to seven years of age. It may be reasonably accurate and it's probably not much worse than what anyone does today. (A study has shown that the elaborate charts that have been produced to determine the age of a horse by his teeth are not very accurate.)

Snape maintains that it's "very necessary" that the surface of the molars remain rough and uneven, like a millstone needs to be for optimum grinding. Contrast this opinion with that of today, which says that the teeth must be level and smooth! (The process of leveling and smoothing the horse's teeth, known as "floating," wasn't done until the 1800s.)

The illustration facing page 211 of the skull and jaw is very well done and quite accurate. Of particular interest is the note occurring in the legends for the illustration under letter *E*.

Sometimes you really have to marvel at the ability of people to create problems. This is of particular concern in medicine. If you can't find a problem, you shouldn't just make one up. Stumbling can be a problem in horses. The seventeenth-century solution for a stumbling horse was to "cut the Cord." This operation must have been barbaric. To Snape's credit, he ridicules the whole idea behind the operation (that there was a cord running from the upper lip to the foot that was too tight and caused the horse to stumble). It's a fascinating historical footnote, however.

CHAPTER 7, PAGE 212

The hyoid bones of the throat are described well enough in this chapter.

CHAPTER 8, PAGES 212–214

The seven vertebrae of the neck are discussed in this chapter. Unfortunately, so is the nonexistent collarbone. (Sometimes you have to wonder how often Snape actually looked at a horse when he wrote this book.)

His discussion of the first two vertebrae of the neck is interesting and accurate. So is his observation that if the rest of the vertebrae were as long as those of the neck, the horse's back would be three times as long as it is!

The neck vertebrae are nicely illustrated in the plate facing page 214.

CHAPTER 9, PAGES 215–219

After another reference to the nonexistent collarbone of the horse, Snape goes on to do a reasonably good job describing the vertebrae of the horse's back and loins. He does get the number of ribs wrong; there are usually eighteen pairs of ribs in the horse (not seventeen) and sometimes a nineteenth rib is found. As Snape states, ribs can be divided into two categories. "True" ribs attach to the sternum while "false" ribs (Snape calls them "bastard" ribs) don't. He misses the count again; there are eight (not nine) true ribs. Snape's reasons for the ribs being shaped the way they are and their uses are teleological masterpieces (although the ribs are really not rough on the outside and smooth on the inside).

CHAPTER 10, PAGES 217–219

This chapter on the sternum and the scapula is fairly well done, although it begins with yet another reference to the collarbone. The illustrations facing page 218 are nice depictions of the areas described in Chapters 9 and 10.

CHAPTER 11, PAGES 219–220

This chapter, devoted to the two large bones of the horse's upper forearm, the "humerus" and the "cubit-bone" (known today as the *fused radius* and *ulna*), opens with a list of the bones of the entire forearm. Curiously, Snape omits five bones of the forelimb, failing to mention the two splint bones, the two sesamoid bones behind the ankle, and the navicular bone of the foot. The remainder of the chapter is a reasonably accurate description of the two bones in question.

This chapter introduces the term *osselets.* In Snape's context, osselets (or "little bones"—*os* being Latin for "bone") were the seven small bones that make up the horse's knee (which is analogous to the human wrist). Today, the term *osselets* has a much different meaning. Used mostly around racehorses, it refers to changes that occur as a result of inflammation in and around the horse's fetlock (ankle) joint.

CHAPTER 12, PAGES 221–227

The lower part of the horse's front limb (from the knee) is responsible for the majority of lameness conditions. While it's therefore appropriate that Snape would spend so much time discussing this area, it's also surprising that he doesn't get the relatively simple anatomy right! Still, the chapter has a number of interesting observations and descriptions and is certainly worth looking at in detail.

Snape opens with a discussion of the osselets. He notes that they are covered with a "membranous and gristly Ligament" that makes them hard to separate (this is apparently the joint capsule, the soft tissue that surrounds every joint). Rather than give names to all of the carpal bones, Snape numbers them; today, the lower row of carpal bones has numbers and the rest have names.

Snape next addresses the three bones that occur immediately below the knee, the "Shank-bone" and the two "Splent-bones." Snape's "shank-bone" (known to anatomists as the third metacarpal bone) is today commonly called the *cannon bone.* (Cannon bone doesn't show up in veterinary literature until the 1800s, however. The term refers to the fact that the bone is cannon-shaped in the sense that it is a tube, that is, a long bone with a cavity in the middle.) It's also interesting to learn the origin of the term "splent-bone" (today it's known as *splint*). Snape describes splints as "bodkin-like"; a bodkin is a short-pointed weapon and the description is reasonable.

The two pastern bones come up for attention next. Snape describes the upper bone as "gibbous," meaning convex, rounded, and protuberant, all of which accurately apply to both of the pastern bones.

Snape's discourse on the coffin bone is, frankly, a bit disappointing, mostly because it's such an important area of the horse and it leaves you wanting to know more about the thoughts of the day. He merely says the bone is called *coffin* from "its hollowness on the underside" (although that's not much of an explanation) and that the bone is "spongy" with many holes for vessels (which it is).

Of far more interest is Snape's brief discussion of horses that have "Founder." The ancient term *founder* (called *laminitis* by today's veterinarians) referred to disease of the horse's foot; it's even found in Chaucer's *Knight's Tale.* It appears to come from an Old French word for "plunging to the bottom" or to "collapse and fall into ruins"; either phrase would be apt in describing the catastrophic end results of severe cases of laminitis.

Snape attributes the condition to bruising of the tendinous fibers that insert into the foot; veterinarians now know that the underlying trouble in laminitis is a derangement of the circulation to the foot.

The treatments described by Snape for laminitis are nothing short of barbarous. "Drawing of the Soals" (sole) of the horse's foot involved cutting out the entire bottom of the horse's foot and wrapping it with herbs and the like to help "draw out" the distemper. Snape also describes a technique for "rasing" (rasping) the hoof in several spots from the coronary band at the top to the ground until the hoof bleeds and applying "remedies to those places." (That sort of treatment is not unlike hoof wall resection, a "treatment" for laminitis that has only recently fallen out of favor.) It's a wonder that any of these horses survived their treatments.

The illustrations facing page 223 show the bones of the forelimb in quite accurate detail. Although they are not discussed, the illustrations at least show the sesamoid bones that occur on the back part of the horse's fetlock joint; the navicular bone of the foot is omitted altogether!

CHAPTER 13, PAGES 227–229

This chapter has a generally good discussion of the bones of the sacrum and the vertebrae of the tail. Snape notes that there are eighteen "rump bones" (*coccygeal vertebrae,* as they are called today); in fact, the number can vary considerably among horses, but eighteen can be considered as an average.

The chapter concludes with a series of very nice illustrations facing page 228. There's an error in Figure IV, which shows seven bones of the loins; there are usually six of these bones. Donkeys, the Arabian horse, mules, asses, and the wild Przewalski's horse sometimes only have five.

CHAPTER 14, PAGES 230–231

Snape's discussion of the pelvis is a bit muddled. To help understand the chapter, an understanding of the relatively simple anatomy is a good idea. There are three bones: the ilium, the ischium, and the pubis. (These are mentioned by name in the chapter.) As Snape correctly states, in the young horse, these are obviously distinct bones; in older horses, they fuse together and so appear as one bone.

Snape begins by asserting that the bone named the *ilium* is so-called because the part of the intestines known as the *ileum* lies under it (note the different spellings used today). This isn't right; actually *ilium* is a Latin word that describes that part of the abdomen extending from the lowest ribs to the groin area; the ilium is the largest bone in the area.

Snape gives the *ischium* the name *os innominatum* (Latin for "unnamed bone"). Interestingly, earlier in the book, he already gave the same name to the small bone behind the eye! To confuse matters for you, rather than call the entire bone the ischium, he decides to call the part of the bone that has the hip sockets the *os coxendici* and leave the rest of the bone as "nameless." This distinction is really nonsensical and makes a mess of a relatively simple set of bones.

The pubis is also called the "Share-bone." It's not called that today; the word *share* refers to the iron blade of a plow; it's also an old term referring to a division or fork in the body. Seeing that the pubis does make a distinct division, perhaps it's not such a bad term.

Snape refers to the entire area of the pelvis as the "Bason"; the spelling is just a variant of *basin,* but the term is reasonably descriptive if you consider the area a receptacle for the various structures that Snape mentions.

The well-done illustrations of this fairly simple "area" face page 231 and should be referred to while perusing this chapter.

CHAPTER 15, PAGES 231–232

As Snape says, the Latin word for thigh is *femur,* but the word has nothing to do with the creature being "born up or sustained" by the bone. The anatomy here is really pretty good. He correctly identifies the anatomy of the upper part of the bone as being covered with a "gristle" used to help facilitate gliding; that "gristle" is called cartilage today.

The chapter closes with a discussion of the patella (kneecap). *Patella* is from the Latin for "pan." Presumably, it describes the shape of the bone.

CHAPTER 16, PAGES 233–235

The stifle joint is well described in the beginning of this chapter. However, Snape mentions that there is a large tibia in horses but no fibula. There is a fibula in a horse, but it's very small, really just a remnant of what may have previously been a larger bone. It serves no obvious purpose but it is there. Snape is correct in asserting that the anatomy of the lower part of the limbs is virtually identical in the front and back legs. The chapter concludes with a fine illustration of the skeleton, which faces page 234.

CHAPTER 17, PAGES 235–236

Without picking a personal favorite, Snape refers to several learned (and fanciful) opinions of how the horse's hoof is generated. His description of how the hoof grows and why it is made of its particular substance is absorbing. His description of how the hoof is attached to the bone of the foot is just inaccurate, however.

CHAPTER 18, PAGES 236–237

Snape's musings on cartilages, or "gristles" as he prefers to call them, are fairly accurate. He also makes a correct observation that in many areas the gristle in old horses hardens into bone (such an example would be "sidebone," which is a hardening of the collateral cartilages of the foot that causes no problems for the horse).

CHAPTER 19, PAGE 237

Given that there are dozens and dozens of ligaments in the horse's body, five paragraphs devoted to their discussion seems painfully little. As you might imagine, it's not possible to cover all of the various types and ligaments and their functions in such a short chapter and Snape doesn't (not that he doesn't give it a go). His third and fourth uses for ligaments are not considered to be uses of ligaments today.

BIBLIOGRAPHY

Boorstin, D. J. *The Discoverers.* Random House, New York, 1983.

The Compact Oxford English Dictionary, 2nd ed., Clarendon Press, Oxford, 1991.

Dorland's Illustrated Medical Dictionary, 25th ed., W. B. Saunders and Co., Philadelphia, 1974.

Getty, R. *Sisson and Grossman's The Anatomy of the Domestic Animals.* W. B. Saunders and Co., Philadelphia, 1974.

Gibson, W. *A New Treatise on the Diseases of Horses.* London, 1751.

Popesko, P. *Atlas of Topographical Anatomy of the Domestic Animals.* W. B. Saunders and Co, Philadelphia, 1977.

Smith, Sir Frederick. *The Early History of Veterinary Literature and Its British Development,* vol. 1. J. Allen & Co., London, 1976.

Smithcors, J. F. *Evolution of the Veterinary Art, a Narrative Account to 1850.* Veterinary Medicine Publishing Company, Kansas City, 1957.

ACKNOWLEDGMENTS

FOR her constant help, support, and enthusiasm, the author would like to especially thank his editor, Madelyn Larsen, who seems to have an uncanny knack for knowing what to suggest and when to leave well enough alone. Thank you to Ed Postal, of Barnaby Rudge books, for finding this wonderful book and offering it to me. Thank you to Rita Wilds, who provided invaluable help in researching the various anatomists and physicians referenced by Snape in the book and made suggestions regarding the introduction and commentary. Finally, thank you to my wife, Elizabeth, for her careful reading, for putting up with the incessant typing noises at night, for her endless support, and for nurturing Jackson, the keeper of the flame.